THE RISE OF AMERICAN PHILOSOPHY

Four Harvard philosophers about 1908. *Left to right:* Josiah Royce, Hugo Münsterberg, George Herbert Palmer, William James. This photograph was made by Winifred Rieber in preparation for a portrait she was to do of the four men. The portrait—of three philosophers—is now on display in Emerson Hall. There is no truth to the legend that Münsterberg was "painted out" of the portrait. When the artist would not put him front center, as Münsterberg desired for "aesthetic reasons," the painting was done without him. See the *Harvard Alumni Bulletin*, vol. 58, no. 9 (18 February 1950), p. 384.

THE RISE OF
AMERICAN
PHILOSOPHY

CAMBRIDGE, MASSACHUSETTS

1860–1930

Bruce Kuklick

New Haven and London

Yale University Press

Designed by Sally Sullivan
and set in Monotype Bembo type.
Printed in the United States of America by
The Murray Printing Co., Westford, Mass.

Published in Great Britain, Europe, Africa, and
Asia by Yale University Press, Ltd., London.
Distributed in Australia and New Zealand
by Book & Film Services, Artarmon, N.S.W.,
Australia; and in Japan by Harper & Row,
Publishers, Tokyo Office.

Library of Congress Cataloging in Publication Data

Kuklick, Bruce, 1941–
    The rise of American philosophy, Cambridge, Massachusetts,
1860–1930.
    Bibliography: p.
    Includes index.
    1.   Philosophy, American—19th century.   2.   Philosophy,
American—20th century.   3.   Harvard University.
I.   Title.
B935.K84   191   76–49912
ISBN   0–300–02039–2 clothbound
          0–300–02413–4 paperbound

For Riki

The pathos of death is this, that when the days of one's life are ended, those days that were so crowded with business and felt so heavy in their passing, what remains of one in memory should usually be so slight a thing. The phantom of an attitude, the echo of a certain mode of thought, a few pages of print, some invention, or some victory we gained in a brief critical hour, are all that can survive the best of us. It is as if the whole of a man's significance had now shrunk into . . . a mere musical note or phrase suggestive of his singularity.

William James

May I, composed like them
Of Eros and of dust,
Beleaguered by the same
Negation and despair,
Show an affirming flame.

W. H. Auden

CONTENTS

Illustrations   xi

Acknowledgments   xiii

Introduction   xv

PART 1: SCOTTISH REALISM AND THE EVOLUTIONARY CONTROVERSY   1

1. Currents of Thought in Nineteenth-Century Cambridge   5
2. Francis Bowen and Unitarian Orthodoxy   28
3. Amateur Philosophizing   46
4. Chauncey Wright: Defender of Science and of Religion   63
5. Fiske and Abbot: Professorial Failures   80
6. Charles Sanders Peirce   104

PART 2: THE GOLDEN AGE AT HARVARD (I)   127

7. Philosophy Rejuvenated, 1869–1889   129
8. Royce and the Argument for the Absolute, 1875–1892   140
9. William James: The Psychologist as Philosopher, 1869–1889   159
10. Psychology at Harvard, 1890–1900   180
11. Hugo Münsterberg   196
12. George Herbert Palmer and Self-Realization Ethics at Harvard   215

PART 3: THE GOLDEN AGE AT HARVARD (II)   229

13. Building a Graduate School, 1890–1912   233
14. James, Royce, and Pragmatism, 1898–1907   259
15. The Battle of the Absolute, 1899–1910   275
16. James and Royce: Public Philosophy, 1902–1912   291

17. Jamesean Metaphysics, 1904–1910   315
18. Ralph Perry and Neo-Realism   338
19. George Santayana   351
20. Royce's Later Work: Logic, Pluralism, and *The Problem of Christianity*   370

PART 4: HARVARD PHILOSOPHY AT MID-CAREER   403

21. The Crisis of 1912–1920   405
22. Edwin Bissell Holt and Philosophical Behaviorism   417
23. Philosophers at War   435

PART 5: PHILOSOPHY AS A PROFESSION   449

24. The Professional Mentality, 1920–1930   451
25. Ernest Hocking   481
26. Harvard Moral Philosophy, 1875–1926   496
27. Alfred North Whitehead   516
28. Clarence Lewis   533

Conclusion: The Triumph of Professionalism   565

Appendixes   573

1. The Separation of History and Philosophy   575
2. Harvard Philosophy after Lewis   577
3. Harvard Doctorates in Philosophy   581
4. Women Philosophers at Harvard   590

Notes   595

   Key to Citations and Abbreviations   596

Essay on Sources   639

Index   653

ILLUSTRATIONS

Four Harvard philosophers about 1908 (Dorothy
   Rieber Joralemon)   *Frontispiece*
Chauncey Wright about 1870 (Edwina Pearson)   3
Francis Bowen in 1858 (Edwina Pearson)   3
Frank Abbot about 1880 (Sydney E. Ahlstrom)   3
John Fiske as a young man (Edwina Pearson)   3
Charles Peirce at Milford (Murray G. Murphey)   4
Hugo Münsterberg in 1893 (Boston Public Library)   128
William James about 1885   128
Josiah Royce about 1885 (Harvard University Archives)   128
George Santayana about 1887   231
Hugo Münsterberg about 1900 (Boston Public Library)   231
Josiah Royce in 1902 (Robbins Library of Philosophy,
   Harvard)   231
William James about 1905 (Harvard University Archives)   231
James and Royce (Harvard University Archives)   232
Private Clarence Lewis in 1918 (Mrs. C. I. Lewis)   404
Major Ralph Perry in 1918 (War Department)   404
Ralph Barton Perry about 1925 (Harvard University Archives)   450
C. I. Lewis (self-portrait) about 1930 (Mrs. C. I. Lewis)   450
Alfred North Whitehead (Harvard University Archives)   450
The Harvard Department of Philosophy in 1929 (Harvard
   Department of Philosophy)   564

ACKNOWLEDGMENTS

I am indebted to the many institutions which funded various parts of this study: Yale University, the University of Pennsylvania, and the American Philosophical Society provided money for summer study; the American Council of Learned Societies financed a year's leave of absence for writing; and Yale University Press advanced funds for various publication expenses.

Many people have helped me with this work and I hope they will forgive this general appreciative note. Among them: Sydney Ahlstrom, Brand Blanshard, Robert Brandom, William Christian, Paul Coates, Larry Dowler, Joseph Ellis, Max Fisch, Richard Hocking, Daniel Howe, Dorothy Joralemon, Alan Kors, Harold N. Lee, Andrew Lewis, Mabel Lewis, Victor Lowe, James W. Miller, Murray Murphey, Leo Ribuffo, Charles Rosenberg, Wilmon Sheldon, H. Standish Thayer, David Watson, Daniel Wilson, Harry Wolfson, and Michael Zuckerman. I am particularly grateful to those who responded to my persistent phone calls and importunate letters for information and criticism; they have never allowed my pugnacious academic discourse to provoke advice that was not sane and balanced. I also want to acknowledge a more special relation. In the last eight years I have made more trips to Boston than I want to remember. Despite his own demanding responsibilities, Richard Freeland unfailingly provided food, shelter, and, most important, intelligent conversation.

R. G. Collingwood has written that historical thinking means nothing else than interpreting all available evidence with the maximum degree of critical skill. If my fellow academics have increased my critical skill, archivists and librarians all over the country have been invaluable in unearthing evidence. They too must receive a general "thank you," but I want to mention specifically Harley Holden and Clark Eliot and their staff at the Harvard University Archives.

For permission to examine, use, and quote various documents or books, I am indebted to Richard Hocking, Andrew Lewis, Israel Sheffer, and Harry Wolfson; the Harvard Department of Philosophy and Harvard University; Charles Scribner's Sons, Publishers. Chapter 16 of this book considerably broadens my previous treatment of Josiah Royce, but much of the rest of my analysis derives from my *Josiah Royce: An Intellectual Biography* (Indianapolis: Bobbs-Merrill, 1972)—especially the view of *The Religious Aspect of Philosophy* and *The Problem of Christianity*—and "The Development of Royce's Later Philosophy," *Journal of the History of Philosophy* 9 (1971): 349–67, portions of which I have used with permission.

Last but not least, there is a group of miscellaneous acknowledgments. Jane Isay, Murdoch Matthew, and the staff of Yale University Press have done a meticulous job in preparing the manuscript for publication. During the period that this book was being completed I took part in the Council of Philosophic Studies' Institute on the History of American Philosophy; I am grateful to the participants, who forced me to rethink some of my assumptions. I should especially mention Fred and Emily Michael, who made me change the chapter on Charles Peirce. Over the past five years a whole battery of work-study students and typists have aided with essential aspects of the research. They have all been guided and organized by Leila Zenderland, Managing Editor of the *American Quarterly*, and I thank her and the *Quarterly* staff. Marcia Wislin Carner selected the photographs.

Henrika Kuklick is a sociologist and historian to whom I am married. She is responsible for many of the analyses in the book that I think are most astute.

Surveying my attempt at synthesizing the thought of fifteen philosophers with the history of an institution, I have become painfully aware of the gaps in the evidence, the failures in my own understanding, and the thin ice of interpretation. I have also become increasingly sensitive to the fact that even a good set of connected historical explanations is lucky to illuminate one-half of what needs explaining; and I uncomfortably accept responsibility for errors and fallings short.

INTRODUCTION

In January 1860 a committee of the Harvard Board of Overseers, a body responsible for the governance of the college, reported on instruction in "Intellectual and Moral Philosophy." The first branch covered roughly what we know today as philosophy, stressing logic, epistemology, and metaphysics; the second covered what we know as the social sciences, although conceived as explicitly normative. The committee lamented the state of both at Harvard, and the overseers considered the report important enough to have it published. There was "a great deficiency in this department," the document declared; it existed in "a neglected and destitute condition"; instruction in metaphysics, logic, ethics, and natural and revealed theology had been "curtailed, cut down, and driven out step by step from . . . [its] proper place in the College course." The problem was that the Alford Professor of Natural Religion, Moral Philosophy and Civil Polity was extraordinarily overworked. Although the number of students had increased in the preceding decade, Harvard had eliminated its University Professorship of Logic and Metaphysics and left vacant the Hollis Professorship of Divinity. One man did almost all the teaching in these areas; and recently the college had assigned him the work in political economy, then in the first phase of becoming a separate area of knowledge. Training in philosophy was consequently "brief and hurried," "an exercise of memory more than of understanding." "The effect of this curtailing and abandonment of the most important studies in the course of a liberal education," the committee declared, was "evident and . . . well known." Without proper drill in moral philosophy, Harvard graduates might succumb to attacks on "the fundamental principles of religion and ethics," and without proper drill in intellectual philosophy they would never attain that mental development and self-discipline necessary for successful work in the world.[1]

Seventy years later, in 1930, the Macmillan Company published *Contemporary American Philosophy*. The three divisions of the American Philosophical Association—Eastern, Western, and Pacific—had each conducted a referendum of its members to select the thirty-four American philosophers whose "personal statements" would represent the state of American thought; the presidents of the three divisions edited the book. All three editors had received their Ph.D.s from Harvard. The professors from across the country had dedicated the book to another Harvard-trained philosopher who had taught at the university for over forty years. Sixteen of the thirty-four contributors had received their highest degree at Harvard, fourteen of them the doctorate. The school's closest rivals were Cornell with three philosophers and Michigan with two; no other institution contributed more than one. Five of the thirty-four, all with Harvard degrees, were members of the Harvard faculty. Columbia's staff had four men, Michigan three, Berkeley and Brown two each; but Harvard had trained six of the latter eleven men, including both from Berkeley.

Despite the striking change from 1860 to 1930, there is a similarity and an irony that we should not overlook. The overworked Alford Professor in 1860 was Francis Bowen, a man whose name has long since ceased to be consequential even in philosophic circles. The three men active at Harvard who contributed to *Contemporary American Philosophy* were Ralph Barton Perry, William Ernest Hocking, and C. I. Lewis. They were philosophers mainly read only within the philosophic community then and largely unread even within that community today. Nor had the growth of philosophy averted the peril feared by the Board of Overseers, that Harvard youth would fall victim to atheism: by 1930 newly trained philosophers had little interest in religious philosophy.

However religion had fared, between Bowen's death in 1890 and the professionals' accession to professorships at about the beginning of the First World War philosophy did achieve a greater importance in Cambridge. A graduate student in those years might have come in contact with, among others, Charles Peirce, William James, Josiah Royce, and George Santayana—figures to conjure with in the history of American thought and in the tradition of western thought. And students would have found much in the work of these men to justify a religious view of the universe.

This book charts the history of philosophic thinking in the United States as typified and dominated by Harvard from 1860 to 1930.. But I mean these dates as only a gross indicator: 1860 produced a report on the moribund state of Harvard philosophy while 1930 produced a book testifying to its potency. Perhaps more significant watersheds—as far as documents are concerned—are 1859 and 1929, the years in which Darwin's *Origin of Species* and Lewis's *Mind and the World-Order* were published. The first changed the structure of problems that philosophers tried to solve; the second marked the coming of age of academic philosophy. Emphasizing dates, however, is misleading. To understand Darwin's impact, I have surveyed the philosophical climate in the middle third of the nineteenth century. To understand the importance of Lewis's work and how his ideas reflected a changed conception of philosophy, I have indicated the orientations of the professional community through the Second World War.

I have tried to answer one central question: How are we to interpret the philosophical ideas promulgated in this period? In answering, I have found it impossible to understand the ideas by concentrating solely on the critical philosophic texts. To make sense of them I have also had to consider a crucial, although secondary, question: How are we to relate these ideas to the society from which they sprang and to the men who espoused them?

Where it has been plausible, I have shown that the side of a given issue on which a philosopher came down was a matter of temperament. In this I have followed William James and, I suppose, other intellectual historians. The most dramatic example is my treatment of Santayana: the temperamental dimension of the analysis stands out because he differed as much as he did from his colleagues. But in all cases temperament was important and played the same structural role of predisposing a philosopher to sympathize with one kind of solution to a problem. I believe, however, that we must discuss the twisting and turning of argument in the context of the philosophical tradition in which the philosophers worked and the implicit demands of logical thinking.

There were constraints on thinkers other than temperamental ones; the society in which they lived determined the kinds of intellectual questions important at any given time (and consequently the kinds of successful philosophic systems—answers to the questions), the types of people who commented on them, and the platform from which they spoke. Here my narrative has focused on the role played by institutions—in this case Harvard University—in supporting thinkers and creating climates of opinion. I have tried to show the power of student-teacher relations in philosophy and the importance of institutions for understanding influence. I have tried to connect changes in the character of philosophizing with its professionalization as a scholarly discipline and the transformation of the philosopher into the philosophy professor. The thought I have interpreted had a life of its own only after the intangibles of personality had created a predisposition for a certain kind of solution to problems the society set for certain people.

It is possible to show that in the nineteenth century the concerns of the cultural elite determined what problems would be philosophically viable and the men who became philosophers did so to resolve personal crises. Religious skepticism troubled them, as it troubled society's leadership, and the outcome of their thinking was predictable. They defended conventional spiritual values, if in chastened form. After Royce and James established a framework for speculation and philosophy became professionalized in the twentieth century, society ceased to be a direct influence in shaping philosophical ideas, and the link between personality and philosophy dissolves.

I do not claim any universality for the methods used in this book. They have evolved from a study of a seventy-year span of American history, and generalizing beyond that period is as dubious as that period is idiosyncratic. Moreover, the intellectual history attempted here is the easiest kind: it sorts out the ideas held by a related group of thinkers and puts aside the difficult questions about the connection of thought with society and personality. Doing this kind of history, however, is a precondition for doing more sophisticated intellectual history. We cannot understand the connection of thought to social and individual variables unless we understand the thought. Obviously, I have not been able to make sense of the thought without some minimal knowledge of social history and biography. But grasping the deeper connections sought by most intellectual historians requires that they move from a limited comprehension of the link between society and personality and ideas to a more complex view. We first must learn, in a straightforward way, what thinkers have said;

we can then try to find out, for example, how they influenced their milieu or expressed its concerns or rationalized the lifestyles of ruling groups.

Although I can succinctly state these intentions, I have carried them out in a long book. It may be useful to outline its substantive structure.

Part 1 shows that the problems of Cambridge philosophy in the middle of the nineteenth century revolved around the intellectual concerns of the Boston gentry. The Unitarian and Transcendentalist controversies disturbed the leaders of southeastern Massachusetts, and they especially valued the philosophical bulwark that Harvard philosophers provided against Emerson's heresies. But the rationale used by men like Francis Bowen to defend religious proprieties from 1830 to 1860 could not meet the challenge of Darwinism. The "Unitarian philosophy," which hinged on arguments dependent on natural and revealed theology, was weakest in defending itself against evolution. As scientists accepted Darwin, the Unitarian philosophers foundered. Believing that natural selection entailed atheism and that man could justify his existence only with religion, they could not integrate the developmental hypothesis into their creed.

At the same time, a group of younger men who had studied at Harvard but were unaffiliated with its philosophic faculty and uncommitted to its doctrines were devising ways to meet the theological crisis without giving up essential religious claims. A mechanistic interpretation of Darwin might destroy religion and lead to a fatalistic atheism. Some thinkers feared that it might eventuate in passivity, suicide, or a mindless absorption with trivia as people tried to preserve their sanity in a meaningless universe. But individuals might understand evolution differently. As the Unitarian credo became moribund, Bowen's students and associates— Chauncey Wright, Charles Peirce, and William James among them— worked out the principle of pragmatism in an informal society called the Metaphysical Club and, individually, different "pragmatic" philosophies. The principle allowed for changes in beliefs over time, defining a belief as a habit of action and not as some abstruse mental entity. By arguing, à la Darwin, that survival was somehow the test of intellectual as well as biological fitness, these men were able to reconcile the new science to a new religion.

Best exemplified in the work of James, "pragmatic" philosophy held that scientific beliefs were those that best enabled us to live in a precarious world. But scientific beliefs did not differ in kind from religious beliefs, and we could justify the latter similarly: they were also true just as far as they adapted us satisfactorily to life. This sort of philosophizing used Darwin in the service of religion, and the men who contrived it had compelling personal reasons for preserving a spiritual commitment. In a sense pragmatism was a form of fideism: it demanded that the world be such as to meet man's deepest needs.

The popular acceptance of these doctrines depended on the intellectual acumen of their defenders and on social support, a public base from which to expound the new principles. Part 1 of the book traces how several members of the Metaphysical Club failed to get a hearing for their work because they never had this sort of base, but part 2 recounts how James received a Harvard position soon after Charles William Eliot became president of the college in 1869 and launched a program that came to symbolize the transformation of American higher education. With shrewd hiring Eliot rejuvenated philosophy at Harvard and added to its ranks not only James but also thinkers of the stature of Josiah Royce, George Santayana, and Hugo Münsterberg. The thirty years that Royce and James spent together, from the 1880s to the First World War, have become known as the Golden Age of American philosophy.

In addition to exploring how Eliot built Harvard's "great department," part 2 begins to examine the point of view enunciated there. The classic problems of philosophy interested all of these men, and they debated both with one another and with the great thinkers of the western tradition. Their involvement with the science-religion controversy was still intimate, and they held similar assumptions regarding it. Personally committed to comprehending man's place in the universe, they conceived of philosophy as the love of wisdom and the guide to the practical affairs of life. It was a systematic study that produced an integrated understanding of the universe and made sense of man's place in it.

In exploring what I call the Harvard Pragmatism of the great department, as well as the earlier doctrines of the membership of the Metaphysical Club and Harvard philosophy after Royce and James, I have stressed a number of recurrent themes. The epistemological problems bequeathed by Kant to succeeding generations of philosophers were central for all of these men, even to classic Unitarians like Bowen. The intellectual optimism of the eighteenth century produced a religious philosophy with its basis in British empiricism: the observed universe was benign and evidenced the deity. But Darwin called forth intellectual pessimism, so that after the Civil War religion was defended on *a priori*, Kantian grounds. Philosophers employed these same grounds to reinterpret the foundations of science as biological advances raised issues that traditional empiricism could not explain. Consequently, Cambridge thought and Harvard Pragmatism, like all forms of pragmatism, had an idealistic character. The truth of a belief was a function of its practical significance. That is, its truth was not independent of the individuals who held it but was relative to the action issuing from it; the objects of which beliefs were true had a relation to individuals, to consciousness.

The working out of this position was complex in the case of each philosopher, but James accepted the cardinal principle of idealism—that existence did not transcend consciousness—and Royce's absolute pragmatism synthesized aspects of Jamesean pragmatism and monistic idealism. Idealistic preconceptions were also essential to the work of three of their successors, William Ernest Hocking, C. I. Lewis, and Alfred North Whitehead. There were clearly personal reasons for the prominence of these preconceptions in the thought of many of the philosophers: idealism provided the means to make individual religious commitment compatible with science and with rigorous philosophical reasoning.

Finally, Cambridge philosophy connected with the growing study of logic in the United States. Bowen was a logician in the traditional sense, as was Royce. Following Peirce, Royce later studied symbolic logic; he introduced it to the Harvard curriculum and made it essential to the philosophy of a number of his best students, Lewis chief among them. Only James stood outside the interest in logic; Whitehead was directly concerned with it.

Part 3 completes the examination of the thought of the Golden Age, and begins an account of the professionalization of philosophy. Eliot slowly became convinced that advanced instruction would be necessary if his generation of scholars was to have successors, and by the turn of the century he had established the pre-eminent American graduate school and an internationally famous university. The major consequence of this development explored in the book is the rise of academic professionalism between 1880 and 1930. Although I have tried to specify it precisely, professionalization is difficult to define concretely. For Cambridge speculation, it encompassed five things: first, the disappearance of the amateur philosopher, the thinker with no institutional affiliation; second, the hiving-off of various areas of study from what was known as philosophy in the 1860s; third, the beginning of a discipline of philosophy, a limited field of knowledge in the university distinguished by special techniques and by an accepted set of doctrines; fourth, the concomitant growth of departmentalism, defining disciplinary integrity by the number of positions in a given field that the university would finance; and fifth, the training and placing of teachers in this field by an intensified apprenticeship leading to the doctorate and appointment as a college professor.

As philosophy became a profession, its nature and the character of the men it attracted changed. James, Royce, and their peers were not unmindful of worldly rewards, but their successors, chiefly Hocking and Ralph Barton Perry, were even more concerned with advancement within the growing university system and the perquisites that went with teaching at Harvard. Impersonal measures of scholarly aptitude—primarily publication—became more important. Although some thinkers still reserved time for concerns outside the discipline, philosophy narrowed to a domain of more arcane interests, competence in which was more subject to expert evaluation. Although his work was still an expression of self, the "professional"—typified by Lewis—tended to specialize in one branch of philosophy. The center of attention shifted from philosophy and life to status in (or the status of) "the profession." The proliferation of universities and enlargement of the scholarly bureaucracy within each university—the codification of professorial grades culminating in tenure grew up at this time—also contributed to a new way of life within which one could climb the ladder of success. Scholarly journals, professional associations, and all the other paraphernalia we associate with the social structure of the modern professoriate came into existence.

Perry, Hocking, and Lewis themselves trained students who had a less personal involvement with philosophy than did their professors; it had less hold on the lives of the third generation, which came to view its study and teaching more as an occupation than as a matter of life and death. By 1930 the narrow professional had emerged; doing philosophy was a job, not a vocation.

Certain important aspects of professionalization are apparent in the Golden Age—most notably in the attitudes of George Herbert Palmer and Münsterberg and in the later writings of Royce. After 1930—in the work of Perry and Hocking—extraprofessional concerns remained alive. But Harvard philosophers mostly abandoned interest in the culture for a preoccupation with technique and with the affairs of their discipline.

In the nineteenth century philosophy was often the province of amateurs. Philosophers had a public function and, whether or not associated with a college, they prepared both their intellectual and moral philosophy for a wide audience, speaking out on issues of concern to the educated upper middle class.

By 1900 philosophy was the activity of the professor. The Harvard Pragmatists argued for a hierarchical view of the various branches of philosophy: intellectual philosophy—which included the "technical branches" of logic, epistemology, and (for a time) metaphysics—was in some sense logically prior to moral philosophy—which included the "practical branches" of ethics, religious, social, and political philosophy, and their applications. The technical provided the ground or justification of the practical; and, for Royce and James, pursuing technical problems was justified only because light was thrown on the practical. Intellectual philosophy was the focus of work and judged only by scholars, but it resulted in the proper end of philosophy, an activist moral and religious creed. Adopting an almost ministerial function among the cultured of their society—in the style of Emerson or their Unitarian predecessors—Royce and James lectured to a wide audience on moral and religious problems, showing that philosophy was relevant to life and popularizing their more fundamental concerns. This was what I call American public philosophy.

By 1930 philosophy's successful practitioners were purely professional; they tended to specialize within the technical areas and even those who specialized in the practical ones lectured only to fellow specialists and did not apply their ideas to the real world; all popularization was suspect.

Professionalization has made my analysis of the philosophers' later repute—or lack of repute—intricate. The analysis hangs both on the intellectual ability of the thinkers and on a matrix of institutional benefits provided by Harvard—the system of rewards and punishments, the stimulation of students and colleagues, a position that commanded an audience, and miscellaneous incentives driving men to produce good work that would win attention. Equally important was the simple prestige and clout attendant on the supreme university affiliation. This factor operated in two ways: employment at Harvard could make a man's career; repudiation by Harvard could destroy it. To take some examples: Royce and James have survived because they had superior abilities and took advantage of the institution and its prestige; Wright and Peirce were philosophers of such extraordinary talent that they are still read despite the lack of institutional support and prestige; the genius of Frank Abbot and Edwin Holt was not great enough to insure later recognition without the benefits or luster Harvard could have brought them; Palmer and Perry are little read despite the benefits and luster because they lacked great gifts, and without institutional advantages John Fiske never receives even the minimal sober respect accorded Palmer and Perry; scholars have forgotten Bowen and Münsterberg because, in effect, Harvard repudiated them despite their gifts and despite employing them.

The changing written style of philosophical work also influenced a philosopher's future audience in ways difficult to pinpoint. As the substance of philosophy changed with its professionalization, the more variable "styles" employed have affected a philosopher's repute. The styles of James and Royce, one popular, the other ministerial, have detracted from their repute, while that of Peirce, technical and anomalous for its time, eventually added to his. Lewis's academic jargon has contributed to a reputation for prowess primarily resulting from his ability and the benefits and prestige of Harvard. Whatever the recognition bestowed on Hocking and Whitehead because of these latter factors, their style— a synthesis of the oracular, ministerial, and technical—has hurt their reputation among many professionals who came after them.

Part 3 investigates the structural changes that professionalization brought about, emphasizing the creation of a graduate program and of various subdisciplines around philosophy. Part 4 continues this story and also charts the reconstruction of the philosophy department after the deaths of James, Royce, and Münsterberg, and the retirements of Santayana and Palmer. Part 4 also considers the waning of extra-professional interests and the politicization of Harvard philosophy during the First World War. The public philosophy of Royce and James did not stress social and political applications, nor did the Harvard philosophers fully engage themselves with social and political problems until the First World War made them proponents of the Allied cause and of American preparedness and belligerency. But the interest in politics did not signify a long-term widening of non-technical commitments; it seems to have been an effect of the wartime hysteria on men who had not been trained to think critically about politics but whose positions impelled them to act in a quasi-ministerial public capacity. After the war the ambiguous role of the philosopher—something between professor and minister—changed, and the full definition of the professional role brought a decline in non-professional interests.

Part 5 examines the mature academic system under President A. Lawrence Lowell in the 1920s. It focuses on the altered character of the philosophers and their philosophizing, both of which changed in conjunction with the structural transformation. Part 5 also elaborates the thinking of the young philosophers who became professors during and after the First World War. The personal needs of thinkers and the concerns of literate society were overt and important for the shape of speculation after the Civil War, but after 1918 personal concerns ceased to mold the substance of a man's thought, and the social order was no longer directly relevant to philosophizing. It seems that once the discipline existed, shaped by its own peculiar techniques and an inherited group of ever more esoteric problems, speculation took on a life of its own.

The paradigmatic achievements of Harvard Pragmatism during the Golden Age insured that students accepted certain premises and did not question the parameters of discussion. In this intellectual context specialization was natural; indeed, it has occurred over and over again in the history of ideas in the wake of distinguished thinking. But professionalization intensified the specialization of philosophy and made its results less revocable than they otherwise might have been. Epistemology became the core area of study within which subspecialities arose, while the other speculative branches atrophied. Philosophy had always been technical, but it became more technical; the non-technical interests of philosophers declined, and they stopped thinking that what they did was significant for public affairs. Philosophy lost its overall synoptic role in the university specifically, and in intellectual life generally; the historical conception of the subject changed. In my Conclusion I link these developments to the advance of symbolic logic.

Because the study revolves around the Harvard department and philosophy during a specific period, I have truncated my treatment in various ways. I have not pursued the work of Peirce and Santayana after their Cambridge connections were severed. The work of Perry, Hocking, and Lewis after 1930 gets short shrift. Although I have tried to recover the most formidable intellects whom others have overlooked —Bowen, Abbot, Münsterberg, and Holt—I have stressed philosophy important for the department and profession, thereby ignoring Abbot's late writings, Münsterberg's early ones, and the thinking of Benjamin Rand and James Houghton Woods—Harvard fixtures for over thirty years. Other men of stature have gone by the boards entirely or received only passing mention because their connection with the department was peripheral or because their careers had just begun by the 1930s; Arthur Lovejoy and Harry Austryn Wolfson are slighted in this way.

The chapters that deal entirely with the complexity of ideas reflect one crucial dilemma of professional philosophy—its inability to communicate with a non-professional readership. There is a tension between these chapters and those that explore how the philosophers made their way in the world. That tension is inevitable and mirrors the increasing disjunction between how these men made their living and how they lived their lives.

These limitations aside, I would not have written this book unless I thought it represented a fruitful approach to the study of philosophers and ideas. The volume is manifestly about philosophy at Harvard, but it is, I think, about much more than that. Of the six classic American philosophers, five are treated here—Peirce, James, Royce, Santayana, and Whitehead. "The whole of American philosophy," one commentator wrote in the 1930s, seemed "but the lengthening shadow of that one great Department."[2] This statement is an exaggeration: whatever Harvard's transcendent importance, John Dewey did not teach there. To some extent I share the unstated low opinion of many contemporary American philosophers and the stated low opinion of the philosophic world outside the United States on Dewey's work, but whatever we make of his thought, the interest in him by liberal intellectuals and some subsequent intellectual historians is an important social phenomenon, and any history of American thought that ignores Dewey, the Chicago school, and Columbia naturalism must be incomplete. Nonetheless, the history of philosophy in Cambridge from the Civil War to the Great Depression illuminates the history of American thought as a whole: *it* is a history of Harvard writ large. Moreover, the story of the professionalization of philosophy at Harvard epitomizes the professionalization of the academy in twentieth-century America.

The attentive reader will note that my own attitudes toward the period are ambivalent. While I regard the narrowing of philosophy's interests as a minor tragedy, much of the Golden Age's wide-ranging speculation was intellectually trivial. The breadth of vision of the classic period was compromised by its lack of restraint; the admirable clarity and precision of professional philosophy is counterbalanced by its narrow scope and the emergence of the narrow professional. Although I think the religious solace James and Royce offered is no longer acceptable, I deplore the *mauvaise foi* of some contemporary philosophers. In part, the book tries to express the complex esthetic feeling I have about these issues.

PART 1

SCOTTISH REALISM AND THE EVOLUTIONARY CONTROVERSY

Chauncey Wright about 1870   Francis Bowen in 1858

Frank Abbot about 1880   John Fiske as a young man

Charles Peirce at Milford

1

CURRENTS OF THOUGHT IN
NINETEENTH-CENTURY CAMBRIDGE

The Unitarian and Transcendentalist Controversies

The cultured classes of nineteenth-century Boston were intensely intellectual. This does not imply, as it would today, that their interests were primarily literary and political; they were also religious. In fact, well-to-do Bostonians were not simply churchgoing and respectable; religion was at the heart of their way of life and theological issues were part of their daily concerns. In the first thirty years of the century, Unitarian religious ideals triumphed over those of Congregationalist Calvinism. The bitter controversy between the two groups occupied both prominent laymen and the large body of clergymen. The major religious dispute concerned the unity or the trinity of the godhead but, more importantly for this discussion, the Unitarians had a moral and social perspective different from that of the Congregationalists.

The product of a more commercial and secular culture, Unitarianism stressed the goodness in man's character and rational or empirical means of sustaining Christian faith. It would be a caricature of Unitarianism, however, to identify it with eighteenth-century Deism. The Unitarians expressed only a qualified optimism in opposing the Calvinists. Unitarianism was a mediating position that avoided both Deistic rationalism and the Calvinist reliance on faith. Good Unitarians did not deny the import of faith; rather, they desired that it be made ever more credible. Miracles were not so much the basis of Christian belief as a further confirmation of it. The scriptures remained essential, but Unitarians subjected them to liberal exegesis molded by nineteenth-century empirical knowledge.

If we consider the scientific views of the Unitarians and their Congregationalist opponents, the differences are clearly matters of degree. The earlier Puritans had interpreted a large class of natural events as divine judgments on human behavior—"special providences"—and therefore no one could explain these events without referring to human conduct. The triumph of the Newtonian model of the universe in the eighteenth century meant that for the nineteenth-century Unitarians this class of events had almost disappeared. Unitarians explained physical occurrences as reflections of universal laws and not as divine rewards or punishments. As Newtonian science became established, there was a growing stress on "natural theology." For religious thinkers, knowledge of God became increasingly dependent on the view that nature was his revelation. That the orderliness of nature implied a first cause was a leading idea among Massachusetts Unitarians.

Of course, natural theology was not new—the Puritans and later Calvinists had conceived of nature as manifesting the deity. And despite decreasing reliance on the supernatural, the reigning Unitarian clerics had not entirely eschewed special providences. Although some of them might question whether God now worked directly in their lives, in the Bible it was plain that he had acted through "secondary causes," for example in Noah's flood. In some cases God had even suspended the laws of nature—as in Christ's walking on water. Miracles, the special acts of God related in the Bible, were still a critical part of the Unitarian system of belief. "Revealed theology" informed divines of the distinctive doctrines of Christianity, of the particular relation of man to God. According to revealed theology, a proper understanding of the New Testament demanded the acceptance of miracles. Scriptural revelation rested on a belief in supernatural intervention.

The Unitarian view suggested two disparate descriptions of nature. Each scientific advance further evidenced the creator's cosmic design and the truths promulgated by natural theology; here, order was the critical concept. The revealed theology sustaining Christian commitment assumed something different: God might suspend the laws of nature at his discretion; it was precisely by a kind of disorder that he revealed his ways to mankind. This inconsistency was initially less vexing than it might seem.

In accepting natural theology, Unitarians believed that nature's laws described the usual mode of action of the divine power; but if the Lord chose, he could express his power in other than conventional ways. Moreover, arguments for natural theology rested on the sciences of physics and astronomy, and their laws were seen to operate in the present. Revealed theology concerned the past and was based on historical documents. Reflecting on the diversity of God's capacities for expressing himself resolved the conflict between these two interpretations of the natural world; the devout rarely questioned whether God had once expressed himself by miracles.[1]

The Unitarians secured control of the religious institutions of eastern Massachusetts in the first quarter of the nineteenth century. But though their victory was capped when the newly-founded Harvard Divinity School emerged as the training ground for their ministry, the Unitarians had no sooner established themselves than they spawned a movement that went beyond what many Unitarians, both clergy and laity, found bearable and that aroused more bitter public argument.[2]

The rise of Transcendentalism is a familiar chapter in American intellectual history. For our purposes we need only to isolate the two criticisms central to the Transcendentalist appraisal of Unitarianism and the locus of the tensions in Unitarian doctrines. For the Transcendentalists religious truth did not depend, as for the Unitarians, on facts—or on tradition or authority for that matter—but on an unerring witness in the soul. Religion transcended the empirical sphere of the senses. For Emerson the faculty of reason had little to do with man's ratiocinative processes or with science as usually understood; reason rather was exercised in feelings and in the emotions. Emerson exaggerated in condemning the "pale negations" of "corpse cold" Unitarianism, but his evaluation summarized the Transcendentalists' belief that Unitarians had lost the aspect of feeling vital to religion.[3]

Emerson was not a consistent expository thinker, but his censure of Unitarianism had obvious consequences. On one hand, Transcendentalists attacked the Unitarian view that empirical knowledge was an essential aid in justifying faith. Emerson was contemptuous of all attempts to ground religion on anything but the intuitive emotional prerogatives of the inner light. On the other hand, but less important to liberal Unitarians, the Transcendentalists attacked the vestiges of Calvinism among the local religious leadership. The miracles for which there was scriptural evidence still counted among Unitarians as the basis for Christian belief about Jesus as the Lord's divine messenger. Through the polemics of Theodore Parker (1810–1860), a gifted exponent of the new religious ideas, the Transcendentalists called into question the revealed theology that Unitarians upheld.

In the 1830s a young German scholar, David Friedrich Strauss (1808–1874), published his *Life of Jesus* and made famous what became known as the higher criticism of the Bible. Scholars like Strauss claimed that the documents which legitimated the revelation of Jesus as the Christ should be subject to the same scrutiny as other historical documents. The conclusion was clear: if Unitarians rejected miracles in the nineteenth century, they must reject the miracles of Biblical times. Strauss effectively extended the action of natural law backward in time and destroyed the theoretical basis for revealed theology.[4]

Although the higher criticism influenced Parker, he was not really concerned with any critique of the gospels based on "scientific" approaches to the study of the past. The Bible might be subject to rough appraisal by historians but why, Parker asked, should Unitarians accept it as an authority at all? Although he did hold that the Bible must be subject to the same skepticism as other works of ancient history—and therefore he could question its miracles—this argument was not critical for Parker, who was a believing Christian. What disturbed him was that Christians should base their faith on this sort of "evidence." In condemning Unitarian revealed theology, Parker and the Transcendentalists were again proclaiming that religion did not rest on our understanding of the world, whether scientific (natural theology) or historical (revealed theology); all nature was miraculous and the appreciation of it as miraculous had no connection with empirical knowledge.[5]

By the middle of the century, Transcendentalism threatened the uneasy coexistence of natural and supernatural modes of reasoning among Unitarians. Conservative Unitarians closer to the older Congregationalism were shocked when Calvinists identified Unitarianism and Transcendentalism as a single non-Christian creed, but Parker's dismissal of scriptural revelation did leave it unclear why his faith was in any sense Christian. Conservatives were quick to call for some doctrinal statement.

Unitarianism had developed as a tolerant and liberalizing faith, but they felt it must have some kind of creed if it were not to degenerate into paganism. Liberal Unitarians were more concerned with the romantic individualism and irrationalism they saw lurking in Transcendentalism than with its critique of the Bible. If Unitarianism were not to become a mystical faith, the liberals contended, it must not discard empirical knowledge as a cornerstone of religion.[6]

My distinction between conservative and liberal Unitarians is perhaps artificial and the labels leave much to be desired. There was no schism among Boston Unitarians—many Transcendentalists even accounted themselves Unitarians—and the notions of *liberal* and *conservative* apply only to the theological accents with which Unitarians spoke. Nonetheless, the response to Transcendentalism increased the tension in the Unitarian marriage of the experiential and the supernatural, and forced progressives more and more to defend their faith empirically.

The Importance of Harvard Philosophy

Many Unitarian laymen were actively engaged in Massachusetts's religious imbroglios, but at the heart of the Unitarian world view was actually a religious philosophy, and Unitarianism had finally to be defended on speculative grounds. In this area both the Boston gentry and its clergy placed their trust in the experts—the philosophers of Harvard College.

Until after the Civil War, philosophy as taught in American schools had a huge significance in the eyes of its practitioners and their supporters. The philosopher connected with an institution was the custodian of certain truths necessary to the successful functioning of civilized society. His job was to convey these truths to the youth who would one day assume positions of leadership. At Harvard, as at many other colleges, philosophic instruction had a practical value greater than other parts of the classical curriculum. The president of the college often taught the final course in moral philosophy in the senior year to insure the insemination of proper beliefs. Schooled in the history of thought and committed to the cultural elite, the philosophers in Cambridge provided the rationale for an entire way of life. Harvard students learned from them the norms of conduct and the justification of the Unitarian view of politics and the arts.

When Transcendentalists attacked the foundation of accepted faith, Unitarian laymen looked to philosophy to buttress the established religion.

The laity were not disappointed. Levi Hedge, James Walker, and Francis Bowen, who controlled speculation at Harvard from the beginning of the nineteenth century until after the Civil War, were acute and able thinkers. A major aspect of the philosophic enterprise for them was interpreting scientific advances and religious doctrines to reconcile competing claims. As philosophic defenders of Unitarianism, they were never mindless adherents of an indefensible creed; they were committed to a scientific, empiricist view of the world and saw no disastrous conflict between it and a moderate and intelligent religion. Adept and knowledgeable in argument, the Harvard thinkers consistently outmaneuvered the Transcendentalists philosophically. Although Emerson and his well-known circle won over a band of converts, the philosophical bases of Unitarianism remained unshaken. While the Unitarian religion itself did not emerge unscathed from the Transcendentalist attack, it persisted as the dominant creed of the Massachusetts leadership through the Civil War, and no small part of its success was due to its worthy philosophical defenders in Cambridge.

The Historical Context of Philosophical Debate

What doctrines did the philosophers espouse? If we consider all American religious movements of the nineteenth century, the views of the numerically unimportant Unitarians were such that many Christians would not have considered them co-religionists. Nonetheless, both the Unitarians and the other denominations that spoke for the socioeconomic elites in various parts of the country found a theoretical rationale in the same philosophy: Scottish realism. This school of thought held great interest for all those in American Protestantism who were concerned with philosophical problems of religion. Scottish doctrines themselves were also the product of a long history.*

*What follows is not meant as an adequate summary of the history of philosophy. It is rather an abbreviated and oversimplified account of the philosophical tradition *as the Cambridge community viewed it*. It is based on the works listed in the Essay on Sources in the section, "History of Philosophy." Appendix 1 also contains relevant material on the philosophers' ideas about their past.

The debate over the sources of knowledge between the rationalists, chiefly Descartes, and the empiricists, Locke, Berkeley, and Hume, had come to a dead end with Hume. Both Descartes and Locke had assumed that the single individual was competent to grasp truths, and that what was indubitable for the individual and, therefore, the only sure basis for knowledge was what was given—the momentarily and immediately present in any instant. These instants in consciousness were somehow internal data and the building blocks of knowledge: sensations or impressions produced by the reactions of the sensory nervous processes— what we saw, smelled, or heard; and images produced by reflection on sensation—memories, imaginings, thoughts, dreams, and so on. For Descartes these instants displayed the entity mind, and mind's self-conscious reflection on its own activity revealed certain principles— "innate ideas"—pertinent to the nature of the world outside of mind. For Locke, mind was only the medium in which the momentarily given presented itself. Locke also held against Descartes that there were no innate ideas; it was impossible for the mind alone to arrive at truths about the world. On the contrary, knowledge came from the immediate contents of the mind—called experience, phenomena, or (discrete) ideas.

Descartes and Locke were representational realists. They believed that a world independent of experience existed and that experience mediated knowledge of it. But Locke's acceptance of the phenomenalistic basis of knowledge and his rejection of innate ideas conflicted with his attempt to assure, as Descartes had, the existence of the external world, the objective world as opposed to the subjective world of appearance. We were presented only with ideas and, for Locke, these were all, ipso facto, presented *to us.* How then could we justify the existence of the non-phenomenal? Descartes relied on indisputable truths about the world which the mind formulated; Locke could rely only on what was experienced, and we never experience the non-phenomenal.

Berkeley took an obvious step: there was no external world, no underlying material substance or matter. All that was was ideal, what was present for minds or minds themselves. On one hand, Berkeley limited the real world to experience. This made the world some grouping of ideas; what existed for minds comprised the world. On the other hand, Berkeley believed that ideas were passive—they passed before the mind. Like Descartes, he believed that there was some sort of intuition—

"notions"—of mind. There were two sorts of ideas: sensations and images. Since all ideas were passive, Berkeley concluded, a mind or spirit more powerful than our own caused the sensations that were forced on our consciousness. This greater spirit ordered and arranged these ideas so that we were able to find our way successfully around the world. Berkeley dismissed the material world as part of a proof for the existence of the deity.

David Hume followed Berkeley. Berkeley's notions of minds, said Hume, were remnants of the Cartesian doctrine of innate ideas and, when Hume exorcised them, he was left merely with a succession of ideas. The phenomenalistic basis common to Descartes and Locke led in Hume to phenomenalism: the mind was only a convenient bundle of ideas, just as Berkeley's so-called external world was a convenient grouping of these phenomena. Most importantly, Hume denied that there was any causal relation among various ideas. Berkeley believed that God's constant activity joined idea to idea, cause to effect. Hume contended that although there might be some power—some material substances—pushing around the ideas he found conjoined, experience never revealed this power. Custom and habit taught us to believe that one kind of experience was the cause of another; examples of various kinds seemed constantly conjoined. Certain "laws of association" based on past experience determined our behavior and our imputations of causality. But we had no reason for believing in cause and effect; we could never justify our faith that the future would resemble the past. This was the problem of induction that Hume bequeathed to succeeding philosophers, but the problem had wider consequences. If we could not ground our faith in induction, the scientific enterprise was irrational. If we could not establish a basis for causality, we must also, as Hume did, renounce religion. The traditional arguments for God collapsed—for example, the "first cause" argument and the "argument from design." The outcome of the rationalist-empiricist debate was a dead end for both religion and science. Neither had any rational basis; neither could warrant belief in either God or the world.

In part Immanuel Kant had designed *The Critique of Pure Reason* to refute Hume. But Kant also adjudicated the claims of empiricists and rationalists concerning the sources of knowledge. He intended to secure a firm base for knowledge in the world of experience while simultaneously avoiding dogmatism about any supra-experiential realm. In Kant's thought, two elements were needed in order to have knowledge of the world: the active constructive powers of mind and the raw data of sense presented to mind. The mind imposed order on raw data, and the product was the "experience" of the world of objects. Mind dynamically structured what we knew so that it could be said that we knew at all.

For Kant, philosophy studied the categorical principles expressed in statements like "Every effect has a cause." Philosophy investigated the nature of these "synthetic *a priori*" propositions whose truth assured that a coherent world of experience was possible; they were necessarily and universally true for all experience and were true independent of experiential corroboration; they expressed the organizing and structural formulas—the categories—by which the mind made experience what it was. We must be justified in applying the categories to the data of sense—and we therefore refuted Hume—for without them we could not constitute experience or render it possible. This was, briefly, the rationale behind what was known as the "deduction" of the categories, the proof that the use made of them in thinking was legitimate and not arbitrary. The deduction assured, said Kant, that Hume's argument about induction was unjustified: we knew that experiences were causally related because causality was involved in the conception of experience.

Kant called his philosophy transcendental, and the only legitimate metaphysics was his own—the examination of the conditions of possible experience and the justification of experiential knowledge. *Transcendent* metaphysics—the attempt to go beyond the limits of experience and make pronouncements about ultimate questions—was impossible. For Kant knowledge was of the phenomenal realm; the world of the noumenal, of the things in themselves, was forever closed to us. We could never know the *Ding an sich*, because the very nature of knowledge involved the activity of mind. To speak of knowing the noumenal was contradictory.

Kant could give no positive answer to a noumenal question like that of the existence of God; at the same time he ruled out a negative answer as well. Moreover, he allowed that whereas the categories were principles constitutive of our knowledge of the phenomenal world, there were other principles that "regulated" within experience our ineradicable tendency to deal with the noumenal. The ideas of God, freedom, and immortality were such regulative concepts; they were ideas toward which knowledge was directed, reminding us that it must always be imperfect. Elsewhere, Kant claimed the regulative principles were "moral postulates" of the rational will which warranted activity; we removed religious and moral concerns from the sphere of knowledge to make way for faith.

This Kantian "constructionalist" position—that existence did not transcend consciousness (and vice versa)—attacked an assumption of all pre-Kantian metaphysics. The dispute between rationalists and empiricists concerned epistemology, the source of knowledge, the way the world was known; the dispute was not primarily metaphysical, over the nature of the real objects. Both rationalists and empiricists agreed that it was at least conceivable that real objects existed independent of consciousness, although there might not be grounds for believing in their existence.

The key to philosophy before Kant was the understanding of representational realism. Confronted only by ideas, we had to find some way to credit the belief that what appeared to us corresponded to what really was. How could we legitimate such a belief? We never got outside our ideas to see if they were caused by the objects we thought caused them or if the ideas were related the way objects were related. The outcome was Hume's dilemma. Kant's deduction of the categories heroically tried to circumvent it: the *Critique* attempted to show that our ways of understanding the world were justified since we had a world only because our ways of understanding were what they were. Representational realism became incoherent: we could not say what it would mean to speak of objects exterior to mind.

Kant shifted discussion for his successors from an epistemological issue—the source of knowledge—to a metaphysical one—the nature of the objects called real.

There was also, however, an epistemological issue on which Kant and his predecessors agreed. Why did we call things the names we called them? We called each of the objects on the shelf a book. Suppose that we said we used the word 'book' as a convenient label to group the things together; the things had nothing in common which justified using the word. This was the epistemological nominalists' position; for them only individuals existed. If we maintained, however, that the things on the shelf had something essential in common—it might be called bookness—that justified using the word 'book' in describing them, we would be epistemological realists: individual things might be real, but "generals" also were real, things like bookness and redness, properties, qualities, or universals. The problem of universals as disputed by epistemological nominalists and epistemological realists concerned the kinds of things known, irrespective of their nature, that is, whether they existed external to consciousness. The British tradition was nominalist, but it might also be argued that nominalism was the position of all modern philosophers from Descartes to Kant. Those who claimed that there were objects independent of consciousness argued that we knew them by means of ideas. And Kant asserted that we never knew things in themselves. None of these thinkers allowed direct knowledge of the world independent of mind. If they were right, we knew only ideas which we associated for various purposes; but ideas were individual existents; accordingly, all modern philosophy was nominalistic. Only on a philosophical basis that did not limit us to the world of individual consciousness would it be possible to believe in epistemological realism, that kinds of things like generals existed. Only if we got directly to the world beyond individual consciousness could we learn if universals existed.

It was one of the ironies of the history of thought that the intent of *The Critique of Pure Reason* was to give a death blow to all systems of metaphysics professing to extend human knowledge beyond experience. For although Kant's German successors—Fichte, Schelling, Hegel, and Schopenhauer—claimed to copy his methods and principles, they all developed philosophies of the absolute which purported to transcend experience and reveal the secrets of the world beyond the realm of sense. The absolute idealists played on the ambiguity of Kant's *Ding an sich*. Mind ordered reality. Correct. But what was this something that mind ordered? Orthodox Kantians did not even allow the question, for the concept of existence was coherent only when applied in the phenomenal order; they could not make sense of the notion of the noumenal existing. But it was then plausible to argue that if they could not conceive of that which mind ordered, it was unnecessary. Mind constructed the world of experience from mind alone; mind was its own raw material.

For Kant, I must conceive the phenomena which I did not now sense as linked in some definable unity that connected them with my present experience. For what was now happening to me I viewed as merely an instance of a process of experience including all physical facts; I also viewed the experiences of everyone else in a unity connected with my present experience—they were all possible experiences of mine and therefore possessed a unity that was the correlate of the unity of my own self. This was, for Kant, just what thinking a world of objects in space and time involved. He regarded all human experience as belonging to a single system, a single unity of possible experience. This "virtual unity" of the consciousness of a single self Kant called the Transcendental Unity of Apperception. For him it was a formal presupposition of the theory of knowledge; for his successors it became a metaphysically knowable entity—an absolute self—and when the *Ding an sich* vanished, this self defined the world.

The Scottish Position and Harvard Thought

The Germans had usurped Kant's methods to go beyond his limits. The Harvard philosophers held that a similar usurpation occurred in the United States where those who came to Kant by way of Coleridge and Carlyle adopted the name Transcendentalists; but Emerson and his circle were really *transcendent* metaphysicians. To circumvent Emerson, the Harvard thinkers adapted the views of Kant to Scottish realism, the "philosophy of common sense."

The Scottish position developed in Aberdeen, Glasgow, and Edinburgh as the first competent British attempt to refute Hume and renew a tradition of Lockeian empiricism. Thomas Reid (1710–1796) and Dugald Stewart (1753–1828) were the two earliest and historically best known advocates of these doctrines, but by the time of the Transcendentalist controversy Harvard thinkers considered Sir William Hamilton (1788–1856) their champion. Hamilton was a man of vast and cosmopolitan learning and was important in making German thought relevant to philosophic debate in Britain. His reputation in the United States derived in part from the recognition that he had brought together Kant and Reid in an attack not only on skepticism but also on claims to supra-empirical knowledge.[7]

Kant and the Scots had much in common: they both attempted to circumvent the religious and the scientific nihilism to which Hume had brought philosophy, and both sought to avoid dogmatism about meta-

physical speculation transcending experience. Hume's conclusions followed from his premise that we were directly aware only of phenomena.
He then went on to argue that the phenomena never revealed causal
connections. In reply, Kant maintained that Hume's notions of phenomena and of causality were incorrect. Causality was a necessary category
of the mind. Although we knew nothing of things in themselves, we
could be sure of relations in the phenomenal world: *it* was a product of
the activity of mind on the data of sense. In refuting Hume, the Scots
denied that we were directly aware only of the contents of consciousnesses. Then, rejecting the representational realism of Descartes and
Locke, they contended that we perceived objects as they are in themselves
and, therefore, as they really interacted. This was Scottish presentational
or "natural" realism.* Kant refuted Hume by disowning his definitions,
Reid and Stewart by disavowing his premise.

This agreement on a common enemy, however, left room for dispute:
did we or did we not know about the noumenal realm, that of things in
themselves? Kant said no; the Scots said yes. Sir William Hamilton tried
to adjudicate this quarrel. He held that knowledge was relative to our
mental faculties. The knowable phenomenon Hamilton called an effect,
and the ground of its reality or its cause the noumenon. The noumenon
must remain unknown. The doctrine of the relativity of knowledge
implied that in knowing, something known (the phenomenon) coexisted
with something unknown (the noumenon).

Hamilton did not understand the distinction between phenomenal and
noumenal to coincide with the distinction between ego and non-ego.
The relativity of knowledge did not mean that the objects of knowledge
were dependent on consciousness. Knowledge consisted of the effects of
noumena, said Hamilton, but it did not follow that these were effects
on us. The "secondary qualities" of the objects of knowledge—for
example, color—were effects of the noumenal world *on us*: they were
essentially connected to consciousness. But the "primary qualities"—for
example, extension—were simply effects *of the noumena*: we immediately

---

*The use of the phrase 'presentational realism' here creates terminological problems.
Scottish realism was not clearly a metaphysical *or* epistemological doctrine. The Scots
believed that things existed as they appeared to an individual, independent of that individual's consciousness. But did things exist independently of all consciousness, that is, was
natural realism metaphysical realism? And what kinds of things existed, for instance, did
generals exist? There were no clear Scottish answers to these questions.

cognized what was external to consciousness, although we still had no knowledge of things as they are in themselves; we knew only their effects. This was Hamilton's version of natural realism: we knew directly what was exterior to mind. We had knowledge of the non-ego (primary qualities) *as immediate as* our knowledge of our own sensations (secondary qualities), and only through phenomena of both sorts were the noumenal (non-ego and ego) known at all. Matter and mind in themselves were not known except as the two real causes or necessary substrata of the phenomena. This union of Kant and Locke—the hero of the Scots—was Hamilton's pivotal idea for philosophers in the United States.

Hamilton also proclaimed what he called the Law of the Conditioned. For Kant it was problematical to speculate on the existence of noumena or on the possibility of their intellectual apprehension. Neither the conditions of possible experience nor the data of sense allowed us to assert or deny anything about the noumenal. Not so for Hamilton. Those possibilities which experience and its conditions determined, he called the Conditioned. What neither possible experience nor intellectual apprehension could conceive was the Unconditioned. For example, we could not conceive the whole of space as either limited or unlimited; knowledge of the nature of space was beyond our understanding. Nonetheless, the two possibilities contradicted one another, and hence one must be true, although we could not know which. The Law of the Conditioned stated that all that could be positively thought, the conditioned, "lies between two opposite poles of thought [the two inconditionates of the unconditioned], which, as exclusive of each other, cannot, on the principles of identity and contradiction, both be true, but of which, on the principle of excluded middle, the one or the other must." One of two alternatives which embraced assertions beyond what was relative (that is, knowledge) must be true although we could never know which one and could conceive of neither as possible. Hamilton went beyond the limits set by Hume and in a sense beyond his own relativism: we knew that one of the inconditionates was true. But Hamilton stopped short of dogma: he asserted nothing positive about the inconditionates.[8]

Because of his particular variety of empiricism, Hamilton became essential to Massachusetts's Unitarianism. For nineteenth-century thinkers, 'empiricism' and 'skepticism' were nebulous words. All used 'empiricism' to describe the British thinkers, who claimed that the source of knowledge was the senses or experience, but Hume was a "skeptical" empiricist—he limited our knowledge to the discrete and momentary data of sense. Indeed, for Cambridge philosophers, 'skepticism' was a word of reproach applied to thinkers suspicious of religious claims: despite Hume's undercutting the warrant for all knowledge, "skeptics" who took Hume as their source of insight often attacked religion while defending a mechanistic, scientific view of the world. "Skeptics" were often materialistic: they dismissed the religious kind of supra-phenomenalistic knowledge and yet clung to another, that of a supra-phenomenalistic world of material atoms that experience could not warrant. Less rigid thinkers of this kind became known as agnostics, withholding judgment about religion while accepting science. Almost all philosophers carelessly gave the opprobrious labels "subjectivism" or "solipsism" to something closer to Hume's position, and tried to pin them on their opponents. Subjectivism was associated with the idea that one could not get beyond the states of consciousness of the self; solipsism that only the individual self existed.

Philosophers at Harvard thought that Hamilton had adopted a more acceptable empiricism, one that asserted that we had knowledge of the phenomenal world of primary and secondary qualities but not of the noumenal. Hamilton's Harvard followers believed in intuitions—undeniable claims philosophers could make—but they also proudly stated that they were empiricists. They based their philosophy on observations that men made in everyday life and that the historical record at any time had transmitted—the ordinary evidence of the senses. The Harvard Unitarians found their empiricism compatible with Hamiltonian doctrine. On one hand, Hamilton allowed a significant place for the realm of phenomena yet did not assert that it was the only realm. On the other hand, Hamilton limited speculation about the noumenal world; he gave the Harvard philosophers a weapon in their fight against the obscurantist doctrines of the Transcendentalists. Simultaneously, Hamilton's insistence on the unconditioned or unknowable demonstrated God's transcendence and the need for scriptural revelation.

Until the time of the Civil War, Scottish ideas were undisputed both at Harvard and in the academic world at large. Despite the popularity of Transcendentalism, the cultured people of New England believed that science and religion were harmonious, that civilized men could avoid both

irrationalism and skeptical empiricism. American thinkers found formidable opposition to their beliefs only in technical philosophy, and the
opposition was in England and not in the United States. John Stuart Mill
(1806–1873) was a talented thinker with wide and sympathetic tastes;
after the publication of his *System of Logic* in 1843, it became apparent that
Mill was a powerful defender of Hume's sort of empiricism. Stimulated
by August Comte's "positive" philosophy, Mill took an austere attitude
toward religion, and few considered him a Christian. His simultaneous
emphasis on the world of science made the word 'positivism'—applied
broadly to Mill, Comte, and others—a term of abuse and contempt in
many circles. In short, the Unitarians interpreted Mill as a champion of
skeptical empiricism; he represented an anti-religious extreme.

In Britain the philosophic dispute centered on the conflicting ideas of
Hamilton and Mill. The controversy reached its height in 1865 when Mill
published his *Examination of Sir William Hamilton's Philosophy*. Mill was
at his intellectual zenith, Hamilton had been dead for almost ten years,
and victory went easily to Mill. The *Examination* damaged Hamilton's
reputation and the position on which it rested. Writing in a masterly
polemical style, Mill exposed the shortcomings and tensions of the
Scottish compromise. If his work lacked sympathy and even justice, the
mature formulation of his own position was strong enough to make most
readers overlook its logical weaknesses. In any event, Mill was most
effective as a critic on just those issues important to American philosophers.
He did not grasp Hamilton's distinction between our knowledge of
primary and secondary qualities, of the effects of the noumena and the
effects of the noumena on us. In this misapprehension Mill was aided by
the scattered and unsystematic quality of Hamilton's writings and the
frequent vaguenesses or even contradictions in his thought. The misapprehension, however, allowed Mill to ridicule what appeared on its face
to be a major failing of Hamilton's position. If knowledge was relative to
the phenomena, Mill asked, how could Hamilton defend his realism, a
claim to direct awareness of noumena? On Mill's analysis, Hamilton's
relativism seemed plainly inconsistent with his realism. Moreover, Mill
tore to pieces Hamilton's Law of the Conditioned; he argued that ignorance of logic had befuddled Hamilton. Hamilton said we had no knowledge of the inconditionates, but then assumed that the principle of
contradiction applied to them. This was a principle, Mill went on, which

on Hamilton's view could only apply to the phenomenal, yet Hamilton used it to show that something must be true of the noumenal.[9]

The critique of Hamilton had a major impact on religious thinkers in America, but the effect is difficult to describe precisely. Hamilton's followers might have warded off Mill's assault had it been all they had to contend with. But while the Civil War undermined the social basis for orthodox optimism, intellectuals in America acquainted themselves with Charles Darwin's *Origin of Species*, published in 1859, six years before Mill's book. Mill's attack on Hamilton reopened debate on epistemological premises. In passing, Darwin contributed to this debate, but more importantly he seemed to deny core religious beliefs directly and to smash all conventional ideas. When the Civil War ended and the science and religion debate began in earnest in America, Mill's denunciation of Hamilton proved a minor injury to his defenders in the United States: Darwin had already dealt them a death blow.

Darwin and His Impact

To explain the development of life on earth Darwin postulated two principles. According to the principle of fortuitous variation, offspring exhibited slight variations from the form of their parents. Because these variations were inheritable, there would be an endless proliferation of forms diverging in every way from the original ancestors. The result was the diversity of species present in the world. To explain the direction of the known succession of these forms, Darwin introduced various means of selection, chief among them a second principle. Following Malthus, Darwin believed that organisms reproduced at a rate far exceeding the increase of their food supply and other vital necessities; a competition, a literal struggle for existence, ensued for the limited necessities available. In the struggle some of the inherited variations paid off and some did not. As Darwin put it, the environment, viewed historically, selected those organisms that were well adapted; they survived and reproduced their kind; the others were eliminated.

Darwin was not the first to hold a view of this kind, nor was his work free from ambiguities, evasions, and real scientific problems—the time span he required was embarrassingly great and his explanation of the transmission of traits equivocal. But the hypothesis accounting for the origin and growth of species was persuasive and cogently reasoned, and a massive array of evidence backed it. There was a controversy over Darwin's theory but the scientific community rapidly accepted its chief tenets. Additionally, the theory lent support to a wide and amorphous set of social, economic, and philosophical doctrines that were vaguely "evolutionary," "developmental," or "Darwinian." In this sense the theory was like other fertile works of the human mind; it spawned any number of offspring and the scientists propounding the theory often looked upon the offspring as legitimate. (In discussing these doctrines, I have not explicitly defined my use of the above words, but have rather let my discussion display the family resemblance among the ideas claiming the theory as a near ancestor.)

So far as the Cambridge scientific community was concerned—and so far as many American naturalists were concerned—the scientific debate was the one that took place between Asa Gray, professor of natural history and director of Harvard's herbarium, and Louis Agassiz, its professor of zoology and geology, director of its Museum of Comparative Anatomy, and a man of immense prestige and learning. The year before the *Origin* appeared, Agassiz wrote an important article, "Essay on the Classification of the Animal Kingdom," in which he defended the special divine creation of species. After Darwin published, Agassiz became his chief American opponent. Gray welcomed Darwin's book to America with a favorable review in the *American Journal of Science and Arts.* Although not convinced that the theory was beyond criticism or its spiritual implications bearable, he worked to insure it a fair hearing, to explain Darwin's idea to the general public, and to convince opponents that the evolutionary hypothesis did not entail religious blasphemy.

Although Agassiz believed that species remained fixed and unchanging and bore no organic relation to one another, his distaste for the developmental hypothesis did not stem from conventional religious views. Rather, he framed his scientific theories within an idealistic philosophy of nature that he had formulated as a young man in Europe (he had been born in Switzerland). Every specific form of plant and animal represented "a thought of God" at the moment of creation; structural affinities among organisms were "associations of ideas in the Divine Mind," not evidences of common ancestry. Believing additionally that God occasionally annihilated old species and created new ones, Agassiz argued that those who objected to repeated acts of special creation ought to consider "that no progress can be made without repeated acts of thinking." Many scholars thought Agassiz's theories peculiar, but his scholarly influence made him a powerful foe of Darwin, and the more conventionally religious seized on his condemnation of evolution and welcomed his battle against Gray. The resources of the deity, Agassiz exclaimed, "cannot be so meagre that in order to create a human being endowed with reason, He must change a monkey into a man."

Gray was less certain of his ground. He became more and more convinced of the truth of Darwin's ideas and helped to convert the scientific community but, although he relinquished cruder versions of natural theology throughout his career, he maintained a religious view. The basis of science, he contended, was faith in an order: without this faith we had no way of understanding the workings of nature. Gray could not sever this faith from a similar faith in an "ordainer." This last faith was the basis of religion: "To us a fortuitous Cosmos is simply inconceivable. The alternative is a designed Cosmos." Because the pursuit of science presupposed a spiritual understanding of the world, it followed that Darwin's theory must also. Although specific adaptations in the natural order lacked evidence of design, Gray asserted, design pervaded the universe as a whole. Chance and contingency were not all there was to Darwin for they operated in such a way that we comprehended their action. In the grand theme of the development of life in the universe there was meaning and purpose, and Gray concluded that natural variation, the struggle for life, and natural selection were only "the order or mode" in which the Creator "in his own perfect wisdom, sees fit to act."[10]

Gray convinced many theologically committed scientists that they could accept both Darwinism and a chastened religion. Agassiz implied that they had to choose. Although he fought the *Origin* with all his resources, when he died in 1873 even his own students had rejected his views. Among scientists some accommodation to the basic principles of evolutionary hypothesizing came quickly.

In those philosophical and religious circles in which Unitarian and Scottish doctrine had come together, there was no such sanguine interpretation of Darwinism. And what happened to Unitarian philosophy exemplified what happened in all religious centers defended by Scottish realism. The debate between science and religion had much graver import for Unitarians than did the squabbles with Congregationalists and Transcendentalists. While the earlier controversies were deep and irreconcilable, they assumed some religious orientation among the participants. Many defenders of Darwin acknowledged no creed at all. Dismissing all meaning to life after death, these atheists rejected religion in toto. Moreover, the Harvard philosophers had effectively blocked the speculative pretensions of Emerson's group, and this achievement had helped to limit the Transcendentalists' religious power. But the reaction against Transcendentalism had oriented Boston clergymen to defend certain sorts of natural and revealed theologies. It concentrated energy on the precise ways thinkers could use these modes of religious reasoning to preserve the conventional faith; it locked Unitarianism into certain patterns of argumentation. But Darwin's hypothesis was strongest against just the arguments that had proved effective against the Transcendentalists. First, along with the higher criticism, it threatened to destroy revealed theology. Indeed the developmental theory substituted blasphemy for miracle. The suspension of natural laws no longer revealed divine purpose; rather, their continuous action produced man from primeval slime. Second, Darwin made the increasingly prominent natural theology unacceptable. Theologians had reasoned from Newton's clockwork universe to a majestic orderly deity. Darwin's order was different:

> he postulated an incredibly wasteful process of random proliferation and ruthless extinction. In place of the benevolent harmony in which all nature conspires to the happiness of the creation, Darwin presented "nature red in tooth and claw." If indeed order bespeaks an orderer, if like produces like, if natural law is but the mode of the divine action, if all effects are intended, what conclusion followed respecting a deity who would design the world on the model of a slaughter house where most perished horribly, where the "saving remnant" was saved by chance adaptation alone, and where the meek would never live to inherit anything? For those who had made the natural theology the foundation of their reconciliation of religion and science, the Darwinian theory suddenly opened the abyss beneath their feet.[11]

The 1860s witnessed the destruction of the philosophical basis of all American religious orthodoxy. But Darwin routed Unitarian philosophy more easily than he did other elite religious groups, and did so mainly because its fight with the Transcendentalists had yoked it to an untenable empiricism. Transcendentalism had made the Unitarians base their religion on a harmonious universe which science evidenced. But evolutionary science was different. Unitarian thinkers could not absorb it, and when scientists accepted Darwin, the Unitarians had no options. He conquered them so quickly and completely that posterity soon forgot them.

The Transcendentalists, without either institutional or scientific support, benefited little from the destruction of Unitarian speculation. As Transcendentalism's exponents grew older, they were not able to transmit their beliefs to a new generation, and their dismissal of science weakened their appeal even for sympathetic intellectuals. More importantly, Darwinism allied itself to the new skeptical empiricism, producing potent anti-religious and anti-Christian world views. Although some thinkers argued that the empiricism of Hume and Mill led to skepticism in science and religion equally, many of the proponents of this empiricism rejected only religion. They asserted that investigation of phenomena showed that the phenomena reflected a universe of ultimate material particles whose relations were described by the laws of science. Some nineteenth-century Humeans argued that Darwin supported this view: he had shown that certain simple combinations of elements could evolve into more complex combinations, death bringing the dissolution of the most complex. The Unitarian thinkers had to fight both the Darwinian materialists and those thinkers who accepted a mechanistic view of the universe but who saw the evolutionary mechanism working in a purposeful direction. Both groups were put into the overcrowded camp of "positivists."

The most important anti-Christian religious thinker was the Englishman Herbert Spencer (1820–1903). Spencer had used evolutionary modes of thought before Darwin to speculate on the nature of the physical, organic, and social world. As people accepted Darwin's theories, Spencer became a philosophic personage and had a vogue in the United States. Basing his speculation on encyclopedic learning and crude analogy, he presented a vision of the universe in which all things had evolved or were evolving according to one progressive formula. The cosmos was part of this evolutionary process, as was the development of the forms of life. Evolution continued within human societies, and from the apogee of Anglo-Saxon civilization, Spencer dispensed wisdom about all the lower orders. In addition to fitting Darwin to an optimistic world view, Spencer even had a modest place for religion. He examined evolutionary processes in the phenomenal world; we knew nothing of the noumenal world, his famous Unknowable, except that it was the ground or cause of the phenomena. Although Spencer did not address the problem of immortality, he managed to write about the Unknowable positively enough that it could be identified with God, or at the very least taken as a surrogate for the deity.

Spencer was frequently denounced as an infidel, but in truth his position was a declension of Kantian religious thought, and to many thinkers the weakness of the Spencerian synthesis of science and religion was its flimsy philosophic support. *The Critique of Pure Reason* was non-committal on claims about the noumenal. In a similar vein, Hamilton argued that we had a minimal sort of knowledge of what transcended our powers of conception. However they appraised his agnosticism, philosophers did not believe Hamilton to be the equal of Kant. In Spencer, they urged, philosophical acumen reached its nadir: in the vagaries of the Unknowable he proposed a ground for religious belief while at the same time attending to the scientific realm where he observed universal evolutionary laws. We must not underestimate Spencer's impact, however, simply because he never sustained a reputation among philosophers. The scope of his work was challenging, and he was an important negative influence; many philosophers sharpened their ideas by demolishing Spencer's.[12]

Pragmatism and the University

With the fundamentals of belief in doubt, the crucial problem for American thinkers was a new understanding of death.[13] Somehow, after Darwin, they had to give existence a meaning that justified human endeavor. Briefly put, the successor to Unitarian philosophy was pragmatism, a set of doctrines able to wed evolutionary science to a religious world view. It had much in common with Scottish ideas, but its philosophical backbone was a sophisticated comprehension of the respectable Kant and not the tarnished Hamilton or the vulgar Spencer;

and it linked Darwin to Kant. The pragmatic analysis of ideas as plans of action applied evolutionary thought to the realm of the mind: theories, beliefs, and ideas were ways of responding to the environment, and they could change over time. In the elaboration of these notions lay the salvation of religion. True ideas were the ones that competed well, that survived and worked. When William James argued that religious ideas enabled us to live well—that they were successful—he meant that they were true.

The story of the fall of one orthodoxy in Cambridge and the rise of another is also a story of institutional change at Harvard. Given the role of the Harvard philosophers in the mid-nineteenth century, the assault on established religion that became critical in the 1860s and 1870s had repercussions beyond those connected with learned disputation. The fight against "positivism" was also a fight for the souls of young men, and control of university positions might have vast consequences for the course of American culture. The normal personnel changes of institutional life took on a different significance. Whereas doctrinal differences had always been significant in determining university appointment, events now forced the Harvard authorities to deal with thinkers who had no religious doctrine. Moreover, as the American college expanded in the last three decades of the nineteenth century, the importance of institutions for the practice of philosophy increased. Philosophers in the schools became the only philosophers, and affiliation with a university became necessary to all those who wished to spend their lives in contemplation. An amateur renegade like Emerson would not gain a following in the new age. In order to understand the successful ideas we must also understand the circumstances attendant to the maturation of the men who espoused them.

2

FRANCIS BOWEN

AND UNITARIAN ORTHODOXY

Appraisals of Bowen and His Philosophy

The Unitarian philosophers have received limited attention from both historians and subsequent philosophers. The Transcendentalists' exciting synthesis of idealistic nature philosophy and public concern has attracted historians at the expense of the conservative and stuffy Unitarians. If philosophers mention the predecessors of Royce and James at all, it is only to disparage the provincial and unsophisticated nature of mid-nineteenth century American thought. One thinker, however, survived from the earlier period to the later Golden Age, and Francis Bowen, Alford Professor of Philosophy from 1853 to 1889, was neither provincial nor unsophisticated. As a historian of modern philosophy he has had no superior at Harvard; his writing was penetrating, deft, and witty; his own constructive work demonstrated that he was a shrewd and able defender of the philosophic underpinnings of Unitarianism; and he left his mark on his students and associates—Chauncey Wright, Charles Peirce, and William James. The contempt shown him by posterity epitomizes the treatment accorded to theorizing that could not meet the challenge of Darwinism.

Bowen's Career

Bowen was born in Charlestown, Massachusetts, in 1811 and, forced to be self-supporting early in life, he clerked in a publishing house and taught school before graduating summa cum laude from Harvard in 1833. Two years later he returned to Cambridge as tutor in intellectual philosophy and political economy, initiating a career that would not end for fifty-four years.

Bowen's life typified the Unitarian and Transcendentalist interest in human affairs. As editor of the *North American Review* from 1843 to 1854 he made the journal a leading organ of informed opinion. During the same period he wrote a series of biographies of American patriots, published an edition of Virgil, and began the study of history and economics. Outspoken in his views and aggressive in promoting them, he denounced the popular Hungarian revolution on historical grounds;[1] for his trouble Harvard denied him its McLean Professorship of History in 1850. His concern with American political culture came to fruition later in the standard translation of Tocqueville's *Democracy in America*.[2] Moreover, worried about American subservience to British economic thought, he urged the publication of "an American treatise of Political Economy . . . that may form a text-book for legislators and statesmen."[3] When no satisfactory volume was forthcoming, he produced a comprehensive work in 1856, *The Principles of Political Economy Applied to the Conditions, Resources, and the Institutions of the American People*. With a few important modifications Bowen was a classical economist linking successful capitalist enterprise to all the moral virtues and defending property rights as essential to civilization. He argued for laissez faire principles because selfish behavior, through the "contrivance" of the deity and a "wise and benevolent arrangement of Providence," led to the public good. Bowen's modifications concerned application of free trade principles between two nations unequal in economic strength, and he advocated an American protective system to offset England's manufacturing advantage. A protective policy was justified only because the United States' fledgling industries were vulnerable; impairing them would leave the nation with a lowered standard of living, dependent on Britain. The United States ought to adopt free trade as soon as its manufacturing system was economically strong enough.[4] Bowen acquired a national reputation as an economist, and some of his contemporaries mistakenly assumed he was simply a high-tariff spokesman. But one of his last public disputes revealed his obstinate integrity: asked for an endorsement of the Republican platform in 1888, he condemned the GOP tariff as a tyranny crushing native industries and taxing the necessities of life.[5]

Bowen's public career was not devoted primarily to economics, however, but to a defense of Christian theism against various forms of agnosticism, materialism, and heresy. For forty years, Bowen wrote toward the end of his life, such a defense had been the thrust of his work. The degraded view of man advanced in "infidel speculations" not only attacked religion but also "those institutions of property, the family, and the state, on which the whole fabric of modern civilization is based." Especially after the publication of the *Origin of Species* he feared the practical consequences of the "dirt-philosophy" and warned that a society "not based upon Christianity is big with the elements of its own destruction."[6]

Unlike the Transcendentalists, Bowen had a consistent philosophy to support his wide concerns. In fact, the Christian theism he considered essential to the social order was virtually equivalent to the philosophy he elaborated from the 1830s through the 1880s. As a young Harvard instructor he wrote a series of articles in the *Christian Examiner* and *North American Review* aimed at discrediting Transcendentalism after Emerson delivered his radical Divinity School Address in 1838. As editor of the *Review* he continued to uphold the Unitarian philosophy and, although he failed to become McLean Professor, his appointment to the Alford chair in 1853 gave him another prominent position from which to disseminate his ideas. In part because of his losing war against Darwinism, Bowen's reputation as a philosopher did not survive the 1860s. He was, moreover, disenchanted with the new ways that Charles Eliot brought to Harvard after 1869. His standing in Cambridge rapidly diminished as he became known for his dated anti-evolutionary philosophic opinions, his opposition to the novel Harvard elective system, and a reliance in his teaching on the older "manuals of instruction" containing barren biographical histories of philosophy and careful orthodox summaries of primary work.[7]

Bowen had strong convictions about teaching. He thought of philosophy as a science, a body of knowledge, whose (Christian) truths must become the property of students. Forced to adopt the "professorial mode of teaching" when it became de rigueur at Harvard, he reckoned it futile. It consisted, he said, of getting up a course of lectures and essentially repeating them year after year; he felt that no one was capable of preparing new lectures every year. He saw the purpose of teaching as the inculcation of information, and this required "the regular use of a text-book or manual of instruction."[8]

The lecture system enabled Eliot's faculty to teach hundreds of students at once and so, indirectly, permitted Eliot to hire more teachers and offer more courses. The result brought into existence the elective program, which allowed undergraduates to choose their own areas of study and to specialize in a variety of fields. As Bowen opposed lecturing, he opposed electives. Part of his argument concerned the merits of "classical" over "utilitarian" studies but what really troubled him was that specialization subverted the proper end of a university education. The goal should be to develop the intellect and form character through general liberal studies (that is, a study of western culture centering on the classics). Bowen doubted that the various specializations could survive if they were isolated and pursued only by their votaries. He was convinced that no one could become a votary without "that very general culture of mind which is nowhere attempted but in college." Young specialists might doom themselves "like each class of artisans in a big workshop, to spend their lives intellectually in making the eighteenth part of a pin."[9]

Bowen's practice reflected his ideas. In addition to preparing editions of Stewart and Hamilton for student use, he wrote four college manuals, one in political economy and three in philosophy. They were all didactic and systematic with synopses of many thinkers, copious extracts from the works of authorities, and confutations of the infidels. Bowen was also wearisome in propagandizing for Christian theism and laborious in his defense of religious fundamentals. Under the best of circumstances he probably would not have been a stimulating teacher. Additionally, during the 1850s and 1860s financial troubles afflicted Harvard. Bowen was constrained to manage most of the instruction in philosophy and teach political economy as well, then on its way to becoming a distinct field. Locked into Harvard's rigid educational system, he spent ten to fifteen hours a week on drill and recitation and at least one morning in listening to essays. In addition to marking essays, computing grades, and administering the college, Bowen delivered various courses of lectures each year.[10]

But to stop here is to shortchange the man. Reid, Stewart, and Hamilton were staples of the curriculum, but two years after Mill published his *Examination*, Bowen was offering a senior elective course on the book. Although the final examinations in this course asked students to refute many of Mill's points, at its best—before and after the economic constraints of 1855–1865—the teaching of philosophy at Harvard was more than indoctrination. The students were acquainted with "a variety of intricate systems and theories, which from age to age have tasked the most acute intellects."[11] The systems and theories treated in detail and treated with favor were those of non-skeptical thinkers, but since these were the thinkers with a hold on the truth, it was in part legitimate that the overseers should describe the purpose of instruction as imbuing students "with the philosophical spirit."[12] When philosophical instruction expanded under Bowen's auspices after the Civil War, he did not ignore controversial ideas. In the early 1870s he introduced courses in German philosophy, mainly Kant, despite the apprehension of many New England newspapers that this would promote agnosticism at Harvard.[13] His textbook "synopses" were skilled and knowledgeable interpretations of modern philosophy; his citations of "authorities" invariably located the heart of philosophic argument; and his "confutations" were detailed critiques that never attacked strawmen.

Bowen's Empiricism

Though Bowen tended to enlist in educational lost causes, his most unfortunate commitment was to an anti-evolutionary religious philosophy. To see why the *Origin* posed such a threat to him, we must investigate his thought as it developed from his assault on Emerson to his diatribes against Darwin in the 1860s and 1870s. But it is not always easy to know what Bowen believed. His texts were no simple compendia of the conventional Unitarian position. The core of his thought was empirical argumentation for natural theology; revealed theology interested him little. While Scottish realism and Hamiltonianism attracted his attention, he used rather than parroted them. During a period that historians have characterized as dominated by "moral philosophy," Bowen—like his Harvard successors—elaborated the technical rationale for practical beliefs. More importantly, his own views were submerged in historical erudition from his earliest writings, papers collected in 1842 under the title *Critical Essays on a Few Subjects Connected with the History and Present Condition of Speculative Philosophy*. This interest was still apparent in his *Modern Philosophy from Descartes to Schopenhauer and Hartmann* (1877), the finest history of modern philosophy produced by a Harvard scholar. He was so steeped in the history of philosophy that we must extrapolate his ideas from his exegeses of the European tradition that nourished his own thinking.

In the *Critical Essays* Bowen's hero was Locke, but Locke seen from the nineteenth century and analyzed in light of Bowen's belief that the central problem of philosophy was to escape skepticism. We had to find a ground for asserting that the external world really existed, that experience accurately replicated the way things were, that the world was as it appeared in consciousness. Bowen gave Locke high marks for his empiricism—his use of the inductive method and reliance on sensory evidence—and for his metaphysical realism. Locke asserted the independent existence of the external world and used common-sense empiricism—"moral" reasoning for Bowen—to justify this assertion. Locke went wrong in his representationalism, "the great mistake of the philosophy of the eighteenth century" (148). By having ideas mediate knowledge of objects, Bowen claimed, Locke made skepticism possible. Once Locke restricted himself to his own consciousness, the external world had to vanish. The further tradition of British empiricism, which Bowen saw as properly proceeding from Locke to the Scottish realists, corrected this aspect of Locke (6–30). Bowen did not, however, explore in any detail his own presentational realism. It was also clear that Bowen's empiricism had room for the intuitive reasoning characterizing Scottish thought: there were certain propositions inwrought in our minds which we saw to be immediately true and true about the world as it is because they were necessary to all experience and their contradiction inconceivable. Some such propositions assured us that the world presented to us in our everyday experience really existed as presented.

As amended by the Scots, Bowen's Locke had refuted the Cartesian doctrine of innate ideas and anticipated what was correct in Kant. Descartes held the mind alone capable of ascertaining the truth of some propositions about the external world. In contradistinction, Locke contended that all knowledge came *through* experience. But in maintaining that experience was the source of knowledge, Locke did not commit himself to believing that knowledge came *only from* experience—he was not a skeptical empiricist. For Locke the mind was the vehicle or avenue of knowledge. Its active constructive nature shaped experience to give us knowledge. Accordingly, in assuming that the mind acting in a vacuum could give us knowledge of the world external to mind, Descartes was wrong. Kant was right in urging that all knowledge began with experience although it did not derive solely from experience, Bowen went on, but Locke said it first. For Bowen (and his Locke) the mind furnished concepts through which we thought about the world, but these concepts merely replicated for us things as they are in themselves, and our intuitive knowledge guaranteed this correspondence between the way the world was and the way it appeared to us via our concepts. In assuming that our conceptual apparatus applied only to the phenomenal world, Kant went off the track (128–30).

Bowen respected Kant—his respect grew over the years—but he always maintained that Kant's strictures on our knowledge of the noumenal world were incoherent. Kant declared that things in themselves, absolutely incognizable, had a real existence apart from experience and that we must distinguish between them and the phenomena. But if noumena were incognizable, asked Bowen, how did Kant know they were distinct from the phenomena? And if they were real, how could they be real except as phenomena?[14] Only a gnarled thinker like Kant, Bowen claimed, could infer the non-existence of space, time, and causality from our inability to conceive their non-existence, could believe they belonged to the mind because we could not imagine their annihilation (302).

Rather than answering Hume, Kant inadvertently had carried philosophy to an even deeper Pyrrhonism. In urging that the noumenal world, the world of things as they are in themselves, was something we never knew, Kant extended the sphere of Hume's arguments, generalizing them to cover the whole field of knowledge; truth about the world was not only unattained but unattainable (301–02). The history of philosophy after Kant, Bowen believed, substantiated this pessimistic appraisal and justified his call for a return to Locke's empiricism. The *a priori* speculations of Kant's successors were monstrous forms of egoism; the German idealists were solipsists, even if absolute solipsists. Moreover, their idealism reduced religion to a matter of conscience or defended it on easily controvertible *a priori* grounds (101–10).

Although he adhered to this position throughout his life, in his youth Bowen's main concern was the impact of the post-Kantians in the United States. Their religion of conscience and *a priori* flights of fancy effected "a forced marriage . . . between poetry and philosophy, the latter borrowing from the former a license to indulge in conceit and highly figurative expressions, and giving in return an abstruse and didactic form to the other's imaginative creations" (6–28). The vagaries of Emersonian nature speculation coming from Germany through England were bad philosophy and bad religion. Emerson's *Nature* contained, Bowen admitted, valuable insights, but its main characteristics were obscurantist language and a substitution of the oracular for the rational. Transcendentalism's dismissal of empirical observation as the basis of proper philosophizing—that is, a dismissal of modified Lockeianism such as Bowen's—"encourages tyros to prate foolishly and flippantly about matters which they can neither master nor comprehend."[15]

Bowen traced these absurdities of the post-Kantians to their reliance on demonstrative or *a priori* reasoning. Indeed, with the exception of Bowen's tradition of empiricism, this sort of reasoning *defined* philosophy (or metaphysics) from Descartes to Hegel. Metaphysicians confused themselves with their belief in the *a priori*. This reasoning was verbal, teaching nothing about the world but only about the relations of ideas. Although some of the proponents of philosophy in this sense had expounded religious systems, Bowen lamented, others had as easily propounded irreligious systems. The only remedy was to forsake the *a priori* and base speculation on empirical reasoning, the observed evidence of the senses (217–58). Only this kind of approach would make our ideas clear, and it was Bowen's approach in his Lowell Lectures of 1848 and 1849, expanded into his popular text, *The Principles of Metaphysics and Ethical Science Applied to the Evidences of Religion.*

Bowen accepted Hume's argument that the succession of events in the natural world did not exhibit causality (73–91). We attributed causality to certain events when they were constantly conjoined with others but observed no causative power in material bodies themselves. The laws of nature, Bowen declared, were "convenient fictions" for grouping certain facts (153–57). But Bowen was no skeptic. Hume and his followers, he argued, had some idea of real cause, otherwise they could not have claimed none had ever been discovered. Since, by their own analysis,

experience did not reveal causality, it must be part of the inherent structure of the mind. Throughout his career Bowen used this insight to attack
first Hume and then John Stuart Mill, who put forward a revised version
of Hume against the Scots.[16]

We had, said Bowen, an intuitive notion of the reality of the self, of our
personal existence. The self was necessary to experience, and we could
not conceive of experience without it. This self, he believed, was indivisible and possessed "the consciousness of activity": what defined the
self for Bowen was will, a primitive power of agency; volition was
essential to the self. Circumstances might limit this power—a person, for
example, might be paralyzed—but the will tended to accomplish its
ends. Under appropriate conditions it furnished us with paradigmatic
cases of efficient causality: I want to get up and I do. The notion of cause
that Hume could not find in the natural world was a mysterious feeling of
effort characterizing the self and its accomplishments, our consciousness
of volition and action. Bowen also pointed out that language pertaining to
causes in the natural world derived from language borrowed from mind
—for example, force, power, agency, and law. We could not really think
of material particles possessing power or force; they were passive, and to
say they had force or power was to use language figuratively (86–121).

In order to explain the causal connections among material bodies,
Bowen hypothesized the direct causative power of a self throughout the
universe, as mysterious in the world as it was in ourselves. As we found
ourselves moving our bodies, so God, an all-powerful self, was the only
true cause of the movements of the material particles of the universe. The
course of nature was nothing but the will of God producing certain effects
in a constant and uniform manner; we always witnessed the immediate
agency of the deity. The succession of events in the universe evinced his
being. On one hand, Bowen implied that the scientific enterprise assumed
this claim: investigations of nature supposed the causal connections the
deity provided. On the other hand, he reckoned that the claim was
empirical: observation of the order in the universe allowed us to infer the
existence of God, and the basis for belief in him was just like that for
belief in everything else—experiential evidence.[17]

Bowen's argument showed the immediate and present existence
of the deity, but in a typical way he went on to elaborate the argument
from design to indicate that God was benign and intelligent. In fact, this

was the central and recurring argument in Bowen's writings.[18] It was an empirical argument par excellence: we found, said Bowen in the *Principles*, that the universe was one vast and complex organism tenanted by creatures living in harmony (134), an indefinitely varied series of beings adapted to their place in the world order and working together by a complex and intricate process to attain a series of ends. We could at least infer from this observation that the cause of the order was personal, intelligent, and good (193–98).

We can gauge the depth of Bowen's optimism and the limited audience he addressed by his statement on human misery:

> How many of those who read this page [of the *Principles*] have been plagued by famines, inundations, earthquakes, the assassination of friends, robbery, ravenous beasts, tyranny, the necessity of slaying fellow creatures for sustenance or the like? And if, which is very improbable, there be an individual who has experienced one of these calamaties, *how small a portion of his whole existence has been immediately saddened by the event* . . . ?

The lives of Bowen's readers probably corroborated this view of a benevolent power controlling the universe, and Bowen took for granted that only the transient ills experienced by genteel Bostonians were important for discussing the quality of human existence.[19]

The *Principles* acknowledged again that Bowen's reasoning was not demonstrative: Hume correctly contended that there were no deductive arguments for God's existence. *A priori* cogitation in general, for Bowen, was suspect, and he was happy to rely on the empirical. Belief in God, he said, was as grounded as scientific belief, and skeptical opponents could not laud science while condemning religion. Both stood or fell together, and the justification for each was sufficient. Bowen consequently allowed that the argument from design might be false: the nature of the deity might not be benign. We were constrained to fathom his nature from empirical evidence, and Bowen only asked if it was credible that his nature could be otherwise, given the beauty and pleasing interaction of the elements of the universe (38–41).

Although preoccupied with natural theology, Bowen left a place for revealed theology (222, 227). It was necessary to prove the immortality of the soul and other doctrines of Christianity (421–44). The concern of revealed theology was not so much the suspension of the laws of nature as an investigation of the purpose for which God observed these laws, making his design more evident to man by a striking change in his mode of operation. The immediate and only cause of all events in the natural world was the deity, and to this extent the cause of any event by another was miraculous and without further explanation. The doctrines of natural theology, Bowen continued, were logically prior to those of revealed theology, but temporally considered, the "suspension" of natural law had prompted man to the study of nature and to the philosophical conclusions concerning the nature of the causal order (444–64).

The explanation of the Biblical miracles at the heart of revealed theology was no stranger than the explanation of the order in the natural world. We observed that certain facts occurred in a certain order. To understand their causal relation in the usual scientific sense, Bowen argued, we must infer the deity's incessant creative work. To consider two successive events as cause and effect when we would not normally do so—that is, to consider certain events as miraculous—was to make a similar inference. He defended the justifiability of this latter inference as necessary to explain such extraordinarily rare conjunctions of phenomena. A man is blind; a word is uttered; the man can see. In this case, as in every case of causal connection, we could not fathom how a word should open blind eyes. We attributed causal power to the spoken word because we needed to explain the conjunction of events. Bowen concluded that, taking into account the scriptural testimony, the ends served by probable miracles, and the circumstances in which they occurred, we had sufficient reason to accept the hypothesis of miracles in Biblical times (465–87).

Bowen and Darwin

The social cataclysm of the Civil War greatly undermined Unitarian optimism, and younger intellectuals would find little in its philosophy to make sense of the conflict and the peace which followed.[20] In the world of ideas, John Stuart Mill's revival of Hume attacked Unitarianism's philosophical rationale. Even if Bowen's kind of thinking could have withstood these social and philosophical changes, it could not withstand the revolution in the life sciences. To understand Bowen's response to

Darwin, we must discuss three issues that came together in his anti-evolutionary polemic: first and most important, the relation of Bowen's empiricism to Darwinian science; second, the relation between some of Darwin's defenders and the empiricism of Hume and Mill; and third, the structure of argument that Bowen had developed in the controversy with the Transcendentalists.

Bowen's analyses were all comprehensible from within his speculative framework, and with hindsight we can see that his failure stemmed from his inability to give up his common-sense empiricism. Bowen adamantly believed in the evidence of his senses. To accept the developmental hypothesis the mind had to make an immense constructive leap. One had to admit the workings of the natural processes in the past far beyond the historical records, and one had also to allow that these same workings, at some time in the past, produced a world very different from that which we presently know, but which changed into this one. And one had to accept these ideas when there were questions about the transmission of traits and the temporal span. Evolution left only a peripheral place for presently verifiable and previously given truths; it could not verify many central truths its adherents felt compelled to believe; and some empirical evidence was inconsistent with it. In short, one could not embrace evolution and continue to accept a common-sense empiricism which relied on what men observed in everyday experience. The new science required one to dismiss the evidence of one's senses.

In a way, Bowen was a strict empiricist. His concern was palpable sensory data and these data did not support Darwin. As Bowen saw it, it was possible to redefine 'empiricism' to stress the non-observed and the postulated. But this view would be only nominally empiricist and would give great weight to the *a priori*, constructive powers of the human mind. Moreover, on this view the empirical evidence suggested that the earth was a charnel house.

Bowen's concept of the empirical becomes clearer if we consider his reaction to the alliance between Darwin and the nineteenth-century skeptical empiricists. Darwin's most militant adherents were often philosophic defenders of Hume. Although Hume's ideas dictated scientific as well as religious skepticism, his nineteenth-century followers frequently forsook religion while adopting anti-religious scientific views. Many of them thought that scientific laws were devised by noting associations among the phenomena; because science could reduce the phenomena to a collection of atoms, the laws finally reflected regularities within a value-less material world. Many thinkers who made this connection between Hume and materialism also assumed that the developmental hypothesis showed *how* our world evolved from a prior universe of simple elements: Darwin made credible the belief that science could construe phenomena as a flux of atoms.

Bowen had long since argued that Humean empiricism presupposed causal connections on one hand and denied them on the other. In his eyes, linking Hume to a materialistic interpretation of Darwin was a further confusion. For Darwin was not an empiricist at all. He spun out ideas without regard for what he saw or felt; he was a metaphysician delighting in *a priori* flights of fancy. Bowen accepted, however, the link between Darwin and skeptical empiricism: Hume led to skepticism in science and religion; correctly understood, Darwin's science was not science at all but a metaphysics justifying religious skepticism.

However Bowen perceived the developmental hypothesis, he could not find a successful way of adapting to it. In meeting the Transcendentalists' attack on Massachusetts orthodoxy, the Unitarians had devised certain modes of argumentation involving natural and revealed theology. This constellation of beliefs conflicted directly with Darwin and could not survive if the *Origin* were accepted. If an argument from design showed the character of the deity, then the evolutionary order showed that the deity was evil: he relished over-production and a bloody, terrifying struggle for existence. If Bowen's argument from the nature of causality proved his existence, God was malevolent. But long before the *Origin* Bowen had assumed that skepticism or atheism would follow the rise of developmental ideas: man came from the brutes, the brutes from simpler creatures, and finally adherents of these theories were left with a swirl of material particles from which, they claimed, the universe came to its present condition.[21] This doctrine led to a belief in no god at all, an outcome better than worship of a god indisputably evil. Bowen feared that believers in evolution finally might become nihilists bent on the destruction of society. If there was no god, existence had no ultimate meaning. The proponents of evolution would accordingly have grounds for believing that human experience was really tragic, that life was not worth living; they might try to abate the misery by reducing civilization to anarchy and ruin.[22]

In a long review of the *Origin*, written within a year of its publication, Bowen began his war on Darwin. The developmental hypothesis stripped creation of "all proof of the incessant creative action of a designing mind, by reducing it to a blind mechanical process, necessarily resulting from inherent mud-born energies and productive power." The worst consequence of evolution by natural selection was its denial of the argument for design, "the principal argument for the being of a God."[23]

Bowen showed that the claims of evolution were tenuous by the standards of reigning philosophical ideas. He attacked the two weak links in Darwin's argument: the hereditary transmission of variation and the vast time required to make the theory go. Referring again and again to observable processes, Bowen reminded his readers that variations of significance to Darwin rarely occurred and, at least as far as we could tell, were not hereditable, that is, they were never regularly transmitted from parent to offspring.[24] Bowen also noted that the "gemmules" which Darwin postulated as the mode of transmission were "descried only by the eye of theory." Their function in Darwin's theory was like that of Leibniz' monads, and this function made the gemmules of doubtful empirical value. Leibniz was frank in propounding the existence of monads as a necessary deduction from his metaphysical axioms, but Darwin showed less candor in claiming that the gemmules were empirical.[25] Even if we accepted the gemmules and the accumulation of inherited variations, Darwin needed a temporal continuum so great that even he was afraid to admit its extent. Bowen wrote:

> the time required for the development of *one* of their Species out of the other would lack no characteristic of eternity except its name. But the theory requires us to believe that this process has been repeated an indefinite number of times, so as to account for the development of *all* the Species now in being. . . .[26]

Bowen granted, however, that Darwin urged his ideas with great ability. For men without intellectual and emotional commitments to common-sense empiricism and anti-evolutionary views, the developmental hypothesis opened up exciting areas of research and investigation.

Bowen was not willing to wait for the confirmation that eventually came. In 1860 he concluded that Darwin was not a scientist but a cosmologist, a metaphysician fond of the *a priori*:

> Such speculations as these appear to be rather exercises of fancy than sober inferences of science. A mere hypothesis of indefinite Cumulative Variation, resting upon analogy in the absence of all direct proof, must be allowed to *create its own evidence* of the inconceivable lapse of time requisite for its development, instead of drawing that evidence from distinct and independent sources.

Such a cosmology or theory of creation was contradictory. It professed to explain the beginnings of things; yet, in assuming that the ordinary succession of phenomena had continued indefinitely, it rejected the notion that there was a beginning. Darwin denied creation, Bowen said, when he pushed it back to an infinite distance.[27]

Bowen believed in the deity's special creation of all species, but because he also believed in God's incessant activity, he did not regard special creation as strange. A direct act of creation was no more inconceivable than an ordinary birth, although the former took place less frequently. As he put it, opponents of special creation believed that "that a horse should create a horse is conceivable; but that God should create a horse is inconceivable."

> The beginning of all life is in a nucleated cell. . . . The original formulation of such a cell . . . [and] its subsequent multiplication . . . are distinct acts of creation . . . whether preceded or not by a generative union of the parents. That the generative act should be ordinarily followed by the vivifaction of such a cell, is a law of nature, which like other natural laws, does not explain the phenomena, nor throw any light on them, but merely describes and classifies them; . . . Whether we call it creation or ordinary generation, the process—the mode in which inorganic particles are suddenly bound together into an organic living whole—is wholly inexplicable. Science throws down her microscope before the process in despair.*

*G, p. 230. Bowen later used this idea to accept evolutionary theories of transmission of traits, but he developed new arguments against Darwin on the basis of the supposed "survival of the fittest" (see G, pp. 362–70).

Bowen's Later Work

Bowen's polemic against evolution won him no future readers, but a second strategy was more respectable from a later perspective, although he received little credit for it. He redefined his position in the 1860s and 1870s, coming to believe that to acknowledge the independent existence of material objects was a concession that might lead to the dismissal of mind from the universe and the triumph of Darwinian materialism. For Bowen, the realist Locke became less important while the constructionalist Kant became more important: mind would contribute to what was real. While Bowen still denounced the post-Kantians, *The Critique of Pure Reason* replaced Locke's *Essay* as his critical text. In addition, he treated Berkeley, the transitional figure between Locke and Hume, with great sympathy.[28]

The existence of an external material world, Bowen said, could only be inferred; we postulated it, at best, as the unknown cause of mind's sensations. In contrast, mind was immediately revealed to us, although we knew directly, as a datum of consciousness, a resisting force, a power not ourselves. This was Berkeley's position, Bowen concluded, and the cause of "ideas" in our minds was, for Berkeley, God. Berkeley was thus a spiritualist: he reduced matter to the ideas God caused in us. But he was not a solipsist like Bowen's loathed German idealists: there were other spirits aside from the individual self. Moreover, Berkeley was a presentational realist in that he claimed we knew the world (of ideas forced on us) directly, as it was.

Was Bowen a Berkeleyan? Not quite. He suggested his agreement with Berkeley in implying

> that matter is nothing but Force; Force is nothing but Will; Will exists only as accompanied and directed by Intelligence and witnessed by Consciousness; and intelligent and conscious Will produces not only order, harmony, and law, but produces also infinite variety, diversity, and change.[29]

But this view did not satisfy Bowen. The nature of the external force was a problem too deep for the finite intellect to solve. We could not ascertain what the external universe was as noumenon, though we knew that the sole reality could not be the physical universe independent of any thought about it.[30]

Locke had given way to Kant. Bowen also saw this position as vindicating Hamilton. Mill maintained that Hamilton could not argue for both presentational realism and the relativity of knowledge: if we had a direct insight into things as they are, Mill claimed, knowledge could not be relative to the human mind. On the contrary, declared Bowen, on his Kant-Berkeley theory we were immediately conscious of an external non-ego: objects were immediately presented to us as existing externally. This was, said Bowen, presentational or natural realism. But we were not concerned on this account with whether these phenomena really existed externally, but "in the mode under which they appear or are presented to our minds." Bowen understood this to be Hamilton's position. Hamilton did not contradict himself, according to Bowen, although external objects might not exist externally as they are presented to us. They were known immediately but not "absolutely," so that presentational realism was compatible with the relativity of knowledge.[31]

Bowen also thought he could defend the objective reality of space and time against some forms of idealism. In his view consciousness need not be limited to the brain; space and time might be the realm of consciousness. Where were its limits?

> If the mind is really present wherever it acts and feels, then all that is inside of the skin is also inside of consciousness. If the sphere of our spiritual activity, instead of being limited to an indivisible point in the brain, is coextensive with our whole nervous organism, then we do not need to go outside of ourselves in order to become *immediately* cognizant both of the extension and the impenetrability of our limbs and muscles. We can become directly conscious of the distinction between void and occupied space; that is, of the resistance which is offered by the several portions of our own embodiment in a material form. Space thus becomes not only a subjective postulate, but an objective revelation. It is apprehended both *a priori* and *a posteriori*; it is known both as a law of thought, and as a manifestation of that which is foreign to our thought—the Power which is not ourselves. If touched on two separate portions of my body, as on the shoulder and the hip, I recognize *immediately* the distinction between *here* and *there*; and the idea of space hitherto undeveloped,

then rises into distinct consciousness. In the effort which is needed in order to effect any muscular movement, as in lifting a weight, we become *immediately* conscious both of our own causal agency, and of the resistance to it which is produced by the inertia of matter. Both the Ego and the non-Ego thus become directly known, each in its contrast with the other, and equally real with that other.[32]

. . . the sphere of knowledge is certainly not limited to what takes place within the thinking Ego, but extends to what lies far outside of it, both in time and space. We know both past and the distant, and we anticipate even the future. Consequently, as the mind certainly, in one sense, extends its sphere of operation out in order to *know*, we may well believe that it exercises an equally transcendent power in order to *act*. . . . the thinking Self (which is the proper designation of what is usually called "mind"), since it is absolutely one and indivisible does not occupy space, and yet is undeniably present to the whole nervous organism which it animates. . . . Granted that we cannot conceive *how* the Ego exercises this marvelous power; still the fact is unquestionable that it *does* exercise it; it is omnipresent to the whole body.[33]

Bowen put forward thesee idas only at the end of his life; they were not elaborated, and so close was his connection with the anti-Darwinian forces that by the 1870s everything he said was safely ignored. Yet in Bowen's mature thought there were all the elements critical to the speculation of Harvard's Golden Age: a shift away from Locke's empiricism to Kant's constructionalism, a renewed interest in Bishop Berkeley, and an attempt to talk about mind by means of the body's activity. Perhaps most importantly Bowen had a self-conscious concern for the practical applications of ideas and a conviction that philosophy had an obligation outside the university. And in his victory over the Transcendentalists he had established that these applications and obligations must receive a reasoned and even technical defense: he had won a jurisdictional battle with Emerson concerning the rights of expertise in the public arena.

These themes dominated Bowen's successors, but it was embarrassing to recognize as a mentor the man who enunciated them, for Bowen had joined his ideas to a denunciation of a cause that prevailed—the *Origin of Species*.

3

AMATEUR PHILOSOPHIZING

Gilded Age Emersonians

Bowen's thought and the synthesis between science and religion he advanced were in trouble as soon as Darwin published. The trouble grew when Mill attacked Hamilton in 1865. At the same time increased duties at Harvard during the 1860s prevented Bowen from either teaching or writing effectively. The trauma of the Civil War also weakened established modes of thinking, but as the study of philosophy declined at the institution, speculative societies of various kinds sprang up all over New England. These eastern clubs were only a fragment of a disorganized and inchoate national group of societies searching for a way to revitalize American intellectual life, sometimes even in quasi-institutional forms. Essentially, however, all the societies sought a solution to philosophical and societal problems in the speculative style of Emerson. Their members were amateurs, not philosophy teachers at American colleges. They had independent sources of income, speculated as an avocation, or mixed literary and philosophical pursuits. From 1870 to 1890 these men searched for their own reconciliation of religion with the new ways of thinking in biological science. They all emphasized the limitations of common-sense empiricism and believed that the philosophic rationale for a defensible religion would have to rely mostly on Kant and the post-Kantians.

This Gilded Age quest for culture and religious solace would not endure. Later commentators would denigrate the amateurs and compare their speculative strength unfavorably, if at all, to the academic philosophers professing in the great universities by the turn of the century. Prominent against the background of moribund college philosophy, the societies disappeared as soon as institutionalized contemplation revived.

Nonetheless, although most of their discourse did not survive, the amateurs created a climate in which the professors could formulate a new and feasible scientific theology. And, although Harvard University would reap the benefit, the amateurs of one of the earliest groups, the Metaphysical Club, also gave to the world the principle of pragmatism.

The Metaphysical Club

William James was abroad in 1867 and 1868. From Berlin, in January 1868, he wrote to his friend Oliver Wendell Holmes, Jr.: "When I get home let's establish a philosophical society to have regular meetings and discuss none but the very tallest and broadest questions. . . . It will give each one a chance to air his own opinion in a grammatical form, and to sneer and chuckle when he goes home at what damned fools all the other members are—and may grow into something very important after a sufficient number of years."[1]

The "society" may not have been formed immediately upon James's return, but it was flourishing in 1871 and 1872. Its members, as one of them remembered, called it "half-ironically, half-defiantly, 'The Metaphysical Club'—for agnosticism was then riding its high horse, and was frowning superbly upon all metaphysics."[2] In February 1872 the club was in full swing. Lacking a social circle himself, William's younger brother Henry wrote his friend Charles Eliot Norton that William and "various other long-headed youths have combined to form a Metaphysical Club, where they wrangle grimly and stick to the question. It gives me a headache merely to know of it."[3] The core of the club consisted of six men: James, Holmes, Charles Peirce, Chauncey Wright, Nicholas St. John Green, and Joseph Bangs Warner. Coming out of a long psychic depression, James had committed himself to teaching in April 1872 by accepting an appointment in physiology at Harvard. Holmes taught at Harvard too, lecturing on jurisprudence at the law school. Peirce had a Harvard connection as assistant at the College Observatory, but he also worked for the United States Coast and Geodetic Survey, spending much time away from Cambridge. These three seem to have been instrumental in organizing the club and providing some forum for discussing philosophical topics of contemporary interest. Wright and Green were older, in their early forties, and seem to have been the group's intellectual leaders. The *Nautical Almanac* employed Wright as a computer, and in 1870–1871 he had given an unsuccessful course of psychology lectures at Harvard. Although Wright was a misfit, Cambridge regarded him as an imposing intellect. Green was a Boston attorney, who also lectured at the law school and maintained an interest in the philosophy of law. Peirce recalled that Wright was the strongest member, "our boxing-master whom we—I particularly—used to face to be severely pummeled";[4] and that Green was a "profound lawyer" and "a marvelously strong intelligence." Warner was twenty-four, a protégé of Peirce and at the time a law student of Holmes and Green.[5]

Six other men were peripherally connected with the club. Frank Abbot, a close friend of Peirce, was not living in Cambridge during the group's most active period, and John Fiske, gaining a reputation as an articulate defender of Herbert Spencer's evolutionary thought, was often away lecturing. John Chipman Gray was another lawyer and friend of Holmes and James. William Montague and Henry Putnam (lawyers) and Francis Greenwood Peabody (a theologian) were friends of Warner or students of the older members.

The men were Harvard educated exclusively; with the exception of William James, each had a Harvard B.A. They were young—the average age was thirty-three—but there were three distinct age groupings: Green and Wright had received their degrees in 1851 and 1852 respectively; five others—Abbot, Fiske, Gray, Holmes, and Peirce (peers of James)—received degrees between 1859 and 1863; the remaining four were all class of 1869. They were practical men: of the six core members three were lawyers, three scientists. Of the wider group, six were lawyers, three scientists, two theologians, and one a librarian (by courtesy only—Fiske's main source of support, in addition to contributions from his family, was writing and lecturing).[6]

The club was an elite group. As James had written to Holmes, the society was "to be composed of none but the very topmost cream of Boston manhood,"[7] and only a few of its members were middle class in origin. Philosophy interested well-to-do professional men.

The Origins of Pragmatism

It is not surprising that a group of brilliant young men with legal and scientific training produced some worthwhile ideas when they jointly set their minds to it. But just what they did is difficult to make out. The club had no secretary and no record of debate. As Peirce later wrote, the proceedings had all been in "winged words."[8] We must consequently reconstruct the history of the club's ideas from very fragmentary evidence, and at best are able to specify three broad sources of the members' opinions: Green's appraisal of the work of the British psychologist Alexander Bain (1818–1903), the legal analyses of Green and Holmes, and the evolutionary theorizing of Wright.

Green relentlessly urged that the membership look to "the practical significance of every proposition," and that "every form of words that means anything indicates some sensible fact on the existence of which its truth depends." Green appears to have derived this view from Alexander Bain. Bain's definition of belief—"of that upon which a man is prepared to act"—was common property. Wright lectured on Bain in his psychology course but, Peirce recalled, Green pushed this definition.[9]

Bain came alive for Peirce and the others as Green and then Holmes applied Bain to the law or saw that Bain's ideas were adequate from the viewpoint of a practicing lawyer. In an erudite article in the 1870 *American Law Review*, "Proximate and Remote Cause," Green traced the genesis and history of that phrase and its shifts in meaning from Lord Bacon's legal principle "In jure non remota causa, sed proxima, spectatur." Analyzing the meaning of the word 'cause', Green concluded that the principle was ambiguous: talking about proximate and remote causes did not clarify our reasoning when what we meant was "only the degree of certainty or uncertainty with which the connection between cause and effect might have been anticipated."[10] When discussing whether an individual was "legally responsible" for certain acts, lawyers did not discuss the "remoteness" of an individual's behavior from its effect; rather they considered if the effects could be predicted from the behavior. Green defined legal concepts by the activities with which the law was actually concerned.

There were other scattered hints in Green's writings of these ideas, but the beliefs implicit in his work were fully articulated by Holmes. In 1871–1872 he was propounding "the prediction theory of law" in his lectures:

What . . . is a statute; and in what other sense law, than that we believe that the motive which we think that it offers to the judges will prevail, and will induce them to decide a certain case in a certain way, and so shape our conduct on that anticipation? A precedent may not be followed; a statute may be emptied of its contents by construction, or may be repealed without a saving clause after we have acted on it; but we expect the reverse, and if our expectations come true, we say that we have been subject to law in the matter in hand. It must be remembered . . . that in a civilized state it is not the will of the sovereign that makes lawyers' law even when that is its source, but what a body of subjects, namely, the judges, by whom it is enforced, *say* is his will. The judges have other motives for decision, outside their own arbitrary will, beside the commands of their sovereign. And whether those other motives are, or are not, equally compulsory, is immaterial, if they are sufficiently likely to prevail to afford a ground for prediction. The only question for the lawyer is, how will the judges act?[11]

Since Holmes did not hold this position two years earlier, we may infer that the doctrine developed in conjunction with the meetings of the Metaphysical Club. In *The Common Law* (1881) and *The Path of the Law* (1897) he stated his position at greater length but it had not essentially changed: to understand the law on a certain subject, we viewed it as would an unscrupulous person who would do anything he could do without incurring legal consequences. The object of study was prediction—predicting the incidence of the use of public force through the courts. What the courts did in fact constituted the meaning of the law; the lawyer's job was to predict for clients what would happen in court as a consequence of acting or not acting in conformity to certain statutes.[12]

Although the legal reasoning of Green and Holmes inspired the members of the club, to understand their thought we must put it in the context of the doctrines of evolutionary science. Holmes was aware of the similarities between legal and evolutionary thinking. His *Common Law* emphasized the evolutionary nature of law: "The law embodies the story of a nation's development through many centuries and it cannot be dealt with as if it contained only the axioms and corollaries of a book of mathematics. In order to know what it is we must know what it has been, and what it tends to become." Wright had adhered to these notions earlier, however, and did so forcefully in the club. His 1873 "The Evolution of Self-Consciousness" declared:

> The judge cannot rightfully change the laws that govern his judgments; and the just judge does not consciously do so. Nevertheless, legal usages change from age to age. Laws, in their practical effects, are ameliorated by courts as well as by legislatures. No new principles are consciously introduced; but interpretations of old ones (and combinations, under more precise and qualified statements) are made, which disregard old decisions, seemingly by new and better definitions of that which in its nature is unalterable, but really, in their practical effects, by alterations at least in the proximate grounds of decision; so that nothing is really unalterable in law, except the intention to do justice under universally applicable principles of decision, and the instinctive judgments of so-called natural law.[13]

In addition to finding evolutionary ideas implicit in legal beliefs, Wright saw that adopting Bain's psychology would buttress Darwin's findings. Suppose beliefs were tendencies to act and not mysterious "intellectual phases of the mind," as some thinkers said. We could then examine changes in the structure of beliefs by examining changes in behavior. Beliefs might then be said to evolve, argued Wright, the most mature and rational resulting "from the survival of the fittest among our original and spontaneous beliefs." Bain's analysis would allow us to confirm this hypothesis empirically; we would investigate any supposed shift in beliefs by perusing changes in action.[14] In linking Bain's doctrine to evolution, Wright supplied the Darwinian context in which the club formulated its lasting contribution, the principle of pragmatism.

The controversial aspect of Darwinian theory was its applicability to the evolution of man, and the controversy concerned not so much the links between the human organism and those of the lower animals but rather between human reason and animal instinct. As we shall see, Wright showed that natural selection could account for man's self-consciousness. What was important was that the pragmatic idea came to fruition in naturalizing the human mind. The principle of pragmatism was one dimension of a defense of Darwin's theory as applied to human evolution: if beliefs were habits of action, Wright could marry intelligence and reason to instinct by analyzing changes in behavior and identifying certain changes as evidence of mind.[15] These were the ideas that William James popularized a few years later:

> The organism of thought . . . is teleological through and through. . . . Far from being vouched for by the past these [our hypotheses and beliefs] are verified only by the future. . . . The survivors constitute the right way of thinking.[16]

> The theory of evolution is beginning to do very good service by its reduction of all mentality to the type of reflex action. Cognition, in this view, is but a fleeting moment, a cross-section at a certain point, of what in its totality is a motor phenomenon.

> . . . the new conceptions, emotions, and active tendencies which evolve are originally produced in the shape of random images, fancies, accidental out-births of spontaneous variation in the functional activity of the excessively instable human brain, which the outer environment simply confirms or refutes, adopts or rejects, preserves or destroys,—*selects* in short just as it selects morphological and social variations due to molecular accidents of an analogous sort.[17]

Within this common framework Peirce formulated "the pragmatic maxim." Rightfully credited as its father, he drew up a paper lest the club be dissolved without a "material *souvenir*."[18] He probably read it, a version of his famous "How to Make Our Ideas Clear," in November 1872, but did not publish it until some six years later, and then in altered form, in the *Popular Science Monthly* as part of a series, "Illustrations of the Logic of Science."[19]

Mill's *Examination* of Hamilton had been a polemical success everywhere, and by the early 1870s Hamilton's reputation as a philosopher had already declined in Cambridge: Mill had weakened the credibility of the Scottish answer to Hume and given new life to skeptical empiricism. Kant and the Scots were one in denouncing Hume, and Mill's book shocked Peirce, who had been taught the Scottish position as an undergraduate and was steeped in Kant even in the early 1860s.[20] Peirce certainly did not adopt skeptical empiricism but he became intrigued with the work of the transitional figure Berkeley, specifically with his premise that things are as they are known as.

In 1871 Peirce wrote a long critique of Berkeley that reasserted his adherence to Kantian and Scottish doctrines but affirmed Berkeley's insistence on avoiding verbalisms. Hamilton's notion that we were immediately aware of the effects of noumenal objects could hardly survive a Berkeleyan examination, and Peirce was on his way to saying that if we had no evidence of noumenal objects, it was verbiage to argue that they must be there to ground certain experiences. Later he made it clear that these objects were no more than their conceivable effects. Said Peirce, "Do things fulfill the same function practically? Then let them be signified by the same word. Do they not? Then let them be distinguished." He later commented that his pragmatism simply represented the unformulated method that Berkeley followed.[21] Peirce was, moreover, doing extended scientific work on stellar photometry, metrology, and geodesy, and these studies inevitably pushed him in a Berkeleyan direction. As a careful and talented experimentalist he would come to believe that the meaning of every scientific statement was that if a given prescription for an experiment was carried out, then an experience of a given description would result. This was only Berkeley's notion applied in the laboratory.[22]

So far as we can recapture discussion, Peirce set down what all his fellows agreed on: practice must define belief; a belief was not a mental entity but a habit of action to be analyzed by examining behavior. Considered as a group product, this idea was not connected to any wider theory, as in Peirce's articles of the late 1870s or James's 1907 *Pragmatism*. For the club, rather, pragmatism was a maxim for investigating the nature of belief consistent with the theory of evolution. What individuals believed was what they would be ready to act on and risk much upon,[23] and scientists could investigate the growth and change of these beliefs empirically. The group concluded that the meaning of a belief consisted (ambiguously) in either its sensible effects, or the rule, habit, or law from which investigators might derive these effects given the occurrence of appropriate antecedent conditions.

The name given to this doctrine—pragmatism—was Kantian and

probably originated with Peirce, although James first put the term into print years later in his 1898 address, "Philosophical Conceptions and Practical Results." In *The Critique of Pure Reason* Kant wrote:

> The physician must do something in the case of a patient who is in danger, even if he is not sure of the disease. He looks out for symptoms and judges, according to his best knowledge, that it is a case of phthisis. His belief is even in his own judgment only a contingent one; someone else might perhaps judge better. I call such contingent belief which still forms the basis of the actual use of means for the attainment of certain ends, *pragmatic belief*. The usual touch-stone or test of whether something is just talk or at least subjective conviction, that is, firm belief, is the *bet*. . . . A bet makes one stop short. . . . If in our thoughts we imagine the happiness of our whole life at stake, our triumphant judgment disappears, we tremble lest our belief has gone too far. Thus pragmatic belief has degrees of strength varying in proportion to the magnitude of the diverse interests involved.[24]

The Kantian word *pragmatisch* stood for the means-ends relation expressed in hypothetical imperatives—for example, counsels of prudence. For the club a connection to definite human purposes and conceivable empirical consequences guided all reasoning. There was an inseparable link between meaningful beliefs and practical activity. Whatever the substantive relations between the Americans and Kant, his *pragmatisch* became the English *pragmatic*, and it did so as an extension of Darwinian ideas.

Other Societies

Holmes's passion for philosophy waned as he threw himself into the law, and he soon dropped out of the club.[25] Wright died in 1875, Green a year later—both in their mid-forties. For the better part of both of these years Peirce was in Europe for the Coast Survey and thereafter ceased even nominally to reside in Cambridge. Nonetheless, the club was still meeting in 1874–1875, and in any event it was reorganized at the start of 1876.[26]

The revived club included some old members and, in addition, Bowen, C. C. Everett of the Harvard Divinity School, George Holmes Howison, then professor at the [Massachusetts] Institute of Technology, and Thomas Davidson and James Elliot Cabot, philosopher-scholars of leisure. This club was more formal—it issued invitations—and there was an assigned text—it began with Hume's *Treatise*. In the following years the emphasis shifted from Hume to Kant, and then to Hegel. Despite the number of its members with permanent Harvard affiliations, the club's leadership came to rest in the hands of Davidson and Cabot.

The second club disintegrated in the spring of 1879. As James wrote, the members were "about talked out," but in the early 1880s two Hegel clubs were formed which continued the emphases of their predecessor. They had little connection with Harvard. Samuel Emery and Edward McClure, two Quincey, Illinois, businessmen who were studying law, first presided over them. Then William Torrey Harris, mentor of Emery and McClure and leader of the famous St. Louis Hegelians, took charge— he was living in Massachusetts from 1880 to 1889. These clubs also drew on Harvard philosophy teachers, a group that now included William James, but the sustaining members were Emery, McClure, Harris, and Charles H. Ames, the general agent for the educational division of Prang and Company. Everyone else seemed to feel the clubs a failure.[27]

Eventually journals printed a number of the papers written for these clubs but, although the new groups were stimulating for their active members, they produced nothing as significant as had their parent. More-over, as amateurs took over their leadership, the Harvard philosophy faculty developed associations more closely connected with the university. George Herbert Palmer, who had started teaching philosophy at Harvard about the same time as James, had initiated a seminar in Hegel that was apparently distinct from either Hegel club. And in 1878 undergraduates, graduate students, and faculty had started a Harvard Philosophical Club.[28] The recruitment of young philosophers to Harvard depleted the ranks of the amateurs and shifted power back to the institution. The recently appointed "assistant" professors got a public platform, and the college got novel ideas.

The growing segregation of the young Harvard philosophers from the migrant amateurs signaled changing times. Harris, Davidson, and Howison were the core of the St. Louis Philosophical Society. Yet despite their serious and unquestioned speculative bent, they were unable to make an impact in Cambridge.

Howison was born in 1834 in Marietta, Ohio, where he was schooled, and found his vocation as a professor at Washington University in St. Louis, where he interested himself in education and the science–religion controversy. Despite fruitful connections with the St. Louis intellectuals Howison was anxious to leave the midwest for any position in Boston. He spent two years there at the English High School; then from 1872 to 1878 he taught at the Institute. When it abolished his professorship because of financial stringencies, he hovered in the Boston area ever hoping that Harvard would call him. He lectured in the Divinity School and offered private philosophic lessons; after two years in Europe, he returned to Boston to give more private lessons; and after an unsuccessful year at Michigan, he returned again to Boston in 1883. Soon thereafter authorities at the University of California established the Mills Professorship in Philosophy and offered the chair to Howison. In 1884, fifty years old, he resigned himself to permanent exile.*

Davidson had been born in northern Scotland and was graduated from the University of Aberdeen in 1860. After spending a few years teaching grammar school in Britain, he came to North America and began a career as a "wandering scholar." In Scotland Davidson had been interested in a university philosophical career but the posts available were few and

---

*Howison's forte was his impressive teaching; from 1884 to 1911 he made Berkeley a center for philosophic discussion and instruction. The Philosophical Union, which he founded, sponsored high level debate, concentrating for a year on the study of a single work and culminating in the appearance of its author. Howison built the symposium that produced the famous *Conception of God* on Josiah Royce's appearance, but he also attracted James, Harris, John Dewey, John Watson, James Ward, J. M. E. McTaggart, and Hastings Rashdall. A Festschrift appearing on his seventieth birthday was the first in a series of distinguished publications by the department he had founded—the *University of California Publications in Philosophy*. Finally, Howison funneled his best students off to Harvard for graduate training. Berkeley remained not only a source of first-rate minds for the Cambridge of Royce and James but also a testing ground for its most promising Ph.D.s: Howison hired Harvard products and for many years after his death Berkeley's Cambridge connections assured its eminence, while Harvard's ability to attract whom it wanted from California attested to the latter's minor league status.

Howison published comparatively little but was much more than a philosophic statesman. A requirement that each faculty member report yearly on his publications incensed him. He blamed the practice on Harvard's Eliot and was careful to put out only his best work. His most significant studies were his portion of *The Conception of God* and essays collected in his 1901 *The Limits of Evolution, and Other Essays Illustrating the Metaphysical Theory of Personal Idealism*. He died in 1916. (Information on Howison comes from John Wright Buckham and George Malcolm Stratton, *George Holmes Howison: Philosopher and Teacher* [Berkeley: University of California Press, 1938].)

oversupplied with applicants. He initially pursued his teaching ambitions in the United States, but his independence and unorthodox religious views made university administrators wary of him. By the time his renown for erudition might have counterbalanced his reputation for unreliability, he no longer relished a university existence. On one hand, he was contemptuous of the academy's increasingly set form and occasional hostility to new lights and progressive ideas. On the other hand, he thought his educational impact would be broader if he could influence the young outside traditional scholarly boundaries. He hoped to be an intellectual missionary who would get at the truth of things and encourage the regeneration of society. In the late 1870s and early 1880s he promulgated his ideas in Boston after a close association with the philosophers in St. Louis.[29]

Harris was the best known St. Louis Hegelian; he was also, as his subsequent fame as United States Commissioner of Education attested, a promoter with his eye on the main chance. He had felt a need for a regular publication on speculative topics, and after the *North American Review* refused to publish his twelve thousand word criticism of Herbert Spencer —Chauncey Wright had damned the manuscript—Harris launched *The Journal of Speculative Philosophy* in 1867. Running until 1893, it was a brilliant success, the first significant technical philosophic magazine in England or the United States. James, Royce, Peirce, John Dewey, Howison, Davidson, and G. Stanley Hall all wrote for it.[30] In 1881 Harris had moved to Massachusetts at the behest of many Transcendentalists. Emerson wanted this man of speculative virility as a counterpoint to the "debility of scholars in Massachusetts."[31] But if Emerson referred to the nascent philosophical community in Cambridge, Harris did not overwhelm it with his vigor; he was unable to transmit his views to those who were all-important at Harvard. By the 1880s the respected speculation was more and more confined to the university.

At this time Harris's protégé Emery began to direct the Concord School of Philosophy. Apparently the idea for such a school had come from Emerson and Bronson Alcott in 1840, but it did not become a reality till forty years later. Its founders conceived this summer school, running in July and August in Concord from 1879 to 1888, as a gathering place for those disturbed by the materialistic tendencies of current science: "by free converse on the deeper questions of the theologico-idealistic philosophy, the men of Concord could emphasize the importance of keeping the mind fixed on the Divine personality of God, on the direct relationship between God and man through man's conscious powers, as the necessary conditions for sound philosophic thinking regarding the principles of right conduct in human life itself."[32] Believing that academic philosophy must become pedantry, the founders of the school insisted that only extra-academic reflection could meet America's religious needs. They also feared that growing secularism in the university would allow men to teach philosophy without answering to theology. Finally, even if speculation in the colleges remained religious, Concord's leaders felt that their own thought was antagonistic to prevailing religious practices and dogmas and needed its own center of influence.

The Concord School was the last gasp of non-professorial philosophy in the Transcendentalist style. Seeing affinities between Emerson's nature philosophy and their own ideas, transplanted St. Louis Hegelians momentarily rejuvenated Transcendental ideals in Concord. But contempt for science characterized the group and weakened its influence even with conservatives like Princeton's President James McCosh.[33] Its members were also amateurs striking out on their own at a time when a revived Harvard faculty was going in another direction. The aging Alcott (he was seventy-nine) was dean, and Emerson initially took part. Franklin Sanborn, a much younger man who had been at Harvard in the 1850s but whose sympathies and friendships were with the older generation, was secretary-treasurer. Harris became a leading teacher and a moving force—he apparently went to Concord with the hope of beginning where Emerson left off.[34]

During the ten years of its existence the school had over fifty teachers, among them Presidents McCosh, Noah Porter (of Yale), and John Bascom (of Wisconsin), Julia Ward Howe, William Henry Channing, Howison, and James. The auditors, mainly college instructors and students, paid a modest fee to listen to lecture courses on a wide range of literary and philosophical topics.[35] The school paid its own way because of Sanborn's wise speculation in railroad securities,[36] but its main purpose was to recreate in Concord the leisured life of the man of letters of an almost vanished era. Harvard scoffed, but in Concord "the best houses were open to the 'philosophers'; Emerson, so long as he could, and Mrs. Emerson always, attending the daily sessions and inviting the lecturers to tea; Miss Riply at the Old Manse giving a tea-party on the lawn in honor of the School, and many parties of pleasure springing up or driving through the village to 'take in' the School."[37]

In 1888 the directors closed the school. Sanborn said the reasons were "partly of sentiment and partly of convenience." Several of the main-stays who had done much of the lecturing were dead and "as the bond of unity at Concord was one of friendship rather than of interest or partisanship . . . the changes wrought by time and chance . . . had an influence on several of the [remaining] faculty."[38]

The pantheistic philosophy of the Transcendentalists was not at the center of the post-Civil War evolutionary controversies. Although it was easily adaptable to developmental modes of thought, as its attraction for the St. Louis Hegelians illustrated, Transcendentalism was left to one side in the task of rebuilding a religious world view. During a period in which institutions were of growing importance, its attitude toward institutions was at best ambivalent. The Emersonian ideal of the philosopher as a gentleman-seer was only practicable for a limited time. By 1890 the independent man of letters could find only minimal social support, and public attention went increasingly to men with university affiliation. When the Transcendentalists died, their ways died with them.

The change was not so abrupt as it might appear. While Harvard was emerging as a great university in the 1880s and 1890s, Davidson—a knight errant of the intellectual life, as William James called him—opened a summer school in Farmington, Connecticut, in the last year of the Concord School's existence. He soon shifted his locale to "Glenmore" in Keene Valley in the Adirondacks. A prospectus read:

> The advantages of spending the summer in this way were so great that it has been proposed this year to extend them to a larger number of persons, that is, to offer them to all serious students, and particularly to teachers, who may desire to pass an agreeable and profitable summer at a very moderate expense. The instruction will consist of private aid to study, and of lectures. The former will be given in the forenoon, or during walks in the afternoon; the latter on four evenings in the week, and on Sunday morning. Three evenings a week—Wednesday, Saturday, and Sunday—will be devoted to music and conversation. For the present the subjects of study will be

limited to what, in contradistinction to the natural sciences, may be called the culture sciences. . . .

Last summer a small number of persons gathered at Glenmore, in the Adirondacks, and freely arranged their days in a way which was found to yield at once rational enjoyment, instruction, and physical exercise. The mornings were devoted to private study and reading, the afternoons to exercise—walking, driving, mountain climbing, tree felling, etc., and the evenings either to the discussion of some important work upon philosophy, art, ethics, or religion, or music. Many of these evenings were spent round a camp fire. . . .

The subject of culture is man's spiritual nature, his intelligence, his affections, his will, and the modes in which these express themselves. This culture includes a history, a theory, and a practice, a certain familiarity with which must be acquired by every person who seriously desires to know his relations to the world and to perform his part worthily in those relations. The aim of the school, therefore, will be twofold,—(1) scientific, (2) practical. The former it will seek to reach by means of lectures on the general outlines of the history and theory of the various culture sciences, and by classes, conversations, and carefully directed private study in regard to their details. The latter it will endeavor to realize by encouraging its members to conduct their life in accordance with the highest ascertainable ethical laws, to strive after "plain living and high thinking," to discipline themselves in simplicity, kindness, thoughtfulness, regularity, and promptness.

In the life at Glenmore an endeavor will be made to combine solid study and serious conversation with reinvigorating rest and abundant and delightful exercise. It is hoped that this may become a place of annual gathering for open-minded persons interested in the serious things of life, so that, being thrown together in an informal way, they may be able to exchange views and initiate sympathies better than in the class room or at the hurried annual meeting. The retirement and quiet of Glenmore seem especially favorable for such things, and the numerous picnics and evening bonfires in the woods offer provision for the lighter moods. Last

year two plays were acted by members of the school, and it is hoped
that a Greek play may be brought out this year. The members of
the school will have access to a large, well-selected library. Every
meal at Glenmore will be opened with a few minutes' reading.[39]

The Glenmore School of the Cultural Sciences attracted as wide and
distinguished a group of people as had gone to Concord, and in addition
to the literary topics emphasized in Concord Davidson stressed formal
philosophy (one course in 1890 was devoted to the work of Thomas
Hill Green) and wide-ranging social and political problems (the same
year John Dewey lectured on the relation of church and state). Nonetheless, Glenmore suffered the fate of the Concord School. It reflected
Davidson's peculiar vision and was oriented to him alone. He died in
1900 and Glenmore soon after. The age of the amateur was over.

Amateurs, Institutions, and the Revolt against Empiricism

It is essential to make two points about this survey of informal philosophizing. First, the loosely organized societies of the last third of the
nineteenth century have received scholarly attention only to the extent
that philosophizing within institutions was moribund. Commentaries
devote space to the amateurs until William James established himself at
Harvard in the 1870s. The later growth of educational institutions and
the support they gave to philosophers soon made it impossible for
free-lance metaphysicians to have any impact at all.[40] The Metaphysical
Club does not hold its place in American intellectual history only because
of its members' towering intellect; they were thinking out matters when
institutional philosophy was at its nadir, and one of them, William James,
became with his Harvard affiliation the most widely known and influential thinker of his generation.

Second, we must not conclude that pragmatism was a first halting but
dramatic step toward twentieth-century empiricism. It is true that the
Metaphysical Club was sympathetic to Darwinian science and that, as
far as the pragmatic maxim was the club's common property, its main
antecedents were in the British tradition. But Berkeleyan and not Humean
empiricism intrigued the members. Moreover, in examining the thought
of each member of the club more fully, we shall find their empiricism mod-

ified by the work of Kant. Like Francis Bowen and the other amateurs, the individual members of the club were concerned with the dispute between science and theology. Although the Metaphysical Club's members did not share Bowen's anti-evolutionism they did share his religious orientation: a positive creed was necessary to human well-being. Indeed, the Unitarian philosophy failed because it relied so heavily on a common-sense empiricist epistemology: arguments for religion based solely on the evidence of the senses could not survive Darwin's analysis of the biological past. Bowen's students not only rejected his anti-evolutionism: to rescue religion and to comprehend the new science they also rejected his empiricism. Darwinian science compelled rejection of sensory evidence and acceptance of the mind's capacity to make great postulational leaps. Kant's philosophy met these demands and simultaneously provided a new basis for religion.

Toward the end of his life Bowen changed his views and haltingly came to terms with Kant, emphasizing Berkeley over Locke. But he could not accept the *a priori* aspects of Kant's philosophy that prohibited access to the noumenal world: the prohibition led away from "natural realism" and, he thought, could easily result in skepticism, however attenuated. Although continuing an interest in the Scots, the members of the club made a more positive appraisal of Kant. Developing Bowen's interest in *The Critique of Pure Reason*, they held that the only religion and the only science defensible in a Darwinian age were those based on Kant's thinking. Bowen showed by observational evidence that God existed; as we shall see, his successors forsook this empiricism for a form of fideism that also undergirded scientific advances.

The next three chapters develop these two points—one institutional, one philosophical—in exploring the careers and thought of some of the young philosophers.

4

CHAUNCEY WRIGHT: DEFENDER OF SCIENCE AND OF RELIGION

Wright and His Commentators

Chauncey Wright was the oldest and the most influential member of the Metaphysical Club. He was also atypical: his younger friends knew Wright as a disciple of John Stuart Mill, who was then giving new life to a skeptical empiricism. With the possible exception of Peirce, Wright was the most talented scientist of the philosophers in Cambridge, and in any event was an accomplished mathematician, biologist, and physicist. He was read in the literature of all the sciences, especially those connected with evolutionary theorizing; and he understood and could apply work in the philosophy of science—for example, Mill's *Logic*—to his understanding of science.[1] At times he described himself as a positivist, having in mind the school surrounding Mill (but also embracing Comte and Spencer for many people).

Wright held no university position and lived inconspicuously, but later commentators have picked him from oblivion, touting the club's leading light as a precursor of anti-metaphysical twentieth-century empiricism and as a source of the younger men's ideas. Wright is worth resurrecting, and there is some truth in describing him as a skeptical empiricist, but if we are to understand his thought, we must place it more carefully in its nineteenth-century context. As vulgar as was its Spencerian component, the positivist movement stressed scientific understanding of the phenomenal world and tended toward skepticism about the non-phenomenal. These emphases were not foreign to Hamilton or to Bowen.

Although intuitions were crucial for Bowen, his philosophy also relied on the evidence of the senses: the argument from design was an argument for God's existence drawn from observed phenomena. The "empiricists," among whom Wright counted himself, did dismiss intuitions as a holdover from rationalism, but Wright allowed that scientists postulated entities and theoretical constructs: in going beyond the bounds of the observed, Wright was as little an "empiricist" as Bowen, who clung to the observed but adopted intuitions. Moreover, Wright began his philosophic career as a Hamiltonian. Hamilton held a modest estimate of the possibility of knowledge of the noumenal realm and as Wright gravitated toward Mill's empiricism, he had only to modify his Hamiltonianism slightly. In short, Wright was not very different from Bowen and his gifted associates in the Metaphysical Club. What has made Wright stand out is the mistaken belief of scholars that he was prophetic of later thinking.

Wright's Early Views

Wright was born in Northampton, Massachusetts, in 1830. The Wrights were respectable but not well-to-do—his father was deputy sheriff and town grocer—and they sent the son to Harvard, where he graduated in 1852. Wright immediately found a job as a computer for the *Nautical Almanac*; it employed him for the next twenty years in Cambridge. The job involved a sort of mathematical piecework, and every year Wright let it go until the last few months and then worked around the clock on the required calculations. The salary was modest but Wright was unmarried and roomed alone, living quietly, almost frugally. Most important to him was the leisure the work gave him to think and write.

Wright was never prolific and he wrote in an impenetrable style; but his essays and reviews were of sufficient quality to earn him a reputation in New England. By the late 1860s and early 1870s he was accounted a philosophic sage in Cambridge and Holmes, James, and Peirce were attracted to his company. A gifted conversationalist, he enjoyed playing Socrates to the younger men, and a sweet and generous nature that belied his intellectual ability increased his impact. When an inheritance enabled him to be free of the *Almanac* in 1872, he devoted himself exclusively to an unhurried contemplative existence.

At Harvard, Wright's interests were scientific and mathematical, but a few years after graduation he turned to philosophy and to Hamilton. Wright was not a voracious reader but used other material as a catalyst for his own thoughts. For years he read the erudite Scot. As a close friend put it, "Chauncey's relation to Hamilton in those days was in a way like that of a devout Christian to his Bible."[2] When Mill published his *Examination* in 1865, Wright was already a convert to scientific Darwinism and had become critical of Hamilton;[3] but he underwent a philosophical crisis when he read Mill's book. He publicly took up its issues three times: an initial notice in the *Nation*; a longer analysis in the *North American Review*; and "a further reflection" in the *Nation* in 1867.[4]

Wright admitted and even applauded the justice of Mill's attack, but he lamented that Mill was unnecessarily polemical and abusive, often nit-picking, and occasionally uncomprehending of Hamilton's position. Mill had "greatly impair[ed] his [Hamilton's] reputation, before unchallenged, for profundity and accuracy, and even for scholarship," but Mill also lacked the sympathy to explicate Hamilton's intentions and failed to appreciate his abilities as a teacher. Mill and Hamilton both agreed that knowledge was relative and limited to the phenomenal world, but Mill repeatedly attacked Hamilton's "realism." Wright protested that Mill did not grasp Hamilton's idea that we knew the *effects* of things in themselves. Nonetheless, Wright allowed that Hamilton was wrong: with Mill, Wright concurred that the phenomenal world consisted of effects *on us* of what must remain unknown; he apparently accepted Mill's definition of substance as the permanent possibility of sensation and its implication that the known world lay within consciousness. Finally, Wright did not dispute Mill's critique of the Law of the Conditioned, but he did so with a bad conscience. Hamilton argued that we knew what was inconceivable although our knowledge could be no more than that one of two inconceivable alternatives was true. Wright believed that Hamilton's reasoning was defective, but wanted to preserve a role for what was beyond the phenomenal.[5]

In a correspondence with Frank Abbot coinciding with the controversy generated by the *Examination*, Wright defended the "gist" of Hamilton's position. As we shall see, Abbot attacked Hamilton in the manner of an apostate. Happy that Hamilton vindicated the existence of the unconditioned, he despaired that Hamilton limited our knowledge of things as they are in themselves, that is, the noumenal world.[6] À la Hamilton,

Wright replied that all we could know were phenomena and their laws; we could not assume or postulate that this order was also "the order of ontological dependence," that it had anything to do with the world of things in themselves. We might contend for "the bare existence" of the noumenal realm as the cause or ground of phenomena, but no more than that, and perhaps not even that. Hamilton, said Wright, was not a strict empiricist but was "opposed equally to the scepticism which would limit faith to the domain of real knowledge and to the dogmatism which would extend knowledge to the horizon of a legitimate faith":

> The purport of his philosophy, . . . so far from being a defense of empiricism, is a defense of faith against empiricism,—not by denying incontrovertible facts on the one hand, the limitations of sense and understanding; nor yet by assuming an indefensible dogma on the other hand, the position of a faculty of absolute knowledge; but by showing how the limits of thought may disclose themselves as such, or prove that thought is limited not simply by ignorance and experience, but by the conditions of its positive activity.[7]

Wright's position was complex. We could have no knowledge of the noumenal realm—*either of its natural or supernatural aspects*—of things existing by themselves, independent of their effects on us. According to "the experiential philosophy," knowledge in this area was "a closed question." With Hamilton, however, Wright allowed that the noumenal might be the object of a faith whose test was "emotional and moral, not intellectual." "Where reason is balanced," according to Hamilton's law, "aesthetic considerations—or perhaps I should say anaesthetic considerations—decide." Wright also called this faith a "belief" in the noumenal although warning that we ought to believe "in a spirit which recognizes the absence of the most perfect proof, however great the interests or the hopes may be which our faith sustains." "Our respects must decide what is worthy of belief. Not what claims our respect, but what gains it is our true faith, and the basis of our religion." And, Wright went on, "nobility of character is the sole end and criterion of its validity." What did this mean? Religion and morality were practical, as opposed to knowledge, which was apparently theoretical. They were concerned with a man's activity, his volitions, his desires, and his duties, and we could not know about the springs of conduct, of the truth of faith; these were non-phenomenal matters. The "criterion of its [faith's] validity" was a man's character: we appraised the truth of a religion by examining the effects it had on its adherents.[8]

Although this notion demonstrated Wright's Hamiltonian concern for the noumenal realm, it would be wrong to infer that Wright had, in effect, made the later distinction between fact and value, the cognitive and the emotive. We have so far analyzed Wright's view of the noumenal aspects of the natural *and* supernatural world. He was never clear whether "faith" was connected with its natural or supernatural dimension, or with both. More importantly, as Mill's disciple he emphasized phenomenal knowledge of the natural world. But couldn't there be phenomenal knowledge of the *supernatural* world? The empiricist need not hold that the world of phenomena was merely the world of *natural* phenomena; he need not identify theology with the noumenal, the supernatural with the non-phenomenal. Against religious apologists attacking Mill's empiricism, Wright hypothesized that knowledge of God's existence or non-existence was possible: phenomenal evidence about his existence or non-existence would yield just that, knowledge.

As a Hamiltonian, Wright distinguished between knowledge of the phenomenal world and faith in the supernatural's noumenal being; at least throughout the 1860s he suggested that this faith was justifiable. But in moving toward Mill, Wright indicated that there might be evidence of the supernatural in the phenomenal world. We could not hold that "evidence" of the supernatural belonged to the realm of faith simply because the evidence was inconclusive. Rather, this evidence belonged to the realm of knowledge because knowledge was the realm of evidence, although the evidence might not be enough to warrant a conclusion.[9]

In 1866 Wright declared that the questions of God's existence and of the immortality of the soul were open and difficult. We must be able to show that the law of nature was or was not universal and that absolute personal agency or uncaused voluntary actions had or had not determined the order or constitution of nature at any time.[10] A year later he wrote that as "scientific doctrines," that is, questions of knowledge, the existence of God and the immortality of the soul were "not proven."[11]

By 1870 Wright had at least tentatively decided. On the immortality of the soul, "there is more reason to believe it than to disbelieve it."[12]

We lack the argumentation that led him to this conclusion, and we are little better off in understanding why he thought he knew of the deity's existence. But here at least there is a connected account. Even before the publication of Mill's attack, Wright devoted himself to defending the claims of science, especially Darwinian science, and explicating its modes of reasoning. In fact, during the 1860s he damned natural theology: we could not, on the basis of the seemingly purposeful adaptation of means to ends in nature, regard the universe as existent for some purpose, for example the glorification of God. Scientists did not consider the causes and effects they explored to be teleological. To stipulate some as ends and others as means would require us to know already that the universe was teleological; but this thesis was just what natural theology attempted to prove. Specifically, the Darwinian theory did not assume, and afforded no evidence for, the belief that nature anticipated any adaptation. We could not claim that any evolutionary change occurred to realize some end simply because the change produced a certain effect. Natural theology was question-begging.[13]

This was not all that Wright had to say on natural theology. He did not find it peculiar that man and his self-consciousness were products of evolution. But, like Bowen, Wright could not see how the phenomenon of life and more particularly that of sensation could arise from the world of matter. The origin of life was an "insoluble mystery." The attempt to reduce sensation to anything but sensation was "gratuitous"; we faced two coexisting substances, matter and mind, and had no way to determine how either could be the cause of the other.[14] Wright briefly put forward an abstruse theory suggesting that mental phenomena were "regulating causes" of the natural world, different from efficient causes, adding nothing to and subtracting nothing from these natural forces. We might not understand how this "regulation" was possible but mental conditions might "restrain, excite and combine the conversions of physical forces in the cycles into which they do not enter." A higher type of this kind of regulation might exist in those laws of nature that determined the order of conversion of nature's physical forces.[15] All this hinted at a spiritual power permeating the natural world, but did not explain how life originated. Yet, said Wright, organisms had come into existence, the living had come from the non-living. Might we not postulate that only the creative power of a deity could bring this miracle to pass?

In the universal order of nature, Wright found a sign, or rather the sign, of an immanent God: the evidence for his existence was the occurrence of an otherwise inexplicable set of events, the emergence of life. Moreover, Wright believed that natural selection was the pervasive working out of Mill's principle of utility. Natural selection, Wright said, achieved the greatest good for the greatest number; viewed historically nature preserved the fit and allowed only the unfit to perish. Consequently, natural selection in the organic realm manifested God just to the extent that he was revealed in the bringing forth of the greatest good for the greatest number; so far natural selection was identical to natural theology.[16]

Wright could dismiss the crude teleology that made means and ends of specific causes and effects in nature. But cosmic history had created and sustained life "by that great alchemic experiment which, employing all the influences of nature and all the ages of the world, has actually brought forth most if not all of the definite forms of life in the last and greatest work of creative power."[17] The whole drama of evolution, the history of the phenomenal world in its wholeness, manifested such evidence as we had of the existence of God.*

Wright's scattered remarks on moral philosophy, written at the time he was defending this restrained natural theology, corroborate this interpretation. The class of intrinsic goods, reckoned Wright, consisted of the ultimate sources of pleasure of whatever rank or intensity: pleasures of various sorts were the immediate sources of human happiness or excellence. Although he did not value them all equally, their value and ranking depended only on preference and varied from individual to individual. The realm of ends was apparently one of faith; the ground of value was non-cognitive. But these values were not moral: in respect to morality Wright was a utilitarian. The principle of utility—the injunction to achieve the greatest good for the greatest number as the end of morality—operated for him in two ways. First, it could order an individual's pleasures so that a person, behaving consistently, would achieve *his* greatest pleasure. Second, however, the principle defined as moral that which maximized the total pleasures of all, based upon the order of preference of each. For Wright moral questions were empirical, and appropriate

*For the relation of Wright's thought to that of his older friend Asa Gray see PD, p. 161; chapter 1; and, for another view, A. Hunter Dupree, *Asa Gray* (Cambridge: Harvard University Press, 1959), pp. 289–90.

calculating techniques could answer them. But he also believed that his natural theology, identical to natural selection, showed that the principle of utility was all-pervasive in nature. The principle that defined the moral also described the history of the cosmos. Although Wright could not rationally determine the preferences which guided individual behavior, in the long run what *ought* to be *is* exactly what occurred in the course of evolution—the maximizing of pleasure "in all sentient beings."[18] In creating life the entire development of the phenomenal world evidenced God; in maximizing pleasure it defined the moral.

Mill's empiricism affected Wright curiously. As a Hamiltonian he relegated theological questions to the world of things in themselves where faith justified belief. After 1865, however, he saw the possibility of obtaining phenomenal evidence to answer theological questions: the question of God's existence had both a phenomenal and a noumenal dimension. Later Wright forswore any talk of a noumenal realm, although he still maintained that faith must determine the practical aspects of our religious life and of our behavior. But regarding theoretical knowledge of morality and religion, he adopted a modest version of natural theology. His strongest arguments against it occurred in the earliest, Hamiltonian, period of his writings. He later contended that whatever evidence there was for the existence of God occurred in the phenomenal world. Although he still rejected the crudities of the usual treatments of natural theology, under Mill's influence he developed a religious view that was untenable on Hamiltonian grounds. By 1870 Wright said that the phenomenal order as a whole manifested deity. This order had produced life from non-life, a feat beyond our capacity to explain and so giving evidence of divinity. While this evolutionary pantheism did not warrant a god who oversaw the world as a moral order, Wright intimated that life itself was absolutely valuable.[19]

Wright's Darwinian Philosophy

To put Wright in proper perspective I have emphasized the speculative dimension of his thought, but in the years after Mill's *Examination* the bulk of his work concerned the defense of science and its method, and he grew increasingly committed to Mill's ideas. The popularizers' distortions of Darwin impelled Wright to champion the rights of science

and urge a proper conception of its role. On one hand, he attacked cari-
catures and misconstruals of the Darwinian hypothesis conjured up by
religious conservatives; he fought the more able opponents of Darwin
with his argumentative powers and the available evidence; and, as we
have noted, he warned against the fallacies that using specific scientific
conclusions to support religion was liable to. On the other hand, Wright
condemned various evolutionary cosmologies that sprang up during this
period. "German Darwinism" was the name he gave to the use of evolutionary doctrine to support systems of metaphysics, and he was contemptuous of the super-scientific claims of its adherents.[20] John Fiske was
one of the objects of his attack, but Wright's treatment of the master,
Herbert Spencer, exemplified his hostility to what he regarded as char-
latanism and revealed his own view of science.

In Spencer's work Wright found "nothing deserving attention . . .
except bad criticism, a perverted terminology, and fanciful discriminations." Spencer's versatility in various fields only equalled his incom-
petency in each of them; his law of evolution was merely a generalized
description of certain facts in abstract language.[21] Real laws were more
than this; they were finders of truth, not merely summarizers. Moreover,
in bringing various facts under the umbrella of his "law," Spencer transferred these terms from their original clear contexts to other obscure
ones. Spencer's view that basic scientific terms were unknowable and
basic laws transcended empirical proof indicated to Wright that Spencer
simply did not understand scientific method.[22] Scientific facts and
theories described the phenomenal character of the world. A fact was
such a description directly verified by experience. But all theories (or
laws) had experiential support:

> a theory . . . if true, has all the characteristics of a fact, except that
> its verification is possible only by indirect, remote, and difficult
> means. To convert theories into facts is to add *simple verification*,
> and the theory thus acquires the full characteristics of a fact. . . .
> Modern science deals then no less with theories than with facts, but
> always as much as possible with the verification of theories,—if
> not to make them facts by simple verification through experiment
> and observation, at least to prove their truth by indirect verifica-
> tion.[23]

The *value* of these theories can only be tested, say the positivists, by an appeal to sensible experience, by deductions from them of consequences which we can confirm by the undoubted testimony of the senses. Thus, while ideal or transcendental elements are admitted into scientific researches, though in themselves insusceptible of simple verification, they must still show credentials from the senses, either by affording from themselves consequences capable of sensuous verification, or by yielding such consequences in conjunction with ideas which by themselves are verifiable.[24]

In stressing the value-neutrality of scientific propositions, Wright pointed out that many of the examples Spencer brought together as his law were not scientific. Teleological conceptions tainted those concerning the character and origin of social progress. Spencer's description of these facts "springs from the [purposeful] order which the mind imposes upon what it imperfectly observes, rather than from that which the objects, were they better known, would supply to the mind."[25]

Two positive contributions to the Darwinian hypothesis, "A Physical Theory of the Universe" and "The Evolution of Self-Consciousness," best illustrated Wright's abilities as a philosopher and scientist. In each article he not only showed scientific skill but also developed his own philosophic position.

Darwin assumed in the *Origin* that evolution had operated through an unlimited temporal span and postulated processes requiring immense periods of time. Lord Kelvin challenged this assumption when, using the nebular hypothesis, he investigated the age of the solar system and the sun's immense annual expenditure of heat. The hypothesis supposed that the system came into being when a rotating nebula cooled, throwing off rings of matter that contracted into planets and their moons, with the great mass of the condensing nebula becoming the sun. The contraction and condensation of the nebula—the planets and the sun—would convert energy into heat and this process offered a means of explaining the sun's thermal expenditure. In 1854 Helmholtz demonstrated that a contraction by the sun of a thousandth of its radius would supply over two thousand years of solar heat. Soon after the *Origin* appeared, Kelvin argued similarly to determine the age of the earth. The figure he reached, around 10 million years, was inconsequential when the Darwinists were asking for at least 300 million. Kelvin's prestige was so great that, although his theories were later cast aside, the age of the earth was the most difficult scientific problem the Darwinists had to meet.[26]

Wright's "Physical Theory of the Universe" was an early and shrewd attempt to answer Kelvin. Wright devised an alternative to the nebular hypothesis from which Kelvin's view followed, given the state of nineteenth-century physics. Wright noted that the fall of solid bodies into the sun would also produce heat. The force of impact would vaporize the solid bodies and the parts of the sun's surface receiving the impact, creating a cloud of gas. When the gas cooled to solid form, gravity would again draw the solids into the sun. These facts, Wright said, would "reverse the nebular hypothesis":

> Instead of, in former ages, a huge gaseous globe contracted by cooling and by gravitation, and consolidated at its centre, we have supposed one now existing, and filling that portion of the interstellar spaces over which the sun's attraction predominates,—a highly rarefied continuous gaseous mass, constantly evaporated and expanded from its solid centre, but constantly condensed and consolidated near its outer limits,—constantly heated at its centre by the fall of solid bodies from its outer limits, and constantly cooled and condensed at these limits by the conversion of heat into motion and the arrest of this motion by gravitation.

He concluded that the planets were successively formed and finally lost in the sun.[27]

Here was an indefinitely old, repetitive cosmic progress. Wright called it a principle of counter-movement or cosmical weather: heat and gravitation acting analogously to the weather constituted "the means and the general mode of operation from which we anticipate an explanation of the general constitutions of solar and sidereal systems." But Wright's article offered more than an alternative to the nebular hypothesis and an attempt to rescue Darwin from Kelvin's attack. Behind the nebular hypothesis, Wright stated, was a primitive teleology. Under certain conditions natural operations appeared directed toward a definite result— the production of the solar system—and when they had effected this result theorists supposed their formative action to cease, the system to be finished.[28] Wright simultaneously attacked Kelvin and Spencer, who used the nebular hypothesis as an example of his law of evolution. On Wright's "physical theory," creation was part of a directionless process that contradicted an evolutionary cosmology.[29] Neither the cosmic weather characterizing physical nature nor the scientific meaning of Darwin's theory supported Spencer's evolutionary doctrine.

Wright wrote "A Physical Theory of the Universe" in 1864 when he was still a Hamiltonian and when his chief concern was to prevent teleological speculation like Spencer's from intruding on the phenomenal realm. His most elaborate piece of research, "The Evolution of Self-Consciousness" appeared in 1873. In it he again displayed his ability to defend Darwin, but he also continued the philosophic thinking engendered by his commitment to Mill.

The origin of life was a mystery displaying the presence of God, but Wright was prepared to tackle the central issue of the evolutionary controversy, the origin of man and his self-consciousness. He first denied the old principle that the effect must resemble its cause. A causal sequence was an event following a certain aggregate of conditions such that whenever the aggregate occurred, the event (or effect) occurred. The causal relation was a species of invariable succession, an unconditional invariable succession enabling us to say not only that actual events followed actual aggregates but also that the succession would always occur. On this analysis of causality the notion of resemblance of cause and effect was useless: the conditions constituting the cause did not constitute the effect; the effect simply followed them and might be wholly unlike the cause.[30] The question of the evolution of self-consciousness was thus one of determining those conditions that would give rise to self-consciousness and of ascertaining how these conditions could have come about; there was no religious question of explaining how something new could emerge.[31]

Wright viewed the behavior of organisms on a continuum ranging from the instinctual to the largely habitual. In habitual behavior a goal mediated the environmental stimulus to the organism's response. The response was instrumental to the goals of the organism; Wright said the organism was motivated, although its response tended to become automatic in the presence of appropriate stimuli. In these cases Wright held that the organism was free, whereas if behavior was instinctive or instrumental to goals the organism did not desire, it was constrained or necessitated. This distinction was his basis for investigating simple consciousness. The ego or self controlled behavior and was distinguished from the non-ego, which was not subject to such control. A more advanced form of consciousness, self-consciousness, occurred with the awareness of this distinction, a consciousness of the self as a cause different from other causes. Wright argued that consciousness existed in the higher animals, who behaved as agents with feelings distinct from those of other organisms and from nature.[32] The problem was to define this phenomenon at the more advanced level.

Habitual behavior implied the presence of what Wright called signs. A habit was a relation between classes of stimuli and of responses. When a habitual response occurred, an organism regarded a stimulus as like the other stimuli which evoked the response; it was a sign representing a class of objects in the presence of which an organism made a response. An organism behaving habitually need not be aware that it was using the stimulus in this way. Wright did not limit signs to perceptual stimuli— anything functioned as a sign if it suggested one of the group of objects to which the organism responded.[33]

Most animals were not aware that habitual behavior involved grouping objects into classes or determining that one member of a group represented the others; the response simply followed the stimulus. But because animals did behave habitually, Wright assumed they had a rudimentary conceptual apparatus: they possessed images representing past experience and permitting them to organize their behavior to achieve goals.[34] For Wright this analysis was equivalent to saying that there was an ego or self, for the concepts which defined habitual behavior simultaneously distinguished the self and its accomplishments from the rest of the world. Consequently, self-consciousness arose when the organism became conscious of its use of signs. Language afforded the most important example of the consciousness of signs leading to self-consciousness, though Wright did not deny that a simple sort of self-consciousness might exist in the higher animals.[35]

Self-consciousness required sufficient strength of memory and imagination to hold a sign before the mind and contrast it with its object so that the representative function might come to the organism's attention. Organisms could most easily achieve this state using linguistic signs, but Wright's argument did not depend on the existence of language, although language and self-consciousness had developed together, the former surely accompanying anything beyond the rudimentary existence of the latter. "The germ of the distinctively human form of self-consciousness" demanded only the power of memory and attention to fix on a vivid outward object without losing a hold on some inner feeling, image, or impression signifying it. The organism then recognized thought (that is, the use of concepts) as such and could reflect upon it.[36]

Natural Realism

Wright had written his essay at Darwin's request, and it spoke to a critical problem of evolutionary science, but Wright also used the occasion to philosophize. When an organism became self-conscious, it became aware of the distinction between itself and the world; it could ruminate on the classification of experience as either subjective or objective, as belonging to either the ego or non-ego. This classification depended on the relation of various portions of experience—on whether an experience functioned as a sign or as what was signified. This discrimination effectively divided experiences on the basis of their subjection to or independence from the will: human beings classified experience in the interests of activity, and in so doing created the distinction between self and the world. The dichotomy between subject and object existed because of observation and analysis; it was not given but developed as consciousness developed, the ego and non-ego being the summa genera into which human consciousness divided.[37]

Considered in itself, a phenomenon in consciousness was neither objective nor subjective, but we never experienced such unattributed or unclassified states of consciousness. We instinctively classified phenomena, but our classifications ultimately derived from the experience of our ancestors whose conceptual framework we inherited.[38]

Many philosophers—the representational realists beginning with Descartes—mistakenly transformed this intra-conscious distinction into one between consciousness and the object causing it. On the contrary, Wright said, we knew the object as it existed, and the object of consciousness was as immediately known as the subject. Knowledge of objects was just as direct as of subjects, while neither was immediate. This view, Wright declared, was that of "natural realism . . . as qualified by the theory of evolution."[39]

With the important exception of his positive use of Darwin, Wright's position was just that of Bowen's later work. We knew the physical object as directly as we knew mind; they were mutually dependent and made distinct through appropriate activity, although we could not fathom the (noumenal) ground of either sort of phenomenon. Unlike Wright, Bowen could not explain the development of self-consciousness but, like Wright, Bowen gave up knowledge of the noumenal. Their positions applied only to the phenomenal realm, both claiming that we knew objects as they are, but that knowledge had nothing to do with "inconceivable substrata."[40] It was also consistent for Wright to call himself "an empirical idealist," a follower of Mill. Wright made all his distinctions within consciousness, within the phenomenal realm.[41]

Wright said little about the time before consciousness existed. His ideas were fragmentary, consistent with his belief in the mystery of the origins of life. He argued that simply because consciousness was necessary to the known cosmos, it did not follow that consciousness was necessary to the absolute existence of the cosmos. But what this "absolute existence" would amount to he could not say, and for him the annihilation of consciousness would be the annihilation of subjects and objects. Nonetheless, the cosmos of the distant past was not necessarily incompatible with the existence of a perceiving mind, however unfit that cosmos might have been for the sustenance of the animal body with its perceptive organs; and Wright considered the cosmos at such a time to be as it would have appeared had minds existed to perceive it.[42]

Wright's Philosophical Temperament

In the early 1870s when Wright was the "boxing master" of the young men in the Metaphysical Club, he had a reputation as an austere empiricist and even called his viewpoint Nihilism: we could only be sure of the discrete and momentarily present data of immediate consciousness. We can dismiss some of this as a pose. He loved philosophic controversy and enjoyed the Socratic stance that encouraged youthful discussion while curbing its exuberance. He even admitted that Nihilism was "rather a discipline than a positive doctrine."[43] But this explanation will take us only so far. By the 1870s Wright had rejected Hamilton's minimal agnosticism about the noumenal world and declared positively, as

William James has made famous, that "behind the bare phenomenal facts . . . there is *nothing*."[44] And like Hume, Wright nearly asserted that the mind passively analyzed these bare phenomena.[45] Moreover, he broadened his notion of cosmic weather to show why a noumenal ground for phenomena was unnecessary: the phenomenal world was itself orderly, having the order of cosmic weather, and he had to posit a ground for it only if he assumed there had been some primeval chaos antecedent to the phenomenal order. But Wright had no reason to assume that the present orderly system itself had a genesis. Only a "metaphysician" would reason that an ancient chaos ever had existed.[46]

William James, who worked himself out of an emotional slump by committing himself to an activist world view, avowed that philosophical positions were a matter of temperament and attributed Wright's intellectual parsimony to "a defect in the active or impulsive part of his mental nature."[47] Wright agreed that philosophical commitment was temperamental,[48] and there was much in his character to justify James's remark. Wright was unambitious and, less fortunately, at times almost pathologically passive. He spoke about his activity as if it had "a kind of fatality." One of his close friends wrote that he allowed the scientific habit of suspending judgment to creep into the region of his conduct. Wright was at times content to have no enterprise at all and to decline to make the effort of ordering his own life. He knew little of the exigencies of practical affairs and appeared as if always on vacation. Sometimes he had no social occupations or correspondence, and without employment to require him to conform to rules and regular hours of work, without a family, and without community duties of any sort, he was often a strange and solitary man.[49] He had never been free from occasional periods of aimless melancholy. At times his depression led to bouts of drunkenness. This occurred once in the early 1860s and then again at the end of the decade when Wright was for a time an alcoholic. At the urgings of friends he recovered control of himself, although over the next few years there were relapses.[50] In 1870 Eliot asked him to teach philosophy at Harvard, and the enthusiasm with which he responded and the eagerness with which he prepared testify that he would have enjoyed a permanent attachment, a position that would have commanded regularity in his daily life.[51] But it was not to be. The gifts he displayed in conversation were lost in lecturing and, although he taught again in 1874, he had no career as a professor.

Nineteenth-century American intellectuals needed a faith to live by, and although Wright had a conception of God, it was not enough to sustain a positive orientation to existence—in fact it was deterministic. Fits of gloom continued to overcome him in the early 1870s, especially when friends were absent and he would arrive at his "uninhabited room, where no one waited to welcome."[52] This was the situation one night late in the summer of 1875. Wright suffered some sort of stroke at his desk and died soon after. He was forty-five years old.

5

FISKE AND ABBOT: PROFESSORIAL
FAILURES

Amateurs and Institutions

John Fiske and Francis Ellingwood Abbot were strong thinkers within the ambience of the Metaphysical Club and exemplified its larger concerns: both defended evolutionary theorizing and religion and did so using Kantian and Scottish ideas. But Fiske and Abbot advanced their ideas in Cambridge as independent entrepreneurs and not at Harvard. For different reasons both men were unable to find niches in the expanding university system; in this sense they were forced to be amateurs, men of letters of a sort. The lack of institutional backing and prestige influenced not only their philosophical work but also the reception of the work by contemporaries and by posterity. Their fate demonstrated the increasing importance of university preferment.

Abbot tried for years to obtain a university post. Without the stimulation and visibility a job would have provided, he produced bitter and overstated writing that received little attention during his lifetime or after. Unable initially to get a job at Harvard, Fiske eschewed the university and became one of the era's great popularizers. Lacking the discipline the academy would have brought and a reputable scholarly base, he was ignored and stigmatized by serious thinkers and his writing was forgotten after his death.

Fiske and His Work

Fiske was born in Connecticut in 1842 and spent his youth in Middletown, living with his mother's family in an elderly and indulgent household. He was a precocious child, an omnivorous reader with a prodigious memory. Even as a boy he determined to become a great scholar. Although his youthful studies led him to become known as the town infidel, he eagerly sought broad and synthetic views of the realm of knowledge, perhaps to replace the Calvinist doctrine that could no longer sustain him. As an adolescent, Fiske yearned to leave Middletown, identifying with the world of nineteenth-century speculation. At Harvard, he continued to develop a scheme for mastering all knowledge, but the modes of teaching there seemed provincial to him. The faculty respected his intelligence but were put off by his attitude toward them; he did not make the kind of record he thought he deserved.

When he was graduated in 1863, he wanted a life as a thinker and the fame and fortune he associated with such a life, but he was unable to get a teaching position. A brief and desultory fling at the Harvard law school convinced him that he would have to make his way as a writer. He attached himself to the literary and publishing group in Boston that was making a success of national magazines with cultural and intellectual aspirations, and by the late 1860s he had achieved a minor reputation.

Given Fiske's desire to make a lasting contribution to philosophy, his decision to ingratiate himself with the Boston literati was a mistake, but it is easy to see how he was misled. He had before him the example of Emerson and other philosophic amateurs. Without collegiate affiliation, he needed both a platform and a way to support himself, for he lacked the independent means possessed by many thinkers of the older generation. And even at this stage of his career, public acclaim was as important to him as the intellectual satisfactions of the life of the mind. Fame would come only if he had a large audience, and the magazines offered one. Fiske adopted a popular style even while discussing academic subjects, hoping to gain public attention and scholarly renown at the same time. His manner of living always seemed to outrun his income, and he took on more and more tasks as he became prominent—anything that would bring in extra money.[1]

In one of his first innovations as president of Harvard, Eliot extended the existing university lecture system to give more advanced instruction and to bring Harvard into the swirl of contemporary controversy. Because Fiske was a lucid expositor of Herbert Spencer's evolutionary cosmology, Eliot thought Fiske might be useful in reinvigorating the college and appointed him in 1869–1870 and in 1870–1871 to give lectures in "the positive philosophy." Three years later, in 1874, Fiske published his two-volume *Outlines of Cosmic Philosophy*. This large work had grown out of his lectures and was the main philosophic book he wrote, the basis on which his standing as a thinker would rest.

The *Cosmic Philosophy* surveyed all knowledge,[2] but its main thrust was outlining how the Spencerian law of evolution worked not only in the creation of the natural world but also in the world of man. There was a world of phenomena, "the effects produced upon our consciousness by unknown external agencies" (1 : 20); the task was to discover the laws governing these phenomena (1: 40–44). Dismissing Wright's critique of 1864, Fiske believed that Spencer had uncovered a law that made sense of all human experience, and he proposed to apply it in the *Cosmic Philosophy*. This "law of evolution" claimed "precisely . . . the universality claimed for the law of gravitation" (1 : 267–75). It was not, however, merely an abstract formulation but supplied an explanation "of any given order of concrete phenomena." As Fiske stated the law, "the integration of matter and concomitant dissipation of motion, which primarily constitutes Evolution, is attended by a continuous change from indefinite, incoherent homogeneity to definite coherent heterogeneity of structure and function, through successive differentiations and integrations" (1 : 337).

Spencer and Fiske thought they had described a universal process of evolution and dissolution. The concentration of material units and the development of an unlikeness among the units that made up any aggregate characterized the former; diffusion and sameness marked the latter. Evolution was "coherent," dissolution "incoherent." The two processes rhythmically took place in both general and local spatio-temporal segments of the universe, but considered as a whole, that part of the universe inhabited by humanity was evolving—the most important, enduring, and large-scale segments of experience were becoming coherent and heterogeneous (2 : 367–68). Fiske located all empirical knowledge within this framework: he covered the beginning of the planetary system, the development of the earth, and the growth of living organisms, but his most interesting speculation concerned the evolution of consciousness and of society.

With Spencer, Fiske defined life as the adjustment of inner relations to outer relations; he posited an external environment and an organism whose reactions maintained an "equilibrium" between it and the environment (2 : 67–70). Fiske defined conscious life further: the "psychical" came into existence with the increase in the spatio-temporal extension of the organism's adaptations to its environment; mind arose when an organism habitually adjusted to future and geographically distant contingencies (2 : 88–93). An organism responding to its environment in this way, Fiske said, was increasing the heterogeneity of its responses and was thus more highly evolved (2 : 95–97). Although the argument was much less developed, he also found the physiological ground of consciousness in the brain's capacity for comparing present phenomena with those remembered. An organism able to use the past to react to the future had a memory, and Fiske associated this capacity with the dawn of self-consciousness (2 : 154–56):

> intellectual superiority . . . is summed up in his [civilized man's] superior power of representing that which is not present to sense. . . . this superiority . . . shows itself . . . in all those combinations of present with past impressions which accompany the extension of the correspondence in space and time, and its increase in heterogeneity, definiteness, and coherence. It is his ability to reproduce copies of his own vanished states of consciousness (2 : 312).

Fiske dabbled with the mechanistic interpretation of mind popularized by Spencer, but he never attempted to reduce the psychical to the physical; like Wright, he denied that this reduction was possible. Two parallel and correlative series existed, one of neural, the other of mental processes. Materialism was false, and the reduction of thought to the motions of matter was impossible. All that Fiske could do was to show the transformation of one kind of "material motion" into another; no conceivable advance in the physical sciences would enable man to identify the most minute "modes of motion" with the thought and feeling parallel to them. Rather, Fiske inferred that there was an "ultimate unit of which Mind is composed, a simple *psychical shock* answering to the simple *physical pulsation* which is the ultimate unit of nervous action." The "manifold and diverse compounding" of myriads of these primitive psychical shocks formed elementary sensations and finally what Fiske called intelligence.[3]

Fiske's most significant discussion analyzed human society. Many animals, the higher mammals especially, evidenced intelligence, but man's cultural development or civilization distinguished him. Fiske attributed this to a social impulse distinct from the gregariousness of other animals. The intelligence defining man's emergence demanded a long period during which "the nervous connections involved in ordinary adjustments are becoming organized"; in some animals they were organized after birth; in man the dependency period extended much longer than a few months and, if the young were to survive, required a protective mechanism. The intelligence enabling man to triumph over the beasts entailed a rudimentary family structure becoming more elaborate as growing mental complexity lengthened the dependency period. In the family, Fiske hypothesized, the parental feelings and affections developed. They were more and more associated "with anticipations and memories," and this situation was the basis for inherited social propensities and the progress of civilization that Fiske identified with the transition from primitive to European man.[4]

The social instinct essentially displayed in the first families was "*the continuous weakening of selfishness and the continuous strengthening of sympathy*," the gradual supplanting of egotism by altruism. For Fiske this change meant a difference in the way an organism was self-pleased, and examining the history of mankind, he found this kind of evolution in the mode of self-pleasing (2 : 201–03). Sympathy extended from the family to the tribal community to larger and larger groups (2 : 353). Displaying Spencer's law, these groups became heterogeneous, definite, complex, and interdependent (2 : 164).

In light of this evolving social instinct, Fiske commented on philosophical problems. He said that the rationalists and empiricists had misconceived the debate on the source of knowledge. Descartes was wrong in defending a kind of intuitional knowledge not due to experience, but Locke was also wrong in believing that each human being built up a conceptual set anew. In learning, experience acted as a catalyst on minds that tended to respond in certain ways under certain conditions; our conceptual framework initially took shape as an untutored response to experience, but in the course of evolution those elements making for survival—those that gave us truth—became hereditary. Similarly, Fiske dismissed the dispute in ethics between intuitionists and utilitarians. The moral sentiments were based on a rule of utility related to the unselfish and sympathetic responses that had enabled us to survive and progress. But we now legitimately described these sentiments as intuitions: we had inherited them from our ancestors and were inherently disposed to respond in certain ways irrespective of any conscious estimate of pleasure or utility (2:326).

Fiske was working in the tradition of those philosophers of history—Vico, Turgot, Condorcet—who saw world history as a drama of human progress. But to this vision he linked a Darwinian notion of change by natural selection. The result was a perfect example of what Chauncey Wright had called German Darwinism. Certainly when he came to the evolution of man, Fiske assumed that "more evolved" meant "better" and "more civilized," and that man progressed from lower to higher forms (2 : 209–28). After admitting that history in many cases was a story of retrogression, Fiske wrote, "progress has been on the whole the most constant and prominent feature of the history of a considerable and important portion of mankind." He did not explicitly conceive natural selection teleologically but it is difficult to see how he could deny it purposive characteristics (2 : 192–93).

There is one other argument of the *Cosmic Philosophy* that we cannot neglect. Fiske saw himself as a positivist, disdainful of metaphysics and beholden only to science. But the word 'positivist' had a negative connotation in many circles, associated as it was with Auguste Comte (1798–1857), whose "Positive Philosophy" denied supernatural religion. Comte's law of the three stages—theological, metaphysical, and positive—purported to show that man had slowly forsaken the supernatural and finally, in the last stage, overthrown it in embracing a religion of humanity. Spencer and Fiske were close to this kind of theorizing, but in the *Cosmic Philosophy* Fiske determined to show that Spencer was far more important and subtle than Comte and that Comte's atheism was indefensible. Throughout the book Fiske disputed Comte, whose central failing was believing in the metaphysical adequacy of the phenomenal world. Comte was correct in believing that the phenomena were all that we could know, but he did not consider "our ineradicable belief in the absolute existence of Something which underlies and determines the series of changes [the world of phenomena] which constitutes our consciousness." In some fashion, Fiske had to make room for the "unknowable Cause or causes of phenomena." Except for the supposed inconceivability of its alternative, there was little to support Fiske's belief in what Spencer made famous as the Unknowable, but Fiske's meaning was patent in his appraisal of Berkeley.

Fiske agreed with Berkeley that the phenomenal world was the world as known and related to consciousness. Berkeley went on to declare any supposed noumenal world a figment of the imagination and the cause of the phenomena the deity. This doctrine, said Fiske, assumed that "the possibilities of our thinking are to be taken as the measures of the possibilities of existence." Berkeley identified the Unknowable with a personal God, while Comte ignored its existence. Although the advance of knowledge had rightfully been one of a gradual "deanthropomorphization" of the Causal Agency, Fiske argued that we could not rid ourselves of the concept altogether (1 : 74–78). He had to locate this agency on our cognitive map even though it was indescribable and incognizable.

Fiske's thought was always religious. Even while emphasizing the limitations of anthropomorphism in the *Cosmic Philosophy*, Fiske was a "cosmic theist," a believer in "a Power which is beyond Humanity and upon which Humanity depends . . . [and] which Cosmism refrains from defining and limiting by metaphysical formulas" (1 : 184). But Fiske went beyond this austere conception, while admitting that his suggestion was not scientifically provable. He had already dismissed the reduction of the mental to the material, and at the end of his work he returned to this idea. Fiske was forced to symbolize the Unknowable in terms of experience, but experience of phenomena was of the psychical. Consequently, as far as the exigencies of thinking required signifying the infinite power manifested in the phenomenal world, we were bound to do so in "quasi-psychical" rather than "quasi-material" terms. Fiske had already asserted that the transformation of force into feeling was inconceivable, while it was conceivable that units of feeling might compose the Unknowable. Fiske concluded that it was appropriate to speak of God as Spirit. He called this "the God of the Christian, though freed from . . . illegitimate formulas."[5]

Fiske's Christianity was little more than nominal, but as if to ensure its palatability he anchored it to a respectable social philosophy. With regard to "the time-honoured institutions which are woven into the fabric of modern society, our Cosmic Philosophy is eminently conservative—owning no fellowship either with the radical Infidelity of the eighteenth century or with the world-mending schemes of [Comtean] Positivism." Society grew into higher states, he said, and men were bred into them: they could not be taught civilization or be remade for it. Society would slowly reform itself, and knowledge of evolution could enable us to see what was required and what must come in any event. He thus simultaneously assured his audiences of progress and of the foolishness of strident reformers. This self-satisfaction derived from a correct understanding of evolution "in which science and religion find their reconciliation" (2 : 472–92).

Fiske's Later Views

Fiske shrewdly united his ideas on society with those on evolution and, although his philosophy was a crude variety of Kantianism laced with Darwinism, the *Cosmic Philosophy* made him a highly regarded thinker. In 1874 men did not judge philosophic merit by technical competence, but on the ability to speak to broad cultural issues; this Fiske did well. While his success was short-lived, he initially enjoyed an Emersonian repute. But although he hoped that the lectures and his two-volume opus would land him a Harvard job—he began to grow a beard to look professorial—no permanent and prestigious employment was forthcoming.[6] Eliot's scheme of university lectures did not work out, and when he abandoned it Fiske resorted in earnest to making his living as a free-lance writer and lecturer.

The lost Harvard opportunity was a turning point in his career; thereafter he wrote and spoke in a vein that won a public large enough to support him but left him ignorant of changing patterns of scholarly success. A generation before, Fiske's future reputation would have been secure; historians of Emerson's era have not found profundity and amateur popularization at odds. In the next generation, however, commentators seeking enduring wisdom have looked to the systematic research promoted by the academy and to the thinkers whose expertise was sanctioned by collegiate affiliation. Perhaps Fiske did not have the capacity to do what critics have come to regard as serious work. But without the prestige of university employment or the regimen it would have provided, it proved impossible for him to produce the kind of work that would gain a later readership.

Fiske never again wrote anything philosophically comparable to the *Cosmic Philosophy*, whatever its defects, and turned thereafter to history, particularly that of the United States. Drawing on his ideas of social evolution, he treated the political organization of the Anglo-Saxon countries as the highest mode of nation-building. His grand scheme was to account for the growth of American civilization, placing it within a comprehensive view of the expansion of European thought and culture. Concentrating on the interplay of two factors, militancy and industrialism, he explored the American experience and its future significance.[7] *The Critical Period of American History 1783–1789* (1888) elaborated these themes as they applied to the denouement of the Articles of Confederation and advanced an interpretation important long after his death. Speaking and writing on these topics in the 1880s and 1890s, he gained a wide following and also brought in enough money to live in the style to which he had grown accustomed.[8]

Fiske did not stop philosophizing. In 1884, 1885, and 1899 he wrote three short works reinterpreting his earlier thought—*The Destiny of Man, The Idea of God*, and *Through Nature to God*. He claimed that he had not essentially changed his beliefs, but the troubles he had had in establishing himself and the long illnesses of his children led him to consider religion more positively; and he found that if his philosophy were suitably rhetorical, he would have a broader appeal. While writing his Harvard lectures in 1869, he described himself as "neither a Christian nor a theist"; when the *Cosmic Philosophy* appeared five years later, his position was abstract and severe, but he called it both Christian and theistic; in his later writing he was neither abstract nor austere and undertook to show how evolution led not simply to God but also to a justification of Christianity.[9]

Fiske seriously faced the problem posed by the anti-Darwinians. If evolutionary doctrine was true, then our vision of nature must include "the hawk's talons buried in the breast of the wren, while the relentless beak tears the little wings from the quivering body. . . . "[10] How did we reconcile this picture with the truth of religion? To read off the creator's character from nature "red in tooth and claw" would be appalling. It was more than a platitude, Fiske said, that could we "lift the veil that enshrouds eternal truth," we could understand nature's cruelty. But this consolation was not enough. Not only must we be able to interpret the universe as benign, but human existence must have meaning beyond the grave. The soul's post-earthly career would be "a delusion and a cruel mockery without the continuance of the tender household affections which alone make the present life worth living."[11] Fiske proposed to show that evolutionary thought not only avoided blasphemy but also was congruent with immortality's most comforting hopes.

He now wanted to avoid only vulgar forms of anthropomorphic theism; his view was avowedly anthropomorphic also but "refined and subtle." Fiske recognized a dramatic tendency in the events of the universe, a reasonableness that on its subjective side he called Purpose. The Infinite Power or Omnipresent Energy was definitely psychical, the living God, although it was "impossible to ascribe to Him any of the limited psychical attributes which we know, or to argue from the ways of Man to the ways of God." Despite problems offered by seemingly cruel experience, Fiske knew "that God is in the deepest sense a moral Being."[12] Fiske's notion was "practically identical" to that of the "immanent Deity":[13] "As in the roaring loom of Time the endless web of events is woven, each strand shall make more and more clearly visible the living garment of God."[14]

Fiske's teleological ideas initially appeared only as an expression of his emotional needs:

> The human soul shrinks from the thought that it is without kith or kin in all this wide universe. Our reason demands that there shall be a reasonableness in the constitution of things. This demand is a fact in our psychical nature as positive and irrepressible as our acceptance of geometrical axioms. . . . nothing can persuade us that the universe is a farrago of nonsense.[15]

But Fiske turned this "psychical fact" into an ingenious argument. Spencer defined life as the continuous adjustment of inner relations to outer relations; those creatures whose adjustments were most successful survived. In man the adjustments were largely psychical, guided by various theories about the world. It followed that true theories would also be those that helped us adjust most successfully—they would accurately adjust our ideas to external facts. In the idea of God we had a persistent "theory" that had guided human conduct from the beginnings of civilization. If this theory were not true, we would confront a situation "utterly without precedent in the whole history of creation." How could the race have survived and human progress taken place, how could psychical adjustment have proceeded successfully, if this theory were false? "*Since every adjustment whereby any creature sustains life may be called a true step* . . . the whole momentum of it [our knowledge of nature] carries us onward to the conclusion that the Unseen World . . . has a real existence." Because true beliefs were those that allowed us to adjust successfully and because a measure of successful adjustment was survival, it was likely that belief in God was true, insofar as it was connected with human progress.*

This defense of God's existence was compatible with Christianity. Fiske now reified Natural Selection as the deity or, rather, made Natural Selection the deity's work in the world. Nature's "supreme end" was maintaining human society; the "paramount aim" was civilization. "The cosmic process was aiming at something better than egoism and dinosaurs." The development of man's moral nature was an inseparable part of evolution: "The ultimate goal of the ethical process is the perfecting of human character."[16] What was original sin but man's brute-inheritance; what was the advance toward salvation but evolution applied to man? This message of the modern prophets of Darwin, Fiske said, was Christianity, "not the masses of theological doctrine . . . but the real and essential Christianity which came, fraught with good tidings to men, from the very lips of Jesus and Paul!" He concluded that the divine energy manifested in human evolution would ultimately allow the soul to "survive the wreak of material forms and endure forever." Once again, although he had no proof, his demand that the universe be "reasonable" had a basis in nature, and immortality was a legitimate postulate of rational faith.[17] In the last fifteen years of his life, particularly when he wrote *Through Nature to God*, the cravings of the human soul were a factor in Fiske's philosophic outlook; he had become a fideist.

Fiske and Posterity

Fiske died in 1901, appropriately enough on the fourth of July, his

---

*See JF, 21 : 217–18, 361–71 (italics added). Fiske claimed that this argument, not a "scientific demonstration," first came to him about ten years before he published it in 1899. It was similar to James's argument for religion. The point is not that Fiske and James mutually influenced one another—although they probably did—but rather that the attempt to reconcile science and religion using evolutionary reasoning was likely to produce a "pragmatic" position. Of course, Fiske's arguments were also exaggerated versions of Wright's.

weight of three hundred pounds testifying to the good life he had led. The cultured of the nation mourned the passing of a great man. As Fiske would have wanted, the press extolled him as a philosopher and historian of abiding greatness, but academic circles lamented him only as a warm and genial man, talented as a popularizer and gifted in interpreting more original thinkers to the literate public. In this respect scholarly opinion has not changed, suggesting more recently that in popularizing Herbert Spencer, Fiske was already dealing with a mind that ignored the most difficult theoretical problems. We can add little to this conventional opinion.

Spoiled as a child, Fiske demanded attention throughout his life.[18] He filled his letters written on his many speaking tours with stories of how his lectures captivated his audiences and how his intellectual presence enthralled all with whom he came in contact.[19] But excluded from the growing university system, he could not keep up with the various fields on which he wrote and spoke. The more Fiske worked to earn popular adulation, the more likely it was that the adulation would not last and that his fame would be *only* popular. He acquired the intellectual eminence and wide acclaim of an Emerson when the social role of the New England man of letters was moribund and when success on the lyceum circuit was as evanescent as the notices in the papers.

Yet this appraisal is too harsh. The *Cosmic Philosophy* was a wide-ranging attempt to reconcile religion with the new scientific advances; Fiske's speculations on the growth of "sociality" have lasting value, and there were insights even in his later work. The problem was that he never went beyond his youthful, uncritical adoration of Spencer. Rather than maturing with age, Fiske became more glib and superficial in his writing. He failed to grasp the criticisms of Spencerian doctrine made by philosophers in university circles during his lifetime. And all this was attributable to his failure to perceive that the amateur could no longer chart the course of learned discussion. His history fared better. Although subject to flaws of research and technique, he was ahead of his time in his conception of the place of American history in international history. The evolutionary theorizing provided a framework within which American history took on definite contours: the implicit stress on interpretive devices made him appealing to many students who came after him, and *The Critical Period* had a longer life than most professional historical works. It still represents one standard treatment of the 1780s.

Abbot's Early Life

A more intriguing and philosophically astute man was Frank Abbot. He had a powerful intelligence and was early interested in philosophy, but he was so personally difficult that no university would hire him. He suffered most as a publicist of unconventional religious causes. Radical religious beliefs had helped Emerson's career, but in a more institutionalized world they helped to destroy Abbot's. One scholar has called his life "one of the most colossal failures in American history."[20]

Abbot was born into an old New England family in 1836. His father was a self-righteous and conservative Unitarian schoolmaster who inflicted on his family his own peculiar ideas of how individuals ought to regulate the minute details of their lives. Frank's mother was sweet and mystically pious, yet not without courage and intelligence. She often lived apart from her arbitrary and irascible husband; in 1855 when they sent Frank to Harvard, the family broke up. The difficult family life and his relation to his father were crucial in shaping his personality. Until their deaths he revered his mother and hated his father; during his youth he had a number of ambiguous relations with other men which he acknowledged as attempts at seeking love; he developed a serious and humorless manner; he was strict, honest, and uncompromising in all that he did (he renounced claims to honorable friendship with his Harvard classmates when he confessed to them in his junior year that he had worn a pair of fake glasses to look intellectual); he became a militantly anti-Christian and anti-authoritarian believer in secular religion; and, finally, he devoted himself to a marriage made at twenty-three to a woman who shared none of his concerns and who became chronically ill.

After college Abbot was briefly a Unitarian minister, but he soon left the church and devoted his life to promulgating a "free religion" that eschewed superstition and eulogized science. He was a founder of the Free Religious Association, many of whose members were followers of Fiske's Cosmism, a religious creed only vaguely Christian. More importantly, Abbot edited *The Index, A Journal of Free Religion*, and from 1873 to 1880 he did so in Boston.[21]

By the mid-1860s Abbot's philosophical leanings were intense, and he longed for a university position, but his personality and his fierce and incorruptible anti-Christian ideas led to rejections from Cornell, from

Harvard as assistant to Bowen, from the [Massachusetts] Institute of Technology, and, later, from Johns Hopkins.[22] As the years went by his allegiance to every sort of radical religious organization and his principled and imperious manner made it increasingly unlikely that he would get academic employment. In an earlier era, the lack of a university position would not have hindered Abbot's ambitions as a thinker, as Emerson's success demonstrated; in the 1870s the lack meant a great deal. As it became clear that no institution would recognize his abilities, Abbot proclaimed his own talents with greater fervor and let his ego run wild. He told one friend that "God does not create such an intellect as mine but once in a century."[23] Charles Peirce recalled that at the Metaphysical Club meetings Abbot would intimate with "that matchless tact that was all his own . . . that it was not to be expected that the intellect who was bringing the history of philosophy to its complete and final dénouement should be much interested in the chatter of a parcel of minds such as ours."[24]

By the 1870s he had written a prospectus for a research professorship in philosophy, and later begged Eliot to approve it. Abbot would fund the chair for five years and then the university would support him for life if, as he predicted, he came up with a book for the ages that would redound to the glory of Harvard and of the United States.[25] Of course Abbot was unsuccessful—Eliot said he would damage the school's reputation—and when he was forced in the 1880s to convert his home into a boarding school for boys preparing for Harvard, his claims became even grander. He received a Harvard Ph.D. in philosophy in 1881, partially to obtain students for his school. His dissertation, he claimed, was "the gist of the greatest philosophical system since the *Critique of Pure Reason* was published in 1781"; men would value it for "hundreds of years to come."[26] The truth of his philosophy was clear "to anyone who has capacity to comprehend and patience to master the argument" and would lead the way "into the sunlight of the predestined Philosophy of Science."[27]

Abbot's Philosophy

Although Abbot respected the Spencerian attempt at a synthesis of knowledge, his criticism of 1866 followed that of Wright and other Cambridge thinkers. "We find an indistinctness and indetermination on all the fundamental points of philosophy which seriously detracts from the power of Mr. Spencer's speculations as a coherent system."[28] But Abbot had bigger game: in two long articles written for the *North American Review* at about the same time,[29] he made a harsh and detailed analysis of Kant and "his clumsy imitator," Sir William Hamilton.[30] Abbot was concerned, as was his teacher Bowen, about Kant's doctrine that things must conform to our ways of knowing and that the noumenal world must be unknown to us. It was Bowen who had unsuccessfully pushed for Abbot at Harvard in the 1860s. He appraised Abbot's abilities highly on the basis of these articles, although Abbot may have impressed his teacher because both of them at that time found the same fault in *Critique of Pure Reason*. Against Kant and with Bowen, Abbot upheld what I would describe as a provisional presentational realism. The position was presentational realism because, Abbot claimed, objects, as we knew them, existed independently of our consciousness. It was provisional in that Abbot finally analyzed the objects of knowledge and the knowing relation by means of one another: objects of knowledge were not ultimately exterior to mind.[31] The articles revealed a penetrating insight and a taste for sustained argumentation that he never equalled again, but they were negative and critical so that his own ideas were difficult to fathom. We can best understand his thought by looking at his most important later pieces of writing, *Scientific Theism* (1885) and *The Way Out of Agnosticism* (1890), where Abbot approached Kant from the different but related standpoint of epistemological realism.

What is the status of the predicates we use to talk about various objects? Why do we designate any number of objects, for example, by the term 'black'? For the epistemological nominalist only individuals are real, and the predicates we use to talk about them are only convenient names to pick out groups of individuals we wish to treat together for some reason or other. For the epistemological realist we cannot justifiably use the predicates we do use unless they truly refer to some common quality that objects—let us say a group of cows—actually possess; consequently, whatever other things there are, predicates refer to qualities, properties, or generals (like blackness) that really exist. The epistemological problem of universals disputed by realists and nominalists concerns the kinds of entities that the universe contains.

Abbot's books attacked nominalism and Kant, its most gifted and, therefore, most pernicious expositor. But in *Scientific Theism* Abbot began with Descartes, whom he and other Cambridge thinkers regarded not merely as the originator of modern philosophy but as the first purveyor of pervasive error. According to Abbot, both the Continental rationalists and the British empiricists accepted nominalism, and the dispute between them over the source of knowledge—whether it was the mind or experience—assumed that we never experienced external objects but confronted phenomena alone; we associated discrete ideas, individual entities, for our convenience (32–37). The logical outcome of modern philosophy, said Abbot, was Hume's skepticism. Emphasizing that aspect of Kant's philosophy which suggested that the *Ding an sich* was the unknowable cause of phenomena, Abbot stated that Kant's rebuttal to Hume was also nominalistic. In arguing that objects must conform to the mind's mode of organization, Kant held that universals had only a mental existence; we could never know the noumenal world of things in themselves. It was a tribute to the subversive power of nominalism that even Kant's majestic philosophy could not circumvent Hume. With Bowen, Abbot agreed that the result of *The Critique of Pure Reason* was also skepticism, or what Abbot called the absolute solipsism of the German idealists—they did not escape the consciousness of a single individual (3–7). Nominalism was "an excrescence upon modern philosophy, a cancerous tumor feeding upon its life" (14). In the late 1880s when the *Harvard Monthly* asked him to write an article on philosophy at Harvard, Abbot attacked these Kantian assumptions of the Cambridge professionals: Harvard philosophy, he warned, must lead to skepticism.[32]

The alternative offered by *Scientific Theism* was a form of epistemological realism based, said Abbot, on the reasoning implicit in science and opposed to Kant. Against Kant, science proceeded on the assumption that we knew things, although incompletely, as they are in themselves and that cognition conformed to them. In natural scientific classifications, Abbot continued, we assumed that universals were objective relations of resemblance among objectively existing things. He called this view that of *universalia inter res*: objects and the universals which defined them as the kinds of objects they were were distinguishable in thought but inseparable in existence. Blackness was real if black things were, and these were real if blackness was (11–25). Scientists assumed that we knew really existing black things and that we could truly classify these things through the universal blackness. Abbot adopted this scientific position as his own: presentational (metaphysical) realism guaranteed epistemological realism and, consequently, avoided skepticism.

On one hand, a thing was a set of internal forces manifesting itself by specific qualities, actions, or motions; these constituted it as phenomenon. The system of relations in which these qualities, actions, or motions appeared constituted it as noumenon, that is, the thing's real unity and its intelligible character. For example, a black cow was a black cow because, in part, it was related to other black cows via the universal blackness. Perception, the mode of phenomenal knowing, never exhausted or discovered all the relations although it discovered more and more of them and, so far, we knew the thing noumenally, as it was. But only its "immanent relational constitution" completely defined it, and things did not exist apart from this constitution (128–29). On the other hand, universals did not exist as substances or entities; nor did they exist *in* particular things, although a relational structure defined a particular thing. Rather, universals "subsisted" as the relations among various kinds of things (27–28). We could legitimately speak of relations whenever experience verified a proposition that asserted them to be true. "This cow is blacker than that one" was true if this cow was indeed blacker than that one, and the relation of being blacker than subsisted if we ascertained that one cow was blacker than the other. Both cows existed as we knew them to exist, but the relation of being blacker than and so the universal blackness which allowed us to compare the cows in respect to blackness did not exist apart from the related things: the objectivity of a relation "*is simply the known objective truth of the proposition which states it.*" But the relation itself was objectively real before we conceived the proposition stating it: it determined the proposition, not the proposition it. Objects and universals were mutually determinative. Abbot also said that we knew truths to be true because they commanded the "unanimous assent of all experts": truths were those propositions affirmed by "the universal experience and reason of mankind, voiced in the unanimous consent of the competent" (60–63).

The achievements of science showed us that knowledge was possible, said Abbot, but scientists presumed that we knew things as they are and that there were real classifications giving us knowledge. We had the alternative of embracing modern philosophy and its nominalism and skepticism, or science and its premise that we knew things in themselves (noumena) and their real classifications. If we accepted science, Abbot said, we must throw away Kant's distinction between phenomena and noumena; we must hold that cognition conformed to things and that we could determine their relations (39–53).

Abbot's critique of nominalism was convincing; his defense of his own position was less so. The way we obtained knowledge (of noumena) was unclear. Knowledge was a correlation of object and subject that had two origins, cosmos and mind. These two "origins" united inseparably but distinguishably in experience (39–40). Experience, Abbot claimed, was a central conception in his thought. "All human knowledge arises in experience" (105); it included all mutual interaction of real existences (cosmos) and the mind and was "the one proximate origin of knowledge," "the beginning and the end of the scientific method," "the chemical union, so to speak, of the noumen-object and the noumen-subject" (61–68). Abbot suggested that experience itself originated "in the influence of that which can be known upon that which can know." The distinction between Being and Thought was seemingly ultimate, and knowing or consciousness arose in experience, in their temporary union (105). But as Abbot continued it appeared that this dualism was not ultimate. Scientific knowledge proved "that the constitution of the universe and the constitution of the human mind are fundamentally one" (61). The primary thrust of Abbot's writing was that something like experience was the final reality; it contained within it two dimensions, Being and Thought, whose interaction yielded consciousness and knowledge—these two signifying mind's awareness of being. In experience the constitution of the world was revealed and the knower was defined (134).

The existence of science guaranteed knowledge of things as they are, but how did we get this knowledge? Abbot had said that thought was the measure of being (and vice versa), but that on the scientific premise knowledge and consciousness in no way conditioned objects. Accordingly, "there must be in the human mind some adequate and appropriate intellectual faculty, or function" "capable of apprehending . . . indubitably discovered objective relations" (108). Because the noumenal universe was known to man, we must postulate such a "Perceptive Understanding": it apprehended the data of sense as they were related (136–37). *Scientific Theism* was not entirely comfortable with this postulate and Abbot's exposition was cautious. We simply could not deny that we knew things as they are and must exert our ingenuity to explore the postulate's meaning, finally enlarging the concept of experience to include it (109–10). Five years later *The Way Out of Agnosticism* was even more circumspect. Either we had knowledge of things as they are or we gave up science. If we accepted science, we must be able to grasp the relations of objects; and Abbot connected this process to observation. He did not mention the Perceptive Understanding; he simply wrote, "*How* we observe may be doubtful; that we observe is indubitable."[33]

In the Middle Ages epistemological realism was the orthodoxy of the Roman Church, which grounded its philosophy in Plato and Aristotle. Abbot was not surprised but still lamented that, in disavowing Scholastic realism, the nominalism of modern philosophy had become identified with intellectual and religious freedom. On closer examination he found that nominalism was incompatible with the scientific revolution with which it was associated. It also created skepticism about science; along with nominalism went the doctrine of the relativity of knowledge to human faculties. The upshot of this misalliance, said Abbot, was that scientists held philosophy in contempt and that philosophy ceased to have any relevance to human existence—the fights of metaphysicians interested only metaphysicians.[34]

On the contrary, Abbot stated, scientists meant by their statements that objective relations existed among phenomena and that objects were dependent on consciousness only for their discovery. Knowledge was relative, but only to the extent that much about the world was still unknown; it was relative to what we might discover in the future. Abbot's philosophical position was just the method of science made explicit, "the philosophized scientific method."[35]

To reconstruct philosophy on the basis of epistemological realism, we must connect speculation with the sciences, and this connection should bring further philosophic advance. More importantly, Abbot held that an understanding of realism "creates the only Real Reconciliation of Science and Religion." As nominalism led to scientific skepticism or, rather, to the denial of science, so in religion nominalism pandered to "the moral lawlessness of an Individualism that sets mere personal opinion above the supreme ethical sanctities of the universe." Making the individual a prisoner of his own consciousness, nominalism ended in solipsism, destroying the rationale for belief in God. "The present philosophical situation has become simply intolerable"; "so far . . . as the social and moral interests of mankind are concerned," the nineteenth century had become "the AGE OF AGNOSTICISM." If philosophers could not vanquish nominalism and resurrect a positive religion, Abbot thought that men would survive only through a "frantic self-absorbtion in the soulless details of life." If religious knowledge were impossible, sublimation would be the only escape from unbearable anguish in the constant presence of pain and death.[36]

The main task of *The Way Out of Agnosticism; or the Philosophy of Free Religion* was to reconcile science and religion. Abbot proposed

> an interpretation of the fact of Evolution which shall be freed from the humiliating and entangling alliance with phenomenism, agnosticism, or know-nothingism, and already ripe for the reception of a thoroughly free philosophy, at once grounded in science and culminating in the loftiest moral and religious ideal. . . . There is no possible redemption of mankind from the political, commercial, industrial, and social immoralities of the present, except in the speedy development of ideals which shall fire the souls of the rising generation to give battle to this hydra-headed monster of corruption, and fight it down in the power of the higher life (2–3).

Abbot's argument for religion analyzed the nature of the universe. Three great categories exhausted the types of being—machine, organism, and person. Epistemological realism guaranteed that as far as we knew objects falling under these classifications, these objects noumenally existed. Because science gave knowledge, if science learned the kind of object the universe was, we could argue that we had knowledge of the universe and that it really was as we thought it.

Abbot cleverly showed that we could not separate conceptions of machine and organism. No machine existed without a purposive use to which it was put, without something that postulated an end for the machine to serve—that was part of being a machine. But no organism—that which had ends—existed without that which could function to achieve its ends. As Abbot put it, there was an *"indissoluble union of cau-*

sality and finality"; both went together, constituting a larger organic whole that Abbot called a self-extended organism or real machine.* In this sort of organism (or real machine), whole and parts simultaneously related reciprocally as cause and effect *and* means and end. The real machine had a twofold organic end: its "indwelling" end was self-evolution, epitomized by self-preservation; its "outgoing" end was the devotion of the self-extended organism to the higher self of species. The indwelling end gave to this organism its self, the outgoing its external others or a higher self in the not-self. Roughly speaking, these ends in man corresponded to egoism and altruism (69–70). All finite real machines had these two equally essential elements of the organic end, equally wrought into a constitution with a separate but necessary "not-self" complementary to its own being (to enable it to fulfill its outgoing end). But suppose the universe as a whole did not fall under the category of person; then it must be a real machine. In this case the organic end could not be dualistic, or separable into indwelling and outgoing end, because the universe could have no external others. The distinction could remain as that between the self as a whole (self-evolution) and the self as many parts or internal others (self-devotion), although in the whole, the self and its parts would be numerically identical. But this identity of subject and object was the personal unity of self-consciousness: the universe as a whole must be a person as well as a self-extended organism or real machine. And in the universe as a whole considered as a person, there was a harmony of egoism and altruism (70–71). The universe as machine was the eternal, organic, and teleological self-evolution of the universe as person, the everlasting realization and fulfillment of an infinitely self-conscious intellect.

Modern evolutionary science was working out just this conception of the universe (nature); it had not successfully formulated the "law" of evolution, nor was the conception adequately developed; but whatever the outcome of investigation, evolution would be compatible with a religious view of the universe:

*Abbot pointed out that another error consequent to nominalism was its attempt to analyze nature causally and not teleologically, that is, to separate the inseparable. As a result, Hume and Mill rejected real causation and reduced the causal nexus to invariable antecedence and consequence, that is, they accepted skepticism about the natural world (WO, p. 60).

the system of Nature, self-evolved as the objectified divine thought, has risen with incalculable slowness from the unconscious to conscious; but the whole process remains utterly unintelligible, nay, an absurdity or self-contradiction, unless the evolution of the universe as Divine Object is viewed as the work of the universe itself as Divine Subject,—that is, as the Infinite Life of God in Time and Space.[37]

Abbot defended his conception of God as theistic. He did not deny personality to the universe as did pantheists. The pantheistic conception of God as immanent in the universe confounded God with matter. Abbot's God was immanent only as far as the universe was known. He was immanent in the world of human experience and transcendent in the world which lay beyond actual human experience—transcendent as far as the universe remained unknown.[38] If this was so, Abbot came close to the idealism that he rejected as absolute solipsism insofar as it was connected with nominalism. Finite minds came to know a universe that Abbot called Infinite Person and Absolute Spirit. But in asserting the identity of Being and Thought and the triune unitary universe of machine, organism, and person, Abbot was on his way to pantheism, whose hallmark was obliterating metaphysical distinctions.

Abbot's Death and Later Repute

Abbot's brother had been killed at Gettysburg in 1863; his father had died in 1873, and his mother in 1883. When finally his wife died in 1893, he resolved for her sake to finish a philosophical magnum opus. Toward the end of 1903 he had completed a manuscript of over a thousand pages. On September 29 he wrote in his detailed personal diary, "A life-task done. . . . At a quarter past twelve, midnight, I finished the last page. . . . I shall never reap a harvest from this seed—may it feed a world famine-struck for truth! . . . I have fought the good fight. *Nunc Dimittis*." On October 22 he took a bouquet of carnations to his wife's grave and there, sometime in the early morning of October 23, exactly ten years after her death, he poisoned himself.[39]

Three years later in 1906 Abbot's son published the two-volume *Syllogistic Philosophy; or Prolegomena to Science.* He sent the book to every major library in the land. Though it was "the burden of his life," Abbot's work, filled with his own terminology, did not make the slightest impact on philosophical or theological tendencies in the United States. Only a narrow circle of thinkers—particularly his college classmate, Charles Peirce, whom a later generation would lift from obscurity—still spoke of the keenness of Abbot's philosophical analysis.[40] He was a sophisticated and able thinker and, despite his isolation and bitterness, he wrote originally and acutely on an important cultural concern. But no community mourned his passing or eagerly awaited his posthumous book. As his biographer has written, Abbot failed because his persecution complex and his delusions of grandeur made him insufferable. It was not adversity that brought about his downfall: "he would have won university preferment as a thinker and teacher; his ideas would have been heeded; men would have recognized his capacity to cut through nonsense, to comprehend, to interpret, and to go beyond the greatest thinkers. But he spent his life fighting minor battles, proofreading the *Index*, teaching grammar to pupils, and then trying to think straight during the last twenty years of his life when he was tortured by grief, pain, disappointment and remorse."[41]

Abbot's personal quirks—especially his religious antipathies—made it impossible for him to get collegiate employment. He consequently never received the perquisites, honor, and intellectual stimulation a university position would have brought. Had he compromised his vicious dislike for organized religion and learned tact—basically if he had learned to keep his mouth shut—he might have held a job, and students now might remember him as a major American philosopher.

Fiske, Abbot, and Their Predecessors

The thought of Fiske and Abbot had its sources in Kant and the Scottish realists, and its conclusions had much in common with Transcendentalism.[42] Although both men deprecated Emerson's contempt for logic and scientific reasoning, they admitted that his pantheistic conceptions were hospitable to Darwinism and a deanthropomorphic religion. Their unorthodox conceptions of religion began where Transcendentalism left off.[43] Just as Harvard would have nothing to do with Emerson, so too it would have nothing to do with Fiske and Abbot. It is a measure of what had happened to speculation in the United States that the religious unorthodoxy that contributed to Emerson's fame helped bar Abbot from institutional employment, so that posterity would forget him despite his intellectual strength. Although Fiske's unorthodoxy only initially prevented his gaining an academic job, it set him out on an Emersonian career—that of popular seer and amateur sage—that precluded the later renown it had secured for Emerson.

6

CHARLES SANDERS PEIRCE

Peirce's Early Career

Fiske, Abbot, and Wright all suffered because no university supported their speculation. None suffered more than Charles Peirce, the most powerful modern American thinker, who died penniless and deeply in debt, unable to afford even the necessities of life.

Peirce was born in Cambridge in 1839, the second son of Benjamin Peirce, professor of mathematics and astronomy at Harvard and the most famous mathematician of his generation. Benjamin recognized his son's genius early and exercised the boy's aptitude for abstract thought in various ways. He also indulged his favorite by using his position at Harvard to secure Charles's advancement, and the son was regarded as an offensive and disagreeable young man. Charles's unconventional sexual behavior—he once lived with a woman not his wife—also made him suspect, and he had the reputation of being spoiled, hostile, and neurotic.

When he received his B.A. from Harvard in 1859, he graduated seventy-first in a class of ninety-one. We may attribute this undistinguished performance to Peirce's idiosyncrasies, which became more pronounced as he grew older, but the rote system of teaching did not inspire him. It was in his senior year that the overseers, visiting his classes under Bowen, pronounced the curriculum in logic and philosophy "destitute." After three years he entered the new Lawrence Scientific School in 1862, and there the demanding work under Louis Agassiz, Jeffries Wyman, and Asa Gray called forth Peirce's best efforts. In 1863 he graduated with a B.S. in chemistry, summa cum laude.

For the next fifteen years Peirce led a successful scholarly and scientific life: the father's academic influence insured that others did not penalize the son for his peculiarities. Benjamin had long been a consulting geometer for the United States Coast and Geodetic Survey and became its superintendent in 1867. The son had jobs with the Survey and continued to work part-time for it after his employment as an assistant to the director of the Harvard Observatory, another job made possible by his famous father, but one in which Charles's original grasp of photometrics justified his claim to the position. When Benjamin became the Survey's head, Charles served as his assistant and established a reputation throughout the 1870s for inventive and pioneering study in the exact measurement of the earth's shape. He continued, however, to plague superiors and subordinates with erratic work habits as well as unpleasant social behavior. On the basis of his original philosophical research, however, President Daniel Coit Gilman of Johns Hopkins appointed Peirce part-time lecturer in logic in 1879. Although he had temporarily lectured at Harvard in the mid- and late-1860s, and had already published respected articles, the Hopkins post was the closest Peirce came to a formal academic position. For four more years Gilman reappointed Peirce, and he looked forward to a professorship at the end of that time.[1]

Kantian Philosophizing

When Peirce arrived at Hopkins he was a mature thinker, but the roots of his philosophizing are difficult to trace. He grew up in the midst of the Transcendental movement, and most of the Transcendentalists were friends of his father, often entertained at the Peirce house on Quincy Street. The romantic strain in his early work, as well as his belief that nature symbolized spiritual truth, might both have derived from Emerson's teaching. More important perhaps was his father's religiosity. Benjamin's Unitarian battles with Calvinists dismayed Charles, and he never adopted one of the respectable creeds as his father had, but the son did accept his father's view of the theological implications of science. Deeply religious, the elder Peirce believed that nature exemplified the deity's wisdom. He once gave a lecture series entitled "On the Manifestation of the Intellect in the Construction and Development of the Material Universe."[2] Science was the means for understanding the deity, Benjamin thought, and mathematics, which nature realized, was the key discipline for investigating the mind of the "Divine Geometer." Like the Transcendentalists, Benjamin believed that knowledge of nature gave us insights into God's plan for the world and he consequently held that the discovery of scientific truth was a religious duty. Charles Peirce's philosophizing would also conclude that science and religion were compatible.

Whatever these early influences and their effect on Peirce's philosophical predispositions, concrete evidence about his first studies makes apparent their Kantian sources. While Bowen was trotting his undergraduates through overcrowded recitations, Peirce read *The Critique of Pure Reason*. In the early 1860s, he recalled, he spent three hours a day for two years mastering the text.[3] When he took up philosophical issues, especially with the members of the Metaphysical Club in the early 1870s, he sported impressive philosophic armor. When the "dispute" between science and religion engaged all thinkers, Peirce's commitment could have been predicted: he had a philosophical anodyne for Wright's "Nihilism," an anodyne that he had compounded after his study of Kant.

For Kant knowledge consisted of the mind's synthesis of the data of sense by means of a fundamental set of categories. The categories were *a priori* true of all possible experience. The years Peirce spent in reading *The Critique of Pure Reason* led him to philosophize in this mold, and the position he developed in the 1860s and advanced against Wright in the Metaphysical Club proceeded along Kantian lines. But Peirce's work was more complex. Kant's list of categories classified by way of the logical form of statements, and Peirce believed that the significance of the logical form of any statement depended upon the statement's role in inference. The clue to refining Kant's position lay in the structure of argument, and so Peirce studied the syllogism's traditional classifications. This investigation, however, led to a broader concern. The connections holding between a statement's subject and predicate and a syllogism's premises and conclusion were both variants of what Peirce called the sign relation. Subjects and premises were signs, respectively, of predicates and conclusions. These various forms of inference involved signhood, the relation of representation. To advance on Kant's understanding of the categories, of the nature of the basic ways in which we structure the world, Peirce asked how representation was possible and in what it consisted.[4] His answers to these questions appeared in a group of articles published in 1867 and 1868 in *The Proceedings of the American Academy of Arts and*

Sciences and the *Journal of Speculative Philosophy*, the central one being "On a New List of Categories."

Peirce dissected the sign relation as statements exhibited it. Following the tradition of formal logic, he believed that statements were all of the subject-predicate type, for example, "The cow is black." In this statement we affirmed the predicate 'black' of the object, a cow, for which the subject, the word 'cow' stood: we connected the quality (blackness) and object (the cow) by affirming the predicate of the subject ('cow') by the copula 'is'; and we affirmed that the subject and predicate referred to the same object. Peirce defined a sign as that which stood for something to someone in some respect, and believed that a sign relation connected subject and predicate. If we asserted that the cow was black, the predicate 'black' stood for the cow in respect to blackness. This complex was the irreducible relation of signification.

Signhood was triadic—it embraced what Peirce called the ground (blackness), the correlate (the object that is black), and the interpreting representation (the predicate 'black'). These three conceptions were central to his new list of categories: they designated the chief *a priori* modes that gave us knowledge of the world.[5]

Kant argued that the categories arose to unify sense data. These data did not refer, they simply were, and in order to refer, the mind must attend to and recognize them as something, as It. Peirce claimed this operation already displayed rudimentary conceptualization. To speak of "It," of "the present in general," used the broadest perhaps vaguest concept, but it was nonetheless a concept. We must assume sense data, but no data were immediately known or given. Peirce directed his animus against the British empiricist doctrine that we could begin with a sense given (impressions). Neural stimuli might precede our conceptualization, but whenever we spoke of knowledge it was impossible to distinguish what was given from what was interpreted: all "phenomena" were interpretations of the data and so were to some degree conceptual. We could pursue these cognitions, as Peirce called them, as far back as we wanted and never reach a first impression or intuition: we would always find that prior cognitions of the same object had determined any cognition. Moreover, every cognition might call forth a further cognition, and Peirce concluded that our series of cognitions, or interpretations of the data of sense, formed an infinite series without beginning or end.[6]

Because the categories involved in the sign relation were fundamental to all conceptualization, to all cognitions, Peirce stated that the sign series was also infinite. Every sign itself functioned as a sign and must itself be interpreted. The series of signs had no beginning and no end. Death or other factors might interrupt it, but of itself the series went on forever. Thus, thinking was an endless process of interpretation.

Every cognition contained a conceptual element; none was an intuition. But could any cognition function as a sign of an intuition, of something that lay outside of experience? Obviously not: all signs or cognitions led to further signs or cognitions; no cognitions were intuitions or could function as signs of them. What was for Peirce must have a conceptual dimension, and "the incognizable," what was not cognized, could not exist—as reflection on the concept's meaning showed. "Over against any cognition, there is an unknown but knowable reality; but over against all possible cognition, there is only the self-contradictory. In short, *cognizability* (in its widest sense) and *being* are not merely metaphysically the same, but are synonymous terms."[7] Peirce was an idealist.

Peirce believed that we had no direct perception of the given (intuitions), that all cognitions were interpretations, and that thinking consisted in never-ending sign interpretation. But if we had no intuitions we could not have them of ourselves, and so, *contra* Descartes, there was no direct introspection or immediate knowledge of ourselves as self-conscious—a position consonant with those of Wright and the later Bowen. Sensations, volitions, and thoughts first occurred as a response to external stimuli; we became aware of them afterward by abstraction and inference from experience of the rest of the world; self-consciousness arose as a hypothesis to explain error and ignorance. Peirce could bolster his claim that all thinking was in signs: overthrowing intuition eliminated one "non-sign" candidate that might have contributed to thinking, and elaborating this belief eliminated another, introspection.[8]

From these principles Peirce concluded that man was a series of signs. If thinking was a series of signs, there were no mental phenomena aside from the sign series, and "the content of consciousness, the entire phenomenal manifestation of mind" was a sign series.[9] But what of consciousness itself? Peirce said it was a "material quality" of a thought-sign: just as 'cow' was composed of the letters 'c', 'o', and 'w' which were its material cause, so consciousness was included in the series of signs as a component of their material cause.[10]

The Review of Berkeley

Peirce made his speculative framework explicit in the 1868 *Journal of Speculative Philosophy* series. Descartes symbolized for him, as for Abbot, much that was wrong with modern philosophy.[11] In stressing that an individual could doubt everything and overcome this doubt as an individual, Descartes trivialized doubt and overlooked the importance of cooperative thinking on a problem. The reliance on personal ratiocination emphasized individuality and armchair reflection at the expense of scientific experimentation dependent on a community of investigators. More importantly, Peirce charged, Descartes's conclusions were suspect: he posited a metaphysical substance, independent of consciousness, that was the cause of cognitions. Like Abbot, Peirce would come to attribute these dubious characteristics to all modern philosophy and its nominalistic bias that must eventuate in skepticism. Peirce had also accepted, however, that he must build his theories on cognitions, the momentary syntheses of data and concept. In a measure, this admission allied him to Descartes, his nominalistic descendents—Berkeley and Hume—and consequently to skepticism. Indeed, Peirce's theory of knowledge and his notion of signs had much in common with Berkeley's theory, and Peirce's concern was to wed some form of phenomenalism, his reliance on the building blocks of cognition, to what he thought was Kant's anti-nominalistic position. He took this step in 1871 in a long review of a new edition of Berkeley's works. The review showed that Peirce's anti-Cartesian idealism was not simply an argumentative exercise. Like his fellows in the Metaphysical Club, the scientific onslaughts on religion obsessed him, but he expressed his concern with great subtlety. His idealistic commitment initiated a reconstruction of the bases of science on a congenial metaphysical foundation, a form of absolute idealism, but he approached this problem by investigating epistemological nominalism and realism.

In his review, Peirce declared his allegiance to epistemological realism. But the practice of science, he believed, had become more and more identified with nominalism:

> The doctrine of the correlation of forces, the discoveries of Helmholtz, and the hypotheses of Liebig and Darwin have all that character of explaining familiar phenomena apparently of a peculiar kind by extending the operations of simple mechanical principles, which belongs to nominalism.[12]

The scientific discoveries of the nineteenth century apparently accorded with epistemological nominalism. Their basis appeared to be what we might call a simple positivism: scientists explored a series of discrete phenomena, the interaction of individual entities, and correlated the behavior of groups of phenomena to produce that body of knowledge and those laws identified with science. Occult entities like universals were unnecessary. Scientists needed only to observe individual phenomena closely and calculate the relations among them carefully.

In examining the philosophic underpinnings of science, Peirce found the situation more complex. Establishing laws and predicting on their basis, he said, were central to laboratory science, and to establish laws an experimentalist assumed that certain groups of objects had similar structures, enabling him to move from what was true of one (examined) object to other (non-examined) similar objects; he assumed that a warrant existed for his belief that the future resembled the past, that induction was justified. For example, a scientist identified properties of a piece of copper—its atomic weight and structure—allowing him to predict that a previously untested piece of copper would behave similarly to his first piece. Suppose a scientist discovered on his desk a black pencil, hat, typewriter, and book, and called them, because they were on his desk, patwrooks. If he were a bad scientist he might conclude, on the basis of existing evidence, that all patwrooks were black and go on to predict that should something be placed on his desk—that is, if something should be a patwrook—it would be black.[13] The procedure was ludicrous because science did not investigate generalizations based on just any common properties: that four objects had the property of being on the table did not warrant the generalization that anything else placed on the table would also have some further property they happened to possess. Rather, scientists distinguished "law like," justifiable, generalizations from accidental ones, and this attempt committed them to a search for real similarities, like the atomic weight and structure of a piece of copper. If they could justify their generalizations, that is, if the problem of induction were solvable and they could warrant reasoning from past to future, they had to admit that the search for real similarities was legitimate.

Peirce contended that if nominalism undergirded science, scientists could not distinguish the two sorts of generalizations above or legitimate the search for real similarities. For the nominalist only individuals were real, and predicates were names given to individuals grouped together. There was no common quality whose existence justified the predictions made about copper and whose lack made dealing with patwrooks foolish. Science could circumvent Hume's problem of induction only on epistemologically realistic grounds. Properly understood, science assumed not epistemological nominalism but realism.

Peirce's grasp of the basis of science meant that his review of Berkeley was an extended attack on British empiricism: like Descartes before them, the British were nominalists and, despite Berkeley's own idealism and his argument for God, Hume proved that the logical conclusion of nominalism was skepticism, skepticism in both science and religion. Peirce, on the contrary, would show that epistemological realism was compatible with science, and that this realism supported religion. As Peirce would find in Kant an epistemological realism answering Hume's scientific skepticism, so he would also find in Kant a compelling answer to Hume's religious skepticism.

Peirce described one view of the metaphysical question concerning the nature of existents, whether individuals or universals:

> We have, it is true, nothing immediately present to us but thoughts. Those thoughts, however, have been caused by sensations, and those sensations are constrained by something out of the mind. This thing out of the mind, which directly influences sensation, and through sensation thought, because it is out of the mind, is independent of how we think it, and is, in short, the real. Here is one view of reality, a very familiar one.[14]

This view, metaphysical realism of the Cartesian or Lockeian kind, the belief that objects existed independently of mind, prescribed a nominalist answer to the epistemological question of universals. On this view, to say that two things were both men was "only to say that the one mental term or thought-sign 'man' stands indifferently for either of the sensible objects caused by the two external realities; so that not even the two sensations have in themselves anything in common, and far less is it to be inferred that the external realities have."[15] Metaphysical realism dictated that only individuals and not universals were real; it entailed epistemological nominalism.

Alternatively, epistemological realists argued that universals were "independent of your mind or mine or that of any number of persons," that predicates referred to qualities that individuals "really have in common, independent of our thought." On this view Peirce went on, "all human thought and opinion contains [*sic*] an arbitrary accidental element, dependent on the limitations in circumstances, power, and bent of the individual; an element of error, in short." In the long run, however, "human opinion universally tends . . . to definite form, which is the truth. Let any human being have enough information and exert enough thought on any question, and the result will be that he will arrive at a certain conclusion, which is the same that any other mind will reach under sufficiently favorable circumstances." For epistemological realists, Peirce said, what truly existed was what was believed in "this final opinion"; they believed that the metaphysically ultimate was independent *"not indeed of thought in general,* but of all that is arbitrary and individual in thought; is quite independent of how you, or I, or any number of men think."[16] Epistemological realism implied a metaphysical idealism—the real was what was non-arbitrary in thought but did not exist independently of thought. And just as metaphysical realism implied nominalism, so too did this metaphysical idealism imply epistemological realism. In the final opinion some qualities would characterize individual things and those qualities would be ipso facto real.

Peirce said his idealism was "instantly fatal" to the idea of a thing in itself conceived as a thing existing independent of mind, as the unknowable cause of sensations—instantly fatal to metaphysical realism. But his position would encourage us to regard sense appearance as signs of what was ultimately real. Akin to universals, real objects would be intellectual constructs, Peirce said, devised to give structure and coherence to sensations; the real objects would be *"noumena,* or intelligible conceptions which are the last products of the mental action which is set in motion by sensation," "the unmoving form to which . . . [human thought] is flowing":

> This theory involves a phenomenalism. But it is the phenomenalism of Kant, and not that of Hume. Indeed, what Kant called his Copernican step was precisely the passage from the nominalistic to the [epistemologically] realistic view of reality. It was the essence of his philosophy to regard the [ultimately] real object as determined by the mind. That was nothing else than to consider every

conception and intuition which enters necessarily into the experience of an object, and which is not transitory and accidental, as having objective validity. In short, it was to regard the reality as the normal product of mental action, and not as the incognizable cause of it.[17]

Descartes was wrong; Kant, correctly understood, right.

The same object did not invariably produce an identical effect upon us, for "our sensations are as various as our relations to the external things." But Peirce took into account differing relations to the object and argued that if the object existed, there would be a series of "if . . . , then . . ." hypothetical statements asserting that under certain conditions of sensation, the object would have certain effects on us: if I sat down in the chair, it would not collapse under me; if I lifted it, I would find that it strained my back; and so on. By postulating the object, Peirce gave experience coherence. We could verify that we had the experience under the specified condition; he justified the postulate because it explained how we verified the series of hypotheticals.[18] To say that a universal (quality) existed meant just that there would be a regularity in the future behavior of certain objects and that speaking of the universal explained the regularity.

Both Peirce and Abbot held Descartes responsible for the wayward course of modern philosophy and both saw nominalism as its great evil, agreeing on the relation of epistemological realism to the justification of induction. But Abbot believed that Kant's thing in itself was the cause of phenomena, and so, that Kant was the most fiendish nominalist. Peirce thought that Kant's thing in itself was not a cause but an intellectual postulate, a mental construct, and so, that Kant was an epistemological realist. Unlike Abbot, Peirce did not label all idealists nominalists. Since mind defined all that was real for Peirce, universals were real even if they had only a mental existence—they simply had to exist independently of individual minds.* Peirce consequently could not be a straightforward

---

*My exposition does not take up the intricacies of Peirce's epistemological realism and does not trace its subtleties to their source in Duns Scotus. On these questions see: DPP, pp. 123–40; John F. Boler, *Charles Peirce and Scholastic Realism* (Seattle: University of Washington Press, 1963), passim; Max Fisch, "Peirce's Progress from Nominalism toward Realism," *Monist* 51 (1967): 159–78; and Don D. Roberts, "On Peirce's Realism," *Transactions of the Charles S. Peirce Society* 6 (1970): 67–83. I have tried to show above why it was legitimate for Peirce to conflate his metaphysical and epistemological doctrines. Although the conflation has perplexed commentators, the doctrines were logically equivalent, each implying the other.

absolute idealist, believing that one great self immediately defined the world. What kind of idealist was he?

Science and Religion

Peirce was committed to epistemological realism in order to justify science, and this commitment led him to an idealism that defined the real as the object believed in the final opinion:

> The real . . . is that which, sooner or later, information and reasoning would finally result in, and which is therefore independent of the vagaries of me and you. Thus, the very origin of the conception of reality shows that this conception essentially involves the notion of COMMUNITY without definite limits, and capable of a definite increase of knowledge.[19]

The investigations of a temporally extended community defined the real; its investigations constantly weeded out error and false opinion, always approaching more closely to the truth. Peirce's paradigmatic community was the scientific one, but we should also recall that he had previously analyzed individual self-consciousness as an idea that arose to explain ignorance and error: "Ignorance and error are all that distinguish our private selves from the absolute *ego* of pure apperception."[20] It followed that as the scientific community struggled to reach agreement and eliminate error, it also attempted to establish the kingdom of God on earth. The aim of science was unity with the divine mind, the absorption of all our individual egos into an absolute self.

Like other nineteenth-century idealists, Peirce believed that Kant's notion of a connected order of experience affirmed a single experience of which human experience was a part: for Peirce, Kant's transcendental unity of apperception was the unity of consistency characterizing the universal mind. This unity appeared as an infinite community, a system of consistent signs. For Kant the transcendental unity of apperception grounded all knowledge of objects, and for Peirce the agreement of the community yielded the objectively real—the constructs that served as real objects were ideas in the mind of God. But this universal mind manifested itself to us in time by the ongoing activity of the community. That this mind knew itself meant that the community had a further interpretation, which was a subsequent community of signs. Since all cognitions required further cognitions, this series was infinite, the community of signs unlimited in time.[21]

Peirce argued that metaphysical realism entailed nominalism but that communitarian idealism and the epistemological realism justifying science were logically equivalent; in fact, the scientific vocation was religious in import. But to argue that we could ground science, solve the problem of induction, within a philosophy embracing idealism and epistemological realism was not to solve the problem, "the lock upon the door of philosophy." Peirce had to offer a solution, and his argument was simple: a world in which induction would fail as often as lead to truth was impossible. In such a world we could not associate any two characters significantly, that is, we could not predict any character from the appearance of any other. But this situation could occur only if every possible combination of characters occurred with equal frequency, and that would not reflect disorder, but the simplest order; the world would not be unintelligible but, on the contrary, everything conceivable would be found in it with equal frequency. The notion of a universe in which probable arguments would fail as often as hold true was absurd. "We can suppose it in general terms, but we cannot specify how it should be other than self-contradictory." Since we could not conceive of a world in which induction was not justifiable, and since what was inconceivable was nonexistent, induction was justifiable. Was it not still possible that the nominalist would be able to show that induction was justifiable in his world? Peirce said no: the nominalist's world postulated the existence of incognizable realities, *Ding an sich*, and since they could not exist, the nominalist's world was contradictory, no world at all.[22]

By the late 1860s Peirce was using his epistemological realism to reconstruct science on a basis congenial to religion. As long as scientists mistakenly based their views on nominalism, he said, "doctrines of a debasing moral tendency" would accompany science—"those daughters of nominalism—sensationalism, phenomenalism, individualism, and materialism." Peirce apparently identified materialism with all forms of metaphysical realism. Grant this position, Peirce believed, and the mental became epiphenomenal, a subtle form of matter (the general name given to the independently existing objects). "A man who enters into the scientific thought of the day and has not materialistic tendencies," he wrote, "is getting to be an impossibility." Yet science had no affinity with these views and was antagonistic to nominalism. Moreover, science based on epistemological realism led to a communitarian idealism and a defensible religion:

> though the question of realism and nominalism has its roots in the technicalities of logic, its branches reach about our life. The question whether the genus homo has any existence except as individuals, is the question whether there is anything of any more dignity, worth, and importance than individual happiness, individual aspiration, and individual life. Whether men really have anything in common, so that the *community* is to be considered as an end in itself, and if so, what the relative value of the two factors is, is the most fundamental practical question in regard to every public institution the constitution of which we have it in our power to influence.

In Peirce's position was the crux of the younger men's philosophical dispute with Bowen. For their Harvard instructor, skepticism arose out of representational realism: if the external world became an inference from the data of consciousness, Bowen taught, it would vanish altogether and we would be locked in our own consciousnesses. He proclaimed a kind of presentational realism, Scottish natural realism, a belief that we were directly aware of objects as they are in themselves. Once Bowen's students had digested Kant, however, it was hard for them to defend presentational realism, as Bowen himself learned in his old age. If mind shaped the data of sense to give us knowledge, how could we ever know these data as they are in themselves? If the world of which we had knowledge was the noumenal world, we had to rely on something like Bowen's intuitions or postulate something like Abbot's Perceptive Understanding. For men like Peirce and Wright, this move simply reintroduced Cartesian innate ideas. Peirce rejected both forms of metaphysical realism, representational and presentational, while at the same time avoiding the Germans' absolute solipsism which Bowen had inveighed against. In fact, in toying with Berkeley—a communitarian idealist—in the 1870s, Peirce took, more boldly, the same step as the aging Bowen. Peirce simultaneously—like Wright—absorbed much of the Scottish position, just as Bowen's later work did. Cognitions were signs of noumenal objects. In this sense we

were, perhaps, in Hamilton's language, aware of the effects of the noumena. Moreover, when men reached universal agreement, for Peirce and
for Abbot, they knew the noumena as they were. In such cases, "the very
same objects that are immediately present in our minds in experience
really exist just as they are experienced out of the mind." In the long run,
we could know things as they are in themselves; when we reached the
truth, presentational realism was a correct view. But at such a time, the
objects known did not exist exterior to mind; rather, mind and object
were one.[23]

Collapse of Peirce's System

The statement "John gives the cow to Sally" was not of the subject-
predicate form. Analysis of it required the logic of relations on which
Peirce was working in the 1860s. But Peirce based his theory of the
"New List" of categories on the primacy of subject-predicate logic,
and as he came to see the importance of "the logic of relatives," he revised his theory of knowledge.

If relations were as abstract and as fundamental as the qualities of subject-predicate logic, the meaning of our concept of an object might lie
in its relations to other objects or in the relations among its states at various
times. The relations in which a thing stood to other things might determine its "essential nature" (quality) rather than this nature determining
its relations to other things. Consequently, the meaning of our conception
of an object might depend on the law governing its relations to other
objects and not on the quality it embodied.[24] Peirce had already nearly
said this: his view that sensation varied with the relation to the object
defined an object's qualities by the relations of operations on the object
to perceived effects, that is, the definition involved a law.[25]

When he enunciated the principle of pragmatism to the Metaphysical
Club in 1872, Peirce attempted to elucidate the meaning of a concept in
a way that would take advantage of his logical advance. The pragmatic
maxim was then not an isolated doctrine that Peirce produced because
of its connection with a post-Darwinian naturalistic doctrine of belief
or because of the work of Alexander Bain or Nicholas St. John Green.
The maxim also fit into a system of philosophy on which Peirce was
working. The problem was that within this larger matrix, the maxim

caused insuperable difficulties. These became clear when Peirce published a second series of articles, "Illustrations of the Logic of Science," in the *Popular Science Monthly* in 1877–1878; he designed them to carry forward a scientific philosophy congruent with idealism.

The articles began with a defense of Bain's theories as the Metaphysical Club had accepted them. A state of belief was a satisfied one and indicated that we had formed some habit which determined actions. Believing put us in a condition to behave in a certain way when an appropriate occasion arose. On the other side, doubt was an irritation, a stimulus to action; doubt was a struggle to reach the reposeful state of belief, and this struggle Peirce called inquiry. (The analysis was another swipe at Descartes: "the mere putting of a proposition into the interrogative form does not stimulate the mind to any struggle after belief. There must be a real and living doubt, and without this all discussion is idle.") Peirce had previously stated that truth was what a community obtained in the final opinion and he now asserted that the end of inquiry was the settlement of opinion. If this fixing of opinion occurred, we had truth, and the question became: What was the best means, the best method, to fix opinion and, therefore, reach the truth?

There was little hint of the Darwinian revolution in Peirce's work of the 1860s; he was the one member of the Metaphysical Club who lacked enthusiasm for the developmental view. Although he doubted Darwinian theory later in his career, his early hesitation was explicable: Louis Agassiz was a close friend of the Peirce family, and Peirce was a student and admirer of Agassiz's work. Nonetheless, in the *Popular Science Monthly* series Peirce intimated that evolutionary modes of thinking, if not Darwin, had attracted him, and he wed them to Bain's work and his own ideas of the previous decade.[26] The first article, "The Fixation of Belief," observed that "each chief step in science has been a lesson in logic" and proceeded as if Peirce were drawing out the lesson taught by the *Origin of Species*:

> The Darwinian controversy is, in large part, a question of logic. Mr. Darwin proposed to apply the statistical method to biology. . . . While unable to say what the operation of variation and natural selection in every individual case will be, he demonstrates that in the long run they will adapt animals to their circumstances. Whether

or not existing animal forms are due to such action, or what position the theory ought to take, forms the subject of a discussion in which questions of fact and questions of logic are curiously interlaced.[27]

More importantly, Peirce analyzed the growth of scientific method, of logical modes of thinking, as an evolutionary process. "Logicality in regard to practical matters is the most useful quality an animal can possess, and might, therefore, result from the action of natural selection."[28] The evolution of human culture produced the scientific method, a description of the psychological structure of modern man's reasoning.

Peirce considered four methods of fixing belief: (1) tenacity—believing what we wanted to believe; (2) authority—allowing the state to control belief; (3) the *a priori* method—coming to conclusions via reason's natural light; and (4) the method of science. In a rough way he charted the evolution of rational thinking or "philosophizing"; we had gone from prephilosophic ideas, to the authoritarian speculation of the Middle Ages, to Continental rationalism typified by Descartes, to contemporary scientific theorizing exemplified by Peirce. In any event, he rejected the first three methods because they didn't work. They didn't fix belief and, accordingly, could not lead to truth. The scientific method won his praise—he could not gainsay its achievements in settling opinion—and Peirce made an eloquent appeal for accepting it.

There were tensions in "The Fixation of Belief." If the final opinion defined the real and the determination of this opinion was the end of inquiry, there was no good reason for Peirce to defend science. Authority seems a better candidate to settle opinion, and we might argue that the best bet is to support it. To avoid this sort of rejoinder Peirce switched his emphasis and spoke of existents independent of thought. These existents were only constructs of ours accounting for peculiarities of experience, but in his defense of science he stressed their independence: we would reach truth only if we took account of them, and we could take account of them only if we used the method of science.

Metaphysical realism and nominalism went hand in hand (the former entailing the latter), and their implications were odious: they destroyed the rationale for inductive reasoning and were tantamount to materialism. To justify inductive reasoning Peirce adhered to epistemological realism, which was logically equivalent to a communitarian idealism. So far,

Peirce was committed to science because it was associated with establishing inductive generalizations. But he also believed that science was the only method of establishing inductive generalizations, and to support this view he appeared to invoke metaphysical realism, the independent existence of the objects science studied.

The dilemma became plainer when Peirce examined the scientific method in his celebrated "How to Make Our Ideas Clear," an essay whose attack on *a priori* obscurantism surely derived from Bowen's contempt for verbal, "metaphysical," reasoning. Peirce passed briefly over the Cartesian criterion of true ideas as clear and distinct and went on to analyze the meaning of ideas, beliefs, or conceptions. His model of meaningfulness came from the laboratory. A conception had meaning if it produced experienced effects under controlled conditions; and he defined a conception's meaning by the consequences produced by operating with it. Peirce had already argued that any belief's essence was the creation of a habit. It followed that the different "modes of action" to which beliefs gave rise distinguished different beliefs:

> If beliefs do not differ in this respect, if they appease the same doubt by producing the same rule of action, then no mere differences in the manner of consciousness of them can make them different beliefs, any more than playing a tune in different keys is playing different tunes. Imaginary distinctions are often drawn between beliefs which differ only in their mode of expression. . . . Such false distinctions do as much harm as the confusion of beliefs really different, and are among the pitfalls of which we ought constantly to beware, especially when we are upon metaphysical ground.[29]

This definition of belief was congruent with the presuppositions of laboratory experimentation, and Peirce concluded that we explicated the meaning of a belief by examining the habits it entailed:

> To develop its [thought's] meaning, we have, therefore, simply to determine what habits it produces, for what a thing means is simply what habits it involves. Now, the identity of a habit depends on how it might lead us to act, not merely under such circumstances as are likely to arise, but under such as might possibly occur, no matter how improbable they may be. What the habit is depends on when

and how it causes us to act. As for the when, every stimulus to action is derived from perception; as for the how, every purpose of action is to produce some sensible result. Thus, we come down to what is tangible and practical as the root of every real distinction of thought, no matter how subtle it may be; and there is no distinction of meaning so fine as to consist in anything but a possible difference of practice.[30]

To call a thing hard was to say that other substances would not scratch it. The conception of this quality lay in the conception of the effects that would occur were we to act on the basis of our understanding of the quality: Peirce reduced qualities to relations. In this context he stated his contribution to the Metaphysical Club, what later became known as the pragmatic theory of meaning: "Consider what effects, which might conceivably have practical bearings, we conceive the object of our conception to have. Then, our conception of these effects is the whole of our conception of the object."[31]

As the maxim was written, the conception of an idea's conceivable effects, the possible consequences of acting on it, defined the idea's meaning. Elsewhere in "How to Make Our Ideas Clear" and in his other writings of this period, Peirce equated an idea's meaning with the habits of action it involved. The consequences of acting on an idea did not determine its meaning, but rather the set of statements relating consequences to the conditions under which they occurred. An idea's meaning was exhibited by the set of hypothetical statements, "if . . . , then . . ." statements, relating operations on the object of the concept to experienced effects.

Peirce considered this explication of the meaning of meaning to be the capstone of his thinking, reflecting both the techniques of laboratory science and the logic of relations. Instead, it undermined his attempt to bring together science and religion. He had previously defined the real object as a construct that gave coherence to experience. The object was necessary to understand the relation of experience to conditions of cognition: the existence of the postulated object implied certain experience under certain conditions. Now Peirce made the object definitionally equivalent to the relation of the conditions of cognition to experience. The object was nothing but our ways of operating on experiences. I suspect that the earlier position reflected Hamilton's notion that we were immediately aware of the effects of noumenal objects. This notion did not finally withstand Peirce's reading of Mill's *Examination*. Peirce adopted Mill's rebuttal to Hamilton—and the Berkeleyan rebuttal—that we knew nothing of the noumenal, that objects were no more than all their conceivable "effects." Whatever the background, the result led Peirce to just that phenomenalism he saw lurking in Mill's sort of empiricism.

In "The Fixation of Belief" Peirce's commitment to science as the only workable method of settling opinion drove him close to metaphysical realism. In "How to Make Our Ideas Clear," explaining this method appeared to demonstrate that we could base our conception of objects on nominalism. The analysis of meaning rested only on a study of phenomena and their relation to us: we needed no additional "intelligible construct." But Peirce linked this position, phenomenalism, with nominalism, that individual entities alone existed. This was why "The Fixation of Belief" came close to expressing the view that there was an independently existing object causing the phenomena: nominalism followed from metaphysical realism.

Nothing was possible for Peirce that was not actual or would not become actual. The cognizable was cognized at some time; and since only the cognizable was real, all there was was cognized. Peirce came to see that this idea entailed that the real was reduced to a set of phenomena, and this view left him open to the charge of nominalism. He thought that the infinite future saved his position: the future transformed possibility into actuality without compromising either the inexhaustibility of the possible or the limitations of the actual. The real was both a permanent and inexhaustible possibility of sensation and wholly cognized.[32] Peirce rendered this notion consistent by postulating an infinite future that realized those possibilities of sensation.[33]

But we could not know that inquiry would go on forever. Consequently, that inquiry will go on forever was incognizable, and so for Peirce there was no such thing as infinite inquiry. Even if inquiry did go on forever (and did converge), Peirce had to deny that there were real possibilities of sensation at any time that no one was cognizing them. The infinite future could not exist on Peirce's premises and even if it did, it could not solve his problems.

Another instance of this dilemma was the two different statements of the pragmatic maxim—that meaning was both the set of habits the object involved and an object's effects. Peirce did not distinguish a law from the set of its actual instances, and he did not do so because making the distinction would have required admitting possible instances that were never actualized. Similarly, Peirce tried to identify the universal mind containing those ideas toward which the community gravitated with the infinite community which could contain only actual instances of these ideas. All these troubles stemmed from his attempt to combine a version of phenomenalism with epistemological realism and idealism.

Peirce's attempt to reconcile science and religion had failed. It is a minor irony in the history of philosophy that more recent operationalists and positivists have hailed these articles as the seminal work of their tradition; Peirce conceived them as part of an argument against these modernist doctrines and rejected the nominalistic aspects of his philosophy as soon as he realized they were leading him to scientific and religious skepticism.

Later Life and Work

In January 1884, Gilman abruptly dismissed Peirce from Hopkins. No one knows why. His first marriage had ended in a divorce and a few months later, in 1883, he had married a still mysterious Frenchwoman, Madame Juliette Pourtalai. Throughout this time Peirce had been personally difficult and irresponsible in managing his affairs and in carrying out some of his academic duties, but despite this troublesome behavior and his marital straits, through the end of 1883 he had satisfied Gilman with his teaching and publication record. After 1884 he never held another scholarly post, and the notoriety of having been dismissed from Hopkins did much to destroy his chances in American academe.

Peirce's life and philosophizing, however, did not immediately disintegrate. He still had his job with the Coast Survey, and although the death of his father in 1880 left him without a patron, he managed to stay on, collecting a salary, until asked to resign in 1891. Meanwhile, he had received his family inheritance on the death of his mother in 1887, and with his second wife he moved to Milford, Pennsylvania, a resort town on the Delaware River. He added to the various monies that came to him a small annuity of Juliette's, and they speculated in real estate and built a country home. Peirce named it Arisbe after the colony of Miletus, the home of the first Greek philosophers, Thales, Anaximander, and Anaximines.[34] Many people regarded the Peirces' behavior as improvident, and an irregular income at least made their first years at Milford exciting. They were able to manage until the depression of 1893 bankrupted them. In debt for the rest of his life, Peirce sold off his land, and after 1905 depended on charity. From 1907, William James was instrumental in collecting a fund which provided Peirce, then 68, with minimal money to carry on.

During the years at Milford his repute in Cambridge grew as an extraordinary if eccentric thinker. Through the teaching of James and Royce, he became a legendary figure among Harvard graduate students in philosophy. In the academic years 1897–1898, 1902–1903, and 1903–1904 he appeared in Cambridge to lecture. Despite the philosophers' efforts and the status of his brother—for a time chairman of the mathematics department and dean of the faculty—Charles could get no appointment at Harvard. As James put it, Peirce had "dished himself" there—and at every other university.[35] Whatever it was, the Hopkins scandal followed him to his grave. His way of life and personality—both regarded as intolerable—also convinced strategically placed university men that, although a genius, he would be impossible as a colleague.

Peirce's dismissal from Hopkins guaranteed that the Harvard philosophers would be preeminent. Peirce and Hopkins were perhaps the one combination that could have challenged Cambridge. But after Gilman fired Peirce, philosophy in Baltimore declined. More promoter than thinker, G. Stanley Hall got the chair Gilman had to offer, and the idealist George Sylvester Morris and his protégé John Dewey left soon after Peirce. A few years later Hall went to Clark, thereby depriving Gilman of the man he had picked, however unwisely. Hopkins did not rebuild until 1910, when Arthur Lovejoy took a job there, and by then its leadership had long been lost.[36]

Peirce suffered as well as Hopkins. The institutional base it had given him was gone and it was thereafter impossible for him to have an effective and successful career. Even his early writing was so oblique in its treatment of the science-religion question that he probably would never have acquired the public repute of James or Royce. Nonetheless, as the profession of philosophy grew, he could have expected academic fame and a circle of students. There was only one way, he wrote to James, that his work "could find its way to people's brains": "if I could meet a class of young men for an hour thrice or even twice a week for the bulk of the academical year, even for a single year, that . . . would spread the truth."[37] This was not to be, and Peirce's growing isolation led him to abandon all concern for fluency and good style perhaps as a defensive measure. He consequently expounded his ideas in a way that made it almost impossible even for thinkers like James and Royce to follow him—Peirce himself admitted to being "a very snarl of twine." Turned away from the academy, he also lost the minimal regularity of a scholarly schedule. Aside from a few series of articles in the journals, there were no publications in the thirty years after he left Hopkins— everything remained in the chaos of fragmentary manuscripts. The impact of his work on professional philosophers was greater even during his lifetime than one might have predicted, but he was never well understood, and the work of his that was read by philosophers represented only a part of his thought. Over and over again from the 1890s through the 1930s, American thinkers, particularly those at Harvard, looked to Peirce for insights; but they went almost exclusively to the published series of works that Peirce had produced in the 1860s and 1870s. Peirce labored on his system until his death, but the later work still remains in shadows. As William James despaired, there were "flashes of brilliant light relieved against Cimmerian darkness!"[38]

His system, I should point out, changed substantially during the years that Peirce philosophized alone, always building on advances in logic and the foundations of mathematics. He tried to solve the difficulties presented in his analysis of possible experience by admitting real possibilities into his framework and redefining his idealism to give a place to the first impressions of sense. Perhaps more importantly, he realized that the doubt–belief theory simply based the scientific method on a psychological theory of learning. In the formulation of the 1870s he had merely described those procedures identified with the scientific method. This made science relative to a particular psychological organization that might alter in the course of evolution, and to avoid this consequence Peirce's later work elaborated a normative theory of scientific method. He also revised his commitment to the convergence of inquiry as grounding his epistemology. In his early work the mind's categories could not fail to correspond to reality since reality was nothing but what mind constructed in the final opinion; in the later work he argued, hypothetically, that the characteristics of experience were explicable if there was an absolute mind with categories identical to our own. In both systems man's mind was commensurate with reality and scientific investigation converged to a final opinion if inquiry went on forever, because the real was knowable and the processes of the absolute mind were identical to those of the human mind. But in the later work inquiry was not a matter of escaping doubt but of realizing a universal harmony. The scientific method was the correct means to reach this goal and not merely a psychological description of behavior. Pragmatism explicated the contribution to that goal made by a concept: it stipulated the difference applying the concept would make in fulfilling the world purpose. Pragmatism was not just a tool for exploring the meaning of concepts; it told us something of the purpose we had in formulating them.[39]

There is evidence that Peirce's failure to operate successfully in American society affected not only his own career and the availability of his thought to others, but the substance of his thought as well. Murray Murphey has written:

> From 1887 on, Peirce lived in almost total isolation. Although he kept up a large correspondence and followed the journals at least sporadically, he was not in direct contact with the men who were doing new and exciting work even in his own fields. Many of the difficulties in Peirce's later philosophy could have been avoided if he had known the new developments in logic, mathematics, physics, and other fields. But although Peirce often had the books and journals which contained these new developments, he was too engrossed in his own often erroneous ideas to be bothered with them. Had he been a member of an academic community, that kind of isolation at least would have been impossible, for his students and colleagues would have forced him to keep abreast of the new work.[40]

These were the costs, to Peirce and to American philosophy, of his discharge from Hopkins. Early in the spring of 1914, a strange recluse, he died in a dark unheated room of Arisbe, still searching, like the ancient Greek philosophers, for the Archê, the Principle, the First of things.[41]

PART 2

THE GOLDEN AGE
AT HARVARD (I)

Hugo Münsterberg in the psychology laboratory in 1893

William James about 1885

Josiah Royce about 1885

7

PHILOSOPHY REJUVENATED

1869-1889

Eliot and American Education

The last third of the nineteenth century was a time of enormous growth for American higher education. The Morrill Act of 1862 provided federal aid for agricultural and technical training in colleges, and by 1900 it had established the core of a distinguished group of state universities. Simultaneously, new private universities—Johns Hopkins, Clark, Chicago, and Stanford—sprang up to challenge the leadership of the old colleges. And the clergy lost control of collegiate education to a new breed of academic administrators.

Like their predecessors, these administrators believed that higher education ought to serve the nation, but they had a different vision of the nation's future. Post-Civil War America would be a business culture requiring men skilled in many areas. The universities would train them and act as a repository for the knowledge an advancing and complex society would need. The new academic leadership was composed of businessmen-savants, worldly-wise enough to see that money was the means to scholarly pre-eminence for a school and astute enough to obtain funds from both public and private sources. The old-time college presidents had not been without guile, but their temporal wisdom was not equal to that of Andrew White of Cornell, Daniel Gilman of Hopkins, William Harper of Chicago—he destroyed Clark in an 1892 raid—or David Jordan of Stanford—he had descended on Cornell the year before. Chief among these captains of erudition was Charles William Eliot of Harvard.

When Harvard hired Eliot as tutor in mathematics in 1854 the college faculty had eighteen members; when he became president in 1869 the faculty had grown to twenty-seven, and the university had sixty-four instructors and administrators. When Eliot retired in 1909 after forty years as his generation's most distinguished university head and, perhaps, American history's most important educator, the instructional and administrative staff numbered over seven hundred.[1]

Had anyone else been Harvard's president during this period, the university would still have developed enormously and, in all likelihood, Harvard would have had substantial influence. Before Eliot's time it was distinguished for a small but brilliant circle of scientists and for the literary talents who made their homes in the environs of Cambridge. Although the college then was merely one of many New England schools training a local elite (before the Civil War Yale was the most prestigious), Boston had a tradition of educational leadership and wealth to back expansion. But Eliot was alone among the new university leadership in presiding over an established and prominent institution, and he was the most astute of the group. Only thirty-five when he came to power, trained as a mathematician and chemist, he was secularly oriented and wanted to see Harvard promote the needs of a growing industrial nation. He did not hesitate to exploit the financial resources around him. His ability and energy insured that as the university system was built, Harvard would emerge not just as the foremost school but as a commanding, dominant, and dynamic frontrunner, clearly first in the nation and one of a handful of internationally famous institutions of learning. Cambridge had bestowed power upon a young man early, and he turned out to be an aggressive and gifted administrator.

First Years of Eliot's Presidency

Eliot was born of an old Boston family in 1834, the right side of his face covered by a disfiguring birthmark. He took the familiar route from the Boston Latin School to Harvard College. After his graduation in 1853 he progressed from his tutorship to an assistant professorship in mathematics and chemistry and then in 1861 to charge of the chemical laboratory of the Lawrence Scientific School. He was never an original scholar, but even during his twenties Harvard recognized him as a talented organizer, and his abilities promised him a useful career. But in

1863, in a move presaging the future, President Thomas Hill appointed Wolcott Gibbs over Eliot to a professorship in the sciences. Eliot left Harvard and, after two years examining European educational institutions, he returned to Boston as professor of chemistry at the new [Massachusetts] Institute of Technology. After four years there, he was elected to Harvard's presidency.[2]

Eliot envisioned a group of associated schools where scholars of diverse interests would prepare students for leadership in American life. Believing that social usefulness and truth seeking were compatible, he asked the public not to look for immediate returns from universities; he was convinced that an institution engaged in liberal studies would produce public-spirited, service-oriented men. He believed that education should foster open minds and broad sympathies, not detached scholarship. Although he did not think Harvard should be practical in a shallow sense, he wanted it to be "scientific" in the sense of welding theory and practice.[3]

To achieve his end Eliot expanded the lecture system, enlarged the faculty and the instructional fields, and abolished the old system of required studies. He was best known for the alternative, the elective system, in which undergraduates selected their own courses.[4] This reform by itself made Harvard the most successful and forward looking of the old colleges. Electives meant that Harvard catered to student needs and offered specialized work, and this naturally led to more advanced work. Free from preconceived limitations, the curriculum would meet the demands of a complex and heterogeneous society.[5] Reducing the teaching load attracted better professors. In turn, they challenged sleepier colleagues and brought sophistication into the counsels of the university.[6]

Eliot's break with the past was nonetheless gradual. Undergraduates had "elected" courses at Harvard and elsewhere before 1869. Moreover, Eliot's predecessor had initiated advanced—and therefore specialized— work for graduates and envisioned "a university of a high order" in Cambridge. Finally, the full development of the elective system under Eliot was not immediate, and it was a long time before he understood the importance of graduate training.[7] Still, his administration did quickly depart from many customary procedures. How could it be, said one angry and perplexed member of the medical school, that after carrying on "in the same orderly path for eighty years . . . within *three or four months* it is proposed to change all our modes of carrying on the school . . . it seems very extraordinary, . . . " Eliot blandly answered, "There is a new President."[8]

Eliot's basic innovations lay in administration and fundraising. Implementing his ideas required money and organization, and he did not shrink from the implications. His inaugural address revealed his thought on academic administration: "the principle of divided and subordinate responsibilities, which rules in bureaus, in manufactures, and all great companies, which makes a modern army a possibility, must be applied in the University."[9] From his earliest association with the college its leadership recognized him as a superb organizer and an adroit solicitor of funds, and he assumed that one of his functions was simply to loosen pursestrings. Convinced that applied science was the route to national prosperity, and so to Harvard's, he had supported the founding of the Lawrence Scientific School. He began expanding in the earliest years of his presidency—by 1871 he had used new monies to establish thirteen additional professorships. Later when money from the great American fortunes began to flow into Harvard's coffers, he quickly dispelled any doubts about the university's accepting tainted money.[10]

Eliot believed that private donations were the only way for Harvard to dominate education. In 1873, when a committee of the National Educational Association proposed that a national university be built in Washington, he belligerently defended laissez-faire financing principles. Governmental support of education was "the military, despotic organization of public instruction which prevails in Prussia"; the American way was through endowments to which individuals voluntarily contributed. He viewed not only the national university but also the new public universities as signs of statism. The argument was not merely self-serving: throughout his life he supported laissez-faire policy and associated it with political democracy. It was also true that the new universities could hope to equal the wealth of the older schools only with government aid. In addition to preserving democracy, Eliot's position would guarantee that Harvard would be the true national university. As matters turned out, such a university never got off the ground, although educators discussed the idea for years. In 1901 a committee of the National Council of Education decided there was no need for it, adopting many of Eliot's arguments, but by then Harvard had less to fear from either this school or the already existing public institutions of higher learning: they had not been able to compete with Harvard's wealth.[11]

On his election to the Harvard presidency Eliot said that what Cambridge had "to think about" was "what to build *on top of* the American colleges." Commentators have seized upon this remark and concluded that Eliot wished to build what we now know as a modern university. It is true that the model of German scholarship influenced him. Although he disliked German methods he admired the results; government funding of higher education was an evil, but the Germans had relieved talented men from pedagogical routine and supervising student behavior. Consequently, Eliot advocated importing selected features of the German system, but he was never comfortable with its primary characteristic, an emphasis on research. His ideal university was something like an efficient liberal arts college and affiliated institutions offering instruction in all fields of knowledge. Subjects would be taught at a higher level than anywhere else, but he did not differentiate the inquiry of the student from that of the mature scholar and was slow to rank faculty research equal to teaching.[12] For the first ten years of his administration he had one priority: to convert the Cambridge community to his ideal; and for the first twenty years of his presidency graduate education was secondary.

Eliot and the Philosophers

From 1869 to 1889 the new ways in education benefited philosophy at Harvard. Although Bowen was not a conservative Unitarian, the impact of the clergy on philosophy before Eliot's time was undeniably preponderant. And while the inability of the Unitarians to meet the challenge of evolution contributed to the rise of different philosophies at Harvard before they gained a hearing elsewhere, Eliot's regime was congenial to the unconventional. The elective system and specialization brought to Harvard academic freedom, the freedom of scholars to pursue whatever studies they wanted. This freedom promoted the independence of philosophy from religion, and Eliot himself attacked the narrower aspects of religious orthodoxy. He was religious, to be sure, but as a scientist he thought that the clergy had previously restricted education and limited the inquiry that every man needed to fulfill his potential.[13]

"Philosophical subjects," he said in his inaugural, "should never be taught with authority." "The notion that education consists in the authoritative inculcation of what the teacher deems true may be logical and appropriate in a convent, or a seminary for priests, but it is intolerable in universities."[14] He once audaciously told a gathering of ministers that "intellectual frugality" marked their work.[15] In 1882 the American Institute of Christian Philosophy, whose vice-presidents included college presidents Bascom of Wisconsin, Porter of Yale, and Mark Hopkins of Williams, asked Eliot to endorse what was intended to be an impartial investigation of philosophy and science "with a view of demonstrating the harmony between true Christianity and true Science." Eliot's reply tartly expressed the view that liberated Harvard philosophy: he did not believe "that impartial investigation is possible in any branch of knowledge if the inquiry is made with a view to demonstrate a proposition already assumed to be true."[16]

The University Lectures heralded the coming era in philosophy. President Hill had initiated them in 1863 as something on the order of university extension work but, sensing the ferment in education, Eliot wanted to use them as a vehicle of graduate instruction. In 1869–1870 a group of lecturers gave two courses for graduates and other competent persons, one in modern literature and the other in philosophy. The response was small and after another trial in 1870–1871, Eliot confessed that the scheme had "failed hopelessly"; graduate work received less attention in succeeding years. But the lecturers in the 1869–1870 philosophy course showed how Eliot's mind was working: they included Bowen, Emerson, Peirce, and Fiske. In a stroke Eliot conveyed that his university would be open to orthodoxy, Transcendentalism, the new epistemological studies, and positivism. Ten years earlier President Cornelius Felton had threatened to expel Fiske for disseminating that last doctrine.[17]

The diversity of the university lecturers infused Harvard philosophy with a new intellectual spirit. And it is probably true that Bowen was finally hostile to this spirit. But Bowen was a talented thinker, and the moribund state of philosophy under his headship in the 1850s and 1860s was the result not of the content but of the manner of his teaching. Using the rote system, Bowen spent twelve hours a week conducting recitations and another morning listening to essays, while delivering lectures each year. In addition to his teaching duties and the time consumed by reading themes and computing grades for the complex marking system, he also participated in university administration.[18] After the elective system was introduced, a simple increase in staff was enough to produce a change. Against the background of declining Unitarian philosophy and Eliot's open mind, Harvard rapidly became the place for avant-garde speculation.

In 1872 Bowen's assistant resigned—he had only been around for a few years—and George Herbert Palmer replaced him as an instructor in philosophy. Palmer was just thirty and at the beginning of a fifty-year association with Harvard. He wanted to study speculative systems unencumbered by doctrinal preconceptions of right and wrong. A year later, in 1873, Palmer became an assistant professor and William James joined the faculty as an instructor in anatomy and physiology in the department of natural history. In 1876 James became an assistant professor of physiology, but had already taught a course on the relationship of physiology and psychology.[19] The following year, with Palmer's help and over Bowen's protest, Eliot transferred this course, now titled "Psychology," to the philosophy department. Here was a fresh start: James's formal training was in medicine, but under the auspices of philosophy he was to teach "mental science." Using Spencer as a text in this elective was only the final blow to Bowen's conception of philosophic proprieties; James's naturalistic inclinations were the real sticking point.[20]

By 1880 when James became an assistant professor of philosophy, the Cambridge scene had irreversibly shifted. Josiah Royce's arrival from California in 1882 added a major voice and increased instruction, but Palmer, James, and the elective system had already set a novel tone. Royce's appointment *was* significant as the outcome of a battle among various men for a Harvard position and, it turned out, for a base of operation essential to scholarly renown.

George Holmes Howison, whom we have already encountered as a member of the later philosophical clubs, was also a candidate for the job in philosophy. But in the late 1870s James was committed to having Royce in Cambridge and, when an opening appeared, Eliot asked Royce and not Howison to fill it. A possible reason was Howison's association with the two amateur St. Louis philosophers, William Torrey Harris and Thomas Davidson, both contemptuous of the thinking that went on in institutions. Harris and Davidson were crucial to the initial success of the Concord and Glenmore Schools, each participating in the undertaking of the other, but their influence on academic thinking was minimal. In the early 1870s Eliot had briefly considered Harris for a Harvard professorship, and some years later Davidson's outspoken public attack on the study of Greek frustrated a move to get him appointed in Greek philosophy.[21] In any event the one opening was filled by Royce and not by Howison or Davidson.

The various career patterns of the philosophers in the Boston area in the 1870s and 1880s suggest how critical institutions were to the success of philosophers in this period. Ten men of note had gathered there—Abbot, Davidson, Fiske, Harris, Howison, James, Palmer, Peirce, Royce, and Wright. Of the six with no academic affiliation, only two—Fiske and Harris—had successful careers, while all those with university jobs had successful careers. Moreover, the reputations of Fiske and Harris as philosophers declined appreciably during their lifetimes.

Philosophizing under Eliot

The men who made it at Harvard established themselves in an educational climate fundamentally altered by the elective system. There was a teaching load of three courses per semester. Two introductory classes and a range of intermediate and advanced ones surveyed the history of philosophy and special subjects like logic and ethics. Instead of recitations, philosophy courses now consisted of lectures, although some courses did allow discussion. In examinations the students would regurgitate the material expounded by Palmer, James, Royce, and Bowen as well as what they learned from reading the sources. Theses, lengthy papers critically expounding the argument of a group of texts or the work of a philosophical school, tested powers of writing and reasoning.[22]

The Introduction has already noted that the overseers despaired of philosophy in 1860. Twelve years later its "low estate" still disturbed them, but with Palmer and James in harness in the mid-1870s the overseers saw progress. While urging more emphasis on the history of thought, they noted that philosophy was increasingly popular and that students now read in the original works. And while pleased at the liberalization of teaching, the overseers asked that the philosophers offer at least one epistemological course teaching the truth; in their intellectual adventure the undergraduates must still be able to refute skepticism. The overseers thought that psychology was an appropriate place for students to learn that materialism was consonant only with scientific ignorance.[23]

Eliot's philosophers were young and talented teachers; they were also ambitious. One route to success was service to the university. But the growing number of universities, some of them following Harvard's example, were looking for staff; another way up the ladder would be to jump around the system of higher education, or to threaten to. Using this device meant that one's name and abilities had to become known, and publishing was the easiest way to advertise.

"I am one of several candidates for a psychological chair [at Johns Hopkins] which is to be filled in June," James wrote in early 1878 to the editor of the new English journal *Mind*. "It is therefore of great practical consequence . . . that . . . [the enclosed] paper . . . should appear in your April number." James's plea went unheeded; *Mind* did not publish "The Sentiment of Rationality" until July 1879, but neither did Hopkins fill its professorial post. For three years James was an off-again–on-again candidate for it. Lacking faith in Eliot, he "wanted a base elsewhere from which to exert pressure at home."[24] When James received an assistant professorship in philosophy in 1880, he became more content with Harvard, but his letters to Royce, still in California, must have taught the younger man that simple virtue was not enough to get ahead. Depressed about the treatment of his *Mind* article, James complained that "delays of publication are fearful." He had also decided, he told Royce, never to write again for Harris's *Journal of Speculative Philosophy*: "He refused an article of mine . . . for lack of room."[25]

Two years later James was more secure and even had Eliot's ear. When Royce got his 1882 appointment, it came because James convinced Eliot of Royce's philosophical power. Eliot was apparently suspicious of Royce's teaching ability, however, and for three years the job was temporary. Royce followed James's lead: having been a student and protégé of Hopkins's Gilman, Royce would have returned to Baltimore and ended his transient Harvard status. But no call came from Hopkins, and Royce waited on tenterhooks until Eliot made him an assistant professor in 1885. Comfortable and happy in Cambridge several years later, it was easy for him to turn down a Stanford offer for an informal promise of promotion to full professorship at Harvard.[26]

Palmer's case was different. He was important to Eliot for his value as a teacher, his weight in university affairs, and his reputation for probity. But these alone would not have secured Palmer's rapid rise, and he too benefited from the expansion of higher education. Eliot promoted him to a full professorship in response to an offer from the University of California.[27] Four years later in 1886 Palmer began negotiating with Hopkins after talk of his being unable to continue his teaching in ethics. When Eliot responded by guaranteeing Palmer instructional turf, he dropped Hopkins.[28] In 1889 when Bowen retired, Palmer got the Alford Professorship, a job he and James had coveted for over ten years.[29]

The Intellectual Context

In 1892 Eliot hired Hugo Münsterberg, a Freiburg, Germany, psychologist and brilliant careerist who became the fourth and last full professor in what was known as the great department. Although Münsterberg arrived long after Eliot had set instructional and institutional patterns, his coming symbolized the intellectual concerns that dominated the lives of the young professors. During the 1880s absolute idealism established itself in the United States as the solution to the science versus religion debate; its chief exponent was Harvard's Royce. Royce, however, was only the major spokesman: most academic thinkers and all the Harvard philosophers accepted idealistic tenets. The Cambridge professors also agreed that idealism had to solve a central set of puzzles, and this agreement for a time submerged the concerns of the Cambridge amateurs. If an absolute mind existed, why did it appear to us as a world of physical objects? How was science—particularly biological science—consistent with the truth of idealism? Although the philosophers knew that this "two worlds" problem was solvable because idealism could be proved, they were reluctant to take a purely metaphysical approach to the problem. Rather, they explored its contours by mastering the new science of psychology. Psychology examined the connection of individual consciousnesses with the world; and perhaps here, on a smaller scale, where "scientific" research was possible, lay a solution to the conundrums of idealism.

During the first part of Eliot's presidency the idealistic consensus and the interest in psychology molded Harvard philosophy. Münsterberg's appointment revealed Eliot's commitment to academic scholarship, and

Münsterberg himself quickly learned how to use the tested strategies for advancement. His appointment also signified the importance of the study of psychology within a philosophical context.

The members of Eliot's staff were gentlemen; they negotiated politely and graciously, and kept their agreements. But there is no doubt that they were men on the make. After Eliot had bound them to Harvard, the combination of their political skills and intellectual acumen made Cambridge the undisputed philosophic center in the United States.

8

ROYCE AND THE ARGUMENT
FOR THE ABSOLUTE
1875–1892

Royce's Impact

The thought of Josiah Royce, as that of no other, shaped the emphases of twentieth-century American philosophy until the First World War. His argument for absolute idealism first redirected Harvard speculation in the 1880s and 1890s. Like Bowen and the members of the Metaphysical Club, Royce was a Kantian intrigued by Berkeley. But he was younger than these other men and began studying philosophy after the vogue of Scottish realism had peaked. A provincial Californian who studied in Germany, he was not exposed to the Scottish atmosphere of Cambridge and read the Germans directly. Although many of the threads that run through his works also run through those of Bowen, Wright, and Peirce, the Scottish strands are missing. In the resulting synthesis, absolute idealism finally received a lucid, uncompromising, and logically compelling American statement. At Harvard, William James concerned himself with Royce's views rather than those of the Scottish realists. Then, after 1900, Royce's systematic intelligence made his views central to speculative orthodoxy in the United States.

Royce at Harvard

Royce was born in 1855 in Grass Valley, California. His father was a pious, devout, eccentric man who moved from job to job. He never managed more than a subsistence living for his family, although he frequently absented himself in various quixotic attempts to make his fortune. Especially after the family moved to San Francisco in 1866, the boy's primary companions were his mother and his three older sisters. The mother, Sarah Royce, was a strong and stable woman—she had kept a school in Grass Valley—but fearing for her son's health and safety she was oversolicitous and prevented his making friends. Royce grew up a shy and lonely child, homely, physically frail, and small in stature. When he began to attend the large San Francisco Grammar School, his peers found him "disagreeably striking" in appearance—"countrified, quaint, and unable to play boys' games."

From his youth Royce was introspective and intellectual, and after a successful high school career, he did well enough at the new University of California at Berkeley to convince a group of businessmen to finance his postgraduate study in Germany. Returning in fall 1876, he took advantage of a Johns Hopkins fellowship to which he was appointed by Gilman, who had recently left the presidency of Berkeley for Hopkins. At twenty-two Royce's gifts impressed all he met at Hopkins. Among others, he met James who encouraged and supported him in his bold desire to follow an academic career in philosophy. But although his intellectual ambition was by then discernible, Royce went through a period of preparation. When he received his Hopkins Ph.D. in 1878, there were no jobs in philosophy and few jobs of any kind in higher education. He was forced to return to Berkeley as an instructor in English. The job did not suit him: he regarded California as a philosophical swamp where he might contract intellectual tuberculosis. During his four years there, only prodigious amounts of work assuaged his loneliness and isolation. Finally, in 1882, James went on a sabbatical and persuaded Eliot to give Royce a one-year contract at $1,250, half of James's salary. Within three months of receiving the offer he made the difficult transcontinental trip to the east coast with his wife of less than two years and their infant son.

Royce was determined not to return to California. Berkeley had truly been his errand in the wilderness. He managed to hang on in Cambridge, although for three years he had only temporary status and a meager salary. In 1885 he published his first major treatise, *The Religious Aspect of Philosophy*, and received a five-year appointment as assistant professor.

Some five years later, Stanford, then a new university, offered him its chair of philosophy, but Harvard promised him an early promotion and in 1892 named him Professor of the History of Philosophy.[1]

From then until his death in 1916 Royce's eminence grew. *The Religious Aspect of Philosophy* changed the shape of the science-religion controversy. In it, Royce formulated a "proof" for absolute idealism crucial for understanding late nineteenth-century Cambridge thought. He developed his position with a remorseless rigor and consistency that made him famous. Possessing an enormous array of knowledge, well-versed in logic and the sciences, and resourceful and articulate in argument, Royce was called by one student "the John L. Sullivan of philosophy." The autobiographies of those who studied with him in his famous graduate seminars in logic and the theory of knowledge read like conversions to absolute idealism or struggles in which young men sought to emancipate themselves from an overwhelming dialectic prowess. Working under him was to witness his "intellectual majesty" and to test oneself against his "ponderous cogency." As William Montague put it, even those who rejected the "massive edifice" of his thought "longed to call him master."[2]

Royce's first ten years at Harvard were unbelievable. Despite his being thirteen years younger than Palmer and James and their junior at Harvard by ten years, his important early work antedated theirs. Through the mid-1890s his position was the paradigmatic Harvard attempt at resolving the dispute between evolution and theology. But though *The Religious Aspect of Philosophy* was a large and critical text, Royce said much in addition to it. He gave a lecture series that culminated in a second large book, *The Spirit of Modern Philosophy*; he continued his interest in literature and literary criticism that had first inspired him as an undergraduate and been his field while teaching at Berkeley; he joined William James in investigating psychical phenomena; in 1886 he produced a fine piece of local history, *California from the Conquest in 1846 to the Second Vigilance Committee in San Francisco*, as well as several shorter articles on the past of his native state; and finally he managed to write a disastrous novel, *The Feud of Oakfield Creek*.

The result of this activity was a temporary mental and physical collapse. In fall 1887 he suffered from depression, insomnia, and general exhaustion, and in the spring he took a leave from Harvard and spent five months recuperating on a voyage to Australia. Thereafter, the tempo of his life changed, and while his production remained enormous, he restricted himself to philosophy.

Royce's motive for work, I think, was more than a desire to express his outlook coherently. Despite his teaching and academic success, he was painfully lonely and never learned basic social amenities. Conversations with him, everyone testified, rapidly became monologues: the only form of verbal communication he mastered was the lecture. Moving from an obscure mining camp to the international professional prestige Harvard brought him undoubtedly increased his personal discomfort. His appearance was still strange: "His short stocky figure was surmounted by a gigantic round head well sunk in his shoulders. The top of it was sprinkled with red hair, while the strongly freckled face seemed to himself and to every stranger unparalleled in homeliness. . . . His clothes, of no particular fashion, seemed to have as little to do with him as matter with mind. His slowly sauntering gait was characteristic." As George Santayana, then a student, wrote of Royce's novel, "What a failure . . . ; he knows so much about the Universal Consciousness that he has forgotten what individual consciousness is like."[3] In theoretical work Royce could escape his social anxieties and awkwardnesses and gain the renown that satisfied his ambition.

E. E. Cummings captured a typical scene of Royce's personal life. As a child, said Cummings,

> I myself experienced astonishment when first witnessing a spectacle which frequently thereafter repeated itself at professor Royce's gate. He came rolling peacefully forth, attained the sidewalk, and was about to turn right and wander up Irving street, when Mrs Royce shot out of the house with a piercing cry "Josie! Josie!" waving something stringlike in her dexter fist. Mr Royce politely paused, allowing his spouse to catch up with him; he then shut both eyes, while she snapped around his collar a narrow necktie possessing a permanent bow; his eyes thereupon opened, he bowed, she smiled, he advanced, she retired, and the scene was over.[4]

There is also something about Royce's philosophical system that demands psychological scrutiny. Like his peers, he was caught up in the debate over Darwinism and the justifiability of religion, and his theorizing adequately provided for both evolutionary science and the meaning-fulness of human existence. But the form of his synthesis was peculiar: the absolute was a world-soul that reconciled all the antitheses between individuals and the social order and defined perfection as harmony, tranquility, and sublime peace. Most importantly, as Royce never tired of saying, rigorous logic demonstrated these ideas—they were impervious to any possible counter-argument. Some of his peers noted that Royce occasionally evinced a sense of the irony involved in his long and unrelenting efforts to deduce what must be certain anyway, but his work more often suggested that a frightened man was trying to prove it to himself.

Early Epistemology

At Hopkins and Berkeley Royce expounded his own thought in various lecture series. His dissertation also attempted original philosophy; and after Hopkins accepted it, he started to contribute to the philosophical journals which had come into existence since the Civil War. Soon after he arrived in Cambridge he delivered some evening talks entitled "The Religious Aspect of Philosophy." In them he continued to work out the position espoused more fully in the 1885 book, whose doctrines thus resulted from seven years' reflection. To understand this first book, we must explore the theme pervasive in his early writings, the nature of knowledge.

Kant's influence on Royce was enormous; the young man wrote of him as "the good father," and in *The Religious Aspect of Philosophy*, which Royce described as belonging to the "wide realm of post-Kantian Idealism," he announced his debt to Kant "most of all." Before 1885 Royce's Kantianism was more striking. He came to philosophy as a neo-Kantian troubled by the status of the *Ding an sich*. A reaction to the idealistic speculations of the post-Kantians, neo-Kantianism arose in Germany as an epistemological movement grounded in *The Critique of Pure Reason*; philosophy would avoid the excesses of Fichte and Hegel and return to the master. The effect of the first *Kritik*, Royce wrote in 1881, was that "we all now live, philosophically speaking, in a Kantian atmosphere"; the critical philosophy was fundamental and it must be the philosophy of the future. Although Royce became one of the leading exponents of post-Kantian idealism, his road to this position was not through the post-Kantians. We should study them because "with all their extravagances" they never lost sight of Kant. Some commentators have cited Schopenhauer's voluntarism, rather than any Hegelian doctrine, as an influence on Royce. But neither Hegel nor Schopenhauer challenged Kant. In his formative years Royce considered Schopenhauer an unsatisfactory expositor of Kant and an inadequate speculator in his own right. Schopenhauer's merit was that he led young students "to look for themselves" into Kant. In the more exact thinking of the German neo-Kantian movement the battle "to grasp and to perfect the critical idea in all its meaning and consequence begins afresh."5

As Royce struggled with the problems generated by Kant's view, he elaborated a position that was idealistic but also voluntaristic. Royce analyzed the purpose of thought—to learn the laws of phenomena and to predict experience. Experience, however, had a dual nature. First, something was given, "something that I passively receive and cannot at this time alter. . . . I cannot resist the force that puts it into my consciousness." Second, we contributed something to experience. Every judgment teaching us the laws of phenomena exceeded the given. The notions of past and future were necessary to all these judgments. For example, the judgment "Cows are black" did not help us understand empirical phenomena unless we assumed that cows existed in time, that is, were entities with a past and probably a future. But the given never included the past and future. In a move reminiscent of Peirce, Royce conjectured that the past and future were constructs that we made up to reduce the given to coherence. We interpreted the given as a sign of something not given. For instance, we implied that some aspects of the given were memories, indicating that something not present was once present: "To declare that there has been a past time at all, is to attribute to some element of the present a reality that does not belong to it as present." This active construction defined mind. It expressed the interest we had in "reality" and was subservient to practical inclinations. Knowing was a form of acting. The given and what we added to it by anticipation and completion mutually determined knowledge.6

Like Kant, Royce said that in consciousness there was both a given and the spontaneous activity of thought. Unlike Kant, Royce did not divorce the two and then have thought organize the given; rather, thought constructed from the given what was not given. The thinking activity did not infuse sense with form, but from present sense projected past and future. Yet if knowledge was just a construct which depended on practical needs, why should we accept it? In what sense could we justify knowledge?

Royce answered these questions with a dialectical argument. Consider the sentence "There is no future." Accepting it leads to denying it. To conceive a condition in which time has ceased introduces a time element into the assumed condition, that is, a future time. Thinking of a nonfuture is thinking of something which is after the present and, therefore in the future. Royce had a conception (the assumption that there would be a future) which he said was absolutely true. A dialectical argument demonstrated its truth: its denial implied its assumption. He argued analogously for the absoluteness of the past. To put the position in another way, the momentarily present given necessarily involved the past and future. These constructs were not merely constructs, but constructs expressing the essence of thought itself. The time flow, Royce contended, was not some independent thing-in-itself but indicated that constructs determined the nature of experience: we could not conceive that the basic forms of experience could be other than they were.[7]

When he made this discovery in 1880, he was jubilant:

> I work on Kant in the evening. I reflect on the analogy between Kant's "Ich denke" and the doctrine of the active present moment to which I find myself driven in my efforts.

> I see Kant as I never saw him before. But we must put our problem differently. Thus says Kant: What is the relation of knowledge to its object? Thus say we: What is the relation of every conscious moment to every other? Our question may be more fundamental, and can be made so only through study of him.[8]

The belief that some postulates were necessary as well as practically justified was a major insight, but the argument had a weakness. The future and the past were constructions of ours, however much they were necessary, that is, aspects of thought itself. We meant by past and future what we conceived as past and future, and, for example, *fiat* solved the problem of induction: the future resembled the past because we determined it to be so. Royce's logic had done too much. To doubt anything was impossible, for what we posited to be true must be true. Royce presciently put just this complaint into the mouth of an objector:

> But, says the objector, all this leaves open no place for a difference between truth and error. If by past and future, and by the content of past and future one means only what is conceived as past and future and as the content thereof, then an error in prediction or in history is impossible. And with error disappears whatever is worth calling truth.

As Royce saw later, he handled this difficulty inadequately. We meant by error, he claimed, that an expectation was disappointed when we found a present content of experience contrasting with the expectation conceived as past: error depended on remembering that a past expectation now disappointed us. But Royce defined the reality of the past as our present consciousness of the past, and for error to disappear we needed only to suppose an appropriately bad memory. As Royce admitted, error became the consciousness of error.[9] For a conveniently forgetful person, error would not exist. But without an adequate explanation of error, his theory of truth was unsatisfactory. If he could not distinguish error from truth, Royce had failed to set out the purpose of thought as learning the laws of phenomena: prediction exempt from error was not prediction at all.

Before we can understand how Royce resolved this problem, we must turn to another aspect of his work. While writing his dissertation at Hopkins in 1877, he delivered a series of lectures, "The Return to Kant." In them he took up the postulational basis of knowledge. He could not explain why the assumptions of thought were satisfactory; although experience verified them, we could not inquire why it did. It was inexplicable that "our sensations do occur with such a degree of regularity that the activity of thought has the power of making enough valid hypotheses for practical use." The "critical doctrine" had to rest with this analysis, and Royce stated that if mind were removed from the universe, "the order of inanimate Nature" might still exist, although there would be no knowledge of it, no truth or error. In his dissertation written a year later he went further, proclaiming that his philosophy was a brand of idealism. This did not mean that consciousness constituted existence; rather, existence was "not external or foreign to Consciousness." Then Royce declared that although human selves "are transient in Consciousness . . . Existence remains." But if existence did not transcend consciousness, how could existence remain when human consciousness passed? For Royce this was another question we could not answer: "We cannot in the least determine what and how various kinds of consciousness may exist."[10]

In two essays published in 1880 and 1881, "The Nature of Voluntary Progress" and "Doubting and Working," the tension between individual consciousness and "Consciousness" was explicit. For any individual, Royce wrote,

> beliefs are always the satisfaction of individual wants. . . . The adjective "true" is applied to a belief by the one whose intellectual wants it satisfies, at the time when it satisfies them. . . . A system of beliefs is held, just as a system of government endures, so long as it seems to the men concerned advantageous to cling to it.

But this assertion did not mean that what we found acceptable was true. "My needs are narrow and changing. It is humanity in its highest development to which the truth will be acceptable." An adequate view of truth must substitute the broader view of mankind for the personal view: there must be some measure of truth outside any individual's ideas.[11]

By 1882 Royce had convinced himself that some truths were necessary as well as practically demanded, and he examined the relation between this theory and his two kinds of consciousness. If ideas were true, we could not create reality; it must be independent of our ideas; we could justify them, it seemed, only if they corresponded to it. But this reality simultaneously had to have a relation to our consciousness. The outcome of these insights was a first attempt to harmonize two distinct notions of 'idea': the first, that an idea corresponded to an external object; the second, that an idea fulfilled the purpose that called it forth. In 1882 the result was tentative adherence to a Berkeleyan theory.[12]

There were some past, present, and future experiences that no one experienced; yet we required them to make sense of the reality of the world. We wanted to say that the cows in the field existed when no one of us was experiencing them. Moreover, this possible experience could not be "merely" possible; it could not consist of "empty" possibilities.

When no one was about, the cows were in the field; dinosaurs were not. We could imagine dinosaurs in the field, but the possible experiences defining the external world had a different status; they had a reality beyond our ideas of them. Reasoning led, Royce surmised,

> to the conception of one uniform absolute experience. This absolute experience to which all facts would exhibit themselves in their connection as uniformly subject to fixed law is conceived as "possible." But once again, what does that mean? Is the meaning only the empty tautology that if all the gaps and irregularities of individual experience were got rid of by means of connecting links and additional experience, these gaps and irregularities would disappear? Is the meaning only this, that if there were an absolute experience of an absolutely regular series of facts, this experience would be absolute and uniform? . . . Here then is our dilemma. Matter as a mere possibility of experience is more than any animal's known actual experience. And yet this matter is to be real for consciousness. Nor is it to be real for consciousness simply in so far as the possible experience is represented or conceived. The reality consists not merely in the representation in present consciousness of a possible experience, but in the added postulate that this conception is valid beyond the present consciousness. How is this postulate to be satisfied?

A consistent idealist who postulated an actual absolute experience must also claim that this experience was consciousness, or for some consciousness. Moreover, the consciousness involved could not simply be an individual consciousness, for example, mine. Royce met this problem by postulating a "hypothetical subject."

> This hypothetical subject we shall postulate only as an hypothesis. That is, its existence is not a necessary result of the postulate that there is an external reality [that is, absolute experience]. One can form other hypotheses [to account for this, for example, pan-psychism]. But this hypothesis has the advantage of being simple and adequate. . . . [We have, however, postulated] what of course never can be proven, that all the conceived "possible experiences" are actual in a Consciousness of which we suppose nothing but that

it knows these experiences, or knows facts corresponding in number and in other relations to these experiences. This Consciousness is the Universal Consciousness.[13]

By the early 1880s Royce's thought was in a curious state. Ideas existed in order to fulfill our needs, but because they had to refer beyond us if they were true, he supposed an "impersonal experience" to which true ideas corresponded. To explain the special status of this reality-defining experience, he postulated a hypothetical subject for it; yet he maintained that he could not prove this subject's existence. Epistemological research had so far denied him a firm basis for metaphysics; *it* must proceed by hypothesis. We could not expect to have an "Absolute vision of truth, free from all taint of postulate." Finally, there was still no way for human knowers to be in error about the reality which the hypothetical subject defined beyond them.[14]

"The Possibility of Error"

In *The Religious Aspect of Philosophy* Royce's hypothetical subject became actual. In the famous chapter 11, "The Possibility of Error," he set forth the most significant argument of his career; it was the "steadfast rock" on which he would build an untainted metaphysics.

For Royce as for Peirce the basis of knowledge was phenomenalistic. The finite knower was aware not of a physical object but of what is momentarily present (359–63). We could best, if inadequately, speak about this "given"—what is immediately before the mind—using locutions like "This appears white to me" or "It seems as if there is a white paper in front of me" or perhaps even "White spot, here, now." From this slender basis Royce proposed to demonstrate that we could know a more extensive realm—the external world. He said this world consisted of contents of consciousness or, equivalently, of actual and possible experience: his cardinal principle was that experiences were ideas, internal data, and that these ideas made up the world. It was some sort of arrangement, combination, or synthesis of ideas. It went beyond any we had or could be aware of at any time, but we must account for the world in ideal terms, that is, in ways that ruled out external existents. As Royce expressed himself in *The Religious Aspect of Philosophy*,

Popular belief about an external world is for the first an active assumption or acknowledgment of something more than the data of consciousness. What is directly given in our minds is not external. All direct data are internal facts; and in the strictest sense all data are direct. . . . the external world . . . is actively accepted as being symbolized or indicated by the present consciousness, not as being given in the present consciousness (300–02).

Ideas or perceptions—the present content of consciousness—were true or false of their object in a real, although still ideal, world beyond them. If I saw that the cows were black, I might say that the cows were black and my statement would be correct if my experience was accurate. I might also believe, sitting in my study, that the cows were black. Then the statement "The cows are black" would be true if the cows were black, that is, if my belief were true. Because Royce believed that whatever was before the mind was an idea, he treated both these cases as equivalent, as ones of the thinker having true or false ideas, assimilating states of belief, and so on, to perceptual states, or experiences.

Royce correctly traced aspects of his heritage to Berkeley and formulated Berkeley's claims as he had three years before. But this analysis was only hypothetical, elaborating and clarifying Royce's thought as it had developed before *The Religious Aspect of Philosophy*. To speak of a hypothetical universal consciousness was simple, intelligible, and plausible (339–54). But his commitment to it as anything other than hypothesis depended on more far-reaching considerations.

The first consideration was negative. For Royce as for Peirce, Berkeley attracted only to repel. What was the "correspondence" between the real world—the hypothetical absolute consciousness—and my ideas—immediate experience? According to Royce, Berkeley argued that it was their cause. On one hand, Royce sometimes felt that this theory implied polytheism: if the external consciousness caused ideas, it and my consciousness must be distinct, each an independent center of consciousness. On the other hand, this analysis might construe causality as a relation independent of thought; or, to put the analysis another way, the external consciousness would not be a consciousness but a "power," a cause. Against both positions, Royce contended that the external world could not cause our ideas (perceptions) about it; the correspondence relation must be deeper (341–54).

The belief that the external world caused our ideas necessitated something prior to the principle of causation: our thought demanded that our idea of causality and our idea of the specific causal relation involved corresponded to the truth of things. We could not conceive of a cause of our ideas except as we postulated that our conception of the cause was similar to the cause itself. Royce made this argument more than once, and perhaps made it most neatly in an article written in 1892. Suppose he defined the real object as the cause of present ideas, experience. He must still ask what causation meant: it was a relation between facts, and he must have some idea of this relation before attributing it to the outer object, which was never experienced. Therefore, he must first believe in the objective truth about the relation between the real object and his ideas:

> this means that there is here at least *one* external truth, and so one "object" (viz.:—the external fact of the causation itself), which I believe in, not because it is itself the cause of my idea of the causation, but because I trust that my idea of causation is valid, and corresponds to the truth. And it is only by *first* believing in this objective truth, viz., the causation, that I come to believe in x the cause. Hence it follows that even in case of immediate sense-perception, my belief in the external object is always primarily not so much a belief that my experiences need causes, as an assurance that certain inner beliefs of mine are as such, valid, i.e., that they correspond with that which is beyond them.[15]

In *The Religious Aspect of Philosophy* Royce concluded that the conception of reality entailed by the search for causes was subordinate to another conception—that ideas had something beyond them and like them.

If causality were logically primary, representational realism might be tenable. Although it was not for Berkeley, the cause of our ideas might be something different in kind from them. But if the real world was similar to our ideas, Royce could more easily prove its ideal nature. As he would show, ideas were fragments of the real world.

Royce must answer three questions. The first, which he would not entirely handle, had a catalytic effect on his thinking: What was the nature of the correspondence between our ideas and the real world? The second, which was left over from his earlier ruminations, he would definitely answer: What was the status of the hypothetical external consciousness which served as the real world? The third, which he believed he had dissolved earlier, now took primacy: How was error possible? To answer these questions Royce went to "the very heart of skepticism itself." Extreme skepticism would bring him to absolute truth (385).

What guarantee did we have that ideas, experiences, in any way corresponded to the real world? What basis did we have for saying that what we took to be true was in fact so? The skeptic urged that everything was doubtful and that we might always be mistaken. Even this skepticism implied that error existed. Was there any way to avoid this assumption? Unlike Abbot and Peirce, Royce respected Descartes's method of doubt. Suppose we argued that what was true was true for us, that two assertions met on no common ground, so that neither was "really true" or "really false." This position went further than skepticism and declared the belief in error itself to be erroneous. Royce called this view that of the total relativity of truth, and he had an argument against it. If the statement "There is error" is true, there is error; if it is false, then there is, ipso facto, error (370–76). He could only conclude that error existed; to deny its existence was contradictory. The dialectical argument Royce discovered five years before rescued him from relativism. At least he had one truth—that there was error, and he asked, how was error possible, what were the conditions allowing us to err (390–95)?

Error was commonly defined as a judgment that did not agree with its object. In an erroneous judgment we combined subject and predicate in a way that the corresponding elements in the world were not combined:

> Now, in this definition, nothing is doubtful or obscure save the one thing, namely, the *assumed relation between the judgment and its object.* The definition assumes as quite clear that a judgment has an object, wherewith it can agree or not agree. And what is meant by the agreement would not be obscure, if we could see what is meant by the object, and by the possession of this object implied in the pronoun *its.* What then is meant by its object (397)?

Royce was again investigating thought's "correspondence" to the real world. The statement that the cows were black was not true because the cows caused my perceptions (ideas) of the animals; rather the statement would be true if my perceptions corresponded to the real world in some non-causal sense of 'correspond'. What was this sense?

Royce said his account explicated the common-sense view. Although he felt it correct, it allowed little room for error and pushed him towards absolute idealism. In order to think about an object—even if falsely, even in error—I did more than have an idea resembling the object. I meant my idea to resemble the object. To make the point in another way, I aimed at the object, picked it out; that is, I possessed the object enough to identify it as what I meant. For example, suppose I burned my fingers; I experienced (that is, had an idea of) burned fingers. Another person might also have burned fingers; my idea would then be like his idea, his experience. But I would not necessarily be thinking of his fingers when I said "This thumb is burned." To think of an object I did not merely have an idea that resembled the object, but I meant to have the idea resemble just that object.[16]

The intention of the speaker, Royce noted, picked out the object, and in that there was a paradox. If, in judging, I meant or intended the object to which the judgment would refer, to which a perception might correspond, then I knew the object. But if I knew the object, how could I err about it? If I said falsely that the cows were black, I knowingly referred to some aspect of the situation about which I made the judgment. For example, there were black horses or white cows in the field and I somehow intended to refer to this fact. If I had no knowledge like this, my judgment might just as well refer to the black cows in another field, and then my judgment would be true and not false. But given that I knew all this, how could I err?

> As common sense conceives the matter, the object of a judgment is not as such the whole outside world of common sense, with all its intimate interdependence of facts, with all its unity in the midst of diversity. On the contrary, the object of any judgment is just that portion of the then conceived world, just that fragment, that aspect, that element of a supposed reality, which is seized upon for the purpose of just this judgment. Only such a momentarily grasped fragment of the truth can possibly be present in any one moment of thought as the object of a single assertion. Now it is hard to say how

within this arbitrarily chosen fragment itself there can still be room for the partial knowledge that is sufficient to give to the judgment its object, but insufficient to secure to the judgment its accuracy (399).

Error was possible if an object, on one hand, was not wholly present to mind and, on the other, was yet partially present (405). But however difficult it was to account for the nature of error on this "common sense" analysis of correspondence and reference, it proved impossible to account for specific erroneous judgments.

Royce's greatest fame as a dialectician derived from his skill in urging that errors about the mental states of others were inexplicable. If two people, John and Thomas, were talking together we must really consider four people: the real John, the real Thomas, John as Thomas conceives him, and Thomas as John conceives him. When John made judgments about Thomas, of whom did John judge? Plainly of his Thomas, for nothing else could be an object of John's judgments. But could he err about his Thomas? It would seem not, for his Thomas was not outside his thoughts; John's conception of Thomas was John's conception, and what he asserted it to be, that for him it must be. Moreover, John could not err about the real Thomas, because—as far as John was concerned—the real Thomas was unknown.

The only way to resolve these dilemmas was to regard the matter from the perspective of a third person. Suppose John made a judgment about Thomas. If I was familiar with the judgment, "saw" the real Thomas that John could not see, and "saw" that John's conception was unlike the real Thomas in some critical respect, I could say that John's assertion was in error. Of course, in this case I would have present to my consciousness what normally would be thought of as an external object—the real Thomas—as well as John's consciousness. But since, like John, I was locked in my own consciousness, this recourse to a third person would not seem to do the job. Moreover, the mere perception of the disagreement of thought with an object would not make a thought erroneous. The judgment must disagree with the object to which the judger meant the judgment to refer. If John never had the real Thomas "in mind" how could John even begin to choose the real Thomas as his object? The third person hypothesis again appeared to solve this puzzle. I could suppose that a being existed for whom the real Thomas and John's conception of him were both directly present. Under appropriate circumstances this being could see that John's conception of Thomas meant the real Thomas; or rather, because the being had Thomas and John's conception of Thomas directly present, this being could mean Thomas by John's conception. This being could compare the one to the other. If John's conception of Thomas agreed with the real Thomas, then we could declare John's ideas true; otherwise, erroneous.[17]

Although it solved the problem, we might reject this suggestion because it contradicted the presupposition that John and Thomas were separate beings, external to any person's consciousness. But we could account for error on no other supposition, and it was necessary that we did so. Suppose then, Royce declared,

> we drop the natural presupposition, and say that John and Thomas are both actually present to and included in a third and higher thought. . . . Let us then drop this natural postulate, and declare time once for all present in all its moments to an universal all-inclusive thought. And to sum up, let us overcome all our difficulties by declaring that all the many beyonds, which single significant judgments seem vaguely and separately to postulate, are present as fully realized intended objects to the unity of an all-inclusive, absolutely clear, universal, and conscious thought, of which all judgments, true or false, are but fragments, the whole being at once Absolute Truth and Absolute Knowledge. Then all our puzzles will disappear at a stroke, and error will be possible, because any one finite thought, viewed in relation to its own intent, may or may not be seen by this higher thought as successful and adequate in this intent.

Royce defined an error as an "incomplete thought." A higher thought which included the erroneous judgment and its intended object knew the judgment to have failed in the purpose that it more or less clearly had (422–25).

This position answered two of the three problems plaguing Royce: the status of the hypothetical external consciousness and the conditions allowing us to err. Through the 1890s Royce spent little time on these issues. Rather, he examined the relation between the finite individual and the absolute, a question which involved specifying the way finite ideas corresponded to their objects. His doctrine made intelligible the common-sense view that even an erroneous judgment partially intended its object: the idea that prompted the judgment and the intended object were fragments of a more inclusive thought that compared the idea to its intended object.

Although this position explained error, Royce could not explain for some time the relation between ideas and object, finite and infinite. In *The Spirit of Modern Philosophy*, however, he did draw an analogy to make the connection clearer. If I tried to remember a forgotten name, I was sure all the while that I meant just one particular name and no other. If I found it, I immediately recognized it—it was the name I meant all along. In one sense I knew it all the while: in its hunt my present self presupposed that the "deeper self" of which the name was a part already possessed what was sought. The search for truth was a search for what I already had, and my deepest doubts and profoundest ignorance entailed the larger self. Even in error I could not mean an object, he said, unless it was "already present in essence" to "my larger self," "my complete consciousness." The absolute was the only real or complete self; I and all finite creatures were fragments of the absolute.[18] Consider, Royce said elsewhere, what it meant to be either the self of "this moment" or a being who thought about "this world of objects." We must be organically related to a complete reflective person who was implied by our finite consciousness: only one existent person was possible, namely, the one complete self.[19]

Idealism's Leading Proponent

The argument from the possibility of error in *The Religious Aspect of Philosophy* did much to make Royce's reputation: it established him as one of idealism's leading proponents. Through his logical argument and dramatic postulational leap, he had avoided skepticism about empirical knowledge and provided an obvious basis for a positive religious doctrine. Evolution simply became the form in which finite creatures, constrained to time and space, must perceive the world-self. Although the relation between finite and infinite remained a difficult problem, the proof for absolute idealism guaranteed that the problem was solvable. And the developmental world view hinted at how the temporal constantly

yearned to overreach itself: with the ever-increasing growth of consciousness it strove for the eternal. James thought Royce's book "one of the
very freshest, profoundest, solidest, most human bits of philosophical
work I've seen in a long time."[20] It was also a bit of philosophical work
that oriented professional thinking in Cambridge and the United States
until the First World War.

9

WILLIAM JAMES: THE PSYCHOLOGIST
AS PHILOSOPHER
1869-1889

Early Life and Personal Crisis

William James was born in New York City in 1842, the oldest son of Henry James, a literary and religious writer of independent means. At the center of an exuberant family life, the elder James was a cheerful and enthusiastic man of mild eccentricities. Dominating his children's education, he introduced them to American and European high culture, but otherwise raised William, Henry, Jr., the second son, and three other children in an unorthodox manner. The family was so close that William was a sheltered and immature child. His father's money provided a carefree youth but the elder Henry's irreverence for and bemused ignorance of the world of work hardly equipped his oldest son for deciding what he should do with his life. The family's constant traveling perhaps added to the insecurity about his future that pervaded William's first thirty years.

In 1860 and 1861 he studied painting under William M. Hunt in Newport; in autumn of the latter year he entered the Lawrence Scientific School at Harvard where Charles Eliot taught him chemistry and Jeffries Wyman comparative anatomy. James's affiliation with Harvard then begun was to be lifelong, and until the last decade of the century his focus was scientific. The studies with Wyman first developed his immense talent as a naturalist, and in time he became the most gifted scientific observer America has produced. His early adherence to Darwin's theories and his long-standing commitment to science also stemmed from this early training. But it would be foolish to argue that in 1861 James's career was fixed. What Eliot recalled as "a delicacy of nervous constitution" was already interfering with James's work, and he showed no particular interest in any special science.[1]

In fall 1863, James entered the Harvard Medical School but did not receive his M.D. until 1869. In March 1865, he left the school to go on an expedition to Brazil. Although he learned little from the Amazon journey, his nine months with its leader Louis Agassiz made the Darwinian controversy a personal one. Returning to Harvard he continued at the medical school, but his interests went beyond his studies, and he dabbled with the speculative problems occupying Boston intellectuals. This existence and renewed residence with his family (he had moved in with them when they settled in Cambridge) did not agree with him. In excellent physical condition when he returned from Brazil, he interrupted his medical course again in the spring of 1867: at twenty-five he thought his health required a change, and he planned a trip to Germany to learn German and to study psychology in the German laboratories.

Eighteen months later James came back to his family in worse health than when he left; he spent the next four years as a semi-invalid. "Condemned to sedentary occupations, and without any definite responsibilities," his son wrote, James seemed "to be declining into a desultory and profitless idleness."[2]

Many have speculated on James's ailments. He sometimes could not use his eyes for more than two hours a day and back trouble disturbed him. Accompanying these physical ills were signs of "mental illness"—he suffered periods of depression. Whatever is made of his complaints, we may keep two things in mind. First, he was a pampered child of the upper classes. Until that time he had never had to work and had received from his father—the crucial figure of his youth—no practical help whatever on what to do with himself. And James did not know what to do with himself, as the aimlessness of his first years evidences. Second, James was a gifted intellect, conversant with the philosophic controversies swirling around the nineteenth-century life sciences. Although he never accepted the Nihilism that Chauncey Wright delighted to expound to his young friends, James respected tight argumentation; and Wright's presentation made James confront the dilemma facing all nineteenth-century intellectuals—if Darwinian science were true, how could he justify a spiritual orientation to life; if he accepted the scientific world view, how could he avoid a materialistic philosophy? These were serious questions: for James materialism meant determinism and determinism meant fatalism—he had no power over the course of his life and was, perhaps, destined to lead his aimless existence. But if this interpretation of Darwinian science was the final word, there was no great tragedy in personal failure because human existence had no meaning or significance.

During winter 1869–1870 James labored under a sense of frustration, despair, and impotence. Day after day he awoke with a feeling of "horrible dread." On 1 February 1870, he wrote in his diary:

> Today I about touched bottom, and perceive plainly that I must face the choice with open eyes: shall I frankly throw the moral business overboard, as one unsuited to my innate aptitudes, or shall I follow it, and it alone, making everything else merely stuff for it?

As Ralph Barton Perry has pointed out, "the moral business" meant a life in which one exercised "vigor of will" and lived "a militant existence," and James wrote that he would give this "alternative" to quietism a fair trial. But how could one decide to exercise one's will if the world was deterministic? In a famous diary passage of 30 April 1870, he found the answer:

> I think that yesterday was a crisis in my life. I finished the first part of Renouvier's second Essais and see no reason why his definition of free will—"the sustaining of a thought because I choose to when I might have other thoughts"—need be the definition of an illusion. At any rate, I will assume for the present—until next year—that it is no illusion. My first act of free will shall be to believe in free will.[3]

Philosophic Resolution

Charles Renouvier (1818–1903) was the nineteenth century's leading French neo-Kantian. He thought of himself as working out the true implications of *The Critique of Pure Reason*, against its perversions in the post-Kantians. It is a sign of the Kantian orientation of much of James's philosophizing that he began reading the *Critique* at the time he was pouring over Renouvier.[4]

Renouvier's importance for James lay in the Frenchman's attack on the Kantian distinction between understanding and reason. Kant questioned transcendent metaphysics by arguing that the understanding, applicable to the phenomenal world alone, was bound to become involved in contradictions when applied beyond this limit. For James the best example was the dispute between determinists and indeterminists. As phenomenal creatures we were determined. But we could not apply the constitutive category of cause and effect beyond the limits of the understanding, and Kant argued for indeterminism by analyzing the regulative character of the "rational will" as it confronted noumenal ethical and religious demands. Here, however, we had faith, not knowledge. Renouvier said we could not partition the mind into the faculties of understanding and reason. Both intellectual and moral activity rested on faith. In effect, all guiding principles were regulative. If the rational will was justified in affirming freedom in the moral sphere, then intellectual speculation—Kant's understanding—might also affirm freedom.[5]

This is the insight from which we must understand the development of James's thought. His need to be assured of his own freedom made the texts of Scottish realism peripheral. The primary problem became the mechanistic interpretation of evolution; in attempting to refute it, James would collapse Kantian distinctions while maintaining that mind was active. He would go on to link this idea to a commitment to Darwin and try to steer between skeptical empiricism and the post-Kantians. With this in mind, let us return to the 1870 encounter with Renouvier and the early essays James was inspired to write on the freedom of the will.

What determined ideas or acts in deliberation? According to the scholarly conventions of James's time, the British philosophical psychologists accepted a model of the mind as a complex mechanical system operating on principles similar to those accepted in the physical sciences. For James, Herbert Spencer typified this sort of view and in addition linked it to a metaphysical materialism in which the ultimate atomic particles nonetheless evolved toward "higher" forms. James thought this "evolutionary associationalism" vulgar, but Spencer was a significant target: he stated in exaggerated form a set of ideas that James had to circumvent. Working in the Humean tradition of skeptical empiricism, associationalists analyzed states of consciousness into sensations—derived from the reactions of the sensory nervous processes—and images—impressions of memory, imagination, and so on—derived from sensory origins. The primary job of the psychologist was to describe these atomistic components properly and to show how the basic elements were related in complex states.

The "laws of association" determined under what conditions elements came together. For example, the fundamental "law of contiguity" held that if two ideas came to the psycho-cerebral apparatus together or in immediate succession, the later reappearance of one tended to bring with it a reproduction of the other—hearing a melody might bring to mind the words with which it was sung. Associationalism was mechanistic, reducing consciousness to brain activity. Assume two brain units 'A' and 'B' and some physiological process whereby the stimulation of 'A' excites that of 'B', or vice versa. The associationalist supposed that the connecting path between the two underwent some change; it became a path of reduced resistance, although 'A' and 'B' themselves did not change. If the path on certain occasions was one of least resistance, a stimulation of one carried over to the other. The associationalists identified these brain units with the psychic units (ideas, sensations, impressions, images) or made the brain and psychic units correspond. The laws of association then described the causal relations among the various elements of consciousness.[6]

On this analysis the last idea present to mind before action determined behavior: the laws of association operated so that one idea was sustained in consciousness; this triumphant "representation" occurred with a given intensity of reinforcement, a certain feeling of effort, and this intensity or feeling determined volition. The associationalists—and often James also—used the vocabulary of representational realism, but they added that we were "conscious automata," our minds and ideas a useless accompaniment of our bodies: inner physiological drives maintained certain representations (ideas) in the mind; when these ideas resulted in behavior, they only reflected the original drives.

Following Renouvier, James said that in critical cases of deliberation the associationalists' intensity of effort was unknown beforehand.[7] Was this intensity a potentially knowable quantity? If it was, determinism and the automaton theory were true; if it was not, "our acts are in certain cases original commencements . . . of phenomena, whose realization excludes other . . . [phenomena] which were previously possible," that is, we selected our acts from a possible series of acts.

Which alternative were we to believe? The one indubitable philosophic position, said James, was skepticism or Pyrrhonism: one could only be certain about the content of the present moment of consciousness. From the point of view of "strict theoretical legitimacy," James argued, "the theoretical pyrrhonist . . . is the only theoretically unassailable man." This was the *aliquid inconcussum*, the Nihilism of Wright, that philosophers had sought. But skepticism was barren. If we adopted any non-skeptical philosophy—associationalism or anti-associationalism—certainty eluded us, and doubt was possible. As even Wright admitted, his Nihilism was a discipline and not a positive doctrine.[8] James asserted: "In every wide theoretical conclusion we must seem more or less arbitrarily to *choose* our side." In the sciences, James continued, the assumption that laws governed the universe was an intellectual postulate; we chose it in order to make sense of the world. In the sphere of action we accepted "an ultimate law of indeterminism" as a moral postulate; we adopted indeterminism. Whereas Kant argued that certain principles constituted our knowledge and regulated our activity, James held, with Renouvier and against Kant, that all ultimate principles were regulative, postulates, acts of will.

To take sides in any non-barren philosophic dispute required an element of choice. In all cases, both intellectual and moral, if determinism were true the choice was determined and, specifically, in choosing between determinism and indeterminism in the moral sphere the choice was determined. Suppose James's choice for or against free will was determined: "there is an end of the matter; whether predetermined to the truth of fatality or the delusion of liberty is all one for us." But suppose he was free: "then the only possible way of getting at that truth is by the exercise of the freedom which it implies." James concluded, "the act of belief and the object of belief coalesce, and the very essential logic of the situation demands that we wait not for any outward sign, but, with the possibility of doubting open to us, voluntarily take the alternative of faith."[9]

It is not altogether clear what this last passage meant: it was apparently justifiable to choose between determinism and indeterminism in the moral sphere and, it seemed, only a fool would not choose the latter. It was clear, however, that James could defend his belief in freedom against the determinism and automaton theory of the associationalists.[10] Like their mentor Bowen, both Peirce and James feared the consequences of representational realism: if ideas mediated knowledge of a material substrate, philosophers faced essentially insuperable religious and moral problems. Peirce's concern was ultimately religious skepticism, James's the absence of moral freedom. In affirming free will, however, James had traveled Royce's path: rejecting the skepticism of the present moment—Royce called it relativism—James had arrived at a postulational basis for knowledge and, applying it to moral problems, affirmed freedom as a postulate.

Surely this sort of thinking alone did not lift James from his psychological doldrums and restore his health.* It helped that Eliot appointed James as instructor in anatomy and physiology in 1872. To have "an external motive to work" was a "perfect God-send." "It is a noble thing for one's spirits to have some responsible work to do." And most important, perhaps, was his 1878 marriage to Alice H. Gibbens, a supportive and self-sacrificing woman who devoted herself to keeping James intact. "I have found in marriage," he wrote, "a calm and repose I never knew before."[11]

James on the Will

In 1875 James began to teach psychology and a year later was named assistant professor of physiology. In 1880 his title became assistant professor of philosophy; in a sense the change was proper for, although he began work on *Principles of Psychology* in 1878, much of his published work from then until 1890 expanded and developed his ideas on the will. Could James make his theorizing about postulates consistent? Although he had collapsed a Kantian distinction by making the bases of both knowl-

---

*But consider his notebook entry of 30 April 1870:

> Not in maxims, not in *Anschauungen*, but in accumulated acts of thought lies salvation. *Passer outre*. Hitherto, when I have felt like taking a free initiative, like daring to act originally, without carefully waiting for contemplation of the external world to determine all for me, suicide seemed the most manly form to put my daring into; now I will go a step further with my will, not only act with it, but believe as well; believe in my individual reality and creative power (LWJ, 1: 148).

edge and morality postulational, he had retained a distinction between science and morality as Renouvier did not. For James the deterministic assumptions of science conflicted with the indeterministic assumptions of ethics. Did he have to accept mechanism in science? Or could he ground science, as he did morality, in some form of voluntarism where the mind added something to our understanding of the natural world?

James faced another dilemma, stemming from his ruminations over the nature of the will and the influence of his father. Henry James, Sr., was a Swedenborgian, and in his mystical religious assurance his son saw a danger as great as that offered by perverse interpreters of Darwin. Religious conviction guaranteed salvation and the meaningfulness of existence. But if we were certain that we were saved, what motive had we for action? Like materialism, religion could lead to passivity and the renunciation of the moral life that was, for James, identical with the life of action. James was not merely concerned with the apparent conflict between science and morality; he believed that religion, morality, and science must be made congruent. To salvage all three James became an epistemologist, and we must trace his lines of thought: an expanded examination of the will, a consideration of its relation to knowledge, and arguments for its spontaneity.[12]

After adopting his own postulational view, Royce tried to justify the postulates. When he could not solve the problem of induction on their basis, he rejected postulation. James's thought did not run in this direction; he explored his indeterministic postulate. His great attempt was a long article, "The Feeling of Effort," published in 1880 as the *Anniversary Memoirs of the Boston Society of Natural History*. Renouvier recognized its importance by having it translated into French in his *Revue Philosophique*.

James might have derived the views in "The Feeling of Effort" from the similar but earlier ideas of his colleague Bowen, but he went beyond Bowen.[13] The aim of the article was to identify the mysterious sentiment of power, the will or *fiat*. This was James's way of describing "what makes it easy to raise the finger, hard to get out of bed on a cold morning, harder to keep our attention on the insipid procession of sheep when troubled with insomnia, and hardest of all to say No to the temptation of any form of instinctive pleasure which has grown inveterate and habitual."[14] He argued against the associationalists again. For them the laws of association determined behavior. They distinguished, however, between two sorts of behavior: that caused by ideas determined by factors within the self and that caused by factors external to the self. Free will was self-determined behavior; freedom contrasted with compulsory or constrained behavior. The associationalist identified the will or *fiat* with the nervous discharge correlated with the feeling of effort, the feeling of striving or straining to do something. It followed that the will had a physiological origin; it was just the discharge accompanying voluntary acts.

James argued that the associationalists could not link the will or *fiat* with voluntary acts: freedom could not consist in doing what we willed without constraint. James denied the accepted view that the feeling of effort coincided with the outgoing stream of nervous energy; the nerve process accompanying the feeling of effort was not a discharge from the motor center into the motor nerve; it was not an outward-flowing discharge. Rather, the feeling of effort was a sensation that came from the tense muscles, strained ligaments, contracted brow, clenched jaw, and so on. It is unnecessary to follow James's nineteenth-century psychological reasoning in reversing the usual position; its philosophical import was plain. If the feeling of effort was a sensation flowing inward and not an outgoing stream, then James could relegate the feeling to the vast and well-known class of motor feelings; it could not be a candidate for the mysterious sentiment of power, the will or *fiat*, which must have an internal origin. The associationalist analysis incorrectly located the feeling of effort; identifying it with the will was consequently wrong.[15]

James assumed that every idea of a motion aroused the motion that was the idea's object unless inhibited by some antagonistic idea simultaneously present. It followed that voluntary movements were exactly like the emotions: the latter were discharged immediately by the mere pressure of the exciting idea; the former were, basically, those acts more readily inhibited, but acts that had "motor centers" which their "sensational centers" could easily arouse, that is, acts which thinking could easily although not immediately arouse. But, James said, whether an act did or did not follow upon an idea was inconsequential in regard to the willing of the act:

> I will to write, and the act follows. I will to sneeze, and it does not. I will that the distant table slide over the floor towards me; it also does not. My willing representation can no more instigate my sneezing centre, than it can instigate the table, to activity. But in

both cases, it is as true and good willing as it was when I willed to write.[16]

James urged that volition, the *fiat*, was "a psychic or moral fact pure and simple and is absolutely completed when the *intention* or *consent* is there." The physical act, which might or might not follow, was another phenomenon belonging exclusively to the study of physiology. We were confronted with "an inscrutable psychophysic nexus" that lay outside the will. Will meant literally a *fiat*, "a knife-edge moment" in which a state of mind consented or agreed that certain ideas should continue to be or should for the first time become part of reality. The *fiat* worked with the feeling of effort to bring about the stable victory of an idea. The best example James gave of what he had in mind was moral action. If the drunkard overcame his desire to have another drink, he overcame his habitual desires. James explained this by saying that the man's conscience made the difference: moral action was action, in the line of greatest resistance, secured by the *fiat*.[17]

Voluntaristic Epistemology

The skeptical empiricist or associationalist could still question whether this *fiat* was free, for he might allow that as automata men have consciousness accompanying movement but in no way influencing it. James's further argument in favor of freedom depended on his identification of the *fiat* with mind and his analysis of the mind's role in knowledge. Although his position changed, his analysis showed how central in his epistemology was his "ethical voluntarism." He did not need to maintain that there was one (deterministic) postulate for science and another (indeterministic) for morality: indeterminism might do for science also. Several long articles written in the late 1870s and early 1880s made this point.

James's language during this period was ambiguous—he used several words to convey the same idea; and the same word sometimes conveyed different or overlapping ideas.[18] Basically he adhered to what he called the "fundamental and well established" "reflex theory of mind."[19] The structural unit of the nervous system was a triad of sensation or perception, conveying what was given; of reflection, conception, thinking, or awareness, displaying consciousness; and of action, willing, or the *fiat*, indicating mind. None of these three existed independently:

The sensory impression exists only for the sake of awaking the central process of reflection, and the central process of reflection exists only for the sake of calling forth the final act. All action is thus re-action upon the outer world; and the middle stage of consideration or contemplation or thinking is only a place of transit, the bottom of a loop, both whose ends have their point of application in the outer world. If it should ever have no roots in the outer world, if it should ever happen that it led to no active measures, it would fail of its essential function, and would have to be considered either pathological or abortive. The current of life which runs in at our eyes or ears is meant to run out at our hands, feet, or lips. The only use of the thoughts it occasions while inside is to determine its direction to whichever of these organs shall, on the whole, under the circumstances actually present, act in the way most propitious to our welfare. The willing department of our nature, in short, dominates both the conceiving department and the feeling department; or, in plainer English, perception and thinking are only there for behavior's sake.[20]

In this passage James's 'will' referred primarily to actions, but on other occasions he identified willing more carefully with the *fiat*, the spontaneous activity of selection—mind itself. He usually defined the "middle department" of conceiving as consciousness, the locus or forum for investigating how mind worked on "outward existence," the given. The senses made this given known to us. The contents of consciousness, James wrote, were empirical, and the function of mind was selective attention: it accentuated and emphasized certain items and did the reverse with others. This was the contrast between the empirical (empirical contents of the mind) and *a priori* (the selective attention definitive of mind). Indeed, the given in consciousness was given with the emphases defining mind.[21] "Outward existence" and mind were essentially constructs needed to explain certain features of consciousness; the content of consciousness was actually a product of two elements, the spontaneous activity of selection (mind) and the given. Together they yielded the world as we knew it; the content of consciousness was mind's sustenance of certain elements of the given in a place of transit.[22] James contended that "we are led to a curious view of the relations between the inner and the outer worlds":

> The ideas [consciousness], as mere representatives of possibility, seem set up midway between them [the mind and the given] to form a sort of atmosphere in which Reality floats and plays. The mind can take any one of these ideas and make it its reality—sustain it, adopt it, adhere to it. But the mind's state will be Error, unless the outer force "backs" the same idea. If it backs it, the mind is cognitive of Truth; but whether in error, or in truth, the mind's espousal of the idea is called Belief. The ideas backed by both parties are the Reality; those backed by neither, or by the mind alone, form a residuum, a sort of limbo or no-man's land, of wasted fancies and aborted possibilities.*

The mind constructed the world of objects that we know by allowing certain present elements of our awareness to stand for other selected non-actual elements (of possible awareness). The present functioned as a sign of what was not present, and the representing elements and the elements they represented constituted the real world. Selectivity produced the real from sensation.

Is the *fiat* free? James's theory is consistent with the notion that the *fiat* accompanied every struggle of ideas but that the victorious ideas determined it—the *fiat* might be "a simple resultant of the victory which was a foregone conclusion decided by the intrinsic strength of the conflicting ideas alone." James was adept in his use of the language of the nineteenth-century life sciences, and his central argument for the will's freedom was biological. It occurred in two articles of the late 1870s, "Remarks on Spencer's Definition of Mind as Correspondence" and "Are We Automata?" Evolutionary science taught that if an organ had a use, it was unlikely to be supernumerary: it would contribute to the organism's survival. Consequently, James asked if the mind was useful to human beings. The brain, he said, had an indeterminate nervous system: stimuli could give birth to any number of responses. Mind determined, in light of human needs and interests, which stimuli were attended to. Without a mind's selective activity, an animal with an indeterminate nervous sys-

---

*CER, p. 205. The difference between belief and volition, the name he gave to bodily movements, was not intrinsic. What the mind did in volition and belief was the same: it said let this stand, let this be real for me. In normal cases of volition—raising a hand—the "outer force" obeyed and followed the mind's lead; in belief, the "outer force" was not constrained to back the mind's adoptions (CER, pp. 205–06).

tem could hardly survive. It would succumb in the struggle for existence, unable to act appropriately in its environment. Mind was efficacious. It added something to the strife of representations in awareness; it partially created the real. Moreover, continued James, only if we adopted this position could we meet the strongest criticism made against Darwin. The problem was that the time required for natural selection to lead to the descent of man was far longer than late nineteenth-century science could justify. In a defense of Darwin and free will, James urged that only if mind contributed to the race's survival, could scientists shorten the time necessary for evolution, otherwise dependent on fortuitous variation. The mind was not passive. We were not conscious automata.[23]

> I, for my part, cannot escape the consideration, forced upon me at every turn, that the knower is not simply a mirror floating with no foot-hold anywhere, and passively reflecting an order that he comes upon and finds simply existing. The knower is an actor, and co-efficient of the truth on one side, whilst on the other he registers the truth which he helps to create. Mental interests, hypotheses, postulates, so far as they are bases for human action—action which to a great extent transforms the world—help to *make* the truth which they declare. In other words, there belongs to mind, from its birth upward, a spontaneity, a vote. It is in the game, and not a mere looker-on. . . . [24]

Indeterminism was not only a postulate justifying moral activity; in arguing that the *fiat* helped to create the real, James showed that indeterminism was also adequate in science. He made his postulates consistent.

James also interpreted this "mighty metaphysical problem" of the will's freedom as part of the conflict between metaphysical realism and idealism. If a world independent of knowledge existed, and if we were to know it, then in the context of James's argument mind would be supernumerary or passive. It would have no role in determining which ideas were true but would reflect what was out there, given to it. Because mind was not passive, however, James accepted a variety of idealism: in arguing that mind or will was free, he argued that it in part created the world it came to know, and that no world existed independently of it. Mind was adventitious and contributed to determining what is.[25] The *fiat* was teleological; it acted according to our interests and propensities. And James arrived at this idealism in a manner that also made it fideistic: the world must conform to our deepest needs.[26]

James acknowledged that his position was still postulational. His arguments were finally inconclusive, and his view and that of the determinist and scientific materialist were each possible; the latter might be true, and mind might be determined. One of James's trademarks was his repeated declaration that men assented to philosophic beliefs, definitions of the universe and conceptions of the world, because of subjective, temperamental factors. The great philosophic positions had equal logical merit and only the satisfaction of certain aesthetic demands made us adherents of any one of them. Would we ever learn which was true? James indicated two different criteria for answering this question: the first was that we must slowly and painfully find out which position worked better, the survivor constituting the right way of thinking; the second was his opponents' "objective" criterion, that reality was what coerced thought in the long run. James rebutted that we must then wait to learn if the belief, in this case, in freedom, was coercive, that is, if it commanded assent. In either case, truth was "the fate of thought," and we would only learn this fate in the future.[27] As he was fond of saying, we would learn the truth *ambulando*, where what we were committed to helped to determine the truth.[28]

This doctrine gave James a reputation for philosophic tolerance, but he also defined the limits within which acceptable beliefs would fall. In this enterprise he revealed something less than tolerance. What he assumed to deserve human aesthetic preference were the beliefs congenial to the articulate public of nineteenth-century New England: an optimistic theism was inherently suited to the human animal. The restricted nature of this outlook was plainest when James discussed the beliefs he thought were universalizable if not universal:

> Here in this room, we all of us believe in molecules and the conservation of energy, in democracy and necessary progress, in Protestant Christianity and the duty of fighting for the doctrine of the immortal Monroe, all for no reasons worthy of the name.[29]

And James tried to show that because of man's practical nature and desire for moral action, a theistic God was the only rational and possible object for us to conceive as lying at the root of the universe.[30]

James's investigation in the 1870s reaffirmed the beliefs with which he began in the late 1860s. The *fiat*—the mysterious spiritual spark distinguishing man from automaton—helped to make the world what it truly was; it made consciousness effective and joined the postulates of our moral and intellectual life. Specifically, if we successfully believed in free will, it would exist: belief in freedom was self-validating.

Half-Hearted Idealism

Having defined his position, James drew back in the early 1880s. He compromised the consistency of his thought and again allowed the moral and scientific postulates to conflict. It was not all beliefs, but only a certain class of beliefs, "of whose reality belief is a factor as well as a confessor." Only in this class of truths was faith not only "licit and pertinent, but essential and indispensable":

> Suppose, for example, that I am climbing in the Alps and have had the ill-luck to work myself into a position from which the only escape is by a terrible leap. Being without similar experience, I have no evidence of my ability to perform it successfully, but hope and confidence in myself make me sure I shall not miss my aim, and nerve my feet to execute what without those subjective emotions would perhaps have been impossible.

So far was James now willing to go—he was dealing with an immense class of beliefs—but he did not defend the view that will affected the physical world. His debt to Renouvier and Kant did not now permit him to examine the relation between mind and the physical world. When he considered how the *fiat* effected it, he did not carry forward his idea that the knower helped to make the truth:

> The future movements of the stars or the facts of past history are determined now once for all, whether I like them or not. They are given irrespective of my wishes, and in all that concerns truths like these, subjective preference should have no part. It can only obscure the judgment. But in every fact into which there enters an element of personal contribution on my part, as soon as this personal contribution demands a certain degree of subjective energy which, in its

turn, calls for a certain amount of faith in the result, so that, after all, the actuality of the future fact is conditioned by the actuality of my present faith in it, how trebly asinine would it be for me to deny myself the use of the subjective method of belief based on desire![31]

The acceptance of idealism and the immediate pulling back first illustrated a tension in James's thought that he did not resolve until the end of his life. Why did he argue for idealism and then retreat? Idealism appeared essential to a defense of freedom but forced us to seemingly strange beliefs about the nature of the physical world. Surely individual minds had nothing to do with the constitution of the universe. Only if we took mind as a whole might we argue that it in some way shaped nature; idealism led to absolute idealism. But James equated that doctrine with a monism in which individuals were inconsequential parts of one supreme consciousness. In short, idealism took back with one hand the freedom it gave with the other.

James had always disliked the exposition of the German speculators. Their language invited grotesque and unlimited expatiation; the Germans had an "overweening tendency to theorize"; Hegel was a poseur who promulgated nonsense.[32] These prejudices would have made absolute idealism difficult for James to treat sympathetically under any circumstances, but the inability of its monistic followers to find a true place for free will sealed the matter for him. James began to see his own position as pluralistic. In arguing that man had free will, he also argued that not all the universe's parts were bound up together; there was a plurality of entities, no one of which regulated the activities of the others. And, apparently, mind was passive in respect to the physical universe.

For some British thinkers—Spencer in particular—the consequences of materialism led to the same conclusions as German idealism. In denying individual initiative as a force, Spencer's evolutionary view, James maintained, became vague and lapsed from scientific determinism into oriental fatalism.[33] Spencer's thought, like German idealism and the Swedenborgianism of James's father, was a metaphysical creed, a mood of contemplative pantheism which an activist religious thinker must avoid.

James dissected the dynamic relation between British and German monism in his 1884 "The Dilemma of Determinism." Determinists, he said, were often pessimists: they viewed the passing scene as an immense tragedy. But their regret was inconsistent with their determinism—for regret implied that things might have been different. For their position to cohere they must abandon pessimism, abandon regret. To avoid regret the determinist usually affirmed that all was good. In James's words:

> Our determinism leads us to call our judgments of regret wrong, because they are pessimistic in implying that what is impossible yet ought to be. But how then about judgments of regret themselves? If they are wrong, other judgments, judgments of approval presumably, ought to be in their place. But as they are necessitated, nothing else can be in their place; and the universe is just what it was before, —namely, a place in which what ought to be appears impossible. We have got one foot out of the pessimistic bog, but the other sinks all the deeper. We have rescued our actions from the bonds of evil, but our judgments are now held fast. When murders and treacheries cease to be sins, regrets are theoretic absurdities and errors. The theoretic and the active life thus play a kind of seesaw with each other on the ground of evil. The rise of either sends the other down. Murder and treachery cannot be good without treachery and murder being bad. Both, however, are supposed to have been foredoomed; so something must be fatally unreasonable, absurd, and wrong in the world. It must be a place of which either sin or error forms a necessary part.

The deterministic solution was "gnosticism." Erroneously regretted acts might be good and error in regretting them might be good. On one condition: that we regarded the world as a place whose final purpose was not to make real any good but to deepen the theoretic consciousness of the intrinsic nature of good and evil. This was the German idealist view in which knowing defined being:

> They [the gnostics] all agree essentially about the universe, in deeming that what happens there is subsidiary to what we think or feel about it. Crime justifies its criminality by awakening our intelligence of that criminality, and eventually our remorses and regrets; and the error included in remorses and regrets, the error of supposing that the past could have been different, justifies itself by its use. Its use is to quicken our sense of what the irretrievably lost is.[34]

For James the question of determinism pinpointed the relation between British materialism and German idealism: the pessimism associated with belief in a mechanistic world easily led to pantheistic quietism. Our active moral nature demanded that we avoid both, and the result was indeterminism and pluralism. But James did not precisely define pluralism. Idealism tended to monism; if embracing pluralism meant rejecting idealism, James must then accept metaphysical realism and the passive mind that he associated with realism; and so he was enigmatic, affirming the power of the *fiat* and then denying it power in the natural world while advocating pluralism.

Royce's Influence

The creative nature of will and the active aspect of consciousness so intrigued James that he was unconcerned with the Kantian problem pre-occupying Royce—the justification for any postulational philosophy. But James was too astute a thinker not to realize the importance of the issue. In many asides he showed a consistent attitude to the question.

In 1875, the same year he discussed at greatest length Renouvier's solution to the problem of freedom, he explained to the readers of the *Nation* Chauncey Wright's ideas on the ground of induction. Wright, James recounted, believed that the order we observed in things wanted explaining only if we supposed a preliminary or potential disorder, but this was a gratuitous notion since things were orderly: if there was no antecedent chaos, there was no reason for a cosmic "glue" to prevent things falling asunder.[35] James's sympathetic treatment of Wright suggested that he thought justification of the postulates unnecessary, but on other occasions James was not so sanguine. No philosophy had cleared up the "miracle" that the "given order" lent itself to scientific remodeling, that is, to an interpretation consistent with our postulates—our purposes of simplicity and predictability. But the real miracle was believing that we could reduce the given to a desiderated form. We would not relinquish the postulate that a harmony existed between the world and our desires.[36] The ideal of cognition that we tenaciously upheld, he wrote in 1879, was "the monstrously lopsided equation of the universe and its knower."[37] At worst, James said, we found memory, personal consciousness, time, and space underlying the worst disjointedness. If they endured—but why should they?—they were all that was necessary to legitimate postulation.[38]

In 1885 Royce published *The Religious Aspect of Philosophy*. Its primary intention was to provide an unassailable alternative to a postulational epistemology. Royce showed that, instead of being irrefutable, skepticism (or Pyrrhonism) was contradictory and that to explain its contradictory nature we had to adopt absolute idealism. When we understood that ideas (or perceptions) were fragments of the absolute idea, we could see why sensation was amenable to mind's interpretation and why there was a harmony between the universe and our volitions: sensation was a dimension of the absolute mind and the universe an expression of its volition. Royce needed no postulates. Ideas referred beyond themselves and were true or false because they all intended, more or less clearly, the absolute idea of which they were a part.

James was familiar with Royce's position before publication and it immediately affected him, forcing him to confront the weaknesses in his own thought and to resolve them in Royce's favor, at least temporarily. James based his espousal of free will and a postulational philosophy on his (and Renouvier's) analysis that only skepticism was certain. Since skepticism was philosophically barren, it was legitimate to accept alternatives depending on postulation, an act of faith. Royce demonstrated that skepticism properly understood was not barren and, instead, allowed escape from the vagaries of faith altogether. Royce's work, said James, was "fundamental" on this issue, sweeping beyond that of Renouvier. James could not refute "the transcendentalist position." More than that, he was inclined to think Royce right "and to suspect that his [Royce's] idealist escape from the quandary [of how thought may refer to its object] may be the best one for us all to take." "As formidable a convergence of testimony as the history of thought affords" justified Royce's conclusion.[39]

By his own recollection James was not able to escape Royce's absolute until 1893,[40] but he was not happy as an absolutist. Royce's "pantheistic monism" left little room for freedom; and in "nourishing a fatalistic mood,"[41] it struck at the heart of James's developing philosophic thought and his rationale for a positive existence. But by 1884 James's well-being was not utterly dependent on his ability to give a logical argument for leading an active life. He initially responded by redefining his philosophic conceptions and skirting a development of his pluralism to avoid confronting Royce head on. A shift in James's analysis of the nature of mind aided this redefinition.

The 1884 "On Some Omissions of Introspective Psychology" adopted the analysis of mind for which he became famous. James had held that mind was a *fiat* sustaining, in consciousness, certain elements of the given or supposed "outer force." Mind and consciousness were distinct, and the connection between mind and the outer force was mysterious. Now, the *fiat* was undiscussed, and consciousness embraced mind and outer force. In a famous phrase, consciousness was a stream of flights and perchings:

> Let us call the resting-places the "substantive parts," and the places of flight the "transitive parts," of the stream of thought. We may then say that the main end of our thinking is at all times the attainment of some other "substantive" part than the one from which we have just been dislodged. And we may say that the main use of the transitive parts is to lead us from one substantive conclusion to another.[42]

Although James's admission that "we" isolated portions of the stream for various uses reasserted the existence of distinct *fiat*, his work assimilated mind to consciousness. He also again deprecated the separate Kantian entities called representations; they were a "vicious mode of mangling thought's stream."[43] But now these representations, the given, did not even function as constructs. He had also merged the given to the stream of consciousness and declared the latter central to ordinary experience.[44]

James's hostility at least to the language of Kantian analysis matched a rejection of any lingering attachment to associationalism. The demand for repeatable "atoms of feeling" (discrete ideas) was a vagary, an illegitimate metaphor. Associationalism was at best a schematism which became a mythology when taken literally; it "had much better be dropped than retained." Even as a heuristic device, this view implied a one-to-one causal relation between individual brain irritations and elements of the stream, and James denied this implication. He said only that conscious states taken as a whole corresponded to brain action as a whole.[45]

As many commentators have argued, James's work at this time contained the main presumptions that he later expressed as pragmatism and radical empiricism. The presumptions were more explicit in "The Function of Cognition," a paper read before the Aristotelian Society in 1884, which James later cited as an early account of "the truth function" of his later *Pragmatism*. But there was a difference, clearly traceable to James's wary respect for Royce.

Cognition, said James, was a function of consciousness. We affirmed states of consciousness cognizant of—true of—an external reality if the practical consequences of "operating" on these states were acceptable to other observers. Ideas were plans of action: we assumed ideas knew their objects if acting on the ideas was satisfactory to others whom we supposed confronted the same objects. Knowing the real world commonsensically meant that the consequences of acting on ideas worked. So far, Jamesean pragmatism. But James couched his discussion in terms of Royce's analysis of how thought referred to an external object and admitted that Royce's argument was effective against James's own position, conceived as philosophy. James took refuge in a "practical and psychological point of view"; he would "stick to practical psychology, and ignore metaphysical difficulties"; his paper "is a chapter in descriptive psychology, hardly anything more." His task was not to ask how thought's self-transcendence was possible: Royce's answer was probably correct, and it was possible only if the absolute existed and James's pluralism was unjustified. Rather, James assumed an understanding of thought's self-transcendence and engaged in what he took to be a psychological task. He asked for the criteria used by common sense to distinguish self-transcendent cases from others.[46]

Royce affected James by delaying his attempt to develop a postulational philosophy and to separate, to some extent, psychology and philosophy in his mind. Consequently, James's writings into the 1890s renounced philosophic import and stressed, instead, that they were psychological, an attempt to state the criteria guiding individual and social behavior. His analyses consciously excluded any attempt to justify these criteria. So in *The Principles of Psychology* James was led to his famous disclaimer concerning the philosophic significance of that work. Only after 1893 did he develop again what he thought was a philosophical position. And when he returned to philosophy, Scottish realism was even more a peripheral concern: he would define his work against the threat of absolute idealism to freedom.

10

PSYCHOLOGY AT HARVARD
1890-1900

The Meaning of Psychology

It is difficult to understand what nineteenth-century thinkers meant when they wrote about "the science of psychology." The area seemed to have attracted Cambridge philosophers because of the post-Kantian problem of determining how and why the absolute consciousness appeared as a world of objects existing in space and time. A central theme running through the literature was the need to integrate the noumenal and phenomenal spheres which Kantian metaphysics had made distinct. Psychology attempted this sort of integration: it investigated the relation of the individual consciousness to its world; it dealt with a more manageable problem than philosophy but one that was still critical. Psychology was both more and less than traditional philosophy. More, because it was supposed to be scientific in the sense that physics and chemistry were and that post-Kantian metaphysics was not; less, because as a natural science it had to be content with describing psychic phenomena and not explaining their ultimate relation to the physical world.

This set of interests, set against the Kantian background, shaped Cambridge "psychological" literature. But when the Harvard philosophers first wrote about these concerns, psychology lacked any clearer definition.

Writing The Principles

In 1878 James contracted with Henry Holt to write a "psychology" textbook for student use. Over the years James's conception of the work expanded and, as its completion became more distant, various chapters appeared in learned journals. Through these articles his reputation grew as a man to watch, and he spent several months in 1882–1883 on the Continent meeting European colleagues. Promoted to full professor in 1885, he was determined to secure scholarly esteem, and commentators have observed that a sense of insecurity hounded him, motivating not only his work but also his desire to please. In any event, Holt published *The Principles of Psychology* in 1890 in two volumes of nearly 1,400 pages. It was unshapely and, many reviewers said, unplanned, but its great scope and massive erudition covered the general area as nothing else had done. His recognition was secure. The *Principles* was an instant success, and two years later Holt got the text he wanted when James wrote his *Psychology, Briefer Course*.[1]

We have already examined much of the substance of the *Principles* in examining James's essays of the 1870s and 1880s—they formed the philosophical backbone of the book.* But he put this material in a new context, giving the work an ambiguous and confusing viewpoint upon which many scholars have written.

Before finishing the book James did not separate psychology and philosophy, and his study of the mind had resulted in a postulational epistemology in which the test of the truth was the satisfaction of human needs. But Royce's *Religious Aspect of Philosophy* convinced James that no postulational account was adequate. Focusing on the relation of intentionality that Royce said must hold between thought and its object, James saw no way to escape absolute idealism. The first fruits of this confrontation with Royce were evident in James's articles of the late 1880s and early 1890s: he had forsaken philosophy, he said, and his examination of the truth concept was merely psychological description and not epistemology. In the *Principles* there were further fruits: the book, he insisted, would not be metaphysical—that is, philosophical, epistemological—at all; it would adopt the limited viewpoint of natural science. Psychology assumed the thoughts and feelings—the consciousness—of individual

---

*The *Principles* discussed the following important themes already taken up: the automaton theory in PP, 1: 128–44, 447–54; the stream of consciousness, 1: 224–90; attention, 1: 402–47; the failure of associationalism and Kantianism, 1: 342–73; 2: 276–82; signs and reality, 2: 27–28, 177–85, 237–40; relations, 2: 1–13, 31–43, 76–82, 103–06, 134–282; the feeling of effort, 2: 283–87, 320–21, 487–542.

minds and the external world to which consciousness referred. It also assumed that these thoughts and feelings knew the world. The natural science pursued by James aimed to give an account of the mental life and to examine its conditions. The psychologist described mental phenomena in detail and ascertained "the empirical correlations of the various sorts of thought and feeling with definite conditions of the brain" (1: vi, 1).

In short, natural science took for granted a variety of representational realism. When the psychologist described psychic phenomena and showed the association of thought with brain states, he had done all he could. To explore the causal relations between mind and brain or the "correspondence" between thought and its object was metaphysics—that is, philosophy, epistemology—and outside the scope of James's work.[2] James criticized German thought because, as he construed it, its proofs for idealism rested on a bad analysis: German transcendentalists needed absolute mind to connect the data of the stream of (phenomenal) thought and, as we have already seen, James contended that this was unnecessary because relations were given in the stream. More importantly, according to the *Principles*, this sort of idealistic argument allowed metaphysics to intrude into psychology where James accepted "the relatively uncritical non-idealistic point of view of all natural science" (1 : 272). Simultaneously, however, the transcendentalists had probably divined "ulterior Metaphysical truth." The trouble was not their belief, but their mixing it with psychology (1 : 367–70). As a metaphysician he found "the notion of some sort of an *anima mundi* thinking in all of us to be a more promising hypothesis, in spite of all its difficulties, than that of a lot of absolutely individual souls" (1 : 346); science "may be enveloped in a wider order, on which she has no claims at all" (2 : 576).

So far the division of labor was clear, and James spent the great bulk of the *Principles* at his scientific tasks, describing mental phenomena and their concomitant brain processes. In his second task, James was circumspect, refusing to do more than assert the correlation of consciousness with the entire activity of the brain, whatever that might be, at a given moment (1 : 177). Although he exhaustively discussed nineteenth-century work in brain physiology, attempted to relate changes in neural processes to altered states of consciousness, and summarized experimental work bearing on the topic, James consistently maintained that the present state of his science forbade anything more than a broad statement of mental and physical co-variation.[3] When he described mental processes, he was more positive and deserved his fame as a gifted observer of natural phenomena. The key to his insights was his delineation of the "psychologist's fallacy" and his ability to avoid it. The fallacy was the confusion of the psychologist's standpoint with that of the mental fact about which he made his report. For example, knowing a given consciousness of an object the way he did, the scientist was likely to assume that this cognitive state knew its object the same way he did; in describing the state, he might illicitly attribute to it the qualities of the (psychologist's) object. Another variety of the fallacy assumed that the mental state studied must be conscious of itself as the psychologist was conscious of it (1 : 196–97). In fact, the presumption that states of consciousness were all self-conscious vitiated most psychological description (1 : 274–75). The stream of thought, James held, was just as it seemed to be. It did not consist of repeatable "elements," but of an ever-varied flow. Only rarely did this flow consist in knowing the world and simultaneously reflecting on the knowledge of it. In full command of the literature of his subject and armed with a means for assuring accuracy, James proceeded to describe mental phenomena in rich, precise, and graphic detail. This account remains the strength of the *Principles*.*

Separating scientific and metaphysical responsibilities superficially succeeded, but critics have pointed out that James constantly allowed himself to philosophize, and it is true that he unevenly integrated into the book the older epistemological studies we have examined. By the time James wrote the *Briefer Course*, he admitted the failure of his original plan. Psychology was "particularly fragile, and . . . the waters of metaphysical criticism leak in at every joint" (467). More importantly, his philosophical work obtruded in a way that compromised the position of the *Principles* and muddied its intent.

The dilemma faced by James was that the natural science viewpoint led to a mechanistic and deterministic conception of psychology—the conscious automaton theory against which he fought. Some interpreters have argued that this actually was the position of the *Principles*. James surely denied that the natural science view implied a mechanistic

*The best discussion of this aspect of James's work is John Wild's *The Radical Empiricism of William James* (Garden City, N.Y.: Doubleday and Co., 1969), pp. 33–103, 167–222. I would recommend the discussion of habit (PP, 1: 121–27) and of the self (PP, 1: 291–330).

psychology, but only weakly resisted this implication. For example, when he took up the question of the *fiat*'s freedom in the *Principles*, he said psychology could not answer it, and opted for freedom on ethical grounds (philosophical, metaphysical grounds, I assume). But indicating his retreat from the idealism of the late 1870s, he added that our scientific and moral postulates were at war, thereby conceding that within psychology, he was a determinist (2 : 572–73). In another place he reasoned that adherence to scientific dualism banished mind "to a limbo of causal inertness," from which it followed that if mind was active, there was no dualism (1 : 133–38). The whole doctrine of the *fiat* represented not only an intrusion of metaphysics into natural science but also a doctrine inconsistent with natural science as James viewed it. In short, James's natural science approach committed him to the deterministic psychology he found repugnant. On the other side, he was not a happy convert to Royce's metaphysical monism: lurking within it was another sort of fatalism. In "The Dilemma of Determinism" James had argued that Spencerian psychology and German idealism were identical in adhering to some kind of oriental pantheism, yet in the *Principles* James embraced a version of each of these philosophies.

The disorder of the *Principles* derived from James's assimilation of "The Possibility of Error." It involved him in a doctrine of two worlds, one of science and one of absolute mind, and created more problems for him than it solved. He half-heartedly defended a scientific psychology and a metaphysical idealism, neither of which satisfied him; and he half-heartedly defended a distinction between the two which he did not believe.

There were two excellent examples of these tensions. The first was James's denial of soul substance. The metaphysician might legitimately uphold this notion, but the psychologist must define the self as it appeared in consciousness as the passing conscious state. James quickly added that this theory was not Hume's associationalist doctrine of the self as a bundle of sensations, for each of James's passing states appropriated what came before and after it; each was continuous with the past and future. There were, for James, no discrete moments of consciousness; the stream was a unity in multiplicity.[4]

In this analysis of the self, the "scientific" approach actually married the conscious automaton and idealist traditions. There was a similar synthesis in the development of the functionalist or pragmatic view of mind; it too followed from James's unsatisfactory view of the scientific and real worlds. According to the "motor theory of consciousness," mind mediated between the environment and the organism's needs; the conscious functions accommodated the organism to novel experience. Physiologically considered,

> mental phenomena are not only conditioned *a parte ante* by bodily processes; but they lead to them *a parte post*. That they lead to *acts* is of course the most familiar of truths, but I do not merely mean acts in the sense of voluntary and deliberate muscular performances. Mental states occasion also changes in the calibre of blood-vessels, or alternation in the heart-beats, or processes more subtle still, in glands and viscera. If these are taken into account, as well as acts which follow at some *remote period* because the mental state was once there, it will be safe to lay down the general law that *no mental modification ever occurs which is not accompanied or followed by a bodily change*. The ideas and feelings, e.g., which these present printed characters excite in the reader's mind not only occasion movements of his eyes and nascent movements of articulation in him, but will some day make him speak, or take sides in a discussion, or give advice, or choose a book to read, differently from what would have been the case had they never impressed his retina. Our psychology must therefore take account not only of the conditions antecedent to mental states, but of their resultant consequences as well (1 : 5).

The organism, he stressed, resembled a machine for converting stimuli into reactions, and mind was bound to the "central" portion of the machine's operations as preparation for appropriate action. In many cases the conscious state depended on prior bodily activity.* This theory, he

---

*PP, 1: 5. The James-Lange theory of emotions applied this idea in a specific area. On the usual understanding of emotion, for example, we met a bear, were frightened, and ran, the first two "mental states" (meeting a bear and becoming frightened) inducing the activity. James said, however, that the first mental state induced the activity and it, in turn, determined the emotion (the mental state of becoming frightened). Behavior was a precondition of feeling; we felt what our bodies predisposed us to feel. (See the discussion in PP, 2: 449–74, esp. 449–50, 472–73). James's defense of his theory almost exaggerated. All he had to hold was that emotion (or any conscious state) did not precede behavior and that conscious states and behavior were mutually dependent. For an illuminating psycho-historical treatment of James's theory see Howard M. Feinstein, "William James on the Emotions," JHI 31 (1970): 133–42.

supposed, "makes us realize more deeply than ever how much our mental life is knit up with our corporeal frame, in the strictest sense of the term" (2 : 372, 467).

At the same time that mind was part of this reaction mechanism, there was in the mind, when we acted voluntarily, "*a mental conception made up of memory-images of . . . sensations, defining which special act it is*" (2 : 492). This mental conception was not the *fiat*, the mysterious feeling of effort (2 : 500–01), but it was both a "kinaesthetic idea" and an inner entity, a mysterious intellectual phase (2 : 493). Although this notion might not be consistent with his description of the physiological organism, the existence of this peculiar kind of image was, I think, a consequence of James's joint commitment to the dualism of the automaton theory and an ulterior idealism; it assured that the motor theory of consciousness did not reduce mind to behavior.

Münsterberg Takes Over

The *Principles* established James as the first name in American psychology, and a year of travel in Europe in 1892–1893 secured his reputation on the Continent. But its publication also meant that a period of his life was over. He wanted to go beyond psychology to philosophy, to resolve the tension between science and metaphysics; more specifically, he wanted to give the experimental work to someone else. In the 1870s he had founded one of the world's first laboratories in experimental psychology and subsequently conducted "demonstrations" for his undergraduates. He was determined to rid himself of these duties. After his appointment as professor of psychology in 1889 (he had previously been professor of philosophy), he set out to get money for a new laboratory. By the end of the 1890–1891 academic year he had raised $4,300 for new equipment and facilities, and in fall 1891 moved into larger, more comfortable, and better equipped quarters. Renovated facilities, he thought, would induce an experimentalist to run the laboratory and, incidentally, to replace him when he went on leave in 1892–1893.[5]

In May 1892 he succeeded in luring the twenty-nine-year-old Hugo Münsterberg from Freiburg, Germany. Allowance being made for his age, he was, James wrote, "the ablest experimental psychologist in Germany." Harvard would continue to lead in psychology—Münsterberg "will scoop out all the other universities so far as that line of work goes."[6]

Wilhelm Wundt, Münsterberg's teacher and the founder of experimental psychology in Germany, had emphasized the description and analysis of the contents of consciousness as being sensations, images, and feelings. Introspection was essential, although Wundt used experimental apparatus as an auxiliary to isolate and measure the basic attributes of the elements from which complex states of minds were built.[7] Münsterberg's interest was motor activity and not sensory processes. Like Wundt, Münsterberg stressed experimentation and was a creative, daring, and ingenious investigator; but he denied Wundt's claim that the feeling of effort coincided with the outgoing stream of energy from the central nervous system to the muscles. This feeling was due rather to the sensations coming from the muscles, tendons, and joints (kinaesthetic sensations—sensations flowing inward); and, so Münsterberg held, this feeling could not be identical to *willing* as Wundt had it.

Although Wundt rejected the dissertation in which Münsterberg expressed this view, Wundt shifted his student to another topic that procured him the doctorate. Three years later, however, Münsterberg published his rejected dissertation as his Freiburg *Habilitationsschrift*. This act ruined him with Wundt, although the subsequent controversy earned the young man recognition.[8] *Die Willenshandlung* (*Voluntary Action*) attracted James's attention, and he praised it in the *Principles* as "a little masterpiece." The remark was not surprising, for Münsterberg's views, corroborated by experimental data, were exactly those James argued in "The Feeling of Effort" and repeated in the *Principles*.[9]

James met Münsterberg at a Paris conference in 1889 and they corresponded thereafter.[10] There is no doubt that he admired the quality of Münsterberg's laboratory work—experiments on association, reaction time, and the subjective estimation of time and size. But when James brought him to Harvard, he knew he was also getting someone with sound doctrine, and Münsterberg's agreement with James extended to much more than their analysis of the feeling of effort. Broadly, Münsterberg's conflict with Wundt lay in a commitment to Jamesean ideas.[11]

On the conventional view, impressions and ideas existed in us independent of activity; when they were complete and perfect, they sent their message to some motor apparatus to carry out an order. This notion, said Münsterberg, was "a fancy." His "action theory" reversed the usual order and developed, in effect, James's motor theory of consciousness. As long as psychologists limited themselves to sensation and the laws of association, said Münsterberg, they neglected the characteristic features of mental life such as vividness and inhibition. Some psychologists—at times James—called in a spiritual principle—the *fiat*—to select the ideas that would occupy the mind. In his single disagreement with James, Münsterberg rejected such a metaphysical principle in psychology, where his only concern was the chain of causal connections. Instead, he suggested that the character of experience depended on the anticipated activity to which sensation led. Experience varied with the open or blocked state of the "path" of motor response. I am not likely to hear my wife's car drive up if I am deep into my book, but I will not catch the drift of the book if I am anxiously awaiting the sound of the car. The state of motor processes, said Münsterberg, decided the possibilities of experience, the content of consciousness: "our ideas are the product of our readiness to act." More specifically, he contended, the physical reaction following sensory excitation was fundamental for experience. Muscular tension or preparedness was "almost more important" than incoming stimulation.[12] In fact, it was arbitrary to separate sensation from activity: the organism was a reaction apparatus in which impression and expression belonged together. The brain which "housed" our experience was useful to the individual only because it was part of a larger system. On one hand, it connected with the sense organs and, on the other, with the muscles. The "arc" which led from the sense organs through the motor nerves to the muscle system was a biological unity designed to achieve the survival of the individual: it adjusted the body to the conditions of the surroundings. "The doings of man determine his possibilities of experience . . . our actions shape our knowledge."[13]

This was Münsterberg's action theory: preparedness and unpreparedness for action conditioned the reinforcement and suppression characterizing mental life. We perceived the world just as far as we were prepared to act in it; knowledge depended on the capacity to respond to objects. Cognition was as much a product of action as action was the product of cognition.[14]

Both James and Münsterberg agreed that their respective motor and action theories of consciousness modified the conventional account.

Münsterberg also believed, with James, that willing required that "an end must be reached which is grasped beforehand by the mind. Everything else is secondary. If we do not anticipate the end, we never have a will." The organism might be a reaction mechanism, with the brain coordinating sensory stimuli and muscular activity, but in voluntary action an idea of the result of our activity preceded the activity.[15] Like James, Münsterberg did not reduce mind to behavior:

> outer behavior defined as the biological arc and . . . inner experience then appear to us as merely two different expressions of the same event. The consciousness and the body with its actions are two different aspects of that reality which we want to study. . . . *Hence "mind" means for us both that which everyone finds in himself, in his inner private consciousness, in which nobody else can directly take part, and at the same time the particular kind of bodily behavior in which the personality expresses itself and which is open to everyone's perception.* . . . Whenever the mind is influenced the behavior changes and whenever the behavior shows characteristic traits we refer them to the mind of the personality.[16]

Münsterberg had what one of his students called "a system of double bookkeeping." Regarding psychological science, only behavior concerned him. But the scientific realm did not have an independent existence. It was an aspect of the real world of purposes. The relation between mind as scientific psychology conceived it and inner experience troubled Münsterberg as it had James. Münsterberg, however, was firmer in his dualism and never allowed the *fiat* to violate the realm of scientific psychology. Although he, unlike James, immediately decided to work out the relation between the two worlds in an orderly way, during the 1890s the laboratory occupied him.*

Royce's Work

James had argued that evolutionists could cut the time they needed

---

*Mary Calkins appears to be the only one of Münsterberg's students who understood (or sympathized with) his "double entry" theory. See her *Introduction to Psychology* (New York: Macmillan Co., 1901), pp. vi–vii; and her revision of Münsterberg's ideas in "Psychology as Science of Selves," PR 9 (1900): 490–501. Münsterberg later adopted much of her analysis. See PGA, pp. 304–05, 338, 363–64.

to account for the descent of man by assuming the (free) power of the mind to aid in human adaptation. In the famous last chapter of the *Principles*, "Necessary Truths and the Effects of Experience," he added that the mind's ability to grasp the external world adequately lay in the accumulation of spontaneous variations fortuitously enabling us to cognize objects. The variations which survived provided our conceptual framework, and we measured its cognitional power by looking at its ability to orient us to the world and not by seeing if it was derived from objects. James called this exploration of the categories "psychogenesis," an examination of how far external things accounted for our tendency to conceive them the way we did and of the steps by which the race came to possess its mental attributes.

This work exemplified James's "evolutionary naturalism,"[17] and many later thinkers emulated it. But in the 1890s Royce undertook a more formal analysis of the categories, and his studies, too, would attract future students.

Royce had taught psychology at Harvard in the early 1880s when James went on leave, and he continued to do so thereafter, caught up in the interest in the new science of mind. Jamesean and Münsterbergian notions packed his 1903 text, *Outlines of Psychology*, but in the 1890s Royce saw in psychology the central problem of his own philosophy. He knew from a logically perfect proof that the real world was the world of absolute mind, a world of feelings. Royce called it the "World of Appreciation." Why did this world appear as the "World of Description," the world of objects existing in space and time, subject to causal explanations characteristic of science? To answer this question was to relate finite to infinite, to give the "deduction of the categories." Kant tried to explain how we could legitimately apply the categories to the data of sense. For his absolutist successors, this deduction must show how we "derived" our forms of experience and categories of understanding from the real world of absolute self. Perhaps, thought Royce, psychology held the answer.

Psychology, he said, was in an anomalous position among the sciences, since it purported to make individual consciousness the object of observation. That is, it proposed to describe the World of Appreciation. How was this science posssible? It rested on the belief that there actually exists in the world of truth an intimate correlation between what self-consciousness reflectively discovers in the inner life of the individual, and what the common consciousness of mankind detects somewhere in the describable processes of the physical world. Were there no such correlation discoverable, there would be no psychology possible.

Reasoning with Münsterberg, Royce said that psychology was conceivable only if the World of Appreciation, the metaphysically real, had "actual ties" to changing physical states. Apart from an "embodiment" or "manifestation" of the inner life in a psychophysical process, the science could not exist. Royce believed that we could discover the ties by studying mental disorders, comparing the behavior of men and animals, and experimenting on human beings.[18]

Royce himself was sidetracked before he progressed with this program. But in the mid-1890s, like James and Münsterberg, he did reflect on the World of Description and its connection to psychology. This problem took on enormous importance for him. The link between individual consciousness and the public behavior which "expressed" it paralleled the link between the world of the absolute self and the world of objects which expressed it. A study of psychology promised a deduction of the categories *writ small*, an explanation of the relation of the Worlds of Appreciation and Description that Royce was determined to achieve. Fifteen years would pass before he articulated this relation adequately, and when he did, he had long since forsaken psychology for another tool—logic and the foundation of mathematics. But in the 1890s he thought psychology might solve the problem.

His crucial effort was an 1894 article, "The External World and the Social Consciousness," but we must define some terms before analyzing it. A small child imitated when he strutted about as a soldier or ran on all fours like a dog. The child was aware of a model and found his own body able to repeat movements of the model. Imitation also included those intelligent functions which tended to the voluntary production of external objects "resembling" other objects, that is, models. Drawing, painting, and building were "imitative functions" of this sort. But imitation did not reproduce one set of data by means of another set like the first. In imitating, we got two sets of data whose contrasts instructed us as much as their resemblances. We interpreted the model in imitating it: the main motive of imitation was to interpret perceptions by means of deeds. A parody was an imitation, but its interest lay more in its contrast to that of which it was a parody than in its similarity. This kind of imitation neglected everything about the model except chosen aspects of it and reproduced even those aspects in an exaggerated way. Royce defined the "resemblance" of imitation and model by saying that an imitation meant or intended its model: imitation was teleological and not rooted in similarity.

What distinguished imitation from other motor activities, such as looking, listening, and grasping?

> My interpretation of what I am usually said to perceive outside of my organism, in the external world, is . . . conditioned upon my setting over against my perceptions a series of motor processes, or of perceived results of motor processes, which in its wholeness contrasts with the other series in the one principal fact that the motor processes, the imitative deeds or their results, appear to me relatively controllable, plastic, reproducible at will, while otherwise the two series are largely similar.

Imitation interpreted an uncontrollable perceptive series by setting against it a series that appeared to be similar—at least *meant* the first series—but had its most important contrast in its controllability. The model might be similar to my imitation but was beyond my power, independent of my movements.

In arguing that the resemblance between model and imitation might consist only in the latter meaning the former, and that the important contrast between the two was control, Royce considered imitation's most interesting elements:

> an imitation appears as an adjustment that leads to the emphasizing or interpreting of a train of relatively external experiences, by virtue of the fact that the mental accompaniment of this adjustment is a train of relatively inner experiences . . . while the similarity of the train of internal experiences to the train of external experiences serves, in the midst of the mutual contrasts of the two trains, to make

livelier the consciousness of each series, when viewed side by side with the other.

The consciousness of the imitator was simultaneously a consciousness of his adjustment and of his model. Imitation was "the one source of our whole series of conscious distinctions between subject and object." The differentiation in consciousness between internal and external experience first took place in the contrast between model and imitation.[19]

The child who possessed a "social consciousness" was for the first time in the presence of supersensual reality: this was the argument of "The External World and the Social Consciousness." The child had models beyond him and found himself and his models imitating other objects—friends, playthings, animals, and the like. For a time he might think that his perceptions of an object were numerically identical with those of others, but communication involved differences of opinion, conflict of testimony, and evidence of variety in the experience of others. The child learned that his experiences were not the same as those of others, although he assumed that the experiences were of the same object. What the child saw he came to regard as the object for him; what I saw, as the object for me. But through our ability to verify one another's experiences we found that we were "imitating in common"; and thus Royce explained the origins of representational theories of knowledge. We reconciled the subjectiveness of perception and the commonality of imitation by postulating a tertium quid, the external object as it was for itself. It was directly present neither to me nor to others, but it was our object insofar as we imitated its structure "as we try to imitate each other's thoughts"; an object was external to both of us as we were external to each other.

Royce's language should not distract us. To imitate each other's thoughts evidently meant imitating one another so that others were able to apply to us adjectives like 'intelligent', 'kind', and 'principled'. In these cases we imitated behavior definitive of mind, of thinking beings; we imitated our fellows' thoughts. Even so, we admitted that another's consciousness was beyond us. We did not experience it as he did. Similarly, imitating an object's structure was akin to describing it. These imitations—a kind of activity—were ways of classifying, enabling us to verify our descriptions and those of others. To describe something as five inches long was to be prepared to act in a certain fashion and, if the description was correct, to have others verify it. Royce called this "imitating the structure" of a thing. But just as we were external to one another, so the object was external to us.

Our world was dualistic. Its social aspect consisted of minds whose thoughts we tried to share when we communicated by gestures or the devices of language. Its physical aspect consisted of entities that were also "imitable" but that did not themselves imitate. All we knew of these objects was what we could mutually verify, even less than we knew of our fellows. What objects were in themselves, we could never discover:

> The object, as it is in itself, is indeed unknowable, for it—the object in itself—declines to tell us what its inner life is. If it would speak for itself, we should know something more about it, but it remains the stubbornly silent partner. Hence, we can only speak in common about it. Where we permanently agree, we suppose that we are touching the reality, not as it is for you or for me, but for us. And it is only as existent for us, who are by hypothesis external to one another, that the object shows any persuasive and verifiable indication of existing externally to both and all of us. Thus, the "things-in-themselves" appear to us, on this level, as unknowable.[20]

A rigorous proof showed that the phenomenal world must "reflect" the absolute self. Using psychology, Royce had now shown in some measure how finite selves came to believe in the world of objects. He had written a genetic account of the development of the categories. The World of Description, he said, "is simply the way in which the world of appreciation, the world of the true and spiritual Self, *must needs appear when viewed by a finite being whose consciousness experiences* [the way man's does]. . . . Here is the permanent truth of Kant's doctrine."[21]

Psychology would carry Royce this far. Elaborating the origins of representational realism, he said, defended Kant's formulations at the finite level of consciousness. Royce's essay restated "in rational fullness" "the true spirit of the Kantian deduction."[22] But this "deduction" was incomplete, for Royce did not analyze the precise status of the categories or show how they grew out of our social consciousness. He only elaborated his view that the World of Description was the finite guise of the World of Appreciation. In the 1890s he could go no further: the exact relation of the World of Description to the World of Appreciation was inexplicable from the "human point of view." But from the perspective of the absolute:

> we should see what now is dark to us, namely, why and how the world of appreciation, when viewed under the conditions of our finite experience, has thus to seem a world of matter in motion. As it is, however, we already know that the world of matter in motion is simply an external aspect of the true and appreciable world. That is, in substance, the whole of our philosophical insight into the matter.[23]

Royce would later change his position when he turned from psychology to logic; but by the turn of the century Münsterberg had oriented himself to American life and took up where Royce left off. James had forsaken psychology to devote himself to the philosophical questions raised by the science. No sooner had he made the break than his successor also decided that the real action was in philosophy and in the two worlds' question posed by the study of psychology.

11

HUGO MÜNSTERBERG

Münsterberg's Career

Münsterberg had been born in Danzig in 1863, the son of a well-to-do international lumber merchant. He took his Ph.D. under Wundt at Leipzig in 1885; two years later he received his M.D. from Heidelberg. The same year, 1887, he went to Freiburg as a *Privatdocent* (private lecturer) but by 1891 he was an assistant professor on the faculty. Even in his twenties Münsterberg was an aggressive and brilliant researcher, but his fight with Wundt and his Jewish background—he disowned it because of his German cultural chauvinism—stood in the way of advancement in Germany. Unfortunately, he regarded every place else as inferior and yearned for a celebrated *Gelehrter's* career in the *Vaterland*. After an initial three-year trial stint at Harvard from 1892 to 1895, he was offered the professorship of psychology. Münsterberg, however, was not yet resigned to a career among the barbarians. Harvard would wait two years for his decision, and in that time he returned to Freiburg hoping to use his Harvard appointment for preferment in Germany. But old animosities died hard, and nothing turned up while the two years passed. After dickering unsuccessfully with Eliot for some means to keep a foothold in Germany, Münsterberg accepted a permanent post at Harvard, returning in 1897. James again became a professor of philosophy and left the laboratory for good.

In time Münsterberg's loyalty to his new home increased. Although he never ceased to be patronizing toward the United States, as the impact of Harvard philosophy grew he found in Cambridge the academic sphere of influence he desired and subsequently refused to return to Europe.

His experimental work put him in the first rank of psychologists and gave Harvard the prestige that James had counted on.

Münsterberg had extensive training in traditional philosophy, wrote on the subject before coming to the United States, and turned to it again after teaching a few years at Harvard. But even philosophy and psychology together could not contain him. As soon as his English was adequate, he began to write on American culture and collected and published a group of essays in 1901 as *American Traits*. A plethora of articles followed this volume, and he printed the most important in *Problems of Today* (1910) and *American Patriotism* (1913). The popularity of his writing allowed Münsterberg to pride himself—undeservedly—as an interpreter of American life and as a symbol and bearer of international good will. His great effort was his 1904 *Die Amerikaner*, which his student Edwin Holt translated into English. An attempt to make the United States comprehensible to the Germans, *The Americans* was not an original or penetrating work, but it was not inconsequential: its 600 pages were a historical and cultural tour de force; they surveyed American history, analyzed its politics, commented on the arts, and speculated on social life and character.[1] *The Americans* and the other popular writings often took the point of view of a psychologist and led Münsterberg to apply his psychology more directly. In 1905 he started a series of books on the ways in which psychology could solve the problems of ordinary life. Among these volumes were one on psychology and medicine, one on psychology and law, and three on psychology and business.

Münsterberg was enormously productive; when he died at fifty-three, he had written thirty-one books,[2] an average of two a year for the last ten years of his life, and he had, additionally, edited the four volumes of the *Harvard Psychological Studies* as well as making briefer contributions to various magazines and journals. The year 1909 was busy but not atypical. Between January 2 and February 12 he wrote the 400 pages of his *Psychotherapy*; between February 25 and April 1 he revised and rewrote his 1907 *Philosophie der Werte* for an American philosophical audience in his 400-page masterwork, *The Eternal Values*; and between April 15 and June 20 he wrote *Psychology and the Teacher*. In October he published a reply to critics of *The Eternal Values* and in November and December wrote *Vocation and Learning*. In April 1910 *Problems of Today* appeared, a collection of popular essays written in 1909; other articles went un-collected.[3]

Münsterberg dictated his books; they came, he said, "from his lips." Much of the product of this garrulous man was not worth reading and much was done as a means of self-advertisement. Nonetheless, he de-served more recognition than posterity tendered him. James's first im-pression was apt: Münsterberg was "vain, loquacious, personally rather formal and fastidious, I think, desiring to please and to shine . . . with probably a certain superficiality in his cleverness and lack of the deeper metaphysical humor [but] . . . a man of big ideas in all directions, a real genius."[4]

Just as Münsterberg's early work displayed an experimental flair attractive to James, there was much in his later work that displayed crea-tive power. He developed a system of absolute idealism in which psy-chology had a significant part, and within this system's framework he justified his popular studies. In this chapter I shall locate the place occupied by psychology in his philosophy and show what applications were en-tailed by his speculation.

Münsterberg's View of Psychology

Münsterberg's conception of psychology changed little throughout his career and was articulated in many works both scholarly and popular; the exposition was most lucid in his 1899 *Psychology and Life.* We did not differentiate the real world, the world of our everyday life, into physical and psychical parts. It was rather a world in which human beings acted to achieve certain ends. They acknowledged others with whom they agreed or disagreed and jointly viewed the world as one of tools and helps and obstacles and goals. Münsterberg described this life-world as one of willing subjects and objects of appreciation; it was not one of the mental and physical. We made no distinction between the inner and outer worlds: "in reality the physical thing and our idea of it are one" (24, 27).

The objects of appreciation were material for our will, but in order to act successfully we had to know what to expect from these objects; we required their "cooperation." There arose, Münsterberg claimed, a will "to isolate our expectation about the objects," "to think what we should have to expect from the objects if they were independent of the willing subjects" (28–29). For our purposes—and these he clarified later—we subjected reality to a "transformation." We called possible objects of awareness for every subject physical objects, and possible objects for one subject alone psychical objects. The tree posited by every reflective consciousness as independent of individual experiences of the tree was a physical object, ultimately defined by a concatenation of atoms having no relation to ordinary life. The psychical object was an individual's experience of the tree, an object for that person alone. Our experiences might agree, Münsterberg said, but mine could never be yours, nor yours mine.[5] Münsterberg's argument followed Royce's and, like James, Münsterberg believed that science assumed a variety of representational realism. Science distinguished physical objects from perceptions of them, and just as physical science studied one sort of hypostasized entity, so psychology studied the other. Both sciences considered their material as perceivable objects composed of causally related elements. Neither scientific branch was concerned with the values and teleological relations that governed the real, that is, ordinary life (30).

We abstracted "nature" from the objects that physical science studied as the locus of physical objects; just so "consciousness" was an abstraction from the totality of psychic facts. Consciousness was not personality; it did not do anything but was only the manifold in which psychical facts appeared, the presupposition making possible the existence of the contents of consciousness.

Physical science conceived the world as a mechanism, governed by what Münsterberg called mechanical laws. These laws were not simply empirical summaries of facts, but "axioms" of a different character, the necessary forms of connection which made it possible to think of a connected world. Sciences like physics and chemistry moved from empirical laws stating relations between various groups of facts to mechanical laws. These sciences understood the world as an application and combination of the mechanical laws for special complexes of atoms. What connection had psychology with this aim? The objects it studied existed only for a single subject.

> This definition [of the physical object] makes it logically necessary that the physical object shall not disappear and shall not be newly

created, but must be equal in all changes, while the psychical object, which cannot be the object of two subjective acts, must therefore be created and disappear in every new act. One psychical object can then not contain another, and can hence not be considered its multiple. It cannot be understood, therefore, as a measurable quantity, and is thus eternally unfit for a causal equation and therefore for a connection by necessity (58–59).

With Royce, Münsterberg held that the possibility of psychology's existence as a science depended on a perfect psychophysical parallelism. For purposes of scientific psychology Münsterberg identified a person with the organism and personality with the central set of the contents of consciousness—ideas, volitions, emotions, and judgments. These he further identified with the various stimuli to which the organism responded (31, 51). In short, the psychologist postulated that every psychical fact had a physiological counterpart (42). The psychologist was then in a position, indirectly, to regard the psychical facts as causally connected whenever the corresponding physical processes were causally linked (60–65).

Psychology was physiological. Because the psychical facts as such were indescribable and unmeasurable, the science that described them must at every stage relate the psychical to the physical (126). This presupposition cohered with the "action theory" that framed Münsterberg's laboratory work. Associationalism adopted a physiological approach, but Münsterberg objected to its holding that the brain had a uniform structure; such a structure did not furnish "sufficient manifoldness of functions" for a physiological process corresponding to every experience, to the differing contents of consciousness (81). Countering this view, Münsterberg analyzed the brain as part of a larger system. The brain functioned to connect the stimuli caused by the perceived object and the anticipated motor response. His psychophysical parallelism consequently guaranteed that a variation in the "centrifugal part" of the "brain process" necessarily changed the associated psychical fact (87–94). In this way Münsterberg allowed the alteration in brain processes—the variation in anticipated motor response—to account for the variations of consciousness and made sense of the laboratory procedures whereby the psychologist interpreted mind by measuring behavioral responses to stimuli.

The action theory argued just this idea—that activity determined consciousness.

Münsterberg's sagacity was apparent in examining the subconscious, spiritualism, and history. In the first decade of the twentieth century Freud was not popular in the United States, but scholars knew him and, in any event, discussed entities like the subconscious in dealing with supposedly otherwise unaccountable behavior. Münsterberg argued that the fact that the subconscious was an explanatory construct should not detract from its "scientific reality." He asked, however, if the construction was justifiable, and to this he answered no. Proponents of the subconscious argued that it caused phenomena but, Münsterberg said, the inner life investigated by psychology caused nothing. At best the psychologist correlated the psychical phenomena with brain processes and gave an indirect causal explanation. To talk of the subconscious was, first, to confuse the teleological framework of reality with the causation of science which was always physical. But, second, because consciousness was only an abstraction indicating the existence of mental phenomena, these phenomena could not exist outside of consciousness. The notion of the subconscious was contradictory.[6]

Münsterberg thought that a psychology that toyed with notions like the subconscious represented a half-hearted and confused attempt at science. He deprecated James's attraction to these concepts, and dismissed James's retort that the time had passed "for metaphysical dogmatism about natural phenomena."[7] All such ideas, for Münsterberg, confused the realm of real life which he understood teleologically with that of science which he understood causally. His bête noire was spiritualism, the belief in supernatural connections between the physical world and the psychical world, construed as teleological. This view not only misdescribed the psychical as an aspect of the real when it was actually a scientific construct, but spiritualism also applied teleological explanations in the scientific realm. Spiritualism led only to obfuscation. The real world lost its value and became subject to causality, and the scientific world lost its order and became subject to chaos, both yielding to a new world controlled by inanity and trickery, unfit for ethical ideals and unworthy of scientific investigation.[8]

If *Psychology and Life* adamantly preserved the purity of causal science, it was equally adamant in setting the boundaries of science. The Social

Darwinist movement repelled Münsterberg because it exemplified a misalliance between the real and scientific worlds. What of the scientific approach to history, the attempt to analyze the world's past by means of psychological laws? The aim of history, it was argued,

> must be to find the constant psychological laws which control the development of nations and races, and which produce the leader and the mob, the genius and the crowd, war and peace, progress and social diseases. The great economic and climatic factors in the evolution of the human race come into the foreground; the single individual and the single event disappear from sight; the extraordinary man becomes the extreme case of the average crowd, produced by a chance combination of dispositions and conditions; genius and insanity begin to touch each other; nothing is new; the same conditions bring again and again the same effects in new masks and gowns; history with all its branches, becomes a vast department of social psychology (10).

Münsterberg rejected one objection to this viewpoint: Wilhelm Windelband's distinction between the nomothetic and the idiographic sciences was no argument that history was not subject to law. All sciences sought laws and made judgments about individual facts. No concern for the "unique" would prevent history from following the path of the sciences (179–228). But Münsterberg asked if the meaning of history was encompassed by what psychological, economic, and statistical laws put in its place; did we think historically, he asked, if we considered the growth of nations "as the botanist studies the growth of a mould which covers a rotten apple? Is it really only a difference of complication?" (16) Methodologically, psychology and physics, on one side, and history, on the other, did not differ. The difference was ontological, in the nature of the material studied. The connections examined in history were not causal but teleological: in history systems of individual wills were fulfilled. The historian revealed the connections among these wills. History did not teach us (in the sense of allowing us to predict behavior) but enabled us to understand and appreciate our place in the real world (25–28). The antithesis between nature and history was the difference between perceiving and willing, the causal and the moral, the thing and the man.

Metaphysics

Locating psychology's place in the scientific system was a persistent theme in Münsterberg's writing. His 1907 *Philosophie der Werte* and its 1909 English counterpart, *The Eternal Values*, presented this system and simultaneously elaborated Münsterberg's idealistic metaphysics: a rationale for the system and some sense of the meaning of his two worlds' doctrine. In fact, he regarded *The Eternal Values* as his philosophical magnum opus, and it deserves careful examination.

Münsterberg first asked what was valuable in itself. Was there anything which individuals desired—indeed which all rational beings must desire—without reference to themselves and their wishes (1–6, 28)? Münsterberg dedicated *The Eternal Values* to Josiah Royce and throughout its first section philosophized dialectically to show that such "absolute values" must exist. The scientific world was value-free only because the scientist himself did not possess the passive spectatorial consciousness used in defining scientific objects: he must think science free of values, but his activity itself was always value-laden and incapable of scientific analysis (7–23). In science and everyday life, we never judged capriciously but consistently to insure a judgment's truth. Loyalty to truth bound us without exception, for even denying a commitment to absolute truth reaffirmed that commitment. Truth was a good example of something valuable in itself, a value that was not relative but which everyone "willed."

By willing Münsterberg meant organized, purposeful striving. Values were the objects of this activity; they satisfied our wills, centers of conscious activity (65–70). Without reference to individual goals, all of us did and must seek some of these values—the eternal values—of which truth was one (28). These "overindividual" values

> have unexceptional validity because they are valid for every possible subject who shares the world with us, and who relates his thinking and striving to our world. In such thinking and striving the values remain independent of any particular individual will. . . . The values stand above the individual (49).

The problem was to elaborate what these values were and how they functioned as they did.

We satisfied our individual wills when we realized one of our ideas: for example, we wanted a glass of water and went and got it. Münsterberg described this process as the "remodeling" of a given experience so that its content—a glass of water—remained the same but its form changed—the idea of the glass of water became a reality. The form of the experience was altered so that a special action was possible—drinking the water. We transformed the contents of consciousness (ideas) into realities (identical contents in a new set of relations which allowed new activities) (70–74). In Münsterberg's world of everyday life, there was no physical-psychical dichotomy. *The Eternal Values* indicated that the dichotomy arose in the interests of action and the satisfaction of our wills. The real world was one of actors and the objects of their goals. The bifurcated world of mental and material existents came into being for the achievement of our goals. We reorganized experience so that one aspect was psychical—ideas of what we should strive for—and one aspect physical—the world which fulfilled our striving. But this distinction was not original: it developed to serve our purposes, to fulfill our wills, and we more truly analyzed the world as one of value.

Münsterberg claimed that this examination of willing permitted us to understand what it meant to have a world at all. The orderliness and connectedness of a world was the preservation of identical contents of experience from past to future. Momentary experiences, instants of consciousness, were given but they had no meaning; to have a world was just to attain in our experiences that continuous identity characterizing successful willing. But the activity of will defining our attempt to have a world had no relation to us as individuals, to our personal pleasures or unique ends. Seeking identity in experience was something we could not give up; if we were to have a world at all, we must make this act of affirmation. Münsterberg had a value sought by every rational creature as the object of his activity. He had an eternal, an overindividual value (75–78).

From this insight Münsterberg built a grand system. The will to have a world was actually fourfold: we willed every part of experience to be identical throughout changing events (the value of conservation); we willed the various parts themselves to have a certain identity (the value of agreement); we willed change to belong to the essential meaning of what was changed (the value of realization); and we willed the three preceding values themselves to be one (the value of completion). Within

	Logic (Conservation: self-identity of parts of experience)	Aesthetics (Agreement: identity of various parts)	Ethics (Realization: change belongs to essential meaning of what is changed)	Metaphysics (Completion: unity of values of conservation, agreement, and realization)
Naive (Life)	Existence	Unity	Development	Holiness (Religion)
Outer World	Things	Harmony	Growth	Creation
Fellow World	Persons	Love	Progress	Revelation
Inner World	Valuations	Happiness	Self-development	Salvation
Intentional (Science)	Connection	Beauty	Achievement	Absoluteness (Philosophy)
Outer World	Natural Science (Physics and Psychology)	Fine Arts	Industry	World
Fellow World	History	Literature	Law	Mankind
Inner World	Reason	Music	Morality	Over-self

Chart 11.1: Münsterberg's Eternal Values

these four values Münsterberg distinguished those that were naive and
intrinsic to life and those posited intentionally in the interests of civilization; and within the four he further distinguished those relating to experience of the outer world, of our fellows, and of our inner world. Consequently, the four values defined sets of values—logical, aesthetic, ethical,
and metaphysical (78–83). The relations are clear in chart 11.1.

It is unnecessary to detail Münsterberg's scheme, but his earlier thoughts
fit into the grander system. Previously, he had dichotomized the worlds
of fact and value and, within these two worlds, relations pertaining to
individuals and those transcending individuals. He had

	World of Facts (Causality)	World of Values (Teleology)
Over-individual	Physics	Normative science
Individual	Psychology	History

where "normative science" referred to those purposeful modes of reasoning (such as deductive logic) valid for all individuals [9] *The Eternal Values*
changed this scheme in three ways. First, where the earlier work dealt
only with what the later book called logical values, the later added aesthetic, ethical, and metaphysical values. Second, Münsterberg transformed
the dichotomy between individual relations and individual-transcending
relations into a trichotomy of outer world, fellow world, and self. Physics and psychology came together as branches of natural science studying
the outer world, and the distinction between them implied no systematic
importance. History studied the activities of our fellows, and normative
science (now reason) studied the activities binding on every self (116–61).
Third, Münsterberg distinguished those values arising naively in life and
those arising intentionally in the growth of science, broadly conceived, or
civilization. This was not the earlier distinction between fact and value.
Although Münsterberg continued in his popular work to speak of the
standpoints of causality and teleology,[10] he had altered his position. The
entire framework of values—both those of naive life and those of civilization—presupposed an ultimate purposeful reality. The values of natural
science, of history, and of reason (all scientific values) assumed this more

ultimate reality but so too did the values of everyday life. In some un-specified sense Münsterberg wanted to say that everyday values were closer to this reality than were scientific values; and that within the naive values the values of the inner world reflected ultimate reality more than those of the outer and fellow worlds. He also made his idealism explicit: all of these necessary forms of willing were human forms and lost their significance in relation to the ultimate reality itself.

In *The Eternal Values* one dimension of the willing necessary for a world was a desire to unify the values in the framework. In naive life the religious values realized this desire, and Münsterberg's framework provided at least a rough place for notions associated with Christianity. In reflective life the philosophical values realized this desire, the supreme value being the "over-self." If we had a world at all, we willed its unity in the over-self; the over-self was the necessary value that unified the logical, aesthetic, and ethical values of the inner world. Each self posited the over-self as an absolute value for every thinkable self. The over-self was that timeless surge of activity that we reflectively conceived as ultimately real and that we immediately (naively) recognized as salvation. All experience, Münsterberg argued less cryptically, had to belong to a self but since such a self could not be an individual self, we posited an over-self containing all possible experience and therefore defining the conditions of the possibility of experience (395–99). But in willing the over-self as the unifier of the values of the inner world, of each individual, we recognized that no individual self was ultimately real: "the selves are in the over-self as the drops in the stream, and the total development of mankind is part of the primary over-will itself. . . . [but] the selves do not live outside the deed of the over-self. . . . [nor does] the sum of the drops make up the stream itself" (413). But if the inner world of individual selves was not real, neither was the fellow world: if there were no indi-viduals, there were no fellows. Finally, when Münsterberg eliminated all reference to individuals, the opposition between selves and things, psy-chical and physical, vanished; the outer world, too, had no final signifi-cance. The over-self was the single ultimate reality: "The content of experience has by that ceased to be experience. It has become over-experienceable manifoldness: the self has been expanded to the all" (395). "The I, the fellow-I, and the not-I are in the over-I one and the same;

and the logical, the aesthetic, and the ethical valuation form in the over-I one single unfolding will, and accordingly one single deed: the world-deed" (422).

Psychology in Its Place

Münsterberg's quest after system was essential to his philosophizing. He was trained as a philosopher in nineteenth-century Germany, and, like Royce's philosophical psychology, Münsterberg's work was in the tradition of Kant and Fichte, attempting a deduction of the categories, showing the way in which the absolute became the world organized in the ways it was for human purposes. Psychology had its place among the various sciences that helped finite individuals realize the infinite purpose, a purpose beyond psychology and the realm of causality. Throughout his career Münsterberg formulated and reformulated frameworks of values, various deductions of the categories.* His mania reached its zenith and his influence its apex in 1904 when he served as vice-president of the International Congress of the Arts and Science held in St. Louis. The congress was part of the St. Louis Exposition and drew scholars of international repute from all over the world to speak on scientific methodology. Münsterberg's latest system was the basis for the complicated agenda that gave a place to over four hundred speakers on various divisions of knowledge. On the program were the Europeans Henri Poincaré, Ernst Troeltsh, James Bryce, Ferdinand Tönnies, Max Weber, Werner Sombart, and Ernest Rutherford; and the Americans Abbot Lawrence Lowell, Woodrow Wilson, G. Stanley Hall, Josiah Royce, David Starr Jordan, and William Torrey Harris.[11] Never had Kantian thought received such a stupendous elaboration.

Münsterberg's investigations illuminated the priorities of the Harvard psychologists at the turn of the century, and the affinities of his thought to Royce's were clear. In 1901 Royce wrote Münsterberg that by different roads they had reached "a substantial agreement" on the two

*The formulations may be followed in (1) PYL; (2) "The Position of Psychology in the System of Knowledge," *Psychological Review Monograph Supplement* 4 (1903) (*Harvard Psychological Studies*, v. 1, ed. Hugo Münsterberg): 641–54 and chart facing 654; (3) "The Scientific Plan of the Congress," in [*International*] *Congress of the Arts and Science, Universal Exposition, St. Louis, 1904*, Howard Rogers, ed. 8 vols. (Boston: Houghton Mifflin, 1905–1907), 1: 85–134; (4) EV; and (5) *Vocation and Learning* (Saint Louis: Servis Publishing Co., 1912), esp. p. 81.

worlds' question.[12] James felt differently. He regarded Münsterberg's congress program as "sheer humbug," "self-infatuation"—"the perfectly inevitable expression of the [academic] system . . . an artificial construction for the sake of making the authority of professors inalienable, no matter what asininities they may utter, as if the bureaucratic mind were the full flower of nature's self-revelation." Surely the congress synthesized Münsterberg's passion for systematic thought, his zeal for institutional organization, and his love of authority; and surely his style and James's were far apart:

> I believe [said James] that the wide difference between your whole *Drang* in philosophizing and mine would give me a despairing feeling. I am satisfied with a free, wild nature; you seem to me to cherish and pursue an Italian garden, where all things are kept in separate compartments, and one must follow straight-ruled walks. Of course nature gives material for those four hard distinctions which you make, but they are only centres of emphasis in a flux, for me; and as you treat them, reality seems to me all *stiffened*. The will-attitude which you describe . . . and its postulations, are also really there, but resultantly and tentatively, along with rival tendencies; and the sort of decree-fulminating prior authorities you make of them strike me as monstrously artificial.[13]

Applied Psychology

The scheme of *The Eternal Values* allowed a place for "practical sciences," but in literally creating the field of applied psychology Münsterberg also wanted to show how we could use a natural science, that is, psychology, to bridge from the outer world and the fellow world to the inner world, and begin to connect the naive and intentional human values to salvation in the over-self. He came to speak of the real world as the realm of "purposive psychology." Applied psychology showed us how to use the causal nexus (causal psychology) to achieve our goals (purposive psychology) and so join the human and real worlds.[14] These relations were all vague, and it is perhaps simplest to note that applied psychology was an outlet for Münsterberg's energies that would secure him fame beyond the academy's bounds. He believed that social difficulties were effects of mental conditions that could be relieved by psychology. Psychology could not set the goals of social existence, but once they were set, it could dictate how they could be achieved or point up how our behavior prevented our realizing these ideals.[15] Armed with his notion of the relation of theory to practice and a twin desire to be useful to society and well-known in it, Münsterberg conjured up various ways in which his pet science could help practical men.

His book *Psychotherapy* examined how to treat the sick by influencing mental life. Psychotherapy was not psychiatry, but rather the practice of treating mental and physical ills by manipulating the patient's response to certain stimuli.[16] Münsterberg believed in hypnotism and was convinced that he successfully practiced it. He regarded the hypnotic state merely as one of greatly increased suggestibility. A paradigmatic example of psychotherapy was employing hypnotism to treat alcoholism. The hypnotist used some ideas to inhibit other ideas associated with the craving for alcohol, and so prevented drinking and cured a physical illness.[17]

His *On the Witness Stand* outlined the way psychology could aid the law. The psychologist could assist the lawyer in determining the credibility of witnesses; he might advise about judging the guilt of suspects; and his knowledge of the association and reinforcement of ideas might be indispensable in isolating the factors that hindered or gave rise to criminal propensities.[18]

Münsterberg contributed most in industrial psychology. Experimentally and statistically, he studied problems occurring in business life and showed how businessmen could use his techniques in selecting personnel, increasing efficiency, controlling purchasing habits, and giving vocational guidance.[19] *Vocation and Learning* set forth the relation of various trades to one of his schemes of the realm of knowledge. But his primary concern—for example in *Psychology and Industrial Efficiency* and *Business Psychology*—was for enlarging the businessman's profits. Although he mentioned that business must serve society and that we could scrutinize the business perspective, he spoke from "the business point of view."[20] Marketing men could use psychology in their advertising to sell products, and he illustrated his thought by rehearsing experiments on advertising's effects on purchasing habits. The point was "to enhance the impulse to buy."[21] Münsterberg also advocated vocational testing to get the most efficient employees and the most effective work from them, and devised experiments to test skills as well as personality characteristics. Although he believed that fine gradations of skill were necessary in all jobs and that the psychological laboratory had the requisite machinery to investigate those skills, he noted that businessmen were best qualified to determine "the points at which the psychological levers ought to be applied."[22] Finally, he lobbied for a government bureau that would apply scientific research in commerce and industry. Simultaneously, he called for training psychologists expert in these areas to be part of the management of large firms.[23]

As Münsterberg turned his talents more and more to applied psychology during the second decade of the twentieth century, his reputation with psychologists and with his colleagues at Harvard declined. Some psychologists regarded his popularizations as pseudo-science, but most of them simply resented his crude attempt at drawing public attention to himself through his practical work when their own expert status was uncertain. Even when the First World War drew American psychologists into just the sort of applied work he advocated, they continued to view his studies as vulgarizations mainly because Münsterberg himself was vulgar.[24] Certainly from a later perspective, much of his experimentation and consequent speculation on American life was foolish. For example, he was fond of scientifically demonstrating sexual differences by "careful experiments" and statistics:

> The average female mind is patient, loyal, reliable, economic, skillful, full of sympathy, . . . on the other hand . . . capricious, over-suggestible, often inclined to exaggeration. . . . the chief point is that in man the various contents of consciousness remain separate while in the mind of woman they fuse. Her life, therefore, has more inner unity . . . [but also] a lack of logical discrimination.[25]

From his experiments he concluded that women were less fit to be jurors than men, and that they abstained from stimulants not because of moral superiority but because they inherently possessed the heightened emotions men must seek in alcohol.[26] Knowing the characteristics of the female brain, he often protested against the feminization of American culture resulting from women's prominence in elementary teaching.[27]

Münsterberg was the one Harvard thinker whose applied speculation was extensive enough to warrant him the title of social philosopher, although one of low grade: in hindsight his pontificating was ludicrous. But while the quantity of his work in these areas was greater than that of his contemporaries, it was of no worse quality and, so, deserving of no more contempt. Moreover, he based his speculations on a discerning if disagreeable view of society. Despite his judgment that the female mind was demonstrably inferior to that of the male, he allowed that women could benefit from appropriate education and instruction and even defended graduate training for some women. In fact, his 1901 study *American Traits* lamented that education had made the home and family less attractive to females. Continuing this trend would undermine the nation's health, and the community must train women in ways that would not subvert the sanctity of the established order.[28] Twelve years later in *American Patriotism* he had some answers. First, the United States should avoid coeducation in secondary schools and colleges. If the university were to stress professional training, it should "keep the future wives and mothers and teachers away from such breeding places. . . . " If the university were to remain a place of liberal education, its ideal should remain the inculcation of a "virile culture." Authorities ought to preserve feminine culture in institutions open to women alone. Second, in these women's schools, "the household sciences" should become part of the curriculum. Taught humanistically and related to the Western tradition, home economics would renew women's commitments to the family:

> It is well known that this [drudgery of household work] is the chief reason for much of the dissatisfaction and restlessness in the world of women. . . . A woman who sees the details of her home work in the light of broad knowledge no longer knows it as drudgery; every little piece in the household bristles with interests, every activity of hers is linked with all mankind, aesthetic and moral, hygienic, and economic problems of highest importance suddenly seem involved in apparently little matters, the whole surroundings become luminous and wonderful.[29]

Similarly, Münsterberg argued against sex education. All thought and discussion on these issues aroused feelings and so contributed to degradation. Society should control sexual urges through silence and the fears caused by silence. Control was imperative because the survival of monogamy in civilization depended on regulating the sexual instincts and raising culture above nature's lures.[30]

The Cinema and Idealism

Münsterberg's popular writings were as ephemeral as his theoretical work and much that was worthwhile was forgotten in both. Published in 1916, *The Photoplay: A Psychological Study* had a shorter lifespan than most—Münsterberg died the same year—but it was a fascinating book that deserved more attention.* In it Münsterberg displayed the ingenious and original understanding characterizing his best work. *The Photoplay* was also his last book applying psychology to other fields and illustrated how acute Münsterberg could be even in discussing a popular new entertainment.

America was an individualistic and practical culture in which, he thought, realism and positivism, however mistaken, were significant philosophies.[31] In investigating the film as it had developed in the United States, he wanted to show that it was an art form of its own, deserving aesthetic appreciation (17). But this investigation would also demonstrate that even a civilization that based its chief contemporary art on a technical and mechanical achievement still had to reflect absolute idealism.

Münsterberg analyzed film-making details (19). He argued that the depth and movement we saw in the film were mixtures of fact and symbol: they were present and yet not *in* what we saw. We invested the impressions we received with depth and motion, yet were not deceived and never took them for real depth and motion (23, 30). Attention was the chief element of our "mental mechanism" by which we created the meaning of the world around us; Münsterberg identified the varied use of the close-up with the mental act of attention. The film maker focused on special features, eliminated all that was not interesting, and heightened the vividness of what we were concentrating on. Unlike the drama, the reality of the action in the film lacked "objective independence." The film catered to the "subjective play of attention," Münsterberg said, and we must understand the cinema through the mind's organization and not the laws of the outer world (39).

Other cinematic devices by which film makers produced successful movies were similar to the close-up. The cutback (or flashback) was like memory. The film maker also used the cutback to display the

*There is, happily, a new edition which I have used: *The Film: A Psychological Study* (New York: Dover Publications, 1970).

fantasy life or imagination. Moreover, in flashing from one scene to another going on at the same time, the cinema made us omnipresent: the film maker intended the different alternating scenes to be simultaneous rather than successive. The film overcame physical distances and brought events together just as they might be in our consciousness. Transcending time and space, the photoplay obeyed the laws of the mind rather than those of the outer world (41–58).

The aesthetic disrepute the film enjoyed in 1916, Münsterberg thought, was due to a bad theory of art. If art imitated the world we lived in, then the film—which critics saw as imitating the drama—must compare badly, for the drama better imitated the real. But art was not imitation. Like the German idealists, Münsterberg believed that art did not imitate but transformed and changed the world, selecting and remodeling special features of it (58, 63). Taking one aspect of the world and treating it in isolation, the artist eliminated indifferent features and selected those which suggested or expressed an essential truth. The function of art was to capture the essential qualities of the subject the artist chose to comprehend (68–69).

For Münsterberg the cinema was most successful in showing dramatic narratives, in which the element of the real world isolated for aesthetic expression was "the human story." But the film accomplished this isolation "by overcoming the forms of the outer world, namely, space, time, and causality"; it did not respect the "structure of the physical universe . . . [the] freedom of the mind has triumphed over the unalterable law of the outer world (74, 78).* It followed that in understanding human relationships we acknowledged our freedom from the physical world and the triumph of the forms of our own consciousness (95). We found a new form of beauty in "the turmoil of a technical age, created by its very technique, and yet more than any other art destined to overcome outer nature by the free and joyful play of the mind" (100). Even practical America could not avoid homage to idealism. Since the film reached a mass audience in a receptive mood, Münsterberg thought it might bring an aesthetic influence and all that that meant into the daily life of the American crowd (99). The cultural victory of absolute idealism was a reasonable possibility.

*Münsterberg rejected sound and color as possible cinematic developments: they would bring the film too close to the natural world.

12

GEORGE HERBERT PALMER AND SELF-REALIZATION ETHICS AT HARVARD

Idealism in the United States

The triumph of absolute idealism in the United States had come about after Kantian and post-Kantian ethics had inspired a generation of intellectuals. By the time of the Civil War, German moral philosophy had attracted great interest in all German speculation in Britain and America. Thinkers in both countries subscribed to an ethic of self-realization imported from Germany: goodness lay in the increasing growth of the individual's real self. In British university circles Thomas Hill Green gave credibility to this idea and to neo-Hegelianism generically, and in the United States the young John Dewey championed Green's work. But before Dewey, the St. Louis Hegelians had read the Germans directly and also defended the same kind of moral philosophy. And more conventional defenders of self-realization were rife in the nascent graduate educational system—James Creighton and Jacob Gould Schurman who founded the *Philosophical Review* at Cornell were among them, as was Dewey's mentor at Hopkins and Michigan, George Sylvester Morris. Royce's independent reading of Kant brought these views to Harvard, but before Royce arrived on the scene, the St. Louis group had made its ideas known in the Cambridge clubs, and all the philosophers had read the texts of the British neo-Hegelians.

George Herbert Palmer's self-realization doctrine was not the most sophisticated version of the position nourished at Harvard but it was characteristic. Palmer devoted his entire academic career to his ethics and, unlike his colleagues, he was not led to seek to justify the moral philosophy that inspired him: his ethics was unencumbered by exegesis of technical points. Most importantly, however, throughout his life Palmer applied his views directly and explicitly to education in general and Harvard in particular. In this chapter we shall begin the study of self-realization ethics by exploring Palmer's ideas; in the next chapter we shall examine how he applied these ideas as a teacher and as an educational bureaucrat.

Palmer's Life

Palmer was born in Boston in 1842, one of eight children of an old Puritan family. His father was a businessman—upper-middle class from all accounts—and a deacon in the local church; four of Palmer's uncles served in its ministry. A stress on the intellect accompanied the religious orientation of the household, but until Palmer was a young adult various ailments interrupted his schooling. This early and prolonged experience with illness together with the Puritan background contributed to the self-control, dignity, and sense of inner purpose that others found in his character. Educated at Boston public schools, he subsequently went to Phillips Academy for two years. Ill health prevented his continuing there and after some medical treatment he took a place in a wholesale dry goods store for more than a year. Palmer's background won out, however, and in 1860 he returned to school, this time to Harvard, graduating in 1864. After a year as an instructor in a Salem, Massachusetts, high school, he decided to spend his life teaching philosophy. He recalled that a passion for it had seized him in Cambridge and, indeed, he read John Stuart Mill avidly during his last two years. But his conventional desire to enter the ministry and his knowledge that divinity school was still the best place in the United States to receive advanced philosophical training appear to have led him to enter Andover Theological Seminary in fall 1865. Perhaps analyzing Palmer's motives is foolish: Puritanism identified theology and philosophy, and when colleges in the United States taught philosophy at this time, the teacher was a minister.

Palmer received his B.D. from Andover in 1867, and his philosophic interests now appeared plainly. He spent the next two years in Germany studying with Christian Sigwart. Actually this is an overstatement, for he passed much of his time there in a sickbed. On his return to Boston in 1870 he received an appointment as tutor in Greek from Eliot, then in the second year of his administration. In 1872 Ellis Peterson, assistant professor of philosophy under Bowen, resigned. Eliot appointed Palmer instructor in philosophy, assistant professor a year later. These appointments began a term of service that eventually left Palmer oldest in years and in academic seniority among Harvard officers of instruction. During his long career in Cambridge he was devoted to reforming teaching methods and to creating a university that would be a prestigious center of learning. He retired as an active teacher in 1913 when he was seventy-one, after forty-one years in the philosophy department. He had been named a full professor in 1882, and Alford Professor, succeeding Bowen, in 1889. He served as overseer for six years after his retirement, and for twenty years thereafter, until his death in 1933, he was a familiar figure, continuing his residence in the Harvard Yard, hospitably interested in the university at his door.

From the beginning of his career Palmer had an accurate sense of his intellectual limitations, resolving that he was to be a teacher and critic of philosophy, especially ethics, but no original thinker. He also gauged that the expanding educational system of the last third of the nineteenth century would permit him such a role. To this philosophical ambition, both modest and far-reaching, he added two others. One of his uncles had suggested that the family baptize the child George Herbert so that Palmer would "always have a friend." This event precipitated Palmer's later fascination with the poet, and the upshot was a lifelong absorption in Herbert and English poetry and several respectable volumes on these subjects. While in Germany, at the instruction of one of his professors, he had begun a Ph.D. dissertation on the concept of sin in *Agamemnon* by Aeschylus. Although this work remained unfinished, it gave Palmer a taste for Greek (and Roman) literature that his first teaching assignment augmented. To his collections of English poetry he added a series of credible translations of the classics.

Palmer was twice married, and even his second wife, Alice Freeman, died well before him. She was particularly noteworthy and more talented than her husband. President of Wellesley College at the time of their marriage, she remained intellectually active after her retirement, commuting to the University of Chicago as the first Dean of Women from 1892 to 1895. Both women, but especially Freeman, allowed Palmer marriages that had the quality of friendship as well as domestic attachment, and before and after their deaths he lived a conventional, comfortable, and staid life within the confines of Cambridge.[1] In their Faculty Minute on his life and service, three of Palmer's most famous students, Ralph Barton Perry, William Ernest Hocking, and C. I. Lewis, summarized the man well:

> The form of his living was dominated by a passion for order, which in its larger aspects was of a piece with his sensibility to beauty. . . . His will seemed always on duty, checking excess and even discouraging exploration. . . . Externally his life was one of quiet decorum, definitely circumscribed in its interests. Few have known so well how to make limitations an advantage; few have so deliberately made this idea the leading principle of the art of life.[2]

Moral Philosophy

How did Palmer make a virtue of his defects? To answer this question is to show how the growth of American universities provided opportunities for those whose talents were not intellectual. Palmer was a powerful force during the time philosophy was expanding as a profession, and his sober thoughts on improving teaching and his enterprise and expertise as a bureaucrat explain his academic weight. Nonetheless, his expertise grew out of a set of intellectual assumptions common to his generation, and these we will first investigate.

Between 1901 and 1920 Palmer published four books in ethics—*The Field of Ethics, The Nature of Goodness, The Problem of Freedom,* and *Altruism.* There was little change in the ideas formulated in these works, and he had expressed the same ideas in his teaching from the 1880s on. "Philosophy 4" was famous for years as the standard introduction to moral philosophy at Harvard and the first modern course of its kind offered in the United States. It was constructive as opposed to historical, a systematic exploration of problems and an attempt to solve them.

Satisfied by lecturing in the afternoon when athletes could not attend, Palmer expounded his own beliefs and elaborated a doctrine which got into print years afterward.[3] The doctrine itself was not novel. Kant, Palmer recalled, had long since replaced Mill as a philosophic hero. Palmer found Kant "a liberator" and learned from the German an idealistic method.[4] Moreover, Palmer spent six summers during the early part of his career studying and arguing with Thomas Hill Green's friend and philosophical associate, the Scottish Hegelian Edward Caird. (Palmer thought the visits would give him an edge over James in receiving the appointment to the Alford professorship when Bowen retired.)[5] While avowing that he was neither a Kantian nor a Hegelian, Palmer enunciated an ethics of self-realization and explicitly anchored its premises in nineteenth-century German thought;[6] it was similar to views being voiced by his colleagues Royce, James, and Münsterberg.

Defining science broadly as any area of knowledge, his first book, *The Field of Ethics*, attempted "to fix the place of ethics in a rational scheme of the universe. I wish to see how it is parted off from neighboring provinces of knowledge, and what kind of being he must be who is the object of its study" (3). Palmer's concern was not with the good man, or rather with making his reader a good man, but with the conception of the good man. He believed unquestioningly that ethics was a cognitive study, that we achieved knowledge of right and wrong as we did knowledge of the physical world; but, as he concluded *The Field of Ethics*, his aim was defining the important terms employed in ethics, and not moral exhortation (212).

The book delineated the realm of moral philosophy within the philosophical sciences, those whose essential concern was consciousness. Palmer distinguished those sciences whose principles were descriptive and merely summarized factual regularities from those like ethics and the law whose principles were prescriptive, what ought to be. These sciences were normative: their realm was what was possible in the future as determined by human ends and expectations. Palmer said that their conception of causality was peculiar: they did not analyze the coming of an event by considering its antecedents (this procedure occurred in a descriptive science) but through human appraisals of what could occur in the future. Consequently, the consciousness dealt with by ethical science was incomplete. Man was always in the making as he estimated future courses of action and accepted or rejected them as corporate parts of himself, always leaving the self's full definition in the future.[7]

The Problem of Freedom differentiated these two types of causation—the sequential causation of nature and the antesequential causation governing human beings. Rather than proceeding from a past actuality to a present one, man considered a desired possible future event and brought other events into being to achieve it (93–108). Ideas which appealed to us through their representative character, depicting what might occur in the future, were ideals. They operated through suggested possibilities when individuals decided about their future. Ideals distinguished instinctive behavior, whose causation was sequential, from goal-directed, antesequential, behavior. Palmer held that antesequential causation occurred at the "intersection" of discrete sequentially ordered series of events. Living in a world of objective chance where the interaction of these series produced accidents, we often found a sequential cause unable to account for the intersection. In these instances antesequential causation was possible: we might "coordinate" intersecting series. The field of freedom was the area of chance and co-existing sequential series (128–50).

Having committed himself to the existence of freedom, Palmer circumscribed its range. There was only one free choice: that between the sequential and the antesequential orders. To choose the latter irrevocably committed us to a stringently defined series of actions, since in every situation where we exercised moral choice, proper understanding of ideals entailed one appropriate action:

> We live encompassed by duties, each closing paths in otherwise attractive directions and making it untrue to say that many courses are in the same sense open. Duty restricts. Probably if we were altogether clear-sighted, we should see in each situation of life a single course to which duty summons and should understand that freedom is not equally distributed over the entire field (162–63).

> [The moral man] must abandon ambiguous futures and accept at each step of action a prescribed single issue. Moral choices therefore do not present a multiplicity of ideals among which I am equally free to follow. . . . They are hedged about with obstacles restricting freedom in all directions but one (163).

To choose the sequential order was possible, although Palmer said that it was suicidal, irrational, and therefore not explicable by philosophical, that is, rational, argument. In this case we ceased to be persons and became part of the natural mechanism. In short, Palmer saw any deviation from the strict antesequential order as an irrational commitment to the sequential order. He restricted freedom to choosing between moral suicide and the necessities inherent in the series of antesequential events (151–68).

The difficulties in this analysis were similar to those involved in many libertarian positions on free will, including that of Palmer's colleague, James. Palmer said that many problems were insoluble. For example, he admitted that he could not explain the choice of, or lapse into, the sequential realm: that was irrational. More importantly, he acknowledged that action seemed subject to sequential causation: he could not explain how ideals got their "clutch" on events, how the mental influenced the physical, or the point of contact between the two.[8]

The Nature of Goodness defined goodness as organic adjustment. When an object was appropriately adjusted to something outside itself, it was good *for* something, it had extrinsic goodness. When "the many powers of an object are so adjusted to one another that they cooperate to render the object a firm totality," the object was good in itself, it possessed intrinsic goodness. Both sorts of goodness indicated relationships; but in one case the relations were extra se, in the other inter se. And, Palmer went on, we could never separate the two: "Nothing exists entirely by itself. Each object has its relationships and through these is knitted into the frame of the universe" (18–70):

> The two phases of goodness are thus seen to be mutually dependent.
> Extrinsic goodness or serviceability, that where an object employs
> an already constituted wholeness to further the wholeness of an-
> other, cannot proceed except through intrinsic goodness, or that
> where fullness and adjustment of functions are expressed in the
> construction of an organism. Nor can intrinsic goodness be supposed
> to exist shut up to itself and parted from extrinsic influence. The
> two are merely different modes or points of view for assessing
> goodness everywhere. Goodness in its most elementary form ap-
> pears where one object is connected with another as means to end.
> But the more elaborately complicated the relation becomes, and
> the richer the entanglement of means and ends—internal and ex-
> ternal—in the adjustment of object or person, so much ampler is
> the goodness. Each object, in order to possess any good, must share
> in that of the universe (35).

There were as many varieties of goodness as there were modes of constructing organisms. Palmer analyzed personal goodness, the peculiar variety of goodness important to moral philosophers, by pointing to the conditions defining personality. Roughly speaking, he associated these conditions with the self-conscious, active nature of human beings (58–115). Self-development or self-realization summed up personal goodness, all the moral aims of life (120, 146). The self was incomplete because future actions always helped to define it; for a self to be good, Palmer said, it would adjust continuously to the rest of the world in order to make the self a firm totality. Ethics was then the study of modes of self-realization, the self's attempt to gain fullness of being.

Problems

Unlike many promulgators of self-realization ethics, Palmer's notions did not flow from a careful metaphysical commitment. He was not concerned with the premises of idealistic philosophizing. Nonetheless, he did explore two central problems that confronted a self-realization ethic—the possibilities, on its account, of sin and self-sacrifice.

Palmer did not argue that human beings merely ought to seek self-realization. Rather, he contended "the only possible ultimate aim of action is self-realization."[9] This position had immediate and undesirable consequences. First, the aims of morality became tautological, for any action must be self-realizing. It was logically impossible to act immorally. Second, altruistic behavior, self-sacrificing behavior whose goal was not essentially concerned with the self, also became impossible. To avoid these perplexities, self-realization theorists often discriminated behavior developing the real self from that developing the false or partial self. This move usually resulted in doubtful arguments about the nature of the real self; it might equally result in setting forth another criterion of personal goodness so that self-realization ceased to be the criterion and whatever contributed to the growth of the real self replaced it.

Palmer confronted the problem of immorality—how it was possible to sin—by stating that it was self-contradictory and irrational. Sinning was simply choosing the sequential order over the antesequential. It negated freedom, although choosing the antesequential order that defined self-realization left no further freedom:

Violating a law of duty, I do not so directly expose myself to the contrariety of nature, but I assault that network of human relations on which I myself depend and so deal a savage blow to my own being. Sin is self-contradictory, a mode of action disorganizing to all human life which it touches.[10]

Palmer said more about sin in discussing altruism or self-sacrifice. He distinguished between the separate self and the conjunct self—in effect defining true self-realization. An early interest in Hobbes and English moral philosophy had propelled Palmer to study individual selfhood and its relation to the social order. English theorists looked upon man in his original state as a self-centered being, a distinct ego. Palmer believed this assumption was wrong. "There is no such solitary person. One person is no person."

> Not that it is an error to say "I." This, properly, is our commonest word and commonest thought. Only with reference to it does anything else have value. However interlocked the total frame of things may be, at certain centres where relations converge there are unique spots of consciousness capable of estimating reality and of sending forth modifying influences. Such a centre of consciousness, unlike all else, we rightly call a person, a self or ego; and because of its importance we often fix attention on it, withdrawing notice for the moment from the relations which encompass it. Such an abstraction, if clearly understood, is entirely legitimate. I shall frequently make use of it under the title of the separate or abstract self. But it should be borne in mind that it is an abstraction and that the real person is what I shall call the conjunct or social self, made up of that centre of consciousness and the relations in which it stands. While these two are usefully distinguishable, they are not separable.[11]

With this distinction in mind Palmer resolved the central dilemma of self-realization ethics. Sin was contradictory because the sinner attempted to deny his own reality, to assert the reality of the separate self; and this was impossible. Self-sacrifice was possible and might be one of the highest moral aims because it nobly expressed self-realization. The real self stood in living relation with his fellows; they were really a part of him and he of them.[12] Self-sacrifice was that mode of self-realization in which risking the separate self served the conjunct self.[13]

Yet while I hold that self-sacrifice is thus the very extreme of rationality, grounding as it does all worth in the relational or conjunct selfhood, I cannot disguise from myself that it contains an element of tragedy too. . . . For though it is true that when opposition arises between the conjunct and separate selves our largest safety is with the former, the very fact that such opposition is possible involves tragedy. One part of our nature becomes arrayed against another.[14]

Altruism contended that underdeveloped forms of social life did not emphasize the conjunctive element of the self. There Palmer traced the advance of morality, the stages of moral maturity traversed by men and nations, and charted the declining emphasis on the separate self. Every phase of the historico-moral evolution of human life was altruistic (self-sacrificing) in some degree; but there were higher grades that gave altruism a prominence and scope that the lower lacked (10). What Palmer called "the forms and stages of the conjunct self" (11) passed through manners (basic civility), to gifts (the diminution of ourselves of some possession, pleasure, or opportunity for growth so that another may have more), to mutuality (32). In mutuality altruism reached its highest form, and ego and alter ego were no longer distinct (69). We recognized another and my (separate) self as inseparable elements of one another, each essential to the welfare of each, and only reaching full significance in union (75–90). The most common form of mutuality was love between two persons—their interests became identical, altruism transforming itself into egoism, egoism into altruism (91–110).

Love was restrictive in its selectivity, however, and Palmer gave the name justice to mutuality that had more of its limitations removed. Although even this variety of mutuality was selective in picking out some aspect of the community to serve, justice was displayed in impersonal love or professional responsibility. A just individual was committed to his social calling and the good of the community, and his work was its own reward. Just behavior reached its most sophisticated expression in the service of institutions, those permanent sets of relations among individuals that past experience had established for promoting human welfare and that successive generations had approved. Institutions were intended for the general good—they could hardly have been established if injurious, said Palmer—but they should be open to constructive criticism and slow change (110–34). *Altruism* concluded by emphasizing that men based institutions on the principle that everyone was wiser than anyone and that the individual's first business was to conform to basic institutions. This conformity must precede the study of institutions and any attempt to readjust their working. Maintaining, studying, and reforming institutions all displayed love for our fellow man. This public love, or justice, the fullest human expression of altruism, was "the rational acceptance of our place in a social order where all are dependent on each" (134–38).

Technical Presuppositions

As I have noted, Palmer said little about the idealistic metaphysic that his ethic presupposed. He called himself a "moderate idealist," whose concern for the human personality ruled out monism. But philosophers still disputed the underpinnings of any such system, and he did not feel qualified to enter the dispute. Charles Bakewell judged that Palmer decided to leave these matters to the philosophic powers in the department—particularly to Royce, whose 1913 *Problem of Christianity*, Palmer thought, successfully handled these questions.[15] In any event, there were only hints of a metaphysical position in Palmer's own work. Human life presented itself to him as an unequal struggle between an infinite obligation—the unending realization of the self—and a finite medium. The continuous growth of the "imperfect" toward perfection partially resolved the struggle. We achieved the infinite through the finite, the latter being incorporated in the former. In fact, only in the medium of the finite could we do noble and divine deeds if we did them at all. The limited accomplished what the unlimited could not.[16]

This was the struggle toward the full realization of the conjunct self, and even in institutions human beings fell short. Only in religion did we see the significance of the striving: God was "the only complete wholeness," and every endeavor to unite with other things or persons was a blind seeking after him.[17] The religious sentiment was the ultimate moral one: the identification of one's self with another, in this case the ground of all being. Morality gained from religion a wider horizon, greater stability, and encouragement for right doing.[18]

All this was vague, and Palmer limited his specific examination of religion's justifiability, an examination of God's existence, to a few Roycean paragraphs. God was the intelligence presupposed in the order of nature, the ground of the comprehensibility of the world. We could not "prove" this "principle," but if tested—if we hypothetically denied it and attempted to see what followed—we reinstated it. Action assumed the order of nature, and this "scientific faith" or "working hypothesis" avowed God. Intelligence was inwrought in the framework of things; it was "latent" in all things; "our very constitution" involved God.[19]

Palmer could not have avoided "monism" easily: the distinct centers of consciousness, the separate selves, were not "real" even in Palmer's ethics, and they tried to identify with "the unitary ground of existence." As Palmer put it, the world was not a unit, but we were making it one.[20] Moreover, he was only rhetorically committed to the dualism between the sequential and the antesequential realms. With James, Royce, and Münsterberg, he held that mechanism and teleology were allied. For Palmer, laws of nature were "ideal constructions formulated by man for his convenience and with little reality if parted from intelligent ends." Similarly, the distinction between mind and matter was not final. "For me, a moderate idealist, mind is no accident, projected into an alien world at a comparatively late period and fashioned out of already existing material. I regard it rather as the originating and explanatory factor conditioning all."[21] The Christian ideal, Palmer wrote in *The Nature of Goodness*, was to subjugate matter to mind, nature to spirit; this was the meaning of the struggle for self-realization. Conduct had three stages— the unconscious (or natural, matter), the conscious (or spiritual, mind), and a third reconciling them. Indeed, the moral struggle did not reduce matter to mind, the natural to the spiritual, but transformed both, had both *aufgehoben*. In this third stage action ran to its intended end with no need of conscious supervision. Mechanized but purposeful action ceased to be self-conscious and became "second nature." Palmer said this activity exhibited "negative consciousness"; it was moral habit. As Jesus instructed us, the goal was to become as a child. Our aim was the simplicity of childhood, although our unconsciousness would differ from that of the young; self-consciousness disappeared as we routinized and regularized moral behavior. Palmer appeared to be going in a pantheistic direction—the goal was "negative consciousness" of a place in the whole of being—but he spelled out none of these metaphysical doctrines.[22]

Ethics and Educational Administration

With his colleagues Palmer shared the view that technical philosophy must ground the application of practical philosophy. They were, however, increasingly attracted to the technical while he became involved much further down in the hierarchy of the philosophical sciences, applying his ethics to the Cambridge world around him. In this sense Palmer's significance lay not in his philosophy at all: it lay rather in his commitments to teaching and to building his department. His moral philosophy provided a rationale for these commitments, and we shall examine them in the next chapter.

PART 3

THE GOLDEN AGE
AT HARVARD (II)

George Santayana about 1887   Hugo Münsterberg about 1900
Josiah Royce in 1902   William James about 1905

William James and Josiah Royce

13

BUILDING A GRADUATE SCHOOL
1890-1912

Eliot and the Graduate School

In the first twenty years of his administration Eliot created an undergraduate curriculum that exhibited scholarly diversity and academic freedom; Harvard remained in the forefront of higher education. As we have noted, however, Eliot was slow to see that undergraduate instruction had limitations, and the success of the Johns Hopkins University in training postgraduates challenged Harvard's university leadership. If Harvard were to maintain its first rank and superior prestige in American higher education, it would have to stress graduate study. Eliot did just that during the second twenty years of his administration.

The achievements of German academe in the nineteenth century impressed many American educators. "German scholars and universities," Eliot commented, had for a century "given example and inspiration to the learned world."[1] He would not use German methods to achieve such distinction for Harvard—state control of education was anathema to him —but as George Santayana reflected, "the laurels of Germany would not let Boston sleep."[2] Methods other than government funding lay at hand: growing American fortunes made possible the endowments private institutions needed to become large, diverse universities with the characteristics we associate with twentieth-century centers of learning. The northeast, and New England in particular, had won the Civil War; the struggle against slavery had made its intellectuals nationally prominent; and after 1865 its businessmen and industrialists became a national elite as merely local centers of influence and wealth vanished. The New England tradition of support for higher learning benefited immensely from an expanding capitalist system that had one of its centers in Boston. Some new money was in hand when Eliot became president and enabled him to raise salaries and hire faculty.[3] From 1869 to 1889 the endowment almost trebled, from $2.4 to $6.8 million; by 1909 the 1889 figure had more than trebled, from $6.8 to $22.7 million.[4] Harvard did not lack money. For Cambridge to remain a center of learning, however, it had to produce a research-oriented community.

The man with such a conception was Daniel Gilman, who had become president of Hopkins in 1874. Gilman hired a small group of men committed to research and to instructing advanced students. Although it had a small "collegiate department" Hopkins was a citadel for postgraduate work, and the quest for knowledge motivated its faculty and students. Eliot long did not believe that Hopkins could succeed, and some commentators have argued that he never understood the role of unhindered research in attracting able men to a university. Nonetheless, it is hard to believe that his predecessor's idea of filling professorships with the best minds, even if they belonged to outsiders, did not affect Eliot: he had initially lost out at Harvard when Thomas Hill appointed Wolcott Gibbs to the chemistry chair.[5] In any event, Eliot kept an eye on Baltimore, determined that Cambridge should not fall behind. When Hopkins became a graduate center, Eliot quickly built up advanced training; and although Hopkins initially bested Harvard, its superiority was short-lived.

When Eliot's experiment with the University Lectures failed, he provided for graduate work through the elective system, broadening the field of studies and making it easier for students to specialize; he gradually superimposed a graduate school upon the college. In 1872 he established a "Graduate Department" which reformed the Harvard A.M. and awarded higher degrees. Students in this department often took electives that they had not been able to take in college, but the faculty also offered advanced courses that became listed as "primarily for graduates." It began to be required that the graduates formulate detailed programs of study, the supervision of individual work becoming part of the program. The statement in the catalogue of 1875–1876 of the requirements for the doctorate remained basically unchanged. Although they were "wholly secondary" to obtaining the degree, they usually sufficed: at least two years of work at a high level following a "course of liberal study" that appropriate officials would evaluate by setting a comprehensive examination and appraising the candidate's thesis of original research. A year or two of study in Germany became common between completing the course work and beginning the dissertation.

With the Hopkins example goading him, Eliot began to recognize and reward scholarship, as distinct from teaching. As the endowment increased, he raised salaries and hired distinguished men, limiting their teaching to their specialties. In 1890 he reorganized the graduate department and, with administrative officers of its own, it emerged as the Graduate School of Harvard University. During this period Harvard first competed seriously with Hopkins in the production of doctorates. For the first fifteen years of its existence Hopkins had no peers as a graduate center; by 1900 the two schools were neck and neck; thereafter Harvard led.[6] Santayana put it well:

> These graduates came to form a sort of normal school for future professors, stamped as in Germany with a Ph.D.; and the teachers in each subject became a committee charged with something of the functions of a registry office, to find places for their nurslings. The university could thus acquire a national and even an international function, drawing in distinguished talent and youthful ambition from everywhere, and sending forth in various directions its apostles of light and learning.[7]

Eliot, Palmer, and Philosophy

Philosophy at Harvard shared this growth and no one promoted it more than George Herbert Palmer. His philosophical position grew up with and simultaneously justified an educational theory and an administrative concern. His commitment to teaching followed directly from two beliefs—first, from his reverence for institutions as the structures within which conjunct selves developed and, second, from his view that professional devotion was the best way for a given conjunct self to grow. As he wrote about the role of institutions in human life:

> As they become narrower our acceptance of them changes its character, affectionate loyalty playing a larger part, dutiful obedience less.

A member of a college, for example, comes to think of it almost as a person, symbolized in Alma Mater, and gives to it the loving devotion he would feel for a revered friend. Members of institutions so individual are apt to take their membership as something like a personal trust and to pride themselves on fidelity to it. But because such institutions are of limited range and not applicable to all mankind, failure in allegiance to them is generally regarded not as a moral lapse, but as an error of judgment.[8]

And about Harvard: "She is the intellectual mother of us all, honored certainly by me, and I believe by thousands of others, for a multiplicity of subtle influences far outside her special modes of instruction."[9]

Palmer made the importance of teaching clear in a short essay reflecting his philosophy, *Trades and Professions*. He distinguished trades and professions by noting that in the former the end was money and the trade the means; in a profession money was the means to the end, the practice of the profession itself. He defined this practice as self-fulfillment, service to the community, and furthering professional goals through loyal identification with them. Not the kind of work, Palmer said, but the spirit in which we entered it made work professional.[10] Teaching occupied a special place in the pantheon of professions: the institutions supporting it portended the future forms of organized society. Teachers were not tempted by better paying occupations; their slender financial rewards were offset by the sense of being about important business. Their work separated teachers from the rest of the community and established them in a "consecrated brotherhood." Finally, the teachers' job was to train and expand needy minds, enriching the experience of those under their tutelage. Palmer concluded that when the kingdom of heaven was at hand, the world would realize the ideals of teaching:

> the mad scramble for personal profit will cease to enslave us. Each man will contentedly accept his special task as that in which lies his best opportunity for personal expression. Every man, too, will be studying the needs of his neighbor as inseparable from his own, and will consequently cleave to that neighbor, sharing with him his inherited knowledge, his own experience, and his guiding ideals.[11]

In short, the function of education was self-realization, and educational institutions reflected the development of the kingdom of God on earth. In particular, said Palmer, Eliot designed Harvard education to give students "control of their own minds" and to allow them to judge how far their inherited bank stock of beliefs fitted their case.* Simultaneously, Harvard grew itself. The aim of its education was to overreach itself, and through this "divine discontent" finite life embodied the infinite, the religious. "Harvard University, to its glory be it said, is enormously unfinished; it is a great way from perfect; it is full of blemishes. We are tinkering at it all the time; and if it were not so, I for one should decline to be connected with it. Its interest for me would cease."[12]

The "tinkering" reflected what Palmer believed was the only legitimate method of altering institutions; one reason for his love for Harvard was that it had allowed him to tinker and to redirect the institution's efforts:

> Harvard education reached its lowest point during my college course. When I entered, it was a small local institution with nine hundred and ninety-six students in all its departments and thirty teachers in the College Faculty. C. C. Felton was its President. Nearly all its studies were prescribed, and these were chiefly Greek, Latin, and Mathematics. There was one course in Modern History, one in Philosophy, a half course in Economics. There was no English Literature, but in the Sophomore year three hours a week were required in Anglo-Saxon. A feeble course or two in Modern Languages was allowed to those who wished it. There were two or three courses in Natural Science, taught without laboratory work. All courses were taught from textbooks and by recitations.[13]

This was not the sort of institution where self-realization would take place. Even primary schooling should proceed with greater emphasis on de-

---

*GHP Autobiography, pp. 83–84. Palmer was characteristically and conscientiously modest with respect to how his teaching functioned this way. His field, ethics, dealt self-consciously with the principles of conduct; it theorized about the central concerns of human existence. But Palmer felt that self-conscious appraisal of standards before students came to university was unwise and unwholesome: it might confuse the young. Even in the university, ethics should be an upper-class elective. It might help students who had come to an imperfect awareness about the principles of conduct. Even at this point in an individual's university career, it might be more prudent not to confront him with the perplexities faced in scrutinizing conduct. See George Herbert Palmer and Alice Freeman Palmer, *The Teacher, Essays and Addresses on Education* (Boston: Houghton Mifflin Co., 1908), pp. 31–48.

veloping orderly freedom to build character than did the Harvard of Palmer's youth. It lacked the minimal prerequisites for the effective transmission of knowledge; it did not train the critical faculties, educate preferences, or expand the imagination.[14]

Palmer met these problems with academic and polemical support for the elective system during the first years of the Eliot administration. He believed that the new system fostered the students' independence and encouraged the faculty to forsake rote teaching. He also emphasized that the university had not given up its role as constructive overseer of student development: an advising system, prerequisites, and attendance regulations, as well as other incentives to work, distinguished the Harvard system from one of laissez faire. Moreover, he proposed that awards of distinction be given to students who did well in a series of courses given by a single department in order to strengthen the elective system.[15]

Palmer's belief in the elective system and his leadership in adopting this innovation and others like it balanced two demands. On one hand, the university must limit choice and prevent confusion; on the other, it must encourage individual growth. "I think it an important part of the business of life," he wrote, "to reduce the range of freedom, which is confusingly broad in youth."[16] Lack of acquaintance with the world and inexperience often made the young capricious. The university must structure choices and reduce the chaos that faced students. The restrictions placed by Harvard on the elective system were to accomplish this goal. Simultaneously. students were to be independent and capable of choice, and their teachers had to encourage them to make decisions. That belief, along with his opposition to rote learning, was Palmer's rationale for election. To be sure, electives might lead to abuses—loafing, squandering time, and forming slothful habits. Nonetheless, Cambridge educators must accept these dangers:

> They know that a student forced, as the routine education of the past attempted to force him, is no student at all. They therefore limit themselves to offering opportunities, to making these opportunities attractive, and letting the ultimate guidance, even if erroneous, be in the student's own hands. Men of independent intelligence are therefore trained here today to a degree unknown of old. Our Fa-

ther in Heaven had been using the elective system long before we discovered it.[17]

Palmer's colleagues and students assumed that he would be remembered as a teacher, but his lasting significance has been his success as an academic citizen. He embodied the social conventions Cambridge thought appropriate for the scholar, combining his provincial concern for Harvard with a disposition for gradual change that was exactly right. When he was an undergraduate, philosophy, like other Harvard subjects, did not measure up to his ideals, and he later struggled to make it a discipline that would be attractive to the intelligent, mature students the elective system was to create. Philosophy too must depart from its traditional methods. Although Palmer exaggerated the rote nature of Bowen's teaching and the didactic quality of the courses, Bowen did view the teaching of philosophy as a moralizing exercise and was wearisome in promoting philosophy as the handmaid to Christian theism. Soon after Palmer started to teach in the early 1870s, he substituted original sources for Bowen's manuals, and used the texts to explore philosophers in their own right and not to prove the truth of Unitarianism. Later, he supported James against Bowen when James wished to teach Spencer.

Bowen also began to teach from the texts themselves, but his foray into German idealism was designed to refute infidels. And by the 1880s when Bowen took this step, Palmer went one better by initiating "Philosophy 4," a new kind of "constructive course" in moral philosophy. All of Bowen's courses were constructive in that they expounded his religious thought and disproved the skeptics. But Palmer's "Ethics" was a secular constructive course. He ignored theological issues and argued for philosophy's independence. Although Palmer presented his own self-realization view, unlike Bowen he did not consider the regurgitation of truths learned in the course as the sole indication of merit. Encouraging students to think critically, Philosophy 4 became a model for philosophical instruction in the United States.

After Bowen retired, Palmer was the senior man in philosophy. Eliot's leadership no doubt encouraged the changes for which Palmer worked, but Palmer guided the department both as chairman and as its most devoted member. The department institutionalized the spirit of inquiry that pervaded the philosophy clubs and private homes in Boston and Cambridge. Appreciating divergence of judgment (within certain bounds), Palmer attempted to treat every member of the department as an equal. During this period he succeeded—with the notable exception of George Santayana, who fell outside the bounds. Aside from the issue of promotion, all members had a voice in decisions. There were tensions and personal strains, but until his retirement in 1913, Palmer led in muting and reconciling disagreements.[18]

The graduate school developed as a significant aspect of the department's growth, and through the 1880s Palmer fought it, believing that advanced instruction would dissipate Harvard's limited resources. But Eliot's argument finally convinced him: "It is not primarily for the graduates that I care for this school," Eliot said; "it is for the undergraduates. We shall never get good teaching here so long as our instructors set a limit to their subjects. When they are called on to follow these throughout, tracing them far off toward the unknown, they may become good teachers; but not before."[19] Graduate training insured independent thought among the faculty, and so Palmer came to support it, advanced education finding a place in his framework of self-realization.

Other more practical reasoning was also crucial. Palmer appraised American higher education in 1892 as an expanding field. Not only were new colleges opening, but old ones were enlarging their faculties. Who would fill these positions if not the products of the new graduate schools? Palmer's elitist view of universities led him to predict—accurately—that Harvard could be a chief source of supply.[20] Establishing advanced training would lead to the rise of Harvard's power and prestige. Indeed, Palmer received many attractive offers from other schools, but he chose to remain in Cambridge "in the further advancement of what is here." As he explained to his fiancée in 1887, he had long been "building up an influence" in Cambridge "which I must not lightly abandon."[21]

Palmer's influence was felt in a specific area. Intellectual limitations, he freely said, left him only the field of philosophic criticism. But his candid, honest nature—often expressed regarding his own deficiencies—and his work of explaining and expounding the history of thought led others to request his advice. Palmer's forte became placement—he became universally respected for studied and discriminating reports on prospective teachers, a role that played to his strengths and increased the influence of the Harvard program. His success may have stemmed from consciously applying his idea of self-realization to his students: each had talents which care could uncover and use. "My recommendations," Palmer recalled, "are accepted because they are not generalities but indicate just the work of which a candidate is capable."[22]

We should not underestimate Palmer's importance in this area; he found situations for some students and could prevent others from getting positions. He could be trusted as the exuberant and erratic William James could not. In 1892 James recommended Peirce for a position in the new department at the University of Chicago. In June Palmer wrote to President Harper questioning James's reference: Peirce's "broken and dissolute character" made him suspect. Palmer was sure that Peirce's personal life had caused his dismissal from Hopkins and denied him a place at Harvard. This appraisal effectively knifed Peirce; Harper dropped him from consideration.[23]

The Growth of Philosophy

Although Palmer was a leading departmental force and a close advisor of the president, Eliot still ran the university personally and by the 1890s had hired not only Palmer but a full complement of philosophers. Appointments in the lowest ranks, such as instructor, were always temporary, often without a clear rationale, and occasionally haphazard. But at the professorial grades a set of precedents developed. The college had named Eliot himself the first assistant professor in 1858, but within three decades appointment to that position was a standard first step on the way to a permanent post—the real hurdle was passing from an instructorship to the lower professorial rank. After men had served two five-year terms as assistant professor, Eliot normally promoted them to full professorships without term, although Harvard could deny some men and reward others earlier, especially those whom other universities might "call."

Eliot made Palmer a full professor in 1882, James in 1885. When Bowen retired in 1889, Palmer got Bowen's chair, and James got the title of professor of psychology. In 1892 Eliot gave Royce the second professorship in philosophy. In that same year, Münsterberg came as a full professor for his three-year trial stint in psychology, surely marking Eliot's expanded perception of the scholar's place in university life. When Münsterberg returned permanently in 1897, he became the professor of psychology, and James's title reverted to philosophy. George Santayana had begun as an instructor in 1889 and, as we shall see in this chapter, was still an assistant professor at the turn of the century. In a few years Eliot had doubled philosophic instruction at Harvard and assembled the most significant philosophic group English-speaking society has known. As Bertrand Russell wrote, the Harvard school of philosophy was "the best in the world."[24]

From 1878 to 1891 G. Stanley Hall (1878), Frank Abbot (1881), and Santayana (1889) received Ph.D.s, but these were three of the five doctorates awarded in thirteen years. As chart 13.1 makes clear, things picked up in 1893. During the next twenty years Harvard literally trained the first generation of professional American philosophers. Many of them had a close association with Cambridge, and we will meet them later in this book. In addition, the young degree holders who made names for themselves included C. M. Bakewell (1894) at Yale, John Elof Boodin (1899) at Carleton, William Savery (1899) at Washington, Wilmon Sheldon (1899) at Yale, Harold Chapman Brown (1905) at Stanford, J. B. Pratt (1905) at Williams, Morris Cohen (1906) at CCNY, Horace Kallen (1908) at the New School, DeWitt Parker (1908) at Michigan, Jacob Loewenberg (1911) and G. P. Adams (1912) at Berkeley, and C. J. Ducasse (1912) at Brown.

5-year periods	Average number of Ph.D.s per year
1893–1897	2
1898–1902	5
1903–1907	7
1908–1912	5

Chart 13.1. Philosophy Ph.D. Production, 1893–1912

After 1912 it is more difficult to gauge the growth in philosophy. In that year the Department of Philosophy became the Department of Philosophy and Psychology, and this change only formally signalled the increasing disparity between those who studied one and those who studied the other. In addition, deaths and retirement soon transformed the department which Eliot had assembled, and then the First World

War disrupted scholarship all over the world. After a brief respite, the depression followed. Chart 13.2 indicates the changes.

| 6-year periods | Average number of Ph.D.s per year | |
	Philosophy	Psychology
1913–1918	4	2.5
1919–1924	2	2.5
1925–1930	5.5	3
1931–1935*	8	6
1936–1941	4	3

*5-year period

Chart 13.2. Philosophy Ph.D. Production, 1913–1941

Departmental Specialization

Charts 13.1 and 13.2 deal with two phenomena affecting philosophy from 1890 to 1912, departmentalism and the production of college teachers. Both merit systematic discussion.

In the nineteenth century there was a limited notion of an academic discipline—a branch of knowledge with a certain informational content requiring a special expertise, training in certain methods, the inculcation of appropriate rules of conduct, and perhaps understanding a particular language. Nor did there exist the contemporary notion of a department—a group of scholars set apart by their study of a discipline. The growth of knowledge may have necessitated departments and disciplines in universities, and the conceptions became entrenched in the competition for university resources: like-minded groups of scholars defined their integrity by the "slots" they possessed. But it was not always so.

During much of the nineteenth century the social sciences fell under the rubric of moral science or philosophy. They were taught together with theology and what we know as philosophy proper (intellectual philosophy). Bowen taught political economy in his "department" until 1871, and political economy did not separate from philosophy until 1879.[25] In practice during the next ten years, philosophy studied ultimate questions and embraced theoretical work dealing with the nature and structure of the cosmos and practical work dealing with the worth and conduct of human existence. Other groups of studies had similarly vague and generalized interests, although what we now know as the social sciences were taking shape, most under the aegis of philosophy. A department of the university was not a well-defined entity, but rather a useful association of academics interested in the same sorts of things. Ties of administrative and intellectual convenience rather than allegiance to a discipline bound them together.

In this limited sense there were departments at Harvard before 1891, but few if any had regular meetings or kept records, although senior professors, Bowen in the case of philosophy, acted as heads and served without term. In 1891 Eliot reorganized the faculty into a number of standing committees called divisions, "including all members in one broad field of study." Each division controlled granting honors and administering higher degrees within its instructional sphere. Eliot subdivided most of these divisions into departments, but philosophy was a one-department division encompassing both philosophy and psychology.[26] This new bureaucratic arrangement operated with divisional and departmental chairmen now chosen for a term—Palmer chaired philosophy in 1891–1894 and 1898–1900, Royce in 1894–1898, Münsterberg in 1900–1906—and contributed to the growth of disciplinary boundaries. But as late as 1899–1900 Eliot could comment on the novel but growing phenomenon of departmentalism. On its negative side, it gave too much authority to senior members and made running the university subject to the factional demands of the various departments. On its positive side, it allowed knowledgeable men to select instructors of the lowest rank and the administration to draw on their expertise in appointing men of higher rank.[27]

Philosophy was still a wide-ranging field, however, and in addition to touching on psychology, it also encroached on the affairs of theology, social ethics, and education.

The Divinity School at Harvard was in a low state during much of the period of the Transcendentalist and Darwinian controversies. It began to come out of its doldrums the same year that Eliot became president when Harvard appointed Charles Carroll Everett (1829–1900) the first Bussey Professor of Theology. Everett was an exponent of Fichtean and Hegelian idealism and gave the Divinity School a philosophic cast. As his successor as dean wrote, when Everett became dean in 1878 his instruction moved from a subordinate place to the center of study and assured that a broad philosophical plan defined the school's function. Everett also participated in the philosophy clubs in the 1870s, demonstrating his links with the philosophers, and the catalogue listed his courses with those in philosophy.[28] More important than Everett in the renaissance of the Divinity School and its connection with philosophy was the appointment of Francis Greenwood Peabody to the Parkman Chair in 1881. Peabody had received his B.A. from Harvard in 1869, graduating with a contempt for Unitarianism and rote methods of teaching; he had also been on the periphery of the Metaphysical Club. Offering a course in "inductive ethics" in 1883 made his reputation as an iconoclast. Peabody believed that theology ought to stress man's religious sentiments and not abstruse speculation, and also argued that ethics should be free of metaphysics. He proposed to deal with ethics "inductively," by examining social problems, and the catalogue listed his lectures as "Studies of practical problems: Temperance, Charity, Labor, Prison, Discipline, Divorce, etc."[29]

The philosophers' study of abstract questions (like freedom) and Peabody's more practical views contrasted sharply. In short, Peabody was an early proponent of the social gospel. Stressing the life and character of Jesus, he insisted that his social concerns reflected the teachings of Christ to men as individuals, emphasizing that "the social question" was one of ethics, that is, of personal behavior. Peabody innovated in approaching the reconciliation of science and religion by applying "scientific" procedures to religious concerns, to the betterment of man's state. Other religious reformers interested in "the social question"—Frank Abbot is the best example—made no attempt to use their power to promote practical and specific political and social changes. It is against this background that a proponent of the social gospel like Peabody appeared so untraditional. Like Abbot, Peabody was unconcerned with a historic Christian affirmation and emphasized individual improvement, but his interest in the social gospel grew in part because extreme anti-institutional groups like Abbot's Free Religious Association left little outlet for social or political action to achieve reforms. In this context Peabody's teaching was crucial even though it downplayed any structural analysis of social and political problems. Despite his individualistic bias, he offered concrete social proposals and read German theological scholarship, trying to come to terms with Marxist literature and the thought of the European Christian Socialists.[30]

Peabody offered his 1883 course—he later changed its name to "Social

Ethics"—to students of both the Divinity School and the college, and in 1886, when Eliot appointed him Plummer Professor of Christian Morals, he became a member of both faculties. Increasingly, he taught in the "department" of philosophy. A 1903 gift of $50,000 toward constructing Emerson Hall, a new building to house the philosophers, insured that Eliot would have space to assign for social ethics. Two later gifts, each of $100,000, established the social ethics department in 1906 to "make Professor Peabody's work on the ethical dealing with the grave social and industrial evils which beset our American communities, permanent at Harvard University."[31] The same year Eliot reorganized the Division of Philosophy and defined it as consisting of the departments of social ethics and philosophy.

The attachment of social ethics to philosophy is important. While academics had not yet set departmental boundaries, they had, in philosophy, agreed on a separation of functions. An 1896 report on the department had anticipated the autonomy of an area whose focus would be social ethics. The report noted that the philosophers ought to create "a branch of work" to give "training in habits of philosophic thought with regard not only to special subjects but to all matters of either speculative or practical interest" that might be relevant to students' later life.[32] The philosophers taught no such courses, and after social ethics became a department within the division, they continued to concentrate on their "special subjects"; they instructed in the traditional branches of philosophy and never in social and political philosophy. Although Münsterberg and Palmer could claim to be political and social thinkers, Royce and James were not seriously involved with the social and political dimensions of human experience. Through the work of all the philosophers ran the assumption that logic, epistemology, and metaphysics were somehow logically prior to religion and ethics, although the study of technical topics could be justified only as they grounded practical ones. Accordingly, Royce and James did write extensively for a non-professional readership, applying their religious and ethical theorizing; this public philosophy popularized their ideas on religion and ethics. Social and political thinking did not similarly attract them but they gave it a place in the speculative hierarchy. To go from the applications of philosophy to morality and theology to applications to society and politics was simply to go from philosophy's usefulness to one individual to its usefulness to many. Peabody fit nicely into the new division of philosophy because his work helped Royce and James break up their tasks. The philosophers themselves would provide a technical rationale and examine individual responsibilities and religious duties. Peabody could extend these latter insights to American life in general.*

The relation of education to philosophy at Harvard during this period evidenced the same syndrome. In 1881 G. Stanley Hall (1844–1924), who had received his Ph.D. three years before, lectured on education at Eliot's request and thereafter taught three years as University Lecturer of Pedagogy. This development led no further, apparently because Eliot remained skeptical of "pedagogical science," but in 1890 political pressure renewed Harvard's interest in education.[33] In 1891 Eliot appointed Paul Henry Hanus (1855–1941) as Assistant Professor of History and Art of Teaching. Hanus supposedly headed a program called "Courses of Instruction in Teaching." Eliot had initially told him that he was "the general agent for the Normal Department," but there was no such department and, as "a member of the Philosophical Department," he gave his courses under the auspices of the division of philosophy. The obscurities in Hanus's status existed because the resident academics viewed him with suspicion and perhaps contempt. Harvard initially gave no credit toward its degree for his courses, and in his first years he was a lonely figure, doing his work single-handedly without accumulated aids or professional fellowship. As Palmer put it, "when professor Hanus came to Harvard, he bore the onus of his subject."[34] Nonetheless, the philosophers were not adverse to having education associated with the division: here was a further practical employment for philosophy. Education specialists could work out uses for philosophy while the philosophers attended to technique. Indeed, in the 1890s Royce and

---

*This construction is applicable only to the view of the philosophers themselves, and Münsterberg was an exception. He was contemptuous of social ethics, perhaps because he thought the applications of his own social theorizing so significant. Moreover, although Peabody worked for personal betterment, even with this bias he thought that William James was overly concerned with individual psychology: he felt that James's observation of social life was inadequate and that he was shallow in his unwillingness to face the darker side of politics and society. Finally, shortly before Peabody retired, he lamented to the new president, Lawrence Lowell, that social ethics had declined at Harvard. The reason he gave was its "complete submergence" in the Division of Philosophy. See David Potts, "Social Ethics at Harvard, 1881–1931," in SSH, pp. 113–14; Jurgen Herbst, "Francis Greenwood Peabody," *Harvard Theological Review* 54 (1961): 59, 64.

James themselves delivered lectures on psychological topics of interest to teachers, offering popularized and watered-down versions of their psychologies.[35]

In 1899 education became a department in the division of philosophy. Even after it was made a division in itself in 1906—the same time that Eliot made social ethics a department within the division of philosophy— relations between philosophy and education remained cordial. The example of Walter Dearborn made this clear. Münsterberg's applied psychology suffered his colleagues disesteem because Münsterberg was not a likeable fellow. He sought public attention and did so with little sense of propriety. But the philosophers tolerated and even encouraged applied studies. Dearborn (1878–1955) was an educational psychologist who came from Chicago to Harvard in 1912. He was in the division of education but his interest in intelligence testing and its uses in education took him into the psychological laboratory, where he was accepted by psychologists and philosophers alike. In philosophy, a permissive and benign attitude favoring diversity accompanied the growth of other departments and disciplines.

Manufacturing Graduate Students?

If the history of departmentalism revealed no sharp cleavages, neither did the history of the training of philosophers who would teach and train other philosophers. In examining this transition, we must investigate both William James's analysis of the graduate program and how Harvard coped with the changes the program brought about.

In his 1903 essay "The Ph.D. Octopus" James decried the nation's demands for "doctors" and the resultant creation of an efficient graduate machine emphasizing the degree and not whatever it should stand for. To halt the veneration of a series of letters after a name, James advocated awarding the degree as a matter of course and guaranteeing that meritorious men were rewarded with or without it.[36] A year later he wrote F. J. E. Woodbridge, editor of the new *Journal of Philosophy*, that his publication should forego "doctoring" and "professoring" its contributors. Philosophers, James said, ought not to "increase the tendency to titles and degrees and all sorts of mandarinism that threatens to submerge our poor country."[37] What could be worse, he wrote to Santayana in 1905, than "the gray-plaster temperament of our bald-headed young Ph.D.'s boring each other in seminaries, and writing those direful reports of the literature in the 'Philosophical Review' [the other American philosophical journal]." James had one word for this "desiccating and pedantifying process": "Faugh!" "The over technicality and consequent dreariness" of the philosophy of the young was appalling.[38]

It is easy to sympathize with James's lament, but his complaint was exaggerated. The doctorate certainly grew in importance and, like other academics, philosophers stressed specialization within their discipline in the training of graduate students. But the consequences were mixed. By the turn of the century graduate training had freed philosophy from its dependence on theology although philosophers still took a great interest in and for some time tried to justify the premises of religion. Philosophers were committed to non-sectarian approaches, and the prerequisite for teaching philosophy was now an advanced degree in the subject and not, as it had been previously, ministerial training.

James's concern was not just the overemphasis on degrees but the context in which the overemphasis occurred. During his career he witnessed the development of procedures that still characterize universities. As early as 1878 Harvard had introduced sabbatical years, periodically relieving its faculty of routine burdens. Administrators at well-known institutions started to look more favorably on publication than teaching in measuring the power of their scholars. There followed the practice of raiding for academic stars as a means of promoting prestige, and the academic entrepreneur emerged. The assembling of "staffs" in various areas of knowledge fortified the belief that a field required expertise and training, and increased the pressure to specialize. Teaching itself changed: at Harvard in philosophy a schedule of three courses one semester, two the other, became standard, with one course each semester occupied with graduate research in a "seminary." The introductory courses expanded enormously, enrolling from two to four hundred students, and the department used its graduate students as a source of cheap labor, primarily as graders but also as "assistants," and perhaps as instructors in their own right of a middle-level course. The content of teaching also altered. Even in undergraduate classes the technical aspects of philosophy were stressed over their practical applications. This shift was more pronounced in graduate work, and by the first decade of the century the core of the graduate curriculum was Royce's course in logic and epistemology.*

What disturbed James was that as the university grew, like other American institutions it took as its model the factory or large industrial enterprise. The concept of a scholarly product and all that it entailed conflicted with James's idea of what philosophy was about. He also had to deal personally with skilled and powerful managers of the academic business. Palmer had no equal in placing graduate students. Regarded as a canny evaluator of men, he embodied all the respected conventions of his day. He had his finger on the pulse of the system of higher education and used every opportunity to increase the department's power. Münsterberg was not subtle but did channel some of his energy and brilliance into the politics of scholarship. He used other offers to move rapidly up the Harvard pay scale,[39] and argued incessantly for higher salaries and social rewards for the American professoriate. Only such a system would attract "the strongest minds and . . . the sons of best families."[40] In addition to believing that money would secure men of talent who were not boors, Münsterberg wanted to establish an over-university whose exclusive concern would be research, making scholarly work a national glory and the expert a demi-god.[41]

---

*The denouement of Frank Abbot symbolized the power of this system. In 1888 Abbot had delivered the lectures in Royce's Philosophy of Nature course during the period of Royce's collapse. Two years later Abbot published *The Way Out of Agnosticism* based on these lectures. The book, he felt, would at last get him an academic position and make others recognize "the transcendent value of my thought, its coherency, power, and adaptation to the age." For some reason or other, however, Royce had set out to annihilate Abbot's reputation. He had treated Abbot's *Scientific Theism* as the work of a harmless incompetent; and although he had asked Abbot to lecture in his stead, in the first issue of the new *International Journal of Ethics* he wrote a long and devastating review of *The Way Out of Agnosticism*. He accused Abbot of an unconscious and blundering borrowing from Hegel, but more importantly issued a "professional warning" against Abbot's "philosophical pretensions" to "the general reader" and "the liberal-minded public." Abbot's attempt at vindicating himself dragged on until 1892, culminating in a public appeal to the Harvard Corporation and Board of Overseers. He contended that Royce was using his professorial status as a means of harassment and called for his dismissal. Abbot was surely as excessive in his reaction as Royce was wrong in his evaluation of Abbot's work, but the overseers' response to the controversy was noteworthy. On grounds that I am not able to perceive, they distinguished between Royce as a professional student and writer and Royce as a Harvard professor. Only the latter, they claimed, was a subject for their discussion. Since Royce had issued a *professional* and not a *professorial* warning, they dismissed Abbot's charges. The overseers did not appear to recognize that the distinction between "professional" and "professorial" was without a difference. In the same report they recommended that Harvard promote Royce to full professor. See LJR, pp. 29–31; HUG 1101.56, 57, FEA Papers; Overseers' Reports UA II 10.7.1* ,v. 6, p. 241.

As James's role in building the department illustrated—Royce and Münsterberg were his appointees—he was no naif, yet his attitude toward Palmer and Münsterberg was remarkably guileless. He wrote Eliot that administrative duties were becoming so burdensome that Eliot should delegate to chairmen the power still in the hands of their colleagues and then appoint as chairmen "men who like power."[42] To Münsterberg, an arch wheeler-dealer, James wrote that the philosophy department must take care in its graduate procedures lest "an atmosphere of academic politics" develop in which "individual cases with their interests would easily become mere counters in our academic game." It would be "a plague," James said, if Harvard simply competed with other schools on the basis of its doctoral package without regard for individual merit and a given school's needs.[43]

Harvard institutionalized Palmer's and Münsterberg's ideas in 1906 when Eliot installed the philosophers in Emerson Hall. In 1901 Münsterberg had begun to beat the bushes for funds for a permanent monument to the great department; and with Palmer's warm and indefatigable support, the money was raised and the building readied for commemorating the one hundredth anniversary of the birth of Ralph Waldo Emerson.* James's remark to Münsterberg typified his attitude and was unprevailing: "Philosophy, of all subjects, can dispense with material wealth, and we seem to be getting along very well as it is. . . . I am not sure that I shouldn't be personally a little ashamed of a philosophy hall." "But, of course," James added, "I shall express no such sentiments in public."[44]

Evolving Standards

James's critique of the Ph.D. mill is appealing. But the "manufacture" of new doctorates, their placement in an expanding university system, their movement through the ranks on the basis of technical publications,

---

*The philosophers chose Emerson as the building's namesake because he evoked the spirit of idealism without being considered a partisan thinker or, indeed, a thinker at all. As a "prophet" instead of a philosopher, all parties accepted him. I have been unable to confirm the old story that Eliot vetoed the philosophers' choice of an inscription, "Man is the measure of all things," in favor of the Biblical "What is man that thou art mindful of him?" See File: Emerson Hall, Box 212; HM to CWE, 10 May 1905, HM File, Box 232, CWE Papers; WJ to HM, 9 May 1903, File 1834 A; CWE to HM, 15 May 1905, File 1678, HM Papers.

and the accompanying growth of an academic bureaucracy and its politics did not develop in the steady, planned way that his frequent use of 'machine' suggested. Institutionalized scholarship almost surprised Harvard. Philosophers and administrators did not behave consistently and often fumbled in making the responses James assumed to be second nature to them. The careers of four men associated with Harvard philosophy during this period—Benjamin Rand, George Santayana, Ralph Barton Perry, and James Houghton Woods—illustrated the prevalent confusions.

In 1885 Rand (1856–1934) received the third philosophy doctorate awarded by Harvard. Produced when the department was growing, he became one of Harvard's first teaching assistants, grading all the papers for enormous lecture courses. In 1896–1897 he read the papers of the 338 students who took Philosophy 1, taught by Royce, James, and Palmer. The status and duties of the transient members of the staff were ill-defined in this period, but Rand's position was outstanding. While other men served as assistants for a year or so and then either left or received promotions to the lowest faculty rank of instructor, Rand assisted for over ten years. When other assistants functioned as aides to the faculty or even taught a course, from what I can determine Rand's duties were grading, and he did the job at a minimal salary— $500.[45] Grading was, Palmer said, a dreary business, but Rand was "not brilliant," a "drudge assistant" whose "plodding patience" suited his employment. He had abandoned all ambition because he realized ambition was useless. Besides, Palmer went on, with Rand in this semi-permanent position, his name could appear in the catalogue, making Harvard's staff as large as Cornell's.[46]

As the years passed and Rand stayed on, the philosophers did not know what to do with him. In 1897 Eliot promoted him to instructor, but in 1900 rejected the department's recommendation to raise him to assistant professor, and finally in 1902 refused to renew his yearly instructor's appointment. The philosophers had no scholarly standards for promotion in mind, but no procedure for firing Rand. In desperation they wrote to Eliot in 1902: would the president write a letter they could show to Rand to get them off the hook? In consequence, Eliot denied a "recommendation" to reappoint Rand to his instructorship in 1902–1903.[47]

This action did not settle the matter. Rand hung around and in 1905 received an appointment as librarian of the Robbins Library in Emerson Hall. There he stayed, most of the time at a salary of $1,000, until he retired in 1933.[48]

Rand's case showed that the new ways in education were not well defined, and the case of Harvard's fourth Ph.D., George Santayana, confirmed it. Santayana received his degree in 1889 and in a minor crisis accompanying Bowen's retirement found himself an instructor. Harvard recognized Santayana's talents as exceeding Rand's, but for eight years he remained an instructor. Finally, in 1898, after Santayana had published philosophical articles, *Sonnets and Other Verses* (1894–1896), and *The Sense of Beauty* (1896), Eliot made him an assistant professor. Even then Eliot suspected Santayana's retiring nature and his lack of involvement in university affairs; he did not "lay bricks or write school books." James supported the promotion because Harvard needed "a specimen" of Santayana's type of mind. In recommending the promotion, Münsterberg had to allay Eliot's fear that Santayana was not a textbook man; his promotion would be a sign of Harvard's commitment to productive and innovative scholarship.[49]

In the next five years Santayana continued to publish: in 1899 *Lucifer: A Theological Tragedy*, in 1900 *Interpretations of Poetry and Religion*, in 1901 *A Hermit of Carmel and Other Poems*, and more philosophical articles. In 1903 Eliot rewarded him with a five-year renewal of his assistant professorship.

In 1905 and 1906 Santayana published his five-volume *Life of Reason* and, after he received an invitation to lecture at Columbia in 1906–1907, the department recommended that he receive a full professorship to begin at that time. The philosophers now noted that Santayana had a "very characteristic influence on a large set of Harvard students" but added that only his literary distinction and influence on contemporary philosophical discussion warranted the promotion: their "unanimous opinion" was that his books contained "rather little of new philosophical thought." The corporation decided to take no action.[50] Finally in 1907, when Santayana was forty-four, after nine years as an instructor and nine as assistant professor, the full professorship came: William James had retired, and the way was open, Eliot said, to Santayana's promotion.

Even then Harvard was not gracious. Eliot committed himself only after Santayana declared that an appointment from "outside" "over my head" would be unsatisfactory.[51]

The problems of Santayana and Rand are explicable only if we assume that Harvard's appointment and tenure system was an evolving series of procedures rather than a machine. Nonetheless, rationalization was taking place. Santayana's initial appointment had been a fluke, but by the turn of the century the department was consciously recruiting its ablest graduate students, often after shipping them off for a few years' seasoning elsewhere. Berkeley became the headquarters of the Harvard second string. Its department, Palmer noted, "is made up almost entirely of our old boys."* But Harvard had apprenticed at Williams and Smith College the most important early junior appointee, Ralph Barton Perry.[52]

Born in Vermont in 1876, Perry was an undergraduate at Princeton and got his Ph.D. at Harvard in 1899. After three years at Williams and Smith he returned to Cambridge as an instructor. He taught until his retirement in 1946 and remained on the Cambridge scene until his death in 1957. Perry was the most enduring American philosopher of his generation; and although his career was more successful than most, it was in many respects typical of the first group of young professional men whom Harvard turned out.

James regarded him as "the soundest, most normal all-around man" that the graduate philosophy program had produced at the turn of the century; and James pushed for Perry. When James first thought of retiring he asked Eliot to hire Perry.[53] James wanted a Harvard place for the young man—"I shall use all my efforts," he wrote, "to get a berth for you in the hope that you may now grow up as one of our permanent and illustrious features."[54] When Perry did get his berth, he made the most of it: he got on with his colleagues (Palmer found him "an amiable fellow"),[55] published regularly, and worked hard for the department and the administration. He also benefited from the institution: it lightened his teaching load to foster publication, and as James's star pupil, he quickly became a force in the philosophic community.[56]

---

*GHP to HM, 20 January 1916, File 2023, HM Papers. Philosophy doctorates at Berkeley not called back by Harvard included: Jacob Loewenberg, professor of philosophy; G. P. Adams and Stephen Pepper, Mills professors of philosophy; Victor Lenzen, professor of physics; and Yuen Ren Chao, Agassiz professor of Oriental languages and literature.

Perry was not a deep or original thinker, but he was a versatile and stylish writer and a vigorous and witty polemicist. As he himself acknowledged, his strength was his capacity for hard, sustained work, and the results of his work were always tidy and cogent. As Royce put it, Perry was a retriever: "Throw a stick anywhere and he will fetch it."[57] Before the end of the first decade of the century, he was probably the best-known young American philosopher. In 1905 he presented Eliot with an offer from Princeton, and Harvard promptly promoted him to assistant professor with a salary hike. A little over a year later, as a thirty-one-year-old assistant professor, he became chairman of the department, and stayed at the job until 1914. He was chairman while the typewriter became common at Harvard and no one could have better matched man and machine. Even William James admitted that "the administrative vocation" in Perry's heart would not "abdicate in favor of the philosophical vocation."[58] From his predecessors, Palmer and Münsterberg, Perry learned "the arts of academic diplomacy and politics." During his chairmanship the volume of business correspondence stepped up, and Perry put his secretary's typewriter to good use. He angled for the department in university affairs, placed graduate students, and insured his own influence by his interest in the "profession." At forty-three he was president of the American Philosophical Association's Eastern Division.

Perry, however, was more than a narrow professional. Following James, he acted throughout his career on the premise that philosophy was relevant to life. He had originally begun his studies at Harvard as a short detour on his way to a Presbyterian pulpit; but although the career changed, he reminisced, the vocation did not. His guiding motives were hortatory and his intent always to do good. His most substantial work was in ethics. He even designed his four philosophically thin and overly schematized textbooks so that they might be a positive force among undergraduates. In university affairs he was a workhorse, and additionally invested energy in writing for popular magazines. Until his retirement he combined philosophizing with an active defense of liberal democracy and Christianity, two creeds he thought to typify American civilization.[59]

James Houghton Woods (1864–1935) followed Perry as chairman, and as Perry represented the future, Woods represented the past. He was from a Boston family and after graduating from Harvard in 1887 he studied and traveled in Britain and Europe until he took his Ph.D. from

Strasbourg in 1896. He then returned to Cambridge and until 1908 held a variety of minor academic positions. He was associated with the Divinity School because of his interest in comparative religion but also lectured in anthropology apparently because no one distinguished an interest in comparative religion from one in primitive religions. For two years he "investigated philosophy" in Japan and India. Woods was an academic nonprofessional with wide interests and a taste for travel that only an independent income could fulfill. In 1903, when Eliot appointed him an instructor in philosophy, he received no salary. As Münsterberg wrote to Eliot, Woods did not care about money, but only about the status that university affiliation would bring. When he became an assistant professor in 1908, it was again without salary. Throughout his career he was paid irregularly and was not on a definite schedule of increments as were his colleagues. He spent much of his time traveling, lecturing, and studying, rather than teaching and researching at Harvard.[60]

The philosophers called Woods's appointment as full professor in 1913 a "presidential appointment,"[61] and the best way to explain his rise at Harvard is to note that Eliot and his successor, Lawrence Lowell, could operate as late as the second decade of the twentieth century without regard for the criteria for academic advance that they were codifying. Woods edited and translated work in non-western philosophy, but he was not a thinker of any repute and had little to do with American philosophical trends. His rise would have been common in the nineteenth century; in the twentieth he enjoyed special protection from Eliot and Lowell.[62] When Eliot left the presidency in 1909, Lowell took over America's premier graduate institution, and the development of the scholarly bureaucracy that accompanied Harvard's triumph over Hopkins, the other Ivy schools, and all the universities west of the Appalachians continued to be irregular but steady. Professionalization was neither conscious nor planned. Still, Woods was already an idiosyncrasy; Perry was the man to watch.

Systematic Philosophizing

The growth of the professional system accompanied changes in the pattern of speculation. Out of the idealistic consensus of the early 1890s came what I call Harvard Pragmatism. To some extent this set of beliefs reflected complexities that would justify the need for disciplinary expertise, but it was also a rich and nuanced perspective that defined concerns and fixed the terms of philosophic debate. Harvard Pragmatism was a form of neo-Kantianism whose adherents drew from a set of connected technical doctrines: a constructionalist epistemology stressing the changing character of our conceptual schemes; a commitment to a kind of voluntarism; a concern with the nature of possible experience; a distrust of the tradition of phenomenalistic empiricism; a recognition of the importance of logic for philosophy; discomfort with the dichotomy between the conceptual and the empirical; and a refusal to distinguish between questions of knowledge and of value. From the mid-1890s to James's death in 1910 Harvard Pragmatism controlled American philosophy. The philosophic world looked to Harvard for stimulation, and when the Harvard speculators themselves wanted stimulation from contemporaries, they looked to their departmental colleagues. Within the department itself, Royce and James developed a common vocabulary that set the limits of philosophical discussion in the United States. To put the matter cryptically for the time being, both Royce and James enunciated voluntaristic idealisms, one monistic, the other pluralistic.*

Agreements on fundamentals, of course, did not mean that there were not disagreements on how to connect the fundamentals or on how to work out the details of puzzles. Indeed, once James and Royce established the basics, it was even possible for philosophers to muster attacks on the basics, and these attacks led ultimately—by the First World War—to the decline of absolute idealism.

*James on Royce:

> You are still the centre of my gaze, the pole of my mental magnet. When I write, 't is with one eye on the page, and one on you. When I compose my Gifford lectures mentally, 't is with the design exclusively of overthrowing your system, and ruining your peace. I lead a parasitic life upon you, for my highest flight of ambitious ideality is to become your conqueror, and go down into history as such, you and I rolled in one another's arms and silent (or rather loquacious still) in one last death-grapple of an embrace. Different as our minds are, yours has nourished mine, as no other social influence ever has, and in converse with you I have always felt that my life was being lived importantly (LWJ, 2: 136).

Royce on James:

> William James was my friend from my youth. . . . I was once for a brief time his pupil; I long loved to think of myself as his disciple. . . . if I often oppose his views I owe to him, as teacher, and as dear friend, an unfailing inspiration, far greater than he ever knew, or than I can well put into words (WJOE, pp. 9, ix).

The floruit of Harvard Pragmatism was the ten-year period from 1898, when James went to Berkeley to deliver his famous address "Philosophical Conceptions and Practical Results," to 1907, the year he retired, when he published *Pragmatism*. It was a period unequalled in its philosophic creativity. In addition to *Pragmatism*, James delivered his Gifford Lectures, "The Varieties of Religious Experience," and developed his radical empiricism. Royce gave *his* Gifford Lectures on "The World and the Individual," broke new ground in logic, and worked on ethics. Palmer and Münsterberg were in their primes. Santayana's *Life of Reason* defended an unconventional metaphysical realism. And Santayana's realism accompanied another heresy: talk of neo-realism filled the pages of the journals, and its youthful and most prominent proponents were Perry and Edwin Holt, another member of the Harvard junior faculty. A third young faculty member, Robert Yerkes, was making a name for himself in the psychology lab, experimenting on animals. Never, perhaps, in the history of universities, declared Arthur Lovejoy, had the philosophers of a single institution produced such a quantity of varied work.[63] A dispute between Royce and James stimulated this activity, for Harvard Pragmatism received its impetus when James devised a way of escaping Royce's absolute. Although James did not forego another version of idealism, his disenchantment with monism rescued some of the ideas of the Cambridge amateurs, particularly Peirce's epistemological realism and principle of pragmatism. But, as we shall see, the beneficiaries of James's cogitation were Perry and metaphysical realism.

14

JAMES, ROYCE, AND PRAGMATISM
1898-1907

Royce Shifts His Position

The argument of *The Religious Aspect of Philosophy* convinced James, and he forsook his own philosophy in the years after 1885. Of course, he spent much of this time writing the *Principles* but there, he contended, he was doing psychology, laying the basis of a natural science, and eschewing philosophizing. For all that, James was a Roycean with a bad conscience. Monism offered no easy explanation of individuality and free will and, as we shall see, James could not tolerate its analysis of evil. Royce too was aware of these problems. Not only James but Howison, who held the chair of philosophy at Berkeley, vehemently attacked the same Roycean tenets. When Royce spoke on "The Conception of God" at Berkeley's Philosophical Union in 1895, Howison was his chief opponent in what became known as "the most notable discussion of its kind in the history of American philosophy."[1] Howison charged that Royce's monism left no room for finite personality or freedom. Royce's address itself answered some of the criticisms of James and Howison. More far-reaching emendations appeared in "The Absolute and the Individual," a supplementary essay which grew out of private discussions in California and out of Royce's attempt "to expound some further developments" of the position of "The Conception of God." He did not publish "The Absolute and the Individual" until two years after "The Conception of God," and its 220 pages indicated the first major shift in Royce's thought and a reassertion of his earlier voluntarism.*

*CG, p. 135 (this volume contains both of Royce's essays and those of his critics).

Royce responded to the charges of pantheism and determinism, which were in fact substantiated by much of his work. *The Religious Aspect of Philosophy* proclaimed that the world of life was "an organic total"; individual selves were "drops in this ocean of the absolute truth." The world was no "mass of separate facts," but everything was "fully present in the unity of one eternal moment." The finite individual was in the organic life of God, the "all-pervading thought." This conception was not, prima facie, one in which there was room for freedom. Moreover, Royce was indifferent "whether anybody calls all this Theism or Pantheism." He deprecated those who enunciated a doctrine of "Universal Thought" and tried to foist it on plain people as "the God of our Fathers." He did not care if his notion of God agreed with anyone else's and acknowledged that his was not that of much traditional theology. Some philosophers took Royce at his word. By 1895 he was more a Christian thinker. His conception of God, he believed, was "distinctly theistic, and not pantheistic." Finite individuals did not lose their "ethical independence." "What the faith of our fathers had genuinely meant by God," Royce insisted, was "identical with the inevitable outcome of a reflective philosophy."[2]

The argument for the absolute in "The Conception of God" was the same as that of *The Religious Aspect of Philosophy*. Royce cared more for that book's "critical argument" than for anything else he had done, and against Howison's supposedly more pluralistic idealism, he still maintained that every estimate of the finite individual's place in the universe must be made "*subject to the validity*" of this kind of argument.[3] With this limitation in mind he defined the nature of individuality more closely, changing his conception of the absolute. In *The Religious Aspect of Philosophy* the absolute was thought, the absolute knower. The 1892 *Spirit of Modern Philosophy* stressed this idea. "The Implications of Self-Consciousness" written later in 1892 made the point bluntly:

> I have . . . laid stress upon this character of the divine World-Self as a Thinker, and have labored to distinguish between this his fullness of Being, as idealism is obliged to define it, and those customary notions which define God first of all in "dynamic," rather than in explicitly rational terms. . . . in insisting upon thought as the first category of the divine Person, I myself am not at all minded to lose

sight of the permanent, although, in the order of logical dependence, secondary, significance of the moral categories, or of their eternal place in the world of the completed Self. That they are thus logically secondary does not prevent them from being, in order of spiritual worth and dignity, supreme.[4]

"The Conception of God" weakened this emphasis. The attribute central to God or the absolute was omniscience, "all logically possible knowledge, insight, wisdom." To have all wisdom the absolute possessed the answer to every rational question. To question meant to have ideas of what was not present and to ask if these ideas did express or could express what some experiences not present would verify. The absolute joined these two elements—ideas and experience: "all genuinely significant, all truly thinkable ideas would be seen as directly fulfilled, and fulfilled in his own experience." Although Royce defined the absolute as unifying absolute thought and absolute experience, the two factors "still remain distinguishable." The absolute thought had ideas, and he experienced, that is, he had what we might call feeling, a world of immediate data of consciousness presented as fact (9–15). Although the absolute was still a knower, Royce defined knowledge not as abstract cogitating, but as a certain kind of experience that related, in common-sense terms, ideas and the external world.

In "The Absolute and the Individual" of 1897, Royce, making a concession to James, brought a voluntaristic dimension back into his writing and emphasized the will; he hoped this revision of his monism would rebut Howison's vague pluralism. Attention was essential to will, the favoring of one conscious content against a dim background of other contents. Will involved a preference for data attended to, against data that remained, relatively speaking, merely ideal or possible objects of attention. Finite beings exercised will when they concentrated, as they must, on one or another aspect of what was before their minds. To attend to the work in front of me was to blot out, as it were, the sounds around me or not to notice the color of the paper on which I wrote or the lack of heat in the room.

The absolute had present to it all our contents of consciousness and all validly possible contents of consciousness. This experience answered all the questions posed by absolute thought. But having this experience present involved will; the absolute attended to what was before it; it excluded from actuality the "barely possible"; it chose. The absolute had an individuating element in addition to thought and experience (191 ff.). This element determined that the content of consciousness, the absolute experience, present to absolute thought was this world "rather than any other of the abstractly possible but not genuinely possible worlds" (169). This redefinition was to account for finite individuals, to defend Royce's idealism from the imputation of pantheism.[5]

What was an individual? Uniqueness was the definiens of individuality, and Royce held accordingly that thought—discursive language—could never individualize. For example, no matter how extensively we described a man, we could not do so uniquely: we only defined a type. This type might only be exemplified once, but only further experience could persuade us of this. Could experience individuate? Royce's answer was no: it only presented us with a mass of data. Experience usually came to us individualized into experiences of this moment, this place, this desk, or this pen. In these cases we assumed a previous knowledge of an individual whole or of a determinate fact within which or in relation to which the *this* of passing experience became definable as individual. Most of these *this*'s were so because of one constantly presupposed individual of daily life: I, the self. Everything presupposed a definition of the self's individuality (247–58).

An individual was an object of exclusive interest: to be an individual was for us to regard something as irreplaceable by any other object. Our exclusive interest was a feeling of repugnance for the idea of two objects simultaneously satisfying us. Individuality was a teleological category: Royce identified the principle of individuation with his notion of selective attention, will, or what he also called love. Human individuals were such because God's love, his choice, his selective attention, his will made them the objects of his exclusive interest: the absolute experience contained those objects that were the unique expressions of Divine Will. God's love is

> an exclusive love,—a love that only one world, one Whole, could fulfill. Such a being [like the Absolute] would say: "There shall be but this one world." And for him this world would be fact. The oneness would be the mere outcome and expression of his will. This would then be an individual world, that is, the sole instance of its

universal idea or type. In this individual world, every finite fact, by virtue of its relation to the whole, would be in its own measure individual. And individuality, in such a world, would neither be absorbed in one indistinct whole, nor yet be opaque fact. For the exclusive love of the Absolute for this world would render the individuality of the fact secondarily intelligible, as being the fulfillment of the very exclusiveness of the love (266).

The finite individual was a part, a fragment, of the absolute. The elements of any moment of our consciousness united to form the whole of that moment. Similarly, our consciousnesses formed the "one luminously transparent conscious moment" of the absolute. Our experiences uniquely constituted the absolute; they were represented nowhere else in God's "life." Without the experiences constituting us, God's life would be different; God would not be God, the precise individual he was. Finally, from our perspective—the only one in which it was intelligible to speak of human individuals—God in no way "determined" our individuality. Rather, expressing our wills shaped what was the will of God from the absolute perspective:

> In my grade of reality, I am unique as this element in and of the Divine Will. Nothing else than my will gives my will its essential character. From this point of view, the individual will . . . can say to God in his wholeness: "Were I not, your Will would not be"; for had I not this my unique attentive choice . . . God's Will would be incomplete. He would not have willed just what I, and I alone, as this fragment of his life, as this member of the Divine Choice, will in him, and as this unique portion of his complete Will (294).

The individual self, so defined, was free. It had the kind of freedom characterizing God, and its uniqueness defined this freedom.

From our point of view, individual consciousness contained an element determined by nothing in the whole of God's life except the individual. This element Royce called the ethically organizing interests of a man's life, his exclusive interests; they made a man one self. These interests expressed a man's ideal, life-ideal, or plan of life—what a man most clearly proposed to be. These interests ensured that individuality and selfhood were moral notions.

Because these interests defined freedom, our notion of ourselves as moral creatures and of freedom were one: "in choosing the ideal, which is the one means of giving his life the unity of Self, the individual is free" (295).

James and Pragmatism

A congenial answer to ethical questions was central to James's early thought and he never saw monism as an adequate option. But when Royce first came to Cambridge, James recalled being "overawed by Royce's immense intellect and felt compelled to share his idealism." By the late 1890s, however, James "had managed to break away."[6] At the same time Royce was making amends, James was rejecting the monistic analysis, but his alternative ignored the problems of Scottish realism although resurrecting some of the ideas of the Metaphysical Club. His own concern for free will and his response to Royce's argument reshaped the course of American philosophy.

James's preliminary statement was the 1898 Berkeley address, "Philosophical Conceptions and Practical Results," also read to Howison's Philosophical Union. Citing Peirce's work, James explicated what he called the principle of practicalism or pragmatism and what, he said, Peirce had put forward in Cambridge over twenty years before. Peirce's "maxim" analyzed meaning as a set of consequences, although his more careful analyses used the notion of a set of hypotheticals. James stressed the definition that Peirce used in setting forth the maxim. So, said James:

> To attain perfect clearness in our thoughts of an object, then, we need only consider what effects of a conceivably practical kind the object may involve—what sensations we are to expect from it and what reactions we must prepare. Our conception of these effects, then, is for us the whole of our conception of the object, so far as that conception has positive significance at all.[7]

In time James diverged so radically from Peirce that the latter renounced the child that James had nurtured. In writing about the set of hypotheticals, Peirce had in mind scientific concepts. A concept was clear if we ascertained and verified the effects that followed when we stipulated the conditions for investigating the object of conception; we usually carried out this sort of procedure in the laboratory. Peirce did not write of an individual's psychology, of the immediately felt effects of pleasure or pain, or of the satisfaction or dissatisfaction associated with entertaining ideas.[8] But emphasizing consequences later enabled James to include in a concept's meaning not only "experimental effects" but also the experiential consequences that might follow from belief in the concept, the particular strategic effects this belief might have in benefiting a person's psyche. Even in "Philosophical Conception and Practical Results," however, James argued that the principle of pragmatism ought tc "be expressed more broadly than Mr. Peirce expresses it":

> The ultimate test for us of what a truth means is indeed the conduct it dictates or inspires. But it inspires that conduct because it first foretells some particular turn to our experience which shall call for just that conduct from us. And I should prefer for our purposes this evening to express Peirce's principle by saying that the effective meaning of any philosophic proposition can always be brought down to some particular consequence, in our future practical experience, whether active or passive; the point lying rather in the fact that the experience must be particular than in the fact that it must be active.[9]

James used the pragmatic principle as a statement of method, as a means of clarifying philosophic problems. He subjected statements of various philosophical positions to this pragmatic test. If "opposing" formulations implied no difference in the future detail of experience or conduct, the opposition was trivial and idle. Consider, said James, the 1895 debate between Howison and Royce, the "Great Philosophical Discussion." Apply the pragmatic maxim to the argument between monism and pluralism as it was there defined. Royce and Howison delineated the issues so cloudily that they were irresolvable, that is, as they expounded the positions, James could not differentiate between them. James concluded that these philosophies were different only if Royce and Howison specified more exactly what monism and pluralism amounted to. If they did, James hinted, we would find that we ought to compromise on the extent to which the world was "one" and "many."[10]

James went no further in this address, but from the point of view of his later work, the consequence of adhering to Peirce's maxim was clear.

If Royce's monism meant something so vague as to be indistinguishable from some forms of pluralism, then perhaps there was no more reason to accept the arguments that led to it than those that led to pluralism. At least there were grounds for suspicion—the reasoning might be merely verbal or even fallacious.

Adopting the pragmatic maxim gave James breathing space. Meanwhile, he strove to redefine the connections between psychology and philosophy. His 1884 "The Function of Cognition" had put forward the essentials of his pragmatism and claimed merely to be giving a psychological account of how human beings sought truth and what they called truth. In 1893 James's student, Dickinson Miller, argued that to do this kind of psychology was to give the meaning of truth, an analysis of how ideas could adequately refer to what they were supposed to be true of, of how we warranted claims to truth. James later said that his student's influence led him to his mature position, but even Miller wrote that his theorizing had little to do with metaphysics.[11] By 1895 in "The Knowing of Things Together" James disputed Miller. The aspects of psychology in which he was interested, he said, were not merely fragments of natural science. He had given up the position of the *Principles*: we could not keep metaphysics and epistemology out of psychology. And James added that he was still an idealist.[12] In the 1904 "Humanism and Truth" and in the 1906 Lowell Lectures published as *Pragmatism*, he took a more radical step: his psychological description spoke directly to the philosophical question of truth. He applied the pragmatic maxim to the meaning of the concept of truth, transforming his old psychological position into philosophy.

Ideas and beliefs were plans of action expressed in statements. If we applied the pragmatic maxim to the concept of truth, true ideas or beliefs were those that led us satisfactorily and expeditiously through experience. Truth was what it was "known-as"—a class name for all sorts of working values in experience.[13] As we shall see more fully in a moment, the meaning of truth was exactly what James had previously supposed to be merely a psychological description of how human beings sought truth. To give an exact description answered the philosophic question of truth.

We can only speculate how James would have revised the *Principles* after denying the distinction between (psychological) science and philosophy. But he was at least on his way to clearing up the ambiguities in his own mind about the relation of our consciousnesses to the world. In broadest terms, rejecting the dichotomy between science and philosophy—the study of the physical world and the study of man's place in it—prompted James's acceptance of "humanism"; he overcame the dualism of body and mind by stressing the primacy of persons who defined their environment and themselves through action.

Was James misled by his method to confound psychology with logic, to confuse our ways of arriving at truth with what it meant for a statement to be true, with justifying truth claims? When he was most subtle, James's argument was clear. In this case there was no distinction between the psychological and the logical:

> A favorite way of opposing the more abstract to the more concrete account is to accuse those who favor the latter of "confounding psychology with logic." Our critics say that when we are asked what truth *means*, we reply by telling only how it is *arrived at*. But since a meaning is a logical relation, static, independent of time, how can it possibly be identified, they say, with any concrete man's experience, perishing as this does at the instant of its production? This, indeed, sounds profound, but I challenge the profundity. The logical relation stands to the psychological relation between idea and object only as saltatory abstractness stands to ambulatory concreteness. Both relations need a psychological vehicle; and the "logical" one is simply the "psychological" one disemboweled of its fulness, and reduced to a bare abstractional scheme.[14]

Carefully describing the most impressive of our claims to truth did not differ from justifying these claims. The matrix of circumstance "surrounding" ideas and allowing them to lead to successful action constituted the truth relation.[15]

Royce had argued that we required the absolute as that objective thing external to our consciousnesses, to our ideas, to which our ideas could correspond, could be true *to*: they would be true only if they agreed with the absolute consciousness, where agreement was a teleological notion. Royce erred, James believed, in isolating a thought and then asking how it referred to a thing outside it. Following his analysis of the stream of consciousness, James argued that there was no present thought, but only a passing moment which overreached itself. This "elementary drag" in the passing moment yielded the basic notion of what knowing was, of one thing leading to another. In this process James found the self-transcendence of thought that constituted knowing.[16]

For Royce, it did not matter if an idea worked or if future experience verified it. Workings did not warrant or ground an idea's truthfulness. They only allowed us to act on the idea successfully; they in no way guaranteed that the idea had any relation to anything beyond our consciousness. James replied that even absolutists could point to nothing other than these guiding processes in discussing truth.[17] Returning to Wright's argument, he implied that to ask for the ground of our activity was to indulge "in a piece of perverse abstraction-worship." The absolutist took "the mere name and nature of a fact" and clapped it "behind the fact as a duplicate entity to make it possible."[18] "Definitely experienceable workings" warranted truths just as well as the absolute's intentions, and these workings were verifiable.[19] Knowing fell entirely within experience, and the analysis of knowledge presupposed nothing beyond human experience.[20]

The absolutists, said James, mistakenly assumed that their logic ensured the possibility of possessing truth. But this sort of logical warranting was impossible. We could never be certain that beliefs were true, that truth was "objectively" obtainable, that ideas corresponded to something external to them. James could give the "nominal essence" of the truth relation, its definition; the question of justification, of warranting, was fruitless. We had no way of answering it.[21] To distinguish description from justification was either to make a distinction without a difference or to set a problem that had no solution. Properly understood, the two notions fell together.

In his essays on pragmatism James did not take up at any length the obvious Roycean question: what was the status of the pragmatist's claim? Royce wanted to force James to hold his notion of truth to be true absolutely, without relation to its workings; Royce could thereby convict James of a contradiction. The issue for Royce was not so much whether we possessed truth but whether our ways of thinking enabled us coherently to conceive the truth relation without a referent beyond our consciousnesses. Discussing this issue briefly, James adopted a Peircean solution: the pragmatist maintained his ideas to be absolutely true, but meant by this phrase only that everyone would adopt the pragmatist position in the long run. The meaning of this absolute truth was still defined by its satisfactoriness. James admitted the notion of absolute truth as an "inevitable regulative postulate"—the forever satisfying for all.[22] With Peirce, James wrote,

> The maximal conceivable truth in an idea would seem to be that it should lead to an actual merging of ourselves with the object, to an utter mutual confluence and identification. . . . *Total conflux of the mind with the reality* would be the absolute limit of truth, there could be no better or more satisfying knowledge than that.[23]

The Meaning of Truth

In what, then, did a careful description of how we arrived at truth consist? James sketched his account by speaking of true beliefs satisfactorily leading us in experience, but his view was more complex. What made a belief true for any individual at any moment was satisfactoriness concretely felt at that time. A belief, idea, or hypothesis (belief for short) was true just to the extent that it was useful.[24] But James measured such prima facie truths against what was satisfactory for all of us in the long run: the truth proved satisfactory for all in the long run. James thus allowed for the accumulation of new truths in the future and preserved the common-sense notion that certainty escaped us.

What did the broad term 'satisfying', or its Jamesean equivalents, 'useful', 'expedient', and 'workable', mean? In some places he asserted that truth was a cover term for all sorts of satisfactions to which our beliefs led us. The "workings" differed in every instance.[25] But he could be more specific.

First, a belief was an instrument of action, and its truth consisted in its verification, in having the experiences that the belief predicted we would have:

> It is hard to find any one phrase that characterizes these consequences better than the ordinary agreement-formula—just such consequences being what we have in mind whenever we say that our ideas "agree" with reality. They lead us, namely, through the acts and other ideas which they instigate, into or up to, or towards, other parts of experience with which we feel all the while—such

feeling being among our potentialities—that the original ideas remain in agreement. The connections and transitions come to us from point to point as being progressive, harmonious, satisfactory. This function of agreeable leading is what we mean by an idea's verification.

James also talked equivalently of "validating" and "corroborating" beliefs.

A simple and fully verified leading typified the truth process: I believe the coffee is on the kitchen shelf, and I leave my chair and go and find it. "Experience offers indeed other forms of truth-process, but they are all conceivable as being primary verifications arrested, multiplied or substituted one for another." Indirect verifications, James added, passed muster thereafter; I assume that it is coffee on the shelf from its visual appearance, without tasting it. "For one truth-process completed there are a million in our lives that function in this state of nascency. They turn us *towards* direct verification; lead us into the *surroundings* of the objects they envisage; and then, if everything runs on harmoniously, we are so sure that verification is possible that we omit it, and are usually justified by all that happens." Moreover, he allowed the verifications of others: I believe my wife if she tells me that there is coffee on the shelf. "You accept my verification of one thing, I yours of another. We trade on each other's truth. But beliefs verified concretely by *somebody* are the posts of the whole superstructure."[26]

Did this mean that objects of true beliefs did not exist before verification? James argued that the objects of belief virtually pre-existed when every condition of their realization save one was present—the missing condition being the experiencer who verified. Supposing a belief true before verification was to hold it verifiable:[27]

> The key to this difficulty lies in the distinction between knowing as verified and completed, and the same knowing as in transit and on its way. . . . it is only when our idea of the [Memorial] Hall has actually terminated in the percept that we know "for certain" that from the beginning it was truly cognitive of *that*. Until established by the end of the process, its quality of knowing that, or indeed of knowing anything, could still be doubted; and yet the knowing really was there, as the result now shows. We were *virtual* knowers

of the Hall long before we were certified to have been its actual knowers, by the percept's retroactive validating power.[28]

Verification was not the only criterion of a belief's satisfactoriness. Additionally, a belief "must mediate between all previous truths and certain new experiences. It must derange common sense and previous belief as little as possible." A truth was "pent in" between the coercions of the world of sense and "the whole body of funded truths." Workability or usefulness meant not just that a truth was verifiable but also that it was assimilable, consistent with previous truth, congruent with our residual beliefs:[29]

> The point I now urge you to observe particularly is the part played by the older truths. Failure to take account of it is the source of much of the unjust criticism leveled against pragmatism. Their influence is absolutely controlling. Loyalty to them is the first principle—in most cases it is the only principle; for by far the most usual way of handling phenomena so novel that they would make for a serious rearrangement of our preconception is to ignore them altogether, or to abuse those who bear witness to them. . . . But often the day's contents oblige a rearrangement. If I should now utter piercing shrieks and act like a maniac on this platform, it would make many of you revise your ideas as to the probable worth of my philosophy. "Radium" came the other day as part of the day's content, and seemed for a moment to contradict our ideas of the whole order of nature, that order having come to be identified with what is called the conservation of energy.[30]

Finally, there was a last criterion, a subjective one of elegance:

> sometimes alternative theoretic formulas are equally compatible with all the truths we know, and then we choose between them for subjective reasons. We choose the kind of theory to which we are already partial; we follow "elegance" or "economy." Clerk-Maxwell somewhere says it would be "poor scientific taste" to choose the more complicated of two equally well-evidenced conceptions, and you will all agree with him.[31]

True beliefs satisfied and by 'satisfy' James meant three things: a belief would be (1) verified or verifiable in our experience or in that of others, (2) consistent with our previous beliefs, and (3) subjectively more elegant than any other belief which also met requirements (1) and (2). Truth in science, James concluded, "is what gives us the maximum possible sum of satisfactions, taste included, but consistency both with previous truth and with novel fact is always the most important claimant."[32]

James spoke only briefly of truths true only because they were immediately satisfying to some individual. His analysis generally assumed that the candidates for true beliefs had claim to social acceptability. In short, we did not in practice start de novo, and this insight prompted him to look at the historical development of our conceptual apparatus:

> My thesis now is this, that *our fundamental ways of thinking about things are discoveries of exceedingly remote ancestors, which have been able to preserve themselves throughout the experience of all subsequent time.* They form one great stage of equilibrium in the human mind's development, the stage of *common sense.* Other stages have grafted themselves upon this stage, but have never succeeded in displacing it.
>
> Our nouns and adjectives are all humanized heirlooms, and in the theories we build them into, the inner order and arrangement is wholly dictated by human considerations, intellectual consistency being one of them. . . . We plunge forward into the field of fresh experience with the beliefs our ancestors and we have made already; these determine what we notice; what we notice determines what we do; what we do again determines what we experience; so from one thing to another, altho the stubborn fact remains that there is a sensible flux, what is *true of it* seems from first to last to be largely a matter of our own creation.[33]

Was James, then, a Kantian?

> Superficially this sounds like Kant's view; but between categories fulminated before nature began, and categories gradually forming themselves in nature's presence, the whole chasm between rationalism and empiricism yawns.[34]

There is much to be said for James's denial. The whole of the nineteenth century's emphasis on change and development and the impact of Darwin mediated between him and Kant. But equally certain was James's debt to idealism: his evolutionary Kantianism was clear.

James and Kant

The Kantian aspects of James's thought became crucial as he amplified his pragmatism in the last years of his life. How could truth consist of satisfactory leadings, however widely understood, critics asked, when we always assumed that beliefs were true *of* something? If James did not shift his position in answering this query, he accentuated its Kantian dimensions. In *Pragmatism* "reality" was what truths had to take account of, and its most important aspects were the sensations and relations given in the stream of consciousness. Reality acted as something independent, as a thing found in experience. We had, however, a certain freedom in dealing with this reality: we attended to what we wanted in the flux of sensation. The *that* of sensations was indisputable; we determined its *what*. James wrote elsewhere that there was "an imperfect plasticity of them [realities] to our conceptual manipulations."[35]

The problem was to distinguish the real from the human factors in cognitive experience. In any functioning body of truth, said James, it was impossible to weed out the "subjective" and "objective" factors. But the way a new truth developed showed, by comparison, that subjective factors must have always been active; they were thus potent and in some degree creative.[36] If our beliefs were annihilated, the reality would still be there in some shape, though it might be a shape lacking whatever belief supplied. That reality was independent meant that there was something in experience escaping our arbitrary control. This something might be due to something independent of all possible experience, an extra-experiential *Ding an sich*, but James was only interested in the determinations that asserted themselves within experience. The sanctions of truth, the only guarantee against licentious thinking, occurred within experience.[37]

While pragmatism stressed the "subjective," "creative" elements of the truth relation, it admitted that there was something to which our truths were true. But this admission was trivial for James. The activities of ours that lay within experience were essential; concern with what might be extra-experiential was pointless.

What was important here and what was emphasized in James's last pronouncements on pragmatism—the essays collected in *The Meaning of Truth*—was his closeness to the Kantian tradition. James's pragmatism conceived of truth as synthesizing our active nature and reality—or what we might call the given—although the doctrine put aside all questions about the existence of the given independent of our active nature. Pragmatism was subjectivistic, James said, only to the extent that thinking contributed part of the truth.[38] The later essays in *The Meaning of Truth* added that although satisfactions were necessary to truth building, they were not sufficient; it was reality (the given) to which the satisfactions must lead.[39] Leadings were the *causa existenti* of beliefs, assigning meaning to them. But leadings were not the "logical cue" or "objective deliverance or content." When a belief was true, its object existed and nothing else contradicted belief in it. Take any belief and its object; if the belief was true, understanding the object must include some notion of the belief's functional workings.[40]

James walked a tightrope. When he allied the description of the modes of attaining beliefs with their justification, he talked of satisfactions (in the sense discussed above). But his tack changed when he responded to the retort that he could not then account for our feeling that beliefs were true *of* something. Of course, said James, there was something given in experience which beliefs were about. To mention a belief's content, however, immediately raised the question of justification aside from description. If "reality" had to exist if we were to have truths, whatever our satisfactions, James had somehow to warrant that beliefs could get at this reality. Describing the peculiar characteristics of true beliefs was inadequate as an account of truth once he admitted that they could be true only if they led to the object.[41]

James did not resolve this ambiguity, perhaps because the metaphysical issues centering around absolute idealism overshadowed the connected but distinct epistemological problems. After all, James developed his pragmatic theory of knowledge to avoid monism and a two worlds' doctrine. Although this epistemology remained unfinished, it brought the moral and intellectual together again: attaining scientific truth became a mode of successful activity and so a moral enterprise. Armed with this idea, James would fight the famous "battle of the absolute" and ultimately attempt to counter absolutism in metaphysics.

15

THE BATTLE OF THE ABSOLUTE
1899-1910

Royce's Influence

The World and the Individual, delivered as the Gifford Lectures at the University of Aberdeen in 1899 and 1900, systematically set forth Royce's philosophy; its publication was the high-water mark of the idealistic tide. The two volumes simultaneously revealed the extent to which Royce's absolutism had become pragmatic: "The Conception of God" reintroduced a voluntaristic aspect into Royce's idealism; *The World and the Individual* affirmed this voluntarism; and thereafter Royce adopted the name "absolute pragmatism." Finally, the context in which he argued allowed him to assault Jamesean pragmatism, representational realism, and mysticism. All of these doctrines—not merely Jamesean pragmatism—acquired currency at Harvard in the next two decades, and Royce's discussion was a text for all combatants. In this chapter and the next two, we shall take up Royce's pragmatism and his critique of James, as well as James's counterattack; in succeeding chapters, we shall examine other responses to *The World and the Individual*.

Systematic Idealist Philosophy

The World and the Individual is difficult to read sympathetically. Royce wrote archaically, and he filled the book with theological phrases and conceptions which sound odd today. Moreover, the lectures run to nearly a thousand printed pages, excluding an important supplementary essay, and the discussion is diffuse, wordy, and obscure. But we must understand this study.

Where we might speak of a statement about present facts or of beliefs, Royce spoke of ideas. His favorite expression was "an idea seeking its other"—its object. This notion was less dubious than it might seem for it meant that we made statements about supposed factual relations, or had beliefs about the world, and that we verified the truth of our statements and confirmed our beliefs. For Royce an idea never "found" its other because we never exhausted the verifications to which we subjected beliefs. Empirical knowledge was probable only, and some possible experience might disconfirm our deepest claims. Royce used this premise to construct a new "pragmatic" absolute. He had previously stated that the will was a distinguishable yet inseparable "aspect" of the absolute. He now asserted that separating willing and being in the absolute had no meaning. The distinction was useful in the finite world, but was ultimately unjustified.

Royce first considered habits. Human beings responded to stimuli according to the responses they had made to similar past stimuli. The attention of human beings guided them to states of consciousness associated with those accompanying habitual activity. We were conscious of a *"brief abstract and epitome of our previous experience."* People must be taught how to perceive, and perceived no more than what they had been prepared to see. Interests and purposes partially determined the content of consciousness, and any analysis of thinking—of "having ideas" —involved action, will. As previously noted, selective attention itself was a voluntary act and included a tendency to external expression. Perception of an object was "a fragment of a possible consciousness involving a whole system of feeling and of conduct in the presence of such an object." Thought consisted of processes producing characteristic motor reactions. To have ideas was to have plans of action, or responses, which we would perforce carry out in the presence of the object about which we had ideas. The only test of understanding an idea was the ability to act fittingly: the idea was a disposition to action.[1]

James influenced this discussion, but Royce did not simply take his pragmatism from his older colleague. The younger man's voluntarism had long been apparent, and his work on imitation also suggested this analysis of ideas. Ideas were Jamesean plans of action but also *"conscious imitations of things."* We had exact ideas only so far as we knew how to *"imitatively reconstruct"* objects, that is, how we ought to act to use objects for the purposes we had. We shared ideas because we compared our imitations with those of our fellows. My ideas were true or false not merely because I verified them but because others verified them in the World of Description, because we "imitated in common."

The pragmatic–Kantian insight was, prima facie, innocuous: we participated in constructing the world. Royce and James both identified this participation as attention, an exercise of our wills. Knowing involved activity, but also something foreign to activity. For Royce verifying our knowledge reduced the world to ideas, for we experienced the object in each verification, that is, we might claim that a portion of it occurred in our consciousness, as idea. But verifications never "exhausted" the object; being remained beyond our grasp, beyond the activities which defined our consciousness of being. Royce carried this analysis further. If we knew an object completely, it would not be beyond our will. In imitating, "an idea seeks its Other." If imitation proceeded to its limit, Royce said, then "I shall face being. I shall not only imitate my object as another, and correspond to it from without: I shall become one with it, and so internally possess it."[2] To know an object perfectly was only to verify it exhaustively and so experience it completely. Indeed there was no "it," there was simply "pure activity" which was simultaneously "pure being." In these circumstances we assimilated object, existing externally, to idea, plan of action. The World of Description was nothing other than the absolute's World of Appreciation. In it, being and willing were one.

In distinguishing object from ideas (that is, plans of action) about it, Royce illuminated a single phenomenon divisible only from the human perspective. The disjunction was useful in understanding finite forms of knowing, and *The World and the Individual* emphasized it in examining the internal and external meaning of ideas.

The internal meaning of an idea was that aspect of its purpose which a present idea immediately embodied (1:25), the most elementary aspect of the plan of action. Royce construed it as the immediate and spontaneous effort to create order out of the flux of consciousness, and did not associate it with executing the plan, formulating the tests which will verify the idea's truth, or the verification itself (1:48–50). The essential quality of the internal meaning was not the sensations or images associated with it, but its expression of some purpose (1:31). Royce's internal meaning was the momentary identification of subject (a certain content) and predicate (a certain form) for a given purpose. His favorite example was a melody I sang to myself. Singing the melody or silently listening to it constituted a musical idea, and at least partially fulfilled and embodied my purpose at the same time—my purpose of imagining the melody. Having the (internal) idea and fulfilling an instantaneous purpose were identical; the idea was its own fulfillment.

Royce contrasted this internal meaning (or simply idea) with a "relatively external meaning"—the object or referent of the idea (or simply object or referent). By using "relatively" or "apparently" before his phrase "external meaning of an idea," Royce gave warning of what was coming. But he needed the abstraction of the external meaning to make his view of knowledge plausible. The referent or object made the idea true or false. Suppose the melody I imagined was a theme composed by Beethoven. My melody embodied my purpose the instant I imagined it, but it was an idea that meant its proper object—a Beethoven theme. We directed our plan of action toward the external meaning (1:23–29).

Royce indicated two ways in which teleology entered his analysis of ideas and referents:

> if it [an idea] means to be true, it intends a sort of correspondence with an object. What correspondence it intends is determined, as we saw, solely by the purpose which the idea embodies, *i.e.* by the internal meaning of the idea. Furthermore, the idea intends to attain this correspondence to some particular object,—not to any object you please, not to whatever happens to correspond to the ideal construction in question, but to a determined object. The determination of what object is meant, is, therefore, certainly again due, in one aspect, to the internal meaning of the idea. Nobody else can determine for me what object I mean by my idea.

As in *The Religious Aspect of Philosophy*, he faced "the central dilemma" of epistemology. Despite what he said, ideas could not entirely determine the correspondence of their referents to them. If that occurred, "truth would be mere tautology, error would be excluded in advance, and it would be useless even to talk of an object external in any sense to the idea" (1:319–20).

The inevitable followed—the dialectical argument. The argument's form did not change, although its new setting advanced Royce's description of the world's metaphysical structure. The novelty was the historical framework into which he put the argument. Volume 1 of *The World and the Individual* investigated four historical conceptions of being. Realism—a doctrine never held in its purity by any first-rate thinkers (1:70)—defined the real as independently existing objects. Only those mistakenly satisfied with the World of Description accepted it. Realism's antithesis was mysticism—the view that the real immediately fulfilled the purpose of ideas—and Royce sympathized with its proponents in Indian philosophy. But in concentrating on appreciation to the exclusion of description, Indian mysticism could not account for finite activity; it could not explain the domain of natural science. The "Third Conception of Being," "critical rationalism," asserted that possible experience verified the real. We must analyze each of these conceptions. Here, before we pass over to the "Fourth Conception of Being"—Royce's conception—we shall examine only critical rationalism.

The Third Conception described the real with partial adequacy (1:251) as what *"under conditions . . . would become knowable and known"* (1:196, 251). The real was what we experience, will experience, and would experience, given that certain observational conditions were met. External objects existed as possible experience; they were independent of private individuality but not of "the constitution of our experience" (1:236). Although many of its adherents ignored or refused to recognize their inheritance, Royce traced this ontology back to Kant (1:205), and one of the targets of Royce's argument was the position he attributed to James. This became apparent when he criticized critical rationalism "in one of its most recent forms" (1:202).

Exponents of this view believed that the real was what, "if present, would satisfy or tend to satisfy our conscious needs and meanings." Royce also used more neutral language: "To be is precisely to fulfill or to give warrant to ideas by making possible the experience that the ideas define" (1:203). A true idea led to experiences which verified the expectations that accepting the idea entailed. If I sincerely said, "The cows are in the field," I believed that if I went to the field, I would see the cows. If the cows were there, then I verified this fact by walking to the field and having my expectations warranted. The Third Conception of Being defined the real as the possible experience making ideas true or false or, as Royce put it, valid or invalid. To say that something was real—for example, the cows in the field—was to say that if we behaved in certain ways, under certain circumstances certain consequences would eventuate—for example, that I would see the cows. The real world was no thing in itself; neither was it merely an assemblage of capricious, momentary, actual experiences. The real was beyond any particular experience; we characterized it by well-defined possible experiences:

> You will, under given conditions, see certain sights, hear certain words, touch certain tangible objects—in brief, get the presence of certain empirical facts. This is all that you can find involved in very many of your statements about the Being of social and of physical realities. Having defined such ideas of possible experience, you then test them. If the result conforms to the expectation, you are so far content. You have then communed with Being (1:257–58).

Some of the thinkers who espoused this view were scientists. Others were narrow empiricists, but Royce noted that many condemned only "theoretical constructions" in religion and were satisfied with "a reasonable and chastened moral faith." They believed that we must treat objects "*as if they were* finally real." The "as if" or "as it were" became an ultimate category. Consequently, we no longer proved that God existed but argued only that "*It is as if he were.*" The critical rationalist might still warrant "an impersonal conception of a Righteous Order of the Universe" (1:258).

Whatever the religious proclivities of the critical rationalist, Royce picked out for discussion one tenet of the doctrine:

> there are countless possible experiences that you never test, and that you still view as belonging to the realm of physical and of social validity. In fact, just when you express your own contentment with your tests, you transcend what you have actually succeeded in getting present to your experience. . . . The prices and credits of the commercial world involve far more numerous types of valid possible experience than any prudent merchant cares to test; for, if these facts are valid as they are conceived, their very Being includes possibilities of unwise investment and of bankruptcy, which the prudent businessman recognizes only to avoid. In fact, since our

whole voluntary life is selective, we all the time recognize possibilities of experience only to shun the testing of them (1 : 258).

The critical rationalist's world of possible experience had a twofold character. We verified its reality by testing ideas about it from moment to moment but believed it to have far more "validity"—possible experience verifiable under proper conditions—than we could individually test. Because of these peculiarities, the Third Conception faced problems about the nature of possibility that Royce often examined in the ensuing years. *The World and the Individual* concentrated on the nature of "possible experience" that no human being experienced. What was the status of the cow in the field when no one was experiencing it, what was the status of unactualized possibilities? This question frustrated Charles Peirce, and the dispute between James and Royce, between pragmatism and absolute pragmatism, was also a question of possible experience.[3]

The critical rationalist, said Royce, held that some possible experience was valid; it was different from what was merely conceivable or possible under absurd conditions. If I were to go into the field, I could conceivably see pink elephants there; if the field were in a world of make-believe, it might be the habitat of pink elephants. But these possibilities—the "fantastically" or "barely" possible—differed from "the determinately possible"—"That which would be observed or verified under exactly stateable, even if physically inaccessible conditions." The latter were "really valid and objective physical characters" (1 : 242–43). The critical rationalist must relate "valid" possible experience to actual experience in a way that he did not relate the fantastically possible. Nonetheless, both the validly and barely possible were unactualized experience, and critical rationalists treated them similarly, if they treated them at all. Royce contended that these philosophers considered all possibilities as barely possible. His point was that the critical rationalists joined valid and fantastic possibilities. This view must be wrong, for valid possibilities were real in much the same way as actual experience was real. Unlike critical rationalism, an adequate philosophy must distinguish between the barely and validly possible, and must link the latter to the actual:

What our Third Conception so far fails to explain to us is precisely the difference between reality that is to be attributed to the valid truths that we do not get concretely verified in our own experience, and the reality observed by us when we do verify ideas. In brief, *what is a valid or a determinately possible experience at the moment when it is supposed to be only possible?* What is a valid truth at the moment when nobody verifies its validity? (1 : 260)

We should expect Royce's answer. He had given it in "The Possibility of Error," and never wavered in believing that his argument there had settled the issue. The valid possible experiences were actual—they were parts of the experience of the absolute, as our actual experiences were part of this complete experience—while the barely possible were non-existent.

Our ideas fulfilled purposes incompletely, and if an idea was true, "certain further experience of the fulfillment of the idea is possible." The real object that possible experiences defined was incompletely defined. From Royce's perspective this meant that the critical rationalist never isolated any object as an individual object: its fully determinate nature was ahead in possible experience, in what would happen if we were to do thus-and-such. But since critical rationalists assumed that valid possibilities and fantastic ones had the same status, these philosophers could not state why just the valid possibilities defined an object. If all possible experience had the same status, they could not characterize any object as "fully determinate" (1 : 356–60). Neglecting to analyze possibility, critical rationalism also failed to account for the individuality of objects. These deficiencies led Royce to an idea of the real world which embodied more than finite ideas and defined individuality in its uniqueness.

If an idea selected its referent and determined the correspondence of idea and referent, how, Royce had asked, were error and non-tautological knowledge conceivable? The answer guaranteed the truth of his position: they were conceivable only if the referent fully embodied the purpose which the idea imperfectly and partially fulfilled and if both idea and object were part of a conscious whole. The dialectical argument assured this, although the result was not absolute thought. The external meaning of an idea was the "fully determinate" purpose of the "fragmentary" internal meaning:

the finally determinate form of the object of any finite idea is that form *which the idea itself would assume whenever it became individuated, or in other words, became a completely determined idea, an idea or will fulfilled by a wholly adequate empirical content, for which no other content need be substituted or, from the point of view of the satisfied idea, could be substituted. . . .* [W]ere not only some, but all possible, instances that could illustrate your idea, or that could give it embodiment, now present, even at this very instant, and to your clear consciousness, what would you experience? I answer, first, *the complete fulfilment of your internal meaning,* the final satisfaction of the will embodied in the idea; but secondly, also, *that absolute determination of the embodiment of your ideas as this embodiment would then be present,—that absolute determination of your purpose, which would constitute an individual realization of the idea* (1 : 337–38).

Objects were ideas of the absolute, that appreciative realm where ideas possessed complete internal meanings and realized true purposes just as (finite) internal meanings realized instantaneous purposes (1 : 324–31):

just what the internal meaning already imperfectly but consciously is, namely, purpose relatively fulfilled, just that, and nothing else, the apparently external meaning when truly comprehended also proves to be, namely the entire expression of the very will that is fragmentarily embodied in the life of the flying conscious idea,— the fulfilment of the very aim that is hinted in the instant (1 : 36).

Imagining a melody fulfilled an instantaneous purpose to imagine the melody. Similarly, the moment of divine experience expressed and realized an infinite purpose which from our perspective was the world of objects our ideas sought to know. Royce proved his ideas the same way he had for fifteen years, but his detailed formulation described more clearly the "conscious whole" of which we were a part.

Possible Experience

Even if Royce did not include James among the critical rationalists, James often saw that the issue between him and Royce hinged on their doctrines of possible experience. In *Pragmatism*, he exclaimed that their religious clash was "over the validity of possibility."[4] He argued forcibly against Royce in a letter written a few months before publication of volume one of *The World and the Individual* and the attack on critical rationalism.

The idealistic principle, James said, demanded only that where there was no knowing, there was no fact—that is, no experience—and that as far as we found experience we found knowing. When Royce spoke of valid possible experience, he ignored the principle; he accepted unknown experience. Then he concluded that because he accepted this experience it could not be unknown and that the absolute must know it. All that the idealist had to argue was that "if a thing can't be shown to be a fact [that is, experience] for any finite consciousness, it is no fact [experience] at all." Royce should not consider valid possible experience. For the idealist it was an unintelligible realm:

> Behind the first knowing actually found, Royce says that you need a second knowing to account for the fact [experience] that it is found. But whose is this knowing? It is that of us critics who discuss the first. We then are the second knower, not the Absolute; and so long as nobody discusses us and knows us as such knowers, there is no higher knower in the field. If, later, we proceed to talk about the "fact" of our second knowing, then we should be third knowers, and so on ad infinitum, but no Absolute Knower would ever logically be required.

James confronted the problem in a sophisticated form. He must translate talk of possible experience into more perspicacious language. He hinted that we should not speak of new, non-actual entities at all, but say something new about old actual entities. We should define the possible by means of relations among the actual. He suggested the difficult step of constructing the world through actual experience. In what respect, James asked, could you call an actual egg a "possible chicken"?

> "Possible chicken" is only one way of naming "actual egg" by a mind that considers present and future things together. If there be no such mind, then there is no status for the possibility as such. We have no business to say, with Professor Royce, that since for us discussing critics the possibility is objectively there, the Absolute Mind must be there to support it. What is there in the universe itself apart from us, is the egg—nothing more—and later, the

chicken; distinct facts which may perfectly well be realized in successive steps, each one of which may be a fresh surprise to the learner.[5]

Discussing the same question later, James maintained that, pragmatically, to speak of possibilities is only to speak of the absence of grounds for preventing a thing as well as the actuality of some of the conditions for producing the thing.[6] For James, analyzing possible experience entailed the appropriate construal of the structure of actual experience, not investigation of metaphysical entities.

Both James and Royce equated the possible with the actual. For Royce there was actual experience that none of us experienced—valid possible experience, some of the experiences of the absolute. James ruled out these possible experiences—the possible did not transcend the actual experiences of finite beings. He dismissed experience unverifiable for us.[7] Whatever Royce said of possible experience (defined in the absolute) transcending actual experience (of finite beings), James found the sole value of this transcendence in finite experience: transcendence could only be "known-as" certain actual experience for us.[8] Here we can connect the argument with the dispute over truth. Royce said that in order to justify claims to truth we required possible experience beyond what we experienced and different from human experience. On the contrary, James said, we defined the truth relation by the structure of actual experience to which acting on ideas led us.[9]

To meet James, Royce must show that the pragmatist account of truth failed when stated in this way. He first argued as others had: in his popular *Philosophy of Loyalty* he criticized James for the individual emphasis in his analysis. Royce largely agreed with James. The assertion of truth was a deed, Royce said, "a practical attitude, an active acknowledgement. . . . the effort to verify this acknowledgement by one's own personal experience and the attempt to find truth in the form of practical congruity between our assertions and our attained empirical results, is an effort which in our individual lives inevitably accompanies and sustains our every undertaking in the cause of truth seeking." Royce declared that "all search for truth is a practical activity, with an ethical purpose . . . a purely theoretical truth, such as should guide no significant active process, is a barren absurdity."

A true idea was practically and genuinely successful. But could we define 'success' as what was successful for an individual? Suppose a man was secretly indebted to someone dead, and suppose he testified about the deceased's estate. We did not need to ask what this man's moral duty was, but simply "what it is that he rationally means to do in case he really intends to tell the truth?" The man was not trying to predict the consequences which he expected to result from his testimony. Nor would his statement's truth be equivalent to the expediency or success of the consequences—either to himself or others—that might follow the statement; nor did his belief in the statement or its congruence with his present memories define its truth.

Asserting that something was true, Royce said, meant something different from all of the above. If 'true' meant 'expedient' then it was redundant to ask "That's expedient but is it true?" But this question was not redundant; designating a belief as expedient gave "just a scrap of your personal biography." To define 'truth' in this way defined what "we all alike regard as the attitude of one who chooses *not* to tell the truth." The contrast between James's doctrine and an adequate theory "is not between intellectualism and pragmatism. It is the contrast between two well-known attitudes of will—the will that is loyal to truth as an universal ideal—and the will that is concerned with its own passing caprices."[10]

However crudely and dramatically James sometimes stated his theory, this criticism, as Royce himself realized, was equally crude.[11] A more sympathetic although still inadequate account of James stressed that true statements were not merely verified by an individual. They were statements that others had verified or would verify. Some statements were true because they would be verified "in the long run," although they were not verified now. Royce's most formidable analysis attacked this formulation of Jamesean pragmatism.

In his previous condemnation of the critical rationalists' account of possible experience, Royce had emphasized that we did not verify some possible experience, although we might have. Now he concentrated on related issues: what did we do with statements whose truth depended on the experiences of others? and what was the status of those statements which were theoretically unverifiable, which it was logically impossible for any human knower to verify, given our conception of a human knower? James said that we accepted the verifications of others. Did the totality of men's experience then exist? If so, how, on Jamesean grounds, could we claim that statement true? James said a statement might be true because we assumed it verifiable in the long run. Would "the long run" then verify a statement? If so, how, on Jamesean grounds, were we able to claim that statement true? Royce contended that if James was correct, these statements must be true, but that on Jamesean grounds we could never ascertain their truth.[12]

Examine the assertion, "The testing of ideas by the course of experience as pragmatism presupposes actually takes place." Suppose it was true; if pragmatism was philosophically justifiable, the statement should be verified or verifiable. Yet it was logically impossible for any individual or group of individuals to verify the statement or for it to be verifiable for human individuals or groups of them. Royce assumed that it was improper to call an experience verifiable if it was inconceivable that anyone could verify it. James dealt not with unactualized possibilities that someone could verify, like the cow in the field, but with possible experience that no human knower could have. No man could experience the experience of anyone but himself; he could not verify the experiences of others; nor could he now verify that he had verified something in the past or would do so in the future.[13] But the unverifiable statement had to be true if pragmatism was true. We could be pragmatists only "by constantly presupposing certain assertions about experience, about the order of the interrelations, the significance, and the unity of empirical facts, to be true, although their truth is never verified and could not be verified, in James's sense of an empirical test, at any moment of our experience." Royce concluded that Jamesean pragmatism accounted for how human beings sought truth, but it demanded other truths for which it could not account.[14]

Although we never experienced the unity of experience required by pragmatism, Royce interpreted this fact not as a "defect in the truth, but as a defect in our present state of knowledge, a limitation due to our present type of individuality." Concepts like the objectively real world were constructs, determined by our desire to conform to an absolute standard, but they always went beyond what we could verify.[15]

Suppose we were wrong, that our constructions erred:

Then there is still real that state of facts, whatever it is, which, if just now known to us, would show us this falsity of our various special ideas. Now, only an experience, a consciousness of some system of contents, could show the falsity of any idea. Hence this real state of facts, this constitution of the genuine universe, whatever it is, must again be a reality precisely in so far as it is also a conspectus of facts of experience. . . . For I am in error only in case my present ideas about the true facts of the whole world of experience are out of concord with the very meaning that I myself actively try to assign to these ideas. My ideas are in any detail false, only if the very experience to which I mean to appeal, contains in its conspectus contents which I just now imperfectly conceive. In any case, then, the truth is possessed by precisely that whole of experience which I never get, but to which my colleague also inevitably appeals when he talks of the "long run," or of the experiences of humanity in general.[16]

The possibility of error still ensured the existence of the absolute. In short, Royce accepted James's pragmatism to the extent he did because he saw its outcome as absolute idealism or, as he came to call it, absolute pragmatism.*

Royce could also escape the weaknesses inherent in James's stress on the individual and offer a positive account of the nature of other minds. He admitted that we never directly experienced other individuals, but unlike the critical rationalist, Royce justified using the experiences of others. Other minds were constructs explaining what would otherwise be inexplicable:

Our fellows are known to be real, and to have their own inner life, because they are for each of us the endless treasury of *more ideas*. They answer our questions; they tell us news; they make comments; they pass judgments; they express novel combinations of feelings; they relate to us stories; they argue with us, and take counsel with us.

*In EV (pp. 27–50) Münsterberg made many of the same arguments against James. He was correct in stressing the relation of truth to our wills and a useful opponent of the materialist content with the causal world alone. But James's own relativism about truth, said Münsterberg, was self-refuting. See the discussion in chapter 11 above.

We were faced with ideas that we could not explain as our own ideas; we postulated that they signalled the presence of other minds. In metaphysical language, since my fellows supplemented my ideas, they supplemented my fragmentary purposes. But what helped to complete my finite purposes was truly real and had an appreciative reality.[17]

Royce, James, and Bradley

At this point theoretical discussion reached a dead end. James responded again that neither he nor anyone else could guarantee the truth of a theory:

> The transcendental idealist thinks that, in some inexplicable way, the finite states of mind are identical with the transfinite all-knower which he finds himself obliged to postulate in order to supply a *fundamentum* for the relation of knowing, as he apprehends it. Pragmatists can leave the question of identity open; but they cannot do without the wider knower any more than they can do without the reality, if they want to *prove* a case of knowing. They themselves play the part of the absolute knower for the universe of discourse which serves them as material for epistemologizing. They warrant the reality there, and the subject's true knowledge, there, of it. But whether what they themselves say about that whole universe is objectively true, *i.e.*, whether the pragmatic theory of truth is true *really*, they cannot warrant,—they can only believe it. To their hearers they can only propose it, as I *propose* it to my readers.

Royce's dialectic attempted to secure knowledge that we could not have. James's doctrine was "something to be verified *ambulando*, or by the way in which its consequences may confirm it."[18]

Although the dispute was insoluble, the two men agreed on fundamentals. Royce urged that James's view was incomplete and that the absolute had to supplement it. Without believing that his view was incomplete, James accepted Royce's idea that both had no argument concerning the finite aspects of knowing. To James, his own view was adequate, but he happily acknowledged that the monist could throw his absolute around the pragmatic conception. Royce, James contended, had done just this, and he hoped to persuade Francis Herbert Bradley, the English absolutist, to adopt the same tactic.[19]

Bradley played a fascinating role in locating the differences between James and Royce. In *The World and the Individual* Royce had conducted a long argument with Bradley. Both men thought that the unification of finite experience occurred in the absolute. Bradley had continued that how the absolute effected this was insoluble for us: the absolute transcended self-consciousness and we could not understand how individuals were *aufgehoben* into it. Against Bradley, Royce had to explain how the absolute unified finite creatures and to define the type of self-consciousness it had. To answer Bradley Royce studied the foundations of mathematics, and we shall explore this aspect of his thought later, but in Bradley's agnosticism James saw the promotion of pragmatism.

James denied the absolute's existence because it generated insoluble moral problems. Bradley affirmed its existence, but also affirmed that we could not make sense of its nature or our relation to it. In short, Bradley's conception was so minimal that if he would adopt pragmatism to the extent that Royce had, the Englishman's "absolute idealism" would be almost identical to Jamesean pragmatism.

So, in a series of letters written from 1904 to 1909, James berated Bradley for not allying himself with the pragmatists and cryptically implored him to turn over a new leaf. "The thought of you in the wilderness of error," James finally wrote in exasperation to a bewildered Bradley, "is intolerable" "when you are so near to becoming the Moses that can lead your people out."[20] Bradley never realized that James saw in him the means of a philosophical rapprochement between Jamesean idealism and Roycean pragmatism.

16

JAMES AND ROYCE:
PUBLIC PHILOSOPHY
1902-1912

Priorities in the Golden Age

The battle of the absolute did not end when James and Royce could not agree on technical issues. Throughout the first decade of the century each developed his moral and religious philosophy and applied it to practical problems, communicating the results to audiences outside the academy. Perhaps they could win converts to their alternative forms of pragmatism not only by theorizing but also by using theory to understand man's place in the world; in any event the philosopher had a public duty to speculate on real-life problems. In fact, the illumination that technical expertise shed on less arcane matters justified philosophy for James and Royce, and measured the worth of the technical.

James on Religion

The Will to Believe and Other Essays in Popular Philosophy, published in 1897, assembled various addresses in which James had made his philosophical attitude—James's pragmatism was not a doctrine in 1897—relevant to human life. A more substantial attempt was his 1902 *The Varieties of Religious Experience*. This volume contained James's Gifford Lectures delivered two years after Royce's. The book was immediately successful, and commentators have long recognized it as a classic in the psychology of religion but, more significantly, it defended religious conviction on Jamesean grounds.

James first described the religious propensities. To be religious, he declared, was to believe in a potent unseen order and to be willing to put ourselves at the mercy of this force greater-than-ourselves because our supreme good lay in adjustment to it. Many persons held beliefs of this kind because they claimed to have directly apprehended "quasi-sensible realities" which immediately grounded their beliefs (39–75). This sort of religious experience was not the only kind, but James wanted to show that experience verified some individuals' religion in much the same way that experience verified other people's ordinary empirical beliefs. More generally, the book outlined various kinds of religious experience, that is, experience that grounded belief for individuals, and examined the forms of religious consciousness to which the experiences gave rise. In this context James elaborated his distinction between the religion of the healthy-minded (for whom all was benign and the universe in tune) and that of the sick soul (for whom the awful shadow of death and extinction palled over all life).[1]

James's interest was not merely typological. The crucial religious claim, for both James and those whom he investigated, concerned the unseen world's reality. People accepted religious dogma not because it was emotionally satisfying in any narrow sense, but because they believed it to be true (291). Alluding to Royce's *World and the Individual*, James said the usual philosophic treatments of God's existence failed: they did not convince people that God is (329–37). For James, the difficulty was that most philosophic proofs of God did not affect our lives. The essence of religion lay not in an abstract theological formulation, but in the promise of the richer and more satisfying lives we lived because we were assured that a force greater than ourselves also fought our moral battles (381–83). Royce's "religion" lacked the core of true religion—a sense of the help religion could give us in the living of life. Briefly put, the philosophy of religion had proved superfluous to common men (338–46).

James argued that traditional philosophic theology was neither necessary nor sufficient to justify religion. For this reason he was interested in individuals who had perceptual experience justifying their religion. The most extreme experiences of this sort, mystical ones, were authoritative on good empirical grounds for those who had them. Although they were not authoritative for others, their existence destroyed the sole authority of non-mystical, "rational" evidence for establishing truth claims (323–38). James's idea also explained his long-time concern for psychical research: in part, it investigated the possibility of spirit deeper than finite consciousness and the way in which we might participate in or communicate with this spirit. Finally, his reasoning cohered with his view of the recent findings of psychology: the subliminal realm of consciousness and the whole notion of the unconscious pointed to the shading off of individual consciousness into a wider realm of consciousness. This wider realm might be that of the higher spiritual powers, influencing human existence, that religion demanded.[2]

In the *Varieties* James was playing with the notion of truth he would soon call pragmatic. On a suitable definition of truth we could justify a living religion and not an irrelevant philosophers' creed. The criteria for determining the truthfulness of a belief, James contended early on, were its immediate luminousness, philosophical reasonableness, and moral helpfulness. We accepted as true beliefs that, first, were verifiable and, then, coincided with our moral needs and with the rest of what we held to be true (32). In undeveloped form, James had set forth his view of truth and made his judgment about the truth of religion on its basis.

Religion as a hypothesis, he said, was true insofar as it worked and gave value to existence. But beliefs also essentially referred to existing higher powers. Consequently, a religious creed was true if the demands made by the higher powers created a real effect when we fulfilled them. For the deity to exist was only for us to behave differently on earth because of his existence; if we behaved differently we had evidence for this belief.* A pragmatic argument on such a scale, James concluded, characterized not merely a belief but what he called an overbelief, a perspective on the universe (383–91).

Many of the essays that James wrote on these questions after the *Varieties* eventually appeared in *Pragmatism*. They made it clear that his intent in developing his theory of knowledge was to provide a rationale for a

---

*In his epistemology James vacillated between defining truth as a certain kind of satisfactoriness and postulating an object to which satisfactions must be true. This same vacillation arose in his discussion of God: God existed if we achieved certain satisfactions, but at the same time James hinted that the object must cause these satisfactions if we were truly to say that God existed.

more vital religion than that offered by Roycean absolutism. Monistic religion tended to encourage passivity; Jamesean religion was activist, a creed compatible with the moral life.

Pragmatism made James's scientific and moral postulates consistent: it analyzed the truth of all beliefs by means of their working values in experience, and overcame the dualism between the world of science and that of Royce's absolute. Simultaneously it allowed James to defend a "meliorist" religious position: to believe in God was to believe that there was a spiritual force greater than we were. Allied with this force, we would secure some vaguely defined benefits to all mankind and assure some meaning to life beyond the grave.[3] This view admitted that evil existed, although it might be rationally inexplicable. But evil was not necessary: concerted human effort could overcome it. For James, to believe in God went a long way toward making the belief true. If we acted on the belief, the world would probably become better, and this was exactly the evidence needed to corroborate our belief. We provided the necessary human push to secure the triumph of a melioristic god over evil.[4]

This justification of religion picked up themes that James cherished in the 1880s and 1890s, but they were now part of an epistemology that he could defend against Royce. (As we shall also see, he framed them within a pluralistic metaphysics that he could defend against monism.) Because he was the sort of pragmatist he was, however, James conceded that Roycean absolutism in religion had fruitful consequences for human experience and was true for *so much*. Absolutism could give us a romantic sense of cosmic well-being:

> What do believers in the Absolute mean by saying that their belief affords them comfort? They mean that since, in the Absolute finite, evil is "overruled" already, we may, therefore, whenever we wish, treat the temporal as if it were potentially the eternal, be sure that we can trust its outcome, and, without sin, dismiss our fear and drop the worry of our finite responsibility. In short, they mean that we have a right ever and anon to take a moral holiday, to let the world wag in its own way, feeling that its issues are in better hands than ours and are none of our business. The universe is a system of which the individual members may relax their anxieties occasionally, in which the don't-care mood is also right for men,

and moral holidays in order—that, if I mistake not, is part, at least, of what the Absolute is 'known-as,' that is the great difference in our particular experiences which his being true makes, for us, that is his cash-value when he is pragmatically interpreted.

James continued, however, that a belief had to survive the gauntlet of our other beliefs, and this notion permitted him to reject Royce's monism:

> as I conceive it,—and let me speak now confidentially, as it were, and merely in my own private person,—it clashes with other truths of mine whose benefits I hate to give up on its account. It happens to be associated with a kind of logic of which I am the enemy, I find that it entangles me in metaphysical paradoxes that are unacceptable, etc., etc. But as I have enough trouble in life already without adding the trouble of carrying these intellectual inconsistencies, I personally just give up the Absolute. I just *take* my moral holidays; or else as a professional philosopher, I try to justify them by some other principle. If I could restrict my notion of the Absolute to its bare holiday-giving value, it wouldn't clash with any other truth. But we can not easily thus restrict our hypotheses. They carry supernumerary features, and these it is that clash so. My disbelief in the Absolute means then disbelief in these other supernumerary features, for I fully believe in the legitimacy of taking moral holidays.[5]

James was most persuasive in his discussion of the absolutist view of evil, which became more and more a sticking point for him. Evil was explicable but necessary for Royce. The absolute guaranteed the triumph of goodness in the universe, but Royce consequently defined goodness as the overwhelming of evil, sometimes in our finite experience, always in that of the absolute. On one hand, knowledge of the victory over evil allowed moral holidays. On the other, James found it repugnant that Royce comprehended the unspeakable horrors of human existence—the suffering and death that surround us—in a few pages of dialectic logic.[6] The gravamen of James's charge was that absolute idealism solved the problem of evil grotesquely and, moreover, might sanction passivity in the face of evil—it might allow too many moral holidays. James justified a different sort of religion, the sort that reflected the sense of the educated laymen: it was activist and meliorist.*

Royce's Religious Philosophy

Royce's commitment to absolute idealism made it possible for him to accept the dualism James disliked. For Royce, it was a product of our finitude, and the World of Description merely an aspect of the World of Appreciation. Reconciling science and religion was, moreover, easy enough for him because he postulated that evolution only displayed the absolute in a limited spatio-temporal form. But he also had to show that his religion did not take a shallow view of evil and could be a fighting faith. With the second of these issues, Royce's *Philosophy of Loyalty* achieved a notable success; with the first he struggled until his death.

In 1906 Royce traveled to the University of Illinois to lecture on ethics. The talks initiated his mature attempt at a moral philosophy that was activist but also consistently monistic. Conduct was right or wrong, Royce said, and "the general doctrine of values" formulated the basis of this distinction. An evaluation was an act of will. As facts in the world, these acts all had the same kind of value. In a hypothetical debate with a head-hunter over the goodness of taking his life, Royce said that as far as they both had a "rational consciousness" of human values, he and the head-hunter recognized each other's valuation as facts:

> Herewith, however, I state a sort of first principle of ethics,—a crude principle I admit, but a principle. All sincere valuations of things, by whomsoever made, are themselves facts having value. Whoever wills anything,—that will has its own value. Whoever wants to know the values of things must take account of all values that any will sets upon things. . . . what, in an impersonal sense, is objectively worth doing, depends as much and of course as little upon his private valuation as upon mine. Now just this sort of truth is the sort of truth that we recognize whenever we deal with men dispassionately, justly, fairly.[7]

Could we harmonize these wills? Suppose we adopted some plan which

*As always, James's critique was tentative: he admitted the importance of providing, as Royce had, an explanation of evil. See VRE, pp. 114–16, 138–39.

might change the lives of two moral opponents but would enable each to carry out his "essential will." This situation "possesses more objective value" than the former situation: the cooperation of wills was ipso facto better than their conflict. This was a second principle. In the debate with the head-hunter Royce might alter the conduct of the former's tribe in the direction of customs prevalent "in a well-regulated company of civilized gentlemen." The head-hunter might remain Royce's enemy but obtain the prestige he achieved through head-hunting by victory in philosophical debate or quest for political office. The alteration would satisfy the head-hunter and Royce would retain his head. Believing as did many in his culture that historical change was progress, Royce argued that history offered us examples of the increased harmony of human wills. The evolution from barbarism to civilization had been morally good. In 1906 everyone carried out his purposes with less conflict than was necessary when men were savages. War had given way to commerce, and men gained prestige in peace rather than war.[8]

Royce's two principles were essential for achieving harmony. We might first apply the principles to bring tranquility to the self. We would admit our valuations, present and future, as equally worthy of regard; we would devise a plan to bring them all into concert. That plan of living would be the best way to live, considering the individual alone. This plan of life, a man's ideal, defined the finite self as a moral creature. As in "The Conception of God" and *The World and the Individual*, the true self was a dynamic structure, a conscious life lived according to a plan. But the Urbana Lectures examined which individuals achieved the greatest harmony and what "life styles" brought about the greatest social harmony. Royce investigated the types of personal ideals, the distinctive sorts of selfhood.

Royce philosophized in a Hegelian style, assuming that history demonstrated progress. He analyzed four personality types arranged in an evolutionary order. Each one represented in turn a chronologically more recent kind of self; and each one in turn was, in what I would call its logical development, superior in gaining self-harmony.[9]

The first of Royce's four types was the heroic or stately self whose deeds compelled a community's admiration. Whenever the stately self became prominent as an ideal type, a culture emphasized socially serviceable righteousness. Although this type embodied worthwhile elements,

Royce contended that it could not be an ethical ideal. The hero's success depended on fortune, strength, and the praise of the world. But intuition told us that they were not essential to moral goodness. Consequently, the stately self could not guide us in achieving universal harmony: it was an ideal whose conditions were extraneous to exemplary moral behavior.

Passing to the saintly or self-denying self, Royce argued that we valued this ideal because of its sacrifices: it abandoned worldly goods and sought resignation. This ideal evolved out of the realization that the ethically valuable rose above fortune, and led to the view that renunciation defined the self. Although Royce valued this insight, he saw it as partial. From our notion that moral goodness transcended circumstance, we might also conclude that defiance determined the ideal self; it learned from the wreck of fortune to value the "unconquerable soul." This titanic or defiant self was Royce's third personality type, but he did not accept it as ultimate. The stately self wed virtue to social triumph; it was inadequate because it made social position and not merely the social order essential to moral worth. The saintly self wrongly assumed that social triumph had no place in virtue. And the titanic self mistakenly asserted that the social order itself was unnecessary for the ethical ideal.

Royce found the ideal in the fourth personality type, the loyal self. It synthesized the insights of the previous three, relying on society without sacrificing individual expression.[10] In this context Royce wrote and lectured on his famous philosophy of loyalty, detailing the importance of his fourth personality type.

The loyal individual of *The Philosophy of Loyalty* was willingly, practically, and thoroughly devoted to a cause. The devotion of a patriot to his country, a martyr to his religion, and a robber to his band, exemplified loyalty, but Royce stressed that more common situations also illustrated loyalty—the father's love for his family, the businessman's allegiance to his firm (16–17). In fact, Royce packed into his definition of cause all he needed to make the loyal personality an adequate ideal. To the loyal person the cause was objective, that is, it served more than the individual's self-interests. But the cause was not impersonal; the interests beyond one's own were those of other people, that is, the interests were social. Finally, the cause of the loyal self did not just collect the interests of separate individuals. The cause involved a social unity:

you can be loyal only to a tie that binds you and others into some sort of unity, and loyal to individuals only through the tie. The cause to which loyalty devotes itself has always this union of the personal and the seemingly super-individual about it. It binds many individuals into one service (19–20).

"Where there is an object of loyalty," Royce wrote, "there is . . . [a] union of various selves into one life" (52).

The loyal person achieved tranquility by ordering his desires as loyalty to a cause demanded. The cause preserved morality's social aspect without compromising individuality. Royce hinted that loyalty mediated between the worlds of description and appreciation. How could we fulfill ourselves—express our own appreciative consciousness—in the external world? Our "divided being," he declared, "demands reconciliation with itself"; it had "one long struggle for unity." Its inner and outer realms naturally warred, and only loyalty reconciled them (124–26).

The Philosophy of Loyalty enunciated Royce's principle of "loyalty to loyalty" as the criterion for determining choices among conflicting causes. We should increase loyalty in the world and prevent its destruction. Although any loyalty was good, causes competed, and the principle of loyalty to loyalty yielded a means for resolving disputes (116–22). But Royce reckoned that we must judge the loyalty of others circumspectly. We best applied his "general guiding maxim for conduct" to conflicts of personal loyalties, and even there it offered only a general guide, and could not prescribe specific courses of action (162–66). He also introduced loyalty to loyalty to explain how an individual guided his choice "insofar as he considers not merely his own supreme good, but that of mankind." Here Royce returned to his concern of the Urbana Lectures. He examined the loyal personality not only because it achieved individual harmony, but also because it best contributed to that cooperation of wills that had ultimate value. "Loyalty to loyalty" secured "the greatest possible increase of loyalty amongst men," and was the "supreme good" of mankind (121).

Consider the truth seeker in this context. Whoever spoke of truth presupposed a spiritually unified world whose consciousness was higher than that of individual minds. The world of truth was a world similar to that in which the loyal believed when they believed their cause was real. This world of truth also had a goodness about it like that which the loyal attributed to their causes. "Truth seeking and loyalty," Royce concluded, "are therefore essentially the same process of life merely viewed in two different aspects." The loyal individual served a cause he thought true. The truth seeker—Royce often had in mind the natural scientist—was serving a cause which unified life upon some higher level than the human level. The scientist's work implied the union of his experiences with those of the scientific community. The activity of the scientist was moral, and he was loyal (313–15). This view of truth, Royce maintained, "meets at once an ethical and a logical need" (376). This vaguely stated the relation of the technical and practical, and the way in which the scientist's World of Description was really a World of Appreciation. But Royce muted the science-religion controversy in *The Philosophy of Loyalty*. Its main task was to show that the self was an ethical concept unifying instincts, passions, and interests around a central set of purposes; that in its highest form this union involved loyalty; and that loyalty permitted the self to express its individuality and simultaneously to contribute to its social order (167–79).

The Philosophy of Loyalty demarcated ethics and religion. Moral philosophy defined the moral life and showed why it was the best life. This Royce accomplished after he delineated the loyal personality type and examined how it provided for harmonizing human wills. When he explored the spiritual unities that loyalty presupposed, he did something more. In 1908, relating loyalty to these spiritual unities, he formulated a religion "to help out one's ethics":

> Purely practical considerations, then, a study of our human needs, an ideal of the business of life,—these inevitably lead us into a region which is more than merely a realm of moral activities. This region is either one of delusion or else one of spiritual realities of a level higher than is that of our present individual human experience (355).

This "region of spiritual realities" constituted the religious nature of existence.

With this region in mind, Royce refined his "inadequate" definition of loyalty. Loyalty not only guided our moral lives but also connected us to an everlasting and embracing spiritual unity. Rightly conceived, loyalty manifested an eternal will—a conscious and superhuman unity of being—

in the life of finite persons (356–57). Religion made loyalty comprehensible by appealing to the emotions and to the imagination. It interpreted the "world-life" symbolically (377). In this context Royce redefined the problem of evil in religious language, in terms of salvation or attaining our goal of harmony. Alluded to briefly in *The Philosophy of Loyalty* (394–96), the notion provided the framework for Royce's 1911 Bross Lectures published in 1912 as *The Sources of Religious Insight*.

The definitions Royce gave to the words in his title captured the aim of *The Sources of Religious Insight*. Insight was knowledge making us aware of the unity of many facts in one whole. The point of religious knowledge was man's salvation, for Royce specified man's need to be saved as religion's fundamental concern: religion's interest was "in freeing mankind from some vast and universal burden, of imperfection, of unreasonableness, of evil, of misery, of fate, of unworthiness, or of sin." This idea hung on two simpler ones: first, that human life had some ultimate end; second, that man "*as he naturally is*" was in danger of missing this end and making his life a senseless failure (5–12).

The Sources of Religious Insight investigated man's struggle to reach his highest goal when it appeared that man would lose the battle, and Royce made it clear that the world's evil threatened human success. What was puzzling were his statements that evil imperilled salvation. His analysis of the ultimate value in life was not surprising:

> We need to give life sense, to know and to control our own selves, to end the natural chaos, to bring order and light into our deeds, to make the warfare of natural passion subordinate to the peace and power of the spirit. This is our need. To live thus is our ideal. And because this need is pressing and this ideal is far off from the natural man, we need salvation (31).

> We are naturally creatures of wavering and conflicting motives, passions, desires. The supreme aim of life is to triumph over this natural chaos, to set some one plan of life above all the others, to give unity to our desires, to organize our activities, to win, not indeed, the passionless peace of nirvana, but the strength of spirit which is above the narrowness of each one of our separate passions. We need to conceive of such a triumphant and unified life, and suc-

cessfully to live it. That is our goal: Self-possession, unity, peace,
and spiritual power through and yet beyond all the turmoil of life—
the victory that overcometh in the world (44–45).

The dialectical argument proved that mankind reached this goal and
was saved. Since Royce repeated the argument in *The Sources of Religious
Insight*, he apparently did not question achieving the goal. Since 1885 his
problem had been reconciling the necessity of harmony's triumph with
the world's evil. In urging that we must "hope" for salvation (220–25),
he implied that we could no longer rely on the absolute. His premise that
"damnation" for the species was possible recast the context in which he
examined the problem of evil. It did so, however, only by pretending that
we doubted the basic truth.

Another element of *The Sources of Religious Insight* also merits comment. In part, Royce wrote it to answer *The Varieties of Religious Experience*. Royce took that book to argue that we justified religion because it
explained otherwise inexplicable personal needs and feelings. For Royce
this view made religion non-rational, and watered down doctrine to
vague emotions whose foundation was individual intuition. *The Sources
of Religious Insight* salvaged religion based on reason and metaphysical
truth. Of course, James felt that the alternative to his approach was the
"abstract" theorizing he associated with Royce, and the abstraction James
had in mind was Royce's absolute. Royce's "block universe," James held,
was inadequate for capturing religious experience. *The Sources of Religious
Insight* posed another alternative:

> Must one choose between inarticulate faith and barren abstractions?
> Must one face the alternative: Either intuition without reasoning,
> or else relatively fruitless analysis without intuition? Perhaps there
> is a third possibility. Perhaps one may use one's process of ab-
> straction as a sort of preparation for certain articulate and noble
> intuitions that cannot be approached, by our human sort of con-
> sciousness, through any other way. Perhaps analysis is not the
> whole process which determines demonstrations. Perhaps synthesis
> —the viewing of many facts or principles or relations in some
> sort of unity and wholeness—perhaps a synoptic survey of various
> articulate truths, can lead us to novel insights. In that case inarticu-
> late intuitions and barren abstractions are not the only instru-

ments between which we must choose. For in that case there will be another sort of aid, a more explicit sort of intuition, a more considerate view of our life and its meaning, which we may adopt, and which may lead us to novel results (89–90).

By the time Royce wrote this, he had redefined the foundation of his thought. He had gone so far that he may have rejected the dichotomy between description and appreciation. *The Sources of Religious Insight* merely claimed that there was knowledge other than the experience of the data of sense or feeling and the analysis of abstract ideas. It is impossible to know what Royce meant precisely or how much further he was prepared to go. Since he would not discourse on logic, he said he could not indicate what we could accomplish through this source of insight (89–93). At the center of his system were technical and complex issues which he could not talk about in a popular lecture series. But, as we should expect, he mentioned that they rested on the "revision and transformation of the Kantian theory of knowledge" (123–24).

These two themes—the existence of the absolute and Royce's alternative to James's dichotomy—came together in the discussion of reason. Reason was a source of religious insight because it showed us that life's goal was attained in a higher unity. The argument from the possibility of error demonstrated that "a superhuman type of life is a real fact in the world" (102) and was a paradigmatic religious insight. The novelty of this exposition described his "wider insight" as "*an all-seeing comprehension of facts as they are*" (114). It exemplified the third kind of knowledge that Royce offered as an alternative to James's division between the "non-rational" and "abstract." Although this tertium quid was important, Royce did not discuss its difference from the appreciative absolute of his earlier works. *The Sources of Religious Insight* simply concluded that the "new" absolute justified our religious interest. The need for salvation must be met although, as I have indicated before, I have not been able to see how we were then in danger of damnation: our salvation was certainly not contingent on a Harvard professor's proving God's existence.

Whatever these complications, we must examine the book's other themes—really extensions of *The Philosophy of Loyalty*. Royce judged that morality and religion were separable and even conflicted. Morality defined man's highest ideal and the best means to attain it. That is, morality directed us to a dutiful life. The desire to be sure of salvation aroused the religious motive:

> It [religion] appeals for help, or waits patiently for the Lord, or rejoices in the presence of salvation. It therefore may assume any one of many different attitudes toward the problem of duty. It may seek salvation through deeds, or again it may not, in the minds of some men, appeal to the active nature in any vigorous way whatever. Some religious moods are passive, contemplative, receptive, adoring rather than strenuous. It is therefore quite consistent with the existence of religious interest to feel suspicious of the dutiful restlessness of many ardent souls (170).

Knowing that we were to be saved, could we not renege on the good fight? Was there a morality, essentially religious, that reconciled the need for salvation with the need for moral action? Was there "a consciousness which equally demanded of those whom it inspired, spiritual attainment and strenuousness, serenity and activity, resignation and vigour, life in the spirit and ceaseless enterprise in service?"

The answer was yes—the religion of loyalty. On one hand, loyal individuals were resolute and had wills of their own; they had social motives, and their faithfulness evidenced what in their eyes was an important calling. On the other hand, their causes linked many lives in unity. Causes were superhuman in the same sense in which the "wider insight" presupposed by the necessity of error was superhuman (197–200).

What about the world's evil, which Royce admitted was dreadfully persistent? How did we reconcile knowledge of the triumph of good with the eternal existence of pain and suffering? Royce said that without real and present evil, religion was trivial. We requested redemption only if "evil is deeply rooted in the very nature of reality"; yet if it was rooted, religion failed (219–27). He approached his problem by stating that our deepest ills could become sources of religious insight; they could bring us knowledge of spiritual truth. Some evils, he said, we assimilated or idealized. This at least meant that we were able to live with them and perhaps triumph over them. Royce also suggested that we "take them up into the plan of our lives, give them meaning, set them in their place in the whole" (235). These evils then would enable us to understand (imperfectly) how the "world-embracing insight" took up into its life evils too terrible for us to bear. They might have places as stages and phases of expression in the larger life to which we belonged. The function of lesser evils might be to give us hints—sources of religious insight—into the way the wider insight incorporated greater evils. Royce spoke of the religious mission of sorrow: when we used the evils in our lives to forge the morally good, sorrow and the overcoming of evil awakened us to what the spiritual realm might be (235–41). God triumphed in the world only if temporal existence was riven with evil. Goodness was not the absence of strife and suffering: it was the triumph over strife and suffering (250–51).

Loyalty was a morality and a religion because there were evils to war against, moral goods to win. Loyalty existed only in a world where the loyal met adversities that changed their lives (252–53). Royce defined loyalty in a context where man faced evil—the trials and tribulations of existence—and devoted himself to overcoming it. Because the loyal personality type was his ideal, it was plausible for Royce to say that "the most rational type of life" demanded the existence of adversity (238). The religion of loyalty became a fount of religious insight.

Sorting out the sources of spiritual knowledge grounded our faith in the triumph of goodness when the finite world contained ineradicable evil. This context created a dilemma in the book. Royce's argument was justifiable on a personal level: a given man might need assurance that loyal effort could result in his own salvation, that his particular failures were eventually made good, and that he was not an evil-doer vanquished in the infinite. Royce made damnation worrisome, however, by intimating that the salvation of the species was dubious. But after he had proved the absolute's existence in 1885, he had assumed that mankind's achievement was positive. The absolute's existence was unassuring only if we doubted mankind's salvation, only if we construed the species as an evil overwhelmed in God. Although the interpretation is labored and requires a more precise definition of salvation than Royce gave, this may be the nub of his discussion. Perhaps both the individual and the species were damned. But because the absolute existed, we hoped that both were positive elements in experience and that we could justify moral effort.

Because it was logically necessary that the world be perfect and that evil exist, Royce's position still involved an awful tension: he had to explain why this "best of possible worlds" contained evil.[11] James and others were not convinced that Royce had in part justified some finite evils by saying that they helped us to understand the inexplicable and unutterable horrors of existence. Was a perfect world one in which bearable evils explained the unbearable?

Social and Political Philosophy

Although public philosophizing was ultimately important, James and Royce were not social and political thinkers of any stature. There is an argument that classic pragmatism has a peculiar relation to social and political theorizing—those speculative concerns that largely define our understanding of the collective effort of Plato, Hobbes, Locke, Rousseau, Mill, and Marx—and that the pragmatic political philosophy embodies the rationale behind American political liberalism. The writings of the Chicago and Columbia "pragmatists"—including John Dewey, George Herbert Mead, Jane Addams, and Sydney Hook—may give this argument apparent plausibility, but despite the broader interests of Palmer and Müsterberg, the argument does not accurately grasp or appraise the concerns at Harvard.

Charles Peirce was an asocial and apolitical thinker. With Royce and James the situation was more complex. They were eminent at a time when philosophy was much more than an arcane discipline interesting to only a handful of specialists. The professor lecturing on speculative topics still occupied a social role requiring him to perform in an almost ministerial fashion. The educated elite expected "the philosopher"—perhaps still conceived in the style of Emerson—to reassure it about the basic worth of human existence and traditional institutions and to join mild exhortation with a defense of fundamental verities. Because of this demand and because of their own proclivities, both Royce and James popularized their moral and religious ideas. In effect they buttressed with their thought the more critical moral and religious convictions of literate, upper-middle-class America.

George Santayana put it well, if acerbically, when he said of the Harvard philosophers that they had an acute sense of social responsibility "because they were conscientiously teaching and guiding the community, as if they had been clergymen without a church . . . at once genuine philosophers and popular professors." Harvard philosophy, he went on, "represented faithfully the complex inspiration of the place and the hour." James and Royce were "men of intense feeling, religious and romantic, but attentive to the facts of nature and the currents of worldly opinion; and each of them felt himself bound by two different responsibilities, that of describing things as they are, and that of finding them propitious to certain preconceived human desires."[12]

Whatever their concern for ethics and religion, James and Royce gave little time to social and political philosophizing. Their ouptut in these areas was slight, their analyses lacked intellectual substance, and their applications were conventional and often trivial.

It is not immediately obvious that Royce was not seriously interested in social and political matters, for three interrelated themes run through the corpus of his work—an account of the ethical life of the individual, a description of the potentially ethical community, and an investigation of the cohesive bonds within that larger whole. The last two of these themes were often social and political. In his earliest essays, in the 1890s, in the first decade of this century, and in the last years of his life, he raised these issues: they justified philosophizing, and as Royce grew older the social and political dimension became more prominent. Nevertheless, the corpus of his work in the social and political area did not equal that in more recondite areas of philosophy. Moreover, this work represented a small investment of time. He composed the disparate essays on these topics rapidly for diverse public occasions. And they contained no sustained discussion as, say, did *The World and the Individual*. Finally, his ideas do not withstand examination.

The Philosophy of Loyalty contained a chapter titled "Some American Problems in Their Relation to Loyalty." This chapter and a 1908 collection of essays, *Race Questions, Provincialism, and Other American Problems*, constituted the major part of Royce's contribution to social thought. "A familiar charge against idealism," said Royce in the preface to *Race Questions*, was "that it is an essentially unpractical doctrine." He designed these essays, all applying his doctrine and spirit to American life, to rebut the charge of abstractionalism. They all used the concept of loyalty, "the practical aspect and expression of an idealistic philosophy" (v–ix).

Royce's foray into social philosophizing exemplified the inadequacy of this sort of thinking among the Harvard Pragmatists. One central problem troubled him: the breakdown of community in America and the upsurge, on one hand, of a vicious individualism and, on the other, of anomic masses. Royce pressed into service his principle of loyalty to loyalty as a nostrum for social ills. For example, we could transform selfish individualism if labor unions and captains of industry considered larger goods beyond their own immediate interests. If they were loyal to loyalty, their sense of self would enlarge, and by participating in American politics they would contribute to a better life for all and to a healthy individualism.

Royce believed that unhealthy individualism led to the growth of anomic masses. When people narrowly and belligerently defined their interests, the resulting aggregation of people had destructive or irrational loyalties. This type of selfhood corrupted individuals' real selves. The consequence was a nameless, unhappy citizenry. Again Royce suggested that cultivating a helpful loyalty would solve American problems. He promulgated *provincialism* to overcome the individual's sense of isolation in dealing with a distant and perhaps unintelligible national authority. Provincialism was devotion to smaller regional communities, a loyalty to more immediate social and political units. If we could absorb individuals in issues intelligible to them, we would have the basis for true loyalty. Political activity at the provincial level directed toward specific causes would make the plans of reformers meaningful. In atomistic American society reformer-idealists wasted their talents on grandiose plans serving no purpose but to dissipate energies. The province would provide an arena for useful social reform and bring about the substitution of workable projects for the foolish and unrealistic (111–65). The development of wider-ranging loyalties on the example of provincial loyalty could eventually lead to a healthy political life for the nation (57–108).

First of all, Royce's discussion was uncritical: he failed to find a problem in deciding which loyalties were rational, constructive, and healthy, and which were irrational, destructive, and diseased. More importantly, he took refuge in clichés about the nature of man's alienation that have been the currency of social thinkers since Plato. Royce's ideas were not false, but rather trivially true. There was no analysis of the roots of concrete social problems, no examination of the distribution of power that determined the structure of the economy, no concern with the patterns of interest represented by politics, and no grasp of the history of the American political economy. Royce appears to have derived his knowledge of these matters from what he picked up in the press and popular literature; his view was similar to that of many other educated and literate men. He then interpreted it in the light of his metaphysics. The result was comforting but unilluminating, and its importance, for Royce himself, was measured by the time he spent on it and the bulk it occupied in his corpus.

If we look to James as a pragmatist concerned with American life, our expectations also go unfulfilled. To be sure, he was passionately interested in the welfare of individuals. Underpinning his pragmatism was a commitment to creating the widest possible area of freedom in which people could operate. A major priority was defending a religious attitude that individuals could live by, and James identified this attitude with an activist ethic. As he was famous for saying, "the consequence of such a philosophy is the well-known democratic respect for the sacredness of individuality." Whatever the truth of this sentiment, James did not even develop a reasoned account of moral argument, and his social and political philosophy was negligible.

In briefly treating the "labor question," James did mention that the distribution of wealth must slowly change, and he was doubtlessly a sensitive, humane person. But the unhealthiness of the conflict between rich and poor, he said, "consists solely in the fact that one-half of our fellow-countrymen remain entirely blind to the internal significance of the lives of the other half." The historian might find it remarkable that James thought half the population rich, but the crux of his theorizing was simply that the route to social amelioration was sincerely attempting to grasp the inwardness of other individuals, their unique efforts to join some ideal to their peculiar form of dedication. "If the poor and the rich could look at each other in this way, *sub specie aeternitatis*," James concluded, "how gentle would grow their disputes! what tolerance and good humor, what willingness to live and let live, would come into the world!"[13] This was strictly a sentiment for upper-class consumption.

"The Moral Equivalent of War," the famous essay he wrote near the end of his life, is noteworthy as James's only statement on society. It is not even a sketch of a social philosophy, but it is the only hint we have of how he might have applied his concrete theorizing to the affairs of the polis.

It was unfortunate, although perhaps not accidental, that *The Philosophy of Loyalty* repeatedly used the martial virtues as examples of constructive loyalty. Fealty to a cause and the duty, service, and discipline implied in this fealty are all tellingly illustrated in war. And present-day critics of Royce's ethics have noted that acting on his central virtue might justify the horror and fanaticism associated with twentieth-century war. James was aware of this problem in 1910. Like Royce, he estimated courage, valor, and commitment highly, and thought that war inspired some of their finest and most characteristic expressions. Apologists for war, said James, argued that

> its "horrors" are a cheap price to pay for rescue from the only alternative supposed, of a world of clerks and teachers, of co-education and zo-ophily, of "consumers' leagues" and "associated charities," of industrialism unlimited, and feminism unabashed. No scorn, no hardness, no valor any more! Fie upon such a cattleyard of a planet!

and James admitted:

> So far as the central essence of this feeling goes, no healthy minded person, it seems to me, can help to some degree partaking of it. Militarism is the great preserver of our ideals of hardihood, and human life with no use for hardihood would be contemptible. Without risks or prizes for the darer, history would be insipid indeed; and there is a type of military character which every one feels that the race should never cease to breed, for every one is sensitive to its superiority.[14]

"The Moral Equivalent of War" carried discussion past *The Philosophy of Loyalty*. James did not wish merely to support peace but to suggest that we could achieve it only by sublimating the martial spirit, preserving some of its important elements:

> A permanently successful peace-economy cannot be a simple pleasure-economy. In the more or less socialistic future towards which mankind seems drifting we must still subject ourselves collectively to those severities which answer to our real position upon this only partly hospitable globe. We must make new energies and hardihoods continue the manliness to which the military mind so faithfully clings. Martial virtues must be the enduring cement;

intrepidity, contempt of softness, surrender of private interest, obedience to command, must still remain the rock upon which states are built—unless, indeed, we wish for dangerous reactions against commonwealths fit only for contempt, and liable to invite attack whenever a centre of crystallization for military-minded enterprise gets formed anywhere in their neighborhood.[15]

Further than this expression of insight James did not go.

Explaining the Quality of Public Philosophy

The question is why James and Royce pledged their time and intelligence to justifying technical beliefs and not to applying them in the social and political realm.

At the level of personality James's lack of interest, at least, is easily understood: his concern was the individual. The theme of his writing was religion and morality as they pertained to unique personalities. More than anything else James's temperament explained his point of view. We must also remember, however, that the Darwinian controversy, which occupied intellectual energy in the United States, focused on the capacity of individual minds to do more than reflect the order of nature. James successfully defended an active view of mind against the mechanistic and deterministic interpretation of Darwin that Spencer popularized. In this sense the "pragmatism" of James (and of Royce) had implications for social and political thought; its success transformed the framework of intellectual debate in the United States and made it possible for those later interested in social and political thought, for example Walter Lippmann and Herbert Croly, to argue credibly for collective action of one kind or another. But this sort of thinking had a low priority for James himself.[16]

It is more difficult to assess the role of Royce's personality in shaping his political thought. His loneliness and lack of social grace drove him to spend long, solitary hours at technical philosophizing. But he also yearned for a social order that would reconcile him with the others with whom he could not relate, and he did *lecture* audiences on the need for this harmony-creating polity. However one appraises the conflicting demands of his temperament, they did not result in political or social theorizing of merit.

On another level we must explore the speculative orientation and the social milieu to understand the attitudes of the Harvard philosophers. Three philosophical reasons help to explain the dearth of social theory. First, the Harvard Pragmatists had a hierarchical view of the branches of philosophy. Logic, epistemology, and metaphysics were somehow logically prior, providing the rationale or basis for understanding the world. These technical areas of study grounded beliefs in practical areas— moral, religious, social, and political. The study of the technical was worthwhile because it legitimated practical applications: the end of the philosophic enterprise was the use of philosophy in life. This vision resulted in the Harvard Pragmatists occupying themselves with justifying their practical beliefs: this was the paradigm for philosophic speculation. When they employed their ideas, they did so in a particular form. For various reasons—among them the conflict between Darwin and religion and the Emersonian ideal of the philosopher—the areas of application were in religious and ethical philosophy. With greater or lesser success Cambridge speculators joined their philosophic ideas to their personal moral and religious experiences and gave the product to the world. Further down on their list of applied topics was the study of society and politics, and all the philosophers conceived it simply as an extension of the application of ethical and religious philosophy. To the extent they did political and social theory and applied it at all, it was anti-institutional and concerned largely with the amelioration of personal troubles. Practical matters had no independent stature, and public social and political philosophy, like public moral and religious philosophy, dealt with individuals.

A second related philosophical reason was that logic and the physical and natural sciences were the model for philosophizing at Harvard. The exemplars of knowledge were mathematical proofs, deductive inferences, and the results of experimentation in fields like chemistry and biology. Neither Royce nor James thought of *die Geisteswissenschaften*, so important in Germany, as constituting a fundamental branch of inquiry that might yield insights upon philosophic scrutiny.

A last philosophical reason was that the outlook of Royce and James derived from Kant's *Critique of Pure Reason* and the problems it generated; they consequently emphasized the technical and not the social and political.*

Perhaps more important in understanding the lack of Cambridge social and political philosophy is comprehending the milieu in which Royce and James lived. We are dealing with late nineteenth-century members of the Harvard faculty. The life-style accompanying that position was not conducive to social and political theorizing. Royce and James were in the first generation of successful big-time American academics, ultimately self-satisfied and uncritical of the social order. It is true that some men in their culture showed a restrained and moderate interest in "reform" politics. But Royce and James did not even display this minimal respectable concern. After all, they *were* philosophers. As James wrote to Royce about their careers early in their relationship, "We are all isolated. . . . Books are our companions more than men." Writers on James often cite his vocal opposition to American neo-colonial expansion at the turn of the century. His enduring political and social attitudes and those of Royce, however, although decent and certainly anti-militarist, were best suggested by noting that both men viewed William Jennings Bryan's candidacy in 1896 with alarm.[17] Even the triumph of "Progressivism" in national politics from 1900 to 1912 had a minimal effect on their thought. During the early part of the decade Royce disclaimed an interest in political philosophy—"my business is largely with other branches of philosophy"—and refused to grade essays on social problems, a field that was "not in my province."[18]

When Royce turned to these issues at the end of the decade, his thought was jejune and he proselytized with verbiage that could only undermine his goals. For example, he developed a scheme for international insurance during the First World War and parodied the Gettysburg address to support his plan: "whenever insurance of the nations, by the nations, and for the nations begins, it will thenceforth never vanish from the earth."[19] This was not the rhetoric of an important political thinker.

One may search without success in the work of Royce and James for references to the social theorists who were, in many cases, their contem-

---

*As *The Philosophy of Loyalty* made clear, Royce was also a student of Kant's *Groundwork of the Metaphysic of Morals*. But both men's historical interests revolved around the concerns of the *Critique* and not, say, the political and social dimensions of Hegel's *Phenomenology of Mind*.

poraries. Marx, Tönnies, Durkheim, Veblen, Pareto, and Weber meant
little in the Harvard philosophy department. One can also search the
work of subsequent social theorists—historians, philosophers, and social
scientists—and find no references to Royce and James. A social theorist
might today describe himself as a Marxist, a Weberian, perhaps a Veb-
lenian; but he would never describe himself as a Jamesean or a Roycean
(or a Deweyan).

The quality of Harvard's political and social philosophy was poor;
the structure of the university and of the discipline well-nigh guaranteed
that first-rate work would not be done; and the work that was done
ignored critical texts and has been subsequently ignored by significant
communities of scholars.*

*Royce's interest in international politics inspired by the outbreak of the First World
War does not challenge this conclusion. I discuss this question in chapter 23. I should also
add that in the last years of his life James thought of writing a "Psychology of Jingoism," or
"Varieties of Military Experience," disturbed perhaps by growing national chauvinism.
But this project never materialized except for the essay already discussed, and James's son
reported that it was a vague project turned to occasionally as a diversion. See LWJ, 2: 284;
and see George R. Garrison and Edward H. Madden, "Willian James—Warts and All,"
AQ 29 (1977).

17

JAMESEAN METAPHYSICS
1904-1910

James's Last Years and American Thought

By the end of the nineteenth century William James was a thinker of worldwide repute and one of Harvard's prized possessions. His engaging personality won over scholars on the Continent as he became Cambridge's foremost ambassador of good will; his openness and mildly unconventional behavior prodded his American colleagues and attracted around him young men eager to make a mark. While professional controversy in the United States and Europe centered on his epistemology, he was also well known to educated laymen. Indeed, as he neared sixty he was torn between a desire to write a great synthetic treatise and a need to communicate with a wide circle of readers.

James had for some years vacationed in Keene Valley in the Adirondacks, and in the 1880s he had bought a farm in Chocorua, New Hampshire, where he also spent much of his time. In the summer of 1898 a prolonged two-day climb in the Adirondacks resulted in a valvular lesion, although it did not seriously curtail his activities. A year later he spent another day lost in Keene Valley and, overstrained to the point of collapse, he went to Europe for two years in an unsuccessful attempt to regain his health. When he returned to Cambridge in 1901, he had almost readied for publication his Gifford Lectures, "The Varieties of Religious Experience," but lamented his inability to work up a philosophic "last will and testament." He intended to husband his strength for writing, and until he fully retired in 1907, he taught only one course a year. At the same time he accepted lecturing commitments and met the demands of correspondents and callers from all over the world. More than once his health required that he escape from Cambridge, his desk, and his friendships altogether, but from 1904 to 1910 he did much to round out his position.[1] The lectures that comprised *Pragmatism* (1907) were popular like much of his previous work and drew heavily on his psychological studies of the 1880s and 1890s. But he wrote his metaphysics of "radical empiricism" for a professional audience and its revision, although presented as the public Hibbert Lectures of 1908–1909, signalled new turns in his thinking.

The development of this metaphysics, provoked by the dispute with Royce, pointed up the priorities of late nineteenth-century philosophers. The materialistic interpretation of Darwin forced them to reexamine fundamental epistemological questions. Darwin's skeptical promoters, many philosophers believed, undercut the basis of both science and religion. If philosophy were to defend religious knowledge, it must first analyze anew how we knew anything at all. In this sense epistemology became the key philosophic area, although thinkers often also identified metaphysics with the speculative enterprise: introducing the absolute (a metaphysical notion) was crucial in solving problems in the theory of knowledge.

Although James scorned this entire brand of metaphysics, it fed the religious propensities which had activated philosophers initially. And James worked out his own pluralistic metaphysics in response to these same propensities and to the same sorts of epistemological problems. I shall argue that this pluralism was idealistic and panpsychic, but James's contempt for orthodox metaphysics presaged an important change in American philosophy. Later in the century, as the philosophy of religion went out of fashion, interest in all metaphysics waned. "Practical philosophizing," represented by religion and fortified by the absolute, also went out of style, and philosophers began to conceive the theory of knowledge as self-sufficient.

James and Kant

James's radical empiricism was as indebted to Kant as was his pragmatism, but before I can defend this view I must clarify terminological problems that come from two sources. As we shall see, Ralph Perry was a leading American metaphysical realist and also considered himself a "scientific empiricist." A student, colleague, and friend of James, he later thought himself the bearer of James's spirit at Harvard. Perry had a polemical and oversimplified view of the history of philosophy, and in his great source book and biography, *The Thought and Character of William James*, he contributed such to the notion of Jamesean pragmatism as a brand of Anglo-American empiricism and emphasized how close James was to Perry's own "common-sense realism." Perry's James did not truck with the alien German doctrine of Kant. Perry's ideas aside, it is much more important to note that James himself often deprecated Kant and "Kantism" in print and, if not stressing his allegiance to the British tradition, at least stressed his empiricism. If I am legitimately to call James a neo-Kantian, I must deal with these issues.

The philosophical contrast that James made the most of was between empiricism and rationalism. As Harvard philosophers saw the history of their discipline, this nomenclature designated the divergence between the British—Locke, Berkeley, and Hume—and the Continental tradition—Descartes, Spinoza, and Leibniz—over the sources of knowledge. The British emphasized the senses, their opponents the ratiocinative mind. Kant mediated between these two schools. In James's terminology, however, the rationalist-empiricist distinction did not serve this purpose: rationalism and empiricism designated vaguely different attitudes about the universe, and he identified empiricism with something like a decent respect for science. James treated Royce as an arch-rationalist, but as James himself wrote, Royce was "a first rate empirical mind." And James said that rationalism was always monistic while calling Leibniz, a pluralist, "a rationalist mind."[2] The upshot is that we must use James's classificatory language circumspectly in categorizing him. But even as he used it, we could still make the case for his neo-Kantianism: in discussing the tough- and tender-minded in the famous first chapter of *Pragmatism*, James intended to steer a via media between the tough-minded (empiricists) and the tender-minded (rationalists)—and this was exactly Kant's historic role.

As I have already argued, James's avowal of an active mind and the tension in his thought about the role of the given vouched for his neo-Kantianism. But three other specific issues located James's commitments. First, he said consistently in opposition to Kant that form and content were inseparable and that relations were given in experience. According to James; Kant always spoke of the aboriginal sensible flux, the manifold, which was disconnected. Kant then called in the transcendental ego of apperception to bring about togetherness and the understanding with its synthesizing concepts or categories to bring about definite connections.[3] For over twenty years James repeated this view, most memorably in the *Principles* where he called the "Kantian machineship in my mind" a myth.[4] But James was wrong in thinking his own account contradicted that of Kant's late nineteenth-century transcendentalist successors, Royce and Bradley.[5]

James conceded that Bradley's assimilation of form and content agreed with his own approach.[6] More importantly, Royce explicitly emended Kant in the manner of James. Royce held from the late 1870s onward that in consciousness there was both a given and the spontaneous activity of thought. Kant believed that we could divorce the two and have thought organize the given. For Royce there could be no divorce: the thinking activity did not infuse the given with form but projected the past and future from a present union of form and content. When James argued that experience gave us relations (form), however, he usually identified his doctrine as a modification of British empiricism. Because ideas were discontinuous for the British, James said his denial of discrete ideas made his empiricism "radical." But in concentrating his fire on the absolute, which Bradley and Royce dragged in to justify the mind's constructional activity, James neglected to see that his modification of the British was precisely that alteration of Kant made by his two formidable "rationalist" opponents.

Second, we must remember that from a historical perspective Kant's task was not only to mediate rationalism and empiricism but also to answer Hume. British empiricism had ended in Hume's skepticism; part of the work of the *Critique* was justifying claims to knowledge. However dimly James viewed Kant's answer, the thrust of James's thought, as he saw it, was also to amend empiricism in such a way as to overcome skepticism. James wanted to make empiricism and religion compatible, to transform the skeptical and irreligious dimension of empiricism, performing a Kantian task a hundred years after Kant.

Third, we must note that the historical division between rationalists and empiricists had little to do with the metaphysical dispute between realists and idealists: Locke and Descartes were realists, Berkeley and Leibniz were idealists, and Spinoza and Hume perhaps unclassifiable. Metaphysical idealism became an important issue after Kant: solving Hume's problem implied that existence did not transcend consciousness. The development of German thought after Kant, however, suggested that his mediating position was inadequate. For the post-Kantian idealists, consciousness must constitute existence in order to answer Hume. In time, German idealism became labelled as a form of rationalism (because it made the active mind central) and anti-scientific (because according to the common understanding, it ignored the growth of science and wallowed in a romanticized notion of the absolute). Consequently, realists were able to adopt the honorific title "empiricist" and its associations with science. One reason that Perry made a case for James's "scientific" realism was that James's careful interest in the life sciences was a sure sign that he was not in the idealist, rationalist, tradition. Nonetheless, this emphasis on post-Kantian rationalism ignored the fact that the Continental rationalists were more interested in science and mathematics than were the British empiricists and that Kant carried on this interest. James's scientific pursuits, of themselves, bespoke no penchant for metaphysical realism, and if James was a neo-Kantian we should find, as in Kant, ambiguity and tension in his position, ambiguity and tension leading in the direction of idealism.

Radical Empiricism

James set forth his metaphysical belief in "a world of pure experience" in a series of articles appearing in the 1904 and 1905 *Journal of Philosophy* and later collected as *Essays in Radical Empiricism*. The first, "Does 'Consciousness' Exist?" began by denying that the word 'consciousness' stood for an entity: there was no "aboriginal stuff or quality of being" making up our thoughts which we might contrast to the matter of physical objects. On the contrary, consciousness was a function: when certain portions of pure experience were appropriately related, we said consciousness existed. The function that defined consciousness was knowing, and functioning in the knowledge relation, the pure experiences were thoughts.

James's attack at first merely looked like an argument against "soul substance," and he did carry forward the attack on a substantial self that informed some of the "psychological" parts of the *Principles*. But the larger issues were plain:

> My thesis is that if we start with the supposition that there is only one primal stuff or material in the world, a stuff of which everything is composed, and if we call that stuff 'pure experience,' then knowing can easily be explained as a particular sort of relation towards one another into which portions of pure experience may enter.

The primary emphasis in James's essays was that pure experience had no characteristics; the world's "stuff" was neither mental nor physical. When the neutral data were organized in one fashion, we called the various organized structures physical objects; when the data were organized in another fashion the result was (knowing) consciousnesses. As James suggested, he picked up and extended the stream of consciousness doctrine of the *Principles*. There, consciousness carved out the enduring objects that comprised the world. Now, James said, consciousness itself was only one mode of organizing a neutral realm of experience which carried within it the elements of its construction into consciousness and objects.[7]

A lesser emphasis in the essays was that pure experience had all characteristics. There was, he said,

> no *general* stuff of which experience at large is made. There are as many stuffs as there are 'natures' in the things experienced. If you ask what any one bit of pure experience is made of, the answer is always the same: "It is made of *that*, of just what appears, of space, of intensity, of flatness, brownness, heaviness, or what not!" . . . Experience is only a collective name for all these sensible natures, and save for time and space (and, if you like, for 'being') there appears no universal element of which all things are made.[8]

In either case "pure experience" labelled all that was, and what was was intrinsically neither mental nor physical.

The possibility of overcoming mind–body dualism by analyzing immediate perception fascinated James. When I looked at the desk in front of me, my "content of consciousness" was my mind or consciousness at that moment, and at that moment the content was identical to the being of the physical desk. Of course, my consciousness and the desk were only momentarily identical. The career of the desk was that organization of pure experience determined by its occurrence in various tactile and visual fields of consciousness; my consciousness was that organization of pure experience determined by my perception of opening the deskdrawer, the following perception of a checkbook, a thought of my money flowing from the bank, and so on. The bits of experience received their mental or physical character from the context in which they existed:

> If at this moment I think of my hat which a while ago I left in the cloak-room, where is the dualism, the discontinuity between the hat of my thoughts and the real hat? My mind is thinking of a truly *absent hat*. I reckon with it practically as with a reality. If it were present on this table, the hat would occasion a movement of my hand: I would pick it up. In the same way, this hat as a concept, this idea-hat, will presently determine the direction of my steps. I will go retrieve it. The idea of it will last up to the sensible presence of the hat, and then will blend harmoniously with it.
>
> I conclude, then, that—although there be a practical dualism— inasmuch as representations are distinguished from objects, stand in their stead and lead us to them, there is no reason to attribute to them an essential difference of nature. Thought and actuality are made of one and the same stuff, the stuff of experience in general.⁹

James never spelled out the relation of his epistemological concerns (pragmatism) to this metaphysical discussion of the nature of reality, but the connection existed.* Pragmatism had a place within the metaphysics: the latter was more fundamental. James's theory of truth described human inquiry, that is, what truth amounted to in practice. This description detailed how some experiences—ideas—lead to certain other experiences —the object of the idea. Pragmatism defined a true belief by what it came to practically, as one which terminated successfully in percepts, direct experience, through a series of transitional experiences that the world supplied.¹⁰ Pragmatism explored that aspect of James's world of

---

*For a compendium of James's remarks, see Perry's preface to his edition of *Essays in Radical Empiricism* (New York: Longmans, Green and Co., 1912) and James's own contradictory remarks in the prefaces to P and MT.

pure experience in which one mode of organization (the physical world) interacted with another (consciousness) when things were known.

Just as James mentioned in *Pragmatism* that we might study the evolution of mental categories that enabled us to know the world, he suggested in the *Journal of Philosophy* essays that we might undertake the same kind of enterprise to study the birth of the physical world from pure experience. First, he admitted that his world of pure experience was not chaotic:

> We must make additional hypotheses. We must beg a minimum of structure for them [pure experiences]. The *kind* of minimum that *might* have tended to increase towards what we now find actually developed is the philosophical desideratum here.[11]

Then he said:

> If one were to make an evolutionary construction of how a lot of originally chaotic pure experiences became gradually differentiated into an orderly inner and outer world, the whole theory would turn upon one's success in explaining how or why the quality of an experience, once active, could become less so, and, from being an energetic attribute in some cases, elsewhere lapse into the status of an inert or merely internal 'nature.' This would be the 'evolution' of the psychical from the bosom of the physical, in which the aesthetic, moral, and otherwise emotional experiences would represent a halfway stage.[12]

James elaborated his mention of moral and aesthetic experience as a "halfway stage" in the last *Journal of Philosophy* article, "The Place of Affectional Facts in a World of Pure Experience." Affectional facts, moral and aesthetic evaluations, were not "objective." They were not like the facts associated with physical objects: blue eyes were not beautiful to everyone. But such facts were not exclusively "subjective"; they were not simply personal likings, ascribable only to single individuals: preciousness was well-nigh essential to our conception of diamonds. We could explain this ambiguity through James's metaphysics. The words 'subjective' and 'objective' did not label an intrinsic quality of an experience but the way that we classified the experience. Classification depended on our purposes, and for certain purposes it was convenient to take experiences in one set of relations, for other purposes in another set. In the case of valuations we had no steadfast purpose that demanded consistency. It was easier to let them float ambiguously, sometimes classing them with feelings, sometimes with physical realities, according to convenience.[13]

This "neutral monism" was James's solution to the two worlds' problem that he could not answer in the 1890s: the two worlds became one. In fact, as chapter 11 above hinted, although their literary performances differed, James wrote his *Journal of Philosophy* essays and Münsterberg his *Eternal Values* at the same time and in the same intellectual context. Both showed how a neutral substance was transformed into the physical and psychical worlds. In many respects following Royce, Münsterberg acknowledged that he was "a pragmatist and a realist" "on the second stage," that is, considering the phenomenal world. He was "the most radical of the radical empiricists—in fact a pragmatist of the right, or idealistic wing, for whom truth and natural sciences . . . are purely instrumental constructs totally different from the real world,—i.e., the world of values."[14] The bureaucratized structure he gave to this world made his style the antithesis of James's, but it was only when Münsterberg went on about his real world of the over-soul that the differences became significant, and then only after the turn of the century when James rejected Roycean absolutism. Even so, James, Royce, and Münsterberg shared a common voluntarism. Finally, as we shall see, James also shared, "in comminuted form," the absolutist conception of ultimate reality; his central thesis expressed "the main contention of transcendental idealism."[15]

Unresolved Problems

James's debt to British empiricism was explicit in the *Journal of Philosophy* essays. In construing existents as what things were "known as," James said, the British were the first to use the pragmatic method. He urged that redefining the mind–matter dualism carried out this method.[16] The methodological postulate involved was:

Nothing shall be admitted as fact . . . except what can be experienced at some definite time by some experient; and for every feature of fact ever so experienced, a definite place must be found somewhere in the final system of reality. In other words: Everything real must be experienceable somewhere, and every kind of thing experienced must somewhere be real.[17]

For such a philosophy as radical empiricism, James contended, *"the relations that connect experiences must themselves be experienced relations, and any kind of relation experienced must be accounted as 'real' as anything else in the system."*[18] Elsewhere he wrote:

> The only fully complete concrete data are, however, the successive moments of our own several histories, taken with their subjective personal aspect, as well as with their "objective" deliverance or "content." After the analogy of these moments of experiences must all complete reality be conceived. Radical empiricism thus leads to the assumption of a collectivism of personal lives (which may be of any grade of complication, and superhuman or infrahuman as well as human), variously cognitive of each other, variously conative and impulsive, genuinely evolving and changing by effort and trial, and by their interaction and cumulative achievements making up the world.[19]

Adhering to this postulate presented James with two problems that he was still resolving at the end of his life. The first concerned possible experience and forced him to examine in a different context the questions raised in his dispute with Royce. The second emended his long-standing view of the uniqueness of the passing states of consciousness. Let us consider each in turn.

The world consisted of neutral stuff out of which mind and matter developed. But everything experienced must count as part of the stuff, and only what was experienced would so count. Because things were as they are known as, James refused to admit as real anything that was unknown, outside of experience: to do so would lead to a monism in which we allowed the absolutely unverifiable on grounds of logic. The alternative to his concrete approach was the abstractionalism of the block universe.

What was the status of my desk in the library when neither I nor anyone else was experiencing it? In responding to Royce at the turn of the century in the dispute over critical rationalism—the Third Conception of Being—James had implied that this was not a legitimate question. His later work took it seriously. He wanted to say the desk existed; it did not pass in and out of existence when we entered the library. James's methodological principle permitted him, perhaps, two elucidations. He could say that the desk continued to exist because it was actually experienced. Or, he could say that the desk's existence was guaranteed because possible experience defined the real—it would be possible to experience the desk if someone were to enter the library. A few Jamesean texts justify the second alternative, although he usually defined objects by the experienced (the first alternative) rather than by the experienceable. As James knew, to speak of the experienceable would embroil him in all the problems Royce pointed out in critical rationalism. Even Perry, who wanted to avoid speaking of the experienced, did not believe that "residual existence" consisted for James in the possibility of experience.[20]

As Perry suggested, James almost immediately committed himself to the first alternative. But who experienced the desk when none of us was around? Not the absolute. James's way out lay in panpsychism, the view that mind was in all things. The desk existed when we were not in its vicinity because in some way it was self-conscious, it experienced itself directly:

> The beyond must, of course, always in our philosophy be itself of an experiential nature. If not a future experience of our own or a present one of our neighbor, it must be a thing in itself . . . that is, it must be an experience *for* itself whose relation to other things we translate into the action of molecules, ether-waves, or whatever else the physical symbols may be. This opens the chapter of the relations of radical empiricism to panpsychism . . .[21]

It would follow that James was a pluralistic idealist. Rejecting Royce's absolute as solving philosophic problems, he was nonetheless attracted to its form of solution: "the pure experiences of our philosophy are, in themselves considered, so many little absolutes, the philosophy of pure experience being only a more comminuted *Identitätsphilosophie*."[22]

But in 1904 James was only *almost* committed to panpsychism. It seemed to imply that the desk's experience of itself differed from the direct experience the rest of us had of it: we experienced it as the action of molecules, ether waves, or whatever, whereas it did not seem likely that the desk experienced itself that way. But if this were so, panpsychism did not solve James's problem: when we were not around, it was not the desk as we experienced it that existed, but something else:

> If to be is to be experienced, then every thing can be *immediately* only as it is *immediately* experienced. If not immediately experienced *as* the same or *as* other, how can it in its immediacy have been the same? or other? . . .

> The difficulty for me here is the same that I lay so much stress on in my criticism of Royce's Absolute, only it is inverted. If the whole is all that is experienced, how can the parts be experienced otherwise than as it experiences them? That is Royce's difficulty. *My* difficulty is the opposite: if the parts are all the experience there is, how can the whole be experienced otherwise than as any of them experiences it?

James could not resolve the issue; by 1907, in metaphysics, he was still only "squinting" toward idealism, but that he was doing that, he said, "I have no doubt."[23]

The second major problem raised by radical empiricism—the uniqueness of mental states—derived from one of the essays in the *Journal of Philosophy* series, "How Two Minds Can Know One Thing." For two minds to know one thing was for them both, as certain modes of organization of pure experience, to contain the same bit of pure experience that in another context was the thing. But James allowed that our minds never shared identical percepts. Aside from differences in perceptual acuity of various sorts, each of us experienced the desk, for example, from different perspectives. James continued, however, that we at least had the spatial aspects of the percept in common. On pragmatic grounds we predicated sameness whenever we sensed no assignable point of difference, and no test would show us that the place occupied by my percept of the desk differed from the place occupied by yours. If asked to point to our percepts, we pointed to the same spot:

> All the relations, whether geometrical or causal, of the . . . [desk] originate or terminate in that spot wherein our hands meet, and where each of us begins to work if he wishes to make the . . . [desk] change before the other's eyes. Just so it is with our bodies. That body of yours which you actuate and feel from within must

be in the same spot as the body of yours which I see or touch from without. 'There' for me means where I place my finger. If you do not feel my finger's contact to be 'there' in *my* sense, when I place it on your body, where then do you feel it? Your inner actuations of your body meet my finger *there*: it is *there* that you resist the push or shrink back, or sweep the finger aside with your hand.[24]

James concluded that since the "receptacle" of certain experiences was common, we might someday prove the experiences themselves were common. To show that two minds knew one thing, it was unnecessary to show that we shared percepts, although we could show that we shared spatial aspects of certain percepts. James required only that the percepts that each of us took to be the desk were part of the same organization of percepts that defined the desk, and this he demonstrated by analyzing our common behavior in regard to the desk. If we behaved the same way toward a supposed object, on pragmatic grounds our minds knew the same object. Unless we reasoned that our minds met in common objects, said James, we had no ground for talking of other minds at all. James here followed Royce on imitation. With Royce, again, he had adopted a postulational account of other minds:

Why do I postulate your mind? Because I see your body acting in a certain way. . . . But what is 'your body' here but a percept in *my* field? It is only as animating *that* object, *my* object, that I have any occasion to think of you at all. If the body that you actuate be not the very body that I see there, but some duplicate body of your own with which that has nothing to do, we belong to different universes, you and I, and for me to speak of you is folly. . . . In that perceptual part of *my* universe which I call *your* body, your mind and my mind meet and may be called coterminous. Your mind actuates that body and mine sees it; my thoughts pass into it as into their harmonious cognitive fulfillment; your emotions and volitions pass into it as causes into their effects. . . . For instance, your hand lays hold of one end of a rope and my hand lays hold of the other end. We pull against each other. Can our two hands be mutual objects in this experience, and the rope not be mutual also? What is true of the rope is true of any other percept. Your objects are over and over again the same as mine. . . . If you alter an object in your world, put out a candle, for example, when I am present, *my* candle *ipso facto* goes out. It is only as altering my objects that I guess you to exist. If your objects do not coalesce with my objects, if they be not identically where mine are, they must be proved to be positively somewhere else. But no other location can be assigned for them, so their place must be what it seems to be, the same.[25]

The reasoning of James and Royce uncomfortably ignored solipsism. Both men postulated other minds to account for the world of objects, but they also assumed the world of objects because they believed in finite minds. James's view consequently implied that portions of the realm of pure experience could be common to two different minds, that they could be identical parts of two different wholes. He was anxious at this point to distinguish his position from Berkeleyan nominalism:

> For the Berkeleyan school, ideas (the verbal equivalent of what I term experiences) are discontinuous. The content of each is wholly immanent, and there are no transitions with which they are consubstantial and through which their beings may unite. Your . . . [desk] and mine, even when both are percepts, are wholly out of connexion with each other. Our lives are a congeries of solipsisms, out of which in strict logic only a God could compose a universe even of discourse. No dynamic currents run between my objects and your objects. Never can our minds meet in the *same*. The incredibility of such a philosophy is flagrant. It is 'cold, strained, and unnatural' in a supreme degree; and it may be doubted whether even Berkeley himself, who took it so religiously, really believed, when walking through the streets of London, that his spirit and the spirits of his fellow wayfarers had absolutely different towns in view.[26]

In contradistinction to this position James said he was a "natural realist."[27]

Perry seized on this phrase to urge that James was a metaphysical realist, believing like Perry, that objects existed independently of consciousness. But as James pointed out, his "natural realism" was not a metaphysical doctrine, it was not concerned with the nature of the experienced world. Rather it was an epistemological doctrine concerned with the kinds of things we knew. Berkeley and Kant, said James, required a deus ex machina to assemble our experiences, the discrete data of sense. But as James never tired of urging, relations were a part of what experience gave. As Hume had demonstrated, Berkeley made it impossible to escape from the "world" of disparate sensations, from solipsism. James's "natural" (epistemological) realism proclaimed that experiences were not discrete sensations, but had aspects others could know. Indeed, they had aspects that were shared with others; they had common qualities. James was rejecting nominalism and solipsism, not adopting metaphysical realism:

> On the principles which I am defending, a 'mind' or 'personal consciousness' is the name for a series of experiences run together by certain definite transitions, and an objective reality is a series of similar experiences knit by different transitions. If one and the same experience can figure twice, once in a mental and once in a physical context . . . one does not see why it might not figure thrice or four times, or any number of times, by running into as many different mental contexts, just as the same point, lying at their intersection, can be continued into many different lines. Abolishing any number of contexts would not destroy the experience itself or its other contexts, any more than abolishing some of the point's linear continuations would destroy the others, or destroy the point itself.

James's position resurrected some of the ideas of the Cambridge amateurs. Peirce had rejected Berkeley for similar reasons. If consistently carried out, Berkeleyan nominalism led to solipsism and skepticism. In a much looser way, James made the same move as Peirce, defining real objects as those transcending individual consciousness and going on to argue that physical objects transcended our immediate consciousness of them. But this belief did not entail metaphysical realism, that is, that objects existed independently of all consciousness. James was not a metaphysical realist, as Perry believed. On the contrary, James was on his way to a communitarian idealism. As with Peirce, so with James:

epistemological realism and a communitarian idealism were mutually supportive.*

One of the central doctrines of the *Principles* was that the stream of consciousness was just what it was and not another thing. Each field of consciousness was a unique stream, and to suggest that the field was composed of analyzable units, identical to units in other fields, returned James to the associationalist view. Yet by the end of 1905, less than six months after completing the *Journal of Philosophy* series, James recognized that something like associationalism must be true if radical empiricism were true:

> In my psychology I contended that each field of consciousness is entitatively a unit, and that its parts are only different cognitive relations which it may possess with different contexts. But in my doctrine that the same . . . [desk] may be known by two knowers I seem to imply that an identical part can help to *constitute* two fields. . . . The fields are . . . decomposable into "parts," one of which, at least, is common to both; and my whole tirade against "composition" in the *Psychology* is belied by my own subsequent doctrine. How can I rescue the situation? Which doctrine must I stand by? . . . We must overhaul the whole business of connection, confluence, and the like, and do it radically. . . .[28]

James stood by the later doctrine of radical empiricism. In fall 1906, he had tentatively revised in its favor. "May not the whole trouble be," he ruminated, "that I am still treating what is really a living and dynamic situation by logical and statical categories?" If this was the trouble, how could he state its resolution? The statement, he wrote in early 1908, would entail using logical and statical categories. Discoursing on "the intuitive or live constitution" of consciousness was paradoxical. "One can do so only by approximation, awakening sympathy with it rather than assuming logically to define it; for logic makes all things static."[29]

*ERE, 37–42, 133. For Perry's misconstrual see TCWJ, 2:388; and for what James believed, pp. 536, 545, 549; also Perry's "Preface" to *In the Spirit of William James* (New Haven: Yale University Press, 1938). It is also true that James, like Peirce, tended more to metaphysical realism the less he emphasized epistemological realism. See TCWJ, 1: 525–28, and PP, 1:468–73.

Difficulties Overcome

The two problems generated by radical empiricism—the status of possibilities and the shareability of pure experience—both reduced to one question: what precisely was the nature of neutral experience? In his Hibbert Lectures delivered at Oxford in May 1908 and published the next year as *A Pluralistic Universe* James made his final declaration on the issue. As he had hinted was necessary a few months earlier, James renounced logic. Adopting elements of Henri Bergson's thought, James classified his own metaphysical position: "the constitution of reality which I am making for is of [the] psychic type."[30]

Bergson claimed that the methods and concepts of science, loosely identified with logic, had practical value only; they enabled us to function in the world, but the conceptual framework they employed, indeed employing any conceptual framework whatsoever, distorted the real nature of experience. James accepted this critique of logic and science: neither gave us "insight" "for they quite fail to connect us with the inner life of the flux [that is, concrete experience] or with the causes that govern its direction." James was aware of how strange this sounded to readers for whom he had extolled the practical as the real; but only his language had altered. He was simply reaffirming the primacy of the concrete and immediate over the abstract and the derived.*

If we were to get at the flux, we must, for James, abandon logic and scientific conceptualization. We learned what existed from intuitive sympathy, from a live understanding of reality's movement. Using this understanding we recognized that every minimal pulse of experience was self-transcendent. In itself experience was compounded and continuous with other bits of experience. In sensational immediacy things were both one and many, flowing, coexisting, and compenetrating. We knew from experience of self, for example, that our immediate selves were parts of wider unconscious selves. But to grasp these ideas required us to think without conceptualizing.[31]

*PU, "Bergson and his Critique of Intellectualism" (see esp. n. 1). Bradley had also stressed the impotence of logic in comprehending the absolute, and this stress may have been another element in James's belief that they were brothers under the skin. James would also have found Bergson's critique specifically applicable to Royce's mathematical analysis of consciousness.

James's embrace of the Bergsonian *durée* and the concomitant attack on science and logic were the most novel features of *A Pluralistic Universe*. But he did not discover in Bergson's *Time and Free Will* and *Creative Evolution* anything uncongenial to the drift of his thought: he had always been suspicious of logic as exhibited in Roycean argumentation, and always committed to the interrelatedness of experience.[32] Reading Bergson forced James to bring these commitments to the fore. The doctrine of compenetration was no retreat from the *Principles*; it carried the views of that book to their conclusion and, surprisingly, allowed James to reinstate, on different grounds, the associationalist doctrine that different consciousnesses could have aspects in common. Compenetration also showed him how panpsychism could succeed and answer the troubling questions over possibility.

In *A Pluralistic Universe* James related in an autobiographical section his attempts to circumvent problems that were entailed by accepting logic and science. By "logic" he meant the sort of dialectical theorizing by which Royce proved the absolute. "Intellectualistic logic" and the "logic of identity" were the villains. He had previously rejected the doctrine of absolute mind because he had accepted Roycean logic. On Royce's own grounds, James had held, each thing was self-identical; finite experience could not also be absolute experience. If we were fragments of the absolute experience, then that absolute experience was only a name for all our experiences, and monism a fraud. He accepted throughout much of his career, he said, that each stream of consciousness had no parts and that no other stream included it. Each stream was what it was and nothing else, and the compounding of consciousness was impossible. His god, he continued, had been theistic, another (larger) consciousness of which we were not parts; he did not consist of smaller minds.[33]

Now that *A Pluralistic Universe* had rejected logic, the old arguments against absolutism, based on the acceptance of logic, no longer held. Although James still rejected monistic idealism, ironically he most clearly embraced a form of idealism when he finally gave up logic, idealism's most formidable weapon.

James's new disavowal of monism as a hypothesis rested in part on an old charge—that it did not solve the problem of evil and was pragmatically unsatisfying. But to this charge James added another: if we grasped the flux of experience using intuitive sympathy, we saw that in sensational immediacy things were one and many, that conscious experiences freely compounded and separated themselves.[34] James found it difficult to put into words what he had in mind, appropriately enough if he was going beyond language. If we went beyond conceptualization, however, we found "a pluralistic panpsychic view of the universe."[35] Neutral experience was now not neutral, but throbbing, alive, constantly coalescing and re-coalescing. This conscious experience was not unitary but contained ever-widening spans of consciousness within some of which human consciousness might lie. Using arguments of the *Varieties,* James conjectured that the study of abnormal psychology and of other psychic phenomena evidenced varied realms of consciousness. For example, the existence of the subconscious declared that a consciousness of a wider span included our rational consciousness:

> The drift of all the evidence we have seems to me to sweep us very strongly toward the belief in some form of superhuman life with which we may, unknown to ourselves, be coconscious. We may be in the universe as dogs and cats are in our libraries, seeing the books and hearing the conversation, but having no inkling of the meaning of it all. . . . The outlines of the superhuman consciousness thus made probable must remain, however, very vague, and the number of functionally distinct "selves" it comports and carries has to be left entirely problematic.[36]

James identified human "substance" with the divine "substance," but this divine substance need not be in the "all" form. It was likely that

> there may ultimately never be an all-form at all, . . . the substance of reality may never get totally collected, that some of it may remain outside of the largest combination of it ever made, and that a distributive form of reality, the each-form, is logically as acceptable and empirically as probable as the all-form commonly acquiesced in as so obviously the self-evident thing.

James added that a reality in which various kinds of consciousness compounded, although spiritual, was not theistic, but pantheistic and pluralistic.[37]

The Hibbert Lectures were James's last sustained philosophical writing. Analyzing experience brought him to panpsychism and a view that knowing constituted existence. This position extricated him from the problems of possible experience and the mutuality of experience. James did not need the possible because the actual was mutable: each pulse of experience could, at the same time, be what it was for itself and what it was for us. And these experiences compenetrated: we could share the same pulse of experience. Moreover, he sorted out the issues that had troubled him since the 1880s. Freedom entailed an active view of mind and consequently idealism. But if idealism was monistic, as James often thought, it assured only a spurious freedom. James's way out was to profess pluralism without confronting his vague belief that if monism was idealistic, pluralism was metaphysically realistic, and so would carry him back to a passive mind and determinism. In the first decade of the twentieth century he resolved his dilemma: pluralism need not be realistic, nor idealism monistic; a pluralistic idealism was consonant with the will's freedom. James *had* relinquished a central doctrine of the *Journal of Philosophy* series, that experience was neutral. By the end of his life he was moving in the direction of Royce, from the view that existence did not transcend consciousness to the view that consciousness constituted existence. Denied in the *Principles* and in the *Journal of Philosophy* series, the substantial self reappeared.[38]

Rather than being the least neo-Kantian of the major Cambridge thinkers, James was the most serious neo-Kantian of the group: in his thought the ambiguities and ambivalences of the Kantian position were most apparent. But the importance of these ambiguities and ambivalences only reveals the limitations of the label neo-Kantian. James was working in a Kantian problem matrix, but his own concerns, and the turnings taken by his thought, marked him as a major thinker in his own right for whom all labels must be inadequate.

Tribute

Because James never wrote a comprehensive statement of his philosophy, it is unsatisfying to chronicle the development of his thought. A historical treatment prevents understanding in any brief compass the overall nature of his world view. But although the time devoted to popular lecturing and writing popular books prevented him from producing a systematic treatise, his guiding principles were implicit in all his work. The penchant for popularizing manifested James's need to convey to others his sense of the way the world was; and his ability to speak to successive generations of readers evidences that the man communicated an attitude toward life expressing deep-felt needs.

Darwinian and Spencerian science initially convinced him that man was a product of a mechanistic universe. Purposeful activity was mythic and human life could have no meaning. Existence was absurd, and in the mass grave of humanity James found nothing to justify his flirtations with art, medicine, or the biological sciences. Having convinced himself, however, that the active nature of the human mind made freedom a possibility, James made his professional commitment a lifelong exploration and defense of our right to make commitments. For him, as for all of his generation who explored Darwinian science, a belief in spiritual powers essential to the being of the universe was necessary to make life significant. Absolute idealism offered a means for reconciling the claims of religion with those of science, but James came to believe that monism vitiated any emotional strength that absolute idealism provided: rather than solving the problem of freedom, monism led one into even more perplexing difficulties. He was consequently led to defend a pluralistic idealism and to believe that all events were not connected, that chance and freedom existed.

James also found the religious aspect of his idealism compatible with science. Empiricism and the scientific investigation it entailed meant that we defined the world experientially and if we believed in God, we justified this belief as we justified scientific beliefs, by finding that he made his presence known in our experience. As he wrote at the end of *A Pluralistic Universe*, "Let empiricism once become associated with religion, as hitherto, through some strange misunderstanding, it has been associated with irreligion, and I believe that a new era of religion as well as of philosophy will be ready to begin."[39] James's God was a consciousness greater than ours but not necessarily all-embracing. His spiritual power was such that we would triumph over the evil in the universe and give meaning to human existence if our own powers for good were added to his. This perspective received confirmation within human experience—in the day-to-day vindications of man's humanity to man.

James's primary motive in writing was not professional advancement nor even a desire to contribute to knowledge, but to understand the human predicament. He believed in an activist moral life and believed that this kind of life was meaningful. He designed all his more technical philosophic speculations on psychology, pragmatism, and radical empiricism to elucidate this dual conception, to show it congruent with a scientific outlook. At the heart of his vision was a world where individual striving mattered and where there was hope that man's ideals would prevail.

At the same time there was in James an awful loneliness. Surrounded by family and friends, in correspondence with an ever-widening circle of colleagues in Europe and America, he still felt a terrible isolation, a feeling that individual life was all that counted and that even its joys were fleeting. Much of his optimism was bravado. As he grew older he became more convinced that as the dark closed in on the spirit, it was left alone with its naked courage. Jamesean pragmatism was a form of fideism: "I have no living sense of commerce with a God," he wrote in 1904, but "I need it so that it 'must' be true." What one essentially finds in James *is* courage. "The sanest and best of us," he said, "are of one clay with lunatics and prison inmates, and death finally runs the robustest of us down"; "the skull will grin in at the banquet." He carried with him a sense of impending horror, of madness, illness, and suicide; his awareness of evil was intensely painful; and he wrote out of personal suffering. Yet he reached out to his audiences and heartened them to believe that we shall overcome.[40]

Early in the spring of 1910, James went to Europe, troubled by his heart ailment, seeking relief from a Paris specialist.[41] As the summer progressed his condition worsened. Walking, talking, and writing had all become painful or impossible and, accompanied by his brother Henry, he and his wife returned to the United States. James hoped that the best cure would be to go home to Chocorua. The little group arrived in mid-August, and just a week later, on August 26th, James died. In the Harvard minute on his life and services, George Herbert Palmer wrote:

> By the death of William James this University loses one who brought it high honor in many lands. As a man of science he left his mark on several departments of knowledge, while as a literary man he charmed all who read his lucid and picturesque pages. In

him science and humanism were singularly combined. Learned as he was, he had none of the pedantry of the scholar. His books, besides illuminating their subjects, were creatures of character, and through them he became one of the chief spiritual forces of our time. . . . The universal admiration given him was ever mixed with love. From him men drew their ideals of human character and were grateful to him for being what he was.

18

RALPH PERRY AND NEO-REALISM

Royce and Realism

In the first volume of *The World and The Individual* Royce preceded his argument for absolute idealism by refuting three other "conceptions of being"—realism, mysticism, and critical rationalism. The first conception, realism, viewed real objects as independent of the idea or experience that knew them. Royce argued that this independence must be an absolute independence and concluded that realism was incoherent. For if idea and object were so independent, there was no reason for saying that an idea was an idea of any particular object. Ideas could not refer to objects and knowledge became impossible.

Royce's first volume, "The Four Historical Conceptions of Being," appeared at the end of 1899. In 1901 and 1902 two of his former students attacked their teacher in the learned journals.[1] Harvard had recently placed William Pepperell Montague at Berkeley and Ralph Barton Perry at Smith College, and they seized on the polemical and abstract quality of Royce's analysis. "No first rate thinker" was a realist, Royce remarked, but he named no proponents of the position. In suggesting the absolute independence of idea and object, Royce also had only representational realism in mind. If realism meant that we were presented only with ideas and inferred objects as their cause or ground, he could easily claim their mutual independence: for how could the realist talk about relations between idea and object when limited to ideas alone? Royce never considered the view of the presentational realist, that we were directly presented with objects as they are. Indeed, Montague reckoned Royce's argument collapsed when the "barriers [were] . . .

removed so that the object can confront its idea in the bright light of immediate experience."[2] With a view like this implicit in their reasoning, Perry and Montague contended that no realist had to assert the absolute independence of idea and object; objects could become known as they are and yet not depend on knowing for their existence. But both men refused to state their critiques positively. They simply pleaded for the "lack of finality" of Royce's refutation. As Perry put it, "the great critical epistemology of *a priori* idealism is as yet unanswered; . . . at the same time [I] suggest that it is not unanswerable."[3]

Royce's young opponents were to reject representational realism, yet they had no connection to the Scots. And unlike Hamilton, Montague and Perry would argue a clear metaphysical position, American neo-realism.

James, Perry, and Realism

In 1904, two years after these articles appeared, William James began the *Journal of Philosophy* series outlining his "radical empiricism." Holding that neither consciousness nor its objects were substances, James said that both sorts of "entities" were different organizations of pure experience. Just as a point at the place of intersection occupied a position on two (or more) lines, James averred that in perception the stream of consciousness contained what, in an alternative organization, was the physical object. Perry and Montague had probably heard James say these things in the classroom but his publications impelled the neo-realists to elaborate a full-fledged doctrine. Using James's insights, they argued positively that objects might be independent of ideas and yet enter into relations with them. But as important as James's radical empiricism was, James himself was more important; in his forays against Royce and in the openness of his philosophical vision, he inspired the younger men to what at the time was a bold opinion. After the publication of *Pragmatism* in 1907, the philosophical world seemed new and exciting.

Four others joined Perry and Montague and, of the six, Harvard had trained the three most important. Montague was by then at Columbia, and Perry had returned to Harvard. The third was Edwin Bissell Holt, another student of Royce and James, who had taught in a junior position at Harvard from the time he had received his degree in 1901.* When the *Journal of Philosophy* agreed to become an "organ" of neo-realism, "to the extent of letting us thrash out any topic through its columns,"[4] the work of Royce and James had launched a new movement that would take issue with both variants of Harvard Pragmatism. In 1910 the six men (Royce called them "the six little realists") published "The Program and First Platform of Six Realists,"[5] which stressed their group inquiry and division of labor. Although the scholarly journals printed this effort and most of the controversial literature, in 1912 the realists also produced a joint book of five hundred pages, *The New Realism: Cooperative Studies in Philosophy.*

Although Holt was the most talented of the realists, Perry, their leader, was the most important for philosophical history. Perry was a favorite of William James, and his great biography of James and many earlier essays made clear his enormous sympathy for his subject's wide range of interests. But Perry was also a philosopher who believed that his discipline progressed and that its practitioners corrected old errors and resolved new problems. His writings on James suffered because they tried to show that James was a metaphysical realist. The reason for this misinterpretation was that, for Perry, part of James's greatness lay in his "anticipation" of Perry and the other neo-realists. But whatever distortions were created by Perry's desire for a usable past, he quickly saw that, properly interpreted, James's radical empiricism would liberate American philosophy from its bondage to absolute idealism. His deserved leadership of the neo-realists stemmed from a remarkably astute and justly praised series of articles, many of which antedated the neo-realists' formal proclamation in the 1910 *Journal of Philosophy.* They established Perry as a controversialist to be reckoned with and as an energetic opponent of idealism.†

Perry's target was "the cardinal principle of idealism":[6] that knowledge was an originating or creative process, that it conditioned the nature of things.[7] The chief argument for this principle—Perry gave it the famous name "the argument from the ego-centric predicament"—was

*The other three, non-Harvard and less important, were Walter Pitkin, also of Columbia, Edward G. Spaulding of Princeton, and Walter Marvin of Rutgers.

†The best introduction to Perry is his "Realism in Retrospect," in CAP, 2: 187–209. This article gives the flavor of the man and his arguments against idealism, illustrates his literary ability, and demonstrates his polemical view of the past.

that because all objects were known, knowing constituted objects. This argument proved only that it was uniquely difficult to determine the modification of things by the knowing of them, for we could not construct a situation in which knowledge was not present without destroying the observational conditions. But to infer that objects depended on knowledge from the fact that all objects were known was an elementary example of the post hoc ergo propter hoc fallacy. At best, the idealist defended a tautology, that known objects were known objects, on the misapprehension that it was a self-evident synthetic truth.[8]

Perry also saw two other pseudo-arguments as confusing idealists and, continuing in the style of a scientific logician identifying fallacies, he gave names to these arguments: "definition by initial predication" and "the error of exclusive particularity." Definition by initial predication regarded "some early, familiar, or otherwise accidential characterization of a thing as definitive." For example, I might by an accident of residence first learn of Columbus through the fact that the Columbia River was named for him. It did not follow that we substituted "the man for whom the Columbia River is named" for "Columbus" in historical scholarship. Similarly, Columbus is the man I am now thinking of, but to treat him as such in all subsequent discourse would assume that my thinking of him was the most significant thing about him. I would make an identical error by finding 'a' in the word 'man' and then defining it as the second letter in the word 'man'. The idealist found things as thought of and then mistakenly named them ideas—defining things by initial predication. The error of exclusive particularity supposed that because objects were known they could not exist unknown, as if the letter 'a' could not also be the fourth letter of 'moral' and occur in other words as well. It had a multiple and not an exclusive particularity. Having found an entity in a mental context where it was named 'idea', we could not assert that it belonged only to this context or define it as idea. We discovered objects as known, said Perry, but they moved in and out of the knowing relationship.[9]

To deny idealistic dogmatism we had only to realize that an idea was an office or relationship instead of a substance: a thing could occupy the office or assume the status of idea without being identified with it. When a citizen of the United States became its president, the citizen and president were identical: there was no "presidential" entity substituted for the citizen, no correspondence or representation. Similarly a thing might belong at once to nature and to mind.[10]

Perry and the other neo-realists agreed with Royce that representational realism must lead either to solipsism or absolute idealism: we became trapped in the realm of our own ideas or, if we desired to escape the trap, we postulated an infinite idea which supplemented our fragmentary ideas. But this alternative was also solipsistic. It was absolute solipsism and, the neo-realists claimed, if we did not initially assume that knowing constituted the being of objects known, we avoided solipsism altogether.[11] Perry and his cohorts espoused what he called "epistemological monism": "when things are known, they are identical, element for element, with the idea, or content of the knowing state." There was no division of the world into ideas and things that the philosopher must initially accept and then explain. There was rather the class of things; the sub-class that we knew were ideas.[12] While knowledge did not condition the known thing, the thing, so far as it was known, was still identical with the knowledge of the thing. And Perry defined a person as an organization into which knowledge entered as an essential component.[13]

Perry completed his case with two further observations on idealism. Nineteenth-century science had left faith and revelation unsupported in their demand that spirit subordinate nature. The world which religion conceived as the handiwork of God or the stage setting of the moral drama threatened to swallow up both man and God. Absolute idealism arose, Perry said, against the claim of science to have alienated the world from man. This new German philosophy would redeem nature from mechanism and restore nature's spiritual center:

> It must not be supposed that this was the conscious aim of the idealists and their forerunners, or that the tendency was not in large part due to purely theoretical motives. But it is this that accounts for the great human importance of idealism, for its stimulating power and widely diffused influence. . . . It is a movement of epochal proportions, supported by a wide diversity of thinkers and dominating philosophy from the time of Berkeley down to the present day. Its central motive is the restoration of the supremacy of spirit. Its distinguishing characteristic as a philosophy of religion, is its sub-

ordination of nature to God by means of a preliminary reduction of nature to knowledge. God is declared to possess the world as man possesses his lesser microcosmic experience. That very mechanical cosmos which had served to belittle man, is now made to glorify him through being conceived as the fruit of intelligence. God, the discarded hypothesis of science, is enthroned again as the master-knower of whom science itself is only the imperfect instrument.[14]

Perry claimed that absolutism subverted its own theological ends. The idealist called in an absolute consciousness because finite consciousnesses were limited and fragmentary. But if we recognized consciousness by its relativity, its inadequacy in defining the world about us, what did "an absolute consciousness" mean? If we defined consciousness as experience relative to a point of view, said Perry, "to retain the concept of conscious-ness for a realm defined as free from just that factor of circumscription is sheer absurdity."[15] Idealists who defined the absolute as will faced a similar difficulty. Will was nothing if not activity, but the "absolute will" was neither changing nor active: being was not reduced to doing, but doing to being.[16] Idealists had succeeded, Perry claimed, by using words that "convey a sense of finality, or of limitless and exhaustive application, where no specific object or exact concept possessing such characters is offered for inspection. . . . The desire of philosophers to satisfy the religious demand for an object of worship or faith . . . leads to . . . verbal suggestion in which a technical philosophical conception is given a name that possesses eloquence and power of edification."[17]

Suppose we dismissed the contention that consciousness could not constitute the world because it referred to relativity and exclusion within the world. Suppose in some crucial sense the world was one of absolute consciousness. Perry still said we gained nothing. Religious philosophizing justified immortality and was rooted in the dread of annihilation, in the severance of ties and activities presently good. Faith's chief interest was that certain values survived and were consummated. But if consciousness was the form of all being, it was not vital to religion. If the world was a universal consciousness, teleological through and through, then immor-tality consisted in existence in this whole. We would not consider the conception religiously relevant had not philosophers expressed it in such phrases as "the eternal life." If the world was all good, then our values' triumph was identical to what actually occurred and what, did language not befuddle us, we regarded as the chief impediments to this triumph.[18] A scientific philosophy would avoid obfuscating issues by developing a more antiseptic vocabulary.

Holt and Montague

Perry's work had two effects. On one hand it demolished the claims of absolute idealism to prima facie tenability; on the other it made a presentational variety of realism seem credible. Holt and Montague defended this realism.

Followed by Perry, Holt advocated a quasi-behavioristic theory of mind. The universe consisted of various sorts of entities that had being. Consciousness or mind was a sub-class of these entities, those selected by the body's nervous system. A principle independent of the principles organizing the entire class of entities defined mind, and entities classed in this way were called *contents of consciousness*:

> The elements or parts of the universe selected, and thus included in the class mind, are all elements or parts to which the nervous system makes a *specific response*. It responds thus specifically if it brings the body to touch the object, to point toward it, to copy it, and so forth. . . . [If we look at a red rose] *that color out there* is the thing in consciousness selected for such inclusion by the nervous system's specific response. Consciousness is, then, out there wherever the things specifically responded to are.

Secondary qualities, Holt concluded, were as objective as primary qualities. The inclusion of either in the class of things we name a consciousness depended for both on the specific response of a nervous system.[19]

There was no reason, the neo-realists said, to infer that the object perceived was identical to the intra-organic means by which we perceived it, that because the means was internal the object was also.[20] Arguing from perceptual physiology, Holt added that the nervous system was a complex transmission system making us aware of those aspects of the world defined by consciousness. But this view did not entail that consciousness was within the nervous system. Consciousness was not in the skull but "out there" precisely where it appeared to be.[21]

The question arose for the neo-realists and their opponents of how to account for error on this theory. Holt urged that consciousness was "out there." But where did we locate the objects of any illusory or delusory experience? Were the two desks I perceived when I pressed on my eyeballs both "out there"? Did Holt populate the universe with all the erroneous perceptions, delusory and illusory experiences, fantasies and hallucinations that had occurred? Representational realists argued persuasively that in limiting ideas to the subjective and postulating the objective, we rigidly controlled what existed. Holt had not said that the entities composing the world existed, however; they had being or, as he put it, "subsisted." He contended, first, that perceived things need not be real: their reality depended on classifying them with other sub-classes of entities defined as real. He defined consciousness as that sub-class of entities that the nervous system selected, and this definition did not imply that every entity in that sub-class was real.[22] Second and more important, for any entity in the universe to have a spatio-temporal existence—and therefore reality of the physical sort—it must have certain systematic relations to other elements. In cases of veridical perception, locating a content of consciousness "out there" acknowledged that what we saw had certain relations to other entities. But a hallucinatory experience, say of a black cow, had no such relations, and Holt accordingly believed that this experience had no spatio-temporal location—either across the room or in my head—although it did have a position in my consciousness.[23]

The space we saw in a mirror was a sub-class of the entities of ordinary space and the bodies therein. It had all the spatial properties of the other save for a geometrically definable mode of reversal, and included the surfaces and shapes of the mirrored objects (reversed) with their colors. But it did not include the ponderability and many other physical properties of these objects. Just as consciousness formed a sub-class of entities with unique properties, so "mirror space" and its objects had a unique set of properties. Holt said that examining cases of illusion and hallucination was examining a sub-class of entities which had some properties of the sub-class of physical objects but lacked others. The former sub-class had no spatio-temporal location: it wanted just those properties of physical objects just as mirror space and its objects wanted others. Holt also denied that hallucinations and illusions were subjective or "in the brain"— we did not say this of mirror space.[24]

Montague disclaimed Holt's (and Perry's) "behavioristic" view of consciousness. For him it was "a purely diaphanous medium which in no way supported or altered its objects." If we analyzed this medium as a "specific response," it must then be a motion, simple or complex, of some or all of the material particles composing the organism. Any motion must be up or down, east or west, north or south, or in some intermediate spatial direction. How, asked Montague, could such a motion constitute what we experienced as the "consciousness of "an object? The "peculiar self-transcending thing called *awareness* puts an individual in relation to objects that are either in other places and times or not in space and time at all."[25]

Montague's qualms over the Holt-Perry position reflected the uneasiness of many philosophers who thought consciousness was either too complex or too spiritually fundamental for thinkers merely to reduce to behavior. Montague additionally objected to Holt's explanation of error, and other philosophers echoed this objection. In truth Holt was a bold ontologist who proposed to construct our universe from a system of neutral entities. He was a neo-realist, to be sure, but realism was only one aspect of his philosophical program.* The very audaciousness and complexity of this program made it suspicious, and Montague pointed out that Holt adumbrated only some of its consequences and that others were unreasonable.

For Holt, objects of perceptual illusion or other erroneous experiences did not have spatio-temporal existence either where they appeared to be or in our heads. What did we do with the various perceptions of objects that we had from different perspectives? From the rear platform of a train, I saw the tracks converging; in a place directly above you saw them as parallel. Appearances deceived neither of us—we each saw what we ought to see if we perceived veridically—but I saw something different from what you saw. We wanted to say, Montague contended, that the tracks existed out there, but we could not say that they existed as they appeared in my consciousness—for they did not converge. It was not clear how Holt handled this question, but Montague recalled Holt's believing in "Relativistic Objectivism." According to this theory, all the objects appearing in space due to the effects of perspective existed. An object at each instant had no single position and shape but many posi-

*See chapter 22 below.

tions and shapes, each one of which was relative to some observer. The convergent tracks were objectively in space just as the rails that were parallel, but in each case the objective existence was not absolute but relative. Holt apparently construed certain of these physical-existents-relative-to-an-observer as more convenient than others and as therefore defining the common physical object. But as Montague pointed out, to say that something existed in this way was close to saying that it was relative to or dependent on consciousness: the new realism degenerated into the solipsism or representational realism it had tried to avoid. Montague went on: if the neo-realist "selected," on the basis of convenience, certain physical-existents-relative-to-an-observer as defining the common object, he evolved into a phenomenalist; objects became bundles of sense perceptions.*

If Holt slipped into "subjectivism," Montague did no better. He solved the problem of error by denying a locus of any kind to the non-existent things figuring in experience. Montague set up a dualism between perceptions that directly presented existing things and those identical only to "subsisting" entities without spatio-temporal position. If consciousness was "a purely diaphanous medium," how was it possible that sometimes existing objects directly presented themselves while at other times subsisting entities appeared and led us into error? How did we tell when consciousness presented us with the real and when the unreal? Montague himself was on his way to representational realism in which the real objects themselves caused, as Montague said, "a select aristocracy of appearances" distinct from the illusory perceptions.[26]

Contribution of Neo-Realism

The fratricidal arguments among the neo-realists and their pussyfooting with representational realism in trying to solve the problem of error were not good omens. In fact, although *The New Realism* promised further "cooperative investigations,"[27] no program developed and the six

*See Montague, "The Story of American Realism," *Philosophy* 46 (1937): 151–52. Montague's interpretation of some dimensions of Holt's position was wrong, and, as Montague noted, it is difficult to believe that anyone would hold such a theory. But I cannot find in Holt's work any discussion of perspective effects and their connection to our perception of objects (see especially CC). Consequently, even if Montague's rendition of "Relativistic Objectivism" was suspect, it was still true that Holt never directly faced certain problems.

authors published nothing further together. The concerted attack died out and the group disintegrated.* Aside from their own disagreements and individual ambitions, the problem of error contributed to their downfall: their unsatisfactory handling of this puzzle made it impossible for them to win converts in any number. As we shall see in detail, by 1920 a group of "critical realists" was promulgating many of the doctrines Perry, Holt, and Montague had fought. But although its success was short-lived, neo-realism made two contributions to American philosophy.

"The Program and First Platform" appeared in the *Journal of Philosophy* in July 1910. Two months later William James was dead and the leadership of the anti-monistic forces in philosophy confused. Royce still flourished at Harvard and, exploiting the "subjectivism" and "relativism" attributable to Jamesean pragmatism, proclaimed absolute idealism as the only bulwark of objectivity in philosophy. In this unlikely situation

---

*Even Perry's neo-realism was fragile, and he constantly toyed with a constructionalist view of mind, as a brief history of his opinions shows. His first book, *The Approach to Philosophy* (1905), heralded the convergence of competing philosophical schools into "realistic idealism" or "idealistic realism" (409).We may directly know reality, Perry suggested, and knowledge did not condition it. This "immanence philosophy" would define reality as what was capable of being known, as experience both in and out of selves. This view had affinities with critical rationalism, Royce's Third Conception of Being, but Perry changed it in *Present Philosophical Tendencies* (1912), substituting for it his own realistic version of James. The real object now transcended experience which, Perry claimed, meant only cognition as a whole (213–21, 349–78). But even here he stated that it was not just the real object that warranted the truth of ideas but also our intentions in dealing with the object. "Interest, means, and circumstance" determined truth (326–27), and this subjectivistic bias was also present in his contribution to *The New Realism*. The real object, Perry said, was independent of the knowledge relation into which it entered but he did not deny that in acquiring that relation it changed "by so much" and that the complex "known object," of course, depended on knowledge as one of its parts (113–18, see also 130–36). But by how much, we could ask Perry, did knowledge transform the real object? If all that we knew was the known object, as he pointed out, what could we say of the real object at all? It seems we could have no knowledge of it, and if knowledge was impossible, the neo-realist had not escaped subjectivism.

In his later *General Theory of Value* (1926) Perry appeared to have gone over to some variety of Kantianism: immediate sensory experience was a transformation of what he called the transcendent object. This object was complementary to an anticipatory response, both of which culminated in the experience. The experience was an aspect of the known object, and he connected knowledge to inferring from the present experience what experience was to come: the known object was some pattern of experience. Perry said the transcendent object—his old real object—existed independently of the anticipatory response, but he left open the question of by how much it was transformed in sensory experience (328–35). There was little of the characteristic view of neo-realism here, and C. I. Lewis, Perry's colleague in the 1920s, seems to have influenced him. On this question, see chapter 28 below.

Perry and his friends saw their opportunity: they snatched the banner of objectivism from the idealists.[28] In so doing, the neo-realists widened American philosophic debate. They emphasized doctrinal differences and opened the door to speculative diversity. Suddenly epistemological cal dispute in the United States became triangular: absolute idealism, Jamesean pragmatism, and neo-realism, each one against the other two. Chart 18.1 depicts the agreements and disagreements.

	Neo-realism	Absolute Idealism	Jamesean Pragmatism
Existence transcends consciousness?	Yes	No	No
Pluralism?	Yes	No	Yes
Truth is absolute?	Yes	Yes	No

Chart 18.1. Philosophic Controversy, 1910–1912

From the realist viewpoint the idealists were correct in believing that truth was absolute and not relative to finite minds, but wrong in insisting that facts existed within a single all-embracing experience. From the same viewpoint the pragmatists were right in their pluralism (the realists also rejected the interdependence of all facts) but wrong in supposing that truth about those facts was relative to and dependent upon the changing and conflicting experiences of verification. Although disagreeing on the absoluteness of truth, the idealists and the pragmatists joined forces against the realists to deny that existence transcended consciousness.

The salutary effect of neo-realism was to question the previously unassailable idealistic preconception—that objects did not transcend knowledge—and to dispute the monolithic satisfaction with Kantian ideas and, accordingly, to broaden philosophic opinion. At Harvard Perry catalyzed debate for the younger generation of philosophers: they would spend their professional lives trying to yoke realism to a voluntaristic idealism.

The neo-realists also had another, more subtle effect. Led by Perry, they accepted "natural science as the model and foundation of all knowledge."[29] The idea that philosophy was a cooperative enterprise that ought to proceed within a community of investigators flowed from this scientific commitment. They joined this commitment to a vague but pervasive conception that mathematics and logic provided an adequate philosophic technique. One of Perry's dicta for the movement was "the application of methods of mathematics and natural science to philosophy."[30] Castigating the emotive language of the idealists was not accidental, and he connected it with the scientific emphasis. In order to advance (like the sciences) philosophers must agree to "the scrupulous use of words." Perry admonished philosophy that it would not escape fruitless disputes "save through the creation of a technical vocabulary."[31]

The meaning of Perry's warning was not clear. It was an admirable goal to exhort philosophers to clarity, although one that was perhaps unnecessary if only because philosophy had always been the sanctuary for the most hair-splitting members of every generation.[32] What was peculiar was the mode of Perry's exhortation: imitate the sciences and mathematics, he said; be "technical." Perry never specified what this imitation meant. He had no special expertise in the sciences or logic—in fact he was ignorant of them. In a few places he substituted symbols for his lucid prose, but the result was mathematical mumbo-jumbo; he used letters and numbers to state relations that he stated just as easily without them—but the formulas did give an appearance of increased precision.[33]

It is not much more than an educated guess to hypothesize on the motives of the plea for scientific and mathematical exactitude. I would suggest that we are witnessing nascent professionals calling for a language and special training that would legitimate their expert status and perhaps procure for philosophy the respect accorded science. The love of wisdom was no longer something that men could practice when they took walks with their friends; nor was it doomed to the endless reworking of ancient puzzles; cooperative inquiry, technical expertise, a learned jargon, and a division of labor would win the day. As one of his collaborators wrote Perry, the neo-realists must emphasize that influential thinkers and department chairmen should "narrow the issues" that philosophers discussed at their professional meetings, in their learned journals, and in the classrooms.[34] At least in practice Perry never shared these ideals, but neo-realism did much to inculcate a "professional spirit" in many other members of the new generation.*

*There is more on this issue in appendix 1.

19

GEORGE SANTAYANA

View of His Background

In 1826 Josefina Borrás was born in Glasgow, Scotland, the daughter of a Spanish colonial service officer who never gave the child a permanent home. In 1849, in the Philippines, she married an American from Boston, George Sturgis. She had five children by him before he died in 1857—he was just forty—but two of them died in infancy, including the firstborn male. On a trip to Spain in 1862 Josefina remarried; her husband this time was Augustin Ruiz de Santayana of the Spanish foreign service. A year later they had a son, George Santayana.

Until Santayana was three the entire family lived in Spain. At that time his older half brother, Robert Sturgis, returned to the United States for his education. Two years later when George was five, the mother also went back to Boston with her two Sturgis daughters. Apparently the social position of the Sturgis family in Boston was superior to that of the Santayana family in Spain. George remained with his father in Spain, and an aunt attended to him. But when her daughter died, the aunt turned her affection to her son-in-law and his children. The mental deterioration of Santayana's uncle completed the destruction of this second household; and when George was eight in 1872, his father took him to Boston. A year later the father returned to Spain without his family. George's care fell to his half sister, Susana Sturgis. She was twenty-one and devoted herself to the child who then grew up in a proper Boston family.

Why did Santayana's mother desert her youngest child and then later destroy his third home by refusing to accompany her husband to Spain? And what effects did these repeated traumas have on the boy?

In his memoirs, written when he was in his eighties, Santayana explained that his mother was cold, reserved, and indifferent to the world, regarding all things from a distance. The death of her first son, Santayana wrote, made "a radical revolution in her heart." "It established there a reign of silent despair, permanent, devastating." His mother had surrendered earthly demands and attachments, and thereafter "the most tragic events . . . could not move her deeply, and the most radical outward changes could disturb her inner life and daily habits very little." She regarded the world as beyond her control; she could not influence external affairs. Santayana recounted in his autobiography that he was confident of this explanation because at thirty, at about the same age as had his mother, he "underwent a similar transformation": "the sheer passage of time, the end of youth and friendship, the sense of being harnessed for life like a beast of burden . . . separated the inner self from the outer, and rendered external things comparatively indifferent." The only attitude to take toward the world, Santayana supposed from his experience and that of his mother, was one of passivity or renunciation; he would absorb himself with his own psyche.

Whatever the merits of Santayana's narrative, there was something awry in his account of his mother and of himself at the age of thirty. Josefina Santayana was a strong and dominating woman: she had left her son and second husband to secure the fortune of the rest of her family, and she had not hesitated to break from Augustin again when he refused to live in Boston. She had suffered by her first marriage, and she might have been reserved and distant, but passive she was not; in an era when women were bereft of power she was indomitable in creating an environment beneficial to her interests. Santayana himself was thirty in 1894, and it is true that his change of heart, "metanoia" as he called it, also had emotional causes—the deaths of his father and a close friend and the marriage of his sister. Moreover, we have come to associate emotional letdown, "mid-career crisis," with people at the same stage of life as was Santayana. But consider the young man's position : he had graduated from Harvard in 1886, summa cum laude, spent two years studying philosophy in Germany on a Walker Fellowship, returned to Harvard and completed a Ph.D. under Royce in 1889, and the same year joined the department as an instructor in philosophy. Although he had no more security than the instructorship in 1894, he was a member of a famous department; his repeated reappointment appeared to signify its members' approval; and he was already staking out a reputation as a philosopher with a literary bent. These were not negligible achievements for a man of thirty. Yet Santayana could only see that the passage of time brought loss and frustration; he did not see mature sexual relationships, professional fulfillment, or any of the other satisfactions adult life promised. Are the reasons he cited enough to bring a man to this despairing point?

Santayana's account seems to be not merely a description of past events but also a device for making the traumas of his childhood bearable and for legitimizing a subsequent fear of interpersonal relations. If Santayana believed in his mother's metanoia, then he would not have to ascribe his childhood traumas to her will or to his unworthiness. The reason for the loss of his mother's love would be external to them both: its cause would lie in the nature of things. It was no one's fault that her firstborn died. Loss was unavoidable, part of living; we were not responsible for what happened to us. Given this state of affairs, the man of reason would renounce the fleeting power that a conventionally successful life brought. Santayana also linked his behavior to his mother's, it seems, in order to rationalize what would otherwise present itself as monstrous and cruel: his mother was not unnatural but, like him, found herself powerless.

Early Poetry and Its Context

Santayana's own experience led him to believe in the impotence of consciousness and inclined him to seek a more general warrant for this belief. Rightly or wrongly, he made the tragedy of his family the tragedy of existence itself. Simultaneously, however, it was possible for him to surrender to contemplation. If involvement was dangerous, meditation was not: "The whole world belongs to me implicitly when I have given it all up, and am wedded to nothing particular in it; but for the same reason no part of it properly belongs to me as possession, but all only in idea. Materially I might be the most insignificant of worms; spiritually I should be the spectator of all times and all existence."

By surrendering power in the world of action, Santayana was able to possess the universe in contemplation. He could indulge his aesthetic capacities and concern himself with the imaginative order. This solution to his personal troubles propelled him to creation: he could master ideas, he could write. At Harvard in the 1890s, Santayana expressed his distinctive outlook first in poetry and then in a philosophy that would explain why the will was ineffectual.

Santayana wrote many of his early sonnets during what he later recalled as his period of crisis. They displayed that facet of his metanoia, literally a dying into life, which made his renunciation vital. The sonnets revealed throughout the elements of his later philosophy: rejection of traditional religion, belief that natural causes explained all phenomena, conviction of the aesthetic basis of value, and the sublimation of instinct for intellect. Sonnet 5 epitomized the early stage of his disillusionment with religion. The lack of distinction between sight and vision, dream and truth, waking and sleeping, was a source of anguish:

> Dreamt I to-day of yesternight,
> Sleep ever feigning one evolving theme,—
> Of my two lives which should I call the dream?
> Which action vanity? Which vision sight?
> Some greater waking must pronounce aright,
> If aught abideth of the things that seem,
> And with both currents swell the flooded stream
> Into an ocean infinite of light.
> Even such a dream I dream, and know full well
> My waking passeth like a midnight spell,
> But know not if my dreaming breaketh through
> Into the deeps of heaven and of hell.
> I know but this of all I would I knew:
> Truth is a dream, unless my dream is true.

This inability to separate dream and reality led in succeeding poems to a sense of the vanity of action and a consequent emotional detachment from it. At the same time, denying the active life marked a freeing of energies; the poet affirmed the intellect as he renounced the interpersonal. In Sonnet 19 he showed that the world could belong to him in idea:

> Above the battlements of heaven rise
> The glittering domes of the gods' golden dwelling,
> Whence, like a constellation, passion-quelling,
> The truth of all things feeds immortal eyes.
> There all forgotten dreams of paradise

From the deep caves of memory upwelling,
All tender joys beyond our dim foretelling
Are ever bright beneath the flooded skies.
There we live o'er, amid angelic powers,
Our lives without remorse, as if not ours,
And others' lives with love, as if our own;
For we behold, from those eternal towers,
The deathless beauty of all winged hours,
And have our being in their truth alone.

Formerly confused by its inability to distinguish fact and fancy, the self aroused itself to activity. It reordered life by taking the whole of consciousness as a contemplative realm.

Santayana wrote his first sonnet sequence between 1883 and 1893; the second sequence appeared in 1896, written a year after his 1894 metanoia. These sonnets constituted its expression, Santayana recalled, and carried forward the theme of constructive impotency, this time in the loss of love, reacted to first with despair, then with renunciation and finally detachment. The vehicle of the second sequence was the platonic love sonnet, which traditionally celebrated the love of a good and beautiful woman so great that it opened the heart of the lover to the love of all beauty and goodness, leading him at last to love the perfect beauty and goodness of God. In Santayana's second sequence not all these ideas were present. He wrote only of the frustration of physical love and the lover's spiritual education. Moreover, he did not just disavow physical love but all instinctual drives. In the poems Santayana mastered these drives and turned them to spiritual use. As he later wrote, "The passion of love, sublimated, does not become bloodless or free from bodily trepidation. . . . It is essentially the spiritual flame of a carnal fire that has turned all its fuel into light. The psyche is not thereby atrophied; on the contrary, the range of its reactions has been enlarged."

In Sonnet 30 he begged his mistress to surrender to his passion:

Let my lips touch thy lips, and my desire
Contagious fever be, to set a-glow
The blood beneath thy whiter breast than snow—
Wonderful snow, that so can kindle fire!
Abandon to what gods in us conspire

Thy little wisdom, sweetest; for they know.
Is it not something that I love thee so?
Take that from life, ere death thine all require.
But no! Then would a mortal warmth disperse
That beauteous snow to water-drops, which, turned
To marble, had escaped the primal curse.
Be still a goddess, till my heart have burned
Its sacrifice before thee, and my verse
Told this late world the love that I have learned.

Yielding to passion was yielding to death, an affirmation of mortality and not its consolation. Neither life nor death brought fulfillment—one is vanity, the other despair. But art, in marble and verse, transcended them.

In Sonnet 33 the poet affirmed the gift of love in its ideal form in the octave·

A perfect love is nourished by despair.
I am thy pupil in the school of pain;
Mine eyes will not reproach thee for disdain,
But thank thy rich disdain for being fair.
Aye! the proud sorrow, the eternal prayer
Thy beauty taught, what shall unteach again?
Hid from my sight, thou livest in my brain;
Fled from my bosom, thou abidest there.

The sestet returned love to the senses, but defined it as an appreciation of nature:

And though they buried thee, and called thee dead,
And told me I should never see thee more,
The violets that grew above thy head
Would waft thy breath and tell thy sweetness o'er,
And every rose thy scattered ashes bred
Would to my sense thy loveliness restore.

The despair which threatened to separate the poet from life forced him to art's ideal creations; in turn they restored him to the world. But he sought not to possess or dominate nature, merely to experience it passively.

Santayana's Philosophy

Although the poetic evidence sustains the view that a few critical events determined Santayana's vision of the world, the poetry is not the best evidence that we could wish for. Other documentation indicates that Santayana's perspective evolved over a longer period and that rebuffs to his professional advancement also helped to produce his viewpoint. We can see how these factors operated on Santayana by noting how his thought and his career developed.[1]

When Santayana turned to philosophy proper in the 1890s, his chief mentor was William James and the last chapter of the *Principles* where James took up "psychogenesis," the steps by which human beings acquired their mental categories. Santayana wanted to survey the vicissitudes and progress of human culture and the various spheres of civilized life. He was one of the first of a group of Harvard thinkers with an interest in what I have called evolutionary naturalism: following James, Santayana would use the developmental hypothesis to understand the growth of the mind. Nonetheless, his evolutionary naturalism was more aesthetic than James's: Santayana would contemplate the history of consciousness, and he emphasized the deterministic side of the *Principles*, the book's scientific dualism, and the spectatorial consciousness that dualism countenanced.[2] He was on his way to a philosophy that would justify passivity. But matters were more complex. Determinism was not all there was to the *Principles*. In it James had implied that no philosopher could credit determinism and meant, finally, to rescue an engaged moralism from the traps of some interpreters of Darwin. This side of the *Principles* also influenced Santayana. Moreover, the hints of radical empiricism in James's early writing and teaching attracted him: James's neutral experiences had organized themselves over the ages into the world we knew, and this idea undergirded Santayana's attempt to outline the growth of forms of experiencing. James's position entailed, however, not only that consciousness was active in organizing experience but also that there was no "world" exterior to experience. Santayana imbibed both the conflicting strands in James's work, and the result was inconsistency in Santayana's early thought. It adopted a Jamesean stance but did not coherently link it to the poetry's vision. In *The Sense of Beauty* (1896), *Interpretations of Poetry and Religion* (1900), and especially *The Life of Reason* (1905–1906), there was a fitful enunciation of Santayana's passive "critical realism," but he was more an unhappy pragmatist; and he came to his own realism via pragmatism and neo-realism.

The Sense of Beauty argued that the world was composed of sensations that intelligence grouped appropriately. The sensations sufficient to explain the world constituted the qualities of things; they were objective. We relegated the rest to a subjective sphere, regarding them as being "in the mind of the beholder" (35–41). Among these latter "sensations," which Santayana, roughly, called the emotions, were the feelings of preference or appreciation, immediate and inexplicable reactions of approval. Aesthetic pleasures were one species of these feelings, but Santayana differentiated them among the emotions because they were "objectified." Aesthetic pleasure was a subjective phenomenon, which we nevertheless attributed to the object. Beauty, Santayana held, was objectified pleasure (16–19).

The analysis had much in common with James's view of "the place of affectional facts in a world of pure experience": for James beauty did not belong entirely to the subjective sphere but had some characteristics of the objective. Nonetheless, Santayana contended that as a preference beauty could not have objective existence (35–41). For him the subjective-objective distinction was not clearly functional as it was for James: "sensations," for Santayana, might simply have their subjective or objective character. In fact, his explication distinguished in sensation the realm of "consciousness" (out of which we constructed the fact world) from that of "emotion" (the realm of feeling). But then he said that all consciousness was tinged with emotion and could not be consciousness without being tinged (13–19).

The same ambiguities occurred in *Interpretations of Poetry and Religion*. The book's central idea was that religion and poetry were the same, differing only in the way people connected them with life. Poetry was religion when it intervened in life, and religion merely supervening upon life was poetry (v–vi). At their point of union, poetry lost its triviality and aimlessness while religion surrended its claim to knowledge. Their synthesis expressed ideals giving meaning and value to life but did not refer to what existed (184–90).

In these passages Santayana was consistently a dualist and could easily have wedded a sterile view of mind to his dualism. Both poetry and religion, he said, were aspects of the imagination. They contrasted with understanding, whose job was deciphering the data of sense and framing an idea of reality; understanding produced science, not poetry or religion. But, Santayana continued, imagination and understanding differed not in "origin" but in "validity": the objects of the understanding were useful and abstract; they were serviceable in practice and capable of verification. On one hand, Santayana kept his two faculties apart by arguing, in effect, that unverified "scientific beliefs" were not beliefs at all but imaginings: religion verified would be science. On the other hand, he said, his distinctions were ideal and arose in discriminating various functions in a dynamically unified life. The scientist might be a religious poet of high order.[3] Science might derive from understanding, Santayana continued, but was "symbolic" like the products of the imagination; only its degree of verification and practical usefulness distinguished it from them.

Santayana admitted his dilemma in saying that everything represented to the human mind was relative to it, but he still declared his ability to make sharp distinctions. We could only argue the relativity of all conceptions, he said, by presupposing their lack of worth for or divergence from an absolute reality. But, he concluded, "humanity" also infected this latter conception.[4]

There were similar strains in *The Life of Reason*, the great five-volume work of Santayana's middle age. Subtitled "The Phases of Human Progress," the book was Santayana's major contribution to evolutionary naturalism, a massive attempt to construct a "natural history" of high culture. As the advertising for the original edition read, "Professor Santayana's general view of the universe and its problems is more or less a variant of the most recent and popular phase of philosophy known as 'pragmatism,' but it is altogether the most original and brilliant statement of this general view."

For Santayana every impulse of a conscious being carried with it a sense of the goodness of its object and, for the impulse, the object did embody the good. If the impulse stood alone, the good would be absolute. Within each individual and in society as a whole, however, there were many opposing impulses. In these circumstances, Santayana said, there arose a special impulse—Reason—whose character it was to have as many other impulses as possible harmoniously satisfied. Reason was thus man's capacity for ordering experience, but reason was also rooted in this "flux": the flux was the union of impulses and that which evoked them, and reason worked within this disordered mass to integrate rival impulses. *The Life of Reason* sketched the extent to which the impulse had come to or might dominate the main branches of human thought and activity, common-sense concepts, social and religious beliefs and institutions, art, and science.[5]

Santayana's language in all his philosophic works was metaphoric rather than precise, and at first he seemed to follow James's neutral monism. There was the flux, a brutish chaos of immediate feeling; human experience at its best was the product of this given and reason, the two conjoined in order to check immediate impulses in the service of those more permanent, the life of reason (1:35–47). We divided immediate experience into objects ("concretions in existence") and ideas ("concretions in discourse") (1:161–83), and Santayana hinted that this analysis easily explained how ideas knew objects—in the first instance they were interdependent (1:126, 140). In knowing, present experience cognized something absent. What we called the object that we knew was not identical to any or all sensations, nor did sensations exhaust it. But the object contained nothing assignable but what sensations could conceivably reveal (1:76–83). To know an object, it seemed, was to allow a given appearance to stand for future ones and to be able successfully to predict them on the basis of the one given.

For James the physical world clearly lay within experience; we carved it from experience. For Santayana things were not so simple. He was writing *The Life of Reason* at the same time James was publishing the *Journal of Philosophy* series and wrestling with the problems of panpsychism. Corresponding over their work clarified Santayana's opinions, and C. A. Strong, a former student and friend, helped both men along. Acknowledging his indebtedness to Jamesean neutral monism, Santayana questioned the status of the neutral experiences when no one experienced them. "For instance, if a candle which was nine inches long when left burning in an empty room is found to be six inches long on the observer's return, was it ever really eight inches in length?" Strong was feeding James with panpsychist answers to this question—yes, the candle was really eight inches in length and existed because it was experiencing itself. Santayana could not accept these answers and, in 1905, as we have seen, neither could James. Santayana made two suggestions for countering panpsychism and, apparently, found both in James's work. First, he said we might distinguish between appearance and reality: appearance was the flux; its cause was reality, "imputed being" existing whether or not we were there to experience the flux it caused. Second and more important, Santayana took the tack of Perry and the neo-realists: we perceived the nine- and six-inch candles as they were when observed; when the candle was eight inches long, it existed as an eight-inch candle although we did not observe it. Known things, Santayana implied, passed in and out of the knowing relation, but, when known, were known as they are.

The upshot was that if we were to account for unexperienced but experienceable possibilities (Royce's valid possibilities), Santayana argued we must postulate a material order that made them and actual experience possible. This scientific world was not relative to human thought but "a real efficacious order discovered in the chaos of immediate experience." And like the neo-realists Santayana held that this order consisted "bodily" of experienced elements and of others not experienced.[6] So *The Life of Reason* stated that the whole object was "the parts observed *plus* the parts interpolated" (1:103).

Neo-realism, however, was a passing phase for Santayana. In *The Life of Reason* his concern was to articulate a different sort of realism. Even the "objective" aspect of the flux, he said, symbolized a natural world outside it. All the flux was appearance. To explain it we hypothesized that ideal objects existed—the scientific world beyond the flux which we never experienced was the real. Santayana took a platonic view of the phenomena as appearance and the ideal objects as the intelligible entities adopted to account for and give coherence to appearance (1:9–32). The justification for these external things was "the function and utility which a recognition of them may have in . . . life" (1:1). The external objects were the "principles and sources of experience" (1:77); sensations were the "effects of a permanent substance distributed in a permanent space" (1:108). This substance or matter differentiated essence and existence. Some things had being only in consciousness (essences) while others existed; as distinct from the possible, what we knew as the actual was essence joined to matter; essences alone yielded the possible (1:73–83).

In this representational realism Santayana had his hand on a personally adequate philosophy. What he initially called nature was actually the *idea* of nature; both concretions in existence and concretions in discourse were dimensions of the flux, of what was present to consciousness. External to them was the real. "With the flux observed, and mechanism conceived to explain it, the theory of existence is complete" (1:17–18). Consciousness so constructed was passive, an epiphenomenon, a characteristic associated with organisms of a certain level. Nature was the condition of mind (1:104), and bodily processes guided the mind. It was not active nor did it enable the body to survive; rather, its survival indicated that the organism was agile in its environment (1:62, 202–07). To the extent that this was the thrust of his book, "the life of reason" was something of a fraud. It appeared to be a Jamesean excursion surveying the cultural achievements man painfully fashioned from brute experience over the centuries. But it really analyzed the play of ideas whose biological significance was nil: man depended on irrational forces beyond him. The value of culture was that it somehow made appearance congenial to the spectatorial mind.[7]

Critical Realism

Santayana did not fully develop his position until a second group of realistic philosophers, joined in a second cooperative effort, agreed that neo-realism could not solve the problem of error. The "critical realists" banded together in 1916 and their book appeared in 1920, *Essays in Critical Realism*. Although Santayana was their leading light and their central idea was his, the other six critical realists were also distinguished and the Harvard affiliation dominated. In addition to Santayana, James B. Pratt of Williams was a Harvard Ph.D. Neither C. A. Strong nor Arthur O. Lovejoy had doctorates, but both had studied at Harvard, as had Durant Drake of Vassar who was a Columbia Ph.D. Arthur Kenyon Rogers, formerly of Yale, was a product of Chicago and Roy Wood Sellars studied and taught at Michigan.*

*The critical realists carried on independent careers before and long after their association with Santayana, and their individual strengths as epistemological specialists was one reason that philosophy in America became so balkanized after the First World War. Strong, Sellars, and Lovejoy deserve independent study, and I must say something here of Lovejoy, the finest critical mind in twentieth-century American philosophy, and a man the Harvard philosophers feared and respected. Born in 1873, Lovejoy received a Berkeley B.A. in 1895 and a Harvard M.A. in 1897—apparently at James's urging he did not take a Ph.D. After more postgraduate work in Paris, he taught at Stanford, Washington (at St. Louis), Missouri, and, from 1910 to 1938, at Johns Hopkins. About the time he went to Hopkins,

The crucial concept Santayana gave to the critical realists was that of essence. The given data in experience were "character-complexes, essences, logical entities, which were irresistibly taken to be the characters of the existent perceived or otherwise known." These data did not exist; we could not identify them with mental states; and they did not represent the external object. In perception we jumped to the conclusion that essences were the characters of objects, fusing "the sense of the outer existence . . . with their appearance." But the critical realists distinguished these two aspects of perception: essences immediately appeared; upon reflection we saw that the belief in the physical world was pragmatically justified. Moreover, we could not identify the appearing essences with consciousness; they appeared in consciousness; they were present to the mind. In perception there was an essence "such and such a physical object," not the essence "such and such a mental state."[8] Finally, when we knew an object, we were assigning an essence to some reality existing independently of knowledge. Truth was the identity of this essence with the actual character of the reality referred to, but the essence itself did not exist (117).

The critical realists claimed that their view of essences distinguished them not only from the neo-realists but also from the older representational realists (Descartes and Locke). Making this claim involved specifying the relation of essence to external object:

In the life-economy of the individual the quality-group [the essence] acts as a token of warning of experiences that may be expected and as a stimulus to certain forms of reaction. It *means*, or *immediately implies*, to him the presence and, to a considerable extent, the nature

he launched in the journals a devastating attack on neo-realism, particularly as Perry espoused it. After attempts to secure him a place at Harvard had failed, he became, for the second generation of Harvard philosophers, as Peirce had for the first generation, the one that got away. Lovejoy devoted himself to vindicating the reality of ideas and images as entities in the mind, thereby pitting himself against the whole Cambridge tradition. In his trenchant *Revolt Against Dualism* (1930) he flailed the failures of pragmatism and neo-realism to escape dualism. His belief in the peculiar status of mental existents led him to the study of the history of ideas. His chief work in this area, in which his philosophic view was implicit, were his William James lectures of 1932–1933, published in 1936 as *The Great Chain of Being*. Lovejoy was also an activist intellectual. He helped to found the American Association of University Professors and took special interest in questions of academic freedom. He was a militant internationalist in both World Wars and became aggressively anti-communist in the 1950s. He died in 1962.

of some active entity of which it is well for him to be aware. It is, in short, *the means of his perceiving* the object. Here, then, the divergence of critical realism from the two other philosophical forms of realism plainly emerges. Locke and the neo-realists agree that the object of perception is the quality-group or some part of it, their disagreement arising upon the interpretation of these qualities. Critical realism differs from both in insisting that the quality-group which one finds in perception is not the object of perception but the means by which we perceive. By adopting this view the critical realist is able to avoid the difficulties about perception and error which . . . render neo-realism altogether untenable, and at the same time escape from the falsely subjective Lockian view that we perceive only our perceptions and are thus imprisoned within our ideas (96–97).

There was a neat bit of philosophy here. The critical realists reckoned that the physical objects caused experience (109–10), that is, in some sense they caused essences to appear (200–02). But the realists rejected the Cartesian claim that perceptions (essences) were what we perceived: we perceived objects, essences appeared. Accepting the Cartesian view that we perceived appearances (essences), the neo-realists, to avoid Cartesian subjectivism, had to argue that what appeared was, literally, the object. The critical realist, however, argued that appearance was the means of perceiving objects. "What we perceive, conceive, and remember, think of, is the outer object itself" (4 n.). Essence had "a sort of revelatory identity with the object . . . it contains its structure, position, and changes" (200).

Critical realism was interesting because it introduced an object external to individual experience to warrant truth claims. It was only possible (pragmatically?) to validate knowledge if there were independent objects for judgments to be true of. The concern of the critical realists was the theory of knowledge, and they minimized the extent to which their realism implied anything positive about the nature of the objects postulated to make sense of knowledge claims. They wrote only that some independent elements were necessarily involved in the knowledge relation but admitted to no metaphysical prejudices, no prejudices about the nature of the elements external to our consciousness (104). "The question of the ultimate nature of these nonhuman entities . . . is much more obscure than that of their existence." The nature of this reality might be "neutral entities," "experience," or panpsychical monads. "The critical realist as such has no exhaustive theory upon the subject. For critical realism does not pretend to be metaphysics" (108–09).

The critical realists did not stay together for long, and in their fine distinctions and isolation of epistemology from metaphysics, they contributed to the decline of system-building in American philosophy and the fragmentation of speculative energy. In this sense they were antithetic to Santayana's aims. Nonetheless, his association with them clarified for him the distinction between the ghostly realm of essence where the spirit could be potent, and the realm of matter where more active but deluded men thought they could be effective. In the work of his old age Santayana developed these themes, forsaking completely his Jamesean evolutionary naturalism. *Skepticism and Animal Faith* (1923) introduced the reader to this mature and unambiguous system, and he followed it with four volumes of *The Realms of Being* (1927, 1930, 1938, 1940). He often remarked that his work was merely a return to the classics, contrasting platonic appearances with the void of democritean atoms. But it is more accurate to say that he synthesized what he saw as the essentials of his teachers' views, for he had contended that Royce was easily reduced to solipsism and James to materialism.[9]

Career at Harvard

Santayana had long since left Harvard when he could be called a critical realist. In 1888, the year before he started to teach, he began to save for an independent future, and during his years in Cambridge he led a modest life. His mother left him a small legacy when she died in 1911, and after some indecision about his future, he resigned his professorship, leaving Harvard for good in early 1912. He never returned to the United States and spent the next several years in England.

One of the factors influencing his decision to leave teaching was his relations with Cambridge and his department. A small coterie of students idolized him. His fastidious black dress—he wore an exotic European cape—and his aloof, removed demeanor epitomized for them the only sane style of life. For most others he was supercilious, vain, and offensive. Santayana also had a peculiar belief that he might have been an unconscious homosexual during his Harvard years and, in fact, some students thought he was a homosexual.[10] His colleagues only grudgingly accepted him, and as his view became more distinct they grew more suspicious. The other philosophers had all developed a robust religious orientation—an academic version of nineteenth-century muscular Christianity—in the face of mechanistic interpretations of science. This orientation suited their active temperaments, and they thought that the alternatives to theological conviction were suicide, mindless involvement with trivia, or passivity. They never admired Santayana's aestheticism or his belief that religion was a form of poetry. He was, said James, "unworldly," "a spectator rather than an actor by temperament," and Harvard needed "a specimen" of someone like him. In effect, Santayana was a good example for the students of the accuracy of the Harvard analysis of what would happen to one without religion. If you don't believe us, the philosophers almost seemed to say, just look at Santayana. Santayana himself claimed that Cambridge tolerated him as a sop to academic freedom. "But this official freedom was not true freedom," he ruminated; "there was no happiness to it. A slight smell of brimstone lingered in the air. You might think what you liked but you must consecrate your belief or your unbelief to the common task of encouraging everybody and helping everything on. You might almost be an atheist, if you were troubled enough about it." He had passed years of suppressed irritation, he said, in the midst of a sanctimonious and repulsive Protestantism.[11]

The administration was less sympathetic than the department. Eliot believed that "continual contemplation of himself" ruined Santayana.[12] More than that: Eliot kept Santayana in the junior ranks from 1889 until 1907. He was forty-four when he became a full professor, and wrote that his career as a wide-ranging non-specialist had been "slow and insecure, made in an atmosphere of mingled favour and distrust"; he was "disliked" but "swallowed."[13]

Santayana had every reason to leave Cambridge. Although he was very much a Bostonian and relished the status his professorship conferred, it was not surprising that after he ended his teaching career he was contemptuous of Harvard culture and acerbic in his judgments. What other twentieth-century American academic of major repute spent eighteen years as instructor and assistant professor? Santayana's metanoia would have been more appropriate at forty than at thirty!

Man of Letters

In the years he spent in Europe, Santayana turned not only to philosophic treatises but also to the essay, and his seductive style and epigrammatic gifts made him known to the reading public not only as an aesthete or critical realist but as a commentator on American life. As one of the few men of letters the United States could claim, his writings became authoritative statements on national character and the state of fin de siècle culture. Unfortunately, Santayana's bitterness, however justified, distorted his appraisal of intellectual life, and his narrow range of experience curtailed the usefulness of his comments on the United States.

Santayana acknowledged that he had no contact "with the deeper layers and broad currents of American life . . . there was nothing in them in my time to interest me, nor had I any opportunity to explore them. Harvard College, a part of Boston, an occasional glimpse of New York made up my America."14 His memoirs were touching in their naiveté. His early life at Harvard, he recalled, was "a miracle of economy." His annual allowance of $750 meant that he blacked his own shoes and made minimal use of servants.15 Twenty years later two-thirds of the adult male workers in the United States still made less than $600 a year.16 In 1921 he issued a book which dealt mainly with the speculative climate in Cambridge at the end of the nineteenth century. Only a stylist like Santayana could have gotten away with calling it *Character and Opinion in the United States.*

Santayana only dabbled in social and cultural history. His greatness for historians lay in his interpretation of "the American mind," and here they have taken as truths about American intellectual life what he frankly said were "chiefly expressions of my own feelings and hints of my own opinions."17

In a famous essay entitled "The Genteel Tradition in American Philosophy" and in related critical writing he gave a name to an entire era in thought (and, almost incidentally, the arts). The Genteel Tradition for Santayana consisted of those nineteenth-century Americans who defended religion against encroaching naturalism. Santayana's traditionalists used the thought of German idealism beginning with Kant to defend their creed, and their chief sin, for Santayana, was adhering to "the Calvinist principle" that good was the triumph over evil. Royce exemplified the tradition at work. More than James did, Santayana loathed Royce's "Theodicy," his justification for the existence of evil.[18] And Santayana did not mourn the passing of the traditionalists when he later analyzed them "at bay." There was much more to this analysis, however, than the description of certain beliefs. Santayana wanted to characterize and to damn a way of life. He said that the genteel philosophers were apologists for theological orthodoxy and implied not only that they were perhaps intellectually dim but also hypocritical. In broader terms he condemned the late nineteenth-century (Harvard?) atmosphere of moral earnestness and suggested that the intellectual gentry was conventional, smug, and sanctimonious.[19]

It is difficult to pin Santayana down if only because his language was such a mix of the descriptive and the censorious. The trouble with his indictment may be simply that it was much more an indictment than an exploration of the history of intellectuals. It was true that the absolute idealism which Royce defended was a potent nineteenth-century doctrine and that its power waned in the twentieth. So much of Santayana's thesis was undeniable, but he meant much more than this by "the Genteel Tradition," and the "more" does not bear scrutiny. For example, although Santayana clearly did not like Royce's work, there is no evidence of apologetics among Royce or other followers of Kant. More importantly, Santayana wanted to associate a set of despised social conventions with three other conditions—a certain time period, a certain style of philosophizing (idealism), and religious beliefs. But first, although he was correct in appraising the conventionality of the New England ethos at the end of the century, Harvard academics were comfortably self-satisfied both before and after that era. Second, the gentlemanly qualities were not limited to idealists—all the significant Harvard philosophers in the nineteenth and twentieth centuries shared them, including Santayana. Finally, although late nineteenth-century idealists did defend religion, so did their realistic predecessors and successors, Bowen and Perry. All of these men were orthodox in defending values approved by the eastern Massachusetts upper middle class, but they were always progressive in adapting their theology to the ways of the world. In interpreting religion by emphasizing man's rational and moral powers, they were participating in what the leading American religious historian has called "a perennial aspect of church history," liberalism.[20] And gentility did not decline with the decline of religious beliefs. There is no "genteel tradition in American philosophy," and insofar as the notion of a genteel tradition in intellectual life rests on the existence of one in formal thought, the notion is mythic.

After the First World War Santayana returned to the Continent and lived chiefly in Rome, always writing, ever more concerned with his realms of spirit and essence. While philosophic interest in his aesthetic viewpoint diminished, he achieved enormous recognition in literary circles as a profound poet surveying the fortunes of the human psyche. He died in Rome in 1952, eighty-eight years old. In an essay unpublished at his death he had written, "I can identify myself heartily with nothing in me except with the flame of spirit itself. Therefore the truest picture of my inmost being would show none of the features of my person, and nothing of the background of my life. It would show only the light of the understanding that burned within me and, as far as it could, consumed and purified all the rest."[21]

20

ROYCE'S LATER WORK: LOGIC, PLURALISM, AND *THE PROBLEM OF CHRISTIANITY*

Royce and James

Toward the end of his life James committed himself to idealism and even moved toward monism. In his last major work, *The Problem of Christianity*, Royce moved toward pluralism. To understand this change that brought the two men so close together on details, we must survey the logical studies Royce undertook from the turn of the century, at Peirce's behest, to provide a formal proof of his doctrine.

Royce, Bradley, and Infinite Systems

Royce's logic initially focused on the English idealist Francis Bradley. Royce dissented from Bradley's contention that the absolute transcended self-consciousness and briefly argued against this position.[1] His concern was Bradley's belief that we could not understand the way finite creatures were *aufgehoben* in the absolute.[2] The supplementary essay to *The World and the Individual*, "The One, the Many, and the Infinite," was a more extended attack and assaulted Bradley with recently gained mathematical knowledge. The essay related to "the most fundamental theses" of the book, and was "one of the most serious and important things that ever I shall be able to write, or that ever I have written."[3]

Appearance and Reality stated the impossibility of having "any explicitly and detailed reconciliation of the One and the Many, or any positive theory of how Individuals find their place in the Absolute." Bradley's magnum opus rested on his analysis of any object, o, in the world and the relation R linking o to the world. To R, as itself an object, there existed R*, R's own relation to the world. We were never able to say that o was R-related to the world without becoming involved in an infinite regress, for R* had its R**, R** its R***, and so on. As Bradley put it, "endless fission" broke out. Royce agreed with this statement of the problem, and both Bradley and Royce agreed that finite experiences were unified in the absolute. But Bradley protested that we could not understand how the unification was effected. We would have to approach this puzzle via an endless succession of relations; we would have to enumerate an "actual infinite," and for Bradley an "actual infinite multitude" was contradictory.[4]

The internal meanings of ideas—actual experience—and the validly possible experience, which made our world "determinate," comprised Royce's absolute. The totality of these experiences was infinite. Each time we might suppose we had "collected" every experience, we would have to recall that there was an experience of all of them, and so on forever: the absolute was "infinitely self-conscious." Royce believed that the structure of this infinite set was intelligible and non-contradictory. The regress generated gave him the chance to display a new philosophy of mathematics and, so he thought at the time, to refute Bradley's skepticism.

The crux of Royce's reply in "The One, the Many, and the Infinite" was his definition of a particular system. In it (1) to every element M^r there corresponded a unique element called M^r's image or successor that, taken in its order, was the next element, (2) every image was distinct, and (3) at least one element M, although imaged by another, was itself the image of no other element. The natural numbers exemplified this order: they formed an infinite series beginning with zero in which each term was followed by a next. Most importantly, Royce defined the system "as a single internal purpose, in advance of the discovery that such purpose involves an endless series of constituents." Illustrating this claim, Royce asked his readers to ponder the attempt to draw in England a perfect map of England. This resolve entailed drawing an endless number of maps: when we came to that part of the map which represented the portion of England where we were mapping, we would have to draw another map, and so on indefinitely. We could never carry out the attempt, but "we should see," he explained, "why the one purpose, if it could be carried out would involve the endless series of maps" (1:504–09).

Royce introduced the phrase 'internally Self-Representative' to describe this system, one in which a part or "portion" represented the whole. He said this kind of system was infinite. Citing the work of Richard Dedekind, Royce held that infinite systems existed. Consider the totality S of all things that could be objects of my thought. Let s_0 be some thought, an element of S, and let s'_0, also an element, be the thought "That s_0 can be the object of my thought."

For any thought s_n there could be a corresponding thought s'_n, and hence the set of thoughts S' containing $s'_0, \ldots, s'_n, \ldots$ corresponded in a one-to-one fashion with the elements of S. But S' was a "constituent portion" of S, that is, every element of S' was by definition an element of S, but at least one element of S, s, was not an element of S'. Hence, "my own realm of thoughts" was infinite (1:510–11).

Royce illustrated Dedekind's formulation by showing that various "portions" of the natural numbers, say the powers of 3, represented all the natural numbers:

$$0\ 1\ 2\ 3\ .\ .\ .\ .$$

$$1\ 3\ 9\ 27\ .\ .\ .\ .$$

But Dedekind's emphasis on thought helped to rebut Bradley, for Royce could answer the main question. The "actual infinite" Bradley thought contradictory was an internally Self-Representative system. Just as a single plan defined the production of an infinitude of elements, so the absolute embodied the many. Royce conceived "the realm of Being as infinite in precisely the positive sense [of the internally Self-Representative system], now so fully illustrated. The Universe, as Subject-Object, contains a complete and perfect image or view of itself. Hence, it is, in structure, at once one, as a single system, and also an endless *Kette* [or series]" (1:553). Royce added that the Self was the form of the universe. Accepting Dedekind's result, Royce said the internally Self-Representative system in question was a completely self-conscious self. Let s be any given thought; and let us reflect fully on s. We defined an infinite system: s, s′ (s is a thought), s″ (s′ is a thought), s‴ . . . . We formed an internally Self-Representative system whose structure "is precisely parallel to the structure of an ideal Self." The "formal order" of first, second, and in general of next, "is an image of the life of sustained, or in the last analysis, of complete reflection. Therefore, this order is the natural expression of any recurrent process of thinking, and above all, is due to the essential nature of the Self when viewed as a totality" (1:532–38). The connection between each finite creature and the absolute was structurally identical to that of various "portions" of the natural numbers and the system itself. Each of us as "completed plans of life" and each of the absolute's individuals—our objects—were like the infinite number of partial but endless "fragments" of this system—the powers of 3, the odd numbers, the primes, and so on indefinitely (2:449–52).

The World of Description

Royce delivered the lectures making up the first volume of *The World and the Individual* in early 1899; they went to the publisher that October. But although he gave the second set of lectures in January 1900, he did not get them into print until October 1901. The two-year delay resulted from even more striking mathematical discoveries than Royce had capitalized on in his dispute with Bradley. They necessitated "a reform" in the later lectures.[5] In this lesser-known second volume Royce turned from the World of Appreciation to the World of Description, the world in which our finitude constrained us to live, the world of facts, of likenesses and differences which we discriminated and classified. Although this world did not express the inmost nature of things, it retained enough significance for Royce to announce that he would present a "new deduction" of its categories (2:45). He would investigate why the absolute appeared as a world of external objects.

Likeness and difference were correlative concepts: when we classified two objects as alike, they were ipso facto in some way different; if we classified them as different, they were because of that fact itself also alike. Love and hate were different emotions but they were both emotions. Moreover, the likenesses and differences we heeded were not thrust on us "without our consent or connivance." They were objects of our "attentive interest," and we could largely disregard or ignore that to which we attended. All "the correlated likenesses and differences which appear before us in the observed facts are such as the direction of our attentive interest in some measure favors. The world of facts is thus not merely *given* . . .. it is at any moment *regarded*" (2:46–51).

Royce also defined how we determined likenesses and differences. We discriminated, and comparing two objects by discriminating signified that something was between the two. Royce based his notion of "betweenness" on the work of the mathematician Alfred Bray Kempe (1849–1922). Making use of a broad notion of "between," Kempe argued that within limits the properties of any complete system of logical classes were identical to the properties of a geometrical system of points. Royce did not examine Kempe's monographs or the betweenness relation, but used the latter to investigate discrimination.

Let there be, said Royce, a collection of discriminable objects. But let it also be possible that we did not discriminate two of them, that is, that we regarded the two as equivalent, their differences not counting for a given purpose. Then, following Kempe, he wrote:

> let an object *m* of the system in question be so related to *a* and to *b*, that if you, either by inattention, neglect, or deliberate choice, disregard their difference, so that in any way they blend or become equivalent, *m* thereupon of necessity blends with both or becomes equivalent to both. In this case we shall say that, in the generalized sense, *m* is such a member of the system in question as to lie *between* *a* and *b* (2:77–79).

This procedure represented the logical structure of discrimination. It subsumed three elements, a, b, and something that kept them apart, or illustrated or determined their difference. The relationship was not dual but what "one may technically name a triadic relation." We knew pairs of facts *"through a single possible act of discrimination and comparison."* In discriminating we placed an object m between a and b, and Royce stated that we had begun a series which could proceed indefinitely. Placing m_1 between a and m discriminated between them, and m_2 between m and b between them. Thus: a . . . m_1 . . . m . . . m_2 . . . b. Theoretically this operation could continue ad infinitum, although it would quickly cease because of physical limitations or the satisfaction of interests, or both. Nevertheless, we had generated the first terms of a dense series, a series in which there was no next term, in which between any two there was a third.

Royce maintained that in the World of Description "all understanding of facts in terms of general laws" hinged on discrimination. The "working postulate" upon which "all scientific description of given facts depends" was that between any two there was a third. The better we conceived and verified a series of discriminations, the better we defined stages of "a single process of ideal construction" expressing, for example, how we passed from a to b, how, in mathematical terms, we "transformed" a into b. Discrimination was the means by which, say, the stages connecting two states of a body become the stages transforming the former state to the latter. But since likeness and difference were correlative, a and b were alike in some way throughout the transformation. The like features were "the invariant characters of this system of transformations." Transformational systems made up empirical knowledge. We discriminated systems of facts from one another and linked them by intermediate systems as we linked a and b. In discovering these invariant characters, Royce said, we ascertained the laws governing the systems of facts in question. Moving a body from one part of space to another left the shape of the body unchanged, and that was the discovery of the spatial property defined as the "axiom" or "law" of "free mobility." Another example of law was that all physical and chemical changes left the mass of matter unaltered: the transformations which a gravitating system of bodies underwent left invariant the system of relationships that the law defined (2:80–96).

Royce had so far analyzed the basic categories of the World of Description. We can note the "deductive" nature of his enterprise if we specify the bond between the World of Description and the World of Appreciation. The mathematical relation existing between them was one of the crucial elements to be extracted from *The World and the Individual* (2:x).

The dense series characteristic of discrimination in the World of Description was, for Royce, "less perfect" than the ordinal series characteristic of the World of Appreciation discussed in volume one's supplementary essay (2:72). This series was "well ordered" and each term in the series had a next (1:529–38). This order was the "original type of all order in heaven and upon earth." The World of Description had no such order; no individual could order the possible discriminations: between any two we found a third. The World of Description had the character of "endless fission" which Bradley pointed out, and the discriminations were gathered up into a well-ordered totality only in the absolute. In the World of Appreciation objects would not be discriminated in pairs; they would be "logically given, all at a stroke," an expression "of a single Self-Representative purpose." Were the world comprehended as a Self-Representative system, Royce asserted, "for one who grasped the facts in the order of that system, the recurrent process of the interpolation of intermediate terms in a series already recognized would no longer express the final truth" (2:81–107, 137). Even in the World of Description discrimination "tends to acquire the unity of a single volitional act" and "may always be viewed as having one general direction, that leads from a to b, through the intermediary stages (2:97–99). We *"interpret the simultaneous* [the objects of the World of Description] *in terms of the successive* [the structure of our appreciative consciousness]." For Royce, acting attempted to reduce the World of Description to the World of Appreciation.[6]

Unresolved Logical Problems

When Peirce reviewed *The World and the Individual* for the *Nation*, he wrote Royce that Royce's view of logic was "antagonistic to all that is possible for progressive science" and entreated him to study logic. Why did Peirce think the logic "most execrable"? In the unpublished portions of his review he revealed the grounds of his displeasure. The map metaphor required emendation. As an analogy, it lacked "several of the essential characters of the class of signs to which ideas belong." Royce must apply all "the new conceptions of multitude and continuity, and not merely that of the endless series," and he must apply them in more than a "single narrow way."[7] We do not know if Peirce was more detailed in his deprecation or if he communicated it directly to Royce, but there was an unassailable objection to Royce's presentation consistent with Peirce's ideas.

In contrasting description and appreciation, Royce's strategy was unmistakable. As Gabriel Marcel put it, "there are two worlds, which undoubtedly correspond to one another and penetrate one another for a higher mind, but which philosophical analysis must distinguish and even provisionally oppose to one another."[8] But Royce never gave the "reduction" of the structure of one world to the other. There was a reason for this: the undertaking could not succeed. Although we could achieve a one-to-one correspondence between the members of the series of natural numbers and a dense series, namely, the rational numbers, the mathematician Georg Cantor had shown that we could not preserve order. There was no way for Royce to reduce the logical structure of the World of Description to the World of Appreciation. At best from a dense series he could pick out a subseries isomorphic to the natural numbers.[9]

To comprehend the one and the many, Bradley said, we must appeal to the contradictory "actual infinite." Royce's supplementary essay showed that on one formulation this infinite was not contradictory, but this did not overturn Bradley's claim. Invoking a satisfactory infinite collection was not enough; it did not intimate how we applied this conception to the World of Description. Royce had restated Bradley's riddle in a more sophisticated form: how were we to reconcile the finite world, marked by dense series, with the absolute, marked by a well-ordered series? In short, *The World and the Individual* took up the challenge of *Appearance and Reality* but did not meet it.

There was another equally serious mathematical perplexity in Royce's metaphysics. Royce was not, I think, aware of it at the time, but since it became important later, it is well to isolate it here. The perfect self-consciousness of the absolute, Royce claimed, had the structure of a well-ordered series. A finite individual was not "wholly conscious" of his own consciousness. To be self-conscious in any complete sense "would be to be aware of the completion of an infinite series of presented facts." The absolute, that is, must be self-conscious of its own self-consciousness; it must verify that it was presently verifying (2:18). In the absolute the infinite contents of self-consciousness were "supposed immediately given"; they were "seen, experienced, presented, . . . all at once" (1:583). The supplementary essay showed that mathematical principles expressed how an infinite series was generated in its order of succession, but for the absolute this infinite series was actually present. In *The World and the Individual* Royce never clarified how we could express this formulation mathematically, but he mentioned it elsewhere as the class of all classes.[10] But he could not construe this conception coherently: Cantor had shown that it too led to a contradiction.[11]

Resolution

Royce joined the logical studies he pursued after *The World and the*

Individual not to volume 1 of that work or to its supplementary essay but to volume 2 and its chapter on Kempe's betweenness relation. By 1905 Royce had composed his masterwork in mathematical logic. His interest in Kempe culminated in this lengthy article, entitled "The Relation of the Principles of Logic to the Foundations of Geometry."

Kempe's papers, to which Royce acknowledged his indebtedness, were ambitious. Defining by postulates a set of entities called the "base system" and a relation Royce considered a generalized notion of betweenness, Kempe deduced the Boolean Algebra of Logic from the base system. Then, by selecting a set of the base system's elements and by introducing one further postulate, he sketched the foundations of geometry. Royce elaborated the philosophical significance of this project in his 1905 paper: "The problem of the foundations of geometry," he exhorted, "is only a part of that general problem regarding the fundamental concepts of the exact sciences." Given a certain system of entities which functioned like classes, we would find that their relations were "as rich as the totality of relations known to the exact sciences." This result would interest all those concerned with "the unification of the categories of science."[12]

It is plain from this article and from other references in Royce's work that both he and Kempe were working in the tradition of the "Erlanger Program," the paradigm for geometrical thinking at the time. Formulated by the mathematician Felix Klein through his understanding of Arthur Cayley, the Erlanger Program attempted a hierarchical classification of all geometries and in some of its phases mistakenly assumed that we could deduce the more restricted geometries from the less restricted.[13]

Kempe's scheme had certain inelegancies and limitations in Royce's eyes, and he tried to perfect it, first refining its basic notions. Royce called his system Σ and developed Kempe's theses not from the betweenness relations but from what he named the O-relation. Reintroducing the "betweenness principle" as one of the six postulates of Σ, however, evidenced its vital place.[14] He aimed at a broader and mathematically more sophisticated version of what he had done in the second volume of *The World and the Individual*. There he outlined the way we derived the "laws" of empirical knowledge from a few fundamental concepts. Although he used the betweenness relation, he did not develop his thesis mathematically; but in "The Relation of the Principles of Logic to the Foundations of Geometry" he believed he had elaborated the mathematics of his categories. Σ was a purely formal "order system" containing uninterpreted variables. By appropriately interpreting these variables, we procured specialized "order systems" characterizing the various branches of knowledge.

Although it is now clear that the relation among these systems was not one of deducibility, the logical connections involved were only vaguely understood at the turn of the century. Royce's idea of reducing the axioms of geometry and logic to (or deriving them from) some further set of postulates was wrong but comprehensible. He could regard Σ's postulates as "presuppositions" of all knowledge.[15] Reducing the geometrical axioms to some ideal system of entities meant that the philosopher required a system of entities that existed only in the mind. Royce would have a postulate system which was the precondition of our knowledge of material objects, the logical ground of the possibility of spatial—that is, external—experience; he would reaffirm the primacy of mind and the derivation of matter from it.

But although Royce had mathematically extended his work in volume 2 of *The World and the Individual*, he had insisted that this work applied only to the World of Description. The 1905 paper did not show how the World of Description was an "aspect" of the World of Appreciation, and insurmountable obstacles blocked this approach, at least as Royce conceived it. As we have also mentioned, his notion of the absolute was contradictory. Lastly, there was a wider and more complex issue. Royce was proud that his idealism was a practical philosophy that he could relate to worldly concerns, since he could only justify pursuing his technical philosophy as the ground of his practical thought. Consequently, he felt obliged to "translate" abstruse logical doctrines into positions intelligible to less mathematically-oriented followers and readers. Royce jokingly wrote to James that "his faithful disciples had certainly never understood him."[16] Again and again his other writings of the first decade of the century underscored the critical nature of Kempe's work and stated that a deduction of the categories was in the offing.[17] Royce did no more in any of his popular expositions than speculate on the philosophic millennium that a grasp of symbolic logic would bring, but by the end of 1910 he had evidently finished what he called the equivalent in the algebra of logic of the "harmonic construction." Unfortunately the "harmonic construction" first appeared in German as part of the *Encyclopedia der Philosophischen Wissenschaften* entitled "Prinzipien der Logik"; the English translation was not available until 1913. Royce's marginalia in the German edition evinced distress at the lack of a translation, and he called attention to the article's merit. The sketch of logic as the "Theory of Order," he noted, went back to the second volume of *The World and the Individual* and not the more famous first volume. The "Prinzipien der Logik," however, outlined his position more fully than any previous inquiry. "This paper," Royce concluded, "is thus a programme of a future possible Logic; and as a programme has a place in a fairly extensive plan. The issues discussed have, in J. R.'s opinion, an importance that is greater than the length of the paper indicates."[18]

Royce believed that he had reduced logic and geometry to the entities and relations of Σ. "The Principles of Logic" said something novel about Σ itself. According to his researches and those of Kempe, either transitive or symmetrical relations characterized the exact sciences. In a universe of discourse of logical classes, statements, or acts of will, we reduced these two kinds of relations to one: what Royce called the illative relation—the relation of subsumption between classes or implication between propositions. But we could transform any expression involving the illative relation into the "purely symmetrical relation of opposition." This "relation" was negation, the "not-relation," "one of the simplest and most fundamental relations known to the human mind," but also one of "the most momentous of all relations for the organization not only of all the exact sciences, but to all the systematic study of human experience and of all our knowledge concerning the order of the world and our own conduct." "It is essential to the whole business of thinking that propositions and the judgements which affirm or deny them go in pairs of contradictories." Voluntary action was possible only to a being who understood the meaning of 'not': we were able to act voluntarily only because we were able to refuse to act.[19]

Royce went further. Voluntary activity largely determined that there were objects of a particular sort to relate, that they were related, or that any given relation was present in the world. In this sense relations and classifications were arbitrary—they were our "creations" or "constructions." But relations necessarily existed among propositions, objects, and so on, because without them *no rational activity of any kind is possible.* For example, the not-relation exhibited a mode of activity that was a law of the "rational will." We reinstated the activity in supposing that it did not exist. Take the tautology 'p ≡ (~p ⊃ p)'. Its denial implied it and thus it must be true. We denied it only at the penalty of "the self-destruction of the thought which [its denial] undertakes to violate." Since denial was a form of willing, truth is that form of willing which reasserted itself in the attempt to do away with it:

> In brief, whatever actions are such, whatever types of action are such, whatever results of activity, whatever conceptual constructions are such, that the very act of getting rid of them, or of thinking them away, logically implies their presence, are known to us indeed both empirically and pragmatically (since we note their presence and learn of them through action); but they are also absolute. And any account which succeeds in telling what they are has absolute truth. Such truth is a "construction" or "creation," for activity determines its nature. It is "found," for we observe it when we act.

Those relations essential to Σ, the order system sufficient to yield all scientific concepts, were founded "upon the consciousness of our own activity and some of its necessary characters." In this sense exact knowledge was the "will to act in an orderly fashion, the will to be rational."[20]

Σ codified the necessary forms of willing defining mind. Could we say more of its structure? Royce's 1905 paper claimed only that the elements of Σ were "simple and homogeneous." He now argued that the elements of this "logically necessary system" were "modes of action." The infinitive or present participle of the verb expressed a mode of action in English. For example, 'to sing' and 'singing' were alternate ways of verbalizing a single mode of action. To every mode of action there corresponded a contradictory mode of action (for example, *not singing*); pairs of modes of action had logical products (for example, *singing and dancing*) and logical sums (for example, *singing or dancing*); the implication relationship held among them (for example, *singing and dancing* implied *singing*). Royce said that the modes of action were a set of entities to which we could apply the Boolean Algebra of Logic. But Royce also thought that the modes of action satisfied the primitives and postulates of Σ and defended this thought in two steps. First, he constructed an adequate set of modes of action. The notion that the absolute had actually present to it a completed infinite series involved a paradox in *The World and the Individ-*

ual, and his first step related to this logical problem. Royce had another problem in connecting his World of Appreciation with the World of Description: he could not link the betweenness relation and the dense series characterizing the latter to the ordinality characterizing the former. Royce's second step applied the betweenness principle of Σ to a well-ordered set of modes of action. We shall examine each step, but Royce's strategy should already be obvious: Σ was to reflect the absolute.

In the supplementary essay Royce urged that the absolute had the structure of a perfectly self-conscious self. Now he defined a similar structure using modes of action:

> It is perfectly possible to define a certain set, or "logical universe" of modes of action such that all the members of this set are "possible modes of action," *in case* there is some rational being who is capable of performing some one single possible act, and is also capable of noting, observing, recording, in some determinate way every mode of action of which he is actually capable, and which is a mode of action whose possibility is *required* (that is, made logically a necessary entity) by the *single* mode of action in terms of which this system of modes of action is defined. Such a special system of possible modes of action may be determined, in a precise way, by naming *some one* mode of action, which the rational being in question is supposed to be capable of conceiving, and of noting or recording in some reflective way any mode of action once viewed as possible.

This statement was consistent with Royce's emphasis on negation: determining some one mode of action (such as *willing, choosing*, or *reflecting*) excluded the contradictory mode of action and was reasserted in its denial. This "calculus" of modes of action had a "logical reality" which we could not question "without abandoning the very conception of rational activity itself." Any rational being capable of conceiving any mode of action at all must recognize it.

An absolute defined by all possible modes of action—as it appeared to be in *The World and the Individual*—was paradoxical. Royce recognized this in the later paper:

> it would indeed be impossible to attempt to define with any exactness "the *totality* of all possible modes of action." Such an

attempt would meet with the difficulties which the Theory of Assemblages has recently met with in its efforts to define certain extremely inclusive classes. Thus, just as "the class of all classes" has been shown by Mr. Russell to involve fairly obvious and elementary contradictions, and just as "the greatest possible cardinal number" in the Cantorian theory of cardinal numbers, and equally "the greatest possible ordinal number" have been shown to involve logical contradictions, so (and unquestionably) the concept of "the totality of all possible modes of action" involves a contradiction. There is in fact no such totality.[21]

The absolute chose among the possible modes of action to preserve its infinite reflective structure. This choice helped to resolve the other difficulty in *The World and the Individual*. Royce defined discrimination in the World of Description by a dense series. Nonetheless, as Cantor had shown, we could not preserve the order of the natural numbers and also put them into a one-one relationship with a dense series. But Royce said that the absolute picked out a set of discriminations (modes of action) from the possible discriminations which could occur.

If the discriminations were well-ordered, however, how did they suffice to analyze the World of Description where the betweenness principle applied? Royce asserted that this set of modes of action was "of the form of the foregoing system Σ" "which had an order *determined entirely by the fundamental* laws *of logic, and by the one additional principle thus mentioned.*" The principle in question was "analogous to a principle which is fundamental in geometrical theory. This is the principle that, between any two points on a line, there is an intermediate point, so that the points on a line constitute, for geometrical theory, *at least a dense series.*"

Royce described how the calculus satisfied the "betweenness principle":

What we may here call the Calculus of Modes of Action, while it makes use of all the laws of the Algebra of Logic, also permits us to make use of the principle here in question, and in fact, in case a system of modes of action, such as has just been indicated, is to be defined at all, *requires* us to make use of this principle. The principle in question may be dogmatically stated thus: "If there exist two distinct modes of action p and r, such that $p \prec r$, then there always exists a mode of action q such that $p \prec q \prec r$, while p and q are distinct modes of action and q and r are equally distinct." This principle could be otherwise stated thus "for any rational being who is able to reflect and to record his own modes of action, if there be given any two modes of action such that one of them implies the other, there always exists at least one determinate mode of action which is implied by the first of these modes of action and which implies the second, and which is yet distinct from both of them."

Royce's discussion had that flavor of mystery associated with Fermat's Last Theorem. He concluded that "this principle holds true of the modes of action which are open to any rational being to whom any mode of action is open." But the demonstration hinged on "considerations for which there is here no space."[22]

What had Royce accomplished in his own mind? Σ was necessary to all rational thought. We might say that a set of possible modes of action of a perfectly self-conscious being yielded a consistent interpretation of Σ's variables. As such the modes of action were well-ordered. "Any orderly succession of deeds in which we pass from one to the next has certain of the characteristics of the series of ordinal whole numbers. . . . there is indeed something about the nature of our activity, insofar as it is rational—something which necessitates a possible next deed after any deed that has been actually accomplished." But the set of modes of action which satisfied the postulates of Σ also defined

> an order of entities inclusive not only of objects having the relation of the number system, but also of objects illustrating the geometrical types of order, and thus apparently including all the order-systems upon which, at least at present, the theoretical natural sciences depend for the success of their deductions.[23]

The modes of action calculus was additionally rich enough to provide the types of order typifying the World of Description. Royce finally had circumvented Bradley's dilemma. The interpretation of Σ by the modes of action calculus gave the widest possible order system, and its fundamental notions reflected all rational thought patterns. By restricting Σ's generality in various ways Royce could obtain the more limited order-frameworks necessary in various areas of scientific understanding. Moreover, in Royce's view the modes of action did not merely give a consistent interpretation of Σ; they actually were the entities of Σ; Σ was the absolute. This was the ultimate deduction of the categories; in a mathematically precise way we saw how the constituents of the divine will functioned as the World of Description.[24]

Logic and Christianity

We should read Royce's last major work, the 1913 *Problem of Christianity*, conscious of the mathematical gains he had made. Even then, however, Royce will not satisfy our anticipations. Through logic he had achieved a spectacular deduction of the categories. Since this work was at the center of his system, advances in this area should lead to advances—indeed now solutions—in more comprehensible regions. We might expect *The Problem of Christianity* to reveal the secret of the universe. The scales will drop from our eyes and the glorious truth will emerge, mounted on invincible logic and clad in Pauline grace. Something less occurred. The connection between logic and Royce's less technical concerns was plain, but he did not work out the details. There were good reasons for this failure—among them, Royce's declining health. But the architectonic design remained unfulfilled, and *The Problem of Christianity* did not succeed as an analogue of the "harmonic construction."

The unfinished quality of the book was not surprising considering that Royce made two revisions in a system that had been abuilding for almost thirty years. Both revisions concerned the relation of finite to infinite: one the connection of the individual to the absolute, the other the reconciliation of description and appreciation. The first volume of *The Problem of Christianity* applied these changes to Royce's religious thinking; the second worked out their epistemological and metaphysical rationale. We shall examine the second volume first, beginning with the question of the two worlds.

Interpretation

In the second volume, Royce defended a novel kind of knowledge—interpretation—and it is not paradoxical to say that in explicating interpretation he solved the two worlds problem as James had, by denying it. The antithesis between description and appreciation was a theme in Royce's work from the late 1880s. But his discussion was metaphysical concerning the "grade of reality" attached to each world and the relation between the grades. When he took up epistemological questions, his position was that of an (absolute) pragmatist. He treated the connection between description and appreciation and absolute pragmatism only obliquely. As a pragmatist, Royce argued that verifying our ideas was engaging in activities leading to appropriate experiences if the ideas were true. In an article written during the same period as *The Problem of Christianity*, he described this enterprise as one in which we formulated hypotheses "prevailingly conceptual" and tested them through direct experience—"perceptual knowledge," "knowledge by acquaintance." For the pragmatist knowledge brought percepts and concepts into an "active synthesis"; it depended on "the marriage of the two processes." For certain purposes, we identified knowledge by acquaintance, perceptual knowledge, with appreciation; conceptual knowledge, with description. His epistemology also aimed at bringing together two different realms of experience.[25]

Royce's doctrine of interpretation repudiated the distinction between perception and conception, that is, the two worlds distinction. He had previously contended that Jamesean pragmatism entailed a unity of experience in principle unverifiable in James's terms. Absolute pragmatism accounted for this unity, and the unity had an appreciative reality, that is, it was the absolute. But *The Problem of Christianity* (and less clearly *The Sources of Religious Insight*) claimed that belief in this unverifiable experience was interpretation—the new form of knowledge (327–29). In effect Royce admitted that his formulation of absolute pragmatism was incorrect.[26] The new form of knowledge transformed the two worlds problem. Since it furnished a basis for metaphysical idealism and became "the main business of philosophy," we must examine the idea closely (38, 274, 297).

Knowledge of mind involved interpretation. When a man clarified his interests and meanings and acquired self-knowledge, he interpreted. Interpretation also gave us knowledge of other minds, the social relations between man and man. The comparison of ideas, however, was the most elementary interpretation, and a paradigmatic form. To compare two objects—let us say two cows—we must have in mind a third or mediating idea which specified how the cows were similar or different. It told us, for example, that one was blacker than the other. The third idea interpreted one to, or in light of, the other (229–304). Whereas perception and conception were dyadic relations—of perceiver to immediate datum and conceiver to abstract universal—interpretation was triadic even in its elementary exemplification (286–90).

Interpretation was sign translation. A sign was anything that determined an interpretation, but, hinting at his full doctrine, Royce noted that a sign indicated mind. For example, a road sign in a foreign language expressed a mind, and called for an interpretation by some other mind acting as a mediator between the sign (or its maker) and someone who read the sign. In these circumstances, someone interpreted something to a third. 'Interpretation' denoted both the triadic relation and the mediating term and even the result of the interpretive process. These inelegancies, however, were usually semantic, and his meaning was contextually unequivocal. He also ambiguously called what was interpreted an object (or idea), or mind; similarly he called the interpretation, qua mediating term, a further object (or idea), or mind. But this ambiguity was consistent: the interpreted object or idea expressed mind, and so did the interpretation, addressed to the mind in need of interpretation. Finally, each interpretation (the mediating term) provided a further interpretation, that is, any given interpretation acted as a sign that a further interpreter (sign) interpreted for another. Ideally the social activity involved was endless (289–90, 340). Every interpretation mediated between contrasting ideas, minds, or purposes (344–46). Royce maintained that signs constituted our world and that the "world process" was mental. This became clearer when he used interpretation to define individual selves.

When a man reflected, he interpreted himself to himself. Although in the usual sense of the word there was only one person, the relation was triadic. Suppose I remembered a former promise. I then interpreted this bit of my past self; the present self interpreted signs (= my past self) to my future self. I said, "I am committed to do thus and so" (286–88). Since self-conciousness defined mind and self for Royce, he regarded selves as sign series, series of interpretations: we unified separate ideas and experiences through interpretation. "In brief," he wrote, "my idea of myself is an interpretation of my past,—linked also with an interpretation of my hopes and intentions as to my future" (245). The interpretation defining the self was a series of comparisons of ideas, and self-knowledge was also a paradigmatic form of interpretation.

Royce took many of his ideas from Peirce's articles of the late 1860s on the same subject; he followed Peirce's exposition and freely expressed indebtedness. Their treatments differed in two central ways. First, Royce was clearer and less technical but also less precise. Peirce's ability to inspire others evidenced his influence again: Royce simplified interpretation as James did pragmatism. Second, as we shall see, Royce comprehensibly spelled out the metaphysical implications of interpretation: he joined Peirce's ideas about interpretation and the community and explicitly applied them to religious theorizing.[27]

The most important Roycean sources for interpretation were his logical studies. They required an emendation of the two worlds doctrine; interpretation emended it properly. Consider Σ's modes of action: they were a well-ordered set to which the betweenness principle applied. Interpretation was triadic, each term mediating "between" two others; yet the result of any interpretation had a *next*. To be sure, no interpretation demanded a unique next. Unlike the well-ordered series of natural numbers, any interpretation might have various next interpretations, and so the exact interconnection of the theses of "The Principles of Logic" (or the discrimination of volume 2 of *The World and the Individual*) and *The Problem of Christianity* (or its view of the comparison of ideas) was uncertain. Interpretation at least synthesized features of both the Worlds of Appreciation and Description just as Σ was "an order-system of entities inclusive not only of objects having the relations of the number system, but also of objects illustrating the geometrical types of order."[28]

Community

If someone interpreted a second to a third, Royce said a community of interpretation existed, and the term 'community' was crucial. It signified that the mind interpreted and the mind to which the interpretation was addressed were brought into a unity and became in a sense one individual. Self-knowledge illustrated this aspect of interpretation, but many ostensibly different selves also achieved unity. The interpreter possessing the mediating idea shared this unity and was the most important member of the community. He created and carried out the united will of the two others "in so far as they both are to become and remain members of that community in which he does the work of the interpreter" or, as Royce said in lofty moments, "the Spirit of the Community."[29]

The above community of interpretation was primitive. Even so, it had a future goal—the achievement of satisfactory interpretation. Moreover, because every interpretation demanded another and ideally had one, the community shared past interpretations. Royce did not detail the past of primitive communities of interpretation, but he characterized all communities when he discussed a wider notion of community. A true community, he said,

> is essentially a product of a time-process. A community has a past and will have a future. Its more or less conscious history, real or ideal, is a part of its very essence. A community requires for its existence a history and is greatly aided in its consciousness by a memory (243).

A true community identified features of the past that each of many men regarded as part of himself. This justified saying that these men constituted a community with reference to their common past. The community was of memory: each one interpreted himself to the others by this third idea of a shared history. Royce also discussed communities of expectation or hope, that were defined by the shared expectation of the same future events (247–49).

Through 1908 Royce conceived the absolute as a concrete universal: it did not exist apart from the facts comprising it, and they were facts only as far as they were its parts. The relation of individuals to the absolute was a relation of part to whole, and Royce did not distinguish this relation of subsumption or inclusion from class membership. By 1913, however, there was no ambiguity. The elements comprising a class were distinct from the class itself. In a letter written in 1913, Royce said this distinction was the most elementary logical problem involved in his theory of the community, but one that he had said nothing about in

The Problem of Christianity "because my audience was popular." Royce concluded by saying that his book dealt with a special case of the class-member relation.[30] If we remember this, we will appreciate the impact of another logical point on his philosophy.

All communities of interpretation had the structure of selves, and extended ones had lives of their own:

> we can compare a highly developed community, such as a state, either to the soul of a man or to a living animal. A community is not a mere collection of individuals. It is a sort of live unit, that has organs as the body of an individual has organs. A community grows or decays, is healthy or diseased, is young or aged, much as any individual member of the community possesses such characters. Each of the two, the community or the individual member, is as much a live creature as is the other. Not only does the community live, it has a mind of its own—a mind whose psychology is not the same as the psychology of an individual human being (80).

This "social mind" expressed itself in language, custom, and religion. Individual human minds could not produce these phenomena, nor could a group of people unless they were organized into a community. Communities themselves were organized in composite communities of "higher grades." A group of individuals might form a state; states were united into empires; and many hypothesized about a future world state (80–81). Royce's true communities were almost identical to the causes of the loyal, and the ultimate community was the universal church. Ideally, he said, the community of mankind would be as united "as one conscious self could conceivably become." Membership raised us out of the self's narrowness to participation in a creative and conscious spiritual whole (195). But the relation between man and community was not the old one of finite being to absolute.

There were two levels of human existence: individual and communal. Man's natural existence was predicated on the distinction between these two levels, but his highest good involved a "loving union of the individual with a level of existence which is essentially above his own grade of being" (218). For a person to become a member of a true community, his natural self must be destroyed; the "merely natural relation" of the individual to the community would be transformed and the primal core of the social self would vanish (194).

The self's connections to a community reflected Royce's logic. In *The Problem of Christianity* the connection of individuals to their social, natural communities was not that of part to whole, as it was, most importantly, in *The World and the Individual*. Finite man was now no part of some greater being, but a member of a class. Suppose there was a religious transfiguration of this community, transforming man and raising him to a higher level. At this level Royce viewed mankind as "one conscious spiritual whole of life" (218), but even this unity was not one in which parts compose a whole.

In *The Problem of Christianity* as in his earlier work, Royce postulated other minds because we could not interpret the signs that we assume they expressed in the way that we interpreted our own ideas. The latter interpretation had the basic triadic form of comparison. While the structure of comparison and of the interpretation of signs as other minds was the same, with comparison I achieved a "luminous self-possession." This gave me an ideal of interpretation that my interpretation of my neighbor lacked (313–15). The goal of any interpretation was a unity only self-consciousness exemplified on the finite level. Members of a community extended their present selves to include past and future deeds of their fellows. As human beings this extension took the form of *"acting as if we could survey* in some single unity of insight, that wealth and variety and connection which, as a fact, we cannot make present to our momentary view" (267).

In a religiously transformed community we might achieve this unity, but although this higher union of *The Problem of Christianity* was similar to the old union of selves in the absolute, even when transformed we did not become fragments of a whole. In our lives as human beings and in our transformed lives, the relation of community to member was different from anything Royce earlier expressed either in regard to the World of Description or to the World of Appreciation. In particular, after the natural individual was transformed, interpretation, differing from self-representation or discrimination, defined his relation to the community.

The Problem of Christianity, again, synthesized aspects of *The World and the Individual*'s two realms.[31] To delineate these relations with any more clarity is impossible, and perhaps they were ambiguous in Royce's mind, but out of his mathematics came a redefinition of his position.*

Royce truncated the proof of this position, and like much else in *The Problem of Christianity* it had new twists. Although he omitted previous discussion, he had "repeatedly defended" the principle at the heart of his doctrine with "various dialectical explanations" (357). The real world was the true interpretation of our problematic situation: that is, to determine the real required the comparison of two ideas—for example, present experience and the goal of experience, ignorance and enlightenment, appearance and reality. To understand the contrast defined the real world. But contrasting two ideas demanded an interpretation; the correct interpretation of them was the real world. Suppose we said there was no solution—no true interpretation. If true, we could verify that hypothesis only by "an experience that in itself would constitute a full insight into the meaning of the real contrast, and so would in fact furnish a solution." A true solution must exist, the real world must include its interpreter, and this mediating idea would clarify the contrast between the antithetical pair and exist in unity with them. If we rejected this principle, we did so "only by presenting . . . some other interpretation as the true one. But thus," Royce asserted, "you simply reaffirm the principle that the world has an interpreter" (361).

Because some interpretation defined the real, the appropriate community was also real; because this interpretation was true, Royce said the community reached its goal: the interpreter succeeded in mediating and reconciling the contrasting elements. Unless something interrupted it, any interpretation necessitated an infinite series of interpretative acts; but we knew that the interpretation constituting the real world existed, that is, nothing interrupted it. Hence, this interpretation exhibited itself in an infinite series of individual interpretations. Because the interpretation constituting reality reached its goal, the infinite series must itself be interpreted. Or, as Royce declared, an insight which surveyed the series' meaning spanned it (339–42).

Since interpretation expressed mind, and since one interpretation

---

*The title of chapter 10 of *The Problem of Christianity*, "The Body and its Members" (251), displayed these ambiguities. The members of a (human) body are its parts but the members of a body (of citizens) are elements of a class.

constituted the real world, the dialectical argument insured that what was, was a single ideal synopsis. Royce described it as a self comparing the ideas of all the community's members. He wrote consistently that "a genuinely and loyally united community which lives a coherent life, is in a perfectly literal sense, a person. . . . On the other hand, any human individual person in a perfectly literal sense, is a community."[32]

Christianity and Philosophical Truth

Royce's purpose in *The Problem of Christianity* was to characterize the religion and to show it worthy of modern man's commitment (64). What we have discussed—the second volume of the work—provided the technical background to these issues. He had promised an analysis of Christian belief in *The Sources of Religious Insight*, and one assumes this later analysis was a culminating effort: with the groundwork laid, he could consider the most significant practical problem. Having examined the connections between morality and religion, and indicated that a religion of loyalty could resolve the conflict between the two, he now dealt with his religion of loyalty, defining 'loyalty' as the love of an individual for a community. His new definition suggested that loyalty no longer involved a cause, but a community with a different form. But this technical matter is not our prime concern here. Our task is to see why Royce believed that the religious doctrine associated with Christianity displayed metaphysical truth.

The first volume of *The Problem of Christianity* contrasted with other theological writing of the time. As he had in *The Sources of Religious Insight*, Royce attempted to give a rational basis for religious belief and continued to deprecate James's stress on the non-rational. Royce relegated to a minor place his contemporaries' quests for "the historical Jesus" and their attempts to recover "the religion of Jesus." He said that the historical details of the life of Christ were peripheral to his interests and beyond his competence to investigate. Nor did he believe that more accurate accounts of the work and teaching of Jesus could encompass Christianity's essentials. It was the suffering and death of Christ that were critical to the church. The central perplexity of Christianity had always been understanding the crucifixion. So, Royce contended, the basic Christian ideas were those that occupied the ancient world as it attempted to explain the Kingdom of Heaven. For Royce, Pauline Christianity was "real" Christianity.[33]

Royce organized his presentation of Christianity around three explicit leading ideas, and an implicit fourth one, the conception of grace. The first was that membership in a spiritual community determined the salvation of man. All men belonged "in ideal" to this universal community, and only if one were a member could one achieve life's goal, what religion called salvation. Although there were differences, loyalty to a cause was the ancestor of membership in a community. The members of a religious community loved the community as if it were a person, devoted themselves to it, served it, and lived and died for it. But it was no cause in the sense intended in *The Philosophy of Loyalty*. Rather, Royce emphasized, love within a community had two objects; it occurred at two levels. For example, in the Christian community, the Christian's sincerity, trust in God, and submission to the Lord's will were services rendered the supreme ruler. But there was a second object of love—the neighbor who was (ideally at least) a fellow-member of the (universal) community. The Christian's primary task toward his neighbors was to make them members of this community, lovers of God. He accomplished this task by example, precept, kindliness, patience, and courage—the traditional virtues; but the individual finally left to God the care for the neighbor whom he loved (89–91).

To these teachings Paul added another constituting the meaning of Christian love. We needed something to reconcile the two levels and kinds of love. They were both directed at persons—the human beings who surrounded us and God the supreme ruler. Royce asserted that both they and their relation were mysterious. Paul's doctrine introduced a third entity, the body of Christ, which brought the two other mysterious beings together and made a community. The "divinely exalted Christ" was this "particular corporate entity," the church—a one in many and a many in one. In Royce's metaphysics the "love of Christ" was the mediating idea creating the community and interpreting God to finite individuals; Christ was the spirit of the community who reconciled infinite and finite (92–95).

On this formulation Royce could not claim that God (the absolute) was the ultimate reality. In the mediating Christ "the Community, the

Individual, and the Absolute would be completely expressed, reconciled and distinguished." Qua absolute, God would not be unified with the many (the community). Christ as spirit or interpreter united the many and the absolute, but the real world, the ultimate interpretation, was still an ideal synopsis which had the structure of self-consciousness. If we considered the temporal world in its wholeness, said Royce, "it constitutes in itself an infinitely complex Sign [the infinite series of human interpretations?]. This sign is, as a whole, interpreted to an experience [God? the absolute?] which itself includes a synoptic survey of the whole of time" (346).

Christianity was transformed by Paul's belief that Christ united human beings to God by expressing and creating Christian love or loyalty. This was Royce's first leading idea: the notion of a spiritual life defined by the work of Jesus. In this life loyalty unified God and man through Christ. To explicate this notion, Royce investigated the second leading idea, the moral burden of the individual, articulating his concern for evil and redemption.

Human beings, he said, were naturally subject to a moral burden from which they could not escape unaided. Only divine intervention could save man from spiritual ruin (100). This was Royce's contemporary translation of the doctrine of original sin. Socialization was really the most primitive form of interpretation, comparison; through comparison I observed or estimated myself by interpreting others (106–09). But Royce contended that the more we were trained, and the more sophisticated social behavior we learned, the more we elevated and emphasized *self-consciousness*. Becoming a social being tainted the conscience of man. We were marked "with the original sin of self-will," "a clever hostility" to the social order on which we depended. This sin belonged to the essence of homo sapiens as a social species—the "diseases" of self-consciousness were due to our nature (118). Human beings could never achieve salvation, the supreme good of social harmony and union; socialization was self-defeating. This was the moral burden that attached to the human condition, and that human beings alone could never cast off.

The Philosophy of Loyalty claimed that the way to our highest good was loyal devotion to a variety of causes which need not involve religion, and Royce included a chapter, "Training for Loyalty." In *The Problem of Christianity* the only community to which we could be loyal was one touched by religion. Natural communities and social training could never give rise to loyalty. This doctrine made for an ambiguity in *The Problem of Christianity*. It was never clear if Royce had a community at all without loyalty and love. He sometimes implied that there were no communities without them, but he also spoke of "purely secular forms of loyalty"— seemingly a contradiction. He alternatively wrote that without loyalty or the divine spark we had primitive, lesser, or natural communities. In any event, I distinguish between natural communities and those that loyalty, or love, as Royce often called it, transformed.[34]

Man's relation to any natural community imperfectly resolved the conflict between him and it; the two levels remained distinct.

Paul saw a way out:

> There is a certain divinely instituted community. It is no mere collection of individuals, with laws and customs and quarrels. Nor is its unity merely that of a mighty but to our own will, an alien power. Its indwelling spirit is concrete and living, but is also a loving spirit. It is the body of Christ. The risen Lord dwells in it, and is its life. It is as much a person as he was when he walked the earth. And he is as much the spirit of that community as he is a person (118).

In this community and in this community alone, the natural self would die and man have a new life; he would exhibit a new type of self-consciousness. In this community man was saved, and Royce said that only the miracle of love sufficed for salvation. Although there might be many redemptive communities arranged in increasing complexity and universality, they would all be religious.

Divine Grace created a true community by the gift of loyalty (128–29). Although it was not labelled as such, grace was a leading idea clarifying Christ's relation to the community and to the individual's moral burden. Christ's work was the creation of a mediating idea—the community—between God and man. Jesus appeared as individual and "spirit of the community" because through him the community became the loyal entity it was. For him as for anyone who served as spirit of the community, said Royce,

> his origin will be inexplicable in terms of the processes which he himself originates. His power will come from another level than our own. And of the workings of this grace, when it has appeared we

can chiefly say this: That such love is propagated by personal example, although how, we cannot explain (131).

The creation of loyalty, which the life of Christ expressed and which conversions to Christianity illustrated, was an act of grace, an incomprehensible gift that began our reconciliation with God. This was the clearest version of the Roycean doctrine of the trinity and an impressive analysis of Christianity using his epistemology. The Holy Spirit in the guise of the work of Christ brought together God the Father (the absolute) and God the Son (as finite man) (137).

The third leading idea was atonement. By grace a loyal community came into existence, or an individual not yet a member of a redemptive community attained loyalty. A member of a religious community might, however, lose his relation to this community through disloyalty. As with an individual who was not yet loyal, no act of his own could restore the traitorous individual. The work of Christ—the supreme act of grace—atoned for the sins of mankind, the sins of self-ishness. Similarly, a loyal fellow, someone other than the disloyal member, must atone for him (50–73).

It was unclear why men were guilty for what was inevitably their nature or why other acts of atonement were necessary once the crucifixion had occurred. If we put aside these questions, however, we may see the rationale behind atonement. Royce stated that if a person had a set of principles, it was possible for him to act in a way that would destroy what made his life morally worthwhile. The person could commit moral suicide. He could express this feeling by saying, "If I were to do that, I would never forgive myself" (154–55). Suppose a principled person acted in this way. He would also have betrayed a true community, for in order to have an ideal, a person must be loyal; and the traitor would now be outside a saving community. By his own acts he could not be received into it again or restore it to what it was before his treachery. How was he to be saved?

Royce's answer was complicated. In the passage of time some loyal member of the community atoned for the disloyalty. His act restored the community to its former state and the traitor to his former estate. The betrayal created the conditions for the source of more righteous communal life than would have been possible had the betrayal not occurred.

The loyal member acted as the spirit of the community, and his deed mediated between the traitor and the broken community:

> this creative work shall include a deed, or various deeds, for which only just this treason furnishes the opportunity. Not treason in general, but just this individual treason shall give the occasion, and supply the condition of the creative deed which I am in ideal describing. Without just that treason, this new deed (so I am supposing) could not have been done at all. And hereupon the new deed, as I suppose, is so ingeniously devised, so concretely practical in the good which it accomplishes, that, when you look down upon the human world after the first creative deed has been done in it, you say, first, "This deed was made possible by that treason; and, secondly, *The world, as transformed by this creative deed, is better than it would have been had all else remained the same, but had that deed of treason not been done at all*" (180).

The Problem of Evil

This account contained two complexes of problems. The first required only clarification. The second was more puzzling and reflected Royce's last efforts to understand evil in a perfect world. It might be comprehensible why the traitor never forgave himself. Even this might be dubious, however, if the atoning act made the world better than it otherwise would have been. But Royce did not spell out why the traitor's act could never atone for his sin against the community. Royce simply asserted that no deed of the traitor's could revoke his betrayal; the reconciliation must come from another who "transforms the meaning of that very past which it [the reconciliation] cannot undo" (180–81). Even if the traitor were never reconciled to his act, why should this prevent him from atoning for the past in the sense Royce specified? The impossibility of self-reconciliation was the only reason he gave (163). This issue was not serious. No critical points hung on it, and Royce could maintain that the traitor was no longer in a state of grace and therefore could not create loyalty. Only a possessor of grace might do that, and he would never be the betrayer.

There was a second and harder set of questions for which there was no acceptable answer. Why did disloyalty set the stage for a situation in which some atonement would make the world better than it otherwise would have been? Royce gave no reason to assume this, but if we understand his metaphysics we can see why he supposed that treason played this role. We knew that the universal community "reached its goal," that Christ reconciled mankind with God; implicit in this idea was progress toward the goal. In history good must overcome evil. The world was evolving morally, and as time passed acts of atonement raised the moral quality of civilization. This was so despite the goal's infinite distance. We still did not know why an act of atonement presupposed one particular act of disloyalty, but the view was consistent with Royce's belief that evil was necessary to good.

The statement of this last leading idea occurred in the first volume of *The Problem of Christianity* before Royce offered the proof of his position. He called the belief in atonement a postulate (207–08). After he showed that the Pauline community reflected the structure of the universe, Royce still insisted that we had no knowledge of when and how disloyalty was reconciled. In the course of endless ages every problem had its solution, and every tragedy its atoning triumph, but we could not know when problems were solved or how mankind atoned for tragedies. The endless order of time in which salvation took place "stands in contrast to its ideal goal." Only the final interpretation of the contrast of this time order and its goal atoned for all the evils of temporal existence (382–83).

Royce admitted that reconciling divine perfection and the "infinite" tragedy of temporal existence was the problem of the universe. On one hand, the same difficulties of *The Sources of Religious Insight*, and of most of Royce's work in ethics, remained: why did a perfect world have an evil character? If the reconciliation (interpretation) must occur, why did it make sense to speak of man's need for salvation? On the other hand, there was progress. *The Sources of Religious Insight* indicated only obscurely that *natural* man's salvation was endangered. *The Problem of Christianity* worked out the meaning of this natural state and how men escaped it. Of course, they still must be saved in *The Problem of Christianity* because the Christian vision was true, but the treatment was an advance if only because it was a retreat. Although he had mathematically resolved the problem Bradley had set, Royce's later metaphysics represented a falling back to Bradley's conception. We were not told how the Spirit of the Community interpreted the infinite series of interpretations to its goal. Royce admitted that temporal beings could not know when or how salvation occurred. In so doing, he acknowledged that the problem of evil was beyond his comprehension.

Royce, James, and Peirce

The later work of Royce and James was very similar. Bradley's metaphysics attracted James because the Englishman had argued that we had no idea of how we were *aufgehoben* in the absolute. At last Royce conceded this point. Moreover, in agreeing with James that evil was in some measure unintelligible, Royce yielded on another issue. Finally, *The Problem of Christianity* downplayed monistic absolutism in favor of the community at a time when James had promulgated "the compounding of consciousness" in ever-widening spheres in *A Pluralistic Universe*. It is perhaps only because James died in 1910 that their metaphysical rapprochement—their consensus on a Peircean communitarian idealism—went unnoticed.

Royce concluded his work by returning to Peirce for support (388 ff.). Royce did not want to use this survey to demonstrate his ideas but to illustrate dramatically that time manifested a progressive world-order whose aim was beyond the temporal. The best example of a Peircean community was the scientific one. For Peirce this community attained truth in the infinite future, and in so doing constituted the absolute mind. Although no scientific community possessed truth, science progressively interpreted an infinite series of signs. Scientists presupposed a final interpretation and also believed that it lay beyond their grasp. In actuality, Royce maintained, the Pauline community behaved like this despite the moral disorder which veiled our view. He closed his work by drawing out this analogy: "We can look forward to no final form, either of Christianity or of any other special religion. But we can look forward to a time when the work and insight of religion can become as progressive as is now the work of science"(405).

End of the Golden Age

In the summer of 1910, Royce lost his closest friend when James died. A few weeks later the son who had come with Royce to Cambridge in

1882 was dead of typhoid fever. For someone as lonely and shy as Royce, these personal calamities had a telling effect. An added tragedy was his own sense of incompleteness and failure. Many philosophic doctrines attracted American thinkers in the second decade of the century, but Royce rightfully felt that the power of speculative idealism was spent; and he had been unsuccessful in creating a viable school around him. In early 1912 he suffered a stroke. Although he made a remarkable recovery, producing *The Problem of Christianity* a year later, he never regained his health.

Frustration, bitterness, and even a decline in intellectual achievement marked Royce's subsequent years. He developed no new ideas, and in 1914 he became preoccupied with the war in Europe and poured his energies into a harsh anti-German campaign. He succeeded only in making himself a leading Allied ideologue. By 1916 he verged on senility, and his death that September—six years after the passing of James and two after that of Peirce—closed the most important and productive era of philosophic thinking in the United States.[35] Three months later, in his presidential address to the American Philosophical Association, Arthur Lovejoy delivered a eulogy to Royce:

> American philosophy has lost one of its greatest figures; and from the circle of our own fellowship has passed one of the most loyal, kindly and richly-endowed human beings whom any of us has known. Josiah Royce contributed to philosophy with an intellectual power, and an incomparable learning, that evoked our admiration and our pride; . . . But it was the man himself that meant most to us, as an embodiment of the philosophic temper and an example of the philosophic life—in the completeness of his devotion to man's supreme task of discovering the nature and meaning of things.[36]

PART 4

HARVARD
PHILOSOPHY
AT MID-CAREER

Private Clarence Lewis in 1918

Major Ralph Perry in 1918

21

THE CRISIS OF 1912-1920

Lawrence Lowell

William James began to retire around the turn of the century, but like a politician who wanted to be convinced to run, he allowed Eliot to persuade him to stay at Harvard until 1907. Of course, Eliot was importunate: "We want your name," he bluntly told James in 1904. After his resignation the catalogue listed him as professor emeritus, and it was known that James was still on the Cambridge scene.

Eliot met James's loss by promoting George Santayana, at long last, to a full professorship. Financial problems dictated that there could not be a fourth professorship in philosophy (the administration considered Münsterberg a psychologist), and even Eliot recognized that Santayana's claims were compelling. He joined Palmer and Royce as James's successor.[1]

Much more serious in its consequences for philosophy than James's departure was Lawrence Lowell's accession to the university presidency in 1909 and the actions he took when the other great men retired or died during the next few years. Although Lowell was a strong and capable administrator, he did not have Eliot's ability and was not in Eliot's position. Lowell took over the headship of a going concern, and his job was not to build a university, but rather to keep Harvard number one. It is unfair, however, to imply that he did nothing but administer. Toward the end of the Eliot era, many observers believed that the elective system had gone too far and was contributing to declining standards of undergraduate scholarship; observers acknowledged that the changes effected by Lowell strengthened the entire university.[2]

More broadly, Lowell's correction of elective system abuses bespoke an inclination for intellectual good form and, while this characteristic served him well in dealing with undergraduate studies, it marred wider aspects of his administration. Both Eliot and Lowell were Boston aristocrats, but the challenges that Eliot had to meet were basically technical. He had to adopt strategies that would get a university built, and his strong feeling for intellectual freedom, exemplified by the elective system, insured success. Money contributed to Harvard's dominance, but so too did Eliot's belief that a university must sponsor diversity.[3] In a period when the ministry was still powerful, his leadership was just enough ahead of its time to give Harvard a commanding position. On Lowell's succession, freedom of inquiry was an accomplished fact. The universities faced a social demand: they had to respond to the call for education and training that a more and more variegated population made upon them. Lowell's cultural perspective proved restrictive. His valuing of good form over diversity meant that he would emphasize Anglo-Saxon "character" as much as intellectual excellence.

When Lowell became president, Harvard had no real rivals. The university was not only the center for scholarship in the United States but also an institution crucial to American life. In training American leaders in every sphere of life, Harvard, so Lowell and others thought, shaped the nation's culture, its style of political, religious, and artistic expression. There was no cant in Lowell's speech to a student group on his nomination in January 1909:

> I believe the office to which I have been nominated . . . is the most important in the United States. . . . the future of the country is in the hands of its young men, and . . . the character of its young men depends largely upon their coming to college. . . . We are all working for Harvard, and not only for the Harvard of the present but the Harvard of the future. I feel this very seriously indeed. . . . institutions live after the men who founded them are dead, and . . . institutions are greater than men. We are building up one of the greatest of institutions and we must live here and work here in such a way that our descendants . . . will be better men for having been in Harvard College.*

*Quoted in ALLY, pp. 101–02. Compare this with William James in 1899: "we 'intellectuals' in America must all work to keep our precious birthright of individualism and freedom from these institutions. *Every* great institution is perforce a means of corruption— whatever good it may also do. Only in the free personal relation is full ideality to be found." LWJ, 2: 100–01 (italics in original).

Lowell's attitudes reflected the Cambridge ethos and his position on the role of the ethnic and religious minorities at Harvard best revealed them. He wanted the university to open its doors to minorities in order to assimilate them. What he said of the Irish applied to many other groups: "What we need is not to dominate . . . but to absorb. . . . Their best interests and ours are, indeed, the same in this matter. We want them to become rich, and send their sons to our colleges, to share our prosperity and our sentiments. We do not want to feel that they are among us and yet not really a part of us."[4] In the early 1920s, when he tried to establish a formal quota for Jews, he did so not because he felt any prejudice against the Jew per se, but because Harvard could not assimilate the Jews if their number became too large. One of Harvard's goals was to produce the "pure American" Jew. Harvard had to give "special consideration" to the Jews just as it did to alumni children: the nation would be strong only if both groups received Harvard socialization.[5] Lowell's real problems came with the blacks. He wanted them to receive Harvard's educational advantages but he believed they were not socially assimilable under any circumstances. His troubled ruminations when he banned blacks from the Freshman Halls measured his limitations and his fear of cultural pluralism: "I wish I knew what our Saviour would think it wise to do about the Negro in America," he confided to his wife.[6] Cambridge could make a Jew indistinguishable from an Anglo-Saxon Protestant; but not even Harvard could make a black man white.

Lowell and the Philosophers

Lowell's view was typical and influenced the lives of the Harvard philosophers. He was committed to appointing the best men, but he did not mean by "best men" merely the most outstanding in intellectual capacity. As we have seen, social and moral character was also at issue. A possible professor must be socially acceptable; he had to have been acculturated to the way of life of the Boston Brahmins and had to behave as a gentleman. No appointee could have marked personal idiosyncrasies; he must be morally above reproach and keep his private affairs in order. It is difficult to delineate this non-academic criterion of character more precisely, but from the pattern of Lowell's selections in philosophy, it is clear that the scholar hoping for a place at Harvard had to have "good character." In

Lowell's view, this was just as it should be: a professor in Cambridge not only had to perform intellectually but also to symbolize that ideal of existence to which Harvard youth might aspire.

Lowell always consulted with his chairmen in making permanent appointments but, like Eliot, assumed responsibility.[7] For this reason he must be the focus of attention in analyzing the department that emerged in the 1920s. But many other factors shaped the new character of Cambridge speculation. Financial problems antedating Lowell's inauguration and lasting until several years after the First World War constrained him;[8] the war itself disturbed academic life all around the world; the philosophers he relied on did not always exhibit good judgment; and finally, a crisis in the affairs of Harvard philosophy faced him early in his presidency.

James died in 1910; in 1912 Santayana resigned; a year later Palmer retired at the age of seventy-one; at the beginning of the 1916–1917 academic year Royce died (his growing frailty had worried those around him since his stroke in 1912); and three months after Royce, Münsterberg collapsed and died while lecturing. In just over six years the department lost all five men who had given it international intellectual fame for thirty years. "To be a philosopher," Alfred North Whitehead said, was "to make some humble approach to the main characteristics of this group."[9]

From 1912 to 1920 the administration and those philosophers still active frantically tried to rebuild. For several years they made temporary appointments to test suitable candidates or simply to insure that courses were offered. Lowell wrote desperately for visitors to help out in memory of "the days of our strength and prosperity."[10] The low point was reached in 1914 when five acting appointees taught philosophy, among them Bertrand Russell, who was a brilliant success.[11] The staff was "broken," the department "crumbling," Palmer wrote.[12] In 1913 while Royce was in Oxford delivering the Hibbert Lectures he spent much time, unsuccessfully, inveigling various philosophers to come to Harvard, and with only James, Palmer, and Santayana gone he lamented the "desperate departmental need."[13] Many of the problems fell on Perry, although he was only an assistant professor. Eliot appointed him chairman in 1906 and he served until 1914. It obsessed Perry that the great men were going, and plans for reconstructing filled his correspondence of the second decade of the century. He wrote to the retired Palmer, "we are in large part leaning upon our prestige and . . . if we allow this to be lost we shall have great difficulty in regaining it. Nevertheless, it is a satisfaction that we have not lost it as yet." When Russell spent his semester in Cambridge, Perry wrote to his brother-in-law, Bernard Berenson, that the department must try "by hook or crook [to] attach him [Russell] to ourselves" and thus "accomplish something towards regaining our former glory."[14]

This scheme came to nought, and as the philosophers floundered the administration acted. In 1913–1914 Lowell promoted Perry and James Woods to full professorships. Perry did not publish his *General Theory of Value* on which his reputation must rest until 1926, and through 1913 he was, as Münsterberg noted, merely the master of "critical epigrams and witty negative aphorisms."[15] But Perry was a Harvard man: he was a leading light among the neo-realists and among younger philosophers generally; he had dutifully served as chairman; he had received his assistant professorship when he turned down an offer from Princeton, and Harvard had promised him rapid advance when he turned down another from Stanford; in fact, his promotion had been hanging from early 1910.[16] We cannot fault Lowell here. Woods's promotion is impossible to explain on academic grounds, and the existing records do not explain it at all. He had been an assistant professor only from 1908–1909 but had an impeccable background, and his wealth, geniality, and world-wide contacts made him the equal of William James in his ability to win friends for Harvard philosophy. He took over the chairmanship from Perry in 1914 and had served a total of twelve years in varying stretches when he died in 1935.

Filling the places which Santayana and Palmer left, these two promotions ostensibly brought the department—at least briefly—to full strength, but everyone believed that quality had declined. The department argued that it must have a man of ability to replace William James. The administration countered that three full professors of philosophy (Royce, Perry, and Woods) were the department's limit, that the department had Münsterberg in psychology, and that it had been lucky to have a distinguished philosopher like Santayana so long as an assistant professor. This dickering had gone on from the time of James's retirement, but in 1914 the administration relented, accepting the philosophers' plight if not their argument: the department might appoint another full professor. As chairman, Perry recommended Arthur Lovejoy, "the most eminent and talented American philosopher eligible"; he was "the one man of conspicuous and undoubted ability in the country" and "would distinctly add to the prestige of the university."[17] Lovejoy was indeed without peer, but the department hesitated over his appointment largely because of his hostility to Münsterberg's "pseudovoluntarism." Münsterberg, however, became reconciled to Lovejoy's presence, and all the philosophers agreed that Lovejoy was the best they could get.[18] The agreement did not matter: Lowell rejected Lovejoy because he was active in founding the American Association of University Professors.[19]

Lowell assuaged the philosophers a few months later when he appointed Ernest Hocking to the fourth professorship. Harvard-trained, Hocking taught at Yale and had written a major book in 1912, *The Meaning of God in Human Experience*; he was everyone's second choice. The philosophers had wanted others but were worn down in considering so many possibilities. The administration preferred a visitor until Harvard could get someone better. But the doubts of Lowell and the Corporation proved cheaply allayed. When Richard Clark Cabot, a wealthy friend of the department, agreed to fund part of Hocking's salary, his appointment had clear sailing.[20] When all the politicking and scrambling was over, philosophy reasserted itself. "It is a high task you have set before me," Hocking wrote to Münsterberg, of "maintaining the force of idealism at Harvard."[21]

No sooner had Hocking settled into the fourth professorship than Royce and Münsterberg died. On the day that Royce died, Woods acted: he wrote Russell that he was the only man who could make good Royce's loss.* Russell had consented to come in the spring of 1917, and Woods

*As an administrator Woods was energetic and ingenious. At the same time he was tempting Russell, he came within an inch of getting T. S. Eliot, who had just completed his dissertation under Royce, to come back to Harvard as an instructor. Eliot was apparently set to return from England when a wartime emergency caused the cancellation of his boat. Woods was "bitterly disappointed" and after the war again wanted to offer Eliot a position. But both Perry and Palmer—still a departmental force—appear to have overruled Woods, although they granted Eliot's genius. Perry believed Eliot was a "sort of attenuated Santayana," too "rare and overrefined"; Palmer that "a certain softness of moral fibre" had allowed a "weak aestheticism" to turn Eliot's head. The memory of Santayana appears to have been operating in cases other than this. B. A. G. Fuller, who instructed at Harvard for a time, was also probably dropped because of his "aesthetic" nature. See "Correspondence and Notes Re Plattsburg Movement, 1921," (4683.13), Folder: Miscellaneous, RBP Papers; JHW to T. S. Eliot, 19 September 1919; to H. Eliot, 3 April 1916, Woods Chm. 1914–1915, Loose Material *E*; JHW to T. S. Eliot, 17 March 1920, 1917–1920, *E*, HPD; ALL to Fuller, 13 March 1919, Folder 680, 1917–1919, ALL Papers; and Folder 566, 1919–1920, ALL Papers.

hoped to have him permanently.[22] But in summer 1916 the British government prosecuted and convicted Russell for his pacifistic activities under the Defense of the Realm Act; he could not leave Britain for the duration of the war. Royce's position, one in the first instance reserved for a logician, was still unfilled after the war, and the department wanted to renew a half-time offer to Russell. But Lowell would now have none of it: great as his abilities were, an iconoclast like Russell would not do at Harvard.[23]

In filling Royce's position, Lowell was not at his best. The veto of Russell was not his only decision. He again rejected Lovejoy as a "mischiefmaker"—in this he had the support of Hocking, who thought Lovejoy would be hard to "domesticate."* Finally Lowell squelched consideration of John Dewey: at fifty-nine he was too old.[24]

While the philosophers were trying to push Russell, Lovejoy, or Dewey on a stubborn Lowell, they were also trying to secure a fifth full professorship, for in addition to a great man from outside Harvard they wanted to promote R. F. Alfred Hoernlé from inside the university. Hoernlé had been born in Germany and educated at Oxford, and had taught in Scotland, South Africa, and England before coming to Cambridge as a visitor in fall 1913. The next year when Lowell hired Hocking as a full professor, he hired Hoernlé as an assistant professor with the understanding that if he had made good in five years, he would have a professorship and a permanent place. Hoernlé was an agreeable man and a competent scholar. He took over as chairman during the war when running the department was a fight against chaos, and Perry, Hocking, and Woods soon grew committed to him. He was a good team player, Hocking said, and although politically left-of-center, just the kind of radical Harvard wanted, "assimilable and wise." When Hoernlé's five-year probationary period ended in 1919, however, he had not published and the tenured faculty members did not request his promotion. In 1920 he had a book in press, and then they unanimously recommended an appointment to full professor.[25]

Lowell was as adamant about Hoernlé as he was about the great men

---

*As late as 1931 Lowell forbade the department to invite Lovejoy as a one-semester replacement for absent staff. When he finally came back to Cambridge in 1932–1933, Lowell had retired, and Lovejoy delivered the William James Lectures out of which came *The Great Chain of Being*. See JHW to C. Moore, 6 February 1931, 1927–1938, *M*, HPD.

suggested for professorships. He first argued that the philosophy department's refusal to recommend promotion in 1919 when Hoernlé was to
have "made good" was tantamount to a vote of no confidence: Hoernlé
"had not fulfilled the hopes we had entertained." Second, Lowell reminded the philosophers that the department "not many years ago was
one of very extraordinary distinction." He would not fill the fourth
professorship until "convinced that the occupant will be on a level with
the great figures who have occupied it in the past."* Lowell directed his
blunt opinion at Hoernlé—a good man who was not the best—but the
implications for Hoernlé's colleagues were clear: they were not equal to
the men from whom the department had inherited its reputation, and
Lowell did not want another like them.[26]

The tenured faculty members were in a frustrating position. Lowell
vetoed recommendations for a great man and met their attempt to push
Hoernlé through with the bland intimation that he was only as good as
they and that Harvard had had enough of that. When Lowell then made
it plain that they could make only one (and not two) permanent appointments, the full professors were furious. On one hand, they argued that
there would be a "profound injury to the position of philosophy" at
Harvard if Hoernlé left; they conjured up the nightmare of the university's losing its place of primacy. On the other hand, they used the same
nightmare to justify their request for "a man of distinctly superior
eminence who would at once add to the prestige of the Department."
In addition to Hoernlé, this man would help "restore the prestige which
the Department enjoyed ten years ago."[27]

At the end of 1919–1920 Hoernlé left for England and the University
of Durham in Newcastle, and no one, distinguished or otherwise, filled
the fourth professorship. It is doubtful that Harvard philosophy lost any
prestige during the politics of this decade—its reputation survived the
changes in personnel. But perhaps something more intangible had
vanished.

If there was any loss in prestige, it was remediable. By 1921 C. I. Lewis
filled the assistant professor's post vacated by Hoernlé. Previously at
Berkeley, Lewis had not acquired the "polish, urbanity and social ease"
that Perry had hoped for, but he managed to stick. A thinker of the

*The Alford professorship, the department's only chair, was empty from 1916, when
Royce died, until 1920, when Lowell appointed Hocking.

first rank, Lewis became in time the fifth professor, and in 1924 Lowell appointed the fourth professor, Alfred North Whitehead. He had the intellectual stature of Russell but was as conventional as Russell was unorthodox. Everyone thought Whitehead perfect: he had all of Russell's talent and none of Russell's handicaps. Woods wrote enthusiastically that Whitehead's presence was sure to revivify philosophy in Cambridge because he was "a radiating center of benevolence and creative thinking."[28] He adorned Harvard until 1937.

Psychology under Lowell

In psychology the situation was not remediable. Münsterberg's death in 1916 was the first of three losses that were not made good. Even in 1916 psychologists regarded assistant professor Robert Yerkes as one of the country's leading animal psychologists, but he left in 1917 when no one could convince Lowell that this sub-discipline was worth encouraging. A year later Edwin Holt resigned. Although philosophers recognized his contributions to neo-realism and his speculative talents, his assistant professorship was in psychology and he directed much of the graduate psychological research. Both philosophy and psychology felt his loss. Even before Yerkes and Holt left, Perry had pleaded with Lowell to hire well-known psychologists because "our prestige in psychology is at the lowest ebb in our history."[29]

Despite Perry's plea, the philosophers themselves subordinated psychology to their own priorities and treated rebuilding in psychology as a secondary concern. And Harvard's values did not unhesitatingly encourage excellence. Lowell offered the position in psychology to E. B. Titchener, Cornell's pre-eminent psychologist. Although Titchener provisionally accepted, both Lowell and the philosophers got cold feet. Titchener had a powerful mind and was at the top of his profession. When he asked for independence from the philosophers for himself and his laboratory, neither the department nor Lowell was happy, and Titchener slipped through their fingers.[30]

After Titchener there was James McKeen Cattell, more a promoter and organizer, but an outstanding trainer of graduate students for all that. Nicholas Murray Butler of Columbia had fired Cattell in 1917 on grounds of disloyalty to the United States—he had given vent to pacifistic sentiments—and in early 1919 Cattell wrote to Lowell for a job. Cattell was famous for his crusty integrity and scrappiness, and Lowell's reply was not surprising: there was no opening for which the psychologist qualified. Lowell must have felt justified when he received Cattell's response: everyone knew that "Harvard is in urgent need of a professor of psychology and can obtain none so well qualified. . . . [Universities conducted] by and for the classes of privilege . . . must be brought into the current of service and democracy, or be allowed to dry up like the medieval monasteries."[31] Harvard was not able to reconstruct psychology until the early 1930s. By then the momentum had been lost.

Understanding the Appointment System

Intellectual excellence alone had never been enough to gain a Harvard post—the earlier struggle in the 1870s and 1880s in philosophy should make that clear. But we explain little about the characteristics of Lovejoy, Russell, Titchener, and Cattell by simply attributing their failure to get Harvard places to "politics." During the earlier period Eliot chose his professors from persons he was acquainted with. Although he ruled out men of extreme eccentricity like Peirce and Abbot and wanted gentlemen, he accepted personal variation. Before the establishment of a disciplinary focus, a man's interests were likely to be diverse and not subject to stringent appraisals, but Eliot even tolerated a lack of scholarly ability. A man's education, personal qualities, and scholarly work—good or bad—were secondary. What counted was that a man and his family were known. But as philosophy established itself as an academic discipline and as the university became a large bureaucracy, meritocratic considerations became more important.* Of course, there was no abrupt change from the Eliot to the Lowell administration. Eliot seems to have chosen Palmer, James, and Santayana because he knew them, but he did not know Royce or Münsterberg; and while Lowell downplayed the personal element, he appears to have promoted Woods because he was a useful and proper Bostonian.[32]

Lowell developed a full scheme of academic distinctions. The promo-

---

*Harvard had to have at least the prospect of enough money to fund positions of varying degrees of permanence, but for purposes of this analysis we may ignore this factor, constant in both the Eliot and Lowell administrations.

tion from instructor to assistant professor was still crucial, but it was no longer a tentative commitment to a full professorship. Assistant professors would get two five-year contracts and yet have no certainty of a full professorship and an appointment without term. And in addition to the "tenure" that leading universities now associated with a professorship—a stronger commitment than appointment without term—Lowell introduced an intermediate step between assistant and full professor, the new rank of associate professor. He could wield this third position to give a further term appointment to someone he was not yet sure of, or to let a man who had become burdensome choose between leaving or accepting a permanent job without the prestige of a full professorship. Later, the rank became a standard tenured post, one step away from a professorship.

Within this system Lowell, like Eliot, made his own final decisions on promotion and hiring. Furthermore, almost all of Lowell's appointments were Harvard products, insuring a "known" commodity as had Eliot's method. And Lowell's criteria of selection included matters irrelevant to scholarship. On one hand, appointment and promotion were dependent on scholarly promise or acceptable publications and then on adequate teaching and service to the community—Lowell did not isolate these academic talents. On the other hand, as this chapter has illustrated, "character" also meant a great deal to Lowell: he hired only men whom he thought could measure up to his gentlemanly ideal.

The difference between the procedures of 1870 and those of the emerging meritocracy is that the latter's standards operated within the universe of Harvard doctorates without regard for specific individuals. Lowell filled positions on the basis of his academic and moral criteria without personal acquaintance. First, he achieved a homogeneity of personnel: Lovejoy, Russell, Titchener, and Cattell lost out because they were not the right *type*. Second, Lowell also assured a modicum of intellectual attainment: Perry, Hocking, Lewis, and Whitehead were all acceptable scholars. Together with the growing professional orientation of philosophy, Lowell's decision-making guaranteed that the scholarly work of the second generation would be narrower and more technical than that preceding it and less interesting to the educated public. The men who wrote it conformed to standards more susceptible to expert evaluation; and they were men of no great personal idiosyncrasies.

Philosophy during the War

In the years immediately preceding the appointments of Lewis and Whitehead—the period of the First World War—philosophical concerns at Harvard reached their nadir. In part this state of affairs was caused by the desperate search for staff that occupied the energies of the philosophers who were still on the premises. But other factors also help explain the dearth of speculation. The junior members of the old department and those who joined them had initially no idea of where philosophy should go; they were not only searching for new personnel but also for a new vision of speculation and their place in it. Such was the disarray of the second decade of the century that the philosophers undervalued the only writing of distinction produced in the period—Edwin Holt's books in philosophical psychology. The department's emphasis on professorial prestige and its downgrading of psychology made it easy for Holt to leave and for his writing to escape proper attention.

Uncertainty over goals was not all that crippled the philosophers. The war led them astray. It propelled them into an uncritical patriotism and, with the defeat of Germany, enabled them to create a mythic view of their intellectual heritage—a view that ignored absolute idealism and its exponents and distorted the history of American thought.

22

EDWIN BISSELL HOLT AND
PHILOSOPHICAL BEHAVIORISM

The Suppositions of James and Münsterberg

William James was no experimentalist, and Münsterberg never thought of his scientific psychology as the whole truth. But both Münsterberg's action theory and James's motor theory did stress behavior, conceived in a mechanistic way. Concerned with mind-body interaction, they postulated the mind as mediating between the environment and the needs of the organism, and they analyzed conscious functions as those that accommodated the organism to novel experience. On one hand, they believed that mind was defined by a kind of mechanical interaction between an organism and its environment, and that propensities to act and incoming stimuli mutually determined the contents of consciousness. On the other hand, they believed that inner experience—consciousness—was in some way separate from the "reaction mechanism" and that this separation was fundamental for understanding will and purpose. As a panpsychist James later denounced this distinction between the world of facts and of values—between science and philosophy—and it is unclear what place he would have made for the will in a new psychology. Münsterberg, on his part, always affirmed the distinction; and although he made the inner world an exact correlate of the world of behavior, the former world of purposes was the real world.

To simplify, both men as psychologists defended a variety of functionalism—the kind of psychology that holds that conscious capacities explain the way an organism achieves success in a perilous world. Behaviorism is a narrower variety of functionalism, its proponents arguing that there is no need to postulate consciousness to explain behavior; the behavioral experimenter defines behavior by a stimulus-response nexus and needs nothing behind behavior to explain it.[1] We can regard Münsterberg's applied psychology as behavioristic. Mental testing, psychotherapy, and vocational psychology as he conceived them paid no attention to consciousness or introspection. Indeed, in all laboratory work Münsterberg's position required experimenters to infer the nature of consciousness from behavior.

Both James and Münsterberg conveyed a functionalist view to their students. It culminated in what I call Edwin Holt's philosophical behaviorism. Holt disagreed with his teachers' premises while adopting their aims. He denied that there was anything more than the interaction device but also disputed the mechanistic conception of this device. Holt needed only behavior to define mind but asserted that this behavior could only be described in the language of will and purpose. By broadening the conception of behavior Holt achieved what his teachers thought possible only by making mind supreme. Their wide notion of "mind" encompassed behavior; his wide notion of "behavior" encompassed mind.

Students of James and Münsterberg

In 1895 Edward Lee Thorndike came to Harvard to study with James. When Thorndike's landlady prohibited him from incubating and hatching chicks in his bedroom, James took the outfit into his cellar where Thorndike thereafter conducted his studies on animal intelligence. Thorndike left Harvard with his fowl when Columbia offered him a fellowship and went on there to a Ph.D. and a brilliant career. No sooner had he gone than someone else interested in animals arrived.[2] Robert Mearns Yerkes received his B.A. from Ursinus College in 1897. After he attempted to make philosophy biological at Harvard, Royce steered him to Münsterberg, then ensconced as head of the laboratory. Yerkes would work in the psychology of animals, "comparative psychology." Eliot's presidential report for 1898–1899 noted that the psychology laboratory had started experiments on "the sensations, feelings, memories, instincts and habits of well-cared-for, normal turtles, newts, frogs, and fishes."[3]

Yerkes received his Ph.D. in 1902 and was appointed an instructor in charge of comparative psychology, remaining at Harvard until 1917. He was the most thorough American investigator in his area, pivotal in establishing the sub-discipline of comparative psychology through his volume of work and his indefatigable use of personal influence to organize investigation. He worked his way up from various lower animal forms to the crab, the turtle, the frog, the dancing mouse, the rat, the worm, the crow, the dove, the pig, the monkey, and man. During the First World War he was chief of the psychological services testing the intelligence of the large drafted army. After the war he concentrated on extended and systematic study of anthropoid apes.[4]

Like James, Yerkes worked in the intellectual context created by Darwin, especially in his 1872 *Expressions of the Emotions in Man and Animals.* Yerkes's original purpose apparently was to study the evolution of mind. He called his dissertation topic on animal physiology "The *Psychic Processes of the Frog.*"[5] He would observe and compare mental phenomena at different levels of the animal hierarchy. Even if Yerkes supposed that he was examining the evolution of mind, animal psychology made observation and behavior important in their own right and not merely as aids to studying consciousness. In his *Psychology* James had intended to combat a wholly mechanistic conception of mind, but before he died students were using some of his ideas to support just that conception.

Whatever James may have thought, Münsterberg correctly sensed that psychology was developing in ways he could not fully approve. But as its head, he kept the psychology department at Harvard under the authority of speculative thinkers when in many universities experimentalists were making it a separate discipline. Shortly after James died, Münsterberg advised Harvard's new President Lowell that comparative psychology ought to play a minor role at Harvard. Yerkes was not a real psychologist, Münsterberg argued, because he studied animal movements under stimulation; such work had little to do with studying inner states through behavior. Münsterberg's action theory had always reflected a partial truth, and when applied to animals was not "psychology" at all. He convinced Lowell, or confirmed Lowell's opinion, that animal psychology was unimportant, and for the next several years Yerkes stayed on at Harvard with only limited influence.*

*HM to ALL, 30 January 1911, File 2357 (10), HM papers. Münsterberg was not merely exerting his academic power. It is obvious from his various schemes of knowledge that to

Yerkes was not the only psychologist at Harvard whose work deviated from strict pragmatic–idealistic orthodoxy. From 1895 to 1903 a talented group of men whose prime concern was laboratory behavior took their Ph.D.s under James and Münsterberg. Robert MacDougall (1895), James Lough (1898), Arthur Peirce (1899), Charles Rieber (1900), Roswell Angier (1903), and Knight Dunlap (1903) sustained Yerkes. Their textbooks show a behavioristic emphasis: Yerkes's *Introduction to Psychology* (1911); Dunlap's *System of Psychology* (1912); and (later) Leonard Troland's *Fundamentals of Human Motivation* (1928).* But of all the young Harvard psychologists the most gifted was Holt, Yerkes's colleague for many years.

Holt and His Work

Holt was born in Winchester, Massachusetts, in 1873, receiving his B.A. and Ph.D. from Harvard in 1896 and 1901. A favorite student of James and Münsterberg, and later their close friend, Holt became an instructor upon completion of his degree and seemed embarked on a conventionally successful career. Holt and Perry, James had said, were two of the best young men in the United States.[6] Harvard promoted Holt to assistant professor in 1905 and, as Münsterberg turned to applied psychology, Holt soon controlled all human experimentation in the laboratory. His association with the new realists contributed to the group's effectiveness

him psychology, although physiological, had as its purpose the understanding of man. As far as he was concerned, Yerkes's rightful place was in biology. Similarly, Münsterberg unsuccessfully tried to get Harvard to refuse a fund that the Hodgson family finally donated for psychical research. Later, Lowell had to order him not to interfere with the work of Leonard Troland, who received his degree in 1915 and who became the first Richard Hodgson Fellow in Psychical Research. Independently funded research projects of this sort circumscribed Münsterberg's power as laboratory head, but his protest also had an intellectual rationale: Troland's work was scientifically illicit, bringing together the causal and teleological realms. See Folder 2357 (18), HM Papers, and HPA, 5, pp. 197, 201, 257–59.

*The development of John Watson's behaviorism was not unconnected with Harvard. He had done his degree in 1903 in comparative psychology at Chicago with James Rowland Angell. Angell had studied at Harvard for a year and accepted James as his mentor. When Watson went from Chicago to Johns Hopkins in 1908, Knight Dunlap—whom we have just met as a peer of Yerkes—was there to greet him. Dunlap was apparently crucial in pushing Watson along the road to his famous 1913 statement, "Psychology as the Behaviorist Views It," although Watson was also collaborating with Yerkes from 1910 on. See HEP, pp. 554, 643–45; and John C. Burnham, "On the Origins of Behaviorism," JHBS 4 (1968): 143–51, and the references therein.

and gave him philosophic standing—he was the most astute of the six. For some years after James's death psychologists waited for Holt to fulfill a promise to rewrite and bring up to date *The Principles of Psychology*. But the care of his aging mother made inordinate demands on him, and his continuing half-time appointment was spent in managing the laboratory. Moreover, during the first decade of the century Holt endured a series of personal crises that changed his outlook. His life revolved around a small social group, the "Wicht Club," that he had organized. The close friendships and common interests he shared with its members— among them Angier, Yerkes, and Perry—did much to make Holt's life meaningful, but the group's members went on to careers outside of Harvard. Those that stayed, married and, consequently, no longer shared Holt's bachelor existence. Perhaps these events should have meant little, but Holt was maudlin about his male friendships. When a romance of his own ended unhappily, he felt bereft of both intellectually stimulating comrades and an emotionally supportive companion. At the same time his mother, with whom he lived in Cambridge, demanded more and more of his time. Often ill, she worshipped her son but wanted to dominate him. Holt felt his obligations increased because his two brothers had "gone to hell." After his life with his contemporaries collapsed, his mother's sickness made his existence increasingly strange and isolated, and he grew more bitter as he grew older.[7]

Like Perry, Holt found the sources of his neo-realism in the revered William James. When he died, Holt wrote that "the greatest and best has gone out of my life, and it interests me less than ever to live."[8] It was not, therefore, surprising that Holt's first book, *The Concept of Consciousness* (completed in 1908 but not published until 1914), detailed James's view that consciousness was not a substance but a function. But like Perry, Holt also used James for his own purposes. As James conceived radical empiricism, pure experience was what a conscious being was aware of— James in some sense assumed the reality of consciousness as a sort of entity. He finally resolved the problems surrounding the "sense" of this reality by adopting a panpsychic view of the universe. Holt claimed his view was consonant with James's,[9] but in *The Concept of Consciousness* consciousness as an entity disappeared.

Holt considered the physical objects to which the organism responded. He called them a "cross-section" of the class of physical objects, meaning by cross-section a part collection of any group of entities defined by a law unrelated to the law defining the whole group. This cross-section of physical objects together with the cross-section of "logico-mathematical terms and systems" to which human beings also responded was what we termed consciousness or mind (166–83). If Holt was not following James's path, his including the logico-mathematical realm in his analysis of mind at least indicated that he was no materialist. There was, Holt claimed, one substance, neither mind nor matter, made up of neutral entities. Certain simple combinations of these entities gave us the terms and systems of mathematics and logic; more complicated combinations of the entities gave us the physical bodies; even more complicated combinations, which the mechanism of response selected in living organisms, gave us that aggregate of neutral entities known as mind. This more complex aggregate contained cross-sections of both the combinations defining logic and mathematics and the combinations defining physical bodies (183).

If we are to understand this notion of consciousness, we must go beyond Holt's reconstruction of James. Like other Harvard students— Henry Sheffer and C. I. Lewis, to name the two most important—"The Renaissance of Logic" intrigued Holt, and his monism derived not only from James but also from Royce's conception of logic. As we have seen, Royce thought of logic as the exploration of more and more comprehensive systems of order: he identified the widest one with the absolute and derived from it the more limited order systems defining the world of spatio-temporal objects. Holt accepted Royce's view of logic and the "conceptual" nature of the universe (xiii), but with a neat twist argued from these premises to a neo-realistic conclusion.

The neutral entities, "the ultimate units of being," were propositions and terms (261). Various systems of being arose from "a certain Given" of propositions and terms that "by a sort of logical activity inherent in the propositions" generated the terms constituting the systems in question (16, 261–62). There was, Holt said, "a *structure* to the existing universe, and one that is ultimate, whereby entities are ordered in a series of graded complexities; a true hierarchy of being that may well suggest Plato's 'realm of ideas.'" Deduction, he continued, was the thinker's name for his own act of conforming his thought to the activity of the propositions whose "agency" generated the system. The new use of logic in philosophy was to grasp the structure of the world (11–14).

Holt's notion that the universe's nature was conceptual yet not mental made sense if we recognized the connection between the universe and his primal terms and propositions. The terms and propositions of logic and mathematics, as well as everything else, were built from his primal terms and propositions, so the latter were so far neutral, although also in some platonic sense conceptual. Mental phenomena existed only at a higher level, dependent on lower levels of physical and logico-mathematical entities. In maintaining his neo-realism against Royce, Holt defined consciousness as an advanced sort of combination of neutral entities, a cross-section of simpler combinations including the physical objects. It followed that we were immediately aware of what in another combination we called the physical objects.[10] Holt was moving toward a kind of behaviorism: the combination that defined consciousness was that cross-section of the neutral entities that a body "selectively described" in responding to the environment (338).

After writing *The Concept of Consciousness* and setting down his thoughts on the new logic, Holt interested himself in abnormal psychology. He attended the famous Clark Conference, which brought Freud and his followers to the United States in 1909, and thought Freud the most impressive of the group.[11] Holt also kept up with the people in the Cambridge area studying psychopathology: Boris Sidis had taken his degree with William James in 1897 and later stimulated interest in Freud in Boston; James Jackson Putnam, Harvard's first professor of neurology from 1893 to 1912, and Morton Prince, a physician who specialized in nervous diseases at the Boston City Hospital from 1885 to 1913, were also early devotees of psychotherapy; and finally Walter B. Cannon, the Harvard physiologist, and Elmer E. Southhard, the psychiatrist, were friends and contemporaries of Holt's, well informed in theories of the "abnormal."[12]

The result of Holt's investigations from 1909 to 1914 was *The Freudian Wish and Its Place in Ethics*; it appeared in 1915 with an addendum, his important *Journal of Philosophy* article, "Response and Cognition." In these writings he put the views of *The Concept of Consciousness* into a framework of speculative psychology. Like Santayana's *Life of Reason*, *The Freudian Wish* was a work of evolutionary naturalism, and in his bold eclecticism, Holt captured James's breadth of vision. Obviously enough, Freud's ideas were prominent in the book. Moreover, Holt delighted in using Freud to shock the social conventions of Cambridge: he illustrated the Freudian notion of wish in the first chapter by telling various stories involving himself and thinly disguised Harvard personages.[13] But Freud was only one aspect of the book. Its real flouting of conventions was intellectual, for it joined Freud to those two currents of thought that James and Münsterberg had in one way or another fostered—the defining of mind via behavior and the evolutionary conception of animal psychology —and used the result to defend a "naturalistic" view of ethics.

Holt noted that animal psychologists called their field a science of behavior, dwelling less and less on the subject of consciousness. Human psychology must follow this lead: students of man should study his behavior. This commitment did not imply that human beings were not conscious but that we could observe only behavior (155–56). The problem was to define behavior so that it accounted for human purposes, something the orthodox explained by calling in the occult entity consciousness. It would not do to conceive human or animal behavior as a simple neural process, "the impinging of stimulus on sense-organ, the propagation of ionization waves along a fiber, their spread among various other fibers, their combining with other similar waves, and eventually causing lowered or heightened muscle tonus." These things were happening, said Holt, but the account overlooked behavior's essentials—its organization (160–61).

If asked what a man was doing, I correctly answered, for example, not that he was going past the window, but that he was going to the store. Holt was interested in the systematic relations the man had to his environment enabling him to function as a whole (154–59). We studied his movements to discover that aspect of the world of which his behavior was a constant function. Holt defined behavior as any process of release that was a function of factors external to the mechanism of which the process was a part. It was not necessary that the immediate stimulus to the "process of release" be the object of which the behavior was a constant function. In fact, it was only when behavior began to be differentiated from reflex action that the stimulus was this object. Neither was the process a function of factors internal to the released mechanism: it was different from reflex action because the organism responded to something outside itself (163–69). This was "the specific response relation" Holt offered as crucial to a proper idea of behavior and as capable of circumventing the crudities of reflex-action analyses:

> In order to understand what the organism is doing, you will just *miss* the essential point if you look inside the organism. For the organism, while a very interesting mechanism in itself, is one whose movements turn on objects outside of itself, much as the orbit of the earth turns upon the sun; and these external, and sometimes very distant, objects are as much *constituents* of the behavior process as is the organism which does the turning. It is this *pivotal outer object*, the object of specific response, which seems to me to have been overneglected (155).

Construed in this holistic way, behavior was observable and subject to empirical investigation. Yet Holt also analyzed consciousness and purpose in its terms. Concentrating on the same elements of James as he had previously, Holt contended that consciousness was not a substance but a relation—the relation between the living organism and the environment to which it specifically responded (96). The "contents of consciousness" were just those objects or the aspects of them toward which organisms responded (189). The contents were just that advanced cross-section of entities that Holt had defined as consciousness itself in *The Concept of Consciousness; The Freudian Wish* argued more clearly that the name 'consciousness' was reserved for the structure defining the organization of these contents.

Holt did not distinguish between the object of consciousness and the object of behavior (172–73). Similarly, to say we had purposes was to say what "one's body in the capacity of released mechanism *does*" (174). My will was just that process whereby the body adjusted or assumed a motor attitude so that its activities were some function of an object (178–96). If we described exactly what someone did, if we found the object, situation, or process of which his behavior was a constant function, we described his purposes (163).

Holt did not reduce the will to actual behavior. The essential physiological condition was the "lambent interplay" of motor attitudes in which some one of them became ascendant and went over into conduct, although he allowed little difference between a motor attitude prepared and one touched off (60). If we examined the sensory pattern, the sum of all sense impulses, we saw that it prompted the muscles to many different motions. Some portions of this pattern augmented one another and produced the individual's overt behavior; other portions were too weak to produce "gross muscular contraction," but they did cause "varying degrees of muscular tonus . . . this is that play of motor attitude." It differed from overt behavior in the small degree of muscular action involved (68–69). Holt distinguished thought from will by relegating the former to those motor attitudes whose energy was too small to produce bodily movement (94). The intellect and the will were one, discriminated only as motor attitude prepared and motor attitude touched off (60):

> *thought is latent course of action with regard to environment (i.e., is motor setting)*, or a procession of such attitudes. But we have already found that will is also course of action with regard to environment, so that the only difference between thought and volition is one of the intensity of nerve impulse that plays through the sensory-motor arcs—a difference of minimal importance. . . . From this appears the literal truth of Spinoza's dictum that "The will and the intellect are one and the same " (98).

Spinoza aside, Holt maintained that his view harked back to Aristotle: the soul was not substantial and not corporeal, but the form of a natural body endowed with a capacity for life, a true entelechy (49). It was also concrete, definite, empirically observable, and incorporated in a living body (201).

We should not understand this position, it seems to me, as behaviorism in any simple sense but as a more subtle development of the psychological theories of James and Münsterberg. Holt did not so much exorcise mind as include it in a widened notion of what constituted behavior. He did not reduce mind to behavior so much as show that behavior had a conscious dimension. I call the position philosophical behaviorism, but whatever Holt's relation to pragmatic theories of mind, he went beyond them when linking his views to Freud.

Freud's "wish," said Holt, was a course of action that some mechanism of the body was set to carry out, whether it actually did so or not, with regard to some aspect of its environment. Holt identified the specific response relation and the wish, although 'wish' emphasized the distinction between a course of action executed and one only entertained (3–4). But this distinction was secondary. Freud's work allowed Holt to see how various wishes (or specific responses) interacted in the complex integration constituting an individual's behavior. Although it is unnecessary to examine the justness of his interpretation, Holt made clear his indebtedness to Freud and argued that slips of the tongue and pen, dreams, and humor revealed various failures in the forms of individual integration. In severe cases—suppression—one motor set became organically opposed to another, the two dissociated, and the personality split. In milder cases of suppressed wishes, a dominant group of wishes—an individual's prevailing character—retained control, but the maverick wishes occasionally actualized themselves in ways that ran the gamut from amusing to horrible (3–46).

Holt saw the organism as living in a precarious environment. Its good consisted in responding in ways that avoided harm, and the central problem of its existence was obtaining the knowledge necessary to insure survival. There were at least two elemental appetites—the nutritive and the sexual—and to appease these the organism responded in some way or another more or less automatically, but Holt assumed that there was much more to a satisfactory human existence than appeasing these appetites (108–09). The dilemma was that the responses necessary to achieve a harmonious existence were hard to ascertain and social existence rendered matters more complex. This statement perhaps makes Holt more sensitive to ambiguities inherent in human decision-making than he was. In his examples there was always a simple and reasoned solution to problems concerning the integration of human responses and, in any event, he supposed that there were solutions, whatever our success in finding them.

When we suppressed wishes, that is, failed to integrate them, the cause was lack of knowledge. Contacts with objects presented anomalies, contradictions, and perplexities. Until experience taught us to discriminate further particulars within these objects, we were in some degree victims of "suppression"—we did not function in the environment as adequately as we could. But, Holt went on, to the same extent conduct was "equivocal, immoral": when he examined behavioral integration, he was investigating the sphere of morality. A man acted aright when he thoroughly discriminated the facts, fulfilling all of his wishes at once.

"Truth and the ever-progressive discrimination of truth . . . alone con-
duce to moral conduct" (128–31).

In effect, Holt used his behaviorism and some Freudian insights to propose a self-realization ethics. For the scientific psychologist "there is one
unbroken integration series from reflex action, to behavior, conduct,
moral conduct, and the unified soul" (201). If we described behavior
objectively, we reached a stage where the descriptions were moral appraisals, evaluations based on the individual's ability to comprehend the
world in a way that produced an integrated set of responses:

> There is at any moment of life *some* course of action (behavior)
> which enlists *all* of the capacities of the organism: this is phrased
> voluntaristically as "some interest or aim to which a man devotes all
> his powers," to which "his whole being is consecrated." This matter
> of the unthwarted lifelong progress of behavior integration is of
> profound importance, for it is the transition from behavior to
> conduct, and to *moral conduct*. The more integrated behavior is
> harmonious and consistent behavior toward a larger and more
> comprehensive situation, toward a bigger section of the universe; it
> is lucidity and breadth of purpose. And it is wonderful to observe
> how with every step in this process the bare scientific *description of
> what the organism does* approaches more and more to a description of
> moral conduct. In short, all of the more embracing behavior for-
> mulas (functions) are moral. The behaviorist has not changed his
> strictly empirical, objective procedure one iota, and he has scienti-
> fically observed the evolution of reflex process into morality (197).

Behavior was wrong when it failed to account for consequences: we had
not adjusted to enough of the environment, and we could correct our
behavior by enlarging its scope and reach. The integration of specific
responses effected this moral change and, Holt noted, "the immediate
stimulus . . . recedes further and further from view" (198). Finally, if we
recall that Holt defended his behaviorism as an outcome of the insights of
animal psychologists, it was not strange that "morals evolve and develop;
they grow, and are a part of the general growth and evolution of the
universe" (148).

Holt said we might do things not conducive to our good but we did
not will them, or at least will them with an undivided will. Moreover,

when we acted out of ignorance and so frustrated a part of ourselves, we were not free: those parts of us that were in more or less secret rebellion always hindered us. The upshot was that only the wise man was free to will, that wisdom and virtue were one, and that only the wise and virtuous man was free (199–200). The Freudian ethic—what I have called Holt's philosophical behaviorism—"is a literal and concrete justification of the Socratic [and Platonic] teaching" (140–41). And he modestly urged that the identification of virtue and knowledge and the conception of the soul as an entelechy "has the apparent novelty that any restatement of the views of Plato and Aristotle must have in an age which has forgotten the classics" (95–96).

The Freudian Wish and its appended "Response and Cognition" together made a small two-hundred-page book. But in addition to joining his epistemology to a self-realization ethic via Freud, in this brief compass Holt also took a whack at being a moralist. In showing how parents might use his Freudian insights in raising children, he simplified moral education and, I think, underestimated the complexity of moral problems. He also chose examples that appeared naive, for example, a parent's concern for a son's smoking because it would stunt his growth and a young working girl's perplexity over a theater invitation. Nonetheless, his perspective again revealed his disregard for convention—he denounced supermundane moral sanctions—and his ambiguous nature, at once iconoclastic and conservative.[14]

In learning to respond to physical dangers, a child acted in a quasi-moral way. The parent should work to insure that her offspring's responses were as integrated, that is, as adequate, as possible. Holt suggested two principles to follow in realizing this goal. First, in the face of insignificant and everyday physical dangers, the parent must permit the child to learn from experience. A child learned that the candle burned and avoided it; he organized his response relations to guarantee his safety. If a mother protected her son in these situations, Holt warned, instead of learning ways to protect himself from physical harm, he learned that the parent blocked his desire. "The child is frustrated and not instructed." By arrogating to herself a bit of experience that should be the child's, the parent taught the child that the parent was an object to be manipulated. In the case of the protective mother and the child with the candle, Holt said,

the mother's hand "suppresses" the child's tendency to touch the fire. But the child's withdrawal becomes a withdrawal from the mother's hand and not, as it ought to be, a response to (or a function of)· the flame itself. Freud, like others before him, calls this "dissociation": The precautionary response which should be "associated" with fire is dissociated therefrom, and transferred to something else; in our case to the mother. Take this mother away, and the child knows no caution with regard to fire (105).

Second, when a course of action whose consequences were serious but deferred and perhaps irremediable tempted a child, Holt allowed the parent a more positive role: she could draw on her experience and explain what the consequences were likely to be. From Holt's perspective the parent was telling the child that the proposed action was wrong. The sanction for the "right" decision was that the wrong one would be injurious. (His example was a heart-to-heart chat about the evils of cigarettes.) Holt's second principle was simple: always tell the truth to children. Under these circumstances the parent conveyed to a child not a "parent says" sign but a "tobacco is" sign. The appropriate facts and not considerations of the parent's desire to manipulate informed the child's decision.

Holt related the two principles: parents who thwarted their child's natural impulses—and so muddled his responses and made the parents the objects of these responses—were also likely to lie to the child "for his own good." Contravening the second principle compounded the contravention of the first. Early and keenly cognizant of untruthfulness in his elders, the child became convinced that he must avoid parents and not, in this instance, cigarettes. But if parents followed both principles, Holt was confident that the child would generally do the right thing; he would resolve moral dilemmas by using the facts in a perspicacious manner. It is easy to mock the sanguine character of this moralizing, but it is hard to deny that Holt had hit on some home truths:

> I have talked with many parents of young children and have found but few who trust the truth sufficiently to deem it practicable with children. But parents need not waste breath to dub the truth "sacred," when they themselves do not trust it; and such parents have only themselves to thank when, in order to secure obedience, they have to resort to cajoleries, threats, whipping-posts, and such

superstitions as "abstract Right." A little concrete rightness in the parent will go much further (113–14).

Holt expanded his philosophical behaviorism only imperfectly. He wrote one more book, the first volume of *Animal Drive and the Learning Process*, in 1931. Subtitled "An Essay Toward Radical Empiricism," this book was, Holt stated, "in the spirit, at least" of James, even though Holt proclaimed himself a latter-day materialist. The first volume of *Animal Drive* exhaustively studied experimental work in comparative psychology and carefully interpreted its results as resting on "biological foundations." Man was a machine, Holt said, but he reserved until his second volume an examination of this statement and its philosophical ramifications,[15] and this volume was never published. Nonetheless, Edward C. Tolman (1886–1959), a student of Holt and Münsterberg, developed the same sorts of ideas. Tolman called his position purposive behaviorism and defended it in his important 1932 book *Purposive Behavior in Animals and Man*. Arguing that the data of consciousness, "raw feels," were ineffable and not public, Tolman claimed that science concerned itself only with behavior. But if we looked at the organism's activity as a whole, behavior was purposive. Men and animals acted in respect of ends, but we observed their purposes. More specifically, in saying that action was goal-directed, Tolman meant that behavior was a function of the situation and antecedent causes. The business of psychology was to determine these functional relations by observing behavior when we varied either the situation or antecedent causes independently. Tolman also postulated intervening variables between these determinants of behavior and the behavior itself: some were cognitive, serving as knowledge or wisdom, while others were demand variables, serving as motives. We always dealt with behavior in this scheme, Tolman said, but we looked at wholes. The behavior was "molar," not "molecular"; and when we found appropriate wholes, we might legitimately talk of purpose: goal-directed behavior was simply behavior of a certain sort.[16]

Holt and Professional Scholarship

From 1900 to 1920 Cambridge was not a community for deviants, but Harvard tolerated Holt's idiosyncrasies because of his undisputed talent and his independent thought and criticism. Holt was not so tolerant. He had been at Harvard almost continuously since he had entered as a sophomore in 1893 and did not like the changes he had seen. He came to despise scholarly entrepreneurship and to loathe the self-aggrandizement and quest for position that he believed was becoming characteristic of academics—this was, I suspect, the reason he announced to Ralph Perry that they could no longer be friends.[17] As time went on he became more and more convinced that Harvard stood for the professorial proprieties and a concern for prestige that he thought antithetic to a real love of wisdom. When his mother died in early 1918 and he had no reason to stay in Cambridge, he resigned his position, giving President Lowell a tidy summary of what the professionalization and bureaucratization of the academy had meant.

William James had taught him, Holt told Lowell, that the scholar must "put truth first." To be sure, Holt added, even the searcher for truth must look out for his own personal interests, but the priority given to truth was just what distinguished "the honest and sober scientist to whom some little truth will surely be vouchsafed, and the full-fledged charlatan." Holt had supposed at first that "the game of self-advertisement and charlatanry" did not work at Harvard, but seventeen years of teaching had convinced him otherwise. The academic game offended Holt—Hocking's recommendation to get a degree ("a philosopher without a Ph.D. is like unto a fisherman without any bait"); Perry's admonition to publish quickly ("out in time to impress prospective employers"); and Münsterberg's advice to attend the Christmas meetings.[18] Holt despised all these stratagems:

> From the side of the young instructor the system operates thus;—he is eager to "get on", and so he must become as soon as possible "well-known". He therefore reads immature papers at Christmas meetings of his scientific society, writes others for his professional journals, scrambles old notes and threadbare formulae together into a "textbook", palavers with everybody who has the slightest academic influence, and turns himself generally into a personal publicity bureau. All this he substitutes outright for anything resembling the sober and honest pursuit of truth, and for all save the most perfunctory attention to the instruction and guidance of his students.

Once embarked on his career the scholar then worked his way up:

> Agreeably to the present level of American intelligence, the young man who has advertised himself most loudly is called to the first academic vacancy that occurs. On receiving the call he hastily brushes his hair, waits upon his college president, and blandly presents a cut-throat proposition; of which the impudence is more or less swamped in unctuous verbiage.

These "familiar hold-up manoeuvres," Holt continued, and "a variety of similarly unworthy tricks" had become routine in the scholarly world. He had decided that he could not adjust his academic gait "to appeal to the altogether rudimentary intelligence of American collegiate circles." The real truthseeker must find the American university a hampering and compromising social affiliation. "Professors Woods, Perry, and Hocking," said Holt, "are moderately talented and enterprising young men with whom philosophy is merely a means for getting on in the world. I do not respect them; I will not cooperate with them; and I am happy to be in a position now to wipe out the stigma of being even nominally one of their 'colleagues'." The president could be sure, Holt concluded, that his resignation was no maneuver. Lowell did not implore him to stay.[19]

Holt's letter focused on Harvard and its philosophy department the bitterness he felt about the outcome of his personal life and his dislike of academic cant and hypocrisy. The indictment was exaggerated but not altogether undeserved.[20]

After leaving Harvard, Holt went at first to live on an island off the Maine coast, and for the next few years, generally with a friend, sometimes alone, tried to conduct what he thought was the true scholar's life. In 1926 Herbert Sydney Langfield, a colleague for a time in the Harvard psychology lab, convinced Holt to come to Princeton and for ten years he was a visiting professor there, teaching every other semester. But his heart was not in this commitment and in 1936 he returned to Maine with a friend.[21] When he died in 1946 the academic establishment had its revenge. Remembered as one of the most respected psychologists of "the old days," Holt received a few tributes and was forgotten—only a few students and no institution remained to keep his work alive.

Although Tolman was a significant psychologist, he did not pursue his work at Harvard. After getting his Ph.D. in 1915 he went to Northwestern and then to a distinguished career at Berkeley. A year later Münsterberg died—James had been dead since 1910—and in 1917 Yerkes left for Minnesota and then for Yale, disgusted with the continued unwillingness of the Harvard administration to recognize comparative psychology. When Holt resigned the next year, Harvard psychology hit bottom. For the next ten years it remained subordinated to philosophy, and disputes over the professional ideologies of various candidates for positions, unhappy appointments, and bad judgment prevented psychology from regaining its former prestige or developing its doctrines. Philosophical behaviorism died.

23

PHILOSOPHERS AT WAR

Philosophers Respond to the War

From 1912 to 1920 problems internal to the institution disturbed the tranquility of Harvard thinkers. But for much of that time the First World War was disrupting academic affairs everywhere. From 1914 to 1917 the spectacle of civilized Europeans slaughtering one another preoccupied all thoughtful Americans, and the role of the United States in the conflict dominated public discussion. When the United States became a belligerent in 1917, its role in the peace was just as heatedly discussed, although Americans expressed their real passions in justifying the plunge into war and the break with the tradition of political isolation from Europe. Although Royce and James had not made social and political theorizing a priority during their primes, in their moral and religious concerns they both had stressed the relation of philosophy to life. The war was a major opportunity for the Cambridge community to carry on in this tradition. But speculation in international affairs proved to be another internal political issue. Hugo Münsterberg was a member of the department, and he was a German.

Münsterberg, the Target at Hand

Vain and garrulous, Münsterberg was impressed with his organizational abilities in a variety of fields and with his talent for spreading good will both in and out of the scholarly community. In short, he was an early academic entrepreneur, but his entrepreneurial qualities were unfortunately wedded to bad judgment and political ineptitude. His pompous and authoritarian manner, heightened by his formal dress, waxed mustache, and pronounced German accent, did not contribute to his personal charm. In many respects he embodied what would become the American stereotype of the German. As Royce's wife quipped, "Münsterberg ist unser Gott." Nonetheless, in his first fifteen years at Harvard Münsterberg was an asset. His philosophical acumen could not be denied, and his experimental skill, his youth and exuberance, and his hospitable nature attracted many graduate students and made him their popular "Chief."[1]

The defects in his character began to tell toward the end of the Eliot administration. His popular applications of psychology brought him more and more public attention; and his attempts to promote German-American friendship—he was instrumental in creating the Berlin Amerika-Institut for scholarly and cultural interchange—gave him opportunity for international headline hunting. After corresponding with Münsterberg about his unofficial concern for Harvard's relation to German universities, Eliot wrote him that the Corporation found his activities intolerable and politely ordered him to curtail his non-academic work.[2] Münsterberg apparently complied but proved irrepressible. He soon wrote Eliot:

> Since my last letter to you in which I expressed my intention to be obedient to the wishes of the Corporation, I have received more than fifty letters which I simply could not answer, if I interpret your ruling strictly. I had letters and cablegrams from the Minister of Education, from the Foreign Office, from the Department of the Interior and from the American ambassador in Berlin to all of whom I ought not to reply. In a corresponding way I had plenty of letters from American men seeking informaiton and help as to official German affairs; for instance, two letters from Carnegie with reference to matters of the Ministry of Education, letters from leading political men, or, to point to other regions, from the Association of American Dentists to help them with German government inquiries, from deans of German universities as to American academic affairs, correspondence as to the new German ambassador in Washington, requests from an official bureau to write on the fellowships for German students in Harvard to be published in more than a hundred newspapers, requests for help in a large German undertaking to raise

the English school instruction in Germany and scores of similar communications. I abstract these entirely from the more political matters; for instance, the emperor's suppressed interview brought me letters and telegrams daily as some papers insisted that I had been the agent.[3]

When Lowell became president, Münsterberg's public career was still a nuisance. Lowell wrote him, "Your high standing as a scholar would be more appreciated if you never allowed your name to appear in the press."[4] Later, he condemned Münsterberg for neglecting the psychological laboratory for "indulgence in popular writings and speechmaking, for self-advertisement."[5] Harvard wanted the prestige which accrued to its faculty members as important public figures, but it did not want the vulgar notoriety Münsterberg brought; his clumsy quest for power was ungentlemanly.

Whatever Harvard's right to muzzle Münsterberg, he was a minor irritation until the war in Europe broke out in 1914. From a later perspective the ethical issues separating the Allies from the Central Powers were unclear, if they existed at all. But in 1914 the British were astute and the Germans inept in their use of propaganda, and in the United States opinion leaders supported the Allies. The New England elite was outstanding in its unanimous hostility to Germany. Later historians did not regard the invasion of Belgium and the initiation of submarine warfare as symptoms of Prussian immorality, but to articulate Americans, especially those in the northeast, these actions seemed incontrovertible evidence of barbarism, and the British cultivated other stories of German "atrocities." Americans also linked moralism to their conceptions of the national interest: the United States had a stake in the continued existence of the British Empire, of English and French democracy, and of the open commerce that characterized the diplomacy of Great Britain and profited both Britain and America. Despite the embarrassment of the western Allies' pact with autocratic Russia, after the Germans sank the *Lusitania* in early 1915, a synthesis of righteousness and interest joined the United States to England. Woodrow Wilson fought the 1916 election by delicately balancing the country's fear of war against its desire to express its virtue belligerently. The result was "preparedness"—a position supposedly making America ready for war with Germany while simultaneously avoiding the extreme anti-German pronouncements common to Republicans like Theodore Roosevelt. By 1917, however, the issue of submarine warfare seemingly forced the second Wilson administration to declare war. Just as historians are less than clear about the degrees of wickedness distinguishing the European powers, so they are restrained in interpreting American entry into the conflict: the war was perhaps necessary but not worthy of a crusade. Of course, this was not the view of United States policy makers or molders of opinion, and from 1917 to 1919 America indulged in a patriotic orgy lauding democracy at home and denouncing its enemies wherever they could be found.

Needless to say, Münsterberg never shared the anti-German sentiment. But the Cambridge community was immediately, overwhelmingly, and emotionally committed to the British and the French. Although it could bear Münsterberg in peace, in war it found a German sympathizer intolerable; and the belief that his self-inflating applied psychology was bringing Harvard into disrepute gave the department extra incentive to treat him viciously.

Political Philosophy

In a sense, after the war started Münsterberg was a German propagandist: New England opinion was violently anti-German, and he worked, with little success, to moderate this sentiment. But in a more important sense he was behaving in a dispassionate and intelligent way when Harvard turned on him. His view of the European struggle and what he said about it were almost impartial. Although he grew more prejudiced as the war went on, a sober tone prevailed in the three books he wrote in 1914, 1915, and 1916. *The War and America* asserted that Americans must look at the conflict as one in which there was no right or wrong, in which each nation was responding to the exigencies of its position in the world power system. If there was a moral issue, Münsterberg declared, it was between German culture and Russian barbarism. Britain had made a terrible strategic error, for in weakening Germany, both Russia and Japan would benefit, hastening the decline of the western world. The overriding duty of Americans was fair-play and neutrality in the face of competing global ideals among which no one could reasonably choose.[6]

A year later in *The Peace and America* the conflict between Britain and Germany was more prominent, but Münsterberg insisted that the goal of the United States should be to reconcile the opposing Anglo-Saxon and Teutonic ideals. Americans should synthesize English individualism and German discipline. Declaring that the humbling of Germany would make lasting peace impossible, he feared that the United States would join the war on the side of Britain and pleaded that the nation remain neutral.[7] In *The Peace and America* Britain began to emerge as a villain, and this theme was carried over in *Tomorrow*. But this final book still analyzed the similar drives of all the states in the war, predicting that in the nationalistic globe that would exist in peacetime, American foreign policy would be similar to that of any other great power.[8]

When measured against the war work and attitudes of his colleagues, Münsterberg's attitudes were almost admirable from a later perspective. The other philosophers at Harvard lost all sense of proportion and, before Wilson declared war, were little less than propagandists for the British. After the United States entered the war in 1917, their views were as partial as those of American policy makers. It is difficult to trace the sources of the popular flow of ideas, but the Harvard philosophers were prominent men, and their ideas certainly contributed to the educated public's stereotype of the relation of German thought and politics and the Teutonic national character. Harvard's political analysis also had the appeal of simplicity: nineteenth-century German philosophy led to twentieth-century German chauvinism, and the arrogant, authoritarian Prussian militarist embodied the central defect of German national character.

Royce, Santayana, Perry, and Hocking all put their literary abilities to work for the British and French war effort. Even C. I. Lewis, who was then at Berkeley and who rarely published anything but technical articles in professional journals, stated that "German philosophy . . . is not a negligible affair; it is capable of wrecking nations, of setting the world afire, of renouncing national obligations . . . of providing apologetic for inhumanities more barbarous than the world had thought to see again." But Lewis limited himself to one article, and his point was that the guilty "German philosophy" was perhaps unfathomable and the connection between nationality and doctrine complex beyond analysis.[9]

The other Harvard men were less interested in complexity but more lavish in their efforts. Royce wrote two books, Perry three, and Santayana and Hocking one apiece.*

The invasion of Belgium and the sinking of the *Lusitania* shocked Royce and made him briefly a political thinker. His attachment to German thought and his investigations into the nature of community produced a curious result as he confronted the Berlin war machine. He apparently felt that the Germans had betrayed lifelong intellectual commitments; this betrayal of the community of nations led Royce to spend the last two years of his life preaching about the "international crime" of the Germans. They possessed the spirit of Cain, an enmity to mankind; they were the willful, deliberate enemies of the human race. Congruent with his position in *The Problem of Christianity*, Royce contended that great tragedies—in this case a betrayal of mankind—were great opportunities: the war's evil could produce an atonement and leave the world better off than it otherwise might have been. "The new griefs which today beset the civilized nations," he exhorted, "call for new reflections and new inventions." The future would invent and practice new forms of international activity which might lead the way toward "the united life of the great community." The activity Royce spoke of was his scheme for international insurance, and consistent with his technical work, he clarified his meaning by recourse to the concept of interpretation. Wars resulted from dyadic relations between men and nations: armed conflict involved one group of powers against another, and these kinds of relations were never free from tension. Pairs were "an essentially dangerous community." The insurance relation was triadic: an insurer—the spirit of the community—interpreted the risks of an adventurer or risk-taker to a beneficiary. The insurance community demanded some larger union in the social order. Royce proposed that nations insure themselves against hazards like war. An impartial board would act as the spirit of the community, and he believed that this contribution to the war's dark problem would "*most tend to bring peace on earth and to aid us towards the community of mankind.*" The reparations to be demanded by the victors could provide the resources to fund the "International Board of Insurance Trustees." While in peacetime no thinker could persuade the nations to make the sacrifice, the (Allied) victors might force the Germans to finance the proposal.

*I include Santayana, who had left Harvard in 1912.

Betrayal itself contained within it a possible atonement. Out of the evil of war—and out of it alone—might come the means to eliminate war and *"to make visible to us the holy city of the community of all mankind."*[10]

Royce's powers had diminished by 1914, and his younger colleagues put forward a much more elaborate anti-German position. All believed that the war was, as Perry put it in a book title, *The Present Conflict of Ideals*. German ideals had developed from the speculative thought of the nineteenth century, beginning with Kant and Goethe. Santayana's book *Egotism in German Philosophy* made the case most dramatically: in maintaining that the physical world was in some way the product of the mind, the Germans stressed the primacy of the self. Goethe's romantic notion that the widest development of the self was the primary obligation hinted at this attitude. As Santayana wrote about Goethe's love affairs, "Every pathetic sweetheart in turn was a sort of Belgium to him; he violated her neutrality with a sigh; his heart bled for her innocent sufferings, and he never afterwards said in self-defense, like the German chancellor, that she was no better than she should be. But he must press on."[11] The philosophers traced this subjectivism in Kant, Fichte, and Hegel in the growing commitment to the notion of an absolute self defining the world. Then, as Perry argued, it was a short step to believing that you were like the absolute—"a pride that claims the world in the name of those spiritual powers which are man's prerogatives."[12] The Germans explained that the state embodied the absolute in time, and the German state, in particular, embodied it in the present historical era.[13] This framework of ideas allowed the Germans to make the individual subservient to state power. But because the state was the only true person, at the same time they elevated selfish concerns as its highest ideal. The result, which even Perry and Santayana had difficulty in linking to German idealism, was Nietzsche's superman. In the most vulgar part of this crude history of ideas, Hegel's absolute egotism led to the glorification of men "beyond good and evil" who denounced "the slave morality" of Christendom.[14] The war consequently became a war of autocracy against democracy, as Hocking put it, "the *cause célèbre* of modern history."[15]

It is easy enough to see that the Harvard philosophers examined politics in light of their philosophical biases, and their emphases differed. Royce was surely in the tradition of German idealism and his work did not investigate the philosophical roots of war; but he shared the common view that the German political philosophy was one of evil statism.[16] In his strident denunciation of the Germans hid a fear of a link between the absolute and the Junker. Hocking, the man philosophically closest to Royce, refused to concede that philosophical idealism truly justified Teutonic bellicosity, although he too denounced Germany and its super-organic conception of the state.[17] But the realism of Santayana and Perry had to benefit if idealism were stigmatized, and they joined their wartime political analyses to their philosophical antipathies. For them idealism was speculatively indefensible and the clear cause of German wrongdoing as well. And curiously enough Perry fancied that the philosophy distinctive of the American spirit was the realism underlying individualism, social democracy, and humanitarianism.*

The philosophers all agreed on the character type that dominated Germany in consequence of its national philosophy: the German was pompous but disciplined and dutiful, a master of organization and "scientific management."[18] It could not have helped Münsterberg that he gave a similar description of the model German character, only more positively.[19] Now, the Harvard philosophers were intelligent, well read, and widely traveled, and many others shared their views. Yet Münsterberg was the German with whom they had the most contact; his bureaucratic mania and his love of authority and discipline struck all of them. Moreover, their interpretations of the causes of world conflict reflected their philosophical prejudices. Consequently, it is more than speculation to argue that Harvard's contribution to the American stereotype of German character resulted from generalizing Münsterberg's unhappier personal traits.

Perry and Hocking as Propagandists

Perry and Hocking did more than speculate on the cultural sources of

---

* *The Present Conflict of Ideals* (New York: Longmans, Green and Co., 1918), pp. 364–68, 497–546. At least Perry and Münsterberg, and perhaps all the Harvard philosophers, owed much to nineteenth-century *Lebensphilosophie*: it related the main philosophic tendencies to the interests of life and to the character of nations. As commentators on national character, the philosophers all had difficulty with Bergson. Although James respected Bergson, the other Cambridge thinkers regarded him as an "irrationalist," yet he also spoke for France, a clear-thinking, democratic ally. On this issue see I. Woodbridge Riley, *American Thought from Puritanism to Pragmatism and Beyond*, 2d ed. (New York: Henry Holt and Co., 1923), pp. 408–23.

the global battle. When American entry into the war became a serious issue in 1916, Perry lent his polemical talents to the preparedness campaign. The Plattsburg Movement—about which he wrote a laudatory book—was part of the effort to insure that America would be ready should war occur. Because the Germans were the obvious enemy, it pushed Wilson further along anti-German lines. The movement got under way when the New York City elite initiated a summer military training program at Plattsburg, New York. Recruits came—Perry and Hocking among them—and learned to be "citizen soldiers," as well as receiving lessons in the obligations of intelligent participation in a democracy. Perry publicized the movement, and in his collection of popular essays, *The Free Man and the Soldier*, stressed the more general issue of preparedness. Dismissing pacifism with the argument that its advocate must be able to acquiesce in the violation of his wife or daughter, Perry observed that in an imperfect world we had to fight for principles in order to bring on the day when fighting no longer would be necessary.[20] "Preparedness" followed naturally from recognizing that war might occur, Perry added, but it need not lead to militarism: the universal draft and military training in colleges would make the United States more effective internationally and better able to implement the ends of its national life—democracy and the well-being and happiness of individual men and women.[21]

When the United States entered the war, Perry took leave from Harvard to become secretary of the War Department's Committee on Education and Special Training. After first directing the training of enlisted men, Major Perry dealt mainly with procuring officers through the universities.[22] He helped to establish ROTC. More broadly, his job was to guarantee that higher education cooperated with the war effort. In 1919 the newly formed American Legion tempted him to resign from Harvard to become its permanent secretary-treasurer, but the job fell through.[23] Bertrand Russell mordantly commented that Perry displayed a brand of New England moralism "which caused him to be intellectually ruined by the First War."[24]

Hocking did not leave Harvard but during the war he served under Perry on the educational committee as District Director of the War Issues Course Program. He toured parts of the European war zone in summer 1917 as the guest of the British; as an "inspector" of war issues courses in colleges, his concern was to educate future officers in the problems of maintaining military morale.[25] The outcome of his work was *Morale and Its Enemies*, a sort of psychological handbook that he hoped the military could use to understand and control the army's spirit.[26] Hocking's interest was not just that Americans should fight courageously but that they do so without compromising their ideals. He begged the military to remember that the war was a moral issue and, accordingly, that officers must not only insure morale but also preserve American moral superiority.[27] One chapter, "War and Women," focused on prostitution: how was the army to meet men's "needs" (and, therefore, maintain morale) while "keeping [the soldiers] straight"? One of America's great strengths was its attitude toward women, opined Hocking, and on whatever other grounds prostitution was evil, it was "inconsistent with democracy," implying a stratification and degradation of human relationships. Still, men at war had desires. To meet the problem Hocking advocated canteens in which the soldier could socialize easily with accessible and anonymous women ready for a harmless good time. "The soldier on leave would prefer not to be burdened with the fact that Miss X is the daughter of So-and-So, living in the city of Boston, Mass., and related to the B's and C's. He wishes to take her as a companion, without other history . . . and without future obligations." Such frivolous and respectable pleasures would maintain *esprit*; conjoined with suitable moral exhortation, they would also keep American men pure, Hocking felt, "provided the war does not last too long."[28]

Münsterberg's Travail

After 1914 Münsterberg lived in this intellectual climate. To be sure, he continued to be offensive. He intrigued in international politics and blathered on for the newspapers about "the psychological equation" of Theodore Roosevelt's personality.[29] When one Allied supporter with a former Harvard student threatened to cut off a $10 million bequest unless the university sacked Münsterberg, he tried to manipulate the issue so that Harvard's stand for academic freedom would appear to be support for his politics.[30] But, regarding the war, Münsterberg was torn between the land of his birth and youth and that of his mature life. In consequence, he continued to be fairly reasonable in his analysis of the war and his attitude toward American belligerency. We could not say the same of the Cambridge community.

When the issue of the $10 million bribe for Münsterberg's dismissal came up, President Lowell emphasized and stood behind the tradition of academic freedom. Nonetheless, Münsterberg embarrassed Lowell, and could he have quietly rid Harvard of the man, he would have acted. He implied as much when he wrote that the $10 million threat "certainly would make it impossible for the University to take steps against Professor Münsterberg, even if it were otherwise inclined to do so."[31]

This was only a minor aspect of Münsterberg's travail. In November 1914 former President Eliot, a leader of Allied sentiment, accused Münsterberg of immorality and then insanity because of his political stance.[32] A month later Royce began to sever his ties with Münsterberg, although he had made a sacred pledge of friendship in 1905 when he convinced Münsterberg to stay at Harvard instead of accepting Kant's chair at Königsberg. But after the *Lusitania* crisis, Royce said his conscience was at stake, and he effectively broke with Münsterberg.[33] The war also led his close friend and old student, Edwin Holt, to denounce Münsterberg's politics, friendship, character, and scholarship.[34] And towards the end of 1916 the Visiting Committee of the Board of Overseers advocated cutting off publication funds for the psychological laboratory.[35] A public letter from Hocking implying that Münsterberg was a traitor whom the authorities ought to censor capped these private humiliations. He could not have taken much solace from a perfunctory private note expressing Hocking's "sincere personal regard and gratitude."[36] The public document caused a minor sensation, but Münsterberg's reputation was so tarnished at this point that it made little difference. He had long since ceased to speak in public, or attend faculty meetings and social functions.[37] Under the strain and tension, however, he punctiliously kept up his classroom commitments, and in December 1916 while delivering a lecture to Radcliffe women, he collapsed, toppled from the podium, and died. He was fifty-three.

Philosophical Commitment and Its Results

The metaphysical positions of the Cambridge philosophers certainly shaped their response to the war. We must also explain the intensity of their commitment and the poverty of their political speculation. The latter is perhaps explained by lack of background. Before the war, they had little interest in or knowledge of the structure of politics or political theory; their mentors—notably Royce and James—had not informed the younger men in these areas. When Santayana, Perry, and Hocking wrote, they did not do so out of concern for or reading in political philosophy. They merely wanted to besmirch the Germans and, mixing together their garden-variety political ideas and their philosophical knowledge, promulgated the consequences to the world. For Santayana and Perry it was particularly easy to tar philosophical opponents—idealists—with the brush of German politics.

An easier question to answer is why the war commanded the dedication of the philosophers in the first place, for a thoughtless patriotism swept the culture, and philosophers and other academics were not immune. Almost the entire American professoriate conscripted itself intellectually. Scholars willingly created a campus climate inimical to academic freedom through the pressure of opinion and by ostracizing those who would not conform. They kept silent as trustees assaulted dissenters. When the United States became involved, professors worked officially to formulate and popularize stereotypes and shibboleths, becoming agents of the government war machine. The alacrity with which they turned institutions of higher education over to the military for training courses of various kinds demonstrated their overriding commitment to the prosecution of the war. This commitment compromised their academic integrity by substituting propaganda for scholarship and by transforming the university into a military training institute.

Two other considerations may also help to explain the disappearance of critical intelligence in the academy from 1914 to 1919, and both may help us to understand the specific actions of the Harvard philosophers. On one hand, they wanted to contribute to the war effort and to overcome any suspicion of ivory tower isolation from American life. On the other hand, philosophers were no longer free-lance, independent thinkers; they were employees of an institution that effectively had adopted a social function—the production of wartime propaganda. The philosophers identified with the purposes and fate of that institution.[38] Münsterberg was merely a foil against which the Harvard community could display its ideological purity. He was forgotten with the American declaration of war and the subsequent opportunity for thinkers to show their patriotism in more virile ways.

The principal Harvard philosophers of the war period—Perry and Hocking—were sociologically marginal: they prided themselves on their professionalism—their scholarship, detachment, and "scientific" approach; at the same time they had learned from their predecessors that philosophy was the guide to life. As "expert" critics of the German polity, they maintained objectivity while demonstrating the relevance to the world of their special training and knowledge. This political activism lasted only as long as the terrible social strain that engendered it. Involvement was also surely more a function of the ambiguous status of the wartime philosopher-professor than of a lasting commitment to the affairs of men extending from religious and moral questions to political ones. After the war professorial duties again became all-consuming and the philosophers' interests in the extra-academic diminished. The professional philosopher would cease to be marginal and would subsequently be fulfilled in attending to university duties alone.

The immediate intellectual tragedy at post-war Harvard was not that the philosophers forgot politics but that they forgot Münsterberg. Brand Blanshard recalled that when he went to Harvard in 1920 Münsterberg's memory was already dim.[39] The insight that saw an illustration of the truth of German idealism in cinematic technique was neglected. Self-righteous memories recalled only the worst of his popular psychology and the worst of his personality. Münsterberg's thought was not the only loss. Royce died three months before Münsterberg. I would speculate that the wider philosophic community vaguely equated the ideas of the two because the enemies of philosophic idealism did not hesitate to identify it—successfully—with the culture of the Hun. So Royce too may have suffered from Münsterberg's eclipse. He molded his two most influential students, Hocking and Lewis, only obliquely (if powerfully), and there was no direct heir to carry Royce's banner. He was left as the respectable if overblown and stodgy champion of an outworn, indeed foolish, creed, while Perry heralded a "realistic" James, who needed no boosting, as the stalwart defender of something quintessentially American. Such were the effects of the Great War on Münsterberg, Royce, and James.

PART 5

PHILOSOPHY AS A PROFESSION

Ralph Barton Perry about 1925

C. I. Lewis (self-portrait) about 1930   Alfred North Whitehead

24

THE PROFESSIONAL MENTALITY
1920-1930

The Golden Age and After

The rise of Darwinism provided the impetus for a new wave of synoptic philosophizing at the end of the nineteenth century. The disintegration of the Unitarian philosophy, the rediscovery of Kant, the convergence in Cambridge of a group of talented thinkers, and the prestige of Harvard led to the triumph of a novel philosophical perspective. Harvard Pragmatists made an activist religion compatible with Darwin's work and promulgated their glad tidings to the world. Their ideas offered a way of understanding the natural sciences, provoked speculation in logic, and had implications for moral philosophy. In short, the philosophers framed a vision of the universe that created many opportunities for philosophical scholarship and was also relevant for the world outside the university.

Royce and James set forth a sophisticated model of how the world worked and how philosophers should study it; specialized work which assumed the contours of this model followed naturally and rationally. Of course, specialization was nothing new: we can trace it back at least to the philosophy of the Middle Ages. Medieval thinkers accepted a common network of assumptions and worked diligently within them. What gave the Golden Age its character was that it had to create a new network to assimilate Darwinian science. Those who came after Royce and James were simply working within that network. Establishing paradigmatic modes of thinking was also one component of the professionalization of philosophy as an academic discipline, and professionalization intensified the drive toward speculative specialities from 1880 to 1930.

Specialization within the twentieth-century profession was also different. The same technical problems that exercised the Golden Age exercised succeeding generations; to this extent patterns of thought remained the same. But the philosophers of the earlier era studied logic and epistemology to see what light they cast on the more practical branches of philosophy. Later philosophers tended to specialize *within* logic and epistemology. The other branches eventually became vestigial and, in any case, finally ceased to be applied to real problems; popularization in any branch ultimately became suspect. By the Second World War specialization within the profession had changed the substance of speculation and radically reoriented the traditional meaning of philosophy. It lost its place as the synoptic integrator of the manifold intellectual concerns of human existence.

The Golden Age nonetheless contained the seeds of its own decay. A desire to prove the meaningfulness of man's goals and his ability to reach them motivated—in fact, goaded—the Cambridge amateurs and Harvard Pragmatists. They were *driven* to convey their ideas to the people. In demonstrating their ideas, however, the philosophers increasingly concentrated on logic and epistemology. Royce exemplified this pattern: he pushed himself to explore the foundations of mathematics to secure the ground of God's existence; he was truly a *theo*-logian. But while the Harvard Pragmatists had as their end the defense of religious truths, they taught their students that solving the problems of *The Critique of Pure Reason* was the key to philosophic advance and did their best work in technical areas. Although students flocked to Cambridge to imbibe the religious solace offered by Harvard Pragmatism, they went away concentrating on Royce's epistemological and logical conundrums; the young men adopted the basic premises of their mentors but often were less willing to apply the premises to a "philosophy of life" or to communicate with non-philosophers; the students *they* trained did not pick up the public concerns at all and occasionally thought of their professors' vocation as only a job.

The Second Department and the Silver Age

The department that reconstituted itself after the First World War was transitional, reflecting both the concerns of the Golden Age and the new disciplinary demands. The later department embodied Lowell's bureaucratic values as opposed to Eliot's personal ones. Lowell's men had a more occupationally centered education as evidenced by the doctoral degree in philosophy as preparation for a career, and more were trained at Harvard —after all, it was the best place for graduate work. The personal backgrounds of the men in the new department were more diverse, although their adult life styles were more homogeneous, than those of the old department: Lowell credited not what a man had been but what he could become, and even more than their predecessors the younger men embodied the social and academic conventions of their times. Nor was their way of life without merit. They made strong and stable marriages and participated in happy and successful domestic lives. The mutual devotion within each family reflected the way of a culture secure in its beliefs and sure of its values.

Lowell's men tended to think of themselves as professionals, experts in a certain discipline. They worked to attain a place within this discipline and the university system supporting it. They promoted impersonal criteria of scholarly aptitude; their own work, often concentrating in one particular branch of philosophy, was highly and uniformly competent. It would, however, be foolish to argue that technical experts composed the new department. In fact, the four men who guided speculation during the inter-war period were of enormous and varied professorial distinction, and made Harvard still the place in the United States to study philosophy. Alfred North Whitehead was recognized as a figure from a different era and, like Royce, synthesized interests in mathematics and metaphysics. Two students of Royce carried on his interests more directly. Ernest Hocking was the most distinguished idealist of his generation. Second in seniority, having joined the department in 1914, he was the last exponent of the old conception of philosophy. C. I. Lewis was the junior man. A logician and epistemologist of undisputed ability, he rose from a 1921 assistant professorship. His appointment—along with Whitehead's three years later—assured that Harvard's concern for "prestige" would be satisfied. The historical importance of Lewis's work for the profession was that it signalled the triumph of the new conception of philosophy. Perry was the senior man, the major link to the old department, and in his maturity

he specialized in ethics and continued a tradition of Harvard moral philosophy. He and Hocking combined the careerism and public-spiritedness
typical of the second generation.

With his ambiguous status Perry was also energetic in increasing Harvard's standing in the wider professional arena. It is remarkable that the
department had no professional journal under its aegis. Royce was a
founding and important member of the *International Journal of Ethics* (now
Ethics), but IJE was not a significant publication for long. Münsterberg
was active in setting up the American psychological journals, but as
psychology developed its own interests, its technical work ceased to concern philosophers. The *Philosophical Review* and the *Journal of Philosophy*
were the two significant organs of opinion in the first thirty years of the
century.[1] Cornell began the first in 1892, Columbia the second in 1904.
Possession undoubtedly benefited the departments at both schools. Why
did Harvard not produce a journal? It is perhaps no explanation at all to
suggest that the voice of Cambridge was so strong among philosophers
that it needed no magazine, but the way the *Journal of Philosophy* threw
its pages open to Perry and the neo-realists suggested that obtaining
visibility was a minor problem at Harvard. Moreover, Perry used his
talents as a publicist more subtly.

The journals influenced a comparative handful of elite academics; textbooks reached colleges and universities at the lower depths of the system
of higher education and their masses of students. In writing his own
texts, Perry recognized that the way for Harvard to develop a commanding position was to proliferate its ideas on the widest academic level.
Writing early in his career about his text, *The Approach to Philosophy*,
he told his publishers that they would not merely benefit from his requiring it for undergraduates. "We have a large number of graduate
students," Perry added, "who go out each year to positions elsewhere and
tend to introduce books with which they become familiar here." Pushing
for the quick publication of another of his books, Perry noted it would be
good to have the volume out for his summer school teaching: "Teachers
from all over the country to the number of a thousand or more are in
Cambridge at that time, and this summer there will also be a considerable
gathering of ministers attending the school of theology."[2]

Perry hit the jackpot in the mid-1920s when he became general editor
of Scribner's Modern Students Library in philosophy. The Library con-

sisted of a series of books, each one containing selections from a great philosopher. In selecting editors, Perry put several Harvard doctorates on the map, and provided the first text series of primary sources to have a mass audience. Although the books had general reader sales, their major impact was in colleges "as required or recommended reading in a very broad spectrum of the philosophy course offerings." Originally selling for a dollar when released as hardbacks, Scribner's converted the texts to paper covers in the late 1950s. When these editions were themselves converted to the paperback Scribner Library in the early 1970s, they had sold nearly a million copies.[3] By controlling what material was anthologized, Perry insured that in some measure his wide readership understood the history of philosophy and of philosophical problems as Harvard perceived them.

The philosophers chose as their chairman James Woods. As administrative leader from 1914 to 1916, 1919 to 1927, and 1931 to 1933, he devoted himself to increasing the department's fortunes. Lowell had not rationalized university finances, and Woods was unflagging in using his contacts to round up independent monies for the philosophers. His greatest feat was obtaining money from a private benefactor to fund Whitehead's salary when Whitehead began his Harvard career.[4] Woods did not stop with Whitehead. During the First World War he wrote to prominent Roman Catholics to obtain funds to have Maurice DeWulf from Louvain come to Harvard. The idea was, Woods wrote in a form letter, to establish a chair for DeWulf so that "Harvard may become one of the centers of Scholastic teaching."[5] DeWulf was at Harvard for several years—Woods paid some of his salary—and although the scheme failed, Woods briefly resurrected it when Etienne Gilson, who later headed the Institute of Medieval Studies in Toronto, came to Harvard from Paris for a time in the late 1920s.

Woods's fund raising reflected not only the limitations of the Harvard budget but also a keen appraisal of the aspirations of American minorities. If Harvard would not pay to have a Roman Catholic in the philosophy department, it would at least accept a free one, and Woods might persuade Catholics to pay for the privilege. He failed with them, but American Jews were more responsive.

Hugo Münsterberg was of Jewish parentage but his parents raised him in an assimilative environment which over-glorified Germany. In order to assure his success in the German academic world he was apparently baptized, but whatever his religious affiliation, it played no part in his reception at Harvard.[6] The wealthy assimilationist German Jew did not differ from his Protestant counterparts, and in America he was so rare as not to constitute a social threat. Not until the large migration of lower-class eastern and southern European Jews began to influence American life did prejudice become noticeable. Eliot's 1908 report stated that one of Harvard's functions as an urban institution must be "Americanizing . . . our hardly-assimilable foreign population." He quoted a Harvard philosopher that among "the more aspiring or well-meaning" foreign students, the Jews seemed "strongly attracted to philosophy and notably susceptible to its broadening influences."[7]

There was no discrimination in Harvard's selection of graduate students. Among others, Morris Cohen took his degree in 1906, Horace Kallen in 1908, Jacob Loewenberg in 1911, Norbert Wiener in 1913, Sydney Pressey in 1917, Marvin Farber in 1925, Benjamin Ginzburg in 1926, and Felix Cohen and Paul Weiss in 1929. But as the influx of Jews to the university increased, coincident with Lowell's initiation of a quota system, the situation became more complex. Although the philosophy department invited Jews to study there, it made it difficult for them later to find jobs. Perhaps it is fairer to say that the philosophers did the best they could for men whose names would have invited discrimination in any circumstances, but in the references written for Jews there is the unmistakable flavor of Lowell-like distaste for an unassimilated minority. Perry wrote of candidates that they were Jews without "the traits calculated to excite prejudice," having "none of the unpleasant characteristics which are supposed to be characteristic of the race"; Woods, that a candidate's Jewishness was "faintly marked and by no means offensive"; Hocking, that a man was "without pronounced Jewish traits"; and Lewis, that a young philosopher "of Jewish extraction" had "none of the faults which are sometimes expected in such cases." Lewis once went out of his way to reassure a prospective employer that although a job seeker's name might suggest it, he was *not* a Jew: "I believe that his paternal grandfather was Jewish, but his other three grandparents not. In all that counts he is distinctly not Jewish."[8]

I suspect the philosophers shared Lowell's waspish values, but even if they did not, in placing their Jewish students they participated in, and therefore in some measure reinforced, a vicious system of prejudice. Its fruits were the destruction of many careers, and Jews did not shake the structure of discrimination until they established themselves in the universities of New York City in the 1930s, forming the core of a distinguished group of philosophy departments.*

Even if Perry, Woods, Hocking, and Lewis were unwilling participants, there was no sign that the Lowell administration was likely to hire Jews, and just as Woods appealed to Roman Catholic ambitions he used Harvard's magic name to appeal to Jewish ones. He pushed for two men, Henry Maurice Sheffer (1883–1964) and Harry Austryn Wolfson (1887–1974).

Much the less interesting case, Wolfson received his B.A. in 1911 and his Ph.D. in 1915. Woods raised money for him from outside sources, and after six years as an instructor he was appointed an assistant professor in 1921. The understanding was that he would not be permanent and that he would receive only such salary as "interested persons could contribute."[9] But Wolfson was an erudite and publishing scholar and, perhaps more importantly, did not threaten Cambridge values. Assigned to the faculty committee investigating Lowell's formal quota proposal, he trod softly and refused, he later recalled, to do anything to embarrass the university. He disagreed with Felix Frankfurter, who thought Lowell a bigot who ought to be exposed, and later Wolfson reminisced that he could never understand why the faculty had not placed Frankfurter, a man of much greater prestige, on the committee. In any event, Lucius Littauer established the Nathan Littauer Professorship of Jewish Literature and Philosophy in 1925, stipulating Wolfson as the first incumbent. Secure as this chair was, Wolfson remembered that he had wanted a joint departmental affiliation, in philosophy and semitic studies, because he did not trust the philosophers' intentions.[10]

Henry Sheffer's case is more complex. He received his B.A. in 1905, his Ph.D. in 1908, and after four years as an assistant in the department, he did one-year stints at the University of Washington, Cornell, Minnesota, Missouri, and CCNY. He was a difficult man, but being a Jew did not help his career. A reference of Perry's asserting that Sheffer had no "unpleasant characteristics" also suggested that Harvard would recommend another man if Sheffer's race disqualified him. Woods showed less

---

*Women were worse off. I have considered them in appendix 4.

perception than he might when he wrote to a prospective employer that Sheffer suffered "under the delusion that the world is hostile to him because of his race."[11]

Sheffer's strength was that he was probably the most brilliant logician Harvard produced through 1930. Despite the paucity of publication—Sheffer was a perfectionist—men like Russell, Whitehead, Lewis, and E. V. Huntington recognized him as a thinker of the first rank. He came back to Harvard after Royce's death in 1917 to fill the logic position temporarily. The department's scheme was that Sheffer would go when Russell came, but when Russell never came Sheffer managed to hang on even after Lewis, whose main interest was logic, arrived in 1920 as a visitor.

From 1917 to 1927 Sheffer had an annual and tenuous appointment as lecturer. In 1919 he was, apparently, nearly fired because he was a "sensitive" Jew and because he had a disagreeable wife. (They were later divorced.) Sheffer fortunately had a manuscript on "Notational Relativity," and with letters from Russell, among others, attesting to Sheffer's "high order of original power," the department secured his annual reappointment.[12]

Thereafter Woods diligently worked the Jewish philanthropy circuit on Sheffer's behalf. Using Frankfurter's donations and contacts, Woods first tried to have "Notational Relativity" subvened for publication by Harvard University Press. Hebrew money, he wrote, could help Sheffer "as a faithful worker who will reflect great credit on the Jewish race."[13] Sheffer never put "Notational Relativity" or the "Analytic Knowledge" which was to come out of it into form he thought acceptable for publication; and in 1926 the administration decided that he would no longer drain its funds, even as a lecturer. Woods continued to beat the bushes, however, and with Jewish funding Sheffer became an assistant professor in 1927. In 1929 a combination of much of the same money that was supporting Wolfson and part of the new Edgar Pierce bequest to the department went to promote Sheffer to associate professor.[14] The university contributed nothing to this arrangement, and the funding of Sheffer's position was still irregular when he became a full professor in 1938 at the age of fifty-four.*

*Another logician of a different sort deserves an extended footnote. Ralph Monroe Eaton received his degree in 1917 and went on to teach at Harvard. His first book (*Sym-

Psychology in the 1920s

Although administratively tied to the philosophers, the psychologists did not benefit from Woods's successes. After Münsterberg died and Holt and Yerkes left, Herbert Sydney Langfeld (1879–1958) and Leonard Troland (1889–1932) ran the psychological laboratory. Langfeld was an assistant professor with a 1909 Ph.D. from Berlin, Troland a student of Münsterberg and Holt with the rank of instructor. In this situation the philosophers had William McDougall (1871–1938) appointed to the psychology professorship in 1920. The philosophers wanted a man with a name and a theoretical and philosophical orientation. McDougall and his books, among them *An Introduction to Social Psychology* (1908) and *Body and Mind* (1911), were world-famous but he failed miserably. The American professional climate was experimentalist and positivistic, and McDougall was in the older, more philosophically oriented tradition. (Münsterberg had inspired him at the turn of the century.)[15] His interest in psychical research scandalized psychologists demanding scientific respectability and, merely tolerated once he had arrived in Cambridge, McDougall left in 1927. The story goes that he received a letter from the president of the newly constituted Duke University asking him to

---

bolism and Truth, 1925) was a rich and dense epistemological treatise that used logic to illuminate philosophy in the tradition of Royce's *World and the Individual*, Holt's *Concept of Consciousness*, and Lewis's *Mind and the World-Order*, which appeared four years later. But while Eaton acknowledged that his book had at least "a superficial resemblance" to Wittgenstein's *Tractatus*, in the sustained concern for logic and language and their relation to problems of knowledge, *Symbolism and Truth* was much nearer to Willard Quine's more recent classic, *Word and Object* (1960), than to the work of Eaton's teachers.

In 1931 he published *General Logic*, one of the first of a fine series of logic texts written by Harvard philosophers. *General Logic* dealt not only with symbolic logic but also with the older Aristotelian conception of logic and newer questions of inductive logic. Apparently on the strength of a manuscript of this book and his other work, Harvard promoted Eaton to an associate professorship in February 1930. He was thirty-eight. Shortly thereafter authorities found him drunk in his rooms, depressed over a broken marriage. His companions had decorated his walls with obscenities of one sort or another. In early March Harvard rescinded the promotion, had him declared emotionally unstable, and gave him leave of absence until the 1931–1932 academic year. He was not to be reappointed after the close of his assistant professor's term at the end of that year. Professors still had to be gentlemen at Harvard. Before his term was up Eaton committed suicide, in April 1932. The graduate students attributed it to the professional pressures involved in pursuing contemplation as a career. See Folder 498, 1928–1930; Shaw to Whom it May Concern, 6 March 1930; and Moore to ALL, 20 November 1930, Folder 233, 1930–1933, ALL Papers; Correspondence, 1927–1938, File: Eaton, HPD; interview with Richard Hocking, 18 and 19 July 1973.

recommend a psychology chairman for Duke. McDougall replied, "I accept."[16]

In the meantime E. G. Boring (1886–1968) came from Clark as an associate professor in 1922. Boring was a young, up-and-coming psychologist, unwilling to have the philosophers dominate a sphere about which they knew nothing and tough enough to effect his will. By 1924 he had become director of the laboratory, forcing an unwanted Langfeld to Princeton.[17] Even while McDougall was in Cambridge, Boring was psychology's spokesman, and after 1927 he was undisputed defender of the rights of the junior Harvard psychologists. Noting that Harvard ranked seventh among leading schools in its expenditure for psychology, he pushed for increased funds, especially for the meagerly supported laboratory.[18] More importantly, he was determined that the philosophers should not aggrandize psychology's operation.

There were four full professors in philosophy in the mid-1920s and one associate (Whitehead had joined Perry, Woods, and Hocking in 1924, the same year that they promoted C. I. Lewis to associate). The men in psychology were all junior except for Boring and the isolated McDougall, but this fact, rather than justifying the philosophers' governance, only pointed up its evil consequences. The philosophers, Boring told Woods, who chaired the joint department, had to face psychology's need for larger staffing and for experimentation. The problem, he said bluntly, was to prevent the philosophers from deciding policy for psychology; they just did not understand the discipline's problems. After McDougall left, Boring asserted that, in matters of psychology, his opinion "should far outweigh the opinion of anyone else in the Department."[19]

But who would replace McDougall? True to type, the philosophers again wanted a theoretician and pushed for Wolfgang Köhler (1887–1967), associated with the Gestalt movement in psychology. Boring was furious. "American psychologists who felt that Harvard had made a mistake with both Münsterberg and McDougall," he wrote to the chairman, "would feel that it again erred." For almost two years Boring managed to veto Köhler's appointment until Lowell settled the matter by promoting Boring to the psychology professorship when Cornell offered him a similar position.[20]

When Perry wrote his history of psychology for Samuel Eliot Morison's *Development of Harvard University* in 1929, the philosopher noted that the connections between philosophy and psychology were those "of administration, counsel, and personal association."[21] At the time Boring found it difficult even to be civil to the philosophers; he aimed to get psychology out from under them altogether and dickered for years over a final split. The report of a committee investigating philosophy and psychology in 1933 minced no words; the members of the division did not understand one another and had agreed on divorce. The psychologists were "scientific, with a bias towards things that can be proved and measured"; the philosophers were "dedicated to the study of eternal verities." William James and Josiah Royce, the report concluded, were "distinguished exceptions [to this division of interests] but the viewpoint of psychology has changed much since their time." In 1931 social ethics had left the division and, along with the sociology courses in the economics department, re-formed as the sociology department. Psychology followed in 1934 by becoming a separate department within the division; two years later Harvard abolished divisions. Boring was psychology's first chairman.[22]

In part the philosophers had wanted a role in governing psychology because they were convinced that the study of consciousness had to involve philosophy or, at the very least, could benefit from conceptual criticism.[23] In practice this concern was hollow after Holt's resignation. Strangely enough, however, a rediscovery of behaviorism contributed to psychology's reconstruction in the late 1920s and early 1930s. As philosophy and psychology were splitting up, philosophy again influenced psychology.

In 1930 Herbert Feigl arrived in Cambridge for a year's study of the philosophy of science. Feigl was a young member of the Vienna Circle and an exponent of logical positivism. He had come to Harvard with an interest in its physicist Percy Bridgman, author of the 1927 *Logic of Modern Physics*. Feigl introduced the Harvard psychologists to the work of their colleague in physics and made it intelligible to them. Bridgman was an "operationalist," arguing that we defined scientific concepts by the set of operations by which we conducted experiments. The psychologists picked up this "new" approach and called their experimental work "operationalism." In this milieu B. F. Skinner wrote his dissertation in 1931, and S. S. Stevens wrote his famous articles throughout the 1930s.[24]

These events evidence the quality of the philosophers' concern for psychology and the impact of specialization. In laboratory practice, operationalism differed little from the philosophical position that Peirce, James, Münsterberg, and Holt had successively espoused and that had given the philosophy department world stature. But twelve years after Holt left Harvard, a visiting Austrian had to introduce the institution's psychologists to a crude version of pragmatic ideas by telling them what was going on in physics.

Ranking		Years	Number of degrees
		1894–1903	
1.	Clark		31
2.	Harvard		18
3.	Columbia		14
		1904–1913	
1.	Clark		59
2.	Columbia		27
3.	Chicago		23
4.	Harvard		20
		1914–1923	
1.	Columbia		44
2.	Chicago		40
3.	Harvard		26
4.	Clark		21
		1924–1933	
1.	Columbia		89
2.	Iowa		84
3.	Ohio		79
4.	Chicago		71
5.	Minnesota		47
6.	Hopkins		44
7.	Stanford		38
8.	Harvard		37
		1934–1943	
1.	Columbia		133
2.	Iowa		127
3.	Ohio		64
4.	Yale		54
5.	Minnesota		52
6.	Chicago		51
7.	Harvard		42

Chart 24.1. Number of Psychology Degrees Awarded

In the development of the discipline which Harvard psychologists were so late in formally joining, the result of psychology's dependence on philosophy was disastrous. The one study of academic prestige done in the early 1920s placed Harvard psychology second, philosophy first.[25] But this minor falling away did not reflect the professional damage which the prolonged fighting had done to psychology and which Harvard felt at a much later time. Chart 24.1, comparing the distribution of doctorates in psychology, is more revealing.[26]

Even if we discount the growth of the large mid-western universities, Harvard still did not attract the students to compete with its east coast rivals. Indeed, it is extraordinary that Harvard placed as high as it did when it was so out of touch with other large universities. During the 1920s psychology's subservience to philosophy placed it in the academic backwaters, and throughout this time there was no psychology department to speak of. Yet Harvard continued to attract and place students, demonstrating the magical potency of its name.

Graduate Students

The changes in the outlook of the philosophers and in the substance of their speculation were reflected in the changing character of graduate students. In the departmental files are fragmentary personal records of these students. Among other things, the department asked Ph.D. candidates to give "a brief statement of the *development* of . . . [their] philosophical and psychological interests." From 1907 to 1927 there is usable information for seventy-two of the eighty-nine men, 81 percent, who received their degrees in philosophy.* The young philosophers' statements usually began with the concerns that led them to philosophy. A surprising number from the early part of the period cite religious doubts or problems, and in many cases specifically mention the conflict between science and religion. Later degree aspirants, however, were less likely to mention personal crises and simply remarked that studying philosophy in college gave them a taste for it. Although a few men said that philosophy made their interests more practical, in taking them from logic to religious and ethical questions, the overwhelming number

---

*Appendix 3 contains the data on which I have based the generalizations which follow in this chapter. This appendix also contains an explanation of the categories used in organizing the data.

		Why are you in philosophy?			
Year degree awarded	Number of men on whom there is information compared to number of Ph.D.s awarded	Religious doubts or problems	College studies	Other	Indeterminate
1907	(7 of 7)	2 1 (and education) 2 (practical)	0	1 (law to philosophy) 1 (interest in mathematics)	0
1908	(6 of 8)	2 1 (and temperament)	0	0	3
1909	(1 of 3)	1 (and educational problems)	0	0	0
1910	(11 of 11)	7 1 (ethical problems)	1 (and speculative interests)	1 (introspection)	1
1911	(5 of 6)	1 1 (problems of life)	0	1 (social and economic) 1 (educational problems) 1 (general intellectual interest)	0
1912	(8 of 8)	1 1 (and ethics) 1 (and social concerns) 1 (problems of life)	1	3	0
1913	(4 of 4)	1 (1)	1 1 (and speculative interests)	0	1
1914	(3 of 3)	2	1	0	0
1915	(2 of 2)	0	1	0	1

Year					
1916	(6 of 7)	5 (4)	1	0	0
1917	(3 of 4)	1 (1)	1 1 (and religion)	0	0
1918	(2 of 3)	0	1	1 (intellectual curiosity)	0
1920	(1 of 2)	1	0	0	0
1923	(2 of 3)	1 (1)	1 (and religion)	0	0
1924	(1 of 1)	1 (1)	0	0	0
1925	(5 of 7)	2 (1)	1 1 (and religion)	1 (general interest)	0
1926	(1 of 4)	1	0	0	0
1927	(4 of 6)	0	2	1 (interest in war) 1 (interest always speculative)	0

Chart 24.2. Tabular View of Motives Listed on Questionnaires by Harvard Doctorates

This table excludes all psychology doctorates after 1912. The figures in parentheses in the first column indicate the number brought to philosophy by religious doubts or problems who specifically mentioned the conflict of science and religion. I have also included among those who came because of religious questions those who had other slightly different motives as well *and* those who described their motivation in slightly different terms (e.g., "problems of life"). (I have noted these additional motives or differently described motives.) I have placed the five men who were motivated by studies in college and religious concerns or speculative interests in the "college" category, noting them also. Column three describes other motives. No Ph.D.s were awarded in 1919, and questionnaires are unavailable for the two awarded in 1921 and the two awarded in 1922.

| | | What has philosophy done to your life? | | | |
Year degree awarded	Number of men on whom there is information compared to number of Ph.D.s awarded	Made interests more theoretical	Made interests more practical	Other	Indeterminate
1907	(7 of 7)	4 1 (religion and educational problems to psychology and educational problems)	1	0	1
1908	(6 of 8)	1	3	0	2
1909	(1 of 3)	0	0	0	1
1910	(11 of 11)	2 (to philosophy) 2	1	1 (religion to teaching) 1 (religion to social ethics)	4
1911	(5 of 6)	2	0	0	3
1912	(8 of 8)	4	1	0	3
1913	(4 of 4)	1 (to metaphysics)	1	0	2
1914	(3 of 3)	2	0	0	1
1915	(2 of 2)	1 1	0	0	1
1916	(6 of 7)	3 (to philosophy)	0	0	2
1917	(3 of 4)	0	0	0	3
1918	(2 of 3)	0	0	0	2
1920	(1 of 2)	1	0	0	0

Year					
1923	(2 of 3)	0		0	2
1924	(1 of 1)	0	1	0	1
1925	(5 of 7)	1 (to philosophy)		0	3
1926	(1 of 4)	1 (to philosophy)		0	0
1927	(4 of 6)	0		0	4

Chart 24.3. Tabular View of Outcomes Listed on Questionnaires by Harvard Doctorates

In this table, I have simply counted as a movement to the theoretical any movement from religious or ethical or practical interests to logical or epistemological or theoretical interests. I have counted movements from mathematics or logic to philosophy or from epistemology to religion or ethics as a practical movement. In the "other" column I have listed those movements which I could not determine as either to more practical or to more theoretical interests. In the "indeterminate" column, I have listed all those who did not indicate that any movement had occurred in their "development." No Ph.D.s were awarded in 1919, and questionnaires are unavailable for the two awarded in 1921 and the two awarded in 1922.

indicated that studying at Harvard took them from practical interests to those of logic and epistemology—not surprising since Harvard taught them that the justification of the former rested on the latter. But even the movement from practical interests to theoretical ones became muted for the later Ph.D.s. By the 1920s the study of philosophy appeared to have had no discernable impact on their lives; at least they mentioned no intellectual movement.

Let us treat these biographies as answering two questions. "Why are you in philosophy?" is tabulated in chart 24.2 and "What has its study done to your life?" is tabulated in chart 24.3.

In chart 24.4 the data are summarized in three periods. The conclusions are obvious so far as we can draw them from fragmentary data. Personal crises, of which religious problems were most common, were important in pushing men into the study of philosophy through the 1920–1927 period. But by the latter date this sort of motive for one's life work had declined, and previous study of philosophy in college had become a significant factor stimulating further investigation. Moreover, while the study of philosophy initially changed men's lives, it changed them by shifting interests from problems of life to those of the ivory tower. Brand Blanshard, a 1920 Ph.D. whose record is not included in this survey, had a characteristic recollection:

> You ask what led me into philosophy. I suppose it was the desire to find respectable support for my religious beliefs. My father and grandfather were both Protestant ministers, and in my early years I had vague thoughts of following them into the pulpit. So I read books on the philosophy and psychology of religion, and in my courses in philosophy I studied with particular interest the arguments that bore on belief. But I found my interest gradually shifting from religious questions to those of logic and the theory of knowledge, and before I finished my work . . . it was clear to me that I wanted to teach philosophy. . . . Judging by my experience, philosophy is not at all a safe subject for those who use it for the fortification of religious belief. There are not many of the beliefs with which I started the study of philosophy that have survived that study, though it has supplied me with others that seem to fill the void remarkably well.

	Why are you in philosophy?			
	Religious doubts or problems	College studies	Other	Indeterminate
1907–1912 (38 of 43 Ph.D.s)	23 (1) 62%	2 3%	9 24%	4 11%
1913–1918 (20 of 23 Ph.D.s)	9 (6) 45%	8 40%	1 5%	2 10%
1920–1927 (14 of 23 Ph.D.s)	6 (3) 43%	5 36%	3 21%	0 0%
	What has philosophy done to your life?			
	Made interests more theoretical	Made interests more practical	Other	Indeterminate
1907–1912 (38 of 43 Ph.D.s)	16 43%	6 16%	2 6%	14 35%
1913–1918 (20 of 23 Ph.D.s)	9 45%	1 (in 1913) 5%	0 0%	10 50%
1920–1927 (14 of 23 Ph.D.s)	4 29%	0 0%	0 0%	10 71%

Chart 24.4. Answers to Questionnaires by Harvard Doctorates,
Summarized in Three Periods
(For explanation see charts 24.2 and 24.3.)

"At the beginning," Blanshard said, "I thought of philosophy as the shining Excalibur with which I would stand at the cross-roads and defend the faith. It turned out to be a double-edged sword that in fact pared away from my creed more than it left."[27] From 1913 onward this shift in interest is less perceptible: more and more men perceived their study as having no impact on their intellectual development.

If we think of narrow professionals as those who acquire a certain expertise in order to hold down a certain job but who do not seek this job because of any deep personal commitment, philosophy at Harvard

Why are you in philosophy?

Year degree awarded	Number of men on whom there is information compared to number of Ph.D.s awarded	Religious doubts or problems	College studies	Other	Indeterminate
Psychologists	19 of 21	1 (and educational problems)			
1907	(3 of 3)	1 (practical problems)	0	1 (interest in mathematics)	0
1908	(1 of 1)	0	0	0	1
1909	(0 of 1)	—	—	—	—
1910	(4 of 4)	1 (ethical problems) 1	0	1 (introspection)	1
1911	(1 of 2)	0	0	1 (educational problems)	0
1912	(1 of 1)	1 (problems of life)	0	0	0
1913	(1 of 1)	0	1	0	0
1914	(4 of 4)	1 (origins of life and causes of death)	1	1 (general interests) 1 (poetry and literature)	0
1915	(4 of 4)	0	4	0	0

Philosophers (social ethics not included)				
1907 (3 of 3)	1 (practical problems) (1)	2	0	0	0
1908 (5 of 7)	2	1 (and temperament)	0	0	2
1909 (1 of 2)	1 (and educational problems)	0	0	0	0
1910 (6 of 6)	5	1 (and speculative interests)	0	0	0
1911 (4 of 4)	1 (problems of life) / 1	0	1 (government and economics) / 1 (general intellectual interests) / 0	0
1912 (7 of 7)	1 (and ethics) / 1 (and social concerns) / 1	1 (and speculative interests)	1	1 (unorthodox sources) / 1 (speculative interests) / 1 (science)	0
1913 (4 of 4)	1 (1)	1	0	1
1914 (3 of 3)	2	1	0	0
1915 (2 of 2)	0	1	0	1

Chart 24.5. Tabular View of Motives Listed on Questionnaires by Harvard Doctorates, Psychologists and Philosophers (For explanation, see chart 24.2.)

Year degree awarded	Number of men on whom there is information compared to number of Ph.D.s awarded	What has philosophy done to your life?			
		Made interests more theoretical	Made interests more practical	Other	Indeterminate
Psychologists	19 of 21				
1907	(3 of 3)	1 (religion and educational problems to psychology and educational problems)	1	0	1
1908	(1 of 1)	0	1	0	0
1909	(0 of 1)	—	—	—	—
1910	(4 of 4)	1	0	1 (religion to teaching)	2
1911	(1 of 2)	1	0	0	0
1912	(1 of 1)	0	0	0	1
1913	(1 of 1)	0	0	1 (from philosophy to psychology)	0
1914	(4 of 4)	1 (religion to psychology)	0	1 (poetry and literature to psychology)	2
1915	(4 of 4)	0	0	1 (science to epistemology and ethics)	3

Philosophers	35 of 40 (social ethics not included)				
1907	(3 of 3)	3	0		0
1908	(5 of 7)	1	2		2
1909	(1 of 2)	0	0		1
		1			
1910	(6 of 6)	2 (religion to philosophy)	0	1 (religion to social ethics)	2
1911	(4 of 4)	1	0		3
1912	(7 of 7)	4	1		2
1913	(4 of 4)	1 (to metaphysics)	1		2
1914	(3 of 3)	2	0		1
1915	(2 of 2)	1	0		1

Chart 24.6. Tabular View of Outcomes Listed on Questionnaires by Harvard Doctorates, Psychologists and Philosophers (For explanation see chart 24.3.)

	Why are you in philosophy?				What has philosophy done to your life?			
	Religious doubts or problems	College studies	Other	Indeterminate	Made interests more theoretical	Made interests more practical	Other	Indeterminate
1907–1912								
Philosophers 26 of 30	17 65%	2 8%	5 19%	2 8%	12 46%	3 12%	1 4%	10 38%
Psychologists 10 of 12	5 50%	0 0%	3 30%	2 20%	3 30%	2 20%	1 10%	4 40%
1913–1915								
Philosophers 9 of 10	3 33%	4 45%	0 0%	2 22%	4 45%	1 10%	0 0%	4 45%
Psychologists 9 of 9	1 11%	6 67%	2 22%	0 0%	1 11%	0 0%	3 33%	5 56%
Totals 1907–1915								
Philosophers 35 of 40	20 57%	6 18%	5 14%	4 11%	16 46%	4 11%	1 3%	14 40%
Psychologists 19 of 21	5 26%	6 32%	6 32%	2 10%	4 21%	2 10%	4 21%	9 47%

Chart 24.7. Answers to Questionnaires by Harvard Doctorates, Psychologists and Philosophers
(For explanation see charts 24.2 and 24.3.)

attracted more and more narrow professionals from 1907 to 1927. Private concerns were less relevant in motivating young philosophers, and the study of philosophy became less important in determining perceived intellectual growth. By the third decade of the century the phrase 'professional philosopher' embodied a verbal contradiction: newly minted doctors found that the love of wisdom was only a job.

These developments were also plain in the hiving off of psychology from philosophy. In 1906 when social ethics became a separate department within the division of philosophy, Eliot recognized psychology and philosophy as distinct fields within the other (philosophical) department of the division, and in 1912 the department of philosophy became the department of philosophy and psychology. The professor of psychology, at that time Münsterberg, was the effective and separate head of the psychological component of the department. Although we cannot sharply distinguish philosophers from psychologists during this period, in the preceding tables I have chosen 1912 as the cut-off date for including Ph.D.s in psychology as philosophers, and after 1915 no data on psychology Ph.D.s appeared in the philosophy graduate student folders. Someone had decided that the department should not treat these men as philosophers. For the period 1907 to 1915 there is personal information on almost all the men who received degrees in philosophical subjects, such as epistemology, logic, ethics; and on those in psychology and later listed as Harvard Ph.D.s in psychology. Using the same rationale as in charts 24.2, 24.3, and 24.4, and comparing psychologists to philosophers from 1907 to 1912 and then from 1913 to 1915, we find striking differences, as charts 24.5, 24.6, and 24.7 demonstrate.

The sub-discipline of psychology was already attracting to it a different type of man and becoming narrowly professional, as I have just defined it, more rapidly than philosophy. More than twice the percentage of philosophers as psychologists came to their studies because of a sense of personal crisis. Almost twice the percentage of psychologists as philosophers picked up their interests in college. While almost 60 percent of the philosophers still felt that their work was changing their lives, this was true of just about 30 percent of the psychologists.*

*A retreat to the ivory tower, I should note, did not accompany the professionalization of psychology as it did philosophy. As behaviorism took over the psychological profession, so too did the idea that psychology as a social science could help control the present and future.

Other information on choice of speciality and on age on receiving the doctorate reinforces these inferences from the autobiographies. Of the Harvard Ph.D.s produced from 1893 to 1930, 34 percent had technical interests—logic, epistemology, methodology, and the like. But they were not distributed evenly throughout this period. Through 1906 only 16 percent of the Ph.D.s were in technical fields. From 1907 to 1918—the second half of the Golden Age during which Royce's seminary in epistemology and logic flourished—the figure jumped to 32 percent; and from 1920 to 1930 to 51 percent. Eliminating psychology and classifying the philosophers into three categories, we get the results shown in chart 24.8.

Year	Number and percentage of Ph.D.s					
	Religious and moral philosophy		Metaphysics		Technical	
1893–1906	42%	(14)	42%	(14)	16%	(5)
1907–1918	40%	(21)	28%	(15)	32%	(17)
1920–1930	22%	(10)	31%	(13)	51%	(23)
Totals 1893–1930	34%	(45)	32%	(42)	34%	(45)

Chart 24.8. Fields of philosophic interest, 1893–1930

The growth of a technical expertise becomes more significant if we examine the distinction achieved by philosophers in relation to their field. The rankings are shown in chart 24.9. What do these figures tell us? In the 1893–1906 period, technical philosophers were insignificant, and a disproportionate percentage of those philosophers with the most practical interests (religious and moral) went unplaced. I suspect the reason for this was that these men were originally clerics and returned to the ministry. But both the practical philosophers and metaphysicians shared eminent and well-placed positions—the metaphysicians dominating eminent positions, the philosophers of religion the well-placed ones. In 1907–1918 the situation changed dramatically. The technicians were

Psychologists accordingly represented one variant of the new academic social scientists convinced both of their professional scientific status and their ability to guide the affairs of men. My understanding of this issue has been helped by John Michael O'Donnell, "The Transformation of American Psychology 1890–1924," M.A. thesis, University of Delaware, 1974.

disproportionately successful while the religious philosophers and metaphysicians were disproportionately unsuccessful. Thirty percent of the degrees went to technical thinkers but 57 and 37 percent of the eminent and well-placed positions, respectively, went to them, while only 25 and 20 percent of the placed and not placed men, respectively, were technical. In general the reverse was true for the softer areas of study: they got fewer of the eminent and well-placed positions than might be expected, and a disproportionate number were only placed, or not placed at all. In the 1920–1930 period the same situation held, but the disproportions were less striking.

Care must be taken in drawing conclusions on the basis of this evidence alone. I have deleted information on psychologists, and it is impossible to sort out psychology's technical level in the philosophic hierarchy.

	Rank	Number and percentage of Ph.D.s					
		Religious and moral philosophy		Metaphysics		Technical	
1893–1906	Eminent	17%	(1)	83%	(5)	0%	(0)
	Well-placed	72%	(5)	14%	(1)	14%	(1)
	Placed	40%	(4)	40%	(4)	20%	(2)
	Not placed	57%	(4)	29%	(2)	14%	(1)
	Percent of total/ number in field	47%	(14)	40%	(12)	13%	(4)
1907–1918	Eminent	29%	(2)	14%	(1)	57%	(4)
	Well-placed	26%	(2)	37%	(3)	37%	(3)
	Placed	50%	(10)	25%	(5)	25%	(5)
	Not placed	40%	(6)	40%	(6)	20%	(3)
	Percent of total/ number of field	40%	(20)	30%	(15)	30%	(15)
1920–1930	Eminent	17%	(1)	33%	(2)	50%	(3)
	Well-placed	0%	(0)	33%	(1)	67%	(2)
	Placed	27%	(6)	18%	(4)	55%	(12)
	Not placed	21%	(3)	43%	(6)	36%	(5)
	Percent of total/ number in field	22%	(10)	29%	(13)	49%	(22)

Chart 24.9. Field and Eminence 1893–1930 (I have eliminated psychology throughout. Retaining it does not change the results.)

It was, roughly, at first considered a branch of metaphysics, dealing as it did with the science of mind. By the turn of the century it attracted both experimental scientists and those interested in the rigorous application of philosophy to life (such as educational psychologists). Psychology aside, the First World War and the end of the Golden Age, more or less coincident occurrences, should obviously have affected the life work and choice of specialization of young philosophers, but there is no way of telling how. Nonetheless, the 1907–1918 period contributed distinctively to the growth of a technical speciality at the expense of other specialities: the period showed a great increase in the number of technical experts and these were the men whom the scholarly world rewarded. The men in the 1920–1930 period were generally less distinguished in the profession; Harvard's department was then only *primus inter pares* and no longer the dominating leader. More importantly, the depression made havoc of careers, and it is risky to read off any trends from the 1920–1930 period.

The other factor to be considered is the age at which men received the doctorate. One sign of professionalization would be a constant decline in the age at which men attained their degrees. Presumably a professional knows what he intends to do with his life and makes an early start. The average age at which Harvard awarded the philosophy doctorate did not decrease over time, but there was a connection between doctoral age and professional distinction as chart 24.10 shows.

In the first and third periods there was no important connection between age and eminence. From 1893 to 1906, it seems, the academy was fluid enough so that age was no barrier to professional attainment. In the 1920–1930 period we are dealing with a group that, again, was less distinguished and, apparently, the depression distorted career patterns so that age was not a critical variable. In the middle period, however, the results are once again striking. Approximately half the doctorates were over thirty, half under thirty. Yet the young men received 86 percent and 78 percent of the eminent and well-placed positions; the older men only 14 percent and 22 percent, respectively. The younger men were under-represented at the lower end of the scale; the older men over-represented.

If we examine the age factor—reflecting professional commitment—together with speciality from 1907 to 1918, the results are dramatic. Harvard doctorates produced between 1907 and 1918 who were young

	Rank	Number and percentage of Ph.D.s			
		Under 30		Over 30	
1893–1906	Eminent	83%	(5)	17%	(1)
	Well-placed	87%	(14)	13%	(2)
	Placed	76%	(13)	24%	(4)
	Not placed	78%	(7)	22%	(2)
	% of total/number in age category	82%	(42)*	18%	(9)
1907–1918	Eminent	86%	(6)	14%	(1)
	Well-placed	78%	(7)	22%	(2)
	Placed	42%	(11)	58%	(15)
	Not placed	37%	(7)	63%	(12)
	% of total/number in age category	51%	(33)†	49%	(32)†
1920–1930	Eminent	83%	(5)	17%	(1)
	Well-placed	67%	(2)	33%	(1)
	Placed	55%	(12)	45%	(10)
	Not placed	64%	(9)	36%	(5)
	% of total/number in age category	63%	(29)‡	37%	(17)

*1893–1906—3 men are unclassifiable in respect to rank.
†1907–1918—4 men are unclassifiable in respect to rank.
‡1920–1930—1 man is unclassifiable in respect to rank.

Chart 24.10. Age and Eminence, 1893–1930

| Rank | Number and percentage of Ph.D.s | | | |
	Religious and moral philosophers over 30		Technical philosophers under 30	
Eminent	20%	(1)	80%	(4)
Well-placed	0%	(0)	100%	(2)
Placed	67%	(6)	33%	(3)
Not placed	80%	(4)	20%	(1)
Percent of total/total in category	52%	(11)	48%	(10)

Chart 24.11. Field, Age, and Eminence, 1907–1918

and technically oriented were rewarded disproportionately to their numbers. Older religious and ethical thinkers could not compete with younger technical ones. The years between 1907 and 1918, the tail end of the Golden Age, were crucial in creating a generation of "scientific" professional philosophers. (See chart 24.11.)

The second department represented a synthesis of public and professional concerns that would not survive. Of the stalwarts, Lewis was the only one who received his degree in the formative technical period. The training of both Perry and Hocking antedated this time, and Whitehead's education in Britain had not been in philosophy. But Lewis, Perry, Hocking, and Whitehead socialized their students to professional roles, and the philosophers who would succeed these four men would reflect the values institutionalized during the last part of the Golden Age.

25

ERNEST HOCKING

Hocking's Youth

William Ernest Hocking was born in Cleveland in 1873, the first son of a homeopathic physician of modest means. The constant element in his early life was his family's devout Methodism, and the stress on personal religious experience resulted in Hocking's own conversion and joining the church at the age of twelve. A consuming desire to master the secrets of existence led him away from his provincial faith, but a basic religious conviction remained. His self-identity was a synthesis of this engulfing conviction and his will for rational understanding.

The family lived in Joliet, Illinois, during Hocking's youth; and after he graduated from high school in 1889, he made his way around the midwest taking various jobs with an eye to furthering his education. After working as a surveyor and civil engineer, he spent a semester at the new University of Chicago but dropped out for lack of money. Following his family to Iowa, he taught Latin and economics at the Newton Normal School and then entered Iowa State College at Ames in engineering. While there he read James's *Principles* and determined that he would study with the great man in Cambridge. Some four years later in 1899, after leaving Iowa State and again supporting himself by teaching, Hocking entered Harvard as a special student. He still wanted to do engineering or architecture, but once involved with Harvard philosophy, he forewent his more practical interests. As it happened, it was Royce and not James who appealed to the young man. Although he always respected James's sense of the concrete, Hocking criticized James's lack of method and found himself increasingly attracted to Royce's system-building. Like many other students of the first rank, he began to study the philosophical implications of logic under Royce. Although this foray was short-lived, Royce's logical ideas still provided the framework for Hocking's metaphysics in his 1904 dissertation.

Palmer got Hocking his first job, a two-year stint at the Andover Seminary, and from there he moved to Berkeley for two more years. Hocking took with him to California his bride, Agnes Boyle O'Reilly Hocking. The daughter of a leader in Boston literary circles, she was a strong and intelligent woman who supported Hocking in his work and retained a modicum of independence herself. She was culturally a Boston Irish Catholic; and although her religion was nominal, their marriage—unconventional at the time—widened Hocking's tolerant religious spirit. His devotion to her was well known, and none forgot her own mode of citing ultimate earthly wisdom: "Ernest Hocking says. . . ." She additionally intensified his commitments to practical life: together they were to found in Cambridge the famous Shady Hill School which made Hocking's educational ideals effective; later they served on the Laymen's Foreign Missions Inquiry, the service eventuating in his leadership in many ecumenical developments.

In 1908 the Hockings moved to New Haven; he was among the first of many Harvard products to make the Yale philosophy department.* Six years later, in the crisis during which Harvard lost Santayana and Palmer, Lowell, unwilling to have Arthur Lovejoy in Cambridge but dubious of everyone else's credentials, finally offered a professorship to Hocking. No one refused such an offer, and Hocking returned to his alma mater in fall 1914.[1]

The Meaning of God

It is difficult to understand why Harvard was wary of Hocking. In 1912 while at Yale he had published *The Meaning of God in Human Experience*, a book immediately recognized as a seminal contribution to religious philosophy. It stands as one of the serious twentieth-century theological works, an influential guide, as Palmer wrote Hocking, "of an age which

---

*Among others: Clark Professors Charles Bakewell and Wilmon Sheldon, and Sterling Professors Brand Blanshard, F. S. C. Northrop, and Paul Weiss. Robert Yerkes, director of the laboratory of primate biology, and Roswell Angier, director of the psychology laboratory, were Harvard Ph.D.s dominating Yale psychology.

through increase of knowledge thinks it has lost its old God and cannot of itself lay hold of a new."[2] The volume was to be Hocking's magnum opus for, although he wrote many more large studies, students always returned to this one. It elaborated the core of his theoretical thinking and evinced his long-standing concern for a religious interpretation of life.

The Meaning of God also typified Hocking's opaque and discursive style. He did not believe that philosophers could prove one position against another. There were different perspectives on the place of man in the universe, and the job of the philosopher was not deductive reasoning but conveying a vision of things. Hocking's task was not to demonstrate his "social idealism" but to make the reader realize the truth of it. In attempting to achieve this goal, he did not dismiss argument but wove it into a pattern of narrative and illustration so that, it was hoped, the reader would experience Hocking's insights. He worked on the book for over eight years—his 1904 dissertation contained its central theses—and the result was impressive. Using the dissertation as a guide, we approach the book best by keeping in mind Hocking's debts to the Harvard faculty—Münsterberg, Palmer, Perry, James, and Royce.

Münsterberg's influence was more marked in the 1904 thesis—"Other Conscious Being in Its Relation to Physical and Reflexive Objects"— although it was still apparent in *The Meaning of God*. Hocking took from Münsterberg a concern for the exact relation, whatever it might be, between brain states and consciousness. Hocking did not analyze this relation, but for his own thought the idea of body as an "exact metaphor" of mind had critical importance.[3] From Palmer, Hocking took a concern for the moral dimension of experience and Palmer's idea of the evolution of the "conjunct-self." And like Palmer, Hocking was leery of monistic idealism: the absolute must not envelope the conjunct-selves. The debt to Perry and the six realists was implicit: Hocking respected the given, "realistic" character of experience and agreed with Perry that idealism had not surmounted the problems of solipsism. *The New Realism* appeared the same year as *The Meaning of God*, and realism had been a topic of discussion for ten years. Any idealist, thought Hocking, must find a way of escaping the confines of his consciousness and make a place for experience of the physical world (x–xviii).

The influence of Hocking's "honored masters," James and Royce, was more complex. James's impact was evident in Hocking's "negative pragmatism": if a belief didn't work, it wasn't true. In rejecting the equation of workability with truth, Hocking looked more severe than James, but where James judged that the future would decide what worked, Hocking knew already: atheism would not do. "We must not let reality go, this reality which has produced us, until it satisfies us: it must yield us the idea which unites what we most deeply desire with *what is*" (436). Negative pragmatism was fideistic. Hocking refused to accept any philosophy which failed to make human existence significant:

> if it [a philosophy] lowers the capacity of men to meet the stress of existence, or diminishes the worth to them of what existence they have, such a theory is somehow false, and we have no peace until it is remedied. . . . Any such criterion of truth is based upon a conviction or thesis otherwise founded, that the real world is infinitely charged with interest and value (xiii).

Hocking also accepted James's belief that we must find life's significance in our experience. Both men distrusted the Roycean absolute which made the world valuable at the cost of transcending human experience; hence the title of Hocking's work.* Indeed, as far as *The Meaning of God* surveyed the history of the reasoning involved in man's belief in God, Hocking was an evolutionary naturalist like Santayana and Holt. But his exploration of the evolution of man's reasoning powers on religious questions carried him to the supernatural.

What was left on which Hocking agreed with Royce? He respected Royce because of the latter's powers as a dialectician, and Hocking adopted Royce's method and his belief that philosophy must be not only emotionally but also intellectually satisfying. In Hocking's commitment to

---

*For Hocking, *The World and the Individual* epitomized Royce's thinking, but Hocking also differed with *The Problem of Christianity*, published a year after *The Meaning of God*: "I should say that Royce, in his new work on the problem of Christianity, though he has much to say about Paul and the church in historic vein, is still unhistorical in his view of religion; since he says in his preface that the ideas which he admits were brought into the world by Christianity are still universal truths of nature, human nature, quite apart from their recognition in any particular religion. In contrast with that view, it seems to me an integral part of the creed to indicate the object of faith as a particular historic fact—'born of the Virgin Mary suffered under Pontius Pilate, was crucified, etc.' " WEH to W. A. Brown, 9 May 1912, Box 1912, *Meaning of God*, WEH Papers. See also Hocking's review of PC, *Harvard Theological Review* 7 (1914): 107–12.

Roycean modes of speculation, we can understand the core of his philosophy and of his personality. He developed a religious view of experience but a view with suitable logical grounds.

The question Hocking asked in *The Meaning of God* was, could we directly know God, could we find him in experience? As history had transmitted it to us, the immediate religious experience was of nature somehow alive. In spiritualism the dead took on nature's powers and punished or rewarded their living brethren. In animism man endowed nature itself with spiritual qualities. Both primitive religions amounted to the same thing: they located social experience, the experience of other mind, in nature. In fact, Hocking claimed, the more recent belief in one God knowing nature had legitimated scientific pursuits. That God knew the world completely, although we did not, made it plausible that nature was at least knowable. Moreover, nature had "responded" positively to scientific questioning, showing itself intelligible, and this was further evidence for many that nature was alive with God.

Hocking wanted to know if we could justify this belief in living nature, as somehow other mind, and he first asked whether we knew other minds directly at all. As Perry had pointed out, idealistic thinkers had never avoided solipsism. If only the contents of consciousness confronted Royce, he might claim that these contents and the solitary individuals who "had" the contents were fragments of an absolute self, but what did he mean by these others if only one self truly existed? Hocking thought that Royce's construct or postulate of other minds failed. Idealism could not escape solipsism unless there was direct experience of other minds. Hocking must rescue for idealism the "stinging reality of contact with the human comrade."[4]

Consider ideal knowledge of other minds. The identity and unity of a personality was bound up with its intercourse with nature: other beings were only such as long as they knew definite objects. Nature, Hocking said, was necessary to understanding other minds. The elements of physical experience, the vividness and pungency of sensation, also characterized social experience. We could not separate knowledge of other mind from knowledge of nature. In a passage reminiscent of James's evocations of the immediate, Hocking illustrated his belief:

I have sometimes sat looking at a comrade, speculating on this mysterious isolation of self from self. Why are we so made that I gaze and see of thee only thy Wall, and never Thee? This Wall of thee is but a movable part of the Wall of my world; and I also am a Wall to thee: we look out at one another from behind masks. How would it seem if my mind could but once be within thine; and we could meet and without barrier be with each other? And then it has fallen upon me like a shock—as when one thinking himself alone has felt a presence—But I am in thy soul. These things around me are in thy experience. They are thy own; when I touch them and move them I change thee. When I look on them I see what thou seest; when I listen, I hear what thou hearest. I am in the great Room of thy soul; and I experience thy very experience. For where art thou? Not there, behind those eyes, within that head, in darkness, fraternizing with chemical processes. Of these, in my own case, I know nothing, and will know nothing; for my existence is spent not behind my Wall, but in front of it. I am there, where I have treasures. And there art thou, also. This world in which I live, is the world of thy soul: and being within that, I am within thee. I can imagine no contact more real and thrilling than this; that we should meet and share identity, not through ineffable inner depths (alone), but here through the foregrounds of common experience; and that thou shouldst be—not behind that mask—but here, pressing with all thy consciousness upon me, containing me, and these things of mine. This is reality.*

In experiencing nature an individual actually had part of what constituted ideal knowledge of other minds. But nature experience, it would

---

*MGHE, pp. 2.5–66. Over forty years later when his "comrade," Agnes Hocking, died, he recaptured the intensity of his early illustration in a manner showing the extent to which his thought came from his own experience: "Her death was like the definite flickering out of a candle, not in pain but in growing limitation. She had long been without words; but these silent weeks are to me among the most precious of my memories. For her utterly simplified self, with nothing but a sign language—perhaps a faint smile, perhaps a pressure of the hand—was still so entirely herself: it was she and no other, and she knew that I was there. And now, while there is no 'there' where I can find her, she is still unlosable" (WEH to RBP, 27 May 1955, Important Letters, A–J, File *H*, RBP Papers).

She had taught him, he said, a new historical category, the unlosable. History was made up of unlosable persons and events (D. C. Williams, "William Ernest Hocking, 1873–1966, Biographical Remarks," paper delivered at Harvard memorial meeting, 10 February 1967, WEH Papers).

seem, was only necessary and not sufficient for social experience. Not all nature experiences were experiences of other people; we differentiated the experiences of other selves from experience of the environment. Ideal knowledge of other minds was knowing nature and knowing that another knew nature. I must not only experience nature but know that another was also experiencing it; we must both know the world at once, it must be common. But, Hocking said, this was just what we *meant* by experience of nature: nature *was* the world known in common. If we had nature experience at all, we had experience of other mind. Nature, Hocking said, was made with reference to co-experiencing minds; it was inherently public. Nature experience and experience of other minds were one. Moreover, the shareability of the world of nature implied that it was always shared. What I knew as nature, I supposed that another could verify and experience, but in order that nature should be so experienceable I also supposed some part already experienced. Nature could not be the mutually experienceable unless we already held some part in common and knew that experience could be mutual. Hocking could not just say that nature was what was experienced in common. For how did we know that some objects were experienced in common? "The only way in which I can know an object to be common is by catching it in the act of being common, that is, by knowing it as known by other mind. The social experience must have a prior and original recognizableness" (258).

Against the absolute idealists, Hocking said, Perry rightly polemicized that our experience was "passive" and "empirical"—we knew objects in the world as they were, we knew a not-self. But while this "natural realism" was correct on one level, on another it was not. In order for us to know objects as they were, to experience nature, we must know objects to be known by other mind. The not-self, Hocking said, was other self. Correctly understood, natural realism was a realism of social experience. So Hocking steered between Royce and Perry, between voluntaristic idealism and neo-realism.

Hocking claimed that nature experience and experience of other minds were equivalent. He must go on to argue, however, that we had this experience. Because the existence of other minds entailed nature's existence, the only alternative to claiming that we had knowledge of nature was the claim of solipsism and, accordingly, the problems of idealism. Might it not be that I only experienced my self and all its phases? Might

Philosophy as a Profession

not all there is be the contents of my consciousness? Hocking said no: experience must be social. To suppose that my experience was solipsistic required that I contrast this experience with non-subjective (social) experience. This world was mine alone only if I knew that another did not experience it. That is, I must know that there were others, that there was social experience. For a solipsist merely to have the idea of a presumed non-existent social experience guaranteed social experience's existence. How could I derive the idea of social experience if not from such an experience itself? Consider Leibniz's monadology:

> Leibniz, for example, judges that all experience is monadic, and that monads do not in actuality experience each other, though to themselves they seem to do so. In making this hypothesis, Leibniz presents to himself the world of monads, and *he* knows their relations to be other than they seem: *he* at any rate occupies a non-monadic position, is for the time being an intermonadic Mind. And any one who judges that he—and God—know the actual reach of ideas to fall short of their apparent reach, does thereby assert that *his* idea has not thus fallen short. There is no degree of outwardness of which we can think; no degree of reality which we incline to *deny* to idea; but in that thought we have claimed it for our idea. Let me represent to myself the Other Subject, his living center, as inaccessible to my experience; then either I deny myself nothing conceivable, or else I have that which I deny (274–75).

Hocking wanted to show that we had nature experience, this experience being identical to social experience, and, like Royce, he used a dialectical argument to show its existence (301–16). Our idea of social experience guaranteed its existence; its denial was contradictory. He called this idea *concrete a priori* knowledge: *a priori*, because we knew of social experience not prior to experience but as part of our conception of experience; *concrete*, because our idea of social experience was experience of other mind (278). But if Hocking had not gone wrong, he had also found an actual instance of nature alive, found the aliveness of nature—and so the fundamental religious experience—in the possibility of our experience. Moreover, we must assume that the other self that we all shared in our nature experience was independent of particular selves. We were all empirical—passive—knowers of nature, of the shared other self wherein we all coalesced. It was creative of us—experience of the world was necessary to our constitution as selves. Nature, Hocking concluded, was the intentional communication, "the communicated being," of a wholly active self. "We have made all social experience depend upon a conscious knowledge in experience of a being, who in scope and power might well be identified with God. We have been led by the successive requirements of our logic to the position that our first and fundamental social experience is an experience of God" (295). Our fundamental social experience, our direct experience of the natural world, was immediate knowledge of the divine.

The key to Hocking's view was his Kantian revision of Descartes. *Cogito ergo sum*, said Hocking, went only part way in expressing the basic *a priori* truth. This truth was "I think something, therefore I exist and something else exists." Mind simply did not think, it must think something, and this joint product—experience—was metaphysical. With Kant, Hocking held that experience was an interplay between two mutually dependent kinds of being, self and non-self.[5] Consequently, the world we knew in experience did not transcend self, was not exterior to consciousness. Moreover, the non-self of experience was Other Self, although this Other Self or Consciousness was not our own or that of any other finite beings. We were led to the idea of a greater self or God, but the being of this God was communicated to us and was, therefore, social (285 ff.).

Hocking called his position "a Realism of the Absolute—not far removed from Absolute Idealism" (290). But obviously, since he disputed Royce over the problem of solipsism, he did not accept Royce's notion that other selves were constructs. Equally obviously, Hocking desired to distinguish his idealism by making selfhood social. Here, however, he disappointed. He wrote that God's creations were not apart from God, that God "included" other selves and their objects (298). What was the relation, then, between God, the world, and other selves? Hocking wanted to avoid absolute solipsism, but he never clarified his position, although we again saw the impact of Royce and James.

We have already noted the effect on American philosophy of Royce's analysis of the realist and critical rationalist conceptions of being in *The World and the Individual*. The other rejected conception of being was mysticism, and the influence of Royce's sympathetic inquiries into Indian thought appeared in *The Meaning of God*. Mysticism ignored the scientific world of our activity as finite beings. At the very least, Royce rejected mysticism as speculative thought: it was the antithesis of philosophy. Hocking accepted this criticism while simultaneously developing Royce's interest. The last part of *The Meaning of God* initiated Hocking's sustained theoretical and practical concern for eastern religion. His exposition revealed his differences with Royce's own Fourth Conception of Being.[6]

With Royce, Hocking denied that mysticism could be a positive philosophy, but we could investigate the meaning of mystic experience and, Hocking argued, the ideal form of worship was mystical, a kind of personal communication with God. Mystical experience made immediately sure the foundations of being; it was the act of recalling oneself to being. The mystic combined non-effort and self-assertion, a consciousness of absolute dependence and an attitude of will-fulness to make his present experience significant of the whole. With James, Hocking said the mystic grasped his selfhood anew, *realizing* his relation to other self (341–441). Hocking could not "explain" our relation to God and the world: the reader must experience it. But he used argumentation to make it possible for the reader to have this experience. In describing how he grasped the mind of his comrade, Hocking wanted to jolt us into seeing the significance of everyday intercourse. In this sense the distinctive literary execution of *The Meaning of God* was full of guile: Hocking wanted to use the art of reason to go beyond it and resolve the problems that left reason helpless.

Political Philosophy and Its Religious Dimension

Hocking felt that the impossibility of explicating men's relation to God justified flirting with mysticism. His commitments as a philosopher, however, pushed him into reasoned discussion on these matters; and after coming to Harvard he approached these metaphysical problems indirectly by investigating the connections of finite to infinite in organized social life. Although his thinking on the First World War was undistinguished, it appeared to have galvanized him into serious work on the theory of politics after his 1920 appointment to the Alford professorship. While the work of philosophers in the 1920s drifted away from human affairs, and while even Ralph Perry became enamored of technical ethical questions, Hocking did political philosophy—territory then unknown at Harvard.

Although at Harvard these interests did not survive his retirement, his writings represented the first modern philosophical studies of politics by an American. Hocking articulated the sophisticated viewpoint of the new academic clerisy. As his sympathetic biographer put it, Hocking was "the veritable incarnation of sanity and responsibility, . . . courtly, well-tailored . . . [a] Christian gentleman, . . . [and a] Harvard man." "His dress, his manners, the style and extent of his letter writing, the special quality of his friendships are all those of a Victorian gentleman. . . . his expectation of what life had to offer was almost never extravagant, but he was a successful and genuinely happy man, and optimism came more naturally to his generation than it does to ours."[7] His vigorous support for American entry into the League of Nations, an issue in the 1920 presidential campaign, exemplified his practical politics. In a letter to *The New York Times* he identified himself as one of "the habitual Republican voters who want a prompt and honest entry into the League and who (for that reason) can do no other than vote [against Harding and] for [the Democratic nominee] Cox."[8] In short, Hocking was a conservative but one whose intelligence always tempered his self-satisfaction and uncritical faith in democratic capitalism.

Man and the State and *The Present Status of the Philosophy of Law and of Rights*, both published in 1926, developed his position. The analysis in *Man and the State* rested on his psychological examination of the individual will. A will to power, in a non-invidious sense, defined each of us; there was a vital impulse, a craving for potency and satisfaction basic and essential to human nature. The conditions necessary for the satisfaction of individual wills were just those features distinctive of the state. Some of these conditions were beyond individual control: the need for permanence of effect of one's will, sufficient knowledge to understand one's goals, and impersonal tests of the adequacy of the ideas which were to achieve the goals. Each of us, then, must will something no one of us could attain in willing his own power at all. This something else established the state; it had its origins in the basic instincts of individual psychology (308–24).

Because it was in the nature of individual willing to secure the state, we all willed the state; it existed by a unanimous will and its purpose was to serve the general interest (380–88). This purpose—the state's essence—was the reasoned promotion of social life. The state canalized and unified individuals' "will overflow." Arising in man's historical sense and rational self-contemplation, the state persisted in space and time to supply a necessary condition of durability to what ought to endure and transiency to what ought to perish. The state enabled men to become what they were truly capable of being (103–95). As Hocking wrote, the state established "the objective right," the objective conditions, for securing the will to power in human history (325–36). Consequently, the right of revolution—indeed our ability to be really disenchanted with the state—was limited. The hopeless inability of a society to change in a just direction legitimated revolution but then only when revolution promised to consume itself, to end revolution (445–55).

Although Hocking vouchsafed his conservatism by believing that the state externalized our "practical reason," he was anxious to distinguish himself from the Hegelian "state idolators" (35–52). The justification of revolution indicated that no actual state perfectly exemplified the state's essence, and Hocking admitted that his discussion of "the state" referred to "the ideal state" (190). Because of the complexities of human existence, "the state" was inevitably an abstraction, and in appraising politics, Hocking confessed that existing states always functioned imperfectly because of greed and conflict (404–13). Although we each willed the state, individual wills produced it:

> The psychology we have been working with is individual psychology. It is the needs and the initiative of individuals that have made the state and continue to make it. This implies that the individual is prior to the state; it also implies that the state is prior to the completed individual. He needs the state to become the person that he has it in him to become (339).

There was no over-individual, super-organic state will. The state was not a greater mind in which we all participated. Although each individual willed the state, its properties were attributable to individuals acting severally. The organismic analogy was misleading if taken as more than an analogy (339–62). Of course, there was an over-individual will, a greater self, which the communication of selves in the state presupposed.

This Other Self, however, was the God of religion and his connection to the state was unclear, at best (375–79).

Hocking faced a dilemma. He differentiated his political philosophy—I would call it a reflective Burkean conservatism—from that of the Hegelian idealists by denying a super-organic in political life. His view of the state as the "overflow" of the several wills of individuals deferred to pluralistic American ideals. But this move made it impossible for him to specify man's connection to the absolute. In the state, he said, man's will sought its satisfaction in history; through religion came its satisfaction beyond history (415). But if religion involved what was beyond history, political experience could never teach us of our relation to God, by the very fact that it was political, and political philosophy would not clarify the metaphysical problem unanswered in *The Meaning of God.**

Hocking was not happy with this boundary between the political and the religious. His 1932 *Spirit of World Politics* groped to delineate in a study of international relations the principles of state action which seemingly went beyond what we ordinarily conceived as political. The title indicated his concern. The same emphasis occurred in another book of the same year, *Re-thinking Missions*. Hocking was chairman of a laymen's inquiry into the viability of Protestant missions in the Far East. Continuing his study of non-western religions, he wrote the first four chapters of this book on "general principles." And if the study of politics carried him to religion, the study of religion carried him back to politics. In effect, he advocated that the churches alter traditional missionary activity. The church in distant lands must now function as a sort "of foreign service or ambassadorship";[9] the Christian must stress the commonality of the world churches' work and the catholic precepts of Protestantism. Only this attitude would make missions live in the modern world and give all religion contemporary relevance. The church must have the ecumenical task of creating a sense of man's common goals. Through the will of Jesus and others like him, Hocking said, "God works throughout human history bringing men toward unity in a love which is universal in

---

*Hocking did say that "individual conscience, broadly understood, appears as the middle ground through which religious impulses pass into the life of society and state." But he allowed that the individual's "impulses" in this area were "vague." See MS, pp. 432 ff.

its sweep."[10] Somehow, history was a revelation of man's relation to the divine. .

Hocking continued to work at these politico-religious themes, most notably in *Living Religions and a World Faith* (1940); *The Coming World Civilization* (1956); and *Strength of Men and Nations* (1959). But it proved impossible to connect man to God by examining man's finite experience. Moreover, when he turned again to metaphysics and directly reconsidered the problems raised by *The Meaning of God*, he could not resolve his difficulties. "Fact and Destiny," the Gifford Lectures he delivered in Scotland in 1938–1939, were to be his major effort and promised more of an exposition of self's relation to Self than the mystical personal act of recognition. But Hocking never printed the Gifford Lectures. At his death he was still working on them, and his mature metaphysic was fragmentary, published in bits and pieces, never entirely worked out.[11] *The Meaning of God* remained the fullest statement of his beliefs.

Although Hocking's points of disagreement with absolute idealism were manifest, it is difficult to know how far beyond Roycean conceptions he could have gone. His later work attempted to delineate the infinite in the finite, the signs of the deity in social life. But to the extent that he went beyond mysticism, his early studies had foreshadowed his positive analysis. At the end of *The Meaning of God*, he noted that the mystic acted historically as the "prophetic consciousness": the mystic saw that the perpetual struggle to overcome evil was progress and so, Hocking argued in Roycean accents, gave us such knowledge as we had of the significance of life sub specie aeternitatis (497–99). Through the institutions of Christianity human beings "remade" themselves by attempting to become one with the cooperation of wills which was the absolute. He suggested that the Christian ideal was justifiable because it encapsulated instinctual "life and death" beliefs that have survived; once more he hinted that reality must meet man's deepest aspirations.[12]

Hocking in Retirement

Hocking was due to retire in 1938, but Harvard extended his appointment for five years. His vigor and creative powers were undiminished and he was, undoubtedly, the most important contemporary American exponent of the idealistic tradition. He had, moreover, carried on the public concerns of James and Royce, extending them into the social and political realm. When he stepped down in 1943 it was the end of an era.

Hocking and his family had built a summer retreat looking over the White Mountains in Madison, New Hampshire, and when he retired there as an emeritus professor after the Second World War, he became the ideal of a philosopher. Until his death in 1966 he continued to write: he tried to round out his metaphysics, he carried on his political and social theorizing, and he expanded his studies on world religions and cultures. The visitors who made a pilgrimage to New Hampshire often came away convinced of the truth of his doctrines. As Brand Blanshard observed, Hocking was a commanding personal presence: "He gave the impression . . . of power held in reserve; there was no strain, scarcely even the appearance of effort; he spoke with the quiet, unworried confidence of one who was master of his matter."[13] He had always emphasized the metaphysical import of man's experience of nature, and what better place for contemplation than the isolated and majestic surroundings to which Hocking could introduce his guests? Looking out at the peak of Mount Washington dominating the fierce winter blue, one of them recalled, anybody would have difficulty doubting Hocking's belief in the absolute.[14]

But in truth philosophers thought Hocking a man of the past. Royce had lived to see the high tide of idealism ebb. In the 1920s and 1930s Hocking had again made idealism respectable, but it never recovered permanently from the realist smear of the First World War. After the second great war, the scope and style of Hocking's work, his interest in mysticism, and his concern for the problems of the world marked him as a man out of step with the specialities of his profession. In his last years he could not comprehend that many philosophers in universities made logic the be-all and end-all of their research or were seriously engaged in analyzing the meanings of words. He died in Madison at the age of ninety-three, his philosophy already a footnote in the history books.

26

HARVARD MORAL PHILOSOPHY

1875-1926

Cognitivism and Non-Cognitivism in Ethics

In 1933 a young student, Charles Leslie Stevenson, went to Cambridge University where Continental logical positivism and analytic British empiricism enjoyed a deserved popularity. In 1935 Stevenson received his Ph.D. in philosophy from Harvard; his dissertation, written under Perry, was called "The Emotive Meaning of Ethical Terms." During the late 1930s Stevenson used this work to produce some important articles on moral philosophy and culminated his study in 1944 with a book, *Ethics and Language*.[1]

Seen in historical perspective, Stevenson's position is ambiguous, owing much to Perry and John Dewey, but Stevenson had also picked up the concerns of British philosophy, and these controlled the book. He argued that there was a cleavage between facts and values, our beliefs about the world and our attitudes toward it. Scientific language was distinct from evaluative language; while the former contained true or false statements, the latter expressed emotion. In particular, moral "statements" were persuasive, analogous to imperatives, or they were ejaculations, manifestations of feelings.

Ethics and Language was a major success, the key post-war work in Anglo-American moral philosophy. Stevenson's "emotivism" became the reference point for various forms of "non-cognitivist" ethics dominating professional philosophy in the quarter century after its publication. Stevenson was so successful that many forgot the existing corpus of American "cognitivist" or "naturalist" ethical theory, claiming that moral propositions were true or false, statements about the world. Certainly it took a back seat to emotivism and emotivism's followers, and after *Ethics and Language* few attacked the distinction between the way the world is and the way it ought to be. For the sophisticated, only thinkers like Stevenson could account for cultural relativism; cognitivism was old-fashioned, a relic of a more stable and provincial era. This appraisal may be true, but non-cognitivism won an easier victory than it deserved.

For over fifty years philosophers at Harvard espoused ethical cognitivism. Palmer's self-realization views were best known, but Royce developed a similar position based on a technically cogent argument in his early writings of the 1870s. We will first examine Royce's argument, relating it to Palmer's more popular one and to those of their students—Hocking, Santayana, and Holt. We shall conclude by explicating the work of Perry, Harvard's most important moral philosopher. His 1909 *The Moral Economy* tied some of Royce's ideas to Perry's realism, demonstrating that cognitivism need not be idealistic. His massive *General Theory of Value* of 1926 classically formulated the Harvard position.

Royce's Early Ethics

In developing his ethics in the 1870s Royce assumed a cognitive distinction between right and wrong; it was pretense to deny this distinction. In some 1877 Johns Hopkins lectures, "The Return to Kant," he stipulated that the "Critical Method" in ethics accepted "as a fact given beyond the possibility of dispute . . . the presence of a power among us of a Moral Sentiment." It was wrong, he wrote elsewhere, to roast a man alive on a gridiron, wrong to dynamite a peaceful man's dwelling to display dislike, wrong to beat a dog for the sake of hearing him howl. "These are simple instances of moral distinctions. Everyone competent to speak upon moral questions will make them." Royce sometimes asserted that we possessed a moral sense enabling us to make these distinctions, but his essential claim was that we were aware of the denotation of phrases like 'moral sense' and 'morally right'. For example, the moral sense allowed us to apprehend what was right or wrong, and we could point out what was right or wrong. The problem of "ethical analysis" was to unpack the meaning or connotation of these terms: we must analyze the nature of the moral sense, of the morally right, or—to emphasize Royce's language—

the moral consciousness.[2] This analysis would determine the basis of moral distinctions. Recognition of them did not appear to commit one to act on them; it seemed possible to assert something like, "That may be the right thing to do, but I really don't care to do it; there's nothing in it for me." In dissecting the notion of moral consciousness, Royce hoped to show that understanding morality's dictates yielded a reason for obeying them; the exponent of prudential conduct was his chief enemy.

In working out how we knew right from wrong, Royce was led to epistemology—to questions of how we know anything at all—and he did not have an answer until 1885. Consequently, his early ethics was incomplete. We made moral distinctions, and Royce said that right action contributed to harmonious living and the interest human beings had in experience. But if moral conduct was binding, the "voluntary progress" that it brought must be worth seeking, and Royce had no ironclad argument that it was. If we attained harmony, we might find it "tedious and intolerable." If Royce doubted the value of the goal of conduct, he was more disturbed about reaching the goal. If it was not achievable, why ought it to constrain us? It would be a foolish and irrational end, and we knew that both nature and man himself conspired to thwart man's best efforts. History recounted man's difficulty in making progress, and Royce was not confident that good would triumph over evil:

> According to our present notion of the universe, we stand alone, a few specks of life in the darkness of infinite space, in the midst of natural forces whose resources we shall never more than meagerly estimate, with an unknown future before us, in which what appalling accidents may happen, we can never even with faint show of accuracy foresee.

Lacking an adequate epistemology, we could not know that things would come out all right in the end or that, if they did, we could pronounce the result worthwhile. Under these circumstances it was not easy to justify the moral persuasion. Sometimes Royce was content with paeans to a free man's worship:

> . . . if the triumph of the good is uncertain, if voluntary progress is always a venturing into a mysterious future, there is no reason why we should on that account work less vigorously, or make our aims

less lofty. It is a cowardly soul that needs the certainty of success before it will work. It is a craven who despairs and does nothing because what he can do may turn out a failure. Whatever future growth eliminates from human nature, it is to be hoped that one trace of the era of universal warfare will survive, namely, the courage that can face possible, even probable destruction with the delight of a hero in resisting and planning and working so long as he can raise his arm.[3]

In less optimistic moments he could not rest with eloquence, and examined the Schopenhauerian pessimism that rejected the doctrines he felt so important.

For Schopenhauer, Royce said, life's essence was the active or desiring principle of consciousness—the will. Continual flights from one object of desire to another made up our lives. We were in a constant state of longing. Without this consciousness of desire, this unrest, there was no life. Schopenhauer defined pleasure as satisfied desire, and if a desire did not arise, there was no satisfaction, no pleasure. Pleasure was at best a neutral state. To desire an object was to lack it, to want it, but not to have it; if we obtained it, we were "even"; in the pleasurable state we cancelled the desire. The only positive element in consciousness was longing, the process by which we gained the object of desire. Freedom from desire occurred only in death. Schopenhauer's pessimism rested on this analysis:

> But if attainment of the absolute end means death [Royce explained], then in life the end cannot be attained. Life can, therefore, never have absolute worth. Whatever is a goal with nothing beyond cannot be life, but must be death. Whatever life has no final goal within its reach, must be an eternal failure.

Insofar as Royce accepted this result, the situation was more desperate. On Schopenhauer's view the best life was one in which we satisfied desires, in which we always strove successfully. But this kind of life was rare. Under ordinary circumstances we did not achieve all our goals, and other people thwarted some of our aspirations. Moreover, the fact that others existed meant for Schopenhauer that even the most successful individual tried vainly to equal in his own pleasure "the immense riches of life embodied in these hosts of humanity." No self possessed the knowledge and power in all life. Even if nothing else opposed his desires, consciousness of his own worthlessness in contrast to all around him robbed an individual of self-satisfaction. Happiness was possible only if one was unconscious of how much life there was around him.[4] For Schopenhauer the goal of life had a "neutral" worth at best, but human beings rarely came off "even" and could never do so while alive. In these circumstances there was little reason for the goal to win men's commitment.

These conceptions impressed Royce, but he could not accept pessimism, and the persuasive arguments he used against it led to a solution to the problems of ethics. He first urged that individual satisfaction could not define life's goal:

> The one goal is the rendering as full and as definite as possible all the conscious life that at any moment comes within the circle of our influence. Devotion, then, to universal conscious life, is the goal of conscious life itself; or the goal is the self-reference or self-surrender of each conscious moment to the great whole of life, in so far as that whole is within reach.

He also denied that we calculated the goal's worth by a pleasure and pain arithmetic. We could not carry out this summation, and, more importantly, human beings made their own appraisal of life's value.

When Royce worked at these problems in the late 1870s and early 1880s he could not prove his position, but the idea was clear: more deeply considered, the end of life was perfect union and harmony with the whole of conscious life. It was trivial that unfulfilled desire dominated individual lives since Royce had not defined the goal as Schopenhauer had. Each being achieved union with the whole, Royce contended, if only in moments. Whatever impressed on each of us his own insignificance and "the grandeur of the great ocean of conscious activity" accomplished this end. Self-sacrifice, work for an impersonal end, or even the contemplation of active life might exemplify it. Since we postulated our goal by "independent volition," we might also choose the extent to which occasional success compensated for failures to reach it. Royce asked not for a tally on a set of experiences, but for a verdict on their value. He did not demonstrate that his goal was justifiable or that we could attain it. "Every man," he said, "has to deal with those queries quite by himself, even as with his own eyes he must see colors. It is our province merely to suggest the ultimate questions."[5]

Schopenhauer's pessimism dissatisfied Royce because it did not see beyond individual life. The German correctly maintained that "all life for Self is worthless." But, Royce added, Schopenhauer had not shown that we must construe values as being only individual or that some other valuational process must fail. Pessimism did not touch Royce's argument for "Holy Living": "living not for Self, but for the quelling, the putting down of Self, and for the building up of peaceful, harmonious, but entirely unselfish life."[6] This contrast between the two sorts of ends tentatively solved Royce's problems. His epistemological studies had given a "postulational" basis for knowledge. Assuming moral distinctions as he did, he analyzed the moral consciousness in a way congruent with his epistemology.

What did I mean by *myself*? Royce claimed that I was one being, existent above and through all the changes of consciousness, the subject of my thoughts and experiences. Nonetheless, experience never gave this being; I directly experienced only present consciousness. I posited my own past and future, that which must be to fill out my self conception. Now what did we accept as the basis of prudential conduct? We approved conduct on this basis of "worldly wisdom" if we treated an act's expected consequences with respect to their intrinsic desirableness to the individual in question. A prudent individual calculated both the long- and short-range consequences to himself of proposed actions. He decided not on the basis of the immediate enjoyments promised by some act, but weighed these against more far-reaching consequences. As Royce stated, the prudent man avoided deciding on "the illusion of perspective in time." Prudence demanded that if he knew consequences at all, he estimate them with equal scrutiny however remote they were. But the prudent man's self was never given, and he acknowledged (or postulated) the reality of other selves as well as its reality. For example, I did not know how or why I should postulate my own past and future as real when they were not given, although I did; and I did postulate my neighbor as real like myself. I based my preference for myself on a feeling called the selfish interest. But this interest was emotional; it was not involved in my postulating as real what was not given. Allowing my interest in myself to determine my

conduct paralleled the imprudent man's allowing short-range consequences to govern him. The canon of prudential conduct was that

> my conduct in these cases is approved if I treat all the consequences
> as if they were present, disregarding the prejudice created by my
> momentary interest, and then choose such consequences as are in
> this view intrinsically more desirable. My conduct is not approved,
> if I give myself over to the illusion of time-perspective, or choose a
> conceived consequence, not for its intrinsic desirableness, but
> because I am the slave of my momentary interest. Approved action
> consists in weighing all future consequences according to their
> conceived value, not according to the value that my passion gives
> them.

Carrying out this principle, I should treat the future experiences of my
neighbors in a similar fashion:

> I have not the same selfish interest [in my neighbors], but I do pos-
> tulate them as equally real and unreal with my own conceived
> future. My existence as an enduring entity is not more immediately
> given than is the existence of my neighbor as an enduring entity.
> The same activity that postulates by expectation my future, pos-
> tulates his future as well. The consequences of my act for me, are
> not more real than they are for him. If then, I am to order my con-
> duct according to all future experience regarded as equally an object
> of striving, I must include my neighbor's future with my own and
> order my conduct accordingly.

Prudential activity illustrated the essence of conduct, putting insight
before desire, conceiving all experience as equally worthy of consideration when deliberating. If we admitted this fact we saw that the analysis
of consciousness did not yield *me* as an entity distinct from all the world.
We expected all future consciousness equally. We also acknowledged that
moral distinctions existed, that some experiences were more desirable
than others. Royce concluded that consistency alone brought us to the
following postulate: we ought to act so that the end of conduct was the
good of the whole world of future experience as we conceived the world
at the moment of action; in our conduct we ought to regard all future

consciousness equally because none was given but only expected, and all was real when it came.

This was Royce's early answer to the problem of ethics; his analysis of moral consciousness, of what it was to behave morally, explicated something of the ground of moral distinctions. He stressed, however, that he could not demonstrate his solution, but only state it:

> the rule of conduct is: Act as thou wouldst wish to have acted were all the consequences of thy act for all the world of being here and now given as a fact of thine own present consciousness. Or again: Choose thy deeds so that their outcome shall seem the best possible outcome when all the results are viewed at once as a whole in their intrinsic good or evil. Thus conduct is made absolutely consistent.

Royce argued that his examination of morality proceeded on the claim of consistency. Conduct was action in the present moment for conceived future moments. Consistent conduct esteemed all conceived future moments, and only absolutely consistent conduct met moral approval: it looked to the worth of all expected consequences. We judged each moment of life with regard to the whole of consciousness conceived as one being or, better, as one moment of being.[7]

The Consensus on Cognitivism

After 1885, for Royce, moral conduct would even more clearly be that conduct best realizing the one truly existing being. In his later work, however, the explicit argument from prudential to moral behavior disappeared although the self-realization aspect remained. For example, the 1906 Urbana Lectures on ethics and *The Philosophy of Loyalty* examined the loyal personality because, in the evolution of human types, it was best able to achieve individual harmony and contribute to the supremely valuable cooperation of all wills.

The same sort of argument appeared in Palmer's 1920 *Altruism*: tracing the evolution of selves in successive societies demonstrated the constantly expanding conception of self. For Palmer, prudential behavior properly understood was moral behavior, and in the highest societies the ethically justifiable realized the self through love and justice. The similarities between Royce's and Palmer's theories are instructive in demonstrating the agreement at Harvard on an ethical cognitivism committed to self-realization. Palmer's ruling concept was justice; Royce's was loyalty or (later) love. Palmer saw justice realized in institutions, Royce in loyalty to a cause or (later) love for a community. Both proclaimed that the world was somehow becoming one, Palmer through the growth of the conjoint self, Royce through the linking of ego and other or (later) through individual growth in a community.

In the work of their students these ideas reappeared. In Hocking's metaphysics the individual self was never given but developed in conjunction with Other Mind (nature). The full development considered as a whole was God as far as we knew him. The growth of the self was ipso facto the growth of our fellows, and social growth aimed at a unity with the whole; our joint self-realization approached the deity. But cognitivism and self-realization were not the assumptions of idealists alone. The definition of Santayana's life of reason evidenced that he shared many of these ideas: in such a life we treated the satisfaction of every impulse as a good to be cherished, and we organized our lives to satisfy as many of them as possible. Santayana's five volumes attempted to chart the progress made by this form of life in human society. The self-realization dimension of realistic ethics was more pronounced in Holt's 1915 *The Freudian Wish and Its Place in Ethics*. Holt advised human beings how to adjust practically to the world and, in so doing, to actualize their potential. Although Holt did not elaborate his metaphysical position in his book, he was clearly not an idealist; he "naturalized" self-realization by stressing the organism's relations to its environment as the mode of achieving the self's potential. As Hocking pointed out, Holt's reasoning was identical to that of Royce and Palmer.[8] Their emphasis on the ever-enlarging conceptions of self in successively evolving societies differed little from Holt's outline of the individual's continuous adaptation to a precarious Darwinian universe.

The work of Santayana and Holt signified that cognitivism and self-realization at Harvard need not be idealistic in character, and as idealism ceased to be predominant, Perry developed the most sustained set of arguments for a cognitivist ethics that put traditional self-realization views to work in another context. For at least a time he made cognitivism plausible by showing that it did not presuppose an idealist metaphysics.

Perry's Early Work

Perry's 1909 *Moral Economy* defined an interest as a unit of life acting for its own preservation, and Perry called goodness the fulfillment of interest (9 ff.). Simple interests were the likings governing our activity. I liked eating apples: the actions and objects necessary to eating apples constituted an interest, and my success in so doing, a good. Goodness at this level might be only personal—that is, related to a single individual—but it was not subjective; on the contrary it was objective because we agreed that, for example, my eating an apple in fact satisfied my interest.

With this basis Perry's first aim was investigating "the logic of prudence." We accepted this logic as unimpeachable, he claimed, but in making clear its grounds, we would see that it involved "the whole ethical dialectic": consistency would lead us from prudential norms to moral ones.

Prudence involved checking one interest in consequence of another's presence. I wanted to eat an apple belonging to you; it would be imprudent for me to steal it, for that would jeopardize my interest, let us say, in continuing our friendship. But in buying the apple from you, assuring that I could eat it and retain your friendship, I acknowledged your interest in the apple but did not adopt it: I preserved my interests by acting so that yours were adjusted in a satisfactory way. We did not always act prudently, but Perry said we agreed that it was irrational or foolish to do otherwise, and we all understood the rationale behind admitting and adjusting conflicting interests at this level. Perry also noted that the adjustment of interests required by prudence extended to future interests: it was prudent for me not to satisfy my interest in apples today if I would be sick tomorrow and unable to use my theater tickets. The prudent man recognized that at least some future interests were as real as present interests. Prudence also implicitly demanded a conception of a higher interest than the simple interests we started with. This interest was "higher" in the sense of greater, exceeding a simple (or narrower) interest by embracing it and adding to it: "Your interest in the fulfillment of today's interest *and* tomorrow's, is demonstrably greater than your interest in the fulfillment of either exclusively, because it provides for each and more. In this perfectly definite sense your preference may be justified." Prudence finally entailed that an action conducive to maintaining two or more interests would take precedence over an action which fulfilled one but sacrificed the other (43–53).

Perry recognized that the prudent man made more complex appraisals than these, but the examples did set forth the principle on which prudence rested: there were controlling interests allowing the maximum fulfillment of conflicting interests permitted by circumstances. Moreover, the basis for decision was quantitative. No interest had priority over another simply because of a "qualitative" difference:

> Two good books are not better than one because two is better than one, but because in two of a given unit of goodness there is more of goodness than in one. Two is more than one, but not more good, unless that which is counted is itself good. Nor is two longer or heavier than one, unless the units numbered happen to be those of length or weight. To prefer two interests to one does not imply that one is a lover of quantity, but a lover of good; of that which if it be and remain good, the more the better. At any rate it seems to me a matter of simple candor to admit that "more" is a term implying quantity, whether it be "more room," "more weight," "more goodness," or "more beauty." It seems to me to be equally evident that "more" implies commensurable magnitude; and that commensurability implies the existence of a common unity in the terms compared. Two inches are more than one inch in that they include one inch and also another like unit. Now in moral matters the unit of value is the fulfillment of the simple interest; and in consequence I see no way of demonstrating that one such simple interest is more good than another, as I see no way of demonstrating that one inch is longer than another. But I do see that if I can carry a simple interest over into a compound one, and there both retain it and add to it, I shall have more—more by what I add (56–57).

Perry called the controlling interest in prudence "moral purpose," and declared that his analysis of the basis of prudential conduct sufficed to justify moral conduct. For the prudent man operated on the principle that no interest was entitled to exclusive regard because it happened at any given time to be moving him: an interest was an interest even if it did not coincide with an individual's momentary inclination. Perry's point was akin to Royce's. The prudent man might be prejudiced in favor of interests that he adopted or found satisfactory and, therefore, felt more vividly. But his mode of selection was a matter of psychology; the logic behind the selection was that interests other than those immediately present were real and that higher interests incorporated these simpler interests. The interests of the prudent man were no more rational than those of the imprudent man; what distinguished the two was that the prudent man adjudicated among interests while the imprudent did not. The argument for prudence might be convincing to any given individual because he was in some measure able to identify with certain future interests, but the logic of the argument required only that individuals could and ought to fulfill interests jointly and maximally.

Royce's early ethics hinged on an analysis of consciousness as momentary and the notion of individual selves as constructs, not distinct from the rest of the world. In *The Moral Economy* Perry's view of consciousness was not explicit, and without an epistemological excursion, he rested his case on a brief critique of the ego's substantiality. "There is no term so altogether handy as the term 'I'," Perry noted, "nor is there any so embarrassed when called on to show its credentials in the shape of clear and verifiable experience." If the egoist judged that his interests were all that he truly observed, the reply was that these interests were unknown and that no "I" was a fixed and demonstrable fact (57–58).

The principle of prudence, Perry concluded, did not warrant egoism. Rather, the essence of prudence and of morality was identical: we determined moral goodness by considering the totality of affected interests in order to satisfy and promote them jointly. Just as we dismissed the imprudent man as irrational, so the merely prudent man—the ethical egoist—could not justify his conduct. Perry conceded that moral conflict might be grave and complex, but still maintained that an impartial empirical procedure could reconcile any such conflict (66–71).

As he later made evident, Perry was no exponent of self-realization ethics. Unlike Holt, Perry did not believe that the conflict resolution and interest harmonization which determined the morally good necessarily contributed to each self's realization. Perry's philosophy was utilitarian. *The Moral Economy*'s intent was "to connect ethical theory with everyday reflection on practical matters" (vii), and in applying his theory to government, Perry argued that democracy was the outcome of construc-

tive reform through the ages. The fruition of history's systems of government was one in which men ideally took all interests into account when
deciding policies, in which "the best of life is for all" (158–70). Such
democratic politics required an accessible public forum where men
transacted business under the eyes of those most involved, where findings
were open to doubt, and where the concern was not just with the present
but with increasing the promise and potentialities of life (66, 168).

The English cast of Perry's thought should not blind us to its philosophic underpinnings. Its key premise was that the same principle under-
lay moral and prudential reasoning and that the insubstantiality of the
self supported this identity. The link betwen prudence and morality was
common idealistic currency at Harvard. Perry's colleague Hocking
espoused it (as did Holt) and so did his teachers Royce and Palmer. And,
among others, William James, Perry's chief mentor, had rejected the
self's substantiality. The merit of Perry's position was that it rescued the
cognitivist arguments of idealistic self-realization theorists when idealism
was in decline, and put them within a realist philosophy.

General Theory of Value

Perry described *The Moral Economy* as "the preliminary sketch" of an
ethical system, and seventeen years later, in 1926, the *General Theory of
Value* placed his ethics within the wider framework of his realism. Even
Perry acknowledged, however, that the 1920s had brought changes:

> That element in my composition which inclined me in earlier years
> to the Christian ministry is accountable, no doubt, for my sustained
> interest in moral philosophy, an interest which in recent years has
> broadened to embrace the whole realm of "value." The passing of
> years, the habit of philosophizing, and, perhaps, the changed
> atmosphere of the times, have combined to give this interest more of
> reflective detachment and less of that reforming zeal which once
> burned within me.[9]

Aside from Perry's professionalization, *General Theory of Value* was a
dreary book in other ways. Its seven hundred pages of small type were
closely reasoned and defined their topic by appealing to the contributions
made by biology, psychology, and sociology to the understanding of

value. This analysis of the findings of the life and social sciences was far from lively, but *General Theory of Value* is still the most compelling expression of Harvard cognitivism.

The book explicitly countered his colleagues' self-realization views. Criticizing the work of Palmer and Hocking, Perry disclaimed self-realization as the measure of ethical value and argued that if self-realization was the end, then moral activity lost meaning because all activity became self-realizing (44–80). He noted that attempts to salvage the meaning of moral activity by defining "true" self-realization defeated the position: they implied that morality consisted in the desire for certain objects and not self-realization (601–05). Pointing to Royce as a target, Perry said that personality was the property of individuals of the human species. Idealistic arguments concerning the relation of individuals to society at best showed that personality was "a multiple and mutual affair, social in its context and determining relations, but not social in its seat or locus." We could not suppose that a group of interdependent persons would compose a person, even if they were reciprocally dependent in possessing personality (442–44). Morality's goal was not self-realization, nor would achieving this goal, even theoretically, be union with a deity conceived as immanent sociality.

Perry defined value as that which invested any object of any interest. An interest was any state, act, attitude, or disposition of favor or disfavor: interest was behavioristic, a certain kind of tendency and adaptation (115–21). In an organism, he said, interest consisted in a disposition to behave in a constant manner with respect to consequences that the organism expected to follow its behavior. Interests programmed an organism with a variety of responses to an object. The accompanying expectation of what they would accomplish in a certain situation governed the responses (522–23). Perry's behaviorism was not mechanistic: interest represented intelligent behavior because individuals *acquired* their talent to adjust and adapt when they construed certain situations by what was ulterior to the situations. Even to speak of acquired adaptation was not enough; at work, rather, was adaptability, the capacity of the organism to adapt to new situations. Perry connected interest to an unfulfilled and variable phase of a governing propensity, both of which were appropriate to an accompanying expectation (140–212).

Value was the peculiar relation between any interest and its object, or the special character of an object which interested someone (115–21). Perry accordingly differentiated facts (the characters ascribed to objects) and values (the attitudes of subjects to objects), distinguishing between describing the world and various acts of approving. Both cognition and valuation were dispositions to behave in specified ways to specified objects. But truth and error, associated only with cognition, depended on the presence or absence of appropriate objects for which cognitive activity prepared us. This activity was independent of any attitude of favor or disfavor with which we viewed the presence or absence of the object. Finally, in valuation the object disposed us to bring it into being; in cognition we were only ready to deal with it if it existed; valuing always promoted its object. The difference was that between acting on an event and for it. Although Perry dichotomized fact and value, he maintained neither that valuation was "relative" or "subjectivistic," nor that its study was non-empirical. Where individuals exercised preference, values simply existed; they were not true or false; a motor-affective act conferred value. But, Perry went on, value theory studied judgments *about* interests. Although these might be individual interests, the judgments were nonetheless true or false, empirically verifiable and not mere opinions (306–21). The judgment that X was good might only be true or false for one person—he might or might not value X—but whether X was good for him was empirically ascertainable.

Determining both the true and the good was an "objective" enterprise for Perry. Consonant with his realism, however he had defined it in the 1920s, the being and nature of an object were independent of consciousness and of its possessing value, while its possessing value was consciousness-dependent. Without organisms, the physical world would exist; values would not. Value depended on the appropriate activity of an organism, in fact just that sort of activity which defined mind or consciousness. But although mind and value grew up together, joining value to consciousness did not relativize value: values were "objective" because they were inter-subjectively verifiable.[10]

At the end of his book Perry discussed what he called the critique of value, the attempt to rank some values as better than others. We knew that 'X is good' was true in the sense that someone actually valued X. Perry now wished to know the condition of the object in which interest was taken in order for it to have comparative or superlative value. Perry here returned to the crux of *The Moral Economy*, an analysis of the ground of morality, of how we determined the binding values. At this stage in his argument, Perry's successors contended, he went off the rails by attempting to show that we could adjudicate among different values in a way that would rationally require people to adopt some of them, that is, adopt certain modes of behavior.* Perry intended to discriminate the principles permitting us to rank values. But he was not simply unearthing the standards implicit in our activity but also setting standards that would determine activity's comparative value. Perhaps the fairest thing to say is that he did not distinguish between describing and justifying the principles governing comparative value.[11]

Interest was a quantity for Perry and, therefore, in some respects measurable. In examining "the condition of an object" that made it better than another, he claimed we found more value. Valuing objects in varying ways, we measured the value invested in some cases and said that more or less was involved. Perry discovered three standards of measurement— intensity, preference, and inclusiveness. The last standard connected with the account in *The Moral Economy*: one interest was more inclusive than another if it was the interest of more objects than the other. This quantitative principle did not require that the interests be those of one subject or that their object be the same. Appealing to this dimension alone, Perry said, a man who liked cats and dogs had a more inclusive interest than a woman who liked only canaries and so his interest was more valuable in this respect. Drinking water and using it to bathe were more valuable than merely drinking it, other things being equal.

---

*See Stevenson, *Ethics and Language* (New Haven: Yale University Press, 1944), pp. 268–71. Any discussion of this issue would carry us into more recent controversies, but the interested reader may pursue its history in George C. Kerner, *The Revolution in Ethical Theory* (Oxford: Oxford University Press, 1966), William Frankena, *Ethics* (Englewood Cliffs, N.J.: Prentice-Hall Publishers, 1967), and G. J. Warnock, *Contemporary Moral Philosophy* (New York: St. Martins Press, 1967). A recent collection of articles is W. D. Hudson, ed., *The Is/Ought Question* (London: Macmillan and Co., 1969). Unfortunately, none of these books considers the work of Perry's colleague, C. I. Lewis, in *An Analysis of Knowledge and Valuation* (LaSalle, Ill.: Open Court Publishing Co., 1946). Lewis, developed an empirical theory of value (pp. 365–554) but distinguished it from a theory of obligation. The reader may exhume the latter from Lewis's collected papers found in *Values and Imperatives*, ed. John Lange (Stanford: Stanford University Press, 1969) and in CPCIL, pp. 151–227. The reader might also consult Thomas Nagel, *The Possibility of Altruism* (Oxford: Clarendon Press, 1970), a book to which some attention has been paid because it ably resurrects cognitivism; students of the history of ethics in America will peruse it with a sense of déjà vu.

Perry closely connected the other two standards, preference and intensity. It is best to let him distinguish them:

> Any given concrete interest, such as Robinson's thirst for water, may wax or wane, or vary in degree of excitement. Let us speak of this variable magnitude as the intensity of the thirst. Now suppose Robinson, still governed by thirst, to be solicited by several alternatives, such as wine, cold water and tepid water, all of which are eligible, that is, promise the satisfaction of his thirst. Robinson then prefers wine to cold water, and cold to tepid water. He does not, strictly speaking, desire one *more* than another, but one *rather than* another. Preference expresses itself in the form, "this is more to my taste than that," rather than the form, "my taste for this is stronger than my taste for that." That such an order of preference is distinguished from the scale of intensities seems to follow from several generally recognized facts. In the first place, the minimal point of one series is not the same as the minimal point of the other. The minimal intensity in interest is the point at which the interest rises above the threshold of apathy. Thus, for example, the interest of the thirsty man in tepid water diminishes in intensity as he drinks it, until, beyond a certain point, it ceases to appeal to him at all. When, on the other hand, we speak of his interest in tepid water as least in the order of preference, we mean that he drinks it only in default of cold water or wine. It represents a minimum of interest in the sense that while tepid water displaces none of the class of eligible objects, it is itself displaced by all of the others. This difference between "intenser than" and "preferred to" is further confirmed by their independent variability. As the interest in tepid water rises in the scale of intensity, it does not rise in the order of preference and take the place of cold water or wine. The interest of the very thirsty man in tepid water may reach any degree of intensity, and still remain least in the order of preference. Furthermore, in order to determine the place of an object in the order of preference one attempts to equalize and discount the intensity of their appeal. When finely discriminating preferences are made the alternatives are "considered," so as to hold them at the same distance; or only nascently adopted, so that there may be a rapid oscillation among them (616–17).

Perry showed that we had a limited ability to measure comparative goodness. His ordering was complex, but he argued, for example, that while an intense interest was incommensurable with a preferred one, where there was "equality" in respect of one dimension, increase in the other yielded an increase in total value. Moreover, if interests were equally inclusive, the more intense was the better, or if we preferred two interests equally, the more inclusive was the better. Finally, Perry established priorities for applying his standards (625–28).

This calculus did not allow for solving moral problems through computation, and Perry was now no longer a utilitarian. Consider James's case of millions of people kept permanently happy on the condition that a certain lost soul should lead a life of lonely torture. On the greatest happiness principle, we could not object to the morality of this arrangement. But Perry said: "As co-exclusive, the claims [interests] of the lost soul and of the happy millions are incommensurable." We might assume them to be equally intense but the preferences were opposed and therefore incomparable. "To declare the good of the millions to be greater than the evil of the one would ignore this incomparability" (670–71). Situations like these manifested the need for a "postulate of concurrence." This postulate, added to Perry's three standards, entailed that we moved in the direction of utilitarianism: we persuaded each person to moderate his interests so that we provided for everyone's. The happy millions gave up a portion of their happiness to benefit the lonely soul and won his approval. We resolved moral dilemmas when, and only when, everyone's will was so attuned that each was content with a situation in which all benefited. This postulate's most familiar application, Perry continued, occurred in democratic political conflict. The justification of majority rule lay not in its numerical superiority but in a general willingness to abide by the majority's will (672–73).

In the above case, Perry was not pretending to deal with actual moral conflict but with justifying democratic procedures and constructing an ethical ideal. This construction connected him to previous Harvard moral philosophers. The highest good would exist in a society where, first, each individual developed a harmonious personality. In this situation every person adopted plans of action embracing and synthesizing all conflicting personal interests: the standard of inclusiveness allowed us to say that such a personality was better than a conflicted one. He used the same standard to argue that a harmonious group of individuals was better than a conflicted group. A group like this existed if each person achieved "socially qualified" personal integration—where one achieved personal harmony only if universal benevolence guided him. The "All Benevolent Will" involved was common only in having common objects: the concern for all satisfied each. The result was a cooperative federation in which the community of interests and personal integration were one (659–85).

Perry appeared to say that this peculiar personal accord defined the deity:

> . . . while the perfected will is thus in form and structure a personal will, it is socially qualified in a double sense. On the one hand, it must have all mankind as its preferred object; and, on the other hand, it must be reaffirmed, repeated and reiterated by all individual members of mankind. It is not a social will, but it is a personal will socially directed and socially multiplied. It is a preferred will because it is everybody's good will towards everybody. It is a will in which it is reasonable for all to concur, not because of some occult property or authoritative sanction, but because such general concurrence is reasonable. God is not a glory that justifies the damnation of men, except in so far as men are participants in the glory and are *willing* to be damned for it. This peculiar accord of persons loses nothing from the fact that it cannot properly be termed a person. The demand that God shall be a person is only the last of the anthropomorphisms by which man has compromised God by the desire to worship him. When persons live in accord the total situation is something greater than a person, as truly as an organism is something greater than a cell (685–86).

God was, it seemed, a type of emergence founded on personal life but not adequately conceived as mind or personality. The social order in which he emerged was ideal, a construct which nonetheless expressed a truth. Perry argued against Royce that neither God nor the evil which he overcame was necessary. Rather, God was "a norm of legitimate aspiration." With James, Perry concluded, "God is a being far exceeding and surpassing man, and yet dependent on man's moral effort. The world becomes divine through being willed to be divine, and . . . its being divine is conditioned by the dynamic faith through which high resolves are carried into effect. God's existence may in this sense result from a belief *in* God, though not from a belief that God already exists" (687–89).

General Theory of Value was critical to professional dispute in the 1930s, but Perry was sixty-eight when *Ethics and Language* appeared in 1944—two years from retirement—and had no students the equal of Stevenson. Perry's Jamesean speculations on the deity marked him as a man of another generation, while the technical acumen of *Ethics and Language* satisfied professional standards and seemed applicable to the pluralism and chaos of the post-war world. When an aging Perry published *Realms of Value* in 1954, there was scarcely a ripple of excitement among professional philosophers. Stevenson had won, and Harvard ethics had ceased to be viable.

27

ALFRED NORTH WHITEHEAD

Life, Concerns, and Career at Harvard

Alfred North Whitehead was born in Ramsgate, England, in 1861, the son of a clergyman and a descendant of educators. At fourteen he went to the Sherborne School and then to Trinity College, Cambridge, in 1880. At twenty-four he became a fellow of Trinity and started a successful academic career. Like past generations of his family, Whitehead led an impressively placid and pleasant existence. His marriage braced him, and his wife dedicated herself to making good his fortunes. He reached maturity in all the splendor and security of Victorian England. He once remarked that he never really felt out of step with his culture, and his later life in the United States bore him out: he was serene, kindly, and seemingly imperturbable. Bertrand Russell said that "something of the vicarage atmosphere" always lingered in Whitehead's ways of feeling, but it is fairer to say that he embodied the best and most benign of the Anglo-American social conventions.[1] In 1910 he moved to London and from 1911 to 1923 occupied various positions at University College and the Imperial College of Science and Technology.

Although Whitehead had read much philosophy and was a fellow of Trinity during an intensely creative speculative period, he made his reputation as a mathematical logician and contributor to esoteric work in the conceptual foundations of geometry and relativity theory. His first book, the 1898 *Treatise on Universal Algebra*, was a pioneer survey of the new logic. With his pupil, Bertrand Russell, Whitehead was co-author of *Principia Mathematica* (1912), although in concentrating on the blinding insights of his student, commentators often underemphasized Whitehead's working out of these insights. While he developed an interest in the philosophy of science during the First World War, in 1924 at the age of sixty-three he appeared to be in the twilight of a striking but not dazzling scholarly life.

In 1924, however, Lawrence Lowell made an astutely intelligent administrative judgment. Inspired by the promise of a friend of the department to fund Whitehead's salary, Lowell offered him an initial five-year professorship at Harvard. Whitehead accepted, and in the next decade Cambridge almost exploded with his philosophic activity. He recalled that Harvard "made it possible for me to express ideas which had been growing in my thoughts for a lifetime."[2] In 1925 there was *Science and the Modern World*, in 1929 *Process and Reality*, and in 1933 *Adventures of Ideas*, as well as many more. Harvard waived its retirement rules, and Whitehead did not step down until 1937 when he was seventy-six, and he remained in the United States until his death in 1947. Although very much a contemporary thinker, Whitehead was a giant from another era—he was born two years before Münsterberg and only six years after Royce—and his mere presence did much to reinvigorate philosophy in Cambridge.

For many reasons it is impossible even to sketch Whitehead's development as a thinker or his mature metaphysics. First of all, he was exceptionally productive in a variety of fields. At Trinity he had explored the new logic and its consequences for the foundations of physics. While in London he examined the philosophy of science, both formally and informally. At Harvard he elaborated a comprehensive philosophical system. Moreover, throughout his career he developed what one scholar has called a "philosophy of civilization"—ruminations on the rise of world culture, history, education, and social relations.[3] Second, for a thinker of his genius and stature, Whitehead was careless, even slovenly, in preparing his work for publication. In one part of the *Universal Algebra* he referred the reader to an appendix, but did not attach the appendix. The typographical mistakes in *Process and Reality* created a small scholarly business: Whitehead's negligence in reading proof left over two hundred errors upon many of which experts still disagree; these misprints alone make for interpretive problems. This Whiteheadian habit has compounded the problems of all expositors.

Finally, Whitehead was a writer of inordinate difficulty. Although knowledgeable in philosophy, he came to its study late in life and tended to view received opinions about the source of philosophic tensions, even those with pedigrees, as misguided and off the mark. He consequently invented his own conceptual apparatus and vocabulary which would allow him, he hoped, to avoid the pervasive mistakes of the past. Unfortunately he was inconsistent and often vague in using his neologisms. Whitehead's exposition was also painfully abstract. Although he was greatly concerned that previous philosophy had ignored concrete experience, he wrote in concepts, as he put it, and often seemed unable to illustrate what he had in mind. Whitehead's manner of expression was unusual, too. Although sometimes vigorously epigrammatic, he was occasionally oracular and frequently obscure, almost incomprehensible to all but his most devoted followers. In addition to the difficulties of his language, his style was dense and cryptic. Whitehead himself acknowledged that in pursuing a philosophy so comprehensive as his, something must give: he sacrificed clarity for scope.* The problems of language and vocabulary make it nearly impossible to explicate Whitehead's ideas without embracing his entire framework of thought.

I have not even attempted to give an account of Whitehead's less technical work. It was a current running through the greater part of his writing career and one venerated by some followers. But his remarks on society came from a satisfied and uncritical perspective, and there was nothing in them that could not be found in the work of many undistinguished authors. He based his views on the rise of world civilization on his bedtime reading of history, and philosophers accepted his belief in the importance of thought to culture more because Whitehead affirmed their prejudices than because he presented any evidence for his belief. Whitehead's *Lebensphilosophie* freeloaded from his repute as a metaphysician, and its principal supporters were men who, like Whitehead, had neither lived in the world of affairs nor studied it with any care.

I have tried to suggest Whitehead's main concerns in two periods of his development, the second "London period" in which he took up the

---

*Whitehead's effect on subsequent philosophical discussion has been curious. His impact has been almost exclusively in the United States, and there it has been non-existent in most large graduate schools and extreme everywhere else. The exegetical literature surrounding his work is enormous; the previously mentioned study of the corrigenda for *Process and Reality* is a minor subsidiary of a major industry.

philosophy of science and the third "Harvard period" in which he placed his philosophy of science within a grand speculative system.

In a sense Whitehead does not fit this book because his connection with the Harvard philosophers who came before him was, I think, non-existent;[4] even his connection to the history of modern philosophy was uncertain. But there are two helpful points to keep in mind. First, at the turn of the century Whitehead and Royce worked in the same context of logical investigation. Although Royce did not influence Whitehead, both men saw the study of logic as the study of ever broader relational systems, the broadest one reflecting the processes of rational thought and, somehow, the structural principles governing the order of the universe. We must see Whitehead's philosophy in the context of the architectonic of this early twentieth-century vision of logic. The central idea was to extract from experience a single abstract set of concepts. Although these concepts came from experience and were rooted in it, in large measure they had *a priori* authority over experience. If the philosopher did his job properly, this conceptual set would adequately account for the most fundamental and enduring aspects of experience, and he could "deduce" from it the more limited features of experience.

The relation of Whitehead's thought to Royce's is structural only. In connecting Whitehead to James—the second point—we are still dealing with a structural similarity although there is a slender basis in the texts for arguing that James influenced Whitehead. The evils of philosophic abstractionalism haunted James; to make sense of the world philosophers were compelled to go to concrete experience. This was the message of his radical empiricism, and *A Pluralistic Universe* urged that people must see the *durée* of life and that perhaps the only way to see it was through the mystic's wordless empathy with being. Whitehead followed James's emphasis on the concrete: the Englishman's philosophy of science argued that we must extract the elements of the scientific world view from ordinary experience; his metaphysics gave primacy to experience as lived, as process.

In its broadest contours Whitehead's thought was an attempt to synthesize the tendency to logical architectonic (characteristic of Royce) with the drive to account for the immediate (characteristic of James). Whitehead's connection with his Harvard colleagues symbolized the two poles of his thought. He and Hocking conducted two joint seminars and their good relations stemmed in part from their joint respect for immediate experience. Whitehead and Lewis met on different ground in their mutual respect for the Roycean problem of the categories.[5]

The Middle Period

The three books Whitehead wrote in the period immediately before coming to Harvard—*An Enquiry Concerning the Principles of Natural Knowledge* (1919), *The Concept of Nature* (1920), and *The Principle of Relativity* (1922)—constituted his treatment of the philosophy of science independent of metaphysics. Impressed by the working scientist's view that he discovered truths about nature, that he knew things as they are, Whitehead proclaimed that nature was closed to mind.[6] In one sense this meant that the mind to which nature appeared did not itself contribute in determining the character of events. In cognizing events, mind placed nothing in nature; it rather encountered what was there or exposed by inference what must be there although it was not at once apparent. We knew nature and investigated it without considering how we came to know it. There was a physical world that behaved according to certain principles or laws whether or not men or other conscious beings were present to observe it. In this sense the problem of natural science was to discover the kind of world this was and the relations and laws underlying its functioning.[7]

Whitehead was not just a naive realist. In another sense the point was that we could treat the philosophy of science as a self-contained field for certain limited purposes: "The *values* of nature are perhaps the key to the metaphysical synthesis of existence. But such a synthesis is exactly what I am not attempting." We left the connection of man and nature to metaphysics: "We are concerned only with Nature, that is with the object of perceptual knowledge, and not with the synthesis of the knower with the known. The distinction is exactly that which separates natural philosophy from metaphysics."[8]

The primary target of Whitehead's polemic was the doctrine of.the representational realists. Arguing that we were aware only of the contents of consciousness, Cartesian philosophy postulated the real (scientific) world as the cause or ground of sensations. Consequently, we knew nature only through mind and must believe that what (directly) confronted us existed only "in our heads." Whitehead said this view presupposed a vicious "bifurcation of nature." Causal nature became an unseen Lucretian universe of whirling particles which determined the apparent nature of consciousness. In these circumstances scientists never perceived the nature they investigated; and the nature on which they experimented was not only merely "apparent" but also dependent on the consciousness of the experimenter.

The problem Whitehead confronted was the relation of scientific knowledge to ordinary experience. I saw a black cow in the field; the scientist discovered things as they are, but what he discovered did not resemble the cow I saw. Where I found an animal whose movements were dictated by a desire for food, he found a swarm of atomic particles whose motion was described by some complex physical law. In Whitehead's philosophy of science, we must find in nature everything we observe: "We may not pick and choose. For us the red glow of the sunset should be as much part of nature as are the molecules and electric waves by which men of science would explain the phenomenon. It is for natural philosophy to analyse how these various elements of nature are connected." "The reason why the bifurcation of nature is always creeping back into scientific philosophy is the extreme difficulty of exhibiting the perceived redness and warmth of the fire in one system of relations with the agitated molecules of carbon and oxygen."[9]

Whitehead was also contemptuous of more recent Kantians whom he viewed as followers of Descartes. They argued that the entities of science were our constructions, calculating devices of a sort, used to predict and control our experience. Scientific entities did not really exist in the way that the cow existed, said the constructionalists, but were a way of saying something else true of nature. "But surely," said Whitehead, "if it is something else that you mean, for heaven's sake say it."[10] We must regard the concepts reflecting the systematic and orderly aspect of experience as arising from experience itself, the mind being just the function of the experiencing self which extracted the formal elements. Whitehead had to find the most abstract scientific objects, and therefore the highest structural principles embodying our knowledge, in concrete experience.

Nature was composed of events, what actually happened in nature.

Whitehead viewed the nature we experienced as in a state of passage: events were the *becoming* of nature—they happened then and there, and each one was just itself, unique and unchanging. Events passed, however, and larger events swallowed them up and extended over them. Whitehead said the passage of events was "extension in the making," where extension was spatio-temporal extension. Events *were* the field of extension: passing events defined extension; it was an aspect of events which, considered apart from them, were the continua of space and time; the latter were derived entities.[11]

By 'object' Whitehead meant not only ordinary physical objects, but also something like the peculiar blue situated in a coat and, of course, scientific objects. All objects had a special relation to events called ingression—it helped to make an event what it was. As "ingredient" in events, objects were permanent, although they also changed—they had a series of relations to events. In a sense objects were not really in space and time: they were only derivatively so in virtue of their relation to events; we discriminated or "prescinded" objects from their background of fact.[12] We simply perceived some objects as ingredient in events, but scientific objects were not simply perceived. They were abstractions, Whitehead said, but abstractions found *in* nature, *in* events. Although we did not perceive them, we inferred them because they expressed how it was that events conditioned one another. Scientific objects expressed "the causal character of events." These objects were important because they explained the connection of events throughout nature. The causal relations that scientific objects defined were accordingly implicit in the deliverances of experience. Scientific objects could be the cause of certain phenomena by constituting the phenomena; they were part of the event with which they were causally implicated. This was Whitehead's answer to Hume.

What Whitehead called "the method of extensive abstraction" described how it was that we could find scientific objects in nature; it explained why it was justifiable to claim that scientific objects were ingredients in events, although they were not perceived. To prevent the bifurcation of nature we must exhibit all objects in one relational system, and the method showed how we could derive scientific objects from experience's actual events.[13] Although a complete account of the method involved a great deal of mathematics—as far as Whitehead scholars have successfully explicated it—we must roughly indicate what it was about.

Events included one another, and Whitehead formed a set of events called an abstractive class in which "(i) of any two of its members one extends over the other, and (ii) there is no event which is extended over by every event in the set." He had formed a series of events converging without limit to the small end. An event with no spatial bound was a duration—a time slice of the whole world—and we could consider an abstractive set of durations—they converged to all nature at a moment, an instant.[14]

Drawing on his reformulation of relativity theory, Whitehead held that durations belonging to diverse time systems intersected. Because the durations intersected, their respective moments did also, and the intersection of the intersection of two moments was, Whitehead said, a "level"—the flat plane of Euclidean geometry.[15] But this Euclidean element and the others "derived" from it were ideal elements and just those at the basis of the scientists' investigations. Whitehead developed his method in much greater detail and complexity, but we are in a position to see the point of his enterprise. Like James he was a radical empiricist: everything in the universe was in what we experienced. But working in the same logico-geometrical paradigm as Royce, Whitehead unearthed abstract objects in experience, and he thought this a significant enterprise because these objects were crucial in explaining the conjunction of events. The order of the spatio-temporal world derived from these scientific objects. Against Hume, Whitehead found causal relations in experience.

Whatever the merits of Whitehead's enterprise, it suffered from a central inadequacy as he recognized and as commentators later pointed out: the closure of nature to mind was leaky; some of the natural entities seemed permeated with the mental. In short, he was not able to keep metaphysics out of his epistemology. A good example of Whitehead's trouble was the view that it entailed of scientific progress. Scientific objects—at least the ones Whitehead found by extensive abstraction—were in nature. But unless future science never superseded them he must eventually say they were not really to be found in nature.[16] Or to put it another way: presumably a Greek Whiteheadian should have been able to find the objects of ancient science in nature, but since we have superseded this science, we apparently could not now find them in nature. One easy way to solve this problem was to distinguish between a conceptual framework and raw experience, but this was, in Whitehead's view, constructionalism—an attenuated but still destructive form of bifurcation.

Most broadly, the problem was that in denying the bifurcation of nature, Whitehead wanted to unify the system of ordinary experience (what others identified with consciousness) and of scientific objects (the realm of nature). If he succeeded, however, mind and nature were part of a single system: nature was open to mind. On many interpretations, closing nature to mind and denying nature's bifurcation were contradictory. When conflicts arose within his philosophy of science, Whitehead tended to permit something like a bifurcation but simultaneously to discount it by effectively allowing mind and nature to condition one another. To explain problems connected with scientific change, we might regard scientific objects as hypothetical entities, conceptual constructs. This strategy did not bifurcate nature, for both apparent and real nature were infused with mind: we insured that both apparent nature (what some thought was in our heads) and real nature (conceptual constructs) were of one (mental) piece.[17] But we then gave up the separation of epistemology and metaphysics. In *Science and the Modern World* (1925) and *Symbolism* (1926), Whitehead moved in this direction. *Science and the Modern World* still left open the possibility of treating nature independently of mind, but the ultimate units of his philosophy were "actual occasions" with both physical and ideational factors. Natural events became abstractions of a sort because they excluded certain fundamental non-physical properties, and Whitehead said he was elaborating a metaphysical position.[18] A year later in *Symbolism* he argued there was no proper line between the physical and mental constitution of experience.[19] He rejected the possibility of isolating the philosophy of science from metaphysics.

In *Process and Reality* (1929), Whitehead resolved the problems generated by his epistemology by systematically joining mind and nature. He already had the essential concepts for such a reform in his earlier fundamental idea of events, and in *Science and the Modern World* he had attacked the substantiality of matter by noting the fallacies of "simple location" and of "misplaced concreteness."[20] But in 1929 both substance and consciousness became aspects of something more basic than event—process.

First Philosophy

In *Process and Reality* and Whitehead's other avowedly metaphysical works, the events and objects of his earlier philosophy of science had their descendants in actual entities and eternal objects. But he transformed the earlier conceptions in a complex fashion, and for purposes of this outline it is better to treat the later ones independently.

Process and Reality began with finite actual entities, "actual occasions" (135). Each such microcosmic entity was an organism that grew, matured, and perished. But while each had a unique structure, these atoms were not substances but activities immanent in one another. Whitehead's models for his actual occasions were the instantaneous moments of human experience; he was philosophizing in a Jamesean mode. For like James he believed that acquaintance with reality "grows literally by beads or drops of perception"; "you can divide these into components, but as immediately given, they come totally or not at all" (105–06). But human experience was only the model. The problem was to elucidate the structure and relations of actual entities and then to explain human experience through them. Whitehead was developing his own radical empiricism: his metaphysics would elucidate how actual entities formed the process which was the world.

Concrescence, a "growing together" of various experiential details into a unity, defined the structural activity essential to an actual occasion's being. The actual occasion *prehended* some other entity, making it an object of the actual occasion's experience. This physical prehension initiated each concrescence, and from what was physically felt, a purely conceptual prehension was derived, the potentiality eventually exemplified by the actual occasion (372). The prehension or "concrete fact of relatedness" had a subject (the actual occasion), an object (the other entity prehended), and a subjective form (the manner in which the subject prehended the object—forms of emotion, consciousness, purpose, and so on). The result of prehension fulfilled the occasion's subjective aim, a teleological quest for a unity of experience; achieving this unity satisfied the occasion.

The living experience of an actual occasion was its subjective immediacy. Each occasion had such a moment of life, but it then became an object for succeeding actual occasions; they prehended it and it then had objective immortality. In reference to other things, the actual occasion was not a subject but a superject (443): the objective immortality of an occasion was the superject of its experiences (43). When one occasion prehended another, the first eliminated certain elements in the second's real constitution (321); objectification made the full constitution of the objectified occasion irrelevant (97). The first felt positively some aspect of the second's experience, and although every occasion was so prehended, none was so prehended in its entirety (66, 335, 366). Whitehead said there were two species of prehensions—positive and negative. The positive ones were like those pointed out above whereby the subject definitely included an item of another actual occasion in the subject's own real internal constitution, and he called them feelings. But all items were either positively or negatively prehended, that is, they were included or definitely excluded (65–66).

An occasion's satisfaction was the outcome of its internal process of becoming and led to the transition to the future. Accordingly, the satisfaction stood between two processes, a pause in the midst of flux, an anticipation of the future in the present.[21] To summarize Whitehead's doctrine thus far,

> The individual immediacy of an occasion is the final unity of subjective form, which is the occasion as an absolute reality. This immediacy is its moment of sheer individuality, bounded on either side by essential relativity. The occasion arises from relevant objects, and perishes into the status of an object for other occasions. But it enjoys its decisive moment of absolute self-attainment as emotional unity. As used here the words 'individual' and 'atom' have the same meaning, that they apply to composite things with an absolute reality which their components lack. These words properly apply to an actual entity in its immediacy of self-attainment when it stands out as for itself alone, with its own affective self-enjoyment. The term 'monad' also expresses this essential unity at the decisive moment, which stands between its birth and its perishing.[22]

The satisfactions contained the occasion's temporal duration, Whitehead said, for the process that produced the occasion was not in physical time (105–08, 433–38): "the subjective unity dominating the process forbids the division of that extensive quantum which originates with the primary phase of the subjective aim" (434). In producing their satisfactions, occasions produced the temporally extended world. The drops of experience gave rise to the continuity of physical time by succeeding one another, but duration, as a feature of the occasion's experience, was "time lived," not "time measured."[23] Concrescence was not in time; but time was in concrescence—an abstraction from actual occasions. This was Whitehead's epochal theory of time.

Speaking of actual occasions as occasions of experience uses language more loosely than Whitehead did in *Process and Reality*.[24] The usage prejudices the question whether he was a panpsychist. *Process and Reality* carefully noted that a conscious act of experience was only one sort of prehending entity. An actual occasion need not be conscious of what it prehended or be conscious of itself (35, 83). Prehensive activity permeated all reality—the phrase referred to the being of stones and electrons, and Whitehead did not attribute consciousness to them or the occasions comprising them. Human experience was only one advanced form of organization of actual occasions. At the same time all occasions were teleological structures of activity, and it is difficult to say why 'psyche' would be inappropriate to describe them. Whitehead did maintain, however, that consciousness presupposed (his widened) experience and not experience consciousness. Kant conceived experiential unity, Whitehead argued, "in the guise of modes of thought" (172); "the philosophy of organism is the inversion of Kant's philosophy. . . . For Kant, the world emerges from the [conscious] subject; for the philosophy of organism the [conscious] subject emerges from the world" (135–36).

Before we examine how microscopic actual occasions eventuated in human experience, we must indicate the role that eternal objects, the other basic conception in Whitehead's system, played in an occasion's life.

There were three "formative" elements in his later philosophy—God, creativity, and eternal objects; the universe of actual occasions emerged from their mutual interaction. Eternal objects were pure potentials or forms of definiteness; an actual occasion exemplified an eternal object, and it ingressed or participated in the occasion (63). The second phase of concrescence of an actual occasion, that of conceptual prehension, had as its datum the eternal object that the physical feeling exemplified (372, 379). Basically, eternal objects functioned for Whitehead as the means by which prehension took place: they determined how the world of actual occasions entered into the constitution of each of its members (93). The data of the prehension were absorbed into actual occasions in virtue of eternal objects that the objectified actuality and the experient subject shared (78).

Whitehead said that eternal objects participated in occasions, and we could consider eternal objects in themselves: we abstracted the notion of an eternal object from the ingression of eternal objects in particular actual occasions. As forms of definiteness of actuality, eternal objects existed as pure possibilities of ingression. An eternal object was *in* an actual occasion or, as Whitehead said, it was a form of definiteness.[25]

Transmutation was the operation whereby an occasion prehended an aggregate of actual occasions not as an aggregate—a many—but as a unity. Roughly, a concrescing subject might have a conceptual prehension with a single eternal object as its datum. But this eternal object might characterize an aggregate of past actual occasions from which the conceptual prehension derived; the conceptual prehension had impartial relevance to them all.[26] The resulting actual occasion was aware of one "macrocosmic" entity where before there were many microcosmic entities. The actual entities so transmuted, Whitehead said, formed a nexus:

> A nexus is a set of actual entities in the unity of the relatedness constituted by their prehensions of each other, or—what is the same thing conversely expressed—constituted by their objectifications in each other (35).

> A nexus of many actualities can be treated as though it were one actuality. This is what we habitually do in the case of the span of life of a molecule, or of a piece of rock, or of a human body (439).

Nexūs were normally four-dimensional. A generation of actual entities spatially related in a three-dimensional pattern might compose a rock at any given moment. But we usually considered the rock as temporally extended, and the total nexus that was the rock was temporally thick—composed of succeeding generations of actual entities. Moreover, there was also a limiting type of nexus, a purely temporal kind lacking spatial dimensions; it included no pair of contemporary occasions and defined a thread of temporal transitions from occasion to occasion. Whitehead said this was a personally ordered nexus; nexūs with personal order were central to understanding those aggregates of occasions we referred to as persons.

Whitehead delineated various types of a sub-species of nexūs with "social order," or societies (50–51). Like Royce before him, Whitehead worked out the metaphysical implications of the Erlanger Program as he saw them. There were a hierarchy of societies, of socially ordered nexūs.

From a logical perspective a few defining axioms described the general type of relatedness binding together the occasions of a vast cosmic epoch. Adding axioms defined the characteristics of a more limited society, and within this society, for example, there might be various narrower sub-societies defined by additional axioms (136–57). So Whitehead elaborated the order systems describing how actual entities related to produce the diversity of the world.

We may analyze one aspect of these ideas in more detail. For limited purposes, Whitehead now accepted Hume's analysis of causation. In abstracting nature from life, he believed that the simple correlations of successions of data might be satisfactory for natural science.[27] Whitehead also agreed that Hume was justified in demanding that we analyze causation as an element of experience. If we were interested in understanding the real world's concrete processes, however, Hume's view was inadequate, for we had direct intuition of causality in experience (253). On the microcosmic level physical prehension was a causal act. The actual occasion that was the initial datum was the "cause," the prehension the "effect," an aspect of the conditioning of the concrescing subject by the intitial datum (361). The power of one actual occasion on another was simply how the former was objectified in the constitution of the latter (91). Causality was the presence of one actual occasion in another; as in his earlier work, the whole structure of Whitehead's mature system implied that causality was *in* experience, something primary and basic.

These observations of the microscopic level connected with the causal relations we dealt with in (macroscopic) experience. Whitehead spoke of physical prehension as "perception in the mode of causal efficacy." It was the basic mode of inheritance of feeling from past data, and it transmitted vague, massive, and inarticulate feelings of the efficaciousness of the past (184–85). There was another mode of perception—that of presentational immediacy—in effect, the mode to which Hume limited himself. This mode presupposed the most general kind of social ordering of actual occasions (101–03). Because it confined itself to contemporary actual entities, it was free of causality, although in concentrating on it alone Hume could not justly analyze perception. Hume demonstrated only what Whitehead accepted: actual entities in the contemporary universe were causally independent (188). In ordinary perception we did not experience either of these modes. We experienced a mixed mode compounded from the more primitive ones, the mixed mode of symbolic reference. What was this mixed mode? When we perceived the contemporary nexus in the mode of presentational immediacy, we perceived it "defined by sensa." But we did not perceive the sensa themselves in the mode of presentational immediacy; they were rather donated from the mode of causal efficacy and "projected" onto the contemporary nexus: ordinary experience was a compound of modes.*

Creativity and God

Of the three "formative" elements of *Process and Reality*, we have only touched on one, eternal objects. Whitehead explained the second, creativity, in a few enigmatic passages. It was the principle immanent in the ever-renewed coming-to-be of actual occasions. The universe moved through the unity of a fresh concrescence to overcome the plurality of past actual occasions; but the process of prehension was ongoing and produced a multitude of novel unique occasions. Creativity thus described the unending process in which the movement to transcend the many gave rise to a new many, a new diversity. Actual occasions were not independent of or separate from one another. But the perpetual advance to future occasions constantly transformed the drive toward monistic unity (10–11, 31–32).

The last formative element was God. He was an actual entity exhibiting all the characters of the other (finite) actual entities, the actual occasions, but God also exemplified the analyses of Whitehead's system (521). Whatever else may be said of Whitehead's God, he proved fecund of a scholarly literature, and we can here give only an undetailed summary.

God was a non-temporal actual entity because while actual occasions originated with physical prehensions, God originated with conceptual prehensions of the timeless realm of eternal objects. This was his primordial nature; God had appetition for the realization of—that is, he valued—every possibility in the multiplicity of eternal objects, and they therefore became relevant to one another (48). Unlike other actual entities, God did not have negative prehensions; his subjective forms did not require eliminations from his data. God's primordial nature was responsible

*This is all too brief and cryptic. For one elementary but modestly intelligible account, see *A Key to Whitehead's Process and Reality*, ed. Donald W. Sherburne (Bloomington: Indiana University Press, 1966), pp. 113–14.

for his role as a formative element in Whitehead's system. The subjective aim of actual occasions was the direction taken by each concrescing subject in constituting the being of the occasion: the occasion did not exist before its concrescence; its being was its becoming. Because every concrescence was *causa sui*, its subjective aim formulated the exact sort of entity it would make itself. Nonetheless, the concrescence derived this aim from an objective lure which God provided; the aim was a transformed version of the lure, that is, the aim more or less completely followed the lure in that way of becoming most in line with God's own aim of realizing every eternal object (374). The divine actuality elicited and evoked the self-creativity of the concrescence itself.

As well as being primordial, God was also consequent. Actual occasions proceeded from physical prehensions to conceptual ones. But in God this process was reversed: he was completed as his physical prehensions of actual occasions integrated his conceptual prehensions. The process of physical prehension was his consequent nature. God realized the world in the unity of his nature (523–26), but his satisfaction was in one sense incomplete: it always included appetition for unrealized possibilities, and new data were ever being prehended. But if God was incompletely actualized in this sense, his satisfaction was always complete at any moment.[28]

Whitehead said the religious question was whether the temporal process passed into other actualities, bound together in an order in which novelty did not mean loss (517). In his notion of God, he outlined an answer. Because God was an actual entity, he was not a person—a complex ordering of actual occasions—and so there was no question of losing individuality, the uniqueness of actual occasions, in a personal organic whole. At the same time, while God was always in concrescence (and always satisfied), novel actual occasions were always becoming, and there was no fully actual totality, ruling out other forms of monism. Nonetheless, God preserved past achievements, giving continuity and solidity to the world, and the subjective aim of all actual occasions derived from his primordial nature so that he also grounded the continuity of future becomings. Because God's aim was the maximal intensity of experience for himself and the world, his concrescence resulted in an ordering of possibilities in the divine experience. But nature's course was not necessary: the creative self-determinations of immediately past occasions and God's self-determination jointly effected each new concrescence. We had an order that was always proceeding to completion without loss of novelty.

There is a majesty in the development of Whitehead's system—even when viewed in this abruptly truncated form—and it was not strange that for many professional philosophers he became not merely a major thinker with whom dialogue was possible but even something of a cult figure. Whitehead also wanted to speak to the educated public on larger issues, but he limited his work in these areas, and his technical vocabulary and involuted thought made his philosophy a passing vogue. Intellectuals responded to Whitehead's desire for a wide audience, but perhaps because of what had happened to philosophy, he could not really successfully respond to them: being a philosopher was inconsistent with having a public function. When he died in 1947, Whitehead really belonged to the profession, and despite his belief in the efficacy of ideas in shaping the world, his ideas never went beyond a small department of the academy.

28

CLARENCE LEWIS

Lewis's Career

Clarence Irving Lewis—C. I. Lewis to the profession—was the most talented philosopher in the second department. His "conceptual pragmatism" made him the most influential American thinker of his generation, and his philosophy linked the writers of the classic period with those of the second half of the twentieth century. Lewis was born in 1883 in Stoneham, Massachusetts, and died in Menlo Park, California, in 1964. He received his B.A. from Harvard in 1905 and returned to graduate school there in 1908, after spending a year teaching high school in Quincy, Massachusetts, and two years as instructor in English at the University of Colorado.

While teaching in Colorado Lewis had married a New England woman, Mabel Maxwell Graves, and although their early years were spent in poverty, she was an uncommonly steadfast person who sustained her husband throughout his career. During this period she reinforced his desire to return to Cambridge and his determination to complete his graduate degree. Lewis got his Ph.D. in 1910 and assisted at Harvard the following year because no jobs were available. In 1911 Palmer placed him at Berkeley. As Lewis put it, Palmer "seeemed to know half the college presidents and heads of philosophy departments in the country; and there was no escaping . . . [his] astute persuasiveness." A series of articles in logic launched his career, and its first period ended with his important *Survey of Symbolic Logic* in 1918. Established at Berkeley as an associate professor, Lewis returned to Harvard in 1920 as a visiting lecturer and a year later accepted an assistant professorship. Whatever the charms of California, he felt that "for one who grew up under Royce and James and Perry, no other position in philosophy could have quite the same meaning.as one at Harvard."[1]

Risk taking paid off for Lewis: he impressed everyone and in 1924 his colleagues promoted him to tenured associate professor. Recognized at Harvard, he turned from logic to epistemology and achieved an international reputation with his 1929 *Mind and the World-Order*. The next year he became a full professor. Lewis remained at Harvard until his retirement in 1953, having been named to Perry's chair, the Edgar Pierce professorship, on Perry's retirement in 1946. Lewis achieved his greatest fame in the 1940s with the publication of *An Analysis of Knowledge and Valuation*. Nonetheless, he had spelled out the fundamentals of his position in *Mind and the World-Order*: it represented the culmination of systematic pragmatic thinking, and we shall conclude our history of philosophizing in Cambridge by examining it.

Early Work

Lewis did not escape James's pragmatism, but as a graduate student after James's retirement, he was subject more to the debate between neo-realism and idealism as carried on by Perry and Royce. "There is no one to whom I owe so much as to Royce," Lewis recalled, "though my debt to Ralph Perry is a close second." Royce did not win over Lewis but did become his "ideal of a philosopher." Moreover, Royce introduced Lewis to the study of symbolic logic and gave him a feeling for its philosophic importance. Lewis also admitted that one could find the ground of his mature thought in Royce's insights, but as a student Lewis was no idealist.

On May 1, 1910, he handed in his doctoral dissertation, tied up in a shoestring, to Royce and Perry. "The Place of Intuition in Knowledge" developed ideas that came to fruition in *Mind and the World-Order*. The early work showed Lewis's reliance on Perry and Royce and the impact his apprenticeship had on his thought. He was a conscientious pupil, and the dissertation tried to reconcile the realistic and voluntaristic epistemologies of his teachers. As Royce said, he thought Perry had influenced Lewis, while Perry thought Royce had done so. Together, Royce confessed, they allowed that Lewis had done something original.[2]

In the dissertation Lewis contended against Perry that knowledge transcended what was present to the mind and that the real object was never given in consciousness (133); knowledge depended on our purposes and activities, and a definition of the real object must include the active constructions of mind and the future experiences we would have under appropriate circumstances (89–92). So far Lewis went with Royce: the basis of knowledge was phenomenalistic and we analyzed it as possible experience. But there was also a given, sensuous, brute-feeling element in knowledge. Lewis called it the intuitive element; it was the element Perry pointed out. We distinguished this given, Lewis said, from the activity of thinking: "the will, the thinking activity, requires a first other or matter, and requires also that the opposition or the matter persist and be taken up into the true object of knowledge" (75–77). Intuition "furnishes us with the material of thought without which our thinking would forever be empty" (143).

Lewis formulated this doctrine only after dutifully spending three initial chapters expounding the antithetical views of his teachers—today we would call it a survey of the literature. His role as synthesizer was even more patent in his citation and long discussions of Kant. The epistemologies of both Royce and Perry were inadequate. The real object was neither a product of willing nor immediately given; it had a reality no different from what we apprehended in immediate presentations, but none of them defined it. Although these presentations in possible experience never transcended our ways of knowing, our purposeful activity, the will did not encompass intuition. "Without our activity," Lewis concluded, "intuition has no significance; without intuition, our activity has no ground or meaning" (139–44).

Lewis's synthesis was on the realist side (90). Basic spatio-temporal qualities of real objects were given (109 ff.). Moreover, the qualities revealed in our activity were implicit in the given; "the distinctions are waiting there to be made" (79). Finally, the real object as defined by possible experience consisted of a series of given presentations (139–44). The role of mind was almost limited to selection and organization; despite mind's indispensability to knowledge, its active constructive function was negligible (159).

During the next few years Lewis changed his position. He repudiated the realistic bias of the dissertation and asserted a variety of idealism whose source was undoubtedly Royce. The beginning of a lifelong respect for Hume's skepticism caused this shift. It became all-important to determine why and how the given could be intelligible if it was independent of mind, questions evaded in "The Place of Intuition in Knowledge." Lewis became convinced that mind must condition—in a strong sense—what was presented to it or knowledge would be equivalent only to a lucky guess. The deepest problems of *The Critique of Pure Reason* were at issue. No realist could circumvent Hume's argument; only a version of idealism would suffice. And in two polemical articles Lewis attacked both Perry and the other Harvard realist, George Santayana.

Against Santayana Lewis defended Kant's "fundamental insight"— that reason imposed conditions upon real objects and that reality was intelligible. Consequently, Lewis rejected Santayana's materialism. The substance or matter of *The Life of Reason* distinguished essences from existences. Some things existed while others like them were merely possible. The actual, Santayana held, were essences linked with matter. But this matter, Lewis declared,

> cannot even be imagined. Unlike the matter of science it has no particular nature or properties, has no place in space or time, and is totally incomprehensible. Necessarily so, since to describe it or define it would be to give it an essence—a definition or idea—which *qua* matter it cannot have. Matter is the universal dough which lends itself to every shape, but has no shape itself. It is the great Nothing-in-particular.

Lewis ridiculed Santayana's matter as a mythology, an attempt at conceiving the inconceivable. On Kantian grounds "it is meaningless to call anything real whose nature we can never understand." What was real must be intelligible; Santayana's matter could not be real; to call it real entailed its intelligibility and gave it a definition or essence.[3]

In attacking Perry a year later in 1913, Lewis was more circumspect, although still leaning to idealism. That all real objects were known, said Perry, did not tell us that knowing constituted real objects; the idealist defended a tautology—that known objects were known objects. The argument from "the ego-centric predicament" proved nothing and prohibited escape from our consciousness. Idealism was a form of skepticism: it made knowledge, in the sense of getting outside individual consciousness, impossible. Realism did not deny that when a real object entered the knowing relation the object acquired that relation; realism denied only that this relation constituted the real object.

Lewis agreed that knowledge of a real object must transcend present experience. The problem was just to ascertain how the knowing experience meant something beyond itself, something not present. By "how much," he asked Perry, did the realist's "known object"—all that we had information about—differ from the "real object"? If knowledge was a kind of acting, related to our needs and interests, our active pursuits in some measure transformed the real object; if knowledge was passive then we knew only what was capable of entering the knowing relation, and real objects unfitted to the knowledge relation, or at least those aspects of them that were unfitted, remained unknown.

The idealist urged that real objects depended on knowledge because they did not essentially differ from objects as known, and Perry thought this doctrine skeptical. But if Perry claimed that the real object was independent of the knowledge relation, Lewis said, then realism was skeptical. Perry recognized that he could only experience the object as known. But in contending that the real object transcended knowledge, he admitted that he never knew this independent reality; his own experience confined him. Polemic aside, Lewis concluded his argument cautiously. Although Perry did not prove his case, he showed that the idealist did not prove his: the idealist had not demonstrated that the real object was dependent on knowledge. Skepticism might be true; we might never escape our consciousness. Alternately, while the idealist did not prove his case, he showed that Perry did not prove his: the realist could never show that the real object transcended knowledge.[4]

The problem any realism could not solve was to account for what Lewis called the validity of knowledge. On realistic grounds we had no way of explaining why my idea of the desk in front of me was true—why my idea referred or corresponded to the real desk. For Lewis this was the question of how we *justified* beliefs about the world. For the realist the objects which warranted the truth of ideas were forever inaccessible, for we knew only the known object, and realists distinguished it from the real object. Lewis challenged the realists to answer Hume: they must somehow show that the conception of causality they used was meaningful, that real objects were related as they supposed them to be and that real object and known object were related as they supposed them to be. Lewis thought such a demonstration was impossible on their terms. Perry could never discover the relations existing among real objects when they were not known, or among real objects and known objects, and this was just the discovery he must make to refute Hume.

For the idealist these puzzles were of no immediate concern. If knowledge legislated for whatever we could call the real object, and if the real object was so far dependent on knowledge, then we had the means to argue that knowledge was "objectively valid." We solved the problem "by proving some necessary relation between reality and our ways of knowing." Yet to assert that a solution was possible on idealist grounds was not to solve the problem. The thrust of Lewis's essays was not so much to espouse idealism as to maintain that "valid" knowledge was possible for the idealist but impossible for the realist. "Whoever takes the principles of knowledge to be legislative for whatever can properly be called real . . . will be assured that knowledge is objectively valid" "*if he makes out his case.*"[5]

During the first decade of the twentieth century, Royce believed that the central problem of idealism was what he called the deduction of the categories: an explication of why the world of ideas and values, the world of idealism, should appear as a world of objects in space and time. He formulated this problem by speaking of the Worlds of Description and Appreciation. He must reduce the first, the world of facts, to the second, the world of feeling. Lewis's essays formulated the problem similarly.

For Lewis we could understand reality only if we viewed it in light of some end or goal. In failing to validate knowledge, said Lewis, the realist admitted that teleology was necessary to make sense of the universe. If the world was intelligible, then science and our understanding of causality must be compatible with explanatory principles of value and purpose. Why was this so? Knowledge was valid only if knowing constituted reality and gave its laws to real objects. Accordingly, these laws would reflect the mind of the knower, the self, and be teleological in nature. Idealism "faces, with Kant, the problem of discovering what validity can attach to moral and religious values consistently with the entire truth of science in the realm of phenomena," and the idealist must maintain that the absolute mind in which thought and object were identical was at least a valid ideal. But the situation was problematic: *if* validity attached to these values, we escaped skepticism.[6]

Lewis's relation to Royce was indirect. For Royce, reducing the World of Description to that of Appreciation resembled nothing so much as a trigonometric identity: he knew that the absolute mind, his world of ideals and values, was real; consequently the phenomenal world had to be an aspect of it, and the problem was merely to get from one to the other. For Lewis the question was different. He was not convinced that idealism was true; but rather that we justified our knowledge only if it was. His concern was whether validation was possible, and, if so, what idealist procedure did the job.

Logic and Metaphysics

These early studies demonstrated Lewis's ties to Royce. Thereafter, through the publication of *Survey of Symbolic Logic,* he committed himself to another Roycean endeavor—logic; its study left him inhospitable to idealist speculation. Ironically Lewis shared Royce's view of logic—that it reflected the principles of human reasoning, and that investigating the widest possible systems of order enabled us to grasp these principles. To see why these concerns led Lewis from idealism we must examine his work on material implication.

Lewis found what he took to be a serious flaw in symbolic logic as Russell and Whitehead had developed it in *Principia Mathematica.* They had defined "p implies q" as "either p is false or q is true," that is, $p \supset q = \mathrm{df} \sim p \vee q$, where we treat 'p' and 'q' as propositional variables, and where we read 'p' and '$\sim$p' as "p is true" and "p is false." This analysis led to the theorems of the *Principia* which Lewis called the "paradoxes of implication":

$$*2.02 \qquad q \supset . \, p \supset q$$
$$*2.21 \qquad \sim p \supset . \, p \supset q$$

As Russell and Whitehead put it, any statement implied a true statement and a false statement implied any statement.[7] Lewis asserted—rightly— that this definition of implication—Russell and Whitehead called it material implication—hardly accorded with the ordinary or useful meaning of the term. He went so far as to say that *Principia Mathematica* did not "demonstrate" or "prove" any of its theorems for they were "implied" only in the sense of 'implied' used by the system and this sense was trivial.[8]

He pinpointed the difficulty in various essays, always returning to the distinction between relations of extension and intension. For example, the zero of the calculus of classes denoted the empty class, or class with no members. There were two kinds of such classes. The class of Mondays that were Tuesdays was necessarily a zero class; the class of fair Mondays was a zero class in any month it happened to rain every Monday. Consider the equation '$a\bar{c} = 0$' which we might read "there are no a's which are not c's." If the zero was of the necessary kind, the relation was intensional; we stated an equivalence of meaning—"There are no Mondays which are not the days before Tuesdays," "All Mondays are the days before Tuesdays." If the zero class was one that was only in fact empty, the relation was extensional; the statement happened to be true—"There are no Mondays in this month that are not rainy," "All Mondays in this month are rainy days." While this ambiguity had little relevance in the calculus of classes, it was just the one leading to the paradoxes of material implication. If a material implication was true, we were merely sure that we preserved truth value; but when we validly inferred one statement from another, we were concerned with identity of meaning. A proper logic must distinguish between what was true in fact and what was necessarily true, and limit its notion of inference to the latter.[9]

From our perspective the issue between Lewis and the authors of the *Principia* resulted in part from a confusion between use and mention. Russell and Whitehead read "p implies q" for '$p \supset q$' and their exposition confused the conditional 'if . . . , then . . . ' belonging between statements, and the verb 'implies' belonging between the names of statements. We might say "if he's a bachelor, then he is unmarried" or "he is a bachelor $\supset$ he is unmarried," both of which were about bachelors. Or we might write 'he is a bachelor' implies 'he is unmarried', which was about statements. In the *Principia* this distinction between using an expression and talking about it was unclear.[10] Lewis correctly noted that material implication was not what we had in mind when we validly deduced one statement from another. But while he properly objected to the idea that one statement implied another whenever the first was false or the second true, his own work also failed to distinguish use and mention. He constructed a different interpretation of 'if . . . , then . . .', strict implication, urging that it delineated the usual meaning of 'implies'. For Lewis 'p ⊃ q' (or 'p ⊰ q' as he wrote it to avoid confusion with Russell and Whitehead) meant q is deducible from p: Lewis still treated 'implies' both as a statement connective and as a predicate about statements. He read 'he is a bachelor ⊰ he is unmarried' both as "he is a bachelor strictly implies he is unmarried" and 'he is a bachelor' strictly implies 'he is unmarried'.

Building on Lewis's path-breaking work, subsequent logicians sorted out these issues by distinguishing between the language that was the object of investigation in which '⊃' or '⊰' were symbols, and the language used to talk about the object language. 'Implies' was a predicate of the metalanguage, and logicians raised Lewis's question by asking what we meant by saying 'he is a bachelor ⊃ he is unmarried' was logically true. On the other side '⊰' could function as a new symbol of the object language; as a statement connective it generated a strengthened version of the Russell and Whitehead 'if . . . , then . . .'. This procedure developed an alternative logic to the one in which '⊃' functioned, and Lewis became known for this development.[11]

But to see the matter from this perspective loses sight of what was crucial. In his earliest logical essays Lewis wedded the problem of alternative logics to important philosophic material. In "The Matrix Algebra for Implications" he introduced three connectives: '~', '−', and '&'. Sentence variables, 'p', 'q', 'r', and so on, were formulas of the system as well as those formulas compounded in standard ways from the sentence variables and connectives: for example, '~p', '-q', '~p &-q', and '~(-p)' (ordinarily omitting the parentheses). He wrote about these formulas under two headings, primitive ideas and truth values, but in both he read '-p' as "p is false" and '~p' as "p is impossible" with the result that '-~p' meant "p is possible" and '~-p', "p is necessary." He then used a series of abbreviations called definitions. If 'A', 'B', and so on were names of any formulas, then the most important of these abbreviations were: (1) A ∘ B is to serve as a rewrite of −~(A&B); (2) A ⊰ B as a rewrite for ~(A&-B); and (3) A ⊃ B as a rewrite for −(A&-B). 'p ∘ q' read "p and q are consistent." 'p ⊰ q' was his formula for implication or inference: "it is impossible that p be true and q false"; 'p ⊃ q' was his old enemy, material implication: "it is false that p is true and q false." With the aid of nine postulates, a rule for substitution, and two rules of inference (*modus ponens* and production—if we assert *p* and if we assert *q* then we may assert *p&q*), Lewis proved several theorems in the matrix algebra.

He then noted a "persistent analogy" in the postulates and theorems between relations which figured in material implication, *p&q* and $p \supset q$, and those involving the idea of impossibility, *p∘q* and *p ∹ q*. Thus,

$$\vdash A\&B \dashv B\&A \text{ and } \vdash A\circ B \dashv B\circ A$$
$$\vdash - A \dashv (A \supset B) \text{ and } \vdash \sim A \dashv (A \dashv B)$$
$$\vdash A \dashv (A\&A) \quad \text{and} \quad \vdash - \sim A \dashv (A\circ A)$$

This result led Lewis to suspect that there was a system of possibilities and impossibilities—he called it the calculus of consistencies—which was an analogue to the system of material implication. Indeed, he contended that there was such a calculus that in effect concerned itself only with the kinds of theorems in the right-hand column above. He proved all the theorems of this calculus with the postulates and rules of the matrix algebra. Similarly he showed, as was obvious from the way he had set it up, that he could generate all the theorems of *Principia Mathematica*'s system from the matrix algebra. In short, the calculi of consistencies and material implication were isomorphic, and the theorems of each deducible from the matrix algebra. Finally, Lewis proved in the matrix algebra all the theorems of his own system of strict implication, which he had published a year earlier in 1913. The chief interest of this system of strict implication was that he had excluded all the theorems of *Principia Mathematica* that seemed queer to him by interpreting 'if . . . , then . . .' by the connective '∹' and not '⊃'. The matrix algebra was a wider system in which he derived all the axioms for the strict implication system.[12]

Following Royce, Lewis thought that logic reflected the principles of rational thinking and he made no distinction or an ambiguous distinction between an uninterpreted system and that interpretation depicting these principles and serving as "an organon of proof." What contemporary logicians might call the metalanguage in which they talk about procedures of valid inference was for Royce and Lewis not separable from that interpretation reproducing our reasoning process, and neither man really distinguished this interpretation from the intrinsic meaning of the correct logical system. The best statement of this notion came from Lewis himself:

Pure mathematics is not concerned with the truth either of postulates or of theorems: so much is an old story. But just here a curious reservation seems necessary. Modern geometry—Euclidean or non-Euclidean—is not concerned with the truth either of postulates or of theorems, but it is concerned with the fact that the postulates *truly imply* the theorems. It would seem, then, that pure mathematics must concern itself with the *truth* of the *propositions in logic* which state, in general form, the implications in question. Since the logic, also, does not prove its theorems, but only proves that its postulates imply them—that they are true if the postulates are true —this concern is finally, with the truth of postulates in the logic.

It may be objected that the logic, like any pure mathematics, is concerned only with "mathematical consistency." If so, it must be borne in mind that the algebra of implications ceases, in a sense, to be pure and becomes applied when its propositions are used in proving anything. Indeed, the attempt to separate formal consistency and material truth is, in the case of the logic, peculiarly difficult. For while other branches find their organon of proof in the logic, this discipline supplies its own. Hence, if this system is formally consistent, but contains a primitive proposition which is materially false, we shall have *false proofs* as well as materially false statements of implications, within the logic itself. Also a materially false theorem—either truly or falsely implied by the postulates—may, when used as a premise, lead to other false propositions; and when used as a *rule of inference*, to further *false proofs*. Thus a single materially false assumption in the logic might produce numerous progeny early in life; and a "mathematically consistent" algebra of implications might still contain the basis for false proofs within itself, as well as in other branches.[13]

In effect, Lewis's matrix algebra was the metalanguage in which he talked about the procedures of inference that governed the proofs of the theorems of *Principia Mathematica*. Having deduced the postulates of the *Principia* from the matrix algebra, he wrote:

These are the postulates for material implication. However, the system of material implication, as previously developed, requires an operation [rule of inference] which may be stated: "if *p* is asserted and $(p \supset q)$ is asserted, q may be asserted." We do not assume this operation, because $(p \supset q)$ is not equivalent to "q can validly be inferred from p." But we can prove all the theorems of material implication from the postulates of the matrix algebra in much the same way as we have just proved the postulates. Also, by using the postulates and theorems of the matrix algebra . . . as principles of inference, we can prove that the theorems of material implication *can be inferred from* the postulates of material implication. This has never before been shown. Previous developments of material implication have proceeded by means of numerous "mathematical operations" or have proved only that the theorems are *materially implied by* the postulates.

If, however, the opinion expressed in this paper, that the relation of material implication is not equivalent to valid inference, be correct, then the system of material implication has no value as an organon of proof, and its interest is chiefly mathematical and historical.[14]

We must regard the novel meaning of 'implies' with suspicion, he wrote, because we dealt "with the basic things of human reason."[15] The system of the *Principia* was untrue as applied non-Euclidean geometry was untrue. But because of logic's peculiarities Russell and Whitehead's system was also false per se, as a pure logic. Logical systems must, it seemed, get at the morphology of reasoning and, like Riemann and Lobachevsky, Russell and Whitehead developed a calculus which was consistent but off the mark. What we wanted was a "true" logic—one which depicted rational thinking procedures.[16]

In Lewis's 1918 *Survey of Symbolic Logic* and certainly in the 1932 *Symbolic Logic*, which he wrote with C. H. Langford, some of these concerns vanished; the books did not raise the metaphysical implications of logic, and Lewis's system of strict implication was more clearly an alternative logic. But the irony was that when Lewis worked out these notions, the last thing he had in mind was developing an alternative logic. He was convinced that Russell and Whitehead were wrong and that the true logic mirrored the form of human thinking. In 1912, 1913, and 1914 Lewis's conception of logic was Roycean: the study of ever more general systems of order, the most general (uninterpreted) one reflecting our modes of thought and adequate to all reasoning. "The Matrix Algebra for Implications" proposed a logic more comprehensive than any previously developed. Lewis was not so bold as to state that his matrix algebra mirrored the laws of thought; yet it would prove useful for investigating the interrelations of necessity, truth, possibility, falsity, and impossibility, and would consequently be important not only for logic but also for epistemology and metaphysics.[17]

In this connection of logic with epistemology and metaphysics we penetrate to the core of his thought. If we accepted the *Principia* as the true logic, Lewis said, valid inference must be identical to Russell and Whitehead's material implication. A true logic reflected the laws of thought; the laws of thought indicated how we validly gained knowledge about the world; therefore, if the *Principia*'s system was the true logic, material implication coincided with the correct notion of deducibility. A false statement implied any statement and any statement implied any true statement. Imagine, said Lewis, what kind of world we lived in: "*In such a world, the all-possible must be the real, the true must be necessary, the contingent cannot exist, the false must be absurd and impossible, and the contrary to fact supposition must be quite meaningless.*" Accepting an extensional logic committed us to metaphysical monism and the coherence theory of truth—the world of an absolute mind.[18] So here in logic by a curious and dramatic twist Lewis found an argument against Royce's idealism. Of course, material implication might "apply" to the actual world. Belief in the contingent might be due to ignorance. Nonetheless, on pragmatic grounds we had good reasons for rejecting extensional logic: it did not reflect actual reasoning procedures, and following these procedures made us practical adherents to a system of logic like Lewis's and warranted a prima facie belief in a non-Roycean universe. Lewis's logical studies inspired his first move away from his nascent idealism, although his conception of logic derived from someone who saw the discipline as the culmination of idealism. As Lewis was aware, Royce thought of his work on his logical system Σ as a profound argument for idealism; in his own comprehensive system Lewis found an argument against it.[19]

Logic against Royce

Lewis's study of "alternative" logics was not all that led him from idealism. Two other logical investigations weakened any lingering Roycean commitments. Idealism was monistic for Lewis, as it was for the early James: all truths were interdependent because inferring one truth from any other depended on "systematic unity," derivability within a system. On this view the distinction between necessary and contingent truths failed, and all truth revealed itself as necessary.[20] Lewis's first bit of logical work worth examining demonstrated the falsity of monism.[21]

Any set of possible states of affairs expressed in statements A, B, . . . N constituted a system Σ if (1) if A is in Σ and A implies the falsity of B, then B is not in Σ, (2) if C is in Σ and C implies D, then D is in Σ, and (3) if A is in Σ and B likewise, then the complex statement A&B is in Σ. That is, a system was what Lewis called a group of statements reflecting a mutually consistent set of states of affairs such that if one was in the set then all its consequences were. A possible world was any system in which in addition to (1), (2), and (3) above, for any A, if A is not in Σ, its contradictory $\bar{A}$ is. A given system might be contained in more than one possible world, and the relation of our knowledge— a given system—to reality—a possible world—represented such containment. The actual world was one of many possible worlds, and we possessed truth in a practical sense to the extent to which our systems were contained in, true of, the possible world we believed to be actual.

Consider Σ (0) and any statement A; Σ (0) implied A, $\bar{A}$, or neither. In the last case A was independent of Σ (0), and A and $\bar{A}$ were consistent with Σ (0). Thus, Σ (0) contained A or $\bar{A}$, or we could adjoin one of them to it to form another system, Σ (1), and go on indefinitely constructing new systems by adding one or the other of every pair of self-contradictory statements. We would be able to construct a possible world for any system to be "true of," that is, contained in. But we also knew of systems like the rival geometries (taken as truths about physical space) which were each consistent; yet each could not be true of the actual world. Therefore, if any world was possible, more than one was.

Now suppose it was false that every possible world had something in common with every other. It followed that there were only two possible worlds—the world of actual states of affairs and the world of all their contradictories. The statements expressing the latter, Lewis posited, were not all consistent with each other and could not describe a possible world, and there was then only one possible world, the actual. But since this could not be true, every possible world had something in common with all possible worlds. Assume that $\Sigma_a(0)$ was that part of the actual world $\Sigma_a(n)$ that that world had in common with any possible world $\Sigma_p(n)$, and that $\Sigma_a(1)$ was that part of $\Sigma_a(n)$ which contained those statements true of $\Sigma_a(n)$ and false of $\Sigma_p(n)$. The statements of $\Sigma_a(0)$ implied no statements of $\Sigma_a(1)$ because those of the latter were false in $\Sigma_p(n)$ and those of the former true. And the actual world had mutually independent parts—more or less numerous according to the number of other possible worlds with which it had something in common.

From this analysis Lewis concluded that coherence as a criterion of truth meant only "consistency with" and not "dependence upon." The actual world was one in which some statements might be independent of others. Coherence was a necessary but not a sufficient condition for truth; there was more than one coherent world possible, and only empirical evidence sufficed to pick out the actual one.[22]

We need not investigate this argument any further, but if it showed that Lewis still had a taste for idealist dialectic, it also showed that he would very likely have to disavow an idealistic solution to the problem of the categories: idealism walked hand-in-hand with monism, and he had repudiated monism.

Lewis criticized another idealistic tenet, using a second logical insight. The dialectical argument of reassertion through denial was a favorite weapon in the idealistic arsenal—it was, for instance, the rock on which Royce based his system. If we found statements that it was self-contradictory to deny, argument often went, we had established basic or self-evident truths. So Descartes became convinced that he could not doubt his own existence, and so Royce found that there must be error. Lewis attacked this "veritable foundation stone for the rationalistic procedure."

A statement was self-contradictory only within a given logical system. In fact, we asserted the statement; we denied it only because the inference rules of the system in question were such that the statement implied its negation.

> The question of what an assertion implies is precisely a question of logic. The content of logic is the principles of inference. Whoever, then, denies a principle of logic may either draw his own inferences according to the principle he denies, or he may con-

sistently avoid that principle in deriving his conclusions. If one deny a principle of inference, but inadvertently reintroduce it in drawing conclusions from his statement, he will indeed find that he has contradicted himself and admitted what originally he denied . . . . But this is true only because so long as we remain within our system of logic, we shall use the very principle in question in drawing inferences from the denial of it . . . .

Statements reaffirmed through denial were usually principles of inference —for example, it is false that X is A and X is not A—but if we rejected these principles and reasoned in accordance with our rejection we incurred no contradiction. We reasserted the principle only if we reintroduced it by drawing inferences from it.

Lewis noted more than these limitations on the reassertion through denial argument. Philosophers used the argument to warrant fundamental verities. But since it was limited to showing systematic consistency, it never demonstrated truth: the principles of inference of a "bad" logic might be obviously "false," yet if used consistently, said Lewis, they might, if negated, presuppose their assertion in a way similar to what occurred with a "good" logic.[23]

Royce and the Pragmatic a Priori

The philosophical consequences of Lewis's long study of logic were leading him away from idealism and, it would seem, any solution to the questions his student apprenticeship had saddled him with. When he returned to these questions in the 1920s, however, it was not to enunciate any form of skepticism. His 1929 *Mind and the World-Order* proposed to defend a theory of knowledge without adopting any metaphysical position: his conceptual pragmatism would be free of metaphysical commitment. With the critical realists, Lewis contended that epistemology was independent of an affirmative metaphysics. He would use the idealistic heritage of Kant, Peirce, and Royce to escape skepticism and any form of "rationalism." We shall see the extent to which Lewis succeeded, but whatever its relation to the previous history of philosophy, his conceptual pragmatism was a powerful new synthesis.

First, Lewis took some of Royce's conceptions to develop what he called the pragmatic *a priori*. During the latter part of Royce's life—much of the time that Lewis spent in Cambridge—Royce held that scientific progress depended upon "leading ideas." A leading idea in the natural sciences was a hypothesis, but a hypothesis different from those tested by observation and experience. Rather, a leading idea was a hypothesis that scientists used as a guide—it was too general in nature to test, although it determined the direction of their researches. Royce claimed that leading ideas, in Kant's language, were regulative principles.

In his introduction to Henri Poincaré's *The Foundations of Science* (1913), Royce drew on Poincaré's formulation of the same notion. Leading ideas were valuable "*despite*, or even *because*, of the fact that evidence can *neither* confirm *nor* refute them." They were devices of the understanding, unifying otherwise discrete and confused facts or principles regarding the structure of the world. Euclid's parallel line postulate typified leading ideas. Royce had long since digested the discovery of non-Euclidean geometries and did not think of the postulate as a logical truth; it was simply a leading idea. But unlike the Kantian regulative principles (and perhaps the categories), time might alter leading ideas like Euclid's axiom. They were subject to "suggestions" of experience. Other interpretations of experience, that is, other leading ideas, were conceivable. The ones we used were merely the most convenient. Leading ideas had a dual nature. Although not subjective or arbitrary, they were "pragmatic"; simultaneously, experience (ambiguously) "imposed" them on us. Royce expressed their status in terms of his own work:

> while experience is always the guide, the attitude of the investigator towards experience is determined by interests which have to be partially due to what I should call that "internal meaning," that human interest in rational theoretical construction which inspires the scientific inquiry; . . . the theoretical constructions which prevail . . . are neither unbiased reports of the actual constitution of an external reality, nor yet arbitrary constructions of fancy.

Consider the principle of the nature of disease which the German scientist Rudolph Virchow enunciated in the nineteenth century. "We have learned to recognize," said Virchow, "that diseases are not autonomous organisms, that they are no entities that have entered into the body, that they are no parasites which take root in the body, but that

they merely show us the course of vital processes under altered conditions."
This hypothesis was not testable. When he propounded it in 1847,
Virchow had not yet formulated the empirical principle of cellular
pathology for which he became famous. He also believed that the science
of pathology was in its infancy and the causation of disease unknown.
Moreover, it was difficult to see what would refute the disease principle
if we thought it false. Should we come to recognize bacteria or any of
their products or accompaniments as causing disease or affecting its
course, Virchow could claim that these causes constituted the "altered
conditions" under which "the course of the vital processes" occurred.
Even if the devil caused disease, the principle would remain "unrefuted
and empirically irrefutable." The principle merely stated that the entity
affecting the organism—fire or air or bullet or poison or devil—was not
the disease but rather constituted the changed conditions of the organism.
If the disease principle was stated with sufficient generality,

> it amounts simply to saying that if a disease involves a change in
> an organism, and if this change is subject to law at all, then the
> nature of the organism and the reaction of the organism to what-
> ever it is which causes the disease must be understood in case the
> disease is to be understood.

Virchow's principle was a resolve to search for the connection between any disease and the normal behavior of the organism, to relate the
pathological and the normal states. Without a leading idea of this kind,
the significant empirical findings could never have resulted. Without
leading ideas scientists would never observe the facts relevant to the
hypotheses they did test. The value of leading ideas like the disease principle lay in the sort of experimentation which they led men to undertake and also in the sorts of ideas they discouraged. They organized
science, kept the discipline in touch with the researchers' culture, and
assured its service to humanity.[24]

The heir of Royce's leading ideas was Lewis's pragmatic *a priori*. The
a priori for Lewis was not a collection of mere necessary truths independent of experience. These truths reflected our modes of classification,
definitions, and logical categories with which we interpreted the given
element of knowledge, the immediate data of sense. But the *a priori* did
not compel the mind's acceptance; it was necessary because it prescribed

nothing to the given and because *a priori* alternatives were possible. These truths explicated the way we chose to categorize, and although we never falsified them, we withdrew them if they were inapplicable:

> in all our knowledge—particularly in all science—there is an element of just such logical order which rises from our definitions. An initial definition, as we may see, is always arbitrary in the sense that it cannot be false. In itself it does not tell us whether anything is true or not, or what the nature of existing objects is. It simply exhibits to us a concept or meaning in the speaker's mind which he asks us temporarily to share with him and symbolize by a certain word or phrase.[25]

> Definitions and their immediate consequence, analytic propositions generally, are necessarily true, true under all possible circumstances. Definition is legislative because it is in some sense arbitrary. Not only is the meaning assigned to a word more or less a matter of choice—that consideration is relatively trival—but the manner in which the precise classifications which definition embodies shall be effected, is something not dictated by experience. If experience were other than it is, the definition and its corresponding classification might be inconvenient, fantastic, or useless, but it could not be false.[26]

The *a priori* was, then, the analytic, that which was true in virtue of meaning alone. But the point had greater significance. In the first place, the *a priori* was pragmatic. We developed and selected meanings because of their usefulness and withdrew, although did not refute, them if they failed to help us. Like Royce, Lewis pointed to Virchow's principle as an example of this dimension of the *a priori*.[27] In the second place, we should not assume that the *a priori* was simply verbal and true by definition. Quoting Royce, Lewis noted that the *a priori* designated "our categorical ways of acting."[28] It was an element in knowledge because it formulated the definitive concepts or categorical tests which made investigation possible. Using a conceptual framework implied characteristic ways of acting, and congruent behavior was our practical criterion of common meaning:

> Such concepts are not verbal definitions, nor classification merely;

they are themselves laws which prescribe a certain uniformity of behavior to whatever is thus named. Such definitive laws are a priori; only so can we enter upon the investigation by which further laws are sought. Yet it should also be pointed out that such a priori laws are subject to abandonment if the structure which is built upon them does not succeed in simplifying our interpretation of phenomena.[29]

Perry and the Given

In addition to the *a priori* Lewis admitted a sensuous element confronting us independent of our wills. He called this admission a primitive Kantianism[30] and again picked up Perry's concerns: we must not overlook that a dimension of knowledge was beyond activity. Knowledge consisted in the "intersection" of the *a priori* and given elements. Indeed, Lewis defined his epistemological position by adjudicating the claims of each, and he became famous for maintaining a strict cleavage between the conceptual and the empirical. Exclusive emphasis on the latter—the given or immediate—characterized Bergson or the mystic. Subordinating the empirical to the conceptual meant idealism or some form of "rationalism." Conceptual pragmatism defended the independence of each element and stressed the interpretive act bringing them together.[31] Reminiscent of Royce, Lewis called interpretation the third element of knowledge: our act applied the *a priori* framework to experience and interpreted the given using the framework's concepts. There were two parts to this analysis of the interpretive act: the first involved the content of knowledge and required Lewis to refine Peirce's views; the second involved justifying knowledge and forced Lewis to review the idealist answer to skepticism.

Peirce and the Content of Knowledge

After Peirce's death Royce had the Peirce manuscripts brought to Harvard for study, and when Lewis returned to Cambridge in 1920 there was apparently an informal agreement that he would arrange and catalogue them. Of course, Lewis did not complete the task—other hands were to carry on—but he spent two years living with the material.[32] One of the results was a Peircean operationalism,[33] in effect the view that Royce had criticized as critical rationalism, the Third Conception of Being.

Mind and the World-Order argued that knowledge arose in applying categorical frameworks to the given:

> the whole body of our conceptual interpretations form a sort of heirarchy or pyramid with the most comprehensive, such as those of logic, at the top, and the least general, such as "swans," etc., at the bottom; . . . with this complex system of interrelated concepts, we approach particular experiences and attempt to fit them, somewhere and somehow, into its preformed patterns. Persistent failure leads to readjustment; the applicability of certain concepts to experiences of some particular sort is abandoned, and some other conceptual pattern is brought forward for application. The higher up a concept stands in our pyramid, the more reluctant we are to disturb it, because the more radical and far-reaching the results will be if we abandon the application of it in some particular fashion (305–06).

The meaning of a framework's concepts consisted in their prescribing certain kinds of behavior in appropriate circumstances. In short, a concept was a plan of action, a mode of responding to the environment. Nonetheless, it was not true or false: if it was inapplicable, it was withdrawn. Using it made judgments predicting the conjunction of certain elements of the given. Mere awareness of the given—best but inadequately reported in statements like 'This appears yellow'—was never knowledge. Knowing was ascertaining that some elements of the given related to others in an orderly fashion. It entailed going beyond the immediate, making inferences about temporal patterns: "That which *any* such concept [of a framework] denotes is always something which, in terms of experience, must have a temporal spread. What is required to determine its applicability is some orderly sequence in experience, or some set of such" (300). Employing a categorical framework supposed that elements of the given fell under specific concepts. If the framework was acceptable, then if we responded consistently, certain other elements of the given confronted us. For example, if this yellowish something is a pencil I hold in my hand, then if I attempt to write with it, I will see the appropriate graphite marks.

I credited the resulting judgment—that I had a pencil in my hand—only if my possible future activities eventuated, or would eventuate, in a certain pattern of experience.

Knowledge was predictive: it consisted in choosing a set of concepts which enabled us to use some elements of the given as signs of others. And knowledge was empirical: it required that claims to truth were at least possibly verifiable. But because of this requirement knowledge was also probable only. We never exhaustively verified statements about patterns in the given—in the normal case statements about physical objects. If we were to spell out the full meaning of a statement, we would define an infinite number of possible experiences that would occur provided we acted in specific ways: if this were a pencil, then it would pierce the paper if pushed; appear uni-dimensional if held at a certain angle; need sharpening if used for a long period; and so on. If we verified a modest number of these hypotheticals we became convinced that the statement was true, but it was always possible that future experience would fail to substantiate our claims. So the statement was probable only (274–308).

Royce and the Categories

This analysis assumed that there was a minimal order among temporally disjoint elements of the given. With varying amounts of success we applied alternative categorical frameworks to these elements, each one selecting different patterns for consideration. But if any of them were to yield knowledge, their application must pick out elements which were genuinely related:

> In empirical knowledge there are, thus, two elements concerning which we have certainty: the recognized qualitative character of the given presentation is one and the a priori elaboration of some concept . . . is the other. But the applicability of the concept to the presentation is probable only, because such application is an interpretation which is predictive. The probability, or degree of assurance of such interpretation, reflects a generalization from experience. It is an argument from past to future or from the uniformity of experience (292).

That is, if knowledge differed from the lucky guess, there must be a ground, a valid basis for applying the concepts. Here Lewis investigated his old question: Could we answer Hume? Could we warrant inferences from the past to the future? But in *Mind and the World-Order* Lewis believed idealism need not taint an answer. He could satisfactorily meet the difficulty without overstepping the boundaries of epistemology. He could repudiate skepticism without embracing metaphysics.

The context was still the dispute between realism and voluntaristic idealism and its relation to the deduction of the categories. In his 1918 *Survey* he wrote that someone might rehabilitate Kant's basic arguments as *"arguments concerning the certainty of our knowledge of the phenomenal world,* i.e., as metaphysics of space."[34] Reporting on John Maynard Keynes's *Treatise on Probability* three years later, Lewis said that Keynes was skeptical of solving Hume's problem while epistemology was in its present state. But Keynes made it clear, Lewis concluded, "That what is required for the validity of induction is some independent deduction of the categories."[35] This dilemma, he maintained in 1930, "historically . . . overshadows and colors all the others . . . this question of the ground, basis, validity of knowledge." The difficulty ran "through the whole history of post-Kantian epistemology,"[36] and a solution to it was now a major theme in Lewis's work. His critique of pragmatism was just Royce's: "It was the besetting sin of James's pragmatism to confuse validity with truth; and of Dewey's to avoid the issue by the near absence of any distinction between the two."[37] The last hundred pages of *Mind and the World-Order* tried to atone for these sins.

We were aware of the given but did not create it by thinking and in general could not displace or alter it. To interpret certain given items of experience as signs of other possible experience, the given must have a minimal order, or, Lewis added, we must be able to impose this degree of order on it (196, 230). As the argument evolved, he implied that he was proceeding independent of metaphysical commitment. If we were able to impose order on the given, we could say that it was mental in nature; if we merely discovered order within the given, we could say that it had objective properties independent of mind. But Lewis wished to leave these metaphysical issues open. Although his usual locution—the given must have a minimal order—might predispose an interpreter to designate Lewis a realist, he was anxious to show that his position was compatible with "the characteristic theses of idealism." Idealists rarely asked if thinking created the data of sense. Rather they asked if we could apprehend a real object without the active construction of mind, and both Lewis and the idealists agreed that such apprehension entailed thought. Lewis did not even contest a second idealist thesis that the existence of sense data, as such, was no evidence of an existent independent of mind (45–48). The given might exist outside of mind, "that question should not be prejudged," although Lewis continued that it was difficult to see what such existence could mean. Nonetheless, he would not dispute whether the given existed unknown. We here left "the analysis of experience and plunged into metaphysics" (64–65). He simply wanted to point out that the idealist did not need to maintain that thought created the given (46–47).

Commentators have emphasized that Lewis used the given to procure a basis of certainty for knowledge, and the given might function this way in his later writing. But in *Mind and the World-Order* this function was not primary. His chapter, "The Given Element of Experience," stressed a minimal claim consistent with idealism, and this theme ran through the book. The idealist's point was that the given, when acknowledged, was known, and Lewis happily conceded this point: the given was an abstraction, and the idealist's contention would be unacceptable only to the mystic or other proponent of pure intuition. In a sense the claim was so minimal that Lewis thought it trivial, to be "taken for granted," something idealists "can hardly mean to deny" (45). To question the sensuous in ordinary cognition "is sufficient to put any theory beyond the pale of plausibility" (46–48, 66).

Lewis bridled only at the dogmatic and speculative theses of idealism. The fallacy of the dogmatic idealist lay in arguing that because things as known depended on mind, they could not have characters independent of mind. We could not infer that mind completely determined known objects from the fact that their nature was dependent on it. The dogmatic idealist neglected the possibility that "the object as known may be coincidently determined by two conditions and thus relative to both." The given was a constituent of Lewis's analysis of objects, and they had "independent" characters, most importantly, because of our awareness that we did not create the given. The idealist might, however, try to explain the existence of the given, why we had the particular experiences we did. The speculative idealist argued that the condition of experience was another spiritual being. Lewis said he could not concern himself with this speculation, but he did venture that the "particularity of experience is itself an ultimate—if inexplicable—datum." But both these notions were metaphysical, and he need not explore them in his examination of epistemological problems. On one hand, his views were compatible with essential idealistic claims; on the other, he wanted to show that arguments for dogmatic idealism were fallacious and that he could avoid speculative idealism in his limited discussion. He concluded that it might be that "between a sufficiently critical idealism and a sufficiently critical realism, there are no issues" (184–94).

We might still hold that Lewis was a Kantian, but he thought he could eschew this commitment also. He had to ascertain how the mind validly imposed its modes of interpretation on the given. For the Kantian, requirements of intelligibility must limit experience: our forms of receptivity imposed conditions upon what we could experience. This was another "metaphysical presumption" Lewis wanted to avoid.*

The Kantian or "rationalistic" solution was impossible. If our receptivity imposed conditions on experience, we could only conjecture that these conditions belonged to mind and not to the nature of the independent real or to that portion of reality to which experience had so far been confined. The conditions would appear simply as limitations on what was given, and their continuance in future experience would be as problematic as any empirical generalization (215). Either we attributed these conditions to the nature of the independent real and consequently had no solution to Hume's problem; or we made the dogmatic commitment that these *a priori* conditions were innate to the mind, although we had no reason for doing so. Kant's work resulted in either skepticism or dogmatism; and the dogmatic alternative accepted an aspect of idealism which Lewis could not embrace: it urged that for something to be given, mind must determine it. What, at last, was Lewis's non-dogmatic and non-speculative answer?

In order for empirical knowledge to be valid the connection between certain given elements and their expected sequences must be genuinely

---

*MWO, pp. 213–19; see also pp. 37–38, 198. Lewis equated "experience" and "the given" and chastised Kant for not doing so, but this interpretation was one-sided. See Lewis White Beck's helpful article on both men, "Did the Sage of Königsberg Have No Dreams?" Nahm Lecture, Bryn Mawr College, 1972.

probable. But although experience was independent of mind, he argued, experience could not conceivably lack this order. If experience had a minimal order, then our world would be one of apprehensible things, "and to this we could conceive no alternative whatever" (219–367). His thesis "requires no peculiar and metaphysical assumption about the uniformity of experience to the mind or its categories; it could not conceivably be otherwise. If this last statement was a tautology, then at least it must be true and the assertion of a tautology was significant if it was supposed that it could be significantly denied" (x–xi). In regard to Kant,

> this means that the proof which Kant attempted in his deduction of the categories may be secured without the Kantian assumption that experience is limited by modes of intuition and fixed forms of thought. Because the deduction of the categories consists at bottom in this: that without the validity of categorical principles, no experience is possible. . . . it means that *experience must, a priori, conform to certain principles in order to be pertinent to any particular ivestigation or to the validity of any particular law of nature* (320–21).

Lewis's solution lay in the *a priori* or analytic. For this reason it bears examination.

Having a world of things meant nothing more than attributing a minimal order to the given, and we must conceive the world to be one of things. Suppose 'We must conceive the world to be one of things' was *a priori* and thus, on Lewis's normal construal of the *a priori*, analytic. From this premise Lewis deduced that the given had a minimal order. But this statement was then also analytic, and he had not shown that knowledge was valid. He had only shown that if we explicated our meanings carefully we learned that the given was defined as that which had minimal order. If the statement was synthetic then Lewis might have shown that knowledge was valid, but the price he would have paid would have been to grant the existence of the synthetic *a priori*.* And, indeed, we could reasonably argue that the statement 'We must conceive the world to be one of things' was not *a priori* in Lewis's usual sense. The *a priori* was definitive of concepts, and thus analytic. But he

---

*If this was a synthetic truth *a posteriori*, we might argue that Lewis had then not deduced it from his premise, or that because it was synthetic and probable only it begged Hume's question. But we need not go in these directions.

reiterated that the *a priori* must have conceivable alternatives. This crucial tautology had no alternatives (213–36, 368). As Lewis White Beck pointed out, this was exactly the characteristic of Kant's synthetic *a priori*: "the characteristic that the concepts or principles are necessary in application to experience, and therefore universally applicable to experience be its content what it may."[38] The principle Lewis used to validate knowledge was *a priori* in the metaphysical sense he denied. Accordingly, he presumed that our receptivity imposed conditions on sense. From his perspective this was a dogmatic, rationalistic claim.

Consider the question in a different light. In one place Lewis urged that he would prove that "knowledge is valid by showing that the only alternative is chaos" (321). But this proof was not forthcoming: what he proved—again and again—was that we could not *conceive* of a non-chaotic alternative.* The only alternative to the *conception* of the validity of knowledge was the meaningless conception that there were no things; it was impossible to *conceive* that the given was unintelligible; we could not *imagine* experience that would not validate probable prediction; to envisage such experience was to *conceive* the inconceivable (368–85).

Suppose it was licit to infer the way the world was from the way we must conceive the world. Lewis could not then maintain the conceptual-empirical distinction. He assured the validity of knowledge by appealing to the dependence of the given on mind—the requirements of intelligibility limited the given.[39]

Lewis's unsuccessful attempts to repudiate the idealism bequeathed to him by Royce explained the ambiguities in *Mind and the World-Order*. His early work stressed that only an idealistic position guaranteed the validity of knowledge and saved us from skepticism. *Mind and the World-Order* culminated a movement away from idealism and metaphysics generally; in it Lewis tried to do what he previously argued was impossible—to secure the validity of knowledge without resorting to idealism. He assumed what he later called "some ground in experience, some factuality it directly affords, which plays an indispensable part in the

---

In two places Lewis did permit alternatives. He asserted at one point that it was simply a miracle that an intelligible world existed (145). At another point he admitted that his tautology was such "if we should be possessed of an adequate set of categories," but how we were to get these he did not say (322–23).

validation of empirical beliefs."[40] The distinction between this given and mind's contribution, Lewis contended, coincided with the division between the empirical and the conceptual. But in "proving" the validity of knowledge, Lewis collapsed this distinction: he secured the ground of knowledge only if he did not bifurcate the way the world was from the way we conceived it. Perhaps this is only an admission that Lewis was a pragmatist, but I think it is more accurate to say that Lewis's pragmatic epistemology was not free of metaphysical commitment: it avoided skepticism only by embracing what he called a dogmatic idealism. Just as Royce's possibility of error argument escaped skepticism by building on a statement that was reasserted in its denial, so Lewis refuted Hume by building on a statement whose contradiction was inconceivable. Lewis acknowledged the importance of the history of philosophy to philosophizing, and his major contribution to the history of thought evidenced his original fusion of past doctrines.

Lewis and the Profession

With the exception of Peirce, Lewis was the most capable philosopher in the school we have studied. He was the pre-eminent American thinker of his generation. When Columbia University gave him a Butler medal in gold, it cited him as "an outstanding contributor to modern formal logic, creative systematizer of the pragmatic philosophy of knowledge and distinguished and influential teacher of philosophy." "His vigorous and forthright teachings have profoundly modified the temper of contemporary philosophy."[41] Yet historians of ideas have overlooked Lewis in their attention to the public aspects of speculation originating in the classic period. In so doing they ignore the decisive transformation in American thought in the twentieth century. To understand Lewis's career and the thrust of his work is to understand the growth of professional scholarship and the academic bureaucracy in the twentieth century.

Lewis was a private person. He lost two of his four children. The first was his oldest son; when the second child, a daughter, died suddenly in the early 1930s, he was scarcely able to meet his classes. A disease crippled a third child. But Lewis bore these trials and other vicissitudes stoically. The enduring aspect of his personality was an unwavering, rigid, and almost puritanical adherence to the demands of his lifework, an unsparing honesty and an utter dedication to the rational pursuit of truth. This trait, more than anything else, I think, accounted for his long battle against philosophical skepticism; it also accounted for his lack of interest in his own popularity, in the "relevance" of his speculation, in the affairs of the contemporary world, or in "the philosophy of life." He was equally uncompromising in what he expected of his readers, and as a result wrote for and lectured to a tiny group of scholars. His personal integrity meshed with the rigors of the profession. He published only in its learned journals, and his subject was intelligible solely to the philosophically erudite and the technically educated. When Chicago awarded him a Doctor of Humane Letters degree in 1941, it paid homage to the "shrewd logician whose lucid investigations of symbolic logic and of the theory of knowledge have imbued American philosophy with scientific rigor, scholarly detachment, and philosophical clarity."[42]

Perry retired from Harvard in 1946. During the Second World War he threw off the disinterested air of *General Theory of Value* and became a militant propagandist for the Allied cause, writing even more activist prose for the democracies than he had during the First World War. After the war as an emeritus professor, he continued to defend the American way against enemies of the left and right.[43] Hocking, who had retired in 1943, joined him in applying speculative truths to practical affairs by his work on the religious aspects of global politics. Both men's later careers were clearly in the public tradition of James and Royce. Lewis was just eight years younger than Perry and ten years younger than Hocking but almost of another generation. Although he had strong political feelings, he never considered advancing himself as an expert or taking advantage of qualifications which some might think accrued to him as a holder of an academic position. He did not think himself a "political scientist" and believed that speaking out on public issues would have been untoward. A scholar outside his special field of competence, Lewis said, "can be as much of a Goddamn fool as anyone else."[44] During the war, while Perry lambasted the Nazis and Hocking preached a Christian internationalism, Lewis finished his 1946 treatise, *An Analysis of Knowledge and Valuation.* For over 550 pages he took up the issues he had first broached in *Mind and the World-Order,* and those who came to graduate school after the war read Lewis and not Perry or Hocking.

Yet Lewis was more than a systematic epistemologist. Like those before him, he believed that, although moral and social philosophy were logically dependent on more theoretical speculation, only these "practical" concerns finally legitimated the philosophic enterprise. While he spent almost his entire career doing epistemological spadework, it had an ulterior purpose. The intent of *An Analysis of Knowledge and Valuation* was to elaborate the theory of knowledge he had developed and to show that it could justify an empiricist theory of value: he grounded both science and evaluation similarly.

After retiring from Harvard, he culminated his studies with a moral and social philosophy based on Roycean premises. Disturbed that his own work might have contributed to an over-emphasis on logic, he condemned contemporary philosophy and his Harvard successors for their lack of "moral earnestness." He felt so strongly about the dominant post-war ethical theory—he thought its "subjectivist," "emotivist" views the epitome of irrationalism—that he wanted to write for the general intellectual public, to stem what he felt was the confusion and cynicism of his times.[45] But this fruition of his life's work poignantly revealed the change that had occurred in American thought. Lewis's best work was in logic and epistemology. He gave his time to these fields, and when he turned to ethics and social philosophy, it was too late to give them the attention they deserved. His last studies went unnoticed by the public and unread by his peers. With Lewis specialization within the profession of American philosophy was complete.

CONCLUSION

The Harvard Department of Philosophy in 1929. *Front row, left to right:* Ralph Perry, Alfred North Whitehead, James Houghton Woods, James W. Miller (instructor), John Wild (instructor), Henry Sheffer. *Back row, left to right:* Clarence Lewis, Kerby Sinclair Miller (instructor), Ralph M. Blake (visitor), Ralph Eaton, Ernest Hocking.

THE TRIUMPH OF PROFESSIONALISM

Changes in Philosophy

This book has been concerned with the history of American philosophy and the establishment of the paradigmatic modes of thought used to defend religion against atheistic interpretations of Darwin. In exploring the changing character of these ideas, I have emphasized the development of the American system of higher education and the simultaneous growth of philosophy as a profession, both of them social phenomena linked to an expanding economy and the rise of technology.

For a generation Royce and James vitalized the view that science and religion were compatible. But the Darwinian controversy was not only a fight between science and religion but also a fight between scientists and ministers as cultural arbiters. Royce and James simultaneously played both roles, combining fundamental research in basic fields with popular presentation of their practical philosophy. As science vanquished religion, however, philosophers shifted away from the ministerial role, although still working within the speculative framework created during the Golden Age. They ignored the public work of Royce and James and centered their attention on logic and epistemology. The order of the day was technical specialized research published for technically competent audiences in technical journals, with popularizations in all areas of speculation frequently relegated to hacks, incompetents, and has-beens. The professionalization of philosophy within the American university radically intensified this shift, and philosophy lost its synthesizing, comprehensive function.

During the period between the two world wars the practice of philosophy in the United States evidenced these changes. Nonetheless, it would be inaccurate to assert that after the First World War there were no philosophical generalists. Brand Blanshard, F. S. C. Northrop, and Paul Weiss, all trained at Harvard during the 1920s, went on to distinguished careers at Yale and were ambitious to philosophize in the grand manner. But these men were exceptions, and as "a stronghold of metaphysics,"[1] Yale and a coterie of schools in its orbit were finally isolated among the large graduate institutions. More and more of those trained after the war were narrow professionals: they were expert in one branch of philosophy, they oriented themselves strictly to the affairs of their discipline, and they viewed "doing philosophy" as a job. With the emergence of these professionals during the interwar period, interest in practical areas of philosophy and in the world outside the university declined while interest in the technical areas increased.

The victory of various kinds of realism was crucial in fostering these changes. Realism not only undermined the authority of idealism but also made suspect philosophers who dwelt on the spiritual aspects of life. Its success additionally narrowed philosophy's scope. Neo-realism stressed "scientific" methods. More subtle in its argumentation, critical realism opened up areas of restricted problem solving including, for example, perception, illusion, and the nature of sense data. Of great importance was Lewis's work for, although it was systematic and broached a range of epistemological issues, he posed questions that interpreters tended to answer piecemeal. Both he and the critical realists thought they could pursue the theory of knowledge without much metaphysical commitment. The Americans were also subject to currents of thought from abroad. The analytic work of G. E. Moore, Russell's elegant empiricism, the Vienna Circle's positivism, and the later language philosophy of Wittgenstein—all contributed to the austere problem-solving aura of philosophy in the United States. Finally, immediately after the Second World War "metaethics" was invented, and non-cognitivism made its main branch. The former claimed to have nothing to do with "problems of life"; the latter made these problems mere expressions of emotion.

Ironically, a current of idealism still haunted the profession. Philosophers ignored it in Lewis. In James they misconceived it. He and Royce both adopted idealism to circumvent materialistic science's attack on religion. But James's idealism was independent of the absolute, an obvious religious concept. Philosophers could secularize James's formulations, leaving much intact while dropping religion, whose defense was a losing battle no matter who took it up. What survived of James was a caricature: a pragmatism without religion that appeared as a realistic empiricism adequate to deal with science and its applications. The besmirching of idealism during the First World War fortified this misconception and so did Perry's persuasive but wrongheaded understanding of James. In the 1930s and 1940s this version of pragmatism celebrated its strength by an illicit alliance with the dominant positivist philosophies in *The Encyclopedia of Unified Science*. Although some later pragmatic analysts came to see the error of their ways, the evolution of an areligious pragmatism did much to shape the problematic view of American intellectual history that historians and philosophers came to accept.

The Second Department

During the interwar period Perry and Hocking were marginal men: they played the professional game—indeed, exemplified many of its features to young philosophers—while simultaneously trying, with no great success, to keep alive the public tradition of Royce and James.* The older catalogues had suggested that those who might want to become "teachers of philosophy" were those who were "personally interested in the fundamental questions of human thought."[2] While the later catalogues did not make this association, Perry and Hocking did so in their daily lives. During the First World War both men had skillfully defended preparedness, belligerency, and American entrance into a league of nations. During the 1920s Perry fought isolationism and materialism while Hocking wrote on political and legal philosophy. During the 1930s Hocking developed his interest in Christian missionary work and the impact of European culture on the Far East. Perry concentrated on the West, lambasting both totalitarian government and individuals with little faith in the democracies while, incidentally, completing his brilliant Pulitzer Prize–winning biography of William James. Both men continued

---

*Whitehead, who made overtures to a wider community, wrote in a style that made his important work unintelligible not merely to laymen but also to many of his professional brethren.

these activities into the 1940s (Hocking retired in 1943 and Perry in 1946), but the era when philosophy had been culturally important had passed.

If Perry and Hocking exemplified one stage of professionalization, Lewis epitomized the triumph of professionalism, although not the narrow sort. His life revolved around the world of philosophical scholarship, and within his discipline his books made a magnificent contribution. His *Survey of Symbolic Logic*, the first work of its type in the United States to deal with the "new" logic, appeared as the First World War ended. He published *Mind and the World-Order* in the middle of the interwar period; its immediate influence indicated the direction of philosophic inclinations. *An Analysis of Knowledge and Valuation*, published in 1946, culminated a long and intense period of minute exploration: its significance for academic speculation registered the end of grandiose thinking and foreshadowed the investigations of the professional community for the fifteen years after the war.*

The retirements of Hocking and Perry in the 1940s, preceded by Whitehead's in 1937, entailed another rebuilding of the department. That rebuilding, more a process than an event, is not part of my story, but the successors of James and Royce themselves surely trained men whose specialized professionalism excluded the nineteenth-century commitments altogether. When the Harvard-trained philosophers of the 1930s moved into professorial chairs after the Second World War, they were unaware that American philosophy was once important outside the university; and if they were aware, they were contemptuous of the fuzziness, lack of clarity, and woolly-mindedness of their predecessors whom, in any event, they did not bother to read.

To some extent the demise of the educated public occurred simultaneously with the rise of professionalism in the humanities. But even if we could speak of a literate upper middle class as an entity, its spokesmen after the First World War were not philosophers but journalists like

*I hesitate to go beyond 1960. After this time it is impossible to see historical trends with any clarity. The signs are mixed. Journals like *Philosophy and Public Affairs* suggest that professional philosophy is seeking new directions. Because these new directions, if such they be, were coincident with the upheaval caused by the Vietnam War and because other wars have not brought out the best in American philosophers, I suspect even more strongly that predictions are inappropriate.

At Harvard, John Rawls, in *A Theory of Justice* (Cambridge: Harvard University Press, 1971) and Robert Nozick, in *Anarchy, State, and Utopia* (New York: Basic Books, 1974) encourage different responses to the common claim that philosophy is culturally unimportant.

Walter Lippmann and Herbert Croly. Although philosophers trained these men, neither the academy nor a discipline constrained the new public thinkers, and they spent their time learning about the world and not keeping up with the literature and writing for scholarly publications. After the Second World War academics were again potent as shapers of cohesive articulate opinion, such as it was, but those who shared this power with writers and journalists were not usually philosophers but social scientists from assorted fields. From its pre-eminent nineteenth-century role as the guide of life, mid-twentieth-century Harvard philosophy reflected the irrelevance of speculation to life.

In 1936 Franklin Roosevelt had heartened the Congress by quoting Josiah Royce: "Fear not, view all the tasks of life as sacred, have faith in the triumph of the ideal, give daily all that you have to give, be loyal, and rejoice whenever you find yourselves part of a great ideal enterprise."[3] American philosophy would not get that recognition again.

Logic and Professionalism

Professionalism received its most exaggerated expression in what the department proudly called "the development of a school of logic which has extended its influence throughout the most important universities here and abroad."[4] The philosophers called attention to Whitehead, although he did his logical work before coming to Cambridge, and to Lewis. The peculiarities of professionalism, however, are best exhibited in Henry Sheffer, whose specialty was logic.

Sheffer was a student of Royce and like his master wanted to reconstruct all of philosophy on the basis of modern logic. Sheffer was not an idealist: he recognized the metaphysics implicit in Royce's logical work, rejected the interpretation of Σ as a system of will-acts, and demonstrated the inadequacy of Royce's "reduction" of geometrical principles to logical ones.[5] At the same time Sheffer, like Holt, believed that the world was a system of neutral entities whose relations logic could investigate and state. Using a single notion of inconsistency—similar to the notion of assertion through denial that Royce used time and again in his proof of the absolute—Sheffer showed that he could develop an entire system of logic.[6] In fact, Sheffer's aims were apparently so close to Royce's that the department felt that Sheffer would bring Royce's "half achieved" life work to fruition: Sheffer had seemingly "found out the solution of the problem at which Royce was working up to the last years of his life."[7]

Unfortunately, this feeble reconstruction of what Sheffer was about is the most extensive knowledge we have. His only published work of note was a 1913 article, "A Set of Five Independent Postulates for Boolean Algebras with Application to Logical Constants."[8] Logicians had typically constructed their systems using two connectives '~' (read 'not'), and '∨' (read 'or'). In his paper, Sheffer devised a new primitive notion '/' (read 'neither . . . nor . . .' or 'stroke') from which he could generate the other two.[9] This was an important contribution to formal elegance and made "Sheffer's stroke" a part of every logician's equipment. But no one knew that his primitive notion of inconsistency had a place in a wider philosophical system. It is also fair to say that Sheffer did not present his results so that anyone could recognize the wider ramifications of his work. In the second edition of *Principia Mathematica* Russell and Whitehead acknowledged that Sheffer's logical method would demand "a complete re-writing" of their study, but called on Sheffer to do the job himself since what he had so far published "is scarcely sufficient to enable others to undertake the necessary reconstruction."[10]

Sheffer wrote no more that was helpful. Assorted projects went undone and, paralyzed by an ideal of perfection, he rewrote constantly and committed nothing to print for fear that error might have crept in. Dreading also that others might steal his ideas, he made his manuscripts impossible to use by cutting typescript pages into one-by-eight-inch strips and consolidating them, along with other material of similar size, into a multitude of rubberband-bound packets.

Sheffer was undeniably a powerful intellect, but his claim to genius rested with his teaching; it made him first in the field of logic. His careful work attracted and inspired many of Harvard's best students, and through the 1930s he trained the great majority of people in the field and, as someone added, his students trained those whom he did not train. As Whitehead put it in 1938, "Where Logic is studied, Sheffer is honored."[11]

Whatever Sheffer's intent, for philosophers his work was an end in itself. Many who followed him pursued logic without metaphysical motives, and the end of inquiry was a few pages of symbols in journals unreadable to philosophers who were not logicians but undisputable to those who were. In extreme instances the subdiscipline of logic represented professionalism run amok.

Philosophy and Death

Scholasticism is not a term of approbation today because we are so far away from medieval ways of thought, and it is true that the scholastics depended inordinately on the Greeks. But in the Middle Ages scholastic thought was the central subject of the university community and the basis of the culture common to all those in the traditional professions. Philosophy was specialized but highly respected. The field integrated all areas of knowledge, and higher studies in theology, law, and medicine presupposed it. Philosophy retained this role into the modern period and into the twentieth century. Thereafter dramatic changes occurred in the United States: professionalization within the university destroyed philosophy's historic function as the synoptic coordinator of human knowledge.

In 1948 returning graduate students from years past commented on their Harvard education in a questionnaire. Graduate students are notorious complainers, and we have no way of telling when Harvard educated these people or how representative their summarized comments were. Nonetheless, the remarks of the anonymous young philosophers—perhaps they still wanted to study ultimate questions—indicated the later flavor of Harvard philosophy. Only Lewis, and to a lesser extent Sheffer and Wolfson, were given recognition as thinkers of stature. "Philosophy, as taught here," one young Ph.D. commented, "is more and more a detailed, isolated, academic discipline. Its role as the overall integrator of other fields of intellectual endeavor is increasingly curtailed."

The remarks went on. Philosophy had "abdicated" its realm of inquiry. "Departmentalism" had run wild, leading to an "inbred intellectual dogmatism." The department was "a pedagogical plant" with "too much emphasis on specialization, on marks, and on the scholarly attitude . . . and the prestige of the school." One naive student "from the business world and four years in the navy" had come to Harvard to study philosophy; both of his former employers, he said, "are noted for backbiting, petty jealousy, [and] politics." "I was sickened to find the same practices more insidiously entrenched and pursued in academic life."¹²

William James and his contemporaries had worried about death. Some interpreters of Darwin had claimed that evolution was proof positive that humanity was just another part of nature and that reality was a swarm of chaotic atoms whose existence had no meaning or value. If this interpretation were true, James and his cohorts reasoned, suicide was a legitimate option. If one did not choose suicide (or passivity), the only way to remain sane in a bitterly cruel world was to immerse oneself in the trivial details of existence, to suppress questions about life's meaning, and to get on with day-to-day business. Consequently, in order to justify an authentic life, the pragmatists in Cambridge defended a religious view of the universe. Only in so doing, James thought, could they lead a meaningful existence.

During the same period in which philosophy became a profession, political and social theorizing continued to occupy a minor place and the philosophic defense of religion began to go out of fashion. Like most academics, philosophers spent their time in administration, in committee work, in placing graduate students, in organizing conferences, and in running the journals. When narrow professionals turned to their scholarship, they thought of their work as a game. For a few, professional philosophy had become a way, not of confronting the problem of existence, but of avoiding it.

APPENDIXES

Appendix 1

THE SEPARATION OF HISTORY
AND PHILOSOPHY

Philosophers' interest in the history of thought began to shift at the turn of the century, and the event was exemplified in the first volume of Royce's *World and the Individual*. Royce explored "the four historical conceptions of being" but, uncharacteristically, did little to place these conceptions historically or to relate them to the positions held by any actual thinker. The approach was systematic, an attempt to grapple with a problem assumed to be solvable. The realists who attacked Royce thereafter, Ralph Barton Perry and William Pepperell Montague, rejected his solution but adopted his style. Perry issued a general call for scientific philosophizing with a specific plea for "the separation of philosophical research from the study of the history of philosophy."

Rightly noting that the history of philosophy derived its dignity from the originality of the great philosophers, Perry concluded that, although historical studies were vital for every philosopher, a concern for philosophical scholarship could also lead to complacent pedantry. More important, Perry was sure that the history of philosophy was distinguishable from philosophizing proper, and the latter amenable to definitive problem solving. The difficulties of historical exegesis and the enormous possibilities for interpretive error prompted him to urge separate treatment for philosophy and history to avoid wasted effort.[1] Apparently philosophy could be a science while history could not.

To these ideas Montague added that philosophers must teach the history of philosophy only as it was significant to the present. "In expounding a philosopher, we should not try unsuccessfully to take the viewpoint of his contemporaries but should treat his problems and theories frankly from the standpoint of the present."[2]

It is unfair to suggest that Montague's view was representative, but in the first three decades of the twentieth century, the students of James and Royce tended to teach the history of philosophy by teaching modal kinds of thinking and not history at all. At least this was true of the important Harvard texts used in introductory courses. Montague's *The Ways of Knowing* and *The Great Visions of Philosophy*; Perry's *Approach to Philosophy*, *Present Philosophical Tendencies*, and *The Present Conflict of Ideals*; and William Ernest Hocking's *Types of Philosophy* all put together various brands of philosophizing as differing sorts of answers to the same set of questions. They consequently continued the emphasis on philosophy as a problem-solving discipline. For their best students, the American philosophers who matured after the Second World War, the history of philosophy had the status Montague assigned it—something studied only to the extent that it could contribute to problems of current relevance.[3] In distinction, real philosophical history became a subdiscipline of its own; the *Journal of the History of Ideas* came into existence in 1940 and the *Journal of the History of Philosophy* in 1963. Arthur Lovejoy was the last example of an original thinker also notably concerned with his subject's past. Since his time, "doing history" has been an activity that did not engage most philosophers.

Appendix 2

HARVARD PHILOSOPHY AFTER LEWIS

One purpose in writing an institutional history of philosophy is to show that the philosophers who succeeded those of the classic period have a past. A major failing of the Peirce-James-Dewey principle of organization is that it makes impossible an explanation of subsequent philosophical analysis. This failing corroborates the view of those analysts who believe that "real" philosophy began sometime after the Second World War. On the contrary, if we examine the case of Harvard, there is a tradition—a concern for a similar set of problems—that goes from Peirce to Lewis and, I believe, to the most important pragmatic analysts of the quarter century after the war, Nelson Goodman and Willard Van Orman Quine. Defending this assertion is not the work of this book, but it is possible to indicate some important points.

Goodman and Quine have developed positions distinctively different from other recent empiricisms. For example, Quine's denial of the analytic-synthetic dichotomy and his espousal of what some have called a coherence theory of truth are moves that idealists have made. The viewpoint is less idiosyncratic, however, if we look at it in historical perspective.* Goodman and Quine received their training at Harvard in the late 1920s and early 1930s at the time Lewis was promulgating the ambiguous doctrines we have discussed.[1] As we have seen, he believed that the only alternatives to skepticism were his conceptual pragmatism or "rationalism." And we have noted that, although Lewis believed maintaining the conceptual-empirical distinction to be crucial to his enterprise, his pragmatism avoided skepticism only by embracing a

---

*I have illustrated my point by considering Quine's relation to Lewis and the question of alternative conceptual systems, but Goodman's relation to Lewis and the questions of induction and of counterfactuals are equally revealing if more complex. Lewis's later work, moreover, examined the Peircean epistemological problem of realism and nominalism, and this problem too has been central to Goodman and Quine.

notion inconsistent with this distinction. We might expect the pragmatic analysts to pick up Lewis's vision of philosophic options and the tensions in his own resolution. It is not surprising that Quine subsequently discarded the conceptual-empirical dichotomy in order to circumvent problems in analyzing how conceptual apparatus related to experience. If this view of the historical development is correct, we could also expect to find an idealistic strain in Quine. As he has noted, denying the analytic-synthetic distinction blurred the boundary between speculative metaphysics and natural science.[2] Moreover, where Lewis was irresolute in maintaining the distinction, I think that Quine is irresolute in denying it.

Maintaining the distinction, for Quine, rests in part on the "dogma" of reductionism, that to each synthetic statement "there is associated a unique range of possible sensory events, such that the occurrence of any of them would add to the likelihood of truth of the statement, and that there is associated also another unique range of possible sensory events whose occurrence would detract from that likelihood." But Quine claims that we cannot separate a statement's truth into its factual and linguistic components; the unit of empirical significance is the whole of science.[3] Lewis's distinction between verifying statements within the system and choosing alternative systems goes by the board, and the question is always one of choice among alternative systems. So Quine declares,

> As an empiricist I continue to think of the conceptual scheme of science as a tool, ultimately, for predicting future experience in the light of past experience. Physical objects are conceptually imported into the situation as convenient intermediaries—not by definition in terms of experience, but simply as irreducible posits comparable, epistemologically, to the gods of Homer. For my part I do, *qua* lay physicist, believe in physical objects and not in Homer's gods; and I consider it a scientific error to believe otherwise. But in point of epistemological footing the physical objects and the gods differ only in degree and not in kind. Both sorts of entities enter our conception only as cultural posits. The myth of physical objects is epistemologically superior to most in that it has proved

more efficacious than other myths as a device for working a manageable structure into the flux of experience.[4]

Quine surely emphasizes the pragmatic dimension of choice among various systems—witness his interest (and Goodman's) as far back as the early 1940s in simplicity as a criterion for choosing among alternative theories.[5] But as the above quotation makes clear, both the gods and physical objects are myths, fictions, or cultural posits, and we can speak of myths and fictions only if we have some idea of what is non-mythic, factual, or given. Because Quine recognizes this—that the "quality of myth" is relative to our viewpoint and purposes—we must ask which viewpoint we adopt in philosophy. Among the various conceptual schemes best suited to various pursuits, Quine says that the phenomenalistic one "claims epistemological priority."[6] Apparently, if we concern ourselves with the theory of knowledge, we must take as basic "the disordered fragments of raw experience"[7]—Lewis's immediate data of sense are the elements by which the philosopher must analyze the attaining and justifying of knowledge. Our choice of a conceptual scheme is pragmatic, but once we have made a choice—here to be epistemologists— it is dictated that the given is ultimate. A bit of Lewis lurks in Quine; if Lewis was committed to the given and adopted a phenomenalistic stance with a bad conscience, Quine's anti-phenomenalism is equally wavering.

The kinship of Lewis and Quine is not so much one of position but of concern for the same epistemological puzzles. In his strongest antiphenomenalist polemics, Quine regards Lewis as his bête noire; obviously they are at odds. But live philosophical disputes assume a measure of agreement and a language of discourse. Quine does not argue with Sartre or Heidegger or, to take Lewis's philosophic peers, Dewey or Santayana.

The closeness of the two men is further evidenced in Lewis's rebuttal to Quine's attack on the analytic-synthetic distinction. Toward the end of his life, Lewis urged that his essential philosophic conceptions hinged on the distinction between analytic and synthetic truth. He warned that attacks on this distinction undermined all positive epistemological work and asserted that denouncing the distinction resulted from an equally mischievous mistake—the development of extensional logical theory. Lewis directed his remarks against Quine, the successor in his chair at Harvard. But his attack was misguided. Lewis wrote that "so far as the history of thought suggests, there is no theory of the possible validity of knowledge which is compatible with such a radical empiricism as is implied by repudiation of analytic truth."[8] As he often recognized, however, skepticism was not the only alternative to conceptual pragmatism. We have seen that in 1913 Lewis believed that an extensional logic led straight to absolute idealism—making Quine and Royce, the great defenders of extensional logic, uncomfortable bedfellows.

If Lewis sought to maintain the analytic-synthetic distinction to avoid skepticism and idealism, attacking this distinction might lead to skepticism but might equally carry one to idealism. Attacking Nelson Goodman, Lewis wrote just that: the only non-skeptical alternative to conceptual pragmatism was "rationalism," the extraction of grounds for empirical belief from logical considerations alone, a revival of the coherence theory of truth.[9] As he told his students toward the end of his annual epistemology lectures at Harvard, they must choose between his theory of justification and a coherence theory like that of Bernard Bosanquet. And near the end of his life he expressed the fear that contemporary philosophers were "headed back toward Bosanquet."[10] For a philosopher like Lewis, so indebted to absolute idealism, this appears less a move backward than one in his own footsteps.[11]

Appendix 3

HARVARD DOCTORATES IN PHILOSOPHY

This appendix lists Harvard philosophy doctorates awarded from 1878 to 1930. I have estimated the age of the recipients at the time Harvard awarded the degree by subtracting the birth date from the year of the award. The letters A, B, C, and D stand for their fields of interest as various Harvard catalogues described them. A encompasses aesthetics, ethics, philosophy of religion, theology, theory of value, education, and the philosophy of law; B, psychology; C, metaphysics and the history of philosophy; D, logic, methodology, philosophy of science, and epistemology.

These fields usually reflect interests at the time of the awarding of the doctorate and, in the few cases where the catalogues do not clearly indicate a field, I have determined it from the dissertation. The ranking is from soft to hard fields—essentially from practical ones, the most important being religious, to technical, the most important being logic and epistemology. My notion of softness and hardness reflects the implicit assumptions of the philosophic community then and now. My giving a B label to psychology doctorates reflects my sense of psychology's place in philosophical studies between 1900 and 1915. I have no way of defending this judgment and no results in the book hinge on it. The numbers 1 through 4 are prestige ranking. If a man ended his career at one of the following schools, I ranked him 2, or well placed: Harvard, Yale, Pennsylvania, Columbia, Princeton, Cornell, Brown, Dartmouth, Stanford, Chicago, MIT, Michigan, Johns Hopkins, UCLA, Clark, Illinois, Texas, NYU, CCNY, and Berkeley. If a man had a chair at, or became president of, one of the above schools I ranked him 1, or eminent. A position at any other institution of higher learning I ranked 3, or placed; men who did not have college or university positions I ranked 4, or unplaced; and I considered those few for whom there was no information as unplaced. A few were unclassifiable: U. I have also added a brief description of the man's career. Finally, I have summarized relevant data on the graduate student questionnaire concerning the reasons for studying philosophy and appraisals of what it had done to their lives for those men whose records were available.

Those familiar with the history of American philosophy will spot, I am sure, categorizations which depart from their own judgments; I certainly have. This problem inheres in any supposedly objective system of classification, and I would welcome suggestions for a better classification. I would also welcome information to fill in the gaps in my data, and corrections for the mistakes to which a work of this sort is liable, although I have carefully scoured all the biographic sources available to me. I do not think the text exhausts what can be done with the data, and I hope others will use them to go beyond or revise my conclusions.

1878	Hall, Granville Stanley	32	B	1	(president and professor, Clark)
1881	Abbot, Francis Ellingwood	45	C	4	(secondary education)
1885	Rand, Benjamin	29	C	4	(librarian)
1889	Santayana, George	26	C	2	(professor, Harvard)
1891	Wright, Theodore Francis	46	C	3	(dean, Theological School of the New Church)
1893	Lloyd, Alfred Henry	29	A	2	(professor, Michigan)
	Mezes, Sidney Edward	30	C	1	(president and professor, Texas; president, CCNY)
	Bigham, John	27	B	4	(finance)
1894	Bakewell, Charles Montague	27	C	1	(Clark professor, Yale)
1895	MacDougall, Robert	29	B	2	(professor, NYU)
	Pierce, Edgar	25	B	4	(business)
1896	Logan, John Daniel	27	C	U	(professor, journalist, government)
1897	Cushman, Herbert Ernest	32	C	3	(professor, Tufts)
	Hodder, Alfred Leroy	31	C	4	(writer)
	Sidis, Boris	30	B	4	(medicine)
1898	Lough, James Edwin	27	B	2	(professor, NYU)
	Montague, William Pepperell	25	C	1	(Johnsonian professor, Columbia)
	Solomons, Leon Mendez	26	B	U	(died in 1900)
1899	Boodin, John Elof	30	A	2	(professor, UCLA)
	Horne, Herman Harrell	25	A	2	(professor, NYU)
	Perry, Ralph Barton	23	A	1	(Pierce professor, Harvard)
	Pierce, Arthur Henry	32	B	3	(professor, Smith)

	Savery, William Briggs	24	A	3	(professor, University of Washington)
	Sheldon, Wilmon Henry	24	C	1	(Clark professor, Yale)
1900	Blewett, George John	27	A	3	(professor, Victoria College)
	Norton, Edwin Lee	—	A	4	———
	Rieber, Charles Henry	34	B	2	(professor, UCLA)
1901	Blanchard, Milton Eugene	—	C	4	(secondary education)
	Carson, Lewis Clinton	28	D	U	(psychologist at many schools; has own astronomical laboratory)
	Haines, Thomas Harvey	30	B	4	(writer)
	Holt, Edwin Bissell	28	B	2	(professor, Princeton)
	Stetson, Raymond Herbert	29	B	3	(professor, Oberlin)
1902	Meakin, Frederick	—	B	4	(law)
	Yerkes, Robert Mearns	26	B	2	(professor, Yale)
1903	Angier, Roswell Parker	29	B	2	(professor, Yale)
	Burnett, Charles Theodore	30	B	3	(professor, Bowdoin)
	Dodson, George Rowland	38	C	3	(professor, Washington University)
	Dunlap, Knight	28	B	2	(professor, UCLA)
	Rogers, David Camp	25	B	3	(professor, Smith)
	Shaw, Marlow Alexander	—	B	4	———
1904	Bell, James Carlton	32	B	2	(professor, CCNY)
	Boswell, Foster Partridge	25	B	3	(professor, Hobart College)
	Doan, Frank Carleton	27	A	4	(clergyman)
	Ewer, Bernard Capen	27	D	3	(professor, Pomona College)
	Flaccus, Louis	26	A	2	(professor, Pennsylvania)
	Hocking, William Ernest	31	C	1	(Alford professor, Harvard)
	Hutchison, Percy Adams	—	A	4	———
	Mason, Mortimer Phillips	28	D	3	(professor, Bowdoin)
1905	Baldwin, Bird Thomas	30	B	3	(professor, Iowa)
	Barrow, George Alexander	23	A	4	(clergyman)
	Brown, Harold Chapman	26	D	2	(professor, Stanford)
	Dewing, Arthur Stone	25	C	2	(professor [economics], Harvard)
	Johnston, Charles Hughs	28	B	2	(professor, Illinois)
	Merrington, Ernest N.	—	C	3	(professor, University of Queensland, Australia)
	Miller, Herbert Aldolphus	30	B	3	(professor, Oberlin)
	Moore, Jared Sparks	26	C	3	(professor, Western Reserve)
	Pratt, James	30	A	3	(professor, Williams)
	Sisson, Edward Octavius	36	A	3	(professor, Reed College)
	Vaughn, Clement Leslie	26	B	4	(secondary education)
1906	Buck, Albert Francis	38	D	4	(librarian)
	Cohen, Morris Raphael	26	A	2	(professor, CCNY)
	Fuller, Benjamin	27	C	3	(professor, USC)
1907	Berry, Charles Scott	32	B	3	(professor, Ohio State)

religious and educational interests
changing to educational and
psychological, religious declining

Dresser, Horatio Willis   41   C   4   (writer)
conflict between science and
religion to interest in logic

Emerson, Louville Eugene   34   B   4   (medicine)
interested in mathematics

Gyorgy, John   30   A   3   (professor, Kolozsvar University, Hungary)
interested in law and then
philosophy

LeBosquet, John Edwards   35   A   4   (clergyman)
interested in practical problems
and then theoretical

Thackray, Edgar   31   C   4   (clergyman)
interested in religion and then logic

Waugh, Karl Tinsley   28   B   3   (professor, USC)
practical interests

1908   Caldwell, Morely Albert   31   A   3   (professor, Louisville)
religious interests

Frost, Eliott Park   24   B   3   (professor, Rochester)
theoretical interests to practical ones

Hudson, Jay William   34   C   3   (professor, Missouri)
religious doubts and temperamental
liking of speculation

Kallen, Horace Meyer   26   A   3   (professor, New School for Social Research)

Kloss, Waldemar   40   C   4   (librarian)
from psychology and logic to social
ethics

McConnell, Ray Madding   33   A   U   (died in 1911)

Parker, DeWitt Henry   23   D   1   (Henley professor, Michigan)
religious interests to epistemology

Sheffer, Henry Maurice   25   D   2   (professor, Harvard)
from mathematics to "neutral"
philosophy

1909   Breed, Frederick Stephen   33   B   2   (associate professor, Chicago)
interest in religion and education

Mellor, Stanley Alfred   27   C   4   (clergyman)

Tait, William Dunlop   —   B   3   (professor, McGill)

1910   Cole, Lawrence Wooster   40   B   3   (professor, Colorado)
interest in psychology and
philosophy of education

Cox, George Clarke   45   D   4   (finance)
from religion to logic as the basis
for ethics

Crooks, Ezra Breckinridge *religious doubts*	36	A	3	(professor, Delaware)
Haggerty, Melvin Everett *ethical problems*	35	B	3	(professor, Minnesota)
Jacobson, Edmund *psychology to philosophy to* *epistemology*	22	B	4	(medicine)
Kengott, George Frederick *religion to social ethics*	46	A	4	(clergyman)
Lewis, Clarence Irving *interests in college and general* *speculative interests*	27	D	1	(Pierce professor, Harvard)
McComas, Henry Clay *from "preaching to teaching"*	35	B	4	(business)
Marshall, Troward Harvey *religious interests to a concern for* *their rationale*	33	A	4	(secondary education)
Mitchell, Arthur *religion to philosophy*	38	D	4	———
Robins, Sidney Swain *now decided on religion as* *between religion and philosophy*	27	C	3	(professor, St. Lawrence University)

1911

Costello, Harry Todd *general intellectual interests*	26	D	3	(professor, Trinity College)
Cox, Harvey Warren *educational problems to theoretical* *ones*	36	B	3	(president and professor, Emory)
LaRue, Daniel Wolford *religious problems*	33	D	3	(professor, East Stroudsburg State)
Loewenberg, Jacob *general problems of life*	29	C	2	(professor, Berkeley)
Musgrove, William James	27	B	4	(business)
Washio, Shogoro *social and economic questions to* *philosophy to more purely specula-* *tive interests*	28	D	4	(journalism)

1912

Adams, George Plimpton *religious and social interests to* *those of logic and ethics*	30	C	1	(Mills professor, Berkeley)
Brown, Walter Theodore *interested by college studies*	29	A	3	(president and professor, Victoria University)
Dana, Edmund Trowbridge *scientific interests*	26	A	4	(medicine)
Demura, Teizaburo *religion and ethics to metaphysics*	39	A	3	(professor, Tohoku Gakuin, Japan)
Ducasse, Curt John *all sorts of unorthodox sources*	31	C	2	(professor, Brown)

	MacPhail, Malcolm *speculative interests led to those of* *religion and social ethics*	35	A	4	(clergyman)
	Parker, Willis Allen *doubting minister now interested* *in "pure philosophy"*	37	C	4	(recreation)
	Rouse, John Edward *problems of life*	41	B	U	(died *c.* 1915)
1913	Chandler, Albert Richard *interested by college studies*	29	C	3	(professor, Ohio State)
	Elliott, Richard Maurice *interested by college studies; went* *from philosophy to psychology*	26	B*	3	(professor, Minnesota)
	Fisher, Donald W. *materialistic scientific philosophy* *to more religious metaphysics*	27	D	3	(professor, Stevens Institute)
	Rattray, Robert Fleming *interest in theology; now in* *metaphysics reconciling science* *and religion*	27	C	4	(clergyman)
	Wiener, Norbert *interest in college and general* *speculative interests*	19	D	1	(Institute professor [Mathematics], MIT)
1914	Brogan, Albert Perley *interested by college studies*	25	A	2	(professor, Texas)
	Feingold, Gustave A. *problems of life and death*	31	B*	4	(secondary education)
	Givler, Robert Chenault *interested in poetry and literature*	30	B*	3	(professor, Tufts)
	Hefelbower, Samuel Gring *theological doubts to the philo-* *sophic rationale of theology;* *now philosophy independent*	43	C	3	(professor, Wagner College)
	Kellogg, Chester Elijah *interested by college studies*	26	B*	3	(professor, McGill)
	McIntire, Walter Oscar *doubting minister now interested in* *"empirical and positivist" studies*	39	A	3	(professor, Wheaton College)
	Moore, Henry Thomas *general interests*	28	B*	2	(professor, Dartmouth; president, Skidmore)
1915	Blake, Ralph Mason *interested by college studies*	26	A	2	(professor, Brown)
	Bridges, James Winfield *interested by college studies*	30	B*	3	(professor, McGill)

*Psychology after 1912.

Burtt, Harold Earnest *interested by college studies; now* *psychology with a philosophic* *bias*	25	B*	3	(professor, Ohio State)
Sen Gupta, Narendra Nath *interested in Indian cultural* *philosophy; now specialist in* *epistemology*	26	D	U	(teacher of some kind in India)
Tolman, Edward C. *ultimate questions provoked by* *science; now epistemology and* *ethics*	29	B*	2	(professor, Berkeley)
Troland, Leonard Thompson *scientific studies in college; now* *relation of philosophy to science* *and science to philosophy*	26	B*	U	(lecturer, Harvard; research on film processing)

1916
Chambers, Lawson Powers *religion to philosophy*	33	D	3	(professor, Washington University)
Demos, Raphael	24	D	2	(professor, Harvard)
Headley, Leal Aubrey *conflict between science and religion*	32	C	3	(professor, Carleton College)
Lenzen, Victor Fritz *conflict between science and religion;* *now logic*	26	D	2	(professor [physics], Berkeley)
Pepper, Stephen Coburn *conflict between science and* *religion; now philosophy*	25	A	1	(Mills professor, Berkeley)
Proctor, Thomas Hayes *conflict between science and religion;* *now philosophy*	31	A	3	(professor, Wellesley)
Underhill, Robert Lindley *college studies*	27	A	4	———

1917
Eaton, Ralph Monroe	25	D	U	(died while assistant professor at Harvard)
Robinson, Daniel Sommer *interested by college studies*	29	D	3	(professor, USC)
Wells, Wesley Raymond *the conflict between science and* *religion*	27	A	3	(professor, Syracuse)
Wieman, Henry Nelson *college studies and religion*	33	A	1	(professor [Christian theology], Chicago)

1918
Chao, Yuen Ren *intellectual curiosity*	26	D	1	(Agassiz professor [Oriental languages], Berkeley)
Locke, Alain Leroy	32	A	3	(professor, Howard)

*Psychology after 1912.

	Mursell, James Lockhart *interested by college studies*	25	C	2	(professor, Columbia)
1920	Carpenter, Niles	29	A	3	(professor, Buffalo)
	Chidsey, Harold Russell *interested by religion; now logic*	33	A	3	(professor, Lafayette)
	Kammerer, Percy Gamble	35	A	4	(clergyman)
	Phillips, George B.	25	C	4	————
1921	Blanshard, Brand	29	D	1	(Sterling professor, Yale)
	Taylor, William Sentman	27	D	3	(professor, Smith)
1922	Miller, John William	31	D	3	(professor, Williams)
	Yule, David	23	D	4	————
1923	Brotherston, Bruce W.	46	A	3	(professor, Tufts)
	Hartshorne, Charles *conflict between science and religion*	26	C	1	(Ashbel Smith professor, Texas)
	Wickey, Norman Jay Gould *interested by college studies and* *religion*	32	C	4	(religion)
1924	Glueck, Sol Sheldon	28	A	1	(Roscoe Pound professor of law, Harvard)
	Northrop, Filmer Stuart *conflict between science and* *religion*	31	D	1	(Sterling professor, Yale)
1925	Buchanan, Milross	30	D	3	(dean, St. Johns College, Maryland)
	Farber, Marvin *general interests*	24	C	3	(professor, Buffalo)
	Larrabee, Harold Atkins *interested by college studies and* *religion*	31	C	3	(professor, Union College)
	McGill, Vivian *interested by college studies*	28	D	3	(professor, Hunter College)
	Roelofs, Howard Dykeman *conflict between science and religion;* *now interested in philosophy*	32	A	3	(professor, Cincinnati)
	Shimer, William Allison *religious interests to logic*	31	D	3	(professor, Bucknell)
	Varnum, Daniel Porter	28	D	4	————
1926	Allan, Denison Maurice	29	C	3	(professor, Hampton–Sidney College)
	Baylis, Charles Augustus *religion to philosophy*	24	D	3	(professor, Duke)
	Ginzburg, Benjamin	28	C	4	(writer, journalist, government)
	Van de Walle, William E.	27	D	3	(professor, Rochester)
1927	Brown, Alward Embury *interested by college studies*	31	C	4	————

Given, Phillip Lombard *interested by college studies*	40	A	4	———
Long, Wilbur Harry *interests were always speculative*	32	D	3	(professor, USC)
Miller, Hugh *turned to philosophy after wartime internment*	36	D	2	(professor, UCLA)
Miller, James Wilkinson	25	D	3	(professor, McGill)
Stephens, Ira Kendrick	40	D	3	(professor, SMU)
1928 Fraenckel, Carl Hartwig	29	C	4	———
Hivale, Bhaskar Pandurang	39	A	3	(Wilson College, Bombay)
Kelson, Jacob Coleman	28	D	4	———
Rosinger, Kurt Edward	24	D	U	(professor, Brooklyn College; government)
Stanley, Phillip Edwin	27	D	3	(professor, Union College)
Williams, Donald Carey	29	D	2	(professor, Harvard)
1929 Chan, Wing Tsit	28	C	2	(professor, Dartmouth)
Cohen, Felix Solomon	22	A	4	(law)
Hoover, Hardy	27	D	4	(secondary education)
Nelson, Everett John	29	D	3	(professor, Ohio State)
Thomas, George Finger	30	C	1	(M. Taylor Pyne professor [re- ligion], Princeton)
Weiss, Paul	28	D	1	(Sterling professor, Yale)
1930 Lee, Harold Newton	31	A	3	(professor, Tulane)
Lee, Otis Hamilton	28	C	3	(professor, Vassar)
Minner, Charles Ben	33	D	4	———
Morgan, George Allen, Jr.	25	C	4	(government)

Appendix 4

WOMEN PHILOSOPHERS AT HARVARD

Harvard was never kind to women. When the Woman's Educational Association petitioned the corporation to consider granting degrees to females in 1872, the corporation instructed Eliot to reply "the University does not propose to give its degrees to women."[1] Twenty years later Mary Calkins, the psychologist and philosopher, created a minor scandal by successfully auditing courses in the philosophical department and requesting a doctorate for her work in 1894.[2] Calkins had completed all the degree requirements, and Münsterberg wrote to Eliot in her behalf as his "best pupil." The reply was negative: "The Corporation are not prepared to give any Harvard degree to any woman no matter how exceptional the circumstances may be."[3]

After the turn of the century circumstances had altered to the extent that the new Radcliffe College was offering advanced degrees as the form of the advanced Harvard degree for women. Taught exclusively by Harvard faculty in regular graduate courses, women were able to get a Radcliffe doctorate from 1902. Calkins was not only philosophically gifted but also adamantly convinced of her rights. Münsterberg begged her as the leader of four women who were to receive a Radcliffe degree retroactively to accept the new degree to insure its academic reputation. She refused on the grounds that she deserved and would have a Harvard degree or none at all.[4]

Counting Calkins—who went formally degreeless—ten women received Radcliffe degrees in philosophy from 1902 to 1930 and in psychology through 1912.* Despite the new arrangement with Harvard, no records for them appear in the Harvard Archives, and I have not found a single reference to them in the extensive files of the philosophy depart-

*Five others received degrees in psychology from 1913 through 1930, two in 1924, two in 1925, and one in 1929.

ment. The date for removing the barriers between Radcliffe and Harvard completely is officially given as 1943, and to this date the graduate programs did not attract women. In a study of female psychologists covering the pre-1912 period and extending through 1943, Bryan and Boring found that, of the twenty-four leading universities, Harvard-Radcliffe ranked third in conferring Ph.D.s on men, twenty-third on women. Harvard-Radcliffe also ranked next-to-last in proportion of female psychologists—0.03. In explaining these facts the authors said, "Possibly what happens is that the feminine tradition and subjects get started at a university and then carry on, with instruction and facilities thereafter adjusted so as to favor the fields that women prefer."[5]

In the Schlesinger Library at Radcliffe there is fragmentary information on the ten philosophers. Chart A 4.1 presents this information; A 4.2 summarizes some career and marriage data; and A 4.3 compares the professional achievements of the women with those of the men who received degrees in the same year, using the data and procedures of appendix 3. The data are so sparse and incomplete that it is almost impossible to draw conclusions about them. But what they do say, they say eloquently enough to need no interpretation. Marriage ended a woman's career or, at the very least, severely crimped it. Perhaps it is better to say that by the 1920s women were able to trade marriage for a career. Even then, however, no woman attained professional distinction or was even "well-placed."

My criteria for professional success relate, as I think they should, to placement at institutions influential in the profession, but these criteria should not permit us to overlook the cases of two distinguished women, Mary Calkins and Susanne Knauth Langer. I have already discussed Calkins's difficulties, but she overcame them to become recognized as a first-rate psychologist and philosopher. Although she never went beyond Wellesley, she was elected president of the American Psychological Association (1905) and the American Philosophical Association (Eastern Division) (1918). Always addressed as Miss Calkins, she was the early token American philosophers contributed to the feminist ideal.[6]

Langer was the token of the 1940s and 1950s. Married in 1921 to the luminous Harvard historian, William L. Langer, she spent the first fifteen years after receiving her Ph.D. (1927–1942) as a tutor at Radcliffe. This is a lowly position, at the nether end of the academic ladder if it is on the

		Ph.D.	Age at Ph.D.	Biographical
Mary Calkins	1863–1930	1894*	32	Professor, Wellesley College
Ethel *Puffer* Howes	1872–1950	1902	30	1902–1908, teaches at Simmons, Wellesley, Radcliffe; 1908, marries; thereafter various jobs center on "the development of women's activities."
Eleanor *Wembridge* Rowland	c. 1881–1944	1905	24	1905–1917, teaches at Mt. Holyoke, Reed; 1917, marries; thereafter various part-time jobs as psychologist, secretary to grand jury, court referee—"of necessity," "running household is chief occupation."
Francis *Rousmaniere* Dewing	1877–1964	1906	29	1906–1910, teaches at Mt. Holyoke and Smith; marries 1910; thereafter does not work. To query, Can you have a career and children? responds "I have never seen this done."
Kate *Puffer* Barry		1909	—	Employed 1909
Grace *Iler* Marshall	Died c. 1963	1910	—	Assorted teaching jobs 1899–1905; marries 1906; 1910–1918, various tutoring jobs; principal, Marshall Tutoring School, Rochester, N.Y., 1918–1936; husband dies 1922
Eleanor Robb Paterson	1899–?	1914	25	No information
Suzanne *Knauth* Langer	1895–	1926	31	Married 1921, tutor Radcliffe, 1927–1942; divorced 1942, various visiting professorships 1943–1953; professor, Connecticut College, 1954–1962
Louise P. Heath	1899–	1927	32	Professor, Hood College, Keuka College
Sarah H. Brown	Died c. 1937	1928	—	Professor, Wells College
Mary Coolidge	1891–1958	1930	39	Professor, Wellesley College

*Degree never awarded.

Chart A 4.1. Women Doctorates

The maiden names of the married women are in italics.

Chart A 4.2.

Data on Career and Marriage for Women Doctorates

	Career	No Career	Indeterminate
Married	0	3	2 (Iler, Knauth)
Unmarried	4	0	0
Indeterminate	0	0	1 (Paterson)
Totals	4	3	3

Chart A 4.3.

Comparison of Male and Female Doctorates

	Men		Women	
	Average Age at Ph.D.	Careers	Age at Ph.D	Careers
1894	27	1 eminent	30	placed
1902	26	1 not placed 1 well placed	31	not placed
1905	28	3 well placed 6 placed 2 not placed	24	not placed
1906	30	1 well placed 1 placed 1 not placed	29	not placed
1909	30	1 well placed 1 placed 1 not placed	?	not placed
1910	35	1 eminent 4 placed 6 not placed	?	not placed
1914	32	2 well placed 4 placed 1 not placed	25	not placed
1926	27	3 placed 1 not placed	31	placed
1927	35	1 well placed 3 placed 1 not placed	32	placed
1928	29	1 well placed 2 placed 2 not placed	?	placed
1930	29	2 placed 2 not placed	39	placed

ladder at all, and during this period, with the burdens of raising a family, Langer was able to write only one book, *The Practice of Philosophy* (1930). Upon her divorce in 1942 and the publication of *Philosophy in a New Key*, she left her tutorship, but despite an increasing reputation, she had no permanent employment for twelve years. She was an assistant professor at Delaware in 1943, a lecturer at Columbia from 1945 to 1950, and a visiting professor at NYU, the New School, Northwestern, Ohio, Washington, and Michigan. Two more books were published in 1953 but only in 1954 did she get a professorship at Connecticut College for Women and, consequently, permanent employment. Her work is highly regarded, especially that published after her retirement in 1962 (*Mind: An Essay on Human Feeling*, vol. 1, 1967, vol. 2, 1972).[7]

NOTES

I have used three kinds of citations in this book. First, where I have analyzed the argument of a book at length, page numbers occur in the body of the text in parentheses. Italicized material appearing in any quotation cited in this way has been italicized in the original. Second, in most cases note numbers are given and the citations collected in this notes section. Third, when I have wanted to make substantive remarks not directly related to matters discussed in the text, I have used asterisks and footnoted my remarks; citations to these remarks, if any, appear with them.

When citing articles which appear in standard collections I have always cited that volume and only incidentally the original source. In the case of William James, I have taken even greater liberties. He was a writer of articles and many of them have subsequently appeared in collections and in a variety of editions. Harvard University Press has begun to print a definitive edition of James's works, and I have used those volumes that have been published. In cases where no standard edition is available (his 1908 Hibbert Lectures on a pluralistic universe) I have merely cited the name of the original book, the name of the lecture or essay, and the appropriate section number, if one exists. In citing Peirce's collected papers I have, as indicated below, used the standard formula commentators have adopted, but I have also cited where possible the appropriate pages in Philip Wiener's useful and easily available anthology, *Charles S. Peirce, Selected Writings (Values in a Universe of Chance)*. In citing John Fiske's *Outlines of Cosmic Philosophy* I have used the two-volume edition of 1874 because it is (comparatively speaking) easily available; when I have cited his other philosophical writings, however, I have taken the appropriate reference from the 1902 collected *Writings of John Fiske* because these writings are, separately, difficult to locate.

Key to Citations and Abbreviations

A   George Herbert Palmer, *Altruism* (New York: Charles Scribner's Sons, 1919).

AI   Alfred North Whitehead, *Adventures of Ideas* (New York: Macmillan Co., 1933).

ALL   Abbot Lawrence Lowell

ALL Papers   Abbot Lawrence Lowell Papers, Harvard University Archives, Nathan Marsh Pusey Library, Harvard University, Cambridge, Massachusetts.

ALLY   Henry Aaron Yeomans, *Abbot Lawrence Lowell, 1850–1943* (Cambridge: Harvard University Press, 1948).

ANW   Alfred North Whitehead

AQ   *American Quarterly*

BHA   Hugh Hawkins, *Between Harvard and America* (New York: Oxford University Press, 1972).

CAP   *Contemporary American Philosophy: Personal Statements*, ed. George P. Adams and William Pepperell Montague, 2 vols. (New York: Macmillan Co., 1930).

CC   Edwin Bissell Holt, *The Concept of Consciousness* (New York: Macmillan Co., 1914).

CE   Francis Bowen, *Critical Essays on a Few Subjects Connected with the History and Present Condition of Speculative Philosophy* (Boston, 1842).

CEPH   Henry James, *Charles W. Eliot: President of Harvard University, 1869–1909*, 2 vols. (Boston: Houghton Mifflin Co., 1930).

CER   William James, *Collected Essays and Reviews* (New York: Longmans, Green and Co., 1920).

CG   Josiah Royce et al., *The Conception of God* (New York, 1897).

CIA   Clifford Barrett, *Contemporary Idealism in America* (New York: Macmillan Co., 1932).

CIL   Clarence Irving Lewis

CN   Alfred North Whitehead, *The Concept of Nature* (Cambridge: at the University Press, 1920).

COUS   George Santayana, *Character and Opinion in the United States* (New York: Charles Scribner's Sons, 1920).

CP   *Collected Papers of Charles Sanders Peirce*, vols. 1–6, ed. Charles Hartshorne and Paul Weiss (Cambridge: Harvard University Press, 1931–1935); vols. 7–8, ed. Arthur Burks (Cambridge: Harvard University Press, 1958). In citations the first numeral following 'CP' refers to the volume number, subsequent numerals to the numbered paragraphs in the volume.

CPCIL   *Collected Papers of Clarence Irving Lewis*, ed. John D. Goheen and John L. Mothershead, Jr. (Stanford: Stanford University Press, 1970).

CSPSW   *Charles S. Peirce, Selected Writings (Values in a Universe of Chance)*, ed. Philip Wiener (New York: Dover Publications, 1968).

CW   Chauncey Wright

CW Papers Chauncey Wright Papers, Northampton, Massachusetts.

CWE   Charles William Eliot

CWE Papers Charles William Eliot Papers, Harvard University Archives, Nathan Marsh Pusey Library, Cambridge, Massachusetts.

CWFP   Edward Madden, *Chauncey Wright and the Foundations of Pragmatism* (Seattle: University of Washington Press, 1963).

DHU   Samuel Eliot Morison, ed. *The Development of Harvard University* (Cambridge: Harvard University Press, 1930).

DPP   Murray G. Murphey, *The Development of Peirce's Philosophy* (Cambridge: Harvard University Press, 1961).

EBH   Edwin Bissell Holt

ECR   Durant Drake et al, *Essays in Critical Realism* (London: Macmillan and Co., 1920).

EFP   Philip Wiener, *Evolution and the Founders of Pragmatism* (Cambridge: Harvard University Press, 1949).

EGB   Edwin G. Boring

EGB Papers   Edwin G. Boring Papers, Harvard University Archives, Nathan Marsh Pusey Library, Cambridge, Massachusetts.

ERE   William James, *Essays in Radical Empiricism* (Cambridge: Harvard University Press, 1976).

EV   Hugo Münsterberg, *The Eternal Values* (Boston: Houghton Mifflin Co., 1909).

FB   Francis Bowen

FE   Josiah Royce, *Fugitive Essays*, ed. Jacob Loewenberg (Freeport, New York: Books for Libraries Press, 1920, 1968).

FEA   Francis Ellingwood Abbot

FEA Papers   Francis Ellingwood Abbot Papers, Harvard University Archives, Nathan Marsh Pusey Library, Cambridge, Massachusetts.

FOE   George Herbert Palmer, *The Field of Ethics* (Boston: Houghton Mifflin Co., 1901).

G   Francis Bowen, *Gleanings from a Literary Life 1838–1880* (New York, 1880).

GHP   George Herbert Palmer

GHP Auto-   George Herbert Palmer, *The Autobiography of a Philosopher*
biography   (Boston: Houghton Mifflin Co., 1930).

GHP   George Herbert Palmer Collection, Wellesley College,
Collection   Wellesley, Massachusetts.

GHPMA   Department of Philosophy, Harvard University, *George Herbert Palmer: Memorial Addresses* (Cambridge: Harvard University Press, 1935).

GS   George Santayana

GTV   Ralph Barton Perry, *General Theory of Value* (Cambridge: Harvard University Press, 1926).

H   Francis Bowen, *Modern Philosophy from Descartes to Schopenhauer and Hartmann* (New York, 1877).

HAP   A. A. Roback, *A History of American Psychology* (New York: Library Publishers, 1952).

HAW   Harry Austryn Wolfson

HDS   *The Harvard Divinity School*, ed. George Huntston Williams (Boston: Beacon Press, 1954).

HEP   Edwin G. Boring, *A History of Experimental Psychology*, 2d ed. (New York: Appleton-Century-Crofts, 1950).

HM   Hugo Münsterberg

HM Papers   Hugo Münsterberg Papers, Boston Public Library, Boston, Massachusetts.

HMLW   Margaret Münsterberg, *Hugo Münsterberg: His Life and Work* (New York: Appleton Publishers, 1922).

HPA   *A History of Psychology in Autobiography*, vols. 1–3, ed. Carl Murchison (Worcester, Mass.: Clark University Press, 1930, 1932, 1936); vols. 4–5, ed. E. G. Boring and Gardner Lindzey (New York: Appleton-Century-Crofts, 1947, 1967).

HPD   Harvard Philosophy Department Papers, Harvard University Archives, Nathan Marsh Pusey Library, Harvard University, Cambridge, Massachusetts.

HUA   Harvard University Archives, Nathan Marsh Pusey Library, Harvard University, Cambridge, Massachusetts.

IPR   George Santayana, *Interpretations of Poetry and Religion* (New York: Charles Scribner's Sons, 1900).

IWM   William A. Christian, *An Interpretation of Whitehead's Metaphysics* (New Haven: Yale University Press, 1959).

JF   John Fiske, *The Writings of John Fiske*, 24 vols. (Cambridge: Riverside Press, 1902).

JHBS   *Journal of the History of the Behavioral Sciences*

JHI	*Journal of the History of Ideas*
JHW	James Houghton Woods
JP	*Journal of Philosophy, Psychology and Scientific Methods* to 1920; *Journal of Philosophy* thereafter
JR	Josiah Royce
JR Papers	Josiah Royce Papers, Harvard University Archives, Nathan Marsh Pusey Library, Harvard University, Cambridge, Massachusetts.
JRIB	Bruce Kuklick, *Josiah Royce: An Intellectual Biography* (Indianapolis: Bobbs-Merrill Co., 1972).
L	Francis Bowen, *A Treatise on Logic or, the Laws of Pure Thought* (Cambridge, Mass., 1864).
LCW	*Letters of Chauncey Wright*, ed. James Bradley Thayer (Cambridge, Mass., 1878).
LJR	*Letters of Josiah Royce*, ed. John Clendenning (Chicago: University of Chicago Press, 1970).
LLJF	John Spencer Clark, *The Life and Letters of John Fiske*, 2 vols. (Boston: Houghton Mifflin Co., 1917).
LR	George Santayana, *The Life of Reason*, 5 vols. (New York: Charles Scribner's Sons, 1905–1906).
LWJ	*Letters of William James*, ed. Henry James, Jr., 2 vols. (Boston: Little, Brown and Co., 1920).
ME	Ralph Barton Perry, *The Moral Economy* (New York: Charles Scribner's Sons, 1909).
MF	Murray G. Murphey and Elizabeth Flower, *A History of American Philosophy* (New York: Putnams, 1977).
MGHE	William Ernest Hocking, *The Meaning of God in Human Experience* (New Haven: Yale University Press, 1912).
MS	William James, *Memories and Studies* (New York: Longmans, Green and Co., 1911).
MT	William James, *The Meaning of Truth* (Cambridge: Harvard University Press, 1975).

MWO   C. I. Lewis, *Mind and the World-Order* (New York: Charles Scribner's Sons, 1929).

NAR   *North American Review*

NG   George Herbert Palmer, *The Nature of Goodness* (Boston: Houghton Mifflin Co., 1903).

NR   Edwin B. Holt et al., *The New Realism* (New York: Macmillan Co., 1912).

OCB   William Ernest Hocking, "Other Conscious Being in Its Relation to Physical and Reflexive Objects," Ph.D. dissertation, Harvard University, 1904.

OCP   John Fiske, *Outlines of Cosmic Philosophy*, 2 vols. (Boston, 1874).

OP   Josiah Royce, *Outline of Psychology* (New York: Macmillan Co., 1903).

P   William James, *Pragmatism* (Cambridge: Harvard University Press, 1975).

PANW   *The Philosophy of Alfred North Whitehead*, ed. Paul Arthur Schilpp, 2d ed. (LaSalle, Illinois: Open Court Publishing Co., 1951).

PAR   Alfred North Whitehead, *Process and Reality* (New York: Macmillan Co., 1929).

PAT   Hugo Münsterberg, *Psychology and the Teacher* (New York: Appleton Publishers, 1909).

PBC   William James, *Psychology, Briefer Course* (New York, 1892).

PC   Josiah Royce, *The Problem of Christianity*, intro. John E. Smith (Chicago: University of Chicago Press, 1968).

PCIL   *The Philosophy of C. I. Lewis*, ed. Paul Arthur Schilpp (LaSalle, Illinois: Open Court Publishing Co., 1968).

PD   Chauncey Wright, *Philosophical Discussions*, ed. Charles Eliot Norton (New York, 1877).

PF   George Herbert Palmer, *The Problem of Freedom* (Boston: Houghton Mifflin Co., 1911).

PGA   Hugo Münsterberg, *Psychology General and Applied* (New York: Appleton Publishers, 1914).

PGS   *The Philosophy of George Santayana*, ed. Paul Arthur Schilpp, 2d ed. (LaSalle, Illinois: Open Court Publishing Co., 1951).

PHP   Robert Thompson, *The Pelican History of Psychology* (Middlesex, England: Penguin, 1968).

PIK   C. I. Lewis, "The Place of Intuition in Knowledge," Ph.D. dissertation, Harvard University, 1910.

PL   Josiah Royce, *The Philosophy of Loyalty* (New York: Macmillan Co., 1908).

PM   Francis Bowen, *The Principles of Metaphysics and Ethical Science Applied to the Evidences of Religion*, new ed. revised and annotated for the use of colleges (Boston, 1855).

PNK   Alfred North Whitehead, *An Inquiry Concerning the Principles of Natural Knowledge* (Cambridge: at the University Press, 1919).

PP   William James, *Principles of Psychology*, 2 vols. (New York, 1890).

PPT   Ralph Barton Perry, *Present Philosophical Tendencies* (New York: Longmans, Green and Co., 1912).

PR   *Philosophical Review*

PRCWC   *Philosophy, Religion, and the Coming World Civilization* (W. E. Hocking Festschrift), ed. Leroy S. Rouner (The Hague: Martinus Nijhoff, 1966).

PSS   Hugo Münsterberg, *Psychology and Social Sanity* (Garden City, New York: Doubleday and Co., 1914).

PT   Hugo Münsterberg, *Psychotherapy* (New York: Moffat, Yard, and Co., 1909).

PU   William James, *A Pluralistic Universe*

PYL   Hugo Münsterberg, *Psychology and Life* (Boston, 1899).

RAP   Josiah Royce, *The Religious Aspect of Philosophy* (Boston, 1885).

RBP   Ralph Barton Perry

RBP Papers Ralph Barton Perry Papers, Harvard University Archives, Nathan Marsh Pusey Library, Harvard University, Cambridge, Massachusetts.

RFAH   R. F. Alfred Hoernlé

RLE   *Royce's Logical Essays*, ed. Daniel S. Robinson (Dubuque, Iowa: William C. Brown Co., 1951).

RMY   Robert Mearns Yerkes

RMY Papers Robert Mearns Yerkes Papers, Yale University Medical School, New Haven, Connecticut.

RQ   Josiah Royce, *Race Questions, Provincialism, and Other American Problems* (New York: Macmillan Co., 1908).

SB   George Santayana, *The Sense of Beauty* (New York, 1896).

SEA   Sydney E. Ahlstrom, "Francis Ellingwood Abbot," Ph.D. dissertation, 2 vols., Harvard University, 1954.

SGE   Josiah Royce, *Studies in Good and Evil* (New York, 1898).

SMP   Josiah Royce, *The Spirit of Modern Philosophy* (Boston, 1892).

SMW   Alfred North Whitehead, *Science and the Modern World* (New York: Macmillan Co., 1925).

SRI   Josiah Royce, *The Sources of Religious Insight* (New York: Charles Scribner's Sons, 1912).

SSH   *The Social Sciences at Harvard 1860–1920*, ed. Paul Buck (Cambridge: Harvard University Press, 1965).

ST   Francis Abbot, *Scientific Theism; or Organic Scientific Philosophy* (Boston, 1885).

TCWJ   Ralph Barton Perry, *The Thought and Character of William James*, 2 vols. (Boston: Little, Brown and Co., 1935).

TD   Thomas Davidson

TD Papers Thomas Davidson Papers, Yale University Library, New Haven, Connecticut.

VRE	William James, *The Varieties of Religious Experience* (New York: Mentor Books, 1958).
WAI	Josiah Royce, *War and Insurance* (New York: Macmillan Co., 1914).
WB	William James, *The Will to Believe* (New York, 1897).
WEH	William Ernest Hocking
WEH Papers	William Ernest Hocking Papers, Madison, New Hampshire.
WI	Josiah Royce, *The World and the Individual*, 2 vols. (New York: Macmillan Co., 1899, 1901).
WJ	William James
WJOE	Josiah Royce, *William James and Other Essays on the Philosophy of Life* (New York: Macmillan Co., 1911).
WO	Francis Abbot, *The Way Out of Agnosticism or the Philosophy of Free Religion* (Boston, 1890).
WPD	Nathaniel Lawrence, *Whitehead's Philosophical Development* (Berkeley: University of California Press, 1956).

Introduction

1. Overseers' Report, 1860, UA II. 10. 30. 60. 5, HUA.
2. Harry Todd Costello, *A Philosophy of the Real and the Possible* (New York: Columbia University Press, 1954), p. 82.

1. Currents of Thought in Nineteenth-Century Cambridge

1. MF, "The Evolutionary Controversy."
2. See Sydney E. Ahlstrom, *A Religious History of the American People* (New Haven: Yale University Press, 1972), pp. 388–402.
3. Ibid., pp. 597–614.
4. See Jerry Wayne Brown, *The Rise of Biblical Criticism in America, 1800–1871* (Middletown, Connecticut: Wesleyan University Press, 1969), pp. 140–52.
5. See Perry Miller, "Theodore Parker: Apostasy Within Liberalism," *Harvard Theological Review* 54 (1961): 275–95; Brown, *Biblical Criticism*, pp. 153–70.
6. See Stow Persons, *Free Religion* (New Haven: Yale University Press, 1947), pp. 1–41.

7. See W. R. Sorley, *A History of British Philosophy to 1900* (Cambridge: at the University Press, 1920), pp. 203–10, 239–48.

8. See Chauncey Wright, "Mill on Hamilton," *Nation* 1 (1865): 278–81; Wright, "Critical Notice," NAR 103 (1866): 250–58; CWFP, pp. 112–14; and Francis Bowen, ed. *The Metaphysics of Sir William Hamilton* (Cambridge, Mass., 1862).

9. *An Examination of Sir William Hamilton's Philosophy* (London, 1865), pp. 12–16, 85–87.

10. This discussion depends heavily on Paul F. Boller, *American Thought in Transition: The Impact of Evolutionary Naturalism, 1865–1900* (Chicago: Rand McNally and Company, 1969), pp. 10–13.

11. MF, "The Evolutionary Controversy."

12. On this issue see Robert M. Young's provocative *Mind, Brain, and Adaptation in the Nineteenth Century* (Oxford: Oxford University Press, 1970), pp. 1–8, 194–206, 251–52.

13. On the new religious groupings, see Timothy L. Smith, *Revivalism and Social Reform in Mid-Nineteenth Century America* (Nashville: Abingdon Press, 1957), pp. 95–102.

2. Francis Bowen and Unitarian Orthodoxy

1. See "The War of the Races in Hungary," NAR 70 (1850): 78–136, and "The Rebellion of the Slavonic, Wallachian, and German Hungarians Against the Magyars," NAR 72 (1851): 205–49.

2. See Daniel Walker Howe, *The Unitarian Conscience* (Cambridge: Harvard University Press, 1970), pp. 224–26.

3. G, p. 123.

4. *Principles* (Boston, 1856), pp. 17, 20–27, 209, 457, 465–68, 479, 491–93.

5. "Francis Bowen," in *Dictionary of American Biography*.

6. G, p. vii; H, p. vii.

7. See GHP Autobiography for the source of the conventional (and distorted) view of Bowen.

8. L, pp. vii–viii.

9. G, especially pp. 19–20.

10. See the Harvard College *Catalogue* and *Report* for the years 1855–1862.

11. Overseers' Report on Bowen, January 1854, HUA.

12. Overseers' Report on Intellectual and Moral Philosophy, 4 May 1852, HUA.

13. See the *Catalogue* and *Report* for 1865 and 1879; Sidney Warren, *American Free Thought, 1860–1914* (New York: Columbia University Press, 1943), pp. 215–16, n. 17.

14. L, p. 330.

15. "Transcendentalism" [a review of *Nature*], *Christian Examiner* 21 (1836–1837): 378.

16. See H, p. 202.

17. PM, esp. pp. 95, 102, 126, 147–49, 159; FB to CW, 10 September 1864, CW Papers.

18. PM, p. 407; CE, pp. 197–201, 229, 242–43; G, pp. 368–70.

19. PM, p. 373; see also Howe, *Unitarian Conscience*, p. 81.
20. Howe in *Unitarian Conscience*, pp. 270–305, and George Fredrickson in *The Inner Civil War* (New York: Harper and Row, 1965), passim, discuss, respectively, the response of Unitarians to slavery and of northern intellectuals to the war.
21. Review of "Vestiges of the Natural History of Creation," NAR 60 (1845): 426–78.
22. G, p. 372.
23. G, pp. 221–23, 369–70; see also H, p. 277.
24. G, pp. 199–209, 233, 236–37, 241; see also L, pp. 280–81.
25. H, pp. 120, 122–25; see also G, pp. 195–96.
26. G, pp. 206–07; see also L, pp. 301–02.
27. G, pp. 200, 210–11, 216–17.
28. See H, pp. 30, 42, 150–53, 166, 217, 318–19.
29. H, pp. 77, 150–53, 217, 318–20.
30. G, pp. 139–40.
31. G, pp. 294–97.
32. G, pp. 159–60.
33. G, p. 196.

3. Amateur Philosophizing

1. Quoted in Max Fisch, "Was There a Metaphysical Club in Cambridge?" in *Studies in the Philosophy of Charles Sanders Peirce*, 2d series, ed. Edward C. Moore and Richard S. Robin (Amherst: University of Massachusetts Press, 1964), p. 4.
2. Quoted in EFP, p. 9.
3. Quoted in Fisch, "Metaphysical Club," p. 5.
4. Quoted in Max Fisch, "Justice Holmes, the Prediction Theory of Law, and Pragmatism," JP 39 (1942): 88.
5. Quoted in Fisch, "Metaphysical Club," p. 26, and Fisch, "Justice Holmes," p. 89.
6. Fisch, "Metaphysical Club," p. 22; Fisch, "Justice Holmes," p. 88.
7. Quoted in Fisch, "Metaphysical Club," p. 4.
8. Quoted in ibid., p. 15.
9. See ibid., p. 16; Max Fisch, "A Chronicle of Pragmatism," *Monist* 48 (1964): 458; Max Fisch, "Alexander Bain and the Genealogy of Pragmatism," JHI 15 (1954): 413–44.
10. The article is reprinted in Green, *Essays and Notes on the Law of Torts and Crime* (Menasha, Wisconsin: George Banta Publishing Co., 1933), pp. 1–17; and in Jerome Frank, "A Conflict with Oblivion: Some Observations on the Founders of Legal Pragmatism," *Rutgers Law Review* 9 (1954–1955): 425–63; see also EFP, pp. 152–71.
11. Quoted in Fisch, "Justice Holmes," p. 93.
12. Ibid., pp. 86–87, 93, 94; Frank, "Conflict with Oblivion," pp. 435, 444–46. For John Chipman Gray's views see Fisch, "Justice Holmes," pp. 94–95.
13. Quoted in Max Fisch, "Evolution in American Philosophy," PR 56 (1947): 368–69.

14. Fisch, "Alexander Bain," pp. 430–31.
15. See ibid., pp. 441–42; Fisch, "Evolution," pp. 362–66.
16. Quoted in Fisch, "Chronicle," p. 462.
17. WB, pp. 84, 247.
18. CP, 5: 13 (italics in original). James's "On Nihilism" was another souvenir. See my discussion in chapter 4.
19. See Fisch, "Alexander Bain," p. 440; Fisch, "Chronicle," pp. 453–55.
20. See EFP, p. 252, n. 16; Fisch, "Chronicle," pp. 443–44, 455, 456.
21. Fisch, "Chronicle," pp. 452–53; Fisch, "Metaphysical Club," p. 23. For similar thoughts by James see VRE, p. 338; P, pp. 30, 47; ERE, p. 7; CER, pp. 434–37.
22. Fisch, "Metaphysical Club," p. 16.
23. See Fisch, "Alexander Bain," p. 443.
24. Quoted in EFP, p. 23.
25. Fisch, "Justice Holmes," p. 96; Fisch, "Metaphysical Club," p. 11.
26. Fisch, "Metaphysical Club," p. 19.
27. Max Fisch, "Philosophical Clubs in Cambridge and Boston," *Coranto* 2 (Fall 1964): 16–18; (Spring 1965): 12–23; 3 (Fall 1965): 16–29.
28. Fisch, "Metaphysical Club," p. 8.
29. Information on Davidson comes from William Knight, ed., *Memorials of Thomas Davidson* (Boston: Ginn and Co., 1907).
30. LCW, p. 87; and Kurt Leidecker's biography of Harris, *Yankee Teacher* (New York: Philosophical Library, 1946), pp. 324–25.
31. Leidecker, *Yankee Teacher*, p. 366.
32. LLJF, 2: 307.
33. See Paul R. Anderson, *Platonism in the Midwest* (Philadelphia: Temple University Press, 1963), pp. 189–90; see also pp. 8–13.
34. Fisch, "Philosophical Clubs," *Coranto* 3 (Fall 1965): 18; I owe much of my knowledge here to conversations with Larry Dowler.
35. Franklin B. Sanborn, *Recollections of Seventy Years*, 2 vols. (Boston: Badger Publishing Co., 1909), 2: 485–503.
36. Ibid., 2: 489; Franklin B. Sanborn and W. T. Harris, eds., *Memoir of Bronson Alcott*, 2 vols. (Boston, 1893), 2: 532–33.
37. Sanborn, *Recollections*, 2: 504.
38. Ibid., 2: 499.
39. Knight, ed., *Thomas Davidson*, pp. 58–60.
40. A good example of the amateur decline is found in Josiah Royce's letters to Davidson in the 1890s, declining repeated invitations to Glenmore. See File: Royce, TD Papers, and the citations under the index entry Davidson in LJR.

4. Chauncey Wright: Defender of Science and of Religion

1. CWFP, pp. 3–30.
2. LCW, pp. 363–65.

3. LCW, pp. 43, 82.

4. "Mill on Hamilton"; "Critical Notice"; and "Mansel's Reply to Mill," *Nation* 4 (1867): 27–29. "Mansel's Reply," as reprinted in PD, pp. 350–59, does not contain the note that it is "a further reflection" on the Hamilton-Mill controversy; and see also LCW, p. 84.

5. "Mill on Hamilton"; "Critical Notice."

6. LCW, pp. 61, 77, 104.

7. LCW, p. 62; see also p. 82 and PD, pp. 92–95.

8. LCW, pp. 61, 81, 96–98; also pp. 115–17 and PD, p. 348.

9. For the shift, probably coming in 1865, concerning the role of inadequate evidence see PD, pp. 40–41, 101, 160–61; for the continued role of faith after 1865 see PD, pp. 160–61.

10. PD, pp. 348–49; also pp. 38–39.

11. LCW, p. 133.

12. LCW, p. 122.

13. PD, pp. 36–37, 100–01; LCW, pp. 68–69.

14. PD, pp. 115–18, 164.

15. PD, pp. 122–24.

16. PD, pp. 101, 118, 160–61, 164.

17. PD, p. 167.

18. PD, p. 101. For other citations see CWFP, pp. 51–62, 69–72; MF, "Chauncey Wright"; and J. J. Chambliss's valuable article "Natural Selection and Utilitarian Ethics in Chauncey Wright," AQ 12 (1960): 144–59.

19. For a more ambiguous statement of CW's own position see TCWJ, 1: 531.

20. PD, pp. 398–405.

21. PD, pp. 72, 88, 92; see also "Spencer's *Biology*," *Nation* 2 (1866): 724–25.

22. PD, pp. 56, 72, 76; Morton White, *Science and Sentiment in America* (New York: Oxford University Press, 1972), pp. 129–33; MF, "Chauncey Wright."

23. PD, pp. 44–45 (italics in original).

24. PD, p. 47 (italics in original); see also "Bowen's *Logic*," NAR 99 (1864): 598–600.

25. PD, p. 73.

26. See Loren Eiseley, *Darwin's Century* (Garden City, New York: Doubleday and Co., 1961), pp. 234–44.

27. PD, pp. 25, 29.

28. PD, pp. 9, 10, 17.

29. PD, p. 8.

30. PD, pp. 202, 245, 409–10.

31. PD, p. 199.

32. PD, pp. 222–25.

33. PD, pp. 206–19.

34. PD, pp. 205–09, 216–23; MF, "Chauncey Wright."

35. PD, pp. 209–17.

36. PD, p. 210.

37. PD, pp. 217–19, 224, 227–30; LCW, pp. 292–93.
38. LCW, pp. 270–72; PD, p. 234.
39. PD, pp. 230–34; LCW, p. 131. Wright calls representational realism 'idealism'.
40. PD, p. 234.
41. LCW, pp. 270–71.
42. PD, pp. 347–48; LCW, p. 104.
43. TCWJ, 2: 720.
44. TCWJ, 1: 522 (italics in original).
45. TCWJ, 2: 719–20; contrast PD, p. 247.
46. TCWJ, 1: 521; Fiske, "Review of PD," JF, 20: 98–99.
47. TCWJ, 1: 522.
48. LCW, p. 97; PD, pp. 76, 367.
49. LCW, pp. 137–39, 148, 320.
50. PD, p. xxii; CWFP, pp. 13–14, 20–21.
51. LCW, pp. 159, 175, 220.
52. LCW, p. 175.

5. Fiske and Abbot: Professorial Failures

1. The source of my biographical information is the excellent monograph by Milton Berman, *John Fiske: The Evolution of a Popularizer* (Cambridge: Harvard University Press, 1961), pp. 6–74.
2. Berman, *Fiske*, p. 92.
3. OCP, 2: 130–32, 439–42; see also JF, 21: 245–46, 344.
4. OCP, 2: 342–44, 360–63; see also JF, 21: 34, 46, 207, 299, 304–05.
5. OCP, 2: 375–80, 422, 445–49, 502–03; see also JF, 21: 200–01.
6. Berman, *Fiske*, pp. 77, 117.
7. LLJF, 2: 221–23, 394–95, 456–59, 465–66.
8. Berman, *Fiske*, pp. 199–247.
9. Berman, *Fiske*, pp. 75, 148–57, 167–70, 196–98.
10. JF, 21: 274.
11. JF, 21: 258, 386, 400.
12. JF, 21: 69, 94, 103, 210.
13. JF, 21: 338–39.
14. JF, 21: 118.
15. JF, 21: 188–89.
16. JF, 21: 306, 311–13, 319–23.
17. JF, 21: 72, 73, 83.
18. Berman, *Fiske*, pp. 204, 264.
19. LLJF, 1: 400 ff.
20. Persons, *Free Religion*, p. 32.
21. I have drawn biographical information on Abbot from SEA. On the relation to Cosmism see Sidney Warren, *American Freethought, 1860–1914* (New York: Columbia University Press, 1943), p. 54.

22. SEA, 2: 133–34, 284; *Universal Religion* (Memorial Number in Honor of Francis Ellingwood Abbot, December 1903), 11 (1903): 153.
23. Quoted in SEA, 2: 355.
24. Quoted in Fisch, "Metaphysical Club," p. 16.
25. See "List of Writings," HUG 1101. 29; "Sketch of a plan . . . ," 31 March 1875, FEA Papers; FEA to TD, 8 March 1885, TD Papers; and Box 74, File: 1886 A–B, November, CWE Papers.
26. Quoted in SEA, 2: 35, 281.
27. ST, p. x; WO, p. 72.
28. "Positivism in Theology" [a review of Spencer's *First Principles*], *Christian Examiner* 80 (1866): 245.
29. "The Philosophy of Space and Time," and "The Conditioned and the Unconditioned," NAR 99 (1864): 64–116, 402–48, respectively.
30. Ibid., p. 437.
31. Ibid., pp. 96–106, 115–16; SEA, 2: 134, n. 1.
32. "The Future of Philosophy at Harvard," November 1887 (5, number 2): 43–49; SEA, 2: 398.
33. WO, pp. 36–37 (italics in original).
34. ST, pp. 21, 33, 49.
35. ST, pp. 49, 69, 81, 208; see also WO, pp. 1, 9, 15, 20–21, 33.
36. ST, pp. xxiii, 9; WO, pp. vii, xi.
37. ST, pp. 165–67, 202.
38. ST, pp. 210–13.
39. Quoted in SEA, 2: 298–301.
40. For the Peirce-Abbot relation, see Daniel D. O'Conner, "Peirce's Debt to F. E. Abbot," JHI 25 (1964): 543–64. O'Conner's interpretations of Peirce's and Abbot's realism are incorrect.
41. SEA, 1: iii–iv; 2: 357.
42. See LLJF, 2: 476–81; Persons, *Free Religion*, pp. 106–19.
43. See Bert James Loewenberg, "Darwinism Comes to America, 1859–1900," *Mississippi Valley Historical Review* 28 (1941–1942): 351–55; and John B. Wilson, "Darwin and the Transcendentalists," JHI 26 (1965): 286–90.

6. Charles Sanders Peirce

1. I have taken the biographical information in this chapter from DPP, chapters 1, 4, and 14; and Paul K. Conkin, *Puritans and Pragmatists* (New York: Dodd, Mead, and Co., 1968), pp. 193–207.
2. Corporation Records, 24 October 1868, HUA.
3. CP, 4: 2.
4. MF, "Charles Sanders Peirce."
5. See CP, 1: 545–59; and DPP, pp. 65–92; see also CSPSW, pp. 51–68.
6. CP, 5: 259–63 (CSPSW, pp. 36–38).

7. CP, 5: 213–24, 254–57 (CSPSW, pp. 18–25, 34–35).

8. CP, 5: 225–49 (CSPSW, pp. 25–33).

9. CP, 5: 283–85, 314–17 (CSPSW, pp. 51–52, 71–72).

10. MF, "Charles Sanders Peirce."

11. CP, 5: 264–65 (CSPSW, pp. 39–41).

12. CP, 8: 38 (CSPSW, p. 86).

13. See John F. Boler, *Charles Peirce and Scholastic Realism* (Seattle: University of Washington Press, 1963), pp. 19–32; and for the spirit of my example, Nelson Goodman, *Fact, Fiction, and Forecast,* 2d ed. (Indianapolis: Bobbs-Merrill Co., 1965), passim.

14. CP, 8: 12 (CSPSW, p. 80).

15. CP, 8: 12 (CSPSW, p. 81).

16. CP, 8: 12 (CSPSW, pp. 81–83).

17. CP, 8: 15 (CSPSW, pp. 83–84).

18. MF, "Charles Sanders Peirce."

19. CP, 5: 311 (CSPSW, p. 69).

20. CP, 5: 235 (CSPSW, p. 29).

21. Murray G. Murphey, "Kant's Children: The Cambridge Pragmatists," *Transactions of the Charles S. Peirce Society* 4 (1968): 12.

22. CP, 5: 345–48.

23. CP, 8: 16, 38 (CSPSW, pp. 84, 88).

24. DPP, pp. 153–54.

25. MF, "Charles Sanders Peirce."

26. EFP, pp. 72–81; Fisch, "Alexander Bain," pp. 439–42.

27. CP, 5: 364 (CSPSW, pp. 94–95).

28. CP, 5: 366 (CSPSW, p. 96).

29. CP, 5: 398 (CSPSW, pp. 121–22).

30. CP, 5: 400 (CSPSW, p. 123).

31. CP, 5: 402 (CSPSW, p. 124).

32. CP, 5: 403 (CSPSW, pp. 124–25).

33. DPP, pp. 168–71.

34. Max Fisch, "Peirce's Arisbe," *Transactions of the Charles S. Peirce Society* 7 (1971): 206.

35. TCWJ, 2: 116.

36. Max Fisch and Jackson I. Cope, "Peirce at the Johns Hopkins University," *Studies in the Philosophy of Charles Sanders Peirce,* 1st series, ed. Philip Wiener and Frederic H. Young (Cambridge: Harvard University Press, 1952), p. 286; Jackson I. Cope, "William James's Correspondence with Daniel Coit Gilman, 1877–1881," JHI 12 (1951), esp. pp. 610–12.

37. Quoted in Fisch and Cope, "Peirce at Hopkins," p. 278.

38. P, p. 10.

39. Murphey, "Kant's Children," pp. 13–14.

40. DPP, pp. 292–93.

41. Victor Lenzen, "Reminiscences of a Mission to Milford, Pennsylvania," *Transactions of the Charles S. Peirce Society* 1 (1965): 3–11.

7. Philosophy Rejuvenated, 1869–1889

1. CEPH, 2: 343, 347.
2. For biographical information see CEPH, 1: 1–204.
3. BHA, pp. 200, 204, 212, 284–86.
4. CEPH, 1: 300 ff.
5. BHA, p. 288.
6. BHA, pp. 63–64.
7. BHA, pp. 64, 213–14.
8. Quoted in CEPH, 1: 284.
9. Quoted in BHA, p. 51.
10. BHA, pp. 4, 216; CEPH, 1: 252–57.
11. CEPH, 1: 324–29.
12. CEPH, 1: 200; BHA, pp. 32–33, 53–54, 64.
13. CEPH, 1: 317–19.
14. Quoted in CEPH, 1: 231.
15. F. G. Peabody, *Reminiscences of Present Day Saints* (Boston: Houghton Mifflin Co., 1927), p. 299.
16. CWE to American Institute of Christian Philosophy, 31 March 1882, Box 70, CWE Papers.
17. LLJF, 1: 235; DHU, pp. 453–54.
18. On these matters, see the Harvard College *Catalogues* for the 1850s and 1860s.
19. TCWJ, 1: 359–60; WJ to CWE, 2 December 1875, Box 68, CWE Papers.
20. TCWJ, 2: 373; WEH, "Philosophy at Harvard: Narrow Chances in Building 'The Great Department,' " *Harvard Foundation for Advanced Study and Research, Newsletter*, 15 May 1963; and Sheldon M. Stern, "William James and the New Psychology," in SSH, pp. 185, 188.
21. Leidecker, *Yankee Teacher*, pp. 366–67, 378–79; Fisch, "Philosophical Clubs," *Coranto* 2 (Fall 1964): 20; and see also D. C. Gilman to D. A. Goddard, 24 March 1876, File: Gilman, TD Papers.
22. See student notes, theses, and examinations in various philosophy courses preserved in HUA.
23. See in HUA the reports on philosophy for 1872 (UA II, 10.6* v. 2) and for 1874–1879 (UA II, 10.7.1*).
24. TCWJ, 1: 598 (RBP wrongly implies that the post was at Harvard); Fisch and Cope, "Peirce at Hopkins," pp. 281–83.
25. TCWJ, 1: 782, 786.
26. Fisch and Cope, "Peirce at Hopkins," p. 286; LJR pp. 22–23, 28.
27. GHP to CWE, 31 March, 7 April 1882; Stebbins to CWE, 15 March 1882, Box 71,

File: 1882, P–W; CWE to GHP, 29 March, 19 May 1882, Box 90, pp. 254, 327, CWE Papers.

28. GHP to CWE, 19 May 1886, Box 74, File: 1886, P–R, CWE Papers.
29. GHP Collection, letters of 1887.

8. *Royce and the Argument for the Absolute, 1875–1892*

1. Biographical information on Royce comes from George Herbert Palmer, "Josiah Royce," in CIA, pp. 3–9, and John Clendenning, "Introduction" to LJR, pp. 1–28.
2. See Ralph Barton Perry, *In the Spirit of William James* (New Haven: Yale University Press, 1938), p. 38, and the autobiographical statements in CAP.
3. GS to G. P. Baker, 17 May 1887, Beinecke Library, Yale University, New Haven, Connecticut.
4. *Six Nonlectures* (Cambridge: Harvard University Press, 1954), p. 25.
5. LJR, pp. 59–86; RAP, p. xii; "Before and Since Kant," *Berkeley Quarterly* 2 (1881): 134, 145, 147. For Schopenhauer see PC, p. 39.
6. FE, pp. 199–204; see also pp. 347–48, 373.
7. FE, pp. 249–53; "Kant's Relation to Modern Philosophic Progress," *Journal of Speculative Philosophy* 15 (1881): 378. See also George Dykhuizen's articles, "The Early Pragmatism of Josiah Royce," *Personalist* 18 (1937): 127–28; and "Royce's Early Philosophy of Religion," *Journal of Religion* 15 (1935): 317–18.
8. Quoted in "Introduction," FE, pp. 32–34.
9. FE, p. 256.
10. Quoted in JRIB, pp. 20–21, 244.
11. FE, pp. 112–13, 338; see also Dykhuizen, "Early Pragmatism," pp. 128–29.
12. Dykhuizen, "Early Pragmatism," p. 133; JR, "Mind and Reality," *Mind* 7 (1882): 30–54.
13. "Mind and Reality," pp. 52–53.
14. JR Papers, "Reality and Consciousness" [draft of "Mind and Reality"], Box 79, p. 6.
15. SGE, p. 158 (italics in original).
16. SMP, pp. 369–70.
17. RAP, pp. 407–15; and see JRIB, pp. 35, 245.
18. SMP, pp. 360–74.
19. SGE, p. 162.
20. Quoted in LJR, p. 24.

9. *William James: The Psychologist as Philosopher, 1869–1889*

1. LWJ, 1: 32, 118; CER, pp. 316 ff.
2. LWJ, 1: 140.
3. TCWJ, 1: 322–23; LWJ, 1: 144 ff.

4. LW J, 1: 138.
5. See the discussion in Peter Fuss and Philip Wheelwright, eds., *Five Philosophers* (New York: Odyssey Press, 1963), pp. 277–84; and Wilbur Harry Long, "The Philosophy of Charles Renouvier and Its Influence on William James," Harvard Ph.D. dissertation, 1927.
6. PHP, p. 20; PGA, pp. 111–12.
7. My account follows CER, pp. 4 ff.
8. TCW J, 2: 720.
9. CER, pp. 3–34; LW J, 1: 130–32.
10. LW J, 1: 163, 169–70.
11. LW J, 1: 167, 205.
12. The most explicit statement of the warring moral and scientific postulates is in PP, 2: 573. On his relation to his father's Swedenborgianism, see James's "Introduction" to *The Literary Remains of the Late Henry James* (Boston, 1884), reprinted in F. O. Matthiessen, *The James Family* (New York: Alfred A. Knopf, 1947), pp. 185–87; TCW J, 1: 146–66; and Robert W. Beard, "James and the Rationality of Determinism," JHP 5 (1967): 149–56.
13. For Bowen's attempt to describe "the feeling of effort," a consistent theme in his work, see "Review of *Vestiges of the Natural History of Creation*," NAR 60 (1845): 426–78; PM, pp. 91–94, 119–21; H, p. 303; and G, p. 306.
14. CER, p. 187.
15. CER, pp. 151–81.
16. CER, p. 190.
17. CER, pp. 187, 211–12.
18. See CER, pp. 43–68; "Are We Automata?" *Mind* 4 (1879): 1–22; WB, pp. 111–44; "What the Will Effects," *Scribner's Magazine* 3 (1888): 240–50.
19. WB, pp. 113, 117.
20. WB, pp. 113–14.
21. "Are We Automata?" pp. 6, 11–14.
22. Ibid., p. 11 n; see also "The Spatial Quale," *Journal of Speculative Philosophy* 13 (1879): 86–87.
23. "Are We Automata?" pp. 3–4, 8–9, 14–16, 18–22.
24. CER, p. 67 (italics in original).
25. CER, p. 200.
26. See "Are We Automata?" pp. 10–14; CER, pp. 43–68, 203–09.
27. CER, p. 67.
28. CER, pp. 35, 60–61.
29. WB, p. 9.
30. WB, pp. 115–16.
31. "Rationality, Activity and Faith," *Princeton Review* 2 (July 1882): 74–75.
32. LW J, 1: 87, 94; CER, p. 13; WB, pp. 263–98.
33. WB, pp. 252–54.
34. WB, pp. 163–65.

35. CER, pp. 20 ff.
36. WB, pp. 119–20; see also pp. 125, 130.
37. "Rationality, Activity and Faith," p. 65.
38. WB, pp. 263–76; see also CER, pp. 83–136.
39. CER, pp. 278, 281–82; MT, p. 22 n. 1.
40. MT, p. 23 n. 6; and see chapter 10.
41. CER, p. 283.
42. "On Some Omissions of Introspective Psychology," *Mind* 9 (1884): 3.
43. Ibid., p. 6.
44. CER, p. 260.
45. "On Some Omissions," pp. 11–12.
46. See MT, pp. 13–32.

10. Psychology at Harvard, 1890–1900

1. For initial reactions to PP, see PBC, pp. iv–v.
2. PP, 1: 1–6; PBC, pp. 1–8, 461–68.
3. PP, 1: 158–59, 177; 2: 122–31; and see 1: 14, 28, 30, 81, 103, 176, 180, 243.
4. PP, 1: 224–50, 400–01.
5. Robert S. Harper, "That Early Laboratory of William James" (1949), HUG 1466. 436, HUA; TCWJ, 2: 15; LWJ, 1: 301, 318.
6. LWJ, 1: 318.
7. PHP, pp. 67–74, 84–90.
8. Biographical information here and in chapter 11 comes from HMLW and HAP, pp. 192–208.
9. HAP, pp. 193–94; PP, 2: 486–92, and esp. p. 505 n.
10. HMLW, pp. 29–32; LWJ, 1: 311–13.
11. PHP, p. 133; TCWJ, 2: 138, 154.
12. PGA, p. 143.
13. PAT, p. 116.
14. PGA, pp. 59–69, 122–44, 161–62; PAT, pp. 112–25.
15. PAT, pp. 183–87; PGA, p. 177.
16. Münsterberg, *Business Psychology* (Chicago: LaSalle Extension University, 1915), p. 32 (italics in original).
17. See PP, 2: 316–17 and 617–88, esp. pp. 617, 631, 688.
18. "Can Psychology Be Founded upon the Study of Consciousness Alone or Is Physiology Needed for the Purpose?" *Addresses and Proceedings of the International Congress of Education of the World's Columbian Exposition* (New York, 1894), pp. 691–92.
19. "Preliminary Report on Imitation," *Psychological Review* 2 (1895): 223–30.
20. "The External World and the Social Consciousness," PR 3 (1894): 540–44; and see the discussion in JRIB, pp. 67–98.
21. SMP, p. 411 (italics in original).

22. "External World," pp. 543–44.

23. SMP, p. 417.

11. Hugo Münsterberg

1. *Aus Deutsch Amerikaner* followed in 1908.

2. Two of these were translations of German works, a third a rewritten edition of a German book.

3. HMLW, pp. 382, 409–10, 412–13, 418.

4. TCWJ, 2: 141.

5. For the example see PT, pp. 132–34.

6. PT, pp. 125–57; "The Sub-Conscious—Part I," in *Subconscious Phenomena*, ed. Morton Prince (Boston: Badger Publishers, 1910), pp. 16–32.

7. WJ to HM, 17 November 1899, Folder 1834 A, HM Papers.

8. PYL, pp. 229–82. The relation to Kant's antinomies is obvious here.

9. PT, p. 291.

10. See *The Eternal Life* (Boston: Houghton Mifflin Co., 1905) and PAT.

11. HMLW, pp. 95–117; CWE to HM, 24 October 1902, Folder 1678, HM Papers; HM to CWE, 25 October 1902, Box 16, Folder 231, CWE Papers; A. W. Coats, "American Scholarship Comes of Age: The Louisiana Purchase Exposition," JHI 22 (1961): 404–17; George Haines IV and Frederick H. Jackson, "A Neglected Landmark in the History of Ideas," *Mississippi Valley Historical Review* 34 (1947–1948): 201–20.

12. LJR, p. 423; WI, 2: vii–viii.

13. TCWJ, 2: 471–72 (italics in original).

14. See PGA, pp. 16, 351; and note on p. 189 above.

15. See PSS, pp. v–ix.

16. PT, pp. 1–54.

17. PT, pp. 85–124, 278–79, 281, 285.

18. New York: The McClure Co., 1908, passim.

19. See PHP, pp. 133–34.

20. See, for example, *Problems of Today* (New York: Moffat, Yard, and Co., 1910), pp. 156–60, 170.

21. *Psychology and Industrial Efficiency* (Boston: Houghton Mifflin Co., 1913), pp. 255–81, 294.

22. Ibid., p. 116; *Business Psychology*, pp. 165–289.

23. *Psychology and Industrial Efficiency*, pp. 303–08; HMLW, pp. 248–51.

24. See, for example, EBH to WEH, 27 March 1917; Letters Received, 1907–1926, General, J, HPD.

25. *Business Psychology*, pp. 240–43.

26. PSS, pp. 181–202; *Problems of Today*, pp. 103–13.

27. *American Patriotism* (New York: Moffat, Yard, and Co., 1913), pp. 134–35; PAT, pp. 307, 320; *American Traits* (Boston: Houghton Mifflin Co., 1901), pp. 162–72.

28. *American Traits*, pp. 139–72.
29. *American Patriotism*, pp. 119–90.
30. PSS, pp. 3–68.
31. *American Traits*, pp. 173–235; EV, pp. vii–viii.

12. George Herbert Palmer and Self-Realization Ethics at Harvard

1. See Alice F. Palmer, *An Academic Courtship* (Cambridge: Harvard University Press, 1940), and G. H. Palmer, *The Life of Alice Freeman Palmer* (Boston: Houghton Mifflin Co., 1908), pp. 168–310.
2. GHPMA, p. 77.
3. GHPMA, pp. 72–79.
4. Palmer, "Introductory," in *Immanuel Kant, 1724–1924*, ed. E. C. Wilm (New Haven: Yale University Press, 1925), p. 15.
5. GHP Collection, letters of 1887.
6. But see *Academic Courtship*, pp. 235–36.
7. FOE, pp. 20–34; and for ethics' place within the normative sciences, pp. 39–131.
8. PF, pp. 169–81; see also NG, pp. 89–115.
9. GHP Autobiography, p. 87.
10. PF, p. 163.
11. A, pp. 4–10.
12. NG, pp. 151–54, 166–70.
13. NG, p. 173.
14. NG, p. 179.
15. GHPMA, pp. 19–24.
16. Ibid., pp. 56–57.
17. A, p. 107.
18. FOE, pp. 136–201; see also GHPMA, pp. 38–40.
19. GHP Autobiography, pp. 79–88.
20. PF, p. 144.
21. PF, p. 203.
22. NG, pp. 191–240.

13. Building a Graduate School, 1890–1912

1. CEPH, 2: 98–99; see also p. 139. The analysis of Eliot both in this chapter and in chapter 21 is corroborated by that of Robert McCaughey, "The Transformation of American Academic Life: Harvard University 1821–1892," *Perspectives in American History* 8 (1974): 245–46, 278.
2. COUS, p. 41.
3. CEPH, 1: 252–53.
4. DHU, p. xxxix.
5. BHA, p. 38.

6. CEPH, 2: 3–15, 344–45; DHU, pp. 453–55.
7. COUS, p. 57.
8. A, p. 135.
9. *The New Education* (Boston, 1887), p. 54.
10. *Trades and Professions* (Boston: Houghton Mifflin Co., 1915), pp. 3–33.
11. Ibid., p. 34. See also G. H. Palmer and Alice Freeman Palmer, *The Teacher, Essays and Addresses* (Boston: Houghton Mifflin Co., 1908), pp. 3–30.
12. *The Glory of the Imperfect* (New York, 1898), pp. 23–24.
13. GHP Autobiography, p. 12.
14. *The Teacher*, pp. 53–60.
15. *The New Education*, passim.
16. PF, p. 158.
17. GHP Autobiography, pp. 109–10.
18. GHPMA, pp. 59–60.
19. *The Teacher*, pp. 18–19.
20. *The Teacher*, pp. 105, 117–18, 122.
21. GHP to Alice Freeman, 1887, GHP Collection.
22. GHPMA, pp. 58, 74; GHP Autobiography, p. 126.
23. See Darnell Rucker, *The Chicago Pragmatists* (Minneapolis: University of Minnesota Press, 1969), p. 10 n; and *An Academic Courtship*, p. 157.
24. Russell, *Autobiography*, vol. 1 (Boston: Little, Brown, and Co., 1967), p. 326.
25. Robert L. Church, "The Economists Study Society: Sociology at Harvard, 1891–1902," in SSH, pp. 24–26.
26. DHU, pp. xxxv–xxxvi.
27. Harvard College, *Report,* 1899–1900, p. 10.
28. "Report of the Committee to Visit the Divinity School in 1879," UA II, 10.30.79.2, HUA; Sydney E. Ahlstrom, "The Middle Period (1840–1880)," HDS, pp. 137–46. But see also Levering Reynolds, Jr., "The Later Years (1880–1953)," HDS, pp. 171–72.
29. Jurgen Herbst, "Francis Greenwood Peabody," *Harvard Theological Review* 54 (1961): 54–55. For another view see David Potts, "Social Ethics at Harvard, 1881–1931," SSH, esp. pp. 99–103.
30. See my discussion of Abbot in chapter 5; Herbst, "Peabody," 55–58; SEA, 2: 248–49; Reynolds, "The Later Years," p. 181; and Barton J. Bernstein, "Francis Greenwood Peabody: Conservative Social Reformer," *New England Quarterly* 36 (1963): 320–37. On the larger issues of social reform and the social gospel see the citations in chapter 1, n. 13 and chapter 16, n. 17; Warren, *American Free Thought*, pp. 228–31; Persons, *Free Religion*, pp. 138 ff.
31. DHU, p. 225.
32. "Report on Philosophical Department," UA II, 10.7.5.687, HUA.
33. Arthur G. Powell, "The Education of Educators at Harvard, 1891–1912," in SSH, pp. 225–29.
34. DHU, pp. 518–22.

35. Powell, "Education of Educators," pp. 229–40; BHA, p. 254. Münsterberg, an exception, still had contempt for Hanus.
36. MS, pp. 329–47.
37. WJ to Woodbridge, 16 November 1904, "History" File, *Journal of Philosophy* Papers, Columbia University, New York.
38. LWJ, 2: 228–29; PU, "The Types of Philosophic Thinking."
39. File 231, Box 116; CWE to HM, 10 October 1898, File 12, Box 92, CWE Papers.
40. See, for example, HM to CWE, 3 May 1905, HM File, Box 232, CWE Papers.
41. HM, "The Carnegie Institution," *Science*, new series 16 (1902): 521–24; "How Can Endowments Be Used Most Effectively for Scientific Research," *Science*, new series 17 (1903): 571–74.
42. WJ to CWE, 3 July 1891, File: 1891, J–L, Box 80, CWE Papers.
43. WJ to HM [n.d., circa 1906], File: 1834A, HM Papers.
44. TCWJ, 2: 270.
45. Testing of Students, Questionnaires, Box 78; GHP to CWE, 14 September 1890, File: Ma–Py, Box 79, CWE Papers.
46. GHP to CWE, 5 June 1891, File: P–R, Box 80; WJ to CWE, 9 June 1891, 3 July 1891, File: J–L, Box 80, CWE Papers.
47. GHP to CWE, 30 May 1900, File 278, Box 118; HM to CWE, 25 March 1902, File: 1902–1903, Phil., Box 289, CWE Papers; CWE to HM, 7 April 1902, File 1678, HM Papers.
48. Rand, File: R–S, Correspondence, 1927–1945, HPD.
49. BHA, pp. 65, 327 n. 42; TCWJ, 2: 270; File 231, Box 116, CWE Papers.
50. HM to CWE, 1 May 1906, File: 1906–1907, Phil., Box 291; CWE to HM, 4 June 1906, File: HM, Box 232, CWE Papers.
51. Corporation Records, 13 May 1907, HUA; and see chapters 19 and 21.
52. In addition to sources cited, I have taken biographical information on Perry from his own statement, "First Personal" (3 May 1946), 7683.5, Folder: Department Dinner, Correspondence and Papers A–L, RBP Papers.
53. LWJ, 2: 121; WJ to CWE, 24 December 1900, CWE Papers.
54. WJ to RBP, 2 January 1900, 4683.6, *J*, RBP Papers.
55. GHP to HM, 1 December 1902, File 2023, HM Papers.
56. For ironic instances of these points see: HM to RBP, 20 March 1902, General Correspondence, 1902–1914, *M*; Creighton to RBP, 28 June 1902, 4683.6 *C*, RBP Papers.
57. "First Personal."
58. WJ to ALL, File 1291, 1909–1914, ALL Papers.
59. See Andrew Reck, *Recent American Philosophy* (New York: Pantheon Books, 1964), pp. 3–11, 29–40.
60. Corporation Records, 1908–1914, HUA; CWE to JHW, 1 March 1904, File 258, JHW; HM to CWE, 11 February 1904, File HM, Box 232, CWE Papers.
61. Prof. Murdock (Committee of Nine), Li–M, Correspondence, 1927–1938, HPD.
62. On Woods's contribution to Indian thought see Dale Riepe, *The Philosophy of India*

and Its Impact on American Thought (Charles C. Thomas Publishers: Springfield, Illinois, 1970), pp. 91–93; biographical information is in "James Houghton Woods (1864–1935)," by WEH, *Proceedings, American Academy of Arts and Sciences* 72 (1938): 402–03.

63. "Romantic Philosophy," *Nation* 90 (1910): 140.

14. James, Royce, and Pragmatism, 1898–1907

1. John Wright Buckham and George Malcolm Stratton, *George Holmes Howison: Philosopher and Teacher* (Berkeley: University of California Press, 1934), p. 80.
2. RAP, pp. 441, 454, 468, 475–77; CG, pp. 49–50, 135.
3. LJR, p. 326; CG, p. 136 (italics in original).
4. SGE, p. 167.
5. LJR, p. 326.
6. John Elof Boodin, "William James As I Knew Him," *Personalist* 23 (1942): 396–406.
7. CER, p. 411.
8. EFP, p. 92.
9. CER, p. 412.
10. CER, pp. 429–31.
11. Dickinson Miller, "The Meaning of Truth and Error," PR 2 (1893): 408–25; see also "The Confusion of Function and Content in Mental Analysis," *Psychological Review* 2 (1895): 535–50; and C. A. Strong, "A Naturalistic Theory of the Reference of Thought to Reality," JP 1 (1904): 253–60.
12. CER, 371–82.
13. P, pp. 34, 38, 98.
14. MT, pp. 85–86 (italics in original); but see also pp. 132–33.
15. MT, pp. 91–92.
16. CER, pp. 371–82; MT, pp. 81–82.
17. CER, pp. 471–74; ERE, pp. 35–36.
18. P, p. 126.
19. MT, p. 23 n. 6.
20. MT, pp. 80–81, 84.
21. MT, pp. 89, 106–07.
22. MT, pp. 87–88, 130–31, 142–44.
23. MT, pp. 87–88, and see pp. 142–44; and chapter 15 below.
24. P, pp. 32–34; MT, pp. 54–55.
25. MT, p. 129.
26. P, pp. 97, 99–100 (italics in original).
27. P, p. 100; MT, pp. 56–57.
28. ERE, p. 34 (italics in original).
29. P, pp. 104, 111–12.
30. P, pp. 35–36.

31. P, p. 104; see also MT, p. 41.
32. P, p. 104.
33. P, pp. 83–84, 122 (italics in original).
34. P, p. 120.
35. P, pp. 117–20; CER, pp. 451–52.
36. CER, p. 466.
37. P, pp. 119–20; MT, pp. 37–48.
38. MT, pp. 45–51.
39. MT, pp. 105–07.
40. MT, pp. 122, 147, 157–58.
41. MT, pp. 146–48; and see Marjorie R. Kaufman, "William James's Letters to a Young Pragmatist," JHI 24 (1963): 417–18.

15. The Battle of the Absolute, 1899–1910

1. OP, pp. 197–208, 222, 226, 236, 280, 286–90, 367–68 (italics in original).
2. OP, pp. 291–93; WI, 1: 38 (italics in original).
3. On this question see H. S. Thayer, *Meaning and Action: A Critical History of Pragmatism* (Indianapolis: Bobbs-Merrill Co., 1968), pp. 522–26.
4. P, p. 135.
5. TCWJ, 1: 727–28.
6. P, p. 136.
7. CER, pp. 480–81.
8. ERE, p. 36.
9. P, pp. 116, 125.
10. PL, pp. 324–48; RLE, p. 86 (italics in original).
11. RLE, pp. 81–85.
12. PL, pp. 334–48; RLE, pp. 78–81, 116–18; see also WI, 1: 362–68.
13. RLE, pp. 116–17.
14. RLE, pp. 116, 336–37.
15. PL, pp. 341–42; RLE, p. 88.
16. PL, pp. 342–43.
17. WI, 2: 171–72.
18. MT, p. 114 n. 6 (italics in original).
19. MT, pp. 43–44.
20. "Ten Unpublished Letters from William James, 1842–1910, to Francis Herbert Bradley, 1846–1924," ed. J. C. Kenna, *Mind* 85 (1966): 327. Bradley's replies are found in TCWJ, 2: 637–44.

16. James and Royce: Public Philosophy, 1902–1912

1. A good discussion of the connection of this aspect of VRE to James's earlier thought is Gail Thain Parker, *Mind Cure in New England from the Civil War to*

World War I (Hanover, N.H.: University Press of New England, 1973), esp. pp. 157–58.

2. See MS, pp. 173–206; CER, pp. 484–90, 500–13.
3. P, pp. 137–44. For a less important defense of immortality see his Ingersoll Lectures for 1897–1898, *Human Immortality*, 2d ed. (Boston, 1898).
4. P, p. 143; VRE, pp. 114–16, 138–39.
5. P, pp. 41, 43 (italics in original).
6. P, pp. 20–22.
7. "Royce's Urbana Lectures," ed. Peter Fuss, JHP 5 (1967): 64–65, 70–71.
8. Ibid., pp. 72–74.
9. Ibid., pp. 78, 269–70, 274–76.
10. Ibid., pp. 272–86.
11. See LJR, p. 291.
12. COUS, pp. 44, 61–62.
13. William James, *Talks to Teachers* (New York, 1899), pp. v–vi, 264–68, 297–301.
14. MS, p. 276.
15. MS, pp. 287–88.
16. On this question see John W. Petras, "Psychological Antecedents of Sociological Theory in America: William James and James Mark Baldwin," JHBS 4 (1968): 132–42; and Merle Curti's analysis in *The Social Ideas of American Educators* (Paterson, New Jersey: Pageant Books, 1959), pp. 429–58.
17. LWJ, 1: 205; RQ, p. 117; TCWJ, 2: 146, but see also pp. 253, 289 ff. On Mugwump reform see Geoffrey Blodgett, *The Gentle Reformers: Massachusetts Democrats in the Cleveland Era* (Cambridge: Harvard University Press, 1966); Peter J. Frederick, *Knights of the Golden Rule* (Lexington, Ky.: University Press, 1976); Arthur Mann, *Yankee Reformers in an Urban Age* (Cambridge: Harvard University Press, 1954); and John G. Sproat, *The Best Men: Liberal Reformers in the Gilded Age* (New York: Oxford University Press, 1968). For the point of view I am attacking see Robert Beisner, *Twelve Against Empire* (New York: McGraw Hill, 1968), pp. 35–52.
18. RQ, p. 156; JR to HM, 11 April 1902, File 2097, HM Papers.
19. WAI, p. 80.

17. Jamesean Metaphysics, 1904–1910

1. LWJ, 2: 78–79, 90–93, 112, 162, 170–72.
2. "Ten Unpublished Letters from James to Bradley," p. 322; P, pp. 13, 18.
3. *Some Problems of Philosophy* (New York: Longmans, Green and Co., 1911), p. 51 n.
4. PP, 2: 275.
5. CER, p. 492; *Some Problems*, p. 51 n.
6. CER, p. 492.
7. ERE, pp. 3–5.
8. ERE, p. 14 (italics in original).
9. ERE, pp. 264–65 (italics in original).

10. ERE, p. 14.
11. ERE, p. 321 (italics in original).
12. ERE, p. 19.
13. ERE, pp. 70–72, 75–77.
14. Horace Kallen to HM, 22 November 1907, Folder 1849, HM Papers.
15. See HM to RBP, 14 April 1912, 4883. 6 M, RBP Papers; TCWJ, 2: 471; and MT, pp. 72–73.
16. CER, pp. 434–37; VRE, p. 338; ERE, pp. 22–23, 263, 271.
17. ERE, p. 81.
18. ERE, p. 22.
19. CER, pp. 443–44.
20. TCWJ, 2: 591–92.
21. ERE, p. 42 (italics in original); see also TCWJ, 2: 446, 749, 756.
22. ERE, p. 66; also p. 100.
23. TCWJ, 2: 549–50, 751–52 (italics in original).
24. ERE, p. 41 (italics in original).
25. ERE, pp. 38–39 (italics in original), TCWJ, 2: 746; for the relation of these ideas to pragmatism see MT, pp. 117–18.
26. ERE, pp. 37–38 (italics in original).
27. ERE, pp. 37, 40, 41 and see MT, pp. 59 n. 8, 117.
28. TCWJ, 2: 750 (italics in original). For the development of James's thought see pp. 588–89.
29. TCWJ, 2: 760, 763–64.
30. TCWJ, 2: 764.
31. PU, "Bergson and his Critique of Intellectualism"; "The Continuity of Experience."
32. PU, "The Types of Philosophic Thinking"; "Bergson and his Critique of Intellectualism."
33. PU, "The Compounding of Consciousness"; TCWJ, 2: 589; ERE, pp. 66–67.
34. PU, "Hegel and His Method"; "Concerning Fechner"; "Bergson and his Critique of Intellectualism"; "The Continuity of Experience." For earlier expressions see ERE, pp. 25–27, 42–43; P, pp. 76–78.
35. PU, "The Continuity of Experience"; "Conclusions"; see also *Some Problems of Philosophy*, pp. 217–19.
36. PU, "Conclusions"; James's more speculative utterances in PU were due to his reading of G. T. Fechner, see esp. "Concerning Fechner."
37. PU, "The Types of Philosophic Thinking"; that James has shifted his position is indicated by the different, earlier, statement in MT, p. 72.
38. In "The Reappearance of the Self in the Last Philosophy of William James," PR 62 (1953): 526–44, Milic Capek usefully treats these developments from a different but complementary perspective as well as supplying detailed bibliographic information.
39. PU, "Conclusions."
40. Parts of this paragraph paraphrase Craig R. Eisendrath's tribute in *The Unifying*

Moment: The Psychological Philosophy of William James and Alfred North Whitehead (Cambridge: Harvard University Press, 1971), pp. 213–14.

41. LWJ, 2: 332.

18. Ralph Perry and Neo-Realism

1. Montague, "Professor Royce's Refutation of Realism," PR 11 (1902): 43–55; Perry, "Professor Royce's Refutation of Realism and Pluralism," *Monist* 12 (1902): 446–58.
2. Montague, op. cit., pp. 49, 50–52, 54–55.
3. Perry, op. cit., p. 458.
4. Walter Pitkin to RBP, 20 January 1910, 4683.82, Box III, File: 6 Realists, RBP Papers.
5. JP 7 (1910): 373–401.
6. He summarizes the arguments in PPT, esp. pp. 113–93, 271–347.
7. Perry, "The Cardinal Principle of Idealism," *Mind* 19 (1910): 326.
8. "The Ego-Centric Predicament," JP 7 (1910): 8–9.
9. PPT, pp. 127–28.
10. Perry, "Cardinal Principle," 330–31.
11. Montague, "The Story of American Realism," *Philosophy* 12 (1937): 146–47.
12. Perry, "Cardinal Principle," p. 331.
13. Perry, "A Division of the Problem of Epistemology," JP 6 (1909): 716.
14. Perry, "Cardinal Principle," p. 325.
15. Perry, "Conceptions and Misconceptions of Consciousness," *Psychological Review* 11 (1904): 292.
16. Perry, "The Life of Reflection and Energy," Ph.D. dissertation, 1899, pp. 74–76, 119.
17. Perry, "Realism as a Polemic and Program of Reform, I," JP 7 (1910): 35–51.
18. Perry, "Conceptions and Misconceptions," pp. 295–96; PPT, pp. 172, 191; but see pp. 164–93.
19. NR, pp. 353–55, 358.
20. Montague, "Story of American Realism," p. 146.
21. NR, pp. 328, 346–55.
22. NR, p. 358.
23. CC, pp. 231–34.
24. NR, pp. 368–70.
25. Montague, "Story of American Realism," pp. 150–51.
26. Ibid., pp. 151–55.
27. NR, p. v.
28. Herbert Schneider, *Sources of Contemporary Philosophical Realism in America* (Indianapolis: Bobbs-Merrill Co., 1964), p. 17.
29. Perry, "William Pepperell Montague and the New Realists," JP 51 (1954): 606.
30. RBP to W. T. Marvin, 12 January 1910, 4683.82, Box III, File: 6 Realists, RBP Papers.

31. Perry, "Realism as a Polemic and a Program for Reform, II," JP 7 (1910): 371–72.

32. On this see Royce's "On Definitions and Debates," JP 9 (1912): 85–100.

33. See, for example, "The Ego-Centric Predicament," pp. 5–14.

34. Pitkin to RBP, as in note 4 above.

19. George Santayana

1. The treatment of Santayana's life and poetry depend in analysis and language on a convincing article: Lois Hughson, "The Uses of Despair: The Sources of Creative Energy in George Santayana," AQ 23 (1971): 725–37. See also Hughson's *Thresholds of Reality* (Port Washington, N.Y.: Kennikat Press, 1977). Also helpful: Douglas L. Wilson, "Santayana's *Metanoia*: The Second Sonnet Sequence," *New England Quarterly* 39 (1966): 3–25. For the longer view of the growth of Santayana's thought and personality see Herbert W. Schneider, "Crises in Santayana's Life and Mind," *Southern Journal of Philosophy* 10 (1972): 109–13 and *Dialogue on George Santayana*, ed. Corliss Lamont (New York: Horizon Press, 1959), passim; and Maurice F. Brown, "Santayana's American Roots," *New England Quarterly* 33 (1960), pp. 435–51.

2. PGS, p. 8.

3. IPR, pp. 1–11, 270–72; see also SB, pp. 124–44.

4. IPR, pp. 11–23; for similar signs of tension see pp. 75, 137–38 and SB, pp. 105–06.

5. LR, 1: 1–8; Timothy L. Sprigge, *Santayana: An Examination of his Philosophy* (London: Routledge and Kegan Paul, 1974), pp. 15, 209.

6. TCWJ, 2: 395–405, 534–52.

7. The best way to follow the ambiguities of *The Life of Reason* is to read it along with the 1922 "Preface" to the second edition (New York: Charles Scribner's Sons) and the 1953 one-volume edition (New York: Charles Scribner's Sons) revised by Santayana in collaboration with Daniel Cory. See also: Andrew J. Reck, "Realism in Santayana's *Life of Reason*," *Monist* 51 (1967): 238–66; and George Santayana, "System in Lectures" (Santayana's extensive lecture notes for fall 1909, edited by Daniel Cory), *Review of Metaphysics* 10 (1956–1957): 626–59. There is at least one passage in which Santayana puts neo-realism and representational realism together. He calls the external reality "this hybrid object, sensuous in its materials and ideal in its locus" (LR, 1: 82). Also useful is Gary R. Stolz, "The Reception of Santayana's *Life of Reason* among American Philosophers," JHP 14 (1976): 323–35.

8. ECR, pp. 4–5, 20–21, and notes thereto for disagreements among the seven.

9. PGS, p. 8.

10. See Hughson, "The Uses of Despair," pp. 734–35; information on students' ideas comes from an interview with Wilmon Sheldon, 15 June 1972.

11. COUS, p. 59; TCWJ, 2: 270, 321.

12. CWE to RMY, 4 May 1921, RMY Papers.

13. *The Middle Span* (vol. 2 of *Persons and Places*) (New York: Charles Scribner's Sons, 1945), p. 159.

14. PGS, p. 602.

15. *The Background of My Life* (vol. 1 of *Persons and Places*) (New York: Charles Scribner's Sons, 1944), p. 187.
16. Harold U. Faulkner, *The Quest for Social Justice 1898–1914* (New York: Macmillan Co., 1931), p. 22.
17. COUS, "Preface," n. p.
18. PGS, p. 10.
19. "The Genteel Tradition in American Philosophy," *University of California Chronicle* 13 (1911): 357–80; COUS; and *The Genteel Tradition at Bay* (New York: Charles Scribner's Sons, 1931). The essays are collected in Douglas L. Wilson, ed., *The Genteel Tradition: Nine Essays by George Santayana* (Cambridge: Harvard University Press, 1967).
20. Sydney E. Ahlstrom, ed., "Introduction" to *Theology in America* (Indianapolis: Bobbs-Merrill Co., 1967), p. 58.
21. *The Idler and His Works*, ed. Daniel Cory (New York: George Braziller, 1957), p. 20.

20. *Royce's Later Work: Logic, Pluralism, and* The Problem of Christianity

1. PR, 3 (1894): 216–17.
2. CG, pp. 141, 298, 302.
3. LJR, p. 473.
4. WI, 1: 472–82, 493. And see Bertrand P. Helm, "The Critical Philosophy and the Royce-Bradley Dialogue," JHP 11 (1973): 229–36.
5. WI, 2: v; Notebooks on Logic, Box 2, Notebook; Psychology Lectures ["Note," 5 February 1901], p. 49, JR Papers.
6. OP, pp. 251–57 (italics in original).
7. CP, 8: 117 n. 10, 125, 131, 277.
8. *Royce's Metaphysics*, trans. Virginia and Gordon Ringer (Chicago: Henry Regnery Co., 1956), p. 95.
9. William and Marthe Kneale, *The Development of Logic* (Oxford: Oxford University Press, 1963), p. 438; JRIB, pp. 147–49.
10. CG, pp. 207–08; "The Sciences of the Ideal," in [*International*] *Congress of the Arts and Science, Universal Exposition, St. Louis 1904*, 8 vols., ed. Howard Rogers (Boston: Houghton Mifflin Co., 1905–1907), 1: 164–65.
11. See Bertrand Russell, *The Principles of Mathematics*, 2d ed. (New York: W.W. Norton and Co., 1938), pp. 362 ff.
12. RLE, pp. 381–84.
13. For full discussion and complete citations, see JRIB, pp. 149–53, 179–209.
14. RLE, p. 386.
15. "Kant's Doctrine of the Basis of Mathematics," JP 2 (1905): 206–07.
16. TCWJ, 1: 819.
17. "Sciences of the Ideal," pp. 157, 160, 168; "Kant's Doctrine," p. 207; "The Present State of the Question Regarding the First Principles of Theoretical Science," *Proceedings of the American Philosophical Society* 45 (1906): 91.

18. Quoted in Daniel S. Robinson, *Royce and Hocking: American Idealists* (Boston: Christopher Publishing House, 1968), pp. 149, 153–55.
19. "Sciences of the Ideal," pp. 164–65; RLE, pp. 182, 184, 187, 188.
20. RLE, pp. 354, 363–67; "Primitive Ways of Thinking with Special Reference to Negation and Classification," *Open Court* 27 (1913): 584. The original appears in italics.
21. RLE, pp. 374–78, 388 (italics in original).
22. RLE, pp. 373–77 (italics in original).
23. RLE, pp. 367–68, 377.
24. See the discussion in JRIB, pp. 175–209.
25. RLE, pp. 149–50, 156.
26. See RLE, pp. 158–59.
27. On this question see also John Boler's "Habits of Thought," in *Studies in the Philosophy of Charles Sanders Peirce*, 2d series, pp. 382–400.
28. RLE, p. 377; and JRIB, pp. 214–17.
29. WAI, pp. 52–54.
30. LJR, pp. 604–09; JRIB, pp. 149–51, 221.
31. See JRIB, pp. 223–24.
32. LJR, pp. 645–46.
33. SRI, p. 10; PC, pp. 41–45, 64–70, 187.
34. See JRIB, pp. 230–31.
35. See JRIB, pp. 236–40.
36. Arthur O. Lovejoy, "On Some Conditions of Progress in Philosophical Inquiry," PR 26 (1917): 123–24.

21. The Crisis of 1912–1920

1. Eliot is cited in Lawrence Vesey, *The Emergence of the American University* (Chicago: University of Chicago Press, 1965), p. 325; for Santayana see GS to CWE, 16, 19 February 1907, Box 245, GS; CWE to GS, 18 February 1907, Box 96, p. 46, CWE Papers.
2. See ALLY, pp. 121–25.
3. See CEPH, 1: 169.
4. Quoted in ALLY, p. 214.
5. ALLY, pp. 212–15; and Norbert Wiener on Lowell in *Ex-Prodigy* (New York: Simon and Schuster, 1953), pp. 125–26.
6. ALLY, pp. 175–77; for women see p. 96.
7. ALLY, pp. 288–90.
8. ALLY, pp. 245–53.
9. *Modes of Thought* (New York: Macmillan Co., 1938), p. 174.
10. ALL to Charles Bakewell, 22 March 1912, Folder 1283, 1909–1914, ALL Papers.
11. RBP to ALL, 2 January 1914, Folder 1291, 1909–1914, ALL Papers.

12. GHP to RBP, n.d., 4683.6 *P*. RBP Papers; GHP to ALL, 5 March 1913, Folder 1259, 1909–1914, ALL Papers.

13. JR to ALL, 10 February 1913, Letters Received, General, 1907–1926, *R*, HPD; see also LJR, pp. 587–92.

14. RBP to Henry James, Jr., 1 May 1914, RBP to GHP, 20 March 1914; RBP to Berenson, 20 March 1914, Letters Sent, 12/1910–11/1914, HPD. In addition to these files see also Correspondence, Second File (UAV687.7.2), HPD.

15. HM to ALL, 3 January 1913, Folder 2357 (16), HM Papers.

16. See Folder 1291, 1909–1914, ALL Papers.

17. RBP to ALL, 2 January 1914; and to R. Robbins, 28 January 1914, Letters Sent, 12/1910–11/1914, HPD.

18. HM to ALL, 9 November 1912, Folder 1289; ALL to JR, 9 February 1913, Folder 1293, 1909–1914, ALL Papers.

19. Prof. Murdock (Committee of Nine) Memorandum, 3 November 1937, Correspondence, 1927–1938, Li-M, HPD.

20. ALL to RBP, 13 January 1914, Letters Received, General, 1907–1926, *L*; RBP to R. C. Cabot, 6 April and 18 September 1914; Letters Sent, 12/1910–11/1914, HPD; Folders 1281 and 1285, 1909–1914, ALL Papers.

21. WEH to HM, 6 April 1910, Folder 180, HM Papers.

22. JHW to RBP, 11 September 1916, Woods Chm., 1914–1915, Loose Material, *P*; to B. Russell, 23 September 1916, Woods Chm., Letters Sent and Rec., 1914–1916, Russell, HPD.

23. ALL to R. Robbins, 13 February 1917, Folder 236, 1914–1917; Folder 1883, 1919–1922, ALL Papers. The best account of Russell's association with Harvard is in Barry Feinberg and Ronald Kasrils, *Bertrand Russell's America* (New York: Viking Press, 1974), pp. 39–81.

24. ALL to R. Robbins, 18 February 1917, Folder 236, 1914–1917; WEH to ALL, 15 June 1920, Folder 636, 1919–1922; RFAH to ALL, 19 November 1917, Folder 1883, 1917–1919; RFAH to ALL, 3 August 1919, and ALL to RFAH, 26 August 1919, Folder 558, 1917–1919, ALL Papers.

25. R. Robbins to ALL, 7 June 1920, Folder 637, 1919–1922, ALL Papers; for information on Hoernlé see his statement in *Contemporary British Philosophy*, 2d series, ed. J. H. Muirhead (New York: Macmillan Co., 1925), and the Hoernlé Festschrift, *Studies in Philosophy*, ed. with a memoir by D. S. Robinson (Cambridge: Harvard University Press, 1952).

26. ALL to WEH, 6 January 1920, RFAH to ALL and ALL to RFAH, 19 January 1920, Folder 304, 1919–1922, ALL Papers; ALL to RFAH, 22 January 1920, 1917–23, *H*, RBP Papers.

27. The dispute may be followed in 1917–1923, *H*, RBP Papers; RBP to ALL, 2 December 1919; ALL to RBP, 3 December 1919; WEH to ALL, 18 December 1919, Folder 304; Department of Philosophy to ALL, 4 June and 10 June 1920, Folder 637, 1919–1922, ALL Papers.

28. RBP to RFAH, 3 February 1919, "Correspondence and Notes Re Plattsburg Move-

ment, 1921" (4683.13), Folder: Miscellaneous, RBP Papers; JHW to R. Eaton, 30 August 1924, Woods Chm., 1924–6/1925, *E*, HPD.

29. RBP to ALL, 9 May 1917, Folder 115, 1914–1917, ALL Papers.

30. Titchner to WEH, 26 June 1917, Letters Received, General, 1907–1926, *T*, HPD; WEH to ALL, 3 May 1917, Folder 1372, and Folder 1493, 1914–1917, ALL Papers.

31. Quoted in Carol Gruber, "Mars and Minerva: The American Intellectual Community and World War I," Ph.D. dissertation, Columbia University, 1968, p. 250.

32. On this issue see McCaughey, "Transformation," passim. My analysis relates only to the early part of the Eliot administration, but I also think McCaughey exaggerates the change in Eliot's views (pp. 294, 305).

22. Edwin Bissell Holt and Philosophical Behaviorism

1. HEP, pp. 552, 557, 634.

2. HEP, pp. 561–64, 626.

3. Harvard College *Report*, 1898–1899, p. 36; and see also HEP, p. 626, and Yerkes, "Testament," 2: 388–89, RMY Papers.

4. HEP, pp. 626–28.

5. Ibid. (italics added).

6. WJ to CWE, 20 July 1907, Box 223, WJ, CWE Papers.

7. See RMY Papers, EBH File, especially EBH to RMY, 15 September 1906.

8. EBH to Ada Yerkes, n.d., EBH File, RMY Papers. For an expression of his later bitterness see "The Whimsical Condition of Social Psychology, and of Mankind," in *American Philosophy Today and Tomorrow*, ed. Sydney Hook and Horace Kallen (New York: Lee Furman, 1935), pp. 170–202.

9. CC, p. xiii. For a late view of James see "William James as Psychologist," in *In Commemoration of William James, 1842–1942*, ed. Brand Blanshard and Horace Kallen (New York: Columbia University Press, 1942), pp. 34–47.

10. On this question, see also "The Program and Platform of Six Realists," JP 7 (1910), reprinted in NR, p. 472.

11. EBH to RMY, 1909 Letters, EBH File, RMY Papers.

12. See Nathan G. Hale's references to these men in *Freud and the Americans* (New York: Oxford University Press, 1971).

13. Pages 38–39 were notorious in publicizing Holt's break with Münsterberg; the "Miss Z" of pp. 40–46 is Ethel Puffer, an early Radcliffe Ph.D.; and the Mrs. A. and Mrs. B. of pp. 36–37 are, very likely, the wives of James and Royce.

14. On this point see Hale, *Freud*, pp. 426–30, an astute discussion that misses Holt in its concentration on Freud; and for the ambience in which Holt wrote, John Burnham, "Psychiatry, Psychology and the Progressive Movement," AQ 12 (1960): 457–65, a good article that relies overly on the notion of "Progressivism."

15. *Animal Drive* (New York: Henry Holt and Co., 1931), pp. v–viii, 233–34, 252–56. And see also for some sense of his ideas: "Professor Henderson's 'Fitness' and the Locus of Concepts," JP 17 (1920): 365–81; "The Argument for Sensationism as

Drawn from Dr. Berkeley," *Psychological Review* 41 (1934): 509–33; "Materialism and the Criterion of the Psychic," *Psychological Review* 44 (1937): 33–53; and "William James as Psychologist."

16. This discussion derives from HEP, pp. 647–48, 719–21; for a bibliography of Tolman's work, see p. 662.

17. Holt to RBP, 11 September 1914, EBH File, RBP Papers.

18. WEH to RMY, 11 May 1903, Hocking File, RMY Papers; RBP to H. Sheffer, 5 October 1910, Letters Sent, Second File 1907–1917, Carbons, 1909–1910, HPD; EBH to ALL, 25 January 1918, Folder 4, 1919–1922, ALL Papers.

19. EBH to ALL, 25 January 1918; and ALL to EBH, 29 January 1918, Folder 4, 1919–1922, ALL Papers.

20. For a discussion of the issues surveyed here and in chapters 13, 21, and 24, see Frederick Rudolph, *The American College and University* (New York: Alfred A. Knopf, 1962), pp. 394–439.

21. For biographical data see Leonard Carmichael, "E. B. Holt," *American Journal of Psychology* 59 (1946): 478–80; and H. S. Langfeld, "E. B. Holt," *Psychological Review* 53 (1946): 251–58.

23. Philosophers at War

1. See letters from EBH to HM, HM Papers, File 1913, and letters in EBH, HM, and RBP files, RMY Papers. Mrs. Royce was quoted to me by Richard Hocking in an interview, 18 and 19 July 1973.

2. HM to CWE, 17 December 1906, Box 232; Box 97, 98, pp. $69\frac{1}{2}$, $70\frac{1}{2}$, 78, $88\frac{1}{2}$, $116\frac{1}{2}$, CWE Papers.

3. HM to CWE, 7 December 1908, Box 97, CWE Papers.

4. ALL to HM, 8 March 1911, Folder 495, 1909–1914; ALL to Richard Dana, 8 March 1916, File 231 A, 1914–1917, ALL Papers.

5. HM to ALL, 3 May 1916, File 231, 1914–1917, ALL Papers.

6. *The War and America* (New York: Appleton Publishers, 1914), pp. 45, 83–107.

7. *The Peace and America* (New York: Appleton Publishers, 1915), pp. 59–86, 158–208.

8. *Tomorrow* (New York: Appleton Publishers, 1917), pp. 1–73.

9. CPCIL, pp. 55, 65.

10. See JRIB, pp. 236–37.

11. *Egotism in German Philosophy* (New York: Charles Scribner's Sons, 1915), pp. 49–50.

12. *The Present Conflict of Ideals* (New York: Longmans, Green and Co., 1918) pp. 233–34.

13. Ibid., pp. 101, 174.

14. Ibid., pp. 398–433; Santayana, *Egotism*, pp. 114–43.

15. *Morale and Its Enemies* (New Haven: Yale University Press, 1918), p. 63.

16. *The Hope of the Great Community* (New York: Macmillan Co., 1916), p. 4.

17. See Hocking's "Political Philosophy in Germany," *JP* 12 (1915): 584–86; John Dewey's "In Reply," pp. 587–88; and *Morale*, pp. 3, 53–92.

18. See Hocking, *Morale*, pp. 14–23, 93–130; Perry, *Present Conflict*, pp. 398–433; Santayana, *Egotism*, pp. 11–21; Royce, *Hope*, p. 97.

19. Münsterberg, *Peace and America*, pp. 59–118.

20. *The Free Man and the Soldier* (New York: Charles Scribner's Sons, 1916), pp. 82–94.

21. Ibid., pp. 15–43; RBP to Cosby, 1 March 1919, HUG, 4683.6, *C*, RBP Papers.

22. Perry, *The Plattsburg Movement* (New York: E. P. Dutton and Co., 1921), pp. 211–13, 231–32.

23. See John Clifford, *The Citizen Soldiers* (Lexington, Kentucky: University of Kentucky Press, 1972) for an account of the movement; for Perry's role, pp. 256, 268 n.

24. Russell, *Autobiography*, 1: 326.

25. Hocking, *Morale*, pp. vii–ix; Leroy Rouner, *Within Human Experience: The Philosophy of William Ernest Hocking* (Cambridge: Harvard University Press, 1969), p. 326; Carol S. Gruber, *Mars and Minerva: World War I and the Uses of the Higher Learning in America* (Baton Rouge: Louisiana State University Press, 1975), pp. 297–98.

26. Hocking, *Morale*, "Dedication," pp. vii–xiv.

27. Ibid., p. 69.

28. Ibid., pp. 68–88.

29. See C. J. Child, *The German-American in Politics* (Madison, Wisconsin: University of Wisconsin Press, 1939), pp. 114–15; HM to Lansing, 31 January 1916, File 570b, HM Papers.

30. Files 231, 231a, 1914–1917, ALL Papers; Viereck to HM, 15 October 1914, File 495Q, HM Papers.

31. ALL to von Mack, 13 October 1914, File 2499b, HM Papers; see also ALLY, pp. 308–16.

32. CWE to HM, 27 March 1915, Box 370, 1915 A–M, CWE Papers; CWE to HM, 16 November 1914, 21 November 1914, File 1678, HM Papers.

33. LJR, pp. 619–21; JR to HM, 12 May 1915, File 414b; File 596, HM Papers.

34. Files 559b, 559c, 559d, 2496, HM Papers; EBH to HM, 17 April 1916, File 637, 1914–1917, ALL Papers.

35. HM to Chairman, 21 November 1916, File 554; Robbins to HM, 22 November 1916, File 407a, HM Papers.

36. WEH–HM correspondence, Files 233a, 233b, 527n, HM Papers.

37. HM–RFAH correspondence, File 1803, HM Papers.

38. Gruber, *Mars and Minerva*, pp. 243–44, 251, 253–59.

39. Interview with Brand Blanshard, 1 June 1972.

24. *The Professional Mentality, 1920–1930*

1. M. S. Lackner, "American Philosophy Periodicals: A Survey" (1965), manuscript in Lackner's possession.

2. RBP to Scribner's, 4 February 1905, 31 March 1909, File: Perry, Scribner's Papers, Princeton University, Princeton, New Jersey.
3. P. C. Coleman (of Scribner's) to author, 18 January 1972.
4. JHW to H. O. Taylor, 7 January 1924, Woods Chm., 1924–June 1925, File: I, HPD; File 576, 1925–1928; Mrs. H. O. Taylor to Murdock, 27 July 1932, File 785, 1930–1933, ALL Papers.
5. DeWulf Fund, 1915–1920, HPD.
6. HAP, pp. 204–06.
7. Harvard College, *Report*, 1908. For Jacob Loewenberg's experiences see his autobiography, *Thrice Born* (New York: Hobbs, Dorman and Co., 1968).
8. RBP to Lexington Kentucky State University, 3 February, to D. M. Gordon, 31 March 1911, Gen. Corr., 1902–1914, RBP Papers; JHW to Mecklin, 16 February 1916, Woods Chm. 1914–15, File: *M*; WEH to Sabine, 11 December 1936, C–G, Cl–Cu, File: Cornell, Corr., 1927–1938; CIL to J. H. Farley, 2 March 1928, to C. H. Langford, 3 April 1930, LA–LY, File: Lawrence College, Langford, Corr., 1927–1930, HPD. See also Herbert Feigl, "The Wiener Kreis in America," *Perspectives in American History* 2 (1968): 650.
9. F. W. Hunnewell to HAW, 27 September 1922, 1921–1923, File: *G*, HAW Papers.
10. Interview with HAW, 24 January 1973; see also HAW, "Remarks on Proposed Changes in Admission Policy at Harvard, 1922," May or June 1922, HUG 4879.325, HAW Papers.
11. RBP to D. M. Gordon, 31 March 1911; JHW to E. H. Lindsay, 1914, File: *L*. Woods Chm., 1914–1915, HPD.
12. See the correspondence in File: *S* (Sheffer), Letters Received, Gen., 1907–1921, HPD; also RBP to ALL, 14 January 1920, File 530, 1919–1922, ALL Papers; ALL to RBP, 15 January 1920, File: *L*, Letters Rec. Gen., 1907–1920, HPD; and Feinberg and Kasrils, *Russell's America*, pp. 77–79.
13. JHW to Sol Rosenbloom, 21 May 1921, File: *R*; JHW to Frankfurter, 28 January 1924, File: *F*, 1921; File: Sheffer's Logic, 1922, Woods Chm., HPD.
14. Moore to JHW, 24 March 1926, File 281; File 796, 1925–1928; File 258, 1928–1930, ALL Papers; File: Sheffer, 1927–1945, HPD.
15. See the letters from McDougall to HM, File: 1920, HM Papers.
16. Jerome Bruner, "Preface" to *Body and Mind* (Boston: Beacon Press, 1961), p. xiii; HEP, pp. 465–66.
17. WEH to RBP, 23 April 1922, 1917–1923, *H*, File: Hoernlé, RBP Papers.
18. EGB to Members of Psychology and Philosophy, 1 March 1924, File 681, 1922–1925, ALL Papers.
19. EGB to JHW, 3 December, 19 December 1924, File: JHW, 1923–1924; EGB to RBP, 15 November, File: RBP, 1928, EGB Papers.
20. EGB to CIL, 7 December 1927, A–B, File: Boring, Corr. 1927–1938, HPD; Memorandum on Edgar Peirce Fund (1929) by E. G. Boring, 30 December 1954, Miscellaneous Material, EGB Papers. The best discussion of the philosophical bias

of Harvard psychology is Frank Albrecht, "The New Psychology in America, 1880–1895," Johns Hopkins, Ph. D. dissertation, 1960, pp. 186–220.

21. DHU, p. 217.

22. 1933 Report of Committee to visit Department of Philosophy and Psychology, UA II.10.7.5.678; Church, "The Economists Study Society," in SSH, p. 53. There is an excellent memoir of Boring: Julian Jaynes, "Edwin Garrigues Boring: 1886–1968," JHBS 5 (1969): 99–112.

23. For suspicions of "scientific" psychology see WEH, *Man and the State* (New Haven: Yale University Press, 1926), pp. 200 ff.

24. HEP, pp. 653–57; HPA, *V*, p. 399; Feigl, "Wiener Kreis," pp. 644–46, 661–62; S. S. Stevens, "Quantifying the Sensory Experience," in *Mind, Matter, and Method*, ed. Paul K. Feyerabend and Grover Maxwell (Minneapolis: University of Minnesota Press, 1966), pp. 215–17.

25. P. M. Hughes, *A Study of the Graduate Schools of America* (Oxford, Ohio: Miami University, 1925).

26. I have tabulated these data from Robert S. Harper, "Table of American Doctorates in Psychology," *American Journal of Psychology* 62 (1949): 579–87. On wider aspects of the professionalization question see: Joseph Ben-David and Kendall Collins, "Social Factors in the Origins of a New Science: The Case of Psychology," *American Sociological Review* 31 (1966): 451–65; Dorothy Ross, "On the Origins of Psychology," and Ben-David and Collins, "Reply to Ross," *American Sociological Review* 32 (1967): 466–69, 469–72.

27. Blanshard to author, 11 October 1972, "How did you choose your career?" *Yale Alumni Magazine* 37 (1973) (no. 1 October): 12.

25. Ernest Hocking

1. Biographical information comes from Leroy S. Rouner, *Within Human Experience*; his "The Making of a Philosopher: Ernest Hocking's Early Years," in PRCWC; and, most important, D. C. Williams, "William Ernest Hocking, 1873–1966, Biographical Remarks," paper delivered at Harvard memorial meeting, 10 February 1967, WEH Papers.

2. GHP to WEH, October 1911, Box: 1912, Meaning of God, WEH Papers.

3. OCB, pp. 76–97, 122–35; MGHE, pp. 539–57.

4. OCB, pp. i–v.

5. See MGHE, pp. 285 ff; PRCWC, p. 36; on Kant OCB, pp. i–v, 59–66, 76–97, 157, 145–64; and Hocking's "The Ontological Argument in Royce and Others," in CIA, pp. 64–66.

6. See Riepe, *The Philosophy of India*, esp. pp. 82–90, 93–97, but also 77–119.

7. Rouner, *Within Human Experience*, pp. 76, 156.

8. *New York Times*, 15 October 1920; see PRCWC, p. 475.

9. *Rethinking Missions* (New York: Harper and Brothers, 1932), p. 26.

10. Ibid., p. 58.
11. See PRCWC, pp. 484–85, 495.
12. *Human Nature and Its Remaking*, rev. ed. (New Haven: Yale University Press, 1923), pp. 383–428.
13. "William Ernest Hocking," *Yearbook of the American Philosophical Society* (Philadelphia: American Philosophical Society, 1966), p. 153.
14. Rouner, "The Making of a Philosopher," PRCWC, p. 8.

26. Harvard Moral Philosophy, 1875–1926

1. New Haven, Yale University Press.
2. "Lectures on the Return to Kant," p. 165, Box C, JR Papers; FE, pp. 197–98.
3. FE, pp. 96–132, esp. 130–32.
4. FE, pp. 139–40, 148–49, 179–80.
5. FE, pp. 181–86.
6. FE, pp. 152–53.
7. FE, pp. 210–18.
8. Hocking, "The Holt-Freudian Ethics and the Ethics of Royce," PR 25 (1916): 479–506.
9. Perry, "Realism in Retrospect," CAP, 2: 201.
10. GTV, pp. 127–37, 357–68; for complexities in the account see pp. 344–57.
11. GTV, pp. 137–45, 257–59; see also PPT, pp. 329–39 for a similar discussion.

27. Alfred North Whitehead

1. Russell, *Autobiography*, 1: 189; and see Lucien Price, *Dialogues of Alfred North Whitehead* (Boston: Little, Brown and Co., 1954), passim. The best place to start on biographical material about Whitehead is his own statement in PANW, pp. 1–14.
2. Price, *Dialogues*, p. 324 (the original appears in italics).
3. See A. H. Johnson, *Whitehead's Philosophy of Civilization* (Boston: Beacon Press, 1958).
4. On this question see Victor Lowe, "The Influence of Bergson, James, and Alexander on Whitehead," JHI 10 (1949): 267–96.
5. On logic see JRIB, pp. 175–92, and Robert M. Palter, *Whitehead's Philosophy of Science* (Chicago: University of Chicago Press, 1960), pp. 126–40; on Hocking see WEH, "Whitehead as I Knew Him," JP 58 (1961): 505–16; on Lewis see chapter 28 below; PANW, pp. 703–04; Victor Lowe, "Whitehead's Gifford Lectures," *Southern Journal of Philosophy* 7 (1969–1970): 339 n.
6. CN, p. 4.
7. WPD, p. 18.
8. CN, pp. 5, 28; PNK, p. vii (italics added).
9. CN, pp. 29, 32.
10. CN, p. 45.
11. PNK, pp. 61–62; CN, pp. 74–98.

12. PNK, pp. 62–66; CN, pp. 78, 143–73.
13. PNK, pp. 87–88, 99; CN, p. 93.
14. PNK, pp. 104–12.
15. PNK, pp. 112–17; CN, pp. 90–94; WPD, pp. 35–38.
16. See CN, pp. 46–47, 142–48.
17. See PNK, p. 63.
18. SMW, for example pp. 228–46.
19. *Symbolism* (New York: Macmillan Co., 1927), p. 20.
20. SMW, pp. 84–85, 102–05.
21. AI, pp. 247–51.
22. AI, p. 227.
23. IWM, p. 81.
24. In AI 'occasions of experience' usually does service for 'actual occasions'.
25. IWM, pp. 207–08.
26. See Donald W. Sherburne, *A Key to Whitehead's Process and Reality* (Bloomington: Indiana University Press, 1966), pp. 73–74.
27. *Modes of Thought*, pp. 202, 211.
28. IWM, p. 297.

28. Clarence Lewis

1. Sources of biographical data on Lewis are: PCIL, pp. 1–21 (from which I have taken every quotation but one); CPCIL, pp. 3–19; Andrew Reck, *The New American Philosophers* (Baton Rouge: Louisiana State University Press, 1968), pp. 3–43; Donald C. Williams, "Clarence Irving Lewis 1883–1964," *Philosophy and Phenomenological Research* 26 (1965–1966): 159–72. For his early promise see RBP to W. Savery, 19 May 1910, and to G. P. Adams, 13 December 1910, Letters Rec., General, 1907–1926, Carbons-Jobs 1910–1911, 1919; and for his earliest ideas see Graduate Student Folders, Lewis, HPD. I have cited Lewis's recollection of his debt to Royce and Perry from CIL to Morton White, 10 December 1955, Box 1, Folder 2, 39, CIL Papers, Stanford University, Palo Alto, California.
2. PCIL, pp. 9, 15.
3. CPCIL, pp. 21–25; for an ambiguity see p. 22.
4. CPCIL, pp. 35–41.
5. CPCIL, pp. 29, 37–41 (italics added).
6. CPCIL, pp. 25–29, 35–36.
7. See the discussion in Thayer, *Meaning and Action*, p. 211.
8. "Interesting Theorems in Symbolic Logic," JP 10 (1913): 242.
9. "A New Algebra of Implication and Some Consequences," JP 10 (1913): 431–33; see also "The Calculus of Strict Implication," *Mind* 23 (1913): 241–42; "Interesting Theorems," 241–42; and CPCIL, pp. 351–60.
10. Thayer, *Meaning and Action*, pp. 210–12.
11. See Rudolph Carnap, *The Logical Syntax of Language*, trans. Amethe Smeaton (London: Routledge and Kegan Paul, 1937), pp. 250–60; Willard Quine, *Mathematical*

Logic, rev. ed. (Cambridge: Harvard University Press, 1951), pp. 27–33; "Three Grades of Modal Involvement," in *The Ways of Paradox* (New York: Random House, 1966), pp. 163–69; and "Whitehead and the Rise of Modern Logic," in *Selected Logical Papers* (New York: Random House, 1966), pp. 13–17; and, most importantly, Dana Scott, "On Engendering an Illusion of Understanding," JP 68 (1971): 787–807.

12. "Matrix Algebra," JP 11 (1914): 589–600; "The Calculus of Strict Implication," pp. 240–47.

13. "A New Algebra of Implications and Some Consequences," pp. 429–30; also see "The Calculus of Strict Implication," pp. 240–41.

14. "Matrix Algebra," p. 598. I have here deleted a footnote reference and changed Lewis's sign for material implication.

15. "The Issues Concerning Material Implication," JP 14 (1917): 355.

16. CPCIL, pp. 358–59; "The Calculus of Strict Implication," p. 241.

17. "Matrix Algebra," pp. 589, 600.

18. "The Calculus of Strict Implication," pp. 244–46 (italics in original).

19. Ibid., pp. 246–47; Lewis, "Review of *Royce's Logical Essays*," *Philosophy and Phenomenological Research* 12 (1951–1952): 431.

20. CPCIL, p. 10.

21. CPCIL, pp. 383–93.

22. CPCIL, pp. 392–93.

23. CPCIL, pp. 372–75.

24. See JRIB, pp. 132–35, for details and citations.

25. CPCIL, p. 244.

26. CPCIL, p. 233.

27. MWO, p. 268.

28. CPCIL, p. 231; MWO, pp. 101–02. I have used 'categorical' throughout, whereas Lewis sometimes adopts 'categorial'.

29. CPCIL, pp. 234–36.

30. Cited in Thomas English Hill, *Contemporary Theories of Knowledge* (New York: Ronald Press Company, 1961), pp. 379–80.

31. CPCIL, pp. 12–14, 16–17, 240.

32. For a partial history of the Peirce Papers at Harvard see the following articles in the *Transactions of the Charles S. Peirce Society*: Lenzen, "Reminiscences of a Mission"; W. F. Kernan, "The Peirce Manuscripts and Josiah Royce—A Memoir: Harvard 1915–1916," 1 (1965): 90–95; Irwin C. Lieb, "Charles Hartshorne's Recollections of Editing the Peirce Papers," and Richard Bernstein, "Paul Weiss's Recollections . . . ," 6 (1970): 149–59, 161–88; Harold Lee, "Note to the Editor," 7 (1971): 180–81. A more accurate account must be constructed from the relevant correspondence in HPD.

33. MWO, pp. xi, 133–34, 417 n.

34. *A Survey of Symbolic Logic* (Berkeley: University of California Press, 1918), p. 341 n. (italics in original).

35. PR 31 (1922): 185.

36. CPCIL, p. 264.
37. PCIL, p. 11. For a general survey of Lewis's ideas about the book see CIL to EGB, 23 February 1928, EGB Papers, HUA.
38. PCIL, p. 284.
39. See MWO, p. 319. For a similar appraisal see Henry Veatch, *Two Logics* (Evanston: University of Illinois Press, 1969), pp. 136–37.
40. CPCIL, p. 324.
41. Cited in Williams, "Clarence Irving Lewis," pp. 160–61.
42. Ibid.
43. See Andrew Reck, *Recent American Philosophy*, pp. 29–41.
44. Andrew Lewis to author, 17 February 1974.
45. *Our Social Inheritance* (Bloomington: Indiana University Press, 1957), p. 8; *Values and Imperatives*, ed. Lange, pp. xiii–xiv; and John Lange, "The Late Papers of C. I. Lewis," JHP 4 (1966): 235–45. For an idea of what Lewis meant by ethical irrationalism, see my discussion of C. L. Stevenson in chapter 26 above.

29. Conclusion: The Triumph of Professionalism

1. See Brand Blanshard, "Epilogue," in Arthur Pap, *An Introduction to the Philosophy of Science* (New York: Free Press, 1962), p. 429.
2. Compare the sections for the Division of Philosophy in the Catalogues of 1902–1903 and 1930–1931.
3. Quoted in Ralph Barton Perry, *In the Spirit of William James* (New Haven: Yale University Press, 1938), pp. 21–22.
4. "Review of Past Performance," Correspondence and Papers, 1927–1942, A–B, File: Prof. Baxter, HPD.
5. See his 1908 Ph.D. dissertation, "A Program of Philosophy Based on Modern Logic."
6. For a comment on this idea see Whitehead, *The Aims of Education* (New York: Macmillan Co., 1929), p. 52.
7. JHW to Billikopf, 12 January 1922, File: Sheffer's Logic, Woods Chm., 1922 HPD.
8. *Transactions of the American Mathematical Society* 14 (1913): 481–88.
9. See Alonzo Church, *Introduction to Mathematical Logic*, vol. 1 (Princeton: Princeton University Press, 1956), pp. 133–34 n. 207.
10. Cambridge: At the University Press, 1927, p. xv.
11. CIL to Birkhoff, 18 January 1938, A–B, File: Birkhoff, 1937–1938; Correspondence, 1927–1938; ANW to CIL, 11 February 1938, R–S, File: Sheffer, Correspondence, 1927–1945, HPD.
12. See the report, "Returning Graduate Students," UAV 687.488, UHA.

Appendix 1: The Separation of History and Philosophy

1. "Realism as a Polemic and Program of Reform, II," JP 7 (1910): 378–79.
2. "Philosophy in the College Course," *Educational Review* 40 (1910): 495–98.

3. For a recent example see Peter Caws, "Reconsideration: Alfred North White-head," *New Republic* 5–12 August 1972, p. 33.

Appendix 2: Harvard Philosophy after Lewis

1. See Goodman, "Memorial Note," in *The Logical Way of Doing Things*, ed. Karl Lambert (New Haven: Yale University Press, 1969), p. ix.
2. *From A Logical Point of View*, 2d ed., rev. (Cambridge: Harvard University Press, 1961), p. 20.
3. Ibid., pp. 40–42.
4. Ibid., p. 44. The reader will want to compare this quotation to my citation from Lewis on p. 553.
5. My discussion is here indebted to Murphey, "Kant's Children," p. 16.
6. Quine, *Logical Point of View*, pp. 17–19; see also pp. 66, 77.
7. Ibid., p. 16.
8. PCIL, p. 659.
9. CPCIL, pp. 324–25; see also p. 265.
10. Cited in Richard B. Brandt, "Coherence, Certainty, and Epistemic Priority," JP 61 (1964): 545. The same issues recur in CPCIL, pp. 335–47.
11. More recent examples of disputes over the same issues include: Thomas Kuhn, *The Structure of Scientific Revolutions* (Chicago: University of Chicago Press, 1962); Israel Scheffer, *Science and Subjectivity* (Indianapolis: Bobbs-Merrill Co., 1967); David K. Lewis, *Convention* (Cambridge: Harvard University Press, 1969); Gilbert Harman, *Thought* (Princeton: Princeton University Press, 1973). The youngest generation of Harvard philosophers now hold tenured positions at Princeton.

Appendix 4: Women Philosophers at Harvard

1. Corporation Records, 25 March 1872, HUA.
2. WJ to CWE, 23 May 1890, Box 79, 1890 Hi–L; Mary Calkins to CWE and Corporation, 30 December 1892, and to CWE, 10 January 1893, Box 81, 1892 C, CWE Papers.
3. HM to CWE, 27 October 1894, Box 116, File 231, CWE Papers; CWE to HM, 31 October, 1894, Folder 1678, HM Papers.
4. HMLW, p. 76.
5. Alice I. Bryan and Edwin G. Boring, "Women in American Psychology," *American Psychologist* 1 (1946): 72–73.
6. On Calkins see Edna Heidbrider, "Mary Whiton Calkins: A Discussion," and Orlo Stunk, Jr., "The Self-Psychology of Mary Whiton Calkins," JHBS, 8 (1972): 56–68, 196–203; and Raymond Calkins et al., *In Memoriam: Mary Whiton Calkins 1863–1930* (Boston: Merrymount Press, 1931).
7. On Langer see the profile by Winthrop Sargent in the *New Yorker*, 3 December 1960.

ESSAY ON SOURCES

This compendium does not include all work previously cited and includes some work not previously cited. It is intended to supplement the abbreviations, notes, and footnotes by providing a topically arranged survey of manuscript collections, primary works, secondary studies, and bibliographies.

History of Higher Education

For a bibliography of relevant studies see Frederick Rudolph, *The American College and University* (New York: Alfred A. Knopf, 1962), pp. 497–516. Carol S. Gruber, *Mars and Minerva: World War I and the Uses of the Higher Learning in America* (Baton Rouge: Louisiana State University Press, 1975) cites more recent studies, pp. 261–81, and presents an excellent synopsis of the growth of the university, pp. 10–45. Laurence Veysey's *The Emergence of the American University* (Chicago: University of Chicago Press, 1965) is superb. Also noteworthy is Logan Wilson, *The Academic Man* (London: Oxford University Press, 1942).

On the role of the educated public in the nineteenth century there is pertinent material in Richard Arthur Firda, "*The North American Review*, 1815–1860: A Study in the Reception of German-American Cultural Influences," Ph.D. dissertation, Harvard University, 1967. Edwin Stratford Budge's "American Philosophy: Some Aspects of Disagreement about Its Role, 1917–1967," M.A. thesis, University of Maryland, 1968, is a full bibliography of philosophers' writings on professionalization. For a more detailed account of the problems of Harvard's Jews, consult Marcia Graham Synnoit, "A Social History of Admissions Policies at Harvard, Yale, and Princeton, 1900–1930," Ph.D. dissertation, University of Massachusetts, 1974, pp. 111–456.

For this study I have been particularly dependent on the papers of Charles William Eliot, Lawrence Lowell, and the Harvard Philosophy Department, all in HUA. In the case of the latter two collections, the Harvard Corporation waived its fifty-year rule when I did my research in 1972 and 1973 and allowed me to examine material through the early 1930s. Statute requires the United States Department of State, in whose Historical Division I have also worked, to release top-secret documents dealing with international politics after thirty years. The difference between the two rules ought to give the reader some idea of the relative importance Harvard attaches to its affairs.

History of Philosophy

The best place to start the study of the history of American thought is the primary sources themselves. The back issues of the *Journal of Specula-tive Philosophy,* the *Philosophical Review,* and the *Journal of Philosophy* are immensely useful, as are those of the British journal *Mind.* Before the turn of the century, magazines like the *North American Review* and *Popular Science Monthly* are also important; and so are lesser known periodicals like the *Princeton Review* and the *Monist.* After noting the names of those who wrote for these journals and the topics that interested them, readers may consult the catalogue of a good library for book-length works. Herbert Schneider's *A History of American Philosophy,* 2d ed. (New York: Columbia University Press, 1963) contains a com-prehensive bibliography of this material, pp. 527–81. There is also an excellent bibliography in James Ward Smith and A. Leland Jamison, eds., *Religion in American Life,* vol. 4, pts. 3, 4, and 5, by Nelson R. Burr in collaboration with the editors (Princeton: Princeton University Press, 1961), pp. 1017–57, 1109–69. The best secondary work appears scattered in the studies of today's learned journals; the reader should consult the indices of most significant ones, the *American Quarterly* (which has no index until 1974), the *Journal of the History of Ideas, Journal of the History of Philosophy,* and *Journal of the History of the Behavioral Sciences.* A convincing case for treating Peirce, James, and Dewey as a group—to the exclusion of Royce and Lewis and the inclusion of Wittgenstein—is given by Robert Brandom, "Practice and Object," Ph.D. dissertation, Princeton University, 1976, especially chapter 1.

Critical sources for the study of the history of philosophy as viewed in

Cambridge are: Charles Peirce, "Review of the Works of George Berkeley" (1871) in CP, 8.7–8.38; Francis Bowen, *Modern Philosophy* (New York, 1877); Francis Abbot, *Scientific Theism* (Boston, 1885) and *The Way Out of Agnosticism* (Boston, 1890); William James, *The Principles of Psychology*, 2 vols. (New York, 1890), 1:342–73; 2:270–82; Josiah Royce, *The Spirit of Modern Philosophy* (New York, 1892) and *Lectures on Modern Idealism* (New Haven: Yale University Press, 1919); Ralph Barton Perry, *Present Philosophical Tendencies* (New York: Longmans, Green and Co., 1912); and W. P. Montague, "The New Realism and the Old," JP 9 (1912): 39–46. Also useful are Arthur Kenyon Rogers, *A Student's History of Philosophy* (New York: Macmillan Co., 1901); William Longstreath Raub, "Pragmatism and Kantianism," in *Studies in Philosophy and Psychology*, ed. J. H. Tufts et al. (Boston: Houghton Mifflin Co., 1906), pp. 203–17; Theodore and Grace DeLaguna, *Dogmatism and Evolution* (New York: Macmillan Co., 1910); Richard Popkin, "The Skeptical Origins of the Modern Problem of Knowledge," in *Perception and Personal Identity*, ed. Norman S. Care and Robert H. Grimm (Cleveland: Case Western Reserve Press, 1969), pp. 3–24; and Richard Rorty, "Cartesian Epistemology and Changes in Ontology," in *Contemporary American Philosophy*, 2d series, ed. J. E. Smith (New York: Humanities Press, 1970), pp. 273–92.

Readers may also consult John Passmore, "Philosophical Scholarship in the United States, 1930–1960," in *Philosophy* by Roderick Chisolm et al. (Englewood Cliffs, New Jersey: Prentice-Hall, 1964), esp. pp. 3–29, 113–24; *History and Theory*'s Beiheft 5 (1965), "The Historiography of the History of Philosophy," pp. 1–104; Albert William Levy, *Philosophy as Social Expression* (Chicago: University of Chicago Press, 1974); the "Foreword for 1976" to Morton White's *Social Thought in America* (New York: Oxford University Press, 1976), pp. ix-xxviii; and, for more specialized institutional approaches, Andrew Reck's "Nagel, Randall, and Buchler: Columbia University Naturalism," in *The New American Philosophy* (Baton Rouge: Louisiana State University Press, 1968), pp. 120–63; and Darnell Rucker, *The Chicago Pragmatists* (Minneapolis: University of Minnesota Press, 1969). Two biographies take up these issues: Daniel Wilson, "Arthur O. Lovejoy," Ph.D. dissertation, Johns Hopkins University, 1976; David Hollinger, *Morris R. Cohen and the Scientific Ideal* (Cambridge: M.I.T. Press, 1975).

Transcendentalism, Unitarianism, and the Evolution Controversy

The literature on each of these topics is vast, and I recommend the bibliographies in Sydney E. Ahlstrom, *A Religious History of the American People* (New Haven: Yale University Press, 1972), pp. 1097–99, 1113–15; and in Paul F. Boller, *American Thought in Transition: The Impact of Evolutionary Naturalism, 1865–1900* (Chicago: Rand McNally, 1969), pp. 250–61, especially 250–54. Of special help to me were: Stow Persons, *Free Religion* (New Haven: Yale University Press, 1947); Daniel Walker Howe, *The Unitarian Conscience* (Cambridge: Harvard University Press, 1970); A. Hunter Dupree, *Asa Gray* (Cambridge: Harvard University Press, 1959); Edward Lurie, *Louis Agassiz* (Chicago: University of Chicago Press, 1960); William R. Hutchison, *The Transcendentalist Ministers* (New Haven: Yale University Press, 1959); Martin Green, *The Problem of Boston* (New York: W. W. Norton and Co., 1966); and John Spencer Clark, *Life and Letters of John Fiske*, 2 vols. (Boston: Houghton Mifflin Co., 1917), especially 2:169–87. Of particular relevance for the issues this study raises are two paperback anthologies, R. J. Wilson, ed., *Darwinism and the American Intellectual* (Homewood, Illinois: Dorsey Publishers, 1967), and George Daniels, ed., *Darwinism Comes to America* (Waltham, Massachusetts: Ginn and Co., 1968).

The Unitarian philosophers, especially Francis Bowen, were an astute group of thinkers. But though there are many volumes by historians on the "moral philosophy" of these men and other mid-nineteenth-century academic philosophers, there are no sophisticated histories of their ideas. In short, the best sources on Bowen are, unfortunately, his own books, available only in large libraries when available at all. There is a small collection of Bowen material in the Houghton Library at Harvard.

Fiske, Abbot, and Wright

Fiske's complete works have been published in *Writings of John Fiske*, 24 vols. (Cambridge: Riverside Press, 1902). Vol. 21, *Studies in Religion*, contains the philosophical books I have cited, and vols. 13–16 the *Outlines of Cosmic Philosophy*, although I have used the standard two-volume edition (Boston, 1874) when citing that book.

I did not use Fiske's papers in preparing this study, but Milton Berman's *John Fiske, The Evolution of a Popularizer* (Cambridge: Harvard University Press, 1961) has drawn on them extensively and gives complete bibliographical material (pp. 275–82). This book, however, does not really treat Fiske's ideas, for which the best source is Josiah Royce's "Introduction" to vol. 13 of the *Writings of John Fiske*, pp. xxi–cxlix. J. D. Y. Peel's *Herbert Spencer* (New York: Basic Books, 1971) treats Fiske's mentor.

Abbot's papers are in HUA, and Sydney Ahlstrom's "Francis Ellingwood Abbot," 2 vols., Ph.D. dissertation, Harvard University, 1951, is both an excellent guide to the papers and an exhaustive treatment of Abbot's life. There are two others which treat Abbot: William Jerome Callaghan, "The Philosophy of Francis Ellingwood Abbot," Ph.D. dissertation, Columbia University, 1958; Fred Rivers, "Francis Ellingwood Abbot," Ph.D. dissertation, University of Maryland, 1971.

Material on Chauncey Wright is sparse. Some of his personal papers are in the possession of Edwina Pearson, Northampton, Massachusetts, and there is a book by Edward Madden, *Chauncey Wright and the Foundations of Pragmatism* (Seattle: University of Washington Press, 1963). The best sources are still Wright's collected *Philosophical Discussions*, ed. with a biographical sketch by Charles Eliot Norton (New York, 1877), and *Letters of Chauncey Wright*, ed. James Bradley Thayer (Cambridge, Mass., 1878—privately printed, press of John Wilson and Son).

Peripheral Figures

Max Fisch's articles cited in chapter 3 are impeccable sources for study of the Metaphysical Club. That chapter draws extensively on his work and to a lesser extent on Philip Wiener's *Evolution and the Founders of Pragmatism* (Cambridge: Harvard University Press, 1949). Fisch's "Philosophical Clubs in Cambridge and Boston," *Coranto* 2 (1964–1965):12–33, contains information on many of the men I have discussed in chapters 3 and 7. In studying the Concord School of Philosophy, the reader can consult, in addition to the cited references in chapter 3, Austin Warren, "The Concord School of Philosophy," *New England Quarterly* 2 (1929): 199–233, and Warren E. Steinkraus, "Philosophical Conversations at a Summer Colony in the 1870s," *JHP* 12 (1974): 341–46. On Harris there is Kurt Leidecker, *Yankee Teacher: The Life of William Torrey Harris* (New York: Philosophical Library, 1946). Glenmore and Davidson are discussed in William Knight, ed., *Memorials of Thomas Davidson* (Boston: Ginn and Co., 1907) and Charles Bakewell, ed., *The Education of the Wage Earners* (Cambridge: Harvard University Press, 1903). On Howison there is John Wright Buckham and George Malcolm Stratton, *George Holmes Howison: Philosopher and Teacher* (Berkeley: University of California Press, 1934). The works on Davidson and Harris are inadequate. *The American Hegelians*, ed. William H. Goetzmann (New York: Alfred A. Knopf, 1973), contains a good bibliography on the American Hegelians and those related to them, pp. 393–97. The most complete source, however, is Lawrence Dowler's "The New Idealism and the Quest for Culture in the Gilded Age," Ph.D. dissertation, University of Maryland, 1974.

Charles Peirce

The basic source for the study of Peirce is *The Collected Papers of Charles Sanders Peirce*, vols. 1–6 edited by Charles Hartshorne and Paul Weiss (Cambridge: Harvard University Press, 1931, 1932, 1933, 1935); vols. 7–8 edited by Arthur Burks (Cambridge: Harvard University Press, 1958). These volumes publish much in Peirce's papers in the Houghton Library at Harvard. As is evident from the documents in the records of the Harvard philosophy department concerning this publication, the department expended much time on the enterprise, carrying it out under adverse conditions. Nonetheless, the volumes are deficient by contemporary standards and difficult for the historian to use even with the helpful bibliography by Arthur Burks in 8:251–330. A new edition is in the works.

There are a number of paperback collections: Justus Buchler, ed., *Philosophical Writings of Peirce* (New York: Dover Publications, 1955); Edward C. Moore, *Charles S. Peirce: The Essential Writings* (New York: Harper and Row, 1972); Vincent Tomas, *Essays in the Philosophy of Science* (Indianapolis: Bobbs-Merrill, 1957); and the best, Philip Wiener, *Charles S. Peirce: Selected Writings* (New York: Dover Publications, 1966). Although some of its interpretations are wrong, a good introduction to Peirce is W. B. Gallie's *Peirce and Pragmatism* (Middlesex, England: Penguin, 1952). The best book, but written at a difficult level, is Murray G. Murphey's *The Development of Peirce's Philosophy* (Cambridge: Harvard University Press, 1961). For a more extended study of Peirce, the place to begin is *Studies in the Philosophy of Charles Sanders Peirce*, 1st series, edited by Philip Wiener and Frederick A. Young (Cambridge: Harvard University Press, 1952); 2d series, edited by Edward C. Moore and Richard S. Robin (Amherst: University of Massachusetts Press, 1964). The second series has a supplement to Burks's bibliography and a careful bibliography of works on Peirce by Max Fisch, pp. 477–514. More recent bibliographical information is in Fisch, "Supplements to the Peirce Bibliographies," *Transactions of the Charles S. Peirce Society* 10 (1974): 94–129. The *Transactions*, published since 1965, is a journal largely devoted to Peirce scholarship. Fisch will soon be publishing a definitive two-volume biography of Benjamin and Charles Peirce.

William James

The James Papers are in the Houghton Library (I used them selectively); collections and editions of his writings are legion, and I have found most useful John J. McDermott's *The Writings of William James* (New York: Random House, 1967), which contains a comprehensive bibliography of James's writings (pp. 811–58); and Gay Wilson Allen's *A William James Reader* (Boston: Houghton Mifflin Co., 1971), which has the advantage of ordering its material chronologically. None of the many treatments of James is satisfactory, but Ralph Barton Perry's two-volume *Thought and Character of William James* must still be the starting point for all secondary work. There is also a biography of James which avoids his ideas entirely: Gay Wilson Allen's *William James* (New York: Random House, 1967). For a shorter treatment introducing James, the reader might consult McDermott's "Introduction" (*The Writings*, pp. xii–xliv), which cites much of the secondary literature on James and can be supplemented by the bibliography in Bruce Wilshire's *William James and Phenomenology* (Bloomington: Indiana University Press, 1968), pp. 226–30. This book is the best product of what has become a new industry, the attempt by scholars to make James, especially in *The Principles of Psychology*, the founder of the phenomenological movement of Continental Europe. Provoked, I suspect, by the opposite and dominant view that James embodies a peculiarly American empiricism, the Old World interpreters are less off the mark than their opponents: as far as the phenomenologists are part of a Kantian movement, they are to be associated with James. The New World interpretation of James assumes some connection between him and the American national character; historians, if not philosophers, ought to know better. Both the New and Old World interpreters commit the unforgivable mistake of presentism. In attempting to find a usable past, they show no concern for the historical context in which James wrote but philosophize about what in him is significant to them. A favorable survey of the Old World work may be found in James M. Edie, "William James and Phenomenology," *Review of Metaphysics* 23 (1969–1970): 481–526. A work that makes the same sorts of philosophical mistakes as the phenomenologists but tries to rescue James (and Peirce) for contemporary Anglo-American thought is A. J. Ayer's *Origins of Pragmatism* (London: Macmillan and Co., 1968).

I am suspicious of the theories that underlie psycho-history and the methods, inferences, and conclusions of its practitioners, but William James is open to this approach if anyone is, and pertinent to such investigation are Cushing Strout's work, "William James and the Twice-Born Sick Soul," *Daedalus* 97 (Summer 1968): 1062–82; "The Pluralistic Identity of William James: A Psychohistorical Reading of *The Varieties of Religious Experience*," AQ 23 (1971): 135–52; and "Ego Psychology and the Historian," *History and Theory* 7 (1968): 281–97. Pages 287–88 of the last article offer appropriate warnings on the limits of "ego psychology" in intellectual history, but they are warnings that Strout and others forget more often than they observe. A good review of the literature is contained in a later piece of Strout's, "The Use and Abuse of Psychology in American History," AQ 28 (1976): 324–42.

Harvard has begun to print a definitive edition of James's works. This is a godsend to the scholar confronted with a myriad of editions and versions of James's publications which, especially, need to be studied in chronological order with due regard for their original form. But aside from the likelihood that James would be utterly contemptuous of the whole project, the volumes, I think, suffer because there is no James scholar of Perry's stature to offer a comprehensive view of James. The volumes do have authoritative and useful introductions, but the publication of the Perryesque *Essays in Radical Empircism*, despite the fact that the volume does *not* represent James's final intentions (pp. 208–209), underscores the need for students to read James in the order in which he wrote (and rewrote).

Josiah Royce

There are various collections of Royce's writings, none of which seems to me distinctive. Two secondary works are worth reading: John E. Smith, *Royce's Social Infinite* (New York: Liberal Arts Press, 1950); and Bruce Kuklick, *Josiah Royce* (Indianapolis: Bobbs-Merrill Co., 1972). John Clendenning has produced a first-rate edition of *The Letters of Josiah Royce* (Chicago: University of Chicago Press, 1970) and is preparing a biography. There is an excellent bibliography of Royce's writing by Ignas Skrupskelis in *The Writings of Josiah Royce*, ed. John J. McDermott (Chicago: University of Chicago Press, 1969), pp. 1167–1226. Royce's papers are in HUA.

Hugo Münsterberg

Münsterberg's extensive papers are in the Boston Public Library. There is also a valuable memoir, *Hugo Münsterberg: His Life and Work*, by Margaret Münsterberg (New York: Appleton Publishers, 1922), which contains a good survey of his writings, pp. 303–437. There are only a few secondary sources: a chapter in A. A. Roback, *History of American Psychology* (New York: Library Publishers, 1952), pp. 192–208; a broader chapter in Antonio Aliota, *The Idealist Reaction Against Science* (London: Macmillan and Co., 1914), pp. 196–273; and George Sydney Brett, *A History of Psychology*, vol. 3 (New York: Macmillan Co., 1921), pp. 181–84. W. H. Werkmeister has an extended treatment of *The Eternal Values* in *Historical Spectrum of Value Theories*, 2 vols. (Lincoln, Nebraska: Johnson Publishing Company, 1970), 251–86. Dover has reissued *The Photoplay* in a 1970 paperback as *The Film: A Psychological Study*. This and *Psychology and Life* (Boston, 1899) are a good introduction to Münsterberg.

Psychology

Robert Thompson's *The Pelican History of Psychology* (Middlesex,

England: Penguin, 1968) contains an excellent bibliography on the history of psychology, pp. 432–57; there is also the valuable bibliographical account in Robert M. Young, "Scholarship and the History of the Behavioral Sciences," *History of Science* 5 (1966): 1–51. On American psychology during this period there is the bibliography in Frank Albrecht, "The New Psychology in America, 1880–1895," Ph.D. dissertation, Johns Hopkins University, 1960, pp. 221–35. Most useful books are Roback, *History of American Psychology; A History of Psychology in Autobiography*, vols. 1–3 ed. Carl Murchison (Worcester, Mass.: Clark University Press, 1930, 1932, 1936), vols. 4–5 ed. E. G. Boring and Gardner Lindzey (New York: Appleton-Century-Crofts, 1947, 1967); and E. G. Boring, *A History of Experimental Psychology*, 2d ed. (New York: Appleton-Century-Crofts, 1950). Boring has excellent brief accounts of Yerkes, Holt, and Tolman as well as bibliographical material. Yerkes's papers, a rich collection, are located in the library of the Yale Medical School; Boring's papers are in HUA. I have been unable to locate material on Holt other than that cited in my footnotes, except for "Eight Steps on Neuro-Muscular Integration," *Problems of Nervous Physiology and Behavior* (Symposium dedicated to I. Beritashvili, Academy of Science of USSR, Georgian Branch) (Tiflis, 1936), pp. 25–36. Interested readers ought to begin with his book *The Freudian Wish* (New York: Henry Holt and Co., 1915). I have listed other bibliographical material in my sections on James and Münsterberg.

George Herbert Palmer

There is an unpublished biography of Palmer in the Palmer Collection at Wellesley College in Wellesley, Massachusetts, "George Herbert Palmer, Counsellor and Friend," by Constance Grosvenor Alexander (1943). It has a bibliography, pp. 193–96, 201–04, which supplements the books I cite, as does Frances Lee Panchaud, "George Herbert Palmer," Ph.D. dissertation, New York University, 1936, pp. I–VII. Neither is adequate, but it is not clear that Palmer merits full-scale study.

Realism

On neo-realism and critical realism there are two bibliographical sources: Herbert Schneider, *Sources of Contemporary Realism in America* (Indianapolis: Bobbs-Merrill, 1964), should be supplemented by pp. 571–72 of his *History of American Philosophy*; more useful is Victor Harlow, *A Bibliography and Genetic Study of American Realism* (Oklahoma City: Harlow Publishing Co., 1931). Charles Morris, *Six Theories of Mind* (Chicago: University of Chicago Press, 1932), and Lars Boman, *Criticism and Construction in the Philosophy of the American New Realism* (Stockholm: Almqvist and Wiksel, 1955), have excellent chapters on Holt, pp. 102–48 and 97–131 respectively, showing the impact of the Americans on Bertrand Russell. I have been unable to locate Syed Zafarul Hasan, *Realism: An Attempt to Trace Its Origins and Developments in Its Chief Representatives* (Cambridge, Mass., 1928). "British and American Realism, 1900–1930" is the subject of an issue of *Monist*—51 (1967): 159–304.

James's relation to C. A. Strong, Dickinson S. Miller, and Santayana, as well as to mid-century Anglo-American philosophy, can be traced in Dickinson S. Miller, *Philosophical Analysis and Human Welfare: Selected Essays and Chapters from Six Decades*, edited with an introduction by Lloyd D. Easton (Dordrecht-Holland: D. Reidel, 1975).

George Santayana

Of all the philosophers of the Golden Age, none has suffered more than Santayana. While he has attracted a group of aesthetic devotees, posterity has ignored his philosophy and, to that extent, missed a complete understanding of the man. The best volume to start with is *The Philosophy of George Santayana*, edited by P. A. Schilpp (LaSalle, Illinois: Open Court Publishing Co., 1940), which contains critical essays and a bibliography of Santayana's writings to 1940. There are also Santayana's own three-volume autobiography *Persons and Places* (New York: Charles Scribner's Sons, 1944, 1945, 1953); the *Letters of George Santayana*, ed. Daniel Cory (New York: Charles Scribner's Sons, 1955); and four important volumes of essays: *Obiter Scripta*, ed. Justus Buchler and Benjamin Schwartz (New York: Charles Scribner's Sons, 1936); *The Idler and His Works and Other Essays*, ed. Daniel Cory (New York: George Braziller, 1957); the helpful *Animal Faith and Spiritual Life*, ed. John Lachs (New York: Appleton-Century-Crofts, 1967); and *Physical Order and Moral Liberty*, ed. John and Shirley Lachs (Nashville, Tennessee: Vanderbilt University Press, 1969).

The preface of this last book indicates the location of Santayana manuscripts other than those in the Houghton Library at Harvard. I consulted none of these collections for this study. Indiana University Press has published Santayana's dissertation, *Lotze's System of Philosophy*, edited by Paul Grimley Kurtz (Bloomington, Ind., 1971); there is an easily available edition of his poems, *Poems of George Santayana* (New York: Dover, 1970); and paperback collections of his essays abound. Thomas N. Munson, *The Essential Wisdom of Santayana* (New York: Columbia University Press, 1961), has a bibliography of work on Santayana, pp. 119–214; and an issue of the *Southern Journal of Philosophy*—10 (1971): 105–285—is devoted to studies of Santayana. There is one excellent book: Timothy L. S. Sprigge, *Santayana: An Examination of His Philosophy* (London: Routledge and Kegan Paul, 1974).

The best biographical accounts are two undergraduate essays by Patrick Emmet Flynn: "George Santayana and the American Academic Scene, 1882–1912: The Philosophic Background" (Bowdoin Prize, Harvard, 1960), and "Santayana in America: The Harvard Phase" (senior thesis, Harvard, 1960), both in HUA.

Ralph Barton Perry

Secondary material on Perry is limited. There is a bibliography of his writing in his papers in HUA. Other material (I did not consult it) is located at Indiana University under the control of his son, Bernard Perry.

William Ernest Hocking

Leroy Rouner, *Within Human Experience: The Philosophy of William Ernest Hocking* (Cambridge: Harvard University Press, 1969), is the most important work about Hocking, but the study of his life and work is an area almost entirely lacking in competent scholarship. The Hocking Papers, a voluminous collection, are located in his library in Madison, New Hampshire, in the possession of Richard Hocking. There is a full bibliography of his writings by Richard Gilman in the Hocking Festschrift, *Philosophy, Religion, and the Coming World Civilization*, ed. Leroy Rouner (The Hague: Martinus Nijhoff, 1966), pp. 464–504. The best bibliography of work on Hocking is in A. R. Luther, *Existence as Dialectical*

Tension: A Study of the First Philosophy of W. E. Hocking (The Hague: Martinus Nijhoff, 1968), pp. 149–50.

Alfred North Whitehead

Victor Lowe is preparing an important book on Whitehead, "Alfred North Whitehead: The Man and His Work," which will contain full bibliographical information.

Whitehead scholarship is a major industry. The works I have found most helpful as a beginner are: William Christian, *An Interpretation of Whitehead's Metaphysics* (New Haven: Yale University Press, 1959); Nathaniel Lawrence, *Whitehead's Philosophical Development* (Berkeley: University of California Press, 1956); Robert Palter, *Whitehead's Philosophy of Science* (Chicago: University of Chicago Press, 1960); and Donald W. Sherburne, *A Key to Whitehead's Process and Reality* (Bloomington: Indiana University Press, 1966). Indispensable are Lucien Price, *Dialogues of Alfred North Whitehead* (Boston: Little, Brown and Co., 1954), and P. A. Schilpp, ed., *The Philosophy of Alfred North Whitehead*, 2d ed. (LaSalle, Illinois: Open Court Publishing Co., 1951); the latter has a bibliography of Whitehead's writings, pp. 749–78. A corrected edition of *Process and Reality* will soon appear, edited by David Ray Griffin, Ivor Leclerc, and Donald W. Sherburne (New York: Free Press, 1977); and a new Whitehead bibliography is to be published by the Philosophy Documentation Center, Bowling Green University.

C. I. Lewis

Aside from the professional philosophical literature, secondary material on Lewis is meager. The reader might start with Bella K. Milmed's discussion in *Kant and Current Philosophical Issues* (New York: New York University Press, 1961); the articles in P. A. Schilpp, ed., *The Philosophy of C. I. Lewis* (LaSalle, Illinois: Open Court Publishing Co., 1968); and, more recently, Robert I. Halpern, "C. I. Lewis's Conception of the Given and the Problem of Epistemic Justification," Ph.D. dissertation, CUNY-Graduate Center, 1975, which has a useful bibliography, pp. 291–94. Schilpp's volume contains a bibliography of Lewis's work, pp. 677–89. *The Collected Papers of Clarence Irving Lewis*, ed. John D. Goheen and John

L. Mothershead, Jr. (Stanford: Stanford University Press, 1970), is invaluable for gathering Lewis's periodical work. Of Lewis's books, must reading is *Mind and the World-Order* (New York: Charles Scribner's Sons, 1929). The student should also be warned that two historically important chapters of *A Survey of Symbolic Logic* (Berkeley: University of California Press, 1918) are omitted in the Dover paperback edition (New York, 1960). The Lewis Papers are at Stanford University, Palo Alto, California. Two memoirs by his wife, Mabel Lewis, are moving accounts of their personal lives. *As the Twig is Bent* and *C&I* are both in the author's possession.

INDEX

Abbot, Francis, 93–103; and Wright, 65–66, 93; amateurism of, 80, 92–93, 102–03; and the *Index*, 92, 102; career of, 92–93, 101–02; and Hamilton, 93; and Metaphysical Club, 93; and Peirce, 93, 101–02, 113, 116–17; and Bowen, 93–94; on Spencer, 93–94; and Kant, 94–95; and nominalism, 94–99; realism of, 94–99; and Descartes, 95; and Hume, 95; scientific views of, 96–100; religion of, 98–101; later work of, 101–02; and Peabody, 245; Royce on, 250*n*

Absolute: in Abbot, 101; in Peirce, 114–15; in Royce, 156–57, 194–95, 260–64, 275–83, 287–90, 302–06, 394–95; James's argument for, 176–84; in Palmer, 225–26; James's arguments against, 284–85, 332; Perry's arguments against, 340–44; in Hocking, 482–90. *See also* Absolute idealism; Idealism; Monism

"Absolute and the Individual, The" (Royce), 259, 261–64

Absolute idealism: as chief philosophic position, 138, 140, 157–58, 215, 256–57, 566–67; Peirce on, 114–15; Royce's, 156–57, 194–95, 260–64, 275–83, 287–90, 302–06, 370–401; James on, 171–78, 283–87, 332; and psychology, 180; Münsterberg's, 203–09; Palmer on, 225–26; Perry on, 340–44; Hocking on, 482–90; Lewis on, 545. *See also* Absolute; Idealism; Monism

Absolute pragmatism, xxi, 287–89, 386–87

Absolute solipism. *See* Subjectivism

Actual occasions: in Whitehead, 525–30

Adams, G. P., 242, 254*n*

Adams, Jane, 306

Adventures of Ideas (Whitehead), 517

Agassiz, Louis, 104; fights evolution, 22–23; and the Peirces, 118; and James, 160

Alcott, Bronson, 57, 58

Alford Professorship: under Bowen, xv–xvi, 28, 30; coveted by Palmer and James, 138, 217, 219; under Hocking, 413*n;* unfilled, 413*n*

Altruism (Palmer), 218; discussed, 224–25, 503–04

Amateur philosophizing: and institutions, xx, xxiii, 26–27, 46–47, 102–03, 136–38, 239–40; priorities of, xxiii, 61–62; and professionalization, xxiii, 239–40, 414–15; success of, 26–27, 46–47; 61–62; social function of, 46–47; and informal clubs, 46–47, 54–61, 215; Metaphysical Club and, 47–54; Howison and, 55–56; Harris and, 55, 56–59; Davidson and, 55–57, 59–61; and St. Louis Hegelians, 55–58; and Concord School, 57–59; and Emerson, 57–59; Wright and, 78–79; and Glenmore School, 59–61; Fiske and, 80, 87, 90–91; Abbot and, 80, 92–93, 102–03; and Transcendentalism, 102–03; Peirce and, 104, 124–25, 126

American Institute of Christian Philosophy, 134

American Law Review, 49

American Patriotism (Münsterberg), 197, 212

American Philosophical Association, xvi, 255, 591

Americans, The (Münsterberg), 197

American Traits (Münsterberg), 212

Ames, Charles H., 55

Analysis of Knowledge and Valuation, An (Lewis), 534; discussed, 511*n,* 561–62; significance of, 569

Analytic. See *A priori*

"Analytic Knowledge" (Sheffer), 458

Angell, James Rowland, 420n

Angier, Roswell, 420n, 421, 482n

Animal Drive and the Learning Process (Holt), 431

Appearance and Reality (Bradley), 370–71

Applied philosophy. *See* Public philosophy; Technical philosophy

Applied psychology, 209–12, 248, 436, 475–76n

Appreciation. *See* Two worlds problem

Approach to Philosophy, The (Perry), 348n, 454

A priori: synthetic, 13, 557–60; Bowen on, 35, 37, 39–42; in Wright, 76; in Fiske, 84; James on, 169; pragmatic, 549–52; in Lewis, 557–60, 579–80; in Quine, 578–80

"Are We Automata?" (James), 170–72

Arisbe, 124, 126

Associationalism: Spencer's, 162, 170; and James, 162–63, 166–67, 182–84; and Münsterberg, 188–89, 200–01

Atheism: Cambridge philosophers on, 24, 26–27, 366, 571–72; Bowen on, 40–41; Santayana's, 366

Atonement: in Royce, 397–400

Bain, Alexander: and Green, 49; influence on Metaphysical Club, 49, 51; and principle of pragmatism, 49, 51, 117–18; influence on Peirce, 117–18; and Wright, 151

Bakewell, Charles, 242, 482n

Bascom, John, 58, 135

Beck, L. W., 557n, 559

Behaviorism, 459, 461; James's, 184–86, 189, 417–18; Münsterberg's, 188–89, 417–18; in Neo-realism, 344–47; Holt's, 344–47, 425–29, 431; students of the Golden Age on, 420; and professionalization of psychology, 475–76n; Perry's, 509

Berenson, Bernard, 409

Bergson, Henri, 552; and James, 331–32, 442n; role in First World War thought, 442n

Berkeley, Bishop George: Harvard view of, 11–12; Bowen on, 43–45; Fiske on, 86; Peirce on, 109, 111; Royce on, 148–51; James on, 328–29

Berkeley, University of California at, 242; relation to Harvard, xvi, 56n, 254; Philosophical Union at, 56n, 254, 260, 264, 265; Howison at, 135–36; Royce at, 141, 260, 265; James at, 265; Palmer on, 533; Lewis at, 533, 534

Bible, 6, 8–9, 32, 37–38

Bifurcation of nature: in Whitehead, 521–24

Blacks, 407

Blanshard, Brand, 468–69, 482n, 566

Board of Overseers, xvi; on intellectual and moral philosophy, xv, 136–37; and psychology, 445, 461

Body and Mind (McDougall), 459

Boler, John F., 113n

Boodin, John, 242

Bosanquet, Bernard, 580

Bowen, Francis, xiv, 28–45, 63, 368; as Alford Professor, xv–xvi, 28; career of, 10, 28–29, 45, 134–35; and Peirce, 28, 35, 116–120; influence on students, 28, 45; and James, 28, 166; public commitment of, 28–29, 45; economic thought of, 29–30; Christian theism of, 30, 31; and Emerson, 30, 35; responds to evolution, 30, 38–42; educational thought of, 31–32, 134–35; introduces Kant, 32; Scottish realism of, 32–34, 44; as empiricist, 32–37, 39–42; and Hamilton, 33, 44; and Descartes, 33–34; and Kant and Locke, 33–34, 43; on Hume, 34–36; on *a priori* reasoning, 35, 37, 39–42; on God, 36; on the self, 36–37, 44–45; revealed and natural theology of, 36–38; and argument from design, 37, 41; and Berkeley, 43–45; later work of, 43–45, 77; and Wright, 77; and Abbot, 93

Bradley, Francis: and James, 290, 318, 331n; and Royce, 290, 318, 331n, 370–71, 372, 373, 399–400; and logic, 370–71, 372

Bridgman, Percy, 461

Brown, Harold, 242

Brown University, xvi, 242

Bryce, James, 208
Buckham, John Wright, 56n
Burnham, John C. 420n
Business Psychology (Münsterberg), 210–11

Cabot, James Elliot, 55
Cabot, Richard Clark, 410
Caird, Edward, 219
California, from the Conquest . . . (Royce), 142
Calkins, Mary, 189n, 590–91, 592, 593
Calvinism, 5–7
Cannon, Walter B., 423
Cantor, George, 377, 383
Carleton College, 242
Catholics, 455
Cattell, J. M., 413–14, 415
Causality: Cambridge view of, 12; Hume on, 12, 16–17, 35–36; Bowen on, 35–6, 42; Wright on, 74, 78; Fiske on, 86; Abbot on, 99–100; Peirce on, 110–11; Royce on, 151–52; Münsterberg on, 199–202; Palmer on, 219–220; Whitehead on, 523, 529–30; Lewis on, 535–36, 560
Cayley, Arthur, 378
Channing, William Henry, 58
Chao, Yuen Ren, 254n
Character and Opinion in the United States (Santayana), 367
Chicago, University of, xxvi, 306
Chocorua, New Hampshire: James at, 315, 336
Christian Examiner, 30
Christianity: Unitarian view of, 5–9, 24–25; Bowen's, 30, 37–38; Fiske on, 88–90; Abbot on, 92; James on, 173; Palmer on, 226; Royce's, 260, 385–400; Hocking's, 493–94
City College of New York, 242
Civil War: as intellectual watershed, xvii, xxvii, 10, 21, 38, 46, 129, 130, 233
Clark Conference, 423
Clark Professorship (Yale), 482n
Clark University, 129, 462
Cognitions, 107
Cognitivism. *See* Ethics
Cohen, Felix, 456

Cohen, Morris, 242, 456
Columbia University, xvi, xxvi, 306
Coming World Civilization, The (Hocking), 494
Common Law, The (Holmes), 50
Community: Peirce on, 114–17; Royce on, 388–93, 440–41; Perry on, 513–14; Lewis on, 562–62
Comte, Auguste, 20, 63; Fiske on, 85–87
"Conception of God, The" (Royce), 259, 260, 261, 275
Concept of Consciousness, The (Holt): discussed, 347n, 421–23; relation to James, 421–22; relation to Royce, 422–23; and Holt's later work, 425
Concept of Nature, The (Whitehead), 520–24
Concord School of Philosophy, 57–59, 61, 135
Conditioned, Law of the. *See* Law of the Conditioned
Condorcet, Marquis de, 85
Congregationalism. *See* Calvinism
Consciousness: Fiske on, 83–85; Abbot on, 99–101; Royce on, 147–57; James on, 168–73, 178–79, 180–86, 319–34; distinct from self-consciousness in James, 183, 319–34; Holt on, 421–23; Perry on, 509–10. *See also* Self; Self-consciousness
Constructionalism: Kant's, 13–14; Bowen and, 39–42; Harvard pragmatism and, 61–62, 256–57; Whitehead on, 521
Contemporary American Philosophy, (Adams and Montague, eds.), xvi
Cornell University, xvi, 93, 215
Cosmical weather: Wright on, 73–74; Wright broadens notion, 78; James uses broadened notion, 176, 268
Cosmism, 92
Creative Evolution (Bergson), 332
Creativity: in Whitehead, 530
Creighton, James, 215
Critical Essays, on a Few Subjects Connected with the History and Present Condition of Speculative Philosophy (Bowen), 33–35
Critical Period of American History, The (Fiske), 88, 91

Critical rationalism: in Royce, 279–82; relation to James, 324–25; relation to Perry, 348*n;* relation to Lewis, 553

Critical realism: importance in American philosophy, 348, 365, 566; in Santayana, 361–62; discussed, 362–65; as a form of metaphysical realism with minimal commitments, 364–65; Lewis on, 557

Critique of Pure Reason. See Kant, Immanuel; Noumenal and phenomenal; Transcendental Unity of Apperception; Two worlds problem

Croly, Herbert, 311, 569

Darwin, Charles, 565; and Unitarians, xix, 21; and pessimism, xxi; work of, 21–22; and Unitarian philosophy, 23–25; Bowen on, 39–42; and principle of pragmatism, 47–54; Wright defends, 70–74, 76; Peirce on, 118–119; Royce and, 143–44, 157–58; James and, 160–61, 170–71; and psychology, 419. *See also* Evolution; *Origin of Species*

Darwinism. *See* Darwin, Charles; Evolution; *Origin of Species*

Davidson, Thomas: and amateur clubs, 55; and Howison and Harris, 55, 135–36; career of, 56–57, 136; and James, 59; and Glenmore, 59–61; and Royce, 136.

Dearborn, Walter, 248

Death, significance of for this study, xxvii, 571–72; and evolution, 24, 26–27, 40–41; and Abbot, 99; and James, 160–61, 334–37, 571–72; and philosophy, 571–72

Dedekind, Richard, 373

Democracy in America (Tocqueville), 29

Descartes, René, 35; Harvard view of, 11; and Wright, 76; and Fiske, 84; and Abbot, 95; and Peirce, 109, 111, 113, 118, 119, 153; and Royce, 153; and Hocking, 489; Whitehead on, 521; and Lewis, 560

Description. *See* Two worlds problem

Design, argument from: Unitarians on, 5–7, 22–25; Bowen on, 32, 36–38, 41; Wright on, 68–70

Destiny of Man, The (Fiske), 88–90

Determinism: and Wright, 79; and James, 161–76; and Palmer, 219–20; and Royce, 259–64

Dewey, John: significance of, xxvi; and *Journal of Speculative Philosophy,* 57; public philosophy of, 306, 314; ethics of, 496

De Wulf, Maurice, 455

Dialectic argument: in Royce, 146–47, 155–58, 260–61, 278, 282–83, 392–93; James's argument against, 265–66; Perry's argument against, 340–41; in Hocking, 484–45, 488–89; Lewis's argument against, 547–48; in Lewis, 560

Die Amerikaner (Münsterberg), 197

"Dilemma of Determinism, The" (James), 174–76

Divinity School (Harvard), 244–45

Doctorates: dispersion of recipients of, xvi, 56*n,* 242, 254, 482*n,* 566; training of recipients of, 133, 233–35, 463–80; production of, 242–43, 248–51, 463–80; James on, 248–51; list of recipients of, 581–94

"Does 'Consciousness' Exist?" (James), 319–320

Dogmatic idealism, 556, 557, 559

Doubt: Peirce on 118; Royce on, 153–57; James on, 164–79

Drake, Durant, 362

Ducasse, C. J., 242

Duke University, 459–60

Dunlap, Knight, 420

Dupree, Hunter, 69*n*

Durkheim, Emile, 314

Eaton, Ralph, 458–59*n*

Education. *See* Educational philosophy; Graduate education; Teaching; Undergraduate education

Education, Harvard department of, 247–48

Educational philosophy: Bowen's, 31–32, 134–35; Davidson's, 56–57, 59–61; Münsterberg's, 212; Palmer's, 235–41; Dearborn's, 248

Egotism in German Philosophy (Santayana), 441

Elective system: Eliot's institution of, 30, 31, 131–3, 238, 240; Bowen on, 30–32; Palmer on, 237–39; Lowell on, 405–06

Eliot, Charles: career of, xx, 129–34, 405–06; elective system of, 30, 31, 131–33, 238–40; 405–06; and Bowen, 30, 134–35; and Wright, 78–79; and Fiske, 81–82, 87; and University Lectures, 81–82, 87, 134, 234; and James, 135, 136–37; and Palmer, 135, 137–38, 239–40; and Royce, 136, 137; and Münsterberg, 138–39, 196, 436–37, 445; and research, 138–39, 235; and Johns Hopkins, 233–35; and graduate education, 233–35, 239–40; and professionalization, 233–35, 414–15; on Santayana, 366; and First World War, 445; and Jews, 456

Eliot, T. S., 410*n*

Emerson, Ralph: at center of controversies, xix, 7–9, 10, 19–20, 27; amateurism of, xxiii, 27, 47, 87, 90–91, 102–03; and public affairs, 28, 29; Bowen on, 30, 35

Emerson Hall, 246, 251

Emery, Samuel, 55, 57

Empiricism and rationalism: traditional Harvard view of, 11–12, 316–19; in Unitarians and Bowen, 18–19, 32–37, 39–42, 61–62, 64; Wright's, 64; in James and Perry, 316–19; in Lewis, 548, 557, 560, 580; in Quine, 578, 580

Encyclopedia of Unified Science, The, 567

Enquiry Concerning the Principles of Natural Knowledge, An (Whitehead), 520–24

Entrepreneurial skills: and academic success, 136–39; Münsterberg on, 138–39, 196–98, 211; Palmer and, 239–41; James on, 248–51; Perry and, 254–56; Holt on, 431–33

Epistemological realism: defined in relation to nominalism, 14–15; and Scottish realism, 16–17; and metaphysical realism, 94, 104–20, 101, 328, 330; Abbot on, 94–101; Peirce on, 104–20, 329; James on, 328–30. *See also* Metaphysical realism; Presentational realism

Epistemology: in professional philosophy, 249–50, 565–67; in Royce and James, 264; in neo-realism, 342, 349–50; in critical realism, 364–65; in Lewis, 561–62, 566; relation to other philosophical sub-disciplines, 565–67. *See also* Hierarchy of philosophical studies

Erlanger Program: and Royce, 378; and Whitehead, 519, 528–29

Error: Peirce on, 108, 114; Royce on, 147, 150–57; in neo-realism, 345–47

Essays in Critical Realism (Santayana et al.) and Santayana, 362, 363; discussed, 362–65; as peculiar form of realism, 363–64; as epistemology, 364–65

Essays in Radical Empiricism (James), 319, 321*n*

Eternal objects, 527–28, 530–31

Eternal Values, The (Münsterberg): and Royce, 203, 323; discussed, 203–08; schematized, 205; relation to earlier work, 206–07; and James, 209, 323

Ethics: in hierarchy of philosophical studies, xxiii, 215–16, Wright's 69–70; and self-realization, 215, 503–04, 507; Palmer's, 215–16, 218–25, 497, 503–04, 508, 509; James's, 294–96, 309–11; Royce's, 296–300, 497–505, 507, 508, 509; Holt's, 428–29, 497, 504, 508; Dewey's, 496; and cognitivism, 496–97, 504; Perry's, 496–97, 504–15; noncognitivism in, 496–97, 515; Stevenson's, 496–97, 515; Hocking's, 497, 504, 508, 509; Santayana's, 497–504; prudence and, 501–03, 505–08; and realism, 503; Harvard consensus on, 503–04; and evolutionary naturalism, 504; and idealism, 504; and utilitarianism, 507–08, 513–14. *See also* Political philosophy; Moral philosophy; Social philosophy

Ethics and Language (Stevenson), 496–97, 511*n*, 515

Everett, Charles Carroll, 54, 244

Evil, problem of: in James, 294–96; in

Royce, 301–06, 395–400

Evolution: relation to pragmatism, xix–xx, 26–27, 45, 47–54, 61–62, 118–19; Darwin on, 21–23; generalized ideas about, 22, 28, 201–02; scientific problems of, 23–24; and Unitarian philosophy, 23–25; and Mill, 25; and Transcendentalism, 25; and skepticism, 25, 38–42; Spencer's view of, 25–26; Bowen on, 30, 38–42; and Metaphysical Club, 47–54; Wright's view of, 70–74, 76; and German Darwinism, 71, 85; Fiske's view of, 81–87, 88–90; Abbot on, 96–101; Royce's view of, 143–44, 157–58; impact on James, 160–61, 170–71. *See also* Darwin, Charles; *Origin of Species*

Evolutionary naturalism: defined, 189–90; in James, 189–90, 359–62; in Santayana, 359–62, 484, 504; in Holt, 423, 504, 484; in Hocking, 484, 504

"Evolution of Self-Consciousness, The" (Wright), 72; and legal pragmatism, 51; and habit, 74–75; discussed, 74–77; and signs, 75–76; natural realism in, 76–77.

Examination of Sir William Hamilton's Philosophy (Mill), 32; impact on American philosophy, 20–21, 52; Peirce on, 52–53, 122; Abbot on, 65–66; Wright on, 65–66

Expressions of the Emotions in Man and Animals (Darwin), 419

Extensive abstraction, 522–23

"External World and the Social Consciousness, The" (Royce), 191, 193–95

"Fact and Destiny" (Hocking), 494

Farber, Marvin, 456

"Feeling of Effort, The" (James), 166–68, 187

Feigl, Herbert, 461–62

Felton, Cornelius, 135, 237

Fermat's Last Theorem, 384

Feud of Oakfield Creek, The (Royce), 142

Fiat: in James, 166–76, 184–86, 188–89; in Münsterberg, 188–89

Fichte. *See* Post-Kantians

Fideism: defined, xx; in James, xx, 172, 336; in Fiske, 90; in Hocking, 484, 490

Field of Ethics, The (Palmer), 218, 219

Film, The (Münsterberg), 213–14, 447

First World War, 140, 408; Harvard responds to, xxiv–xxv, 438–47; history of, 435, 437–38; attack on Münsterberg during, 435–38, 444–45, 446–47; and impact on idealism, 446–47, 495, 567

Fisch, Max, 113n

Fiske, John, 80–93; and Wright, 71; and Scottish thought, 80; amateurism of, 80, 87, 90–91, 103, 104; career of, 80–81, 87, 90–91; at Harvard, 81–82; evolutionary cosmology of, 81–87, 88–90; and Spencer, 81–87, 91; and positivism, 82, 85–86; and sociality, 83–85; on Descartes and Locke, 84; and Comte, 85–87; Christianity of, 86, 88–90, 92; and Kant, 87; later work of, 87–90; historical writing of, 88, 91; and pragmatism, 88–90; and shorter philosophical works, 88–90

"Fixation of Belief, The" (Peirce), 118–20, 122

Foundations of Science, The (Poincaré), 549

Four Conceptions of Being: Royce discusses, 275, 279–83, 338, 575; and James, 324–25; and Perry, 338, 348n; and Hocking, 489–90; and Lewis, 553. *See also* Critical rationalism; Mysticism; Representational realism

Frankena, William, 511n

Frankfurter, Felix, 457

Freedom. *See* Free will

Free Man and the Soldier, The (Perry), 443

Freeman, Alice, 217–218, 237n

Free will: Bowen on, 36–37, 44–45; in James, 161–76, 335; Palmer on, 219–220; in Royce, 259–64

Freud, Sigmund: and Münsterberg, 201; and Holt, 423, 428

Freudian Wish and Its Place in Ethics, The (Holt), as evolutionary naturalism, 423; and Freudianism, 423–24, 426–27, 428; discussed, 423–31; behaviorism of, 424–28; as moral philosophy, 428–29, 504; moralism of, 429–31

Fuller, B. A. G., 410*n*

"Function of Cognition, The" (James), 179, 266

Fundamentals of Human Motivation (Troland), 420

Garrison, George R. 314*n*

General Theory of Value (Perry), 409, 497, 561; epistemology of, 348*n*; discussed, 348*n*, 508–15; relation to earlier work, 348*n*, 511; relation to other work, 509, 513–14; conception of God in, 514–15

Genteel Tradition, 367–69

"Genteel Tradition in American Philosophy, The" (Santayana), 367–69

Geometry, 549

German Darwinism: Wright on, 71; Fiske's, 85

Gibbs, Wolcott, 131, 234

Gifford Lectures, 258, 275, 291, 494

Gilman, Daniel Coit, 105, 123, 129, 137, 215, 233–35

Gilson, Etienne, 455

Ginzburg, Benjamin, 456

Given: in Royce, 145–46, 318; in James, 168–71, 178–79, 318; in Perry, 339–42; in Hocking, 483, 487; in Lewis, 552

Glenmore School of the Cultural Sciences, 59–61, 135

God: arguments for the existence of, 5–9, 22–26; Bowen on, 36, 38, 42; Wright on, 67–69; Fiske on, 86, 88–90; Abbot on, 98–101; Palmer on, 225–26; Royce on, 260–64, 296–306, 394–95, 514; James on, 294–96, 335–36, 514; Hocking on, 485–94; Perry on, 514–15; Whitehead on, 530–32; Quine on, 578

Golden Age (of American Philosophy): specifically mentioned, xx, xxv, 28, 45, 400–01, 451–52

Goodman, Nelson, 577, 580

Grace: in the later Royce, 396–98

Graduate education, 133, 233–35, 239–40, 405–06; Palmer on, 240–41; and production of doctorates, 242–43, 248–51, 463–80; and teaching, 249–50; Münsterberg on, 250–51. *See also* Educational philosophy; Teaching; Undergraduate education

Grass Valley, California, 140, 141

Gray, Asa, 104; defends evolution, 22–23; and Wright, 69*n*

Gray, John Chipman, 48

Great Chain of Being, The (Lovejoy), 363*n*, 411*n*

Great Visions of Philosophy, The (Montague), 576

Green, Nicholas St. John, 47–50, 54, 117

Green, Thomas Hill, 61, 215

Habit: Wright on, 75–76; Peirce on, 120–21; James on, 184–86; Royce on, 276–77; Holt on, 424–29; Perry on, 509

Hall, G. Stanley, 124, 247

Hamilton, William, 31, 63; and Kant, 17–18; Unitarians on, 18–21; and Mill, 20–21; Bowen on, 33, 44; and Wright, 64–68, 93; Abbot on, 94; and Peirce, 116–17, 122

Hanus, Henry, 247

Harper, William, 129, 241

Harris, William T.: and St. Louis Hegelians, 55, 57–58, 135–36; and amateurs, 55, 57–59, 135–36; career of, 57; and Concord School, 57–59, 135–36; and Davidson and Howison, 135–36; decline of reputation of, 136

Harvard Board of Overseers. *See* Board of Overseers

Harvard Philosophical Club, 55

Harvard Pragmatism: explicitly defined as organizing principle, xx–xxi, 256–58

Harvard University: elective system at, 30–31, 131, 238–40, 405–06; undergraduate education of, 30–32, 131–33, 233, 405–06; and Hopkins, 129; leadership of, 129, 233–35, 405–06; and Eliot, 129–130, 131–35, 233–35, 239–240, 414–15; expansion of, 130, 233–35, 241–42; graduate education at, 133, 233–35, 239–40, 405–06; philosophers at, 133–38, 235–42, 248–56, 407–15; 452–59; hiring policies of, 135–36, 251–56, 407–15; promotions at, 137–39, 241–42, 251–56, 407–15; Santayana on, 235; Palmer on, 235–41; and Lowell, 405–15, 453; Jews at, 407; tenure system at, 414–15; women at, 590–94

Hedge, Levi, 10

Heidegger, Martin, 579

Helmholtz, H. L. F., 72

Herbert, George, 217

Herbst, Jurgen, 247n

Hermit of Carmel and Other Poems, A (Santayana), 253

Hierarchy of philosophical studies, xxiii, 215–16, 227, 311–14

Hill, Thomas, 131, 234

History of ideas: study of, xvii–xviii; 575–76, 577

History of philosophy: in Cambridge, 10–19; Bowen's view of, 32–35; Abbot's view of, 94–95; neo-realists' view of, 349–50, 575–76; Whitehead on, 518–19; Lewis and, 548, 555, 560; Royce's view of, 575; development of study of, 575–76

Hobbes, Thomas, 223, 306

Hocking, Agnes, 482, 485–86

Hocking, Ernest, xvi, 433, 442–44, 481–95; and Perry, xxii–xxiii, 483, 485, 486; as professional, xxii–xxiii, 567; public concerns of, 439, 441–44, 445, 494–95, 561, 567–68; and First World War, 439, 441–44, 445, 495; political philosophy of, 441, 444, 490–94; and Royce, 453, 481–82, 483, 484–85, 488, 489–90; on Jews, 456–67; and James, 481, 483–84, 485, 489, 495; Palmer on, 482; idealism of, 482–83, 485–90; and Palmer, 483; and neo-realism, 483, 485; pragmatism of, 484; fideism of, 484, 494; on *The Problem of Christianity,* 484n; on *The World and the Individual,* 484n, 489; concept of God in, 485–494; and solipsism, 487–90; and mysticism, 489–90; Christianity of, 493–94; later work of, 494; ethics of, 497, 504, 508, 509; and Whitehead, 520

Hodgson, Richard, 420n

Hoernlé, R. F. Alfred, 411–12

Hollis Professorship, xiv

Holmes, Oliver Wendell, Jr.: and Metaphysical Club, 47–51, 54; and principle of pragmatism, 49–51; and Wright, 64

Holt, Edwin, 413, 417–34; and development of neo-realism, 258, 339–40; neo-realism of, 344–47, 422–23; behaviorism of, 344–47, 425–29, 431; and James and Münsterberg, 417–18, 420, 421, 426; career of, 421, 431–34; and Perry, 421, 432, 433; and consciousness, 421–23; logic of, 422–23; and Santayana, 423, 504; evolutionary naturalism of, 423, 504; and Freud, 423–28; ethics of, 428–29, 497, 504, 508; as moralist, 429–30; and Lowell, 432–33; and professionalization, 432–34; on First World War, 445

Holt, Henry, 180, 181

Hook, Sydney, 306

Hopkins, Mark, 134

Howe, Julia Ward, 58

Howison, George Holmes: and amateur clubs, 56, 135–36; career of, 56, 135–36; and Berkeley Philosophical Union, 56n, 260, 264, 265; and Royce, 260, 265; and James, 265

"How to Make Our Ideas Clear" (Peirce): and Metaphysical Club, 52; and Bowen, 120; discussed, 120–23; and James, 264–65

"How Two Minds Can Know One Thing" (James), 326–29

Hudson, W. D., 511n

"Humanism and Truth" (James), 266

Hume, David, 38; Harvard view of, 12, 16–17; and the Scots, 16–17; and Bowen, 34–36; and Wright, 74, 78; Abbot on, 95, 100n; Whitehead on, 523, 529–30; and Lewis, 535–36, 560

Hunt, William M., 159

Huntington, E. V., 458

Idealism: Whitehead's, xxi, 527; Bowen on, 43–45; Abbot's, 101; Peirce's, 109, 114–17; and epistemological realism, 114–17, 328–30; and psychology, 138–39, 180, 190–95, 203; Royce's, 140, 157–58, 392–92; and James, 171–79, 323–26, 331–34; Münsterberg's, 203–06; and First World War, 446–47, 495,

567; Hocking's, 482–83, 485–90; Lewis's, 534, 535–39, 559–60. *See also* Absolute; Absolute idealism
Idea of God, The (Fiske), 88–90
"Illustrations of the Logic of Sciences" (Peirce), 52, 118
Imitation: in Royce, 191–93, 276–77; in James, 326–27; in Lewis, 553–55
"Implications of Self-Consciousness, The" (Royce), 260–61
Index, The, 92, 102
Induction: problem of, stated, 12–14; Wright on, 78; Abbot on, 100*n;* Peirce on, 115; Royce on, 147–48, 176–79; James on, 176–77; Lewis on, 555–560
Inquiry: Peirce on, 118–23; Royce on, 400
Institute of Technology. *See* Massachusetts Institute of Technology
Institutions: and study of philosophy, xviii, 9–10, 23–27, 28, 30–32, 46–47, 61–62, 133–39, 235–57; 407–15, 451–80, 565–67; and amateurs, xx, xxiii, 26–27, 46–47, 102–03, 136–38, 239–40; and Transcendentalism, xxiii, 24–25, 87, 90–91, 102–03; and Bowen, 28, 30–32; and philosophical clubs, 46–47, 54–61, 215; and Wright, 63, 64, 78–79; and Fiske, 80, 87, 90–91, 103, 104; and Abbot, 80, 92–93, 102–03, 104; and Peirce, 123–24; and Eliot, 133–39; and James, 165, 406*n;* Palmer on, 224–25; and professionalization, 235–57; 407–15, 451–80, 561–63, 565–67; and Lowell, 405–15; Holt on, 431–33; and Lewis, 561–62
Institutions: Scottish view of, 17–18; Bowen on, 33, 64
Intellectual philosophy. *See* Moral philosophy
Interest: and Perry's ethics, 505–15
International Congress of the Arts and Science, 208
International Journal of Ethics, 250*n,* 454
Interpretation: Peirce's account of, 107–08; Royce's account of, 385–88; Royce's use of Peirce, 388; in Lewis, 552
Interpretations of Poetry and Religion (Santayana), 253, 357, 358–59

Introduction to Psychology (Yerkes), 420
Introduction to Social Psychology, An (McDougall), 459

James, Alice, 165, 336
James, Henry, Jr., 47, 159, 336
James, Henry, Sr., 159, 166
James, William: xvi, 159–79, 264–74, 311–37; on philosophical temperament, xvii; and development of pragmatism, xix–xx, 176–79, 264–74, 283–85, 292–94; fideism of, xx, 172, 236; and professionalism, xxii, 249–51; creates framework of thought with Royce, xxiii–xxv, 256–58, 291, 316, 370, 451, 565; and Bowen, 28, 166; and Wright, 64, 160, 164, 176–77; temperament of, 78, 159–61, 165, 177, 311, 315–16, 335; and Fiske, 90*n;* and Peirce, 124, 125, 264–65, 269; career of, 135, 136–37, 159–61, 180–81, 315–16, 405; and Royce, 157–58, 176–79, 181–84, 259, 264–69, 279–90, 291–96, 306–14, 324, 325, 327–28, 370, 400; and Nihilism, 160, 164; and Darwin, 160–61, 170–71, 335; and Kant, 161, 272–74, 313*n,* 316–19; and free will, 161–76; and postulation, 161–80, 328; on Spencer, 162, 170; and associationalist psychology, 162–63, 166–67; and representational realism, 162–63, 171–76; and the *fiat,* 166–76, 184–86, 188–89; and analysis of consciousness, 168–73, 178–79, 180–86, 319–34; realism of, 171–79, 323–26, 328–31; idealism of, 171–79, 323–26, 331–34; and monism, 173–79, 265–66, 274, 283–85, 294–96, 320, 332–33; and German idealism, 174, 316–19; and induction, 176–77; on Royce, 176–79, 259*n,* 284–85, 292; and the self, 178–79, 184–85, 508; psychology of, 180–86, 189–90, 266, 417–18; and Münsterberg, 188–89, 196, 208, 209, 212, 250–51, 323; and Palmer, 226; on Perry, 254–55; Royce on, 257*n,* 285; on truth, 266–74; on possibility 283–89; and Bradley, 289–90, 318, 331*n;* religious thought of, 291–96; and problem of evil, 294–96; on God, 294–96,

335–336, 514; social and political philosophy of, 306–14; and Perry, 317, 319, 328–29, 508, 567; radical empiricism of, 319, 334; and panpsychism, 323–26, 331–34; and Berkeley, 328–29; and logic, 331–32; and Bergson, 331–32, 442n; and neo-realism, 339, 348–49; on Santayana, 366; and Holt, 417–18, 420, 421, 426; and Hocking, 481, 483–84, 485, 489, 495; and Whitehead, 519, 523, 525; and Lewis, 533; and death, 572

James-Lange theory of emotions, 185n

Jews: Münsterberg and, 196, 455–56; Lowell on, 407; treatment of at Harvard, 407, 455–58; Eliot on, 456; as graduate students, 456; references for, 456, 457–58; in American academic life, 456–57; Wolfson and, 457; Sheffer and, 457–58

Johns Hopkins University: 129, 137, 215; and Abbot, 93; and Peirce, 105, 123; and graduate education, 233–35

Jordan, David, 129, 208

Journal of Philosophy, 248, 454

Journal of Speculative Philosophy, 57, 137

Journal of the History of Ideas, 576

Journal of the History of Philosophy, 576

Journals: significance of, 29–30, 57, 137, 454, 576

Kallen, Horace, 242, 456

Kant, Immanuel: and Harvard pragmatism, xx–xxi, 26; and religion, xxi; Harvard view of, 12–18, 26; and Hamilton, 17–18, 26; and Locke, 18; introduced at Harvard, 32; and Bowen, 32, 33–34, 43–45; and Peirce, 105–07, 112–114, 115; and Royce, 144–47, 277, 313n; and James, 161, 272–74, 313n, 316–19; and categories, 190–95, 208, 557–59; and Hocking, 489; and Whitehead, 521, 527; and Lewis, 535, 536, 548, 557–59. *See also* Noumenal and phenomenal; Transcendental Unity of Apperception; Two worlds problem

Keene Valley (Adirondacks), 59, 315

Kelvin, William Thompson, Lord, 72–73

Kempe, Alfred, 374, 378–80

Kerner, George C., 511n

Keynes, John M., 555

Klein, Felix, 378

"Knowing of Things Together, The" (James), 266

Kohler, Wolfgang, 460

Lange, John, 511n

Langer, Susanne, 591–94

Langer, William L., 591

Langfeld, Herbert, 433, 459

Langford, C. H., 544

Law of the Conditioned, 18, 19, 65

Lawrence Scientific School, 130, 132

Laws (of nature): Unitarians on, 5–9; Hume on, 12; Spencer on, 25–26, 162, 170; Bowen on, 35–36, 38; Wright on, 68, 71–72, 74; Fiske on, 82–83; Peirce on, 110–11; Münsterberg on, 199; Palmer on, 219–21

Leading ideas: and *The Problem of Christianity,* 394–96; Royce on, 549–50; in Lewis, 550–51

Lebensphilosophie, 442n, 518

Legal pragmatism. *See* Pragmatism

Leibniz: Bowen on, 41; James on, 317; Hocking on, 488

Lenzen, Victor, 254n

Lewis, C. I., xvi, 422, 533–62; professionalism of, xxii, 561–62, 568; and Perry, 348n, 534–35, 536–37, 552; career of, 412–13, 533–34, 560–62; and First World War, 439; and Royce, 453, 533, 534–35, 538–39, 545–48, 559–60, 562; on Jews, 456–57; ethics of, 511n, 562–62; and Russell and Whitehead, 520, 539–45; and James, 533; Palmer on, 533; Royce on, 534; idealism of, 534, 535–39, 559–60; realism of, 534–39; early work of, 534–48; and Kant, 535, 536, 548, 557–59; on Hume, 535–36, 560; and Santayana, 536; logic of, 539–48; and Peirce, 548, 552–53; pragmatic *a priori* of, 549, 550–552; pragmatism of, 549, 550–52, 552–55, 560; on the given, 552; on the categories, 555–59; and dogmatic idealism, 556, 557, 559; social philosophy of, 562

Lewis, Mabel, 533

Life of Jesus (Strauss), 8

Life of Reason, The (Santayana), 253, 258, 357; exemplifies evolutionary naturalism, 359, 422, 524; pragmatism of, 359–60; discussed, 359–62, 504; James's influence on, 360–61; realism of, 360–62; and Lewis, 536

Lippmann, Walter, 311, 569

Littauer, Nathan, 457

Living Religions and a World Faith (Hocking), 494

Locke, John: Harvard view of, 11, 16–17; and Scottish realism, 16–17; Bowen on, 33–34, 43; and Fiske, 84. *See also* Representational realism

Loewenberg, Jacob, 242, 254n, 456

Logic, xxv; and Harvard Pragmatism, xxi; Peirce and, 117; James on, 331–32; ∑ and, 378–85, 388, 545, 569; Royce and, 380–85, 388–90; Holt and, 422–23; Lewis and, 458, 539–48, 580; Russell and Whitehead and, 458, 516, 539–45, 570; Eaton and, 458–59n; material implication in, 539–45, 580; Sheffer and, 569–70; professionalization and, 569–71; Quine and, 580

Logical positivism. *See* Positivism

Lough, James, 420

Love: in the later Royce, 394–95

Lovejoy, Arthur, xxvi; on Harvard productivity, 258; critical realism of, 362–63n; career of, 362–63n, 409–10; on Royce, 401; and professionalism, 414–15; and history of philosophy, 576

Lowell, Lawrence: and Woods, 256; on hiring and tenure, 256, 407–15; on elective system, 405–06; career of, 405–15; and Jews, 407, 456–57; and philosophy, 407–15, 452–53; and First World War, 408, 444–45; and psychology, 413–14, 419, 420n; and Holt, 432–33; and Münsterberg, 437, 443–44

Loyalty, 296–306, 394, 395–96, 503–04

Lucifer (Santayana), 253

Lusitania crisis, 437, 440, 445

McClure, Edward, 55

McCosh, James, 58

MacDougall, Robert, 420

McDougall, William, 459–60

McLean Professorship of History, 29, 30

McTaggart, J. M. E., 56n

Madden, Edward H., 314n

Malthus, Thomas, 21

Man and the State (Hocking), 491–93

Marcel, Gabriel, 376

Marvin, Walter, 340n

Marxism: Harvard's avoidance of, 313–14

Massachusetts Institute of Technology: and Howison, 55, 56; and Abbot, 93; and Eliot, 131

"Matrix Algebra for Implications, The" (Lewis), 544–45

Maxwell, James Clerk, 271

Mead, George, 306

Meaning: in Metaphysical Club, 49–54; Peirce on, 52–54, 120–23, 264–65, 552–53; James on, 264–66; Royce on, 277–83; and operationalism, 461–62; cognitive and emotive, 496–97

Meaning of God in Human Experience, The (Hocking), 410, 493, 494; discussed, 482–90; as evolutionary naturalism, 483; influence of Palmer and Münsterberg on, 483; influence of neo-realism on, 483, 485, 487; influence of Royce on, 483–84, 488, 489–90; influence of James on, 483–84, 489–90

Meaning of Truth, The (James), 274

Metaphysical Club, 245; pragmatism in, xix, 48–54; and Holmes, 47, 49–51, 54; significance of, 47, 61–62; membership of, 47–48; history of, 47–49; and Green, 47–50, 54; Bain and, 49, 51–52; Peirce and, 51, 93, 117–18, 121; and James, 52; Abbot and, 93, 148

Metaphysical realism: representational realism as a form of, 11, 14; and Abbot, 94; presentational realism as a form of, 94, 338–39, 104–17; and Peirce, 104–17; neo-realism as a form of, 338–39

Michigan, University of, 215

Mill, John S., 32, 36, 38, 71; Unitarians on, 20–21, 25; and *Examination of*

Hamilton's Philosophy, 20–21, 52; Bowen on, 36; philosophers on, 52–53, 65–66, 122; and Wright, 63, 65, 67; Abbot on, 100*n*

Miller, Dickinson, 266

Mind, 137

Mind and the World-Order (Lewis), 534; influence of, xvii, 560; influence on Perry, 348*n;* influence of Royce on, 545–48, 559–60, 562; influence of Peirce on, 548, 552–53; discussed, 548–60; influence of Perry on, 552

Miracles: in Unitarianism, 5–6, 8; in Bowen, 36, 38; in Lewis, 559*n*

Modern Philosophy from Descartes to Schopenhauer and Hartmann (Bowen), 33

Modes of action: Peirce on, 113, 117, 121; Royce on, 381–85

Monism: James on, 173–79, 265–66, 274, 283–85, 294–96. *See also* Absolute; Absolute idealism; Idealism

Montague, William, Jr., 142, 344, 348; attacks Royce, 338–39, 575; attacks Holt, 346–47; and history of philosophy, 575–76

Montague, William, Sr., 48

Moore, G. E., 566

Morale and Its Enemies (Hocking), 444

Moral Economy, The (Perry), 511; Royce and, 497, 507; discussed, 505–08; James and, 508

"Moral Equivalent of War, The" (James), 309–11

Moral philosophy, in relation to intellectual philosophy: defined, xv; nadir at Harvard, xv; function of in antebellum America, 9–10, 19, 27, 30–32. *See also* Ethics

Morison, Samuel Eliot, 460

Morrill Act, 129

Morris, G. S., 124, 215

Münsterberg, Hugo: xx, 196–214, 413; career of, xxiii, 138–39, 186–87, 196–98, 414; action theory of, 187–89, 200–01; and two worlds problem, 187–89, 202, 203, 206–08, 208–09; and James, 188–89, 196, 198, 209, 323; and Royce, 195, 203, 208–09, 323; and Eliot, 196, 436–37, 445; and American life, 196–97; temperament of, 196–98; as academic entrepreneur, 196–98, 211, 250–51; on the will, 198–208; and Freud, 201; on scientific and purposive psychology, 201–02, 206–07; idealism of, 203–06; on value, 203–08; and applied psychology, 209–12; reputation of, 211, 213; social philosophy of, 211–12; on the cinema, 213–14, 447; and Palmer, 226; on graduate education, 250–51; and Holt, 417–18, 420, 421, 426; and Yerkes, 419–20; and First World War, 435–39, 444–45, 446–47; and Lowell, 437, 443–44; and Boring, 460

Murphey, Murray, 126

Mysticism: in Royce, 275, 279, 489–90; in James, 331–34; in Hocking, 489–90, 484

Nagel, Thomas, 511*n*

Nahm, Milton, 557*n*

National Council of Education, 132

National Educational Association, 132

Natural realism. *See* Scottish realism

Natural theology: controversy over, 6–9, 24–25; in Bowen, 36–37; in Wright, 66–69

Nature (Emerson), 35

Nature of Goodness, The (Palmer), 218, 221–22, 226

Nautical Almanac, The, 48, 64

Nebular hypothesis: and Wright, 72–74

Neo-Kantianism: Harvard pragmatism and, xx–xxi, 256–58; Royce on, 144–47, 317–18, 497; James's, 273–74, 316–19, 334

Neo-realism: as a form of presentational realism, 338–39; Royce's relation to, 338–39, 348–49; develops at Harvard, 338–350; James's relation to, 339, 348–49; Perry's, 340–44, 348*n;* Holt's, 344–47, 422–23; Montague's, 346–47; and critical realism, 348; Lewis's relation to, 348*n,* 534–35, 536–37, 552; Hocking's relation to, 483–85

Neutral monism: in Münsterberg, 198–209, 323; in James, 209, 319–30; in Perry, 339–44; in Holt, 344–45, 420–23; Miller and Santayana on, 360–61

New Realism, The (Perry et al.), 340, 347, 348*n*

New School of Social Research, 242

Nexus, 528–29

Nihilism: Wright on, 77–78; Peirce on, 106; James on, 160–64

Nominalism. *See* Epistemological realism

Non-cognitivism (in ethics), 496–97, 511*n*, 515

North American Review, 29, 30, 57, 65

Northrup, F. S. C., 482*n*, 566

Norton, Charles Eliot, 47

"Notational Relativity" (Sheffer), 458

Noumenal and phenomenal: 26; in history of philosophy, 12–16 and Scottish realism, 16–21, 32–34, 44–45; and Bowen, 32–34, 44–45, in Wright, 65–67, 76–78; in Abbot, 9498; in Peirce, 111–17; in psychology, 180, 190–95; in Royce, 190–95. *See also* Kant, Immanuel; Transcendental Unity of Apperception; Two worlds problem

Nozick, Robert, 568*n*

"On a New List of Categories" (Peirce), 107

"One, the Many, and the Infinite, The" (Royce), 370–73

"On Some Omissions of Introspective Psychology" (James), 178

On the Witness Stand (Münsterberg), 210

Operationalism: in Peirce, 123, 553; in psychology, 461–62; in Lewis, 553

Origin of Species (Darwin), xvii, 45; discussed, 21–22; response to, 22–26, Bowen on, 30, 32, 41–42. *See also* Darwin, Charles; Evolution

Outlines of Cosmic Philosophy (Fiske), 88, 91; and physical world, 82–83; discussed, 82–87; and social world, 83–85; and Comte, 85–86; conservatism of, 86–87

Palmer, George, 215–27, 408; as academic politician, xxiii, 236–41; career of, 135, 137–38, 216–18, 235–41, 414; and Eliot, 135, 137–38, 239–40; ethics of, 215–16, 218–25, 235–36, 497, 503–04, 508, 509; and hierarchy of philosophic studies, 215–16, 227; technical philosophy of, 215–16, 227; Lewis, Hocking, and Perry on, 218; and causation, 219–20; and free will, 219–20; on the self, 222–25; social philosophy of, 224–25, 236–41; on God, 225–26; on Royce, 225–26; and James, 226; and Münsterberg, 226; as administrator, 226, 236–41; on Peirce, 241; on Santayana, 410*n;* on Hocking, 482; and Hocking, 483; Lewis on, 533

Panpsychism: Royce on, 149; James's 323–26, 331–34; and critical realism, 364–65; Whitehead's, 525, 527

Pantheism: Wright's, 67–70; Abbot's, 101; Royce's, 260; James's, 332–34

Pareto, Vilfredo, 314

Parker, DeWitt, 242

Parker, Theodore, 8

Path of the Law, The (Holmes), 50

Peabody, Francis Greenwood, 244–47

Peace and America, The (Münsterberg), 439

Peirce, Benjamin, 104–06, 123

Peirce, Charles, xvi, xix, 104–26; and Bowen, 28, 116, 120; and Metaphysical Club, 53–54, 93, 117–18, 121; and principle of pragmatism, 53–54, 121, 123; and Wright, 64, 106, 116; and Abbot, 93, 101–02, 113, 116–17; amateurism of, 104, 124–25, 126; career of, 104–05, 123–24; and Hopkins, 105, 123; and Kant, 105–07, 112–14, 115; and categories, 106–07; on signs, 106–18; on cognitions, 107; idealism of, 109, 114–17; and Berkeley, 109, 111; and Descartes, 109, 111, 113, 118, 119; on nominalism and realism, 109–17, 119–20; and laws, 110–11; phenomenalism of, 112; and Transcendental Unity of Apperception, 114–15; on community, 114–17;

synthesizes science and religion, 114–17, 123; and induction, 115; and Hamilton, 116–17, 122; logic of, 117; and Bain, 117–18; and pragmatism, 117–23; on doubt, 118; and Darwin, 118–19; on habit, 120–21; on possibility, 122–23; and operationalism, 123; and institutions, 123–24; later repute of, 123–24; and James, 124, 125, 264–65, 269, 388, 400; and Royce, 125, 388, 400; later work of, 125–26; and Lewis, 548, 552, 553

Pepper, Stephen, 254*n*

Perry, Ralph: xvi, 258, 338–50, 368, 453, as early professional, xxii–xxiii, 254–55, 256, 349–50, 408–14, 567; career of, 252, 254–55, 256, 408–14; careerism of, 254–55, 454; carries on public role, 255, 439, 441–42, 442–44, 561, 567–68; and James, 317, 319, 328–29, 339, 567; and Royce, 338–39, 575; neo-realism of, 340–44, 348*n;* and Lewis, 348*n;* Holt on, 421, 432, 433; in First World War, 439, 441–44; political philosophy of, 439, 441–44, 507–08, 513–14; and Scribner's, 454–55; on Jews, 456–57; and Hocking, 483, 485, 486; ethics of, 496–97, 504–15; interest and value theory of, 505–15; and utilitarianism, 507–08, 513–14; and history of philosophy, 575–76

Pessimism: after Darwin, xxi, 38, 46; in Santayana, 352–53

Peterson, Ellis, 217

"Ph.D. Octopus, The" (James), 248

Phenomenal. *See* Noumenal and phenomenal

Phenomenalism: in the history of philosophy, 11–12; in Wright, 76–78; in Peirce, 109–23; in Royce, 150–57; in James, 323–30; in Lewis, 552–55

Phenomenology of Mind, The (Hegel), 313*n*

"Philosophical Conceptions and Practical Results" (James), 54, 258; and Peirce, 264–65; discussed, 264–66; and Royce, 265–66

Philosophical Review, 249, 454

Philosophie der Werte. See Eternal Values, The

Philosophy, Harvard department of: development of, xvi, xvii, 131–33, 135–39, 241–42; 243–56; 452–59; potency of, xvi–xvii; undergraduate education in, 131–33; graduate education in, 133, 233–35, 463–80; personnel of, 135–39, 239–42, 407–15, 452–59; hiring and promotion policies of, 135–39, 251–56, 407–15, 455–58; teaching in, 136–37, 233–35, 239–40, 249–50, 252; conflict in, 239–40, 413–14, 459–63; doctorate production in, 242–43, 248–51, 463–80; relation to other disciplines, 243–48, 413–14, 459–63, 475; specialization in, 243–48, 414–15, 451–52; chairmen of, 244, 409

Philosophy and Public Affairs, 568*n*

Philosophy 4: model for college courses, 237*n,* 239

Philosophy of Loyalty, The (Royce), 285, 296, 307, 309; criticizes James, 285–86; discussed, 298–301; and *The Sources of Religious Insight,* 300–01, 303; and martial virtues, 309–10; relation to Kant, 313*n:* relation to *The Problem of Christianity,* 395–96

Photoplay, The. See Film, The

"Physical Theory of the Universe, A" (Wright), 72–74

Pierce, Arthur, 420

Pierce, Edgar, 458, 534

Pitkin, Walter, 340*n*

"Place of Affectional Facts in a World of Pure Experience, The" (James), 322–23

"Place of Intuition in Knowledge, The" (Lewis), 534–36

Plato, 306

Pluralism: in Royce's later work, 370, 400; in James, 176, 265, 325, 332–33, 335

Pluralistic Universe, A (James), 335; and Bergson, 331–32; discussed, 331–34; relation to Royce, 332, 400; and Whitehead, 519

Poincaré, Henri, 208, 549

Political economy, xv, 29–30

Political philosophy: discussed in relation to hierarchy of philosophic studies, xxiv–xxv, 311–14, 435, 561–63; in First World War, xxiv–xxv, 439–45; of Royce and James, 306–14, 435, 439–41; appraised, 311–14, 439; in Hocking, 439, 441–42, 442–44, 507–08, 513–14; in Second World War, 561, 567–68; in Lewis, 562

Popularization: Fiske and, 80, 90–91 and professional philosophy, 565. *See also* Hierarchy of philosophical studies; Public philosophy; Technical philosophy

Porter, Noah, 58, 135

Positivism: in Mill, 20, 63; Spencer's, 25–26, 63, 82–83, 85; in Wright, 63, 77; in Comte, 63, 85; in Fiske, 82, 85–86; logical, 461, 566

Possibility: Peirce on, 122–23; Royce and James on, 283–89; and Lewis, 553–55; after Lewis, 577*n*

Possibility of Altruism, The (Nagel), 511*n*

"Possibility of Error, The" (Royce), influence on American philosophy, 138, 157–58; discussed, 150–56, 260, 288, 392–93; influence on James, 157–58, 176–79, 181–84, 332. *See also* Dialectic argument

Post-Kantians, 215, 342, 441; Bowen on, 35, 43; and Royce, 144–45, 297, 449–501; James on, 174, 318–19; and Münsterberg, 208; relation to Abbot and Royce, 250*n*

Postulation: in Bowen, 39, 43, 64; and empiricism, 39, 43, 64; in Wright, 64, 71–72; in Peirce, 111–14; in Royce, 144–48, 288–89, 328, 391, 399, 501–03; in James, 161–80, 328; and other minds, 288–89, 328, 391, 399; and Perry, 507–08

Potts, David, 274*n*

Pourtalai, Juliette, 123

Practical philosophy. *See* Public philosophy; Technical philosophy

Pragmatic *a priori:* in Lewis, 549, 550–52; Royce's relation to, 549–51

Pragmatisch: and derivation of pragmatism, 54

Pragmatism: in Metaphysical Club, xix, 47–54; principle of, xix, 49–54, 121–25,

264–74, 283–85; in Peirce, xix, 52–53, 121–25, 264–65, 269; and Darwin, xix–xx, 26–27, 47–54; in James, xix–xx, 52, 176–79, 264–74, 283–85; defined, xix–xxi; and Kant, xx–xxi, 26–27, 45, 47, 54, 61–62; Harvard, xx–xxi, 256–58; in Royce, xxi, 145–50, 264–69, 278–89, 386–87; at Chicago and Columbia, xxvi, 306; Absolute, xxi, 264–69, 278–89, 386–87; Bain and, 49, 51–52; in Green, 49–50; in Holmes, 49–51; legal, 49–51; nominal derivation of, 54; in Fiske, 89–90; and Münsterberg, 323; in Santayana, 357–61; in critical realism, 361–65; negative, 483–84; Hocking's, 483–84; in Lewis, 549, 550–55, 560; in Goodman and Quine, 577–80

Pragmatism (James), 53, 316, 339; logic and psychology of, 266–68; discussed, 266–73; relation to Royce, 267–68; and meaning of truth, 269–72; Kantian aspects of, 272–74, 322; and possibility, 283; religious aspects of, 293–96; and tough- and tender-minded, 317

Pratt, James B., 242, 362

Prediction theory of law, 49–51

Presentational realism: and Scottish realism, 33–34, 339; and Bowen, 43–45, 77; and Berkeley, 43–45, 328–30; and Abbot, 94; and Peirce, 104–20, 329; and James, 328–30; and neo-realism, 338–39

Present Conflict of Ideals, The (Perry), 441, 576

Present Philosophical Tendencies (Perry), 348*n*

Present Status of the Philosophy of Law and of Rights, The (Hocking), 491

Pressey, Sydney, 456

Primary qualities, in relation to secondary qualities: Hamilton on, 17–18; Bowen on, 44; Wright on, 76–77

Prince, Morton, 423

Princeton University, 433

Principia Mathematica (Russell and Whitehead), 516, 539–45, 570

Principle of Relativity, The (Whitehead), 520

"Principles of Logic, The" (Royce), 380–85

Principles of Metaphysics and Ethical Science Applied to the Evidences of Religion, The (Bowen), 35–38

Principles of Political Economy Applied to the Conditions, Resources, and the Institutions of the American People (Bowen), 29

Principles of Psychology, The (James), 165, 266; as natural science, 179, 181–84, 259; James's writing of, 180–81; substantial self in, 320, 334; ambiguities in, 181–84; discussed, 181–86; relation to Münsterberg, 187–89; and stream of consciousness, 320, 330; relation to James's later work, 320, 330, 332, 334; relation to Holt, 421

"Prinzipien der Logik." *See* "Principles of Logic, The"

Problem of Christianity, The (Royce), 401; Palmer on, 225; pluralism in, 370, 400; incompleteness of, 385; and logic, 385, 388, 389–90; and interpretation, 385–88; discussed, 385–400; and *The Sources of Religious Insight,* 386, 393, 394; and *The World and the Individual,* 388, 391; relation to Peirce, 388, 400; and community, 388–93; and *The Philosophy of Loyalty,* 394, 395–96; love in, 394–95; God in, 395; and problem of evil, 395–400; grace in, 396–98; and Bradley, 400; relation to James, 400; influence on Hocking, 484n

Problem of Freedom, The (Palmer), 218, 219–21

Problems of Today (Münsterberg), 197

Process and Reality (Whitehead): typographical errors in, 517, 518n; and actual entities, 524–27; discussed, 524–32; formative elements in, 527–32; and causality 529

Professionalization: and character of philosophizing, xvii–xxv, 256–58, 413–14, 463–80, 561–62; concept discussed, xviii, xxi–xxv, 233–35, 241–58; 565–72; and amateurs, xx, xxiii, 26–27, 46–47, 61–62, 126–38, 239–40; in the Golden Age, 27–28, 413–14, 451–52;

nascent, 136–39; Eliot's relation to, 233–35, 414–15; Palmer on, 239–41, 250–51; and production of doctorates, 242–43, 248–51, 463–80; in psychology, 243–44, 459–63, 475; and departmentalism, 243–48, 459–63; James on, 248–51; Münsterberg on, 250–51; and hiring and promotion, 251–56, 407–15, 452–53; and tenure procedures, 413–14; in the Silver Age, 413–14, 451–59, 566, 567; Holt on, 432–34; Lowell's relation to, 414–15, 432–34, 452–53; and specialization, 451–52; Perry on, 508; and Lewis, 561–62

"Program and First Platform of Six Realists, The" (Perry et al.), 340, 348

"Proximate and Remote Cause" (Green), 49

Psychologist's fallacy (in James), 183

Psychology: Spencer's, 25–26, 162, 170; Bain's, 49–51, 117–18; and idealism, 138–39, 189, 194–95, 266; and philosophy, 138–39, 244, 413–14, 459–63; and associationalism, 162, 170, 187–89; conception of in early period, 180; as a laboratory science, 180, 186, 196–98, 420, 459–63; James's, 180–86, 189–90, 417–18; history at Harvard, 180–95, 413–14, 459–63; comparisons among James's, Royce's, and Münsterberg's, 186–87, 188–89, 195, 208–09, 417–18; Münsterberg's, 187–89, 198–202, 206, 208–12, 417–18; behaviorism in, 189, 190–91, 344–47, 425–29, 431, 459–63; and evolutionary naturalism, 189–90; and physiology, 190–91; Royce's, 190–95; deduction of the categories and, 190–95, 208; split with philosophy, 244, 413–14, 459–63, 475; Holt's, 344–47, 418, 425–29, 431; professionalization of, 413–15, 459–63, 475; Yerkes's, 418–19; Tolman's 431–34; Boring's, 459–63

Psychology and Industrial Efficiency (Münsterberg), 210–11

"Psychology of Jingoism" (James), 314n

Psychology and Life (Münsterberg), 198–202, 208n

Psychology and the Teacher (Münsterberg), 197

"Psychology as a Science of Selves" (Calkins), 189*n*

"Psychology as the Behaviorist Views It" (Watson), 420*n*

Psychology, Briefer Course (James), 181, 183

Psychotherapy (Münsterberg), 197, 210

Publication: Eliot on, 133, 138–39, 256; role of in philosophy, 137–38, 256, 414–15; Lowell on, 256, 411–12, 414–15

Public philosophy: changing role of, xxiii, xxv, 565, 572; and hierarchy of philosophic studies, 311–14; in Royce and James, 291, 435, 439–41, 445, 565, 567; as social and political philosophy, 306–14; in Perry and Hocking, 442–43, 445–47, 453–55, 567–68; in Lewis, 561–63. *See also* Technical philosophy

Purposive Behavior in Animals and Man (Tolman), 431

Putnam, Henry, 49

Putnam, James, 423

Pyrrhonism, 34, 164–65, 177

Quine, Willard, 459*n*, 577–80

Race Questions, Provincialism, and Other American Problems (Royce), 307–08

Radical empiricism: discussed in James, 319–34; in Perry, 339; in Holt, 421, 431

Rand, Benjamin: xxvi; career at Harvard, 252–53

Rashdall, Hastings, 56*n*

Rationalism. *See* Empiricism and rationalism

Rawls, John, 568*n*

Realism. *See* Critical realism; Epistemological realism; Metaphysical realism; Neo-realism; Presentational realism; Representational realism; Scottish realism

"Realism in Retrospect," (Perry), 340*n*

Realms of Being, The (Santayana), 365

Realms of Value, (Perry), 515

Regulative principles: in Kant, 13–14, 162; in Wright, 68; in James, 161–76; in Royce, 548–52 in Lewis, 550–52

Reid, Thomas, 16, 17, 31

Relativity of knowledge: Hamilton on, 17–19, 20–21; Mill on, 20–21, 44, 65–66; Bowen on, 44; Wright on, 65–66

Religious Aspect of Philosophy, The (Royce), 141; discussed, 150–56; influence on American philosophy, 157–58; influence on James, 157–58, 176–79, 181–84

"Remarks on Spencer's Definition of Mind" (James), 170–72

Renouvier, Charles, 161–63, 166, 177

Representational realism defined as a form of metaphysical realism, 11, 14; and James, 162–63, 171–76; and Royce, 279; and critical realism, 363–64; and Lewis, 534–39. *See also* Locke, John

Reputation (of philosophers): analysis of, xxiii–xxiv, 565–67; Bowen's, xxiv, 28, 45; Wright's, xxiv, 63–64; Abbot's xxiv, 80, 92–93, 101–03; Fiske's, xxiv, 80–81, 87, 90–91, 102–03; Peirce's xxiv, 104, 124–25, 126; Royce's, xxiv, 140, 157–58, 447; James's, 181, 315–16, 334–37, 340, 447; Münsterberg's, 197–98, 211, 213, 447; Palmer's, 239–41; Perry's 254–55; Santayana's, 365–66, 369; Holt's, 431–33; and First World War, 447, 495, 567; Hocking's, 493–95; and ethics, 496–97, 515; Whitehead's, 518*n*, 532, 567*n*; Lewis's, 533, 560–63

"Response and Cognition" (Holt), 423, 429

Re-Thinking Missions (Hocking), 493

Revealed theology: controversy over, 6–9, 24–25; Bowen's, 37–38

"Review of Berkeley" (Peirce), 109–13

Revolt Against Dualism, The (Lovejoy), 363*n*

Rieber, Charles, 420

Riley, Woodbridge, 422*n*

Rogers, Arthur, 362

Roosevelt, Franklin, 569

670   *Index*

Roosevelt, Theodore, 438
Rousseau, 306
Royce, Josiah, xvi, xx, 28, 40, 140–58,
259–64, 409, 413, 497–503 as professional, xxii, xxiii; creates a framework
of thought with James, xxiii–xxv,
256–58, 291, 316, 370, 451, 565; career
of, 136, 137, 140–44; temperament of,
141–44, 311–12; Palmer on, 143; and
evolution, 143–44, 157–58; and Kant,
144–47, 277, 313*n;* and postulation,
144–48, 391, 399; early work of, 144–
50; and justification of knowledge,
144–50, 267–69, 279–89; and skepticism, 144–53, 153–57, 278; and ideas,
144–57, 276–83, 371, 385–86; and Berkeley, 148, 151; and Peirce, 151, 370,
388, 400; and Descartes, 153; on doubt,
153–57; on the self, 156, 386–88, 501–
03, 507; and two worlds problem,
156–57, 181–95, 275–83, 303, 373–85,
388; and James, 157–58, 176–79, 181–
84, 259, 264–69, 279–90, 291–96, 306–
14, 324, 325, 327–28, 370, 400; on the
categories, 190–95, 370–85; psychology of, 190–95; on imitation, 191–93,
276–77; and Münsterberg, 195, 203,
280–09, 323, 445; and Palmer, 225, 226;
on Abbot 250*n;* James on, 257*n,* 284–
85; on James, 257*n,* 285; on God, 260–
64, 296–306, 514; and Jamesean pragmatism, 264–69, 278–89, 386–87; and
four conceptions of being, 274, 279; on
possibility, 283–89; absolute pragmatism of, 287–89, 386–87; and Bradley, 289–90, 318, 331*n,* 370–73, 399;
public philosophy of, 291, 296–314,
435, 439–41, 445; ethics of, 296–300,
497–505, 507, 508, 509; on loyalty,
296–306, 395–98; and problem of evil,
301–06, 395–400; political and social
philosophy of, 306–14, 435, 439–41,
445; and Perry, 338–39, and neo-
realism, 338–39, 348–49; and Santayana, 367–68; logic of, 370–85; later
work of, 370–400; on interpretation,
385–400; on signs, 386–88; and community; 388–93; 440–41; and First

World War, 401, 439–41, 445; and
Hocking, 453, 481–82, 483, 484–85,
488, 489–90, 495; and Lewis, 453, 533,
534, 535, 538–39, 545–48, 559–60, 562;
and Whitehead, 519, 523, 528–29
Royce, Katharine, 141, 436
Royce, Sarah, 141
Russell, Bertrand: and Harvard, 408–09,
410–11, 413, 414, 415; and Sheffer, 458,
570; and Whitehead, 516, 539–45; and
Lewis, 539–45. See also *Principia
Mathematica*
Rutherford, Ernest, 208

Sanborn, Franklin, 58–59
San Francisco Grammar School, 141
Santayana, George, xvi, xx, 258, 351–69;
temperament of, xvii, 351–53, 365–66;
career of, 252, 253–54, 352–53, 357,
365–67, 405; and promotion, 252,
253–54, 366; poetry of, 353–57; and
James, 357–58, 360–61, 368; pragmatism of, 357–61; evolutionary
naturalism of, 359–62, 497, 504; neo-
realism of, 360–61; critical realism of,
361–65; later work of, 365; Eliot on,
366; James on, 366; on Harvard, 366–
68; and Royce, 367–68; on Genteel
Tradition, 367–69; Palmer on, 410*n;*
and Holt, 423, 497, 504; on First World
War, 439, 441–42; and Lewis, 536
Santayana, Josefina Borras Sturgis, 351–
53, 365
Sartre, Jean Paul, 579
Savery, William, 242
Schopenhauer, Arthur. See Post-Kantians
Schurman, Jacob, 215
Science and the Modern World (Whitehead),
517, 524
Scientific Theism (Abbot), 94–98, 250*n*
Scottish realism: impact in America, 10,
18–21; relation to Kant, 16–17; de-
scribed, 16–19; as natural realism, 17,
328–30; and Unitarian philosophy,
18–21, 23–24; and evolution, 23–26;
and Bowen, 33–34, 43–45, 77; and
Wright, 76–77; and Abbot, 94; and
Peirce, 104–20, 329; and Royce, 140;

and James, 140, 328–30; and neo-realism, 339

Scotus, Duns, 113*n*

Scribner's Sons, Charles (publishers), 454–55

Secondary qualities. *See* Primary qualities

Second World War, xvii, 495; and Lewis, 560; and Perry and Hocking, 560, 567–68

Self: Bowen on, 36–37, 44–55; Royce on, 156–57, 370–73, 386–88, 501–03, 507; James on, 178–79, 184–85, 319–34, 508; Palmer on, 222–25; Holt on, 421–23; Perry on, 507–08. *See also* Consciousness; Self-consciousness

Self-consciousness: Wright on, 74, 75–76; James on, 183, 319–34; Palmer on, 222–25; Royce on, 370–73, 395–98; Holt on, 421–23. *See also* Consciousness; Self

Self-realization ethics: dominant at Harvard, 215, 503–04; and Royce, 215, 497–505, 507, 508, 509; and Palmer, 215–16, 218–25; problems of, 222–24; and Holt, 428–29, 504; and Perry, 496–97, 504–15; and Hocking, 497, 504; and Santayana, 497, 504; and realism, 503; as a form of cognitivism, 503–04; and idealism, 504

Sellars, Roy, 362

Sense of Beauty, The (Santayana), 253, 357, 358

Sheffer, Henry, 571; and Royce, 422, 569; as Jew, 457–58; career of, 457–58, 570; philosophy of, 569–70; and Russell and Whitehead, 570; stroke function of, 570

Sheldon, Wilmon, 242, 482*n*

Sherburne, Donald W., 530*n*

Sidis, Boris, 423

Σ: Royce's system, 378–85, 388, 545, 569; Lewis's system, 546–47. *See also* Logic

Signs: Peirce on, 106–08; James on, 170, 181*n;* Perry on, 348*n;* Royce on, 386–88; Holt on, 424–25; Lewis on, 553–54, 557–59

Sigwart, Christian, 216

Silver Age, 452–59, 567–69

Skepticism: and religion, xviii; Cambridge view of, 19; and evolution, 25, 39–42; Bowen on, 33; 35, 39–42; in Hume, 39–42; Wright's, 77; Abbot on, 94–101; Peirce on, 109–17, 119–20; Royce on, 153–57; James on, 164, 176–77. *See also* Subjectivism

Skepticism and Animal Faith (Santayana), 365

Skinner, B. F., 461

Smith College, 254, 338

Social ethics, 244–47

Social philosophy: Münsterberg's, 211–12; Palmer's, 224–25; Royce and James on, 306–11; problems with, 311–14; Whitehead's, 517, 518, 532, 567*n;* Lewis's, 562–63. *See also* Hierarchy of philosophical studies; Political philosophy

Solipsism. *See* Subjectivism

Sombart, Werner, 208

Sonnets and Other Verses (Santayana), 253, 353–57

Sources of Religious Insight, The (Royce): discussed, 301–06; relation to *The Varieties of Religious Experience,* 302; relation to *The Problem of Christianity,* 386, 393, 399

Southhard, Elmer, 423

Spaulding, Edward G., 340*n*

Specialization, 451–52, 565, 571. *See also* Hierarchy of philosophical studies; Professionalization

Speculative idealism, 556–57

Spencer, Herbert: views of, 25–26; influence on American philosophy, 26, 63; Wright on, 71–74; Fiske on, 81–87, 91; Abbot on, 93–94; James on, 162, 170

Spirit of Modern Philosophy, The (Royce), 142, 157, 260

Spirit of World Politics, The (Hocking), 493

Stanford University, 129, 137, 208, 362*n*

Sterling Professorship (Yale), 482*n*

Stevens, S. S., 461

Stevenson, Charles, 496–97, 511*n,* 515
Stewart, Dugald, 16, 17, 31
St. Louis Hegelians, 55, 57–59, 135–36, 215
Stratton, George Malcolm, 56*n*
Strauss, David, 8
Strength of Men and Nations (Hocking), 494
Strong, C. A., 360, 362
Sturgis, George, 351
Sturgis, Robert, 351
Sturgis, Susana, 351, 352
Sub-conscious: Münsterberg on, 201; James on, 201, 292–93, 333; Holt on, 427–28
Subjectivism: in relation to solipsism, 19, 34–35, 94–101; Royce and James on, 327–29; Perry on, 342–43; Hocking on, 483, 485, 494; Lewis on, 536–39. *See also* Skepticism
Suicide, 571–72; James's contemplation of, 165; Eaton's, 459*n*
Survey of Symbolic Logic (Lewis), 533, 539, 544, 568
Syllogistic Philosophy, The (Abbot), 101–02
Symbolic Logic (Lewis), 544
Symbolism (Whitehead), 524
Symbolism and Truth (Eaton), 458–59*n*
Synthetic. See *A priori.*
System of Logic, A (Mill), 63
System of Psychology, A (Dunlap), 420

Teaching: and elective system, 30–31, 131, 238–40, 405–06; undergraduate, 30–32, 233, 405–06, Bowen on, 31–32, 134–35; graduate, 133, 233–35, 239–40, 405–06; Eliot on, 137–38, 233, 235; Palmer on, 235–41
Technical philosphy (in connection with practical or applied philosophy): and hierarchy of philosophical studies, xxiii, 472–80; conception of stated, xxiii–xxv; Palmer and, 215–16; Royce and James and, 291, 311–14; neorealism and, 349–50; Lewis and, 561–63. *See also* Public philosophy

Temperament: James on, xvii, 78; Santayana's, xvii, 351–53, 365–66; and study of the history of ideas, xvii–xviii, 414–15; Wright's, 77–79; James's, 78, 159–61, 165, 177, 312, 335; Fiske's, 81, 91; Abbot's, 92–93, 101–02; Münsterberg's, 96–98; Royce's, 141–44, 311–12; Perry's, 254–55, 340*n;* Holt's, 421, 431–33; Hocking's, 481–83; Lewis's, 560–61
Tenure, 407–13, 414–15, 459*n,* 534
Theism: Fiske's, 88–90; Abbot's, 101; Royce's, 260, 385–400; James's, 292–96, 332–34, 335
Theology. *See* Christianity; God; Natural theology; Revealed theology
Through Nature to God (Fiske), 88–90
Time and Free Will (Bergson), 332
Titchener, E. B., 413, 414, 415
Tocqueville, Alexis, 29
Tolman, Edward C., 431, 434
Tomorrow (Münsterberg), 439
Tönnies, Ferdinand, 208, 314
Tractatus (Wittgenstein), 459*n*
Trades and Professions (Palmer), 236
Transcendentalism. *See* Emerson, Ralph
Transcendental Unity of Apperception: Harvard view of, 15–16; Peirce on, 114–15; Royce on, 148–50, 156–57, 176–78; James on, 176–78, 182; Lewis on, 538–39. *See also* Kant, Immanuel; Noumenal and phenomenal; Two worlds problem.
Treatise on Probability (Keynes), 555
Treatise on Universal Algebra (Whitehead), 516, 517
Troeltsh, Ernst, 208
Troland, Leonard, 420*n,* 459
Turgot, Anne Robert, 85
Two worlds problem: in psychology, 175–95, 198–209; in Royce, 156–57, 191–95, 275–83, 303, 373–85, 388; in James, 175–86, 266–67; in Münsterberg, 186–89, 198–209; in Palmer, 225–27; and deduction of the categories, 190–95, 208–09. *See also* Kant, Immanuel; Noumenal and

phenomenal; Transcendental Unity of Apperception

Types of Philosophy (Hocking), 576

Unconditioned. *See* Law of the Conditioned

Undergraduate eduction: 249–50, 405–06; Eliot and, 30–32, 131–33, 136–37; Palmer and, 135–38, 239–40. *See also* Educational philosophy; Graduate education; Teaching

Unitarianism: controversy with Transcendentalism, xix, 7–9, 19–20, 25, 105; role of philosophy in, xxiii, 28, 38; development of, 5–7; natural and revealed religion in, 6–9, 24–25; and Peirce, 105

Unitarian philosophy, 28; described, xix; importance of, 9–10; historical context of, 10–19; views of, 18–21, 23–25. *See also* Bowen, Francis

United States Coast and Geodetic Survey, 105, 124

Universals. *See* Epistemological realism

University of California at Berkeley. *See* Berkeley, University of California at

Unknowable, 25, 26

Utilitarianism, 507–08, 513–14

"Varieties of Religious Experiences, The" (James), 258, 315, 333; discussed 291–93, 296n; and Royce, 292, 303; relation to *The Sources of Religious Insight,* 303

Veblen, Thorstein, 314

Vico, Giovanni, 85

Virchow, Rudolph, 549–50, 551

Vocation and Learning (Münsterberg), 197, 210

Voluntarism: in Royce, 141–44, 145–48, 259–64, 323; in Münsterberg, 198–208, 323; in James, 208, 323. *See also* Pragmatism; Will

Walker, James, 10

War and America, The (Münsterberg), 438

War and Insurance (Royce), 440–41

Ward, James, 56n

Warner, Joseph Bangs, 47, 48

Warnock, G. J., 511n

Washington University (St. Louis), 362n

Washington, University of, 242

Watson, John, 56n, 420n

Way Out of Agnosticism, The (Abbot), 94, 98–101, 250n

Ways of Knowing, The (Montague), 576

Weber, Max, 208, 314

Weiss, Paul, 482n, 566

White, Andrew, 129

Whitehead, Alfred North, 412, 481, 516–32; and idealism, xxi, 527; later repute, xxiv, 518n, 532; on Golden Age, 408; comes to Harvard, 413, 453, 455; and *Principia Mathematica,* 516, 539–45; and Russell, 516, 539–45; career of, 516–17, 518–19; social philosophy of, 517, 518, 532, 567n; and history of philosophy, 518, 519; relation to James, 519, 523, 525; and Royce, 519, 523, 528–29; and Harvard philosophy, 519–20; and Hocking, 520; and Lewis, 520, 539–45; middle period of, 520–24; and Descartes 521; and Kant, 521, 527; and bifurcation of nature, 521–24; and extensive abstraction, 522–23; and Hume, 523, 529–30; mature work of, 524–32; and panpsychism, 525, 527; and actual occasions, 525–30; and eternal objects, 527–28, 530–31; and nexus, 528–29; creativity in, 530; God in, 530–32; and Sheffer, 570

Wicht Club, 421

Wiener, Norbert, 456

Will: James on, 165–79; Münsterberg on, 198–208; Holt on, 424–31. *See also* Pragmatism; Voluntarism

Williams College, 134, 242, 254, 363

Will to Believe and Other Essays in Popular Philosophy, The (James), 291

Wilson, Woodrow, 208, 437–38

Windelband, Wilhelm, 202

Wittgenstein, Ludwig, 459n, 566

Wolfson, Harry, xxvi, 457

Women: Münsterberg on, 211–12; treatment at Harvard, 457*n*, 590–94

Woodbridge, F. J. E., 248

Woods, James: xxvi, 252, 433, 460; career of, 255–56, 409; as chairman, 409, 410–11, 455; on Whitehead, 413; on Jews, 456, 458

World and the Individual, The (Royce), 258, mysticism in, 275, 489; realism in, 275, 279; discussed, 275–83, 370–78, 379, 380; influence on James, 276–86; critical rationalism in, 279–83; and *The Problem of Christianity,* 388, 391; influence on Hocking, 484*n*, 489; and history of philosophy, 575

Wright, Chauncey: xix, 63–79; and Bowen, 28, 77; and Bain, 51; and pragmatism, 51; and positivism, 63; and science, 63, 64, 71–2; career of, 63, 64, 78–79; appraisals of, 63–64; and Peirce, 64, 106, 116; and James, 64, 160, 164, 176–77; as Hamiltonian, 64–68; and Abbot, 65–66; and natural theology, 66–69; on the origins of life, 66–69, 74; shift in position, 67–70; and Gray, 69*n;* ethics of 69–70; defends Darwin, 70–74, 76; and Fiske, 71; and Spencer, 71–74, 93; cosmic weather of, 73, 78; on causality, 74; on self-consciousness, 74, 75–76; on habit, 75–76; and Descartes, 76; natural realism of, 76–77; Nihilism of, 77–78, 160, 164, 176–77; and Metaphysical Club, 77–78; temperament of, 77–79; on induction, 78, 176–77; amateurism of, 78–79, 104

Wundt, Wilhelm, 187, 196

Wyman, Jeffries, 104, 159

Yale University, 130, 482*n*, 566

Yerkes, Robert, 258, 421, 459; leaves Harvard, 413, 434; career of, 418–19; and Münsterberg, 419–20